Praise for Stephen Book and Improvisation Technique:

*Stephen Book's Improvisation Technique is creatively explosive!
It has heightened my presence with new levels of freedom, authenticity
and generosity. Right after completing Stephen's class I booked
Buffy which led to Angel and films.*
—DAVID BOREANAZ

*A very intelligent and highly skilled teacher of acting. Actors find him exciting to
work with and get a great deal from his particular form of teaching.*
—JOHN HOUSEMAN

*Coming as I did from stand-up comedy—and with a movie part in hand I was
greatly in need of a teacher and a system which could bring out and begin to
develop my natural skills in a short time. Stephen Book and his workshop were
just such a combination. I continue working with him to my great benefit.*
—GEORGE CARLIN

*I was a student in Stephen Book's acting class during the three or so years he was
writing this book, so I have experienced its riches first-hand. I know how much
I gained, and I witnessed the growth of the other actors in the class. I still
remember our first round of scene work and the remarkable transformation
of each actor's work after we did the First-Level Improvisations. It was a startling
demonstration of the transforming power of the Improvisation Technique we
were learning. And the best was yet to come. I was 75 when I began the class,
a professional actor for 50 years. I finished not long after I turned 79, my craft
immeasurably enriched and strengthened, with access to emotional resources
I did not realize I had within me. As I get ready to start rehearsals for
a new play, I have a fresh sense of myself in the work I have been doing
my whole professional life. Priceless!*
—WILLIAM SCHALLERT, President, Screen Actors Guild (1979-81)

D1127713

BOOK ON ACTING

BOOK ON ACTING

Improvisation Technique

for the Professional Actor in Film, Theater & Television

by **Stephen Book**

SILMAN-JAMES PRESS LOS ANGELES

First Edition

10 9 8 7 6 5 4 3 2

Acknowledgment is made to the following for permission to reproduce the material indicated

Excerpts from the script based on Hollywood Pictures' copyrighted feature film *Miami Rhapsody* are used by permission from Disney Enterprises, Inc.; *Frasier.* Courtesy of Viacom Consumer Products; *House Arrest.* Courtesy of Viacom Consumer Products; *Star Trek: Voyager.* Courtesy of Viacom Consumer Products; *Dogma.* Courtesy of STK LLC; From *The Three Sisters* by Anton Chekhov, translated by Lanford Wilson, © 1984 by Lanford Wilson. Reprinted by permission of International Creative Management, Inc.; *Long Day's Journey into Night* 1956© by Eugene O'Neill. Reprinted by permission of William Morris Agency, Inc. on behalf of the author; From *The Glass Menagerie* by Tennessee Williams, copyright © 1945 by The University of the South and Edwin D. Williams, renewed © 1973 by The University of the South. Reprinted by permission of New Directions Publishing Corp. and The University of the South, Sewanee, Tennessee. Published by New Directions; From *House of Blue Leaves* by John Guare, © 1968, 1971, 1972 by St. Jude Productions, Inc. Published by arrangement with the author; Screenplay excerpt from *L. A. Law: The Movie.* Courtesy of Twentieth Century Fox Television. Steven Bochco, Terry Louise Fisher, and William M. Finkelstein. All rights reserved; From *Glengarry Glen Ross* by David Mamet, © 1982, 1983 by David Mamet. Used by permission of Grove/Atlantic, Inc.; *What Dreams May Come.* Copyright © 2002 by Universal Studios. Courtesy of Universal Studios Publishing Rights, a Division of Universal Studios Licensing, Inc. All rights reserved; From *Death of a Salesman* by Arthur Miller, © 1949, renewed © 1977 by Arthur Miller. Used by permission of Viking Penguin, a division of Penguin Putnam Inc. and reprinted by permission of International Creative Management, Inc.; Excerpt from *Target of Suspicion* (aka *Presumed Guilty*). Courtesy of Ellipseanime; *Dangerous Curves.* Excerpt courtesy of Artisan Entertainment; *Melrose Place.* Courtesy of Viacom Consumer Products; Screenplay excerpt from *Love Potion No. 9.* Courtesy of Twentieth Century Fox Film Corporation. All rights reserved; From *Golden Boy* by Clifford Odets, © 1937 by Clifford Odets, renewed © 1965 by Nara Odets and Walt Whitman Odets. Used by permission of Grove/Atlantic, Inc.; Screenplay excerpt from *The Practice.* Courtesy of Twentieth Century Fox Television. David E. Kelley and Christopher Mack. All rights reserved; From *The Children's Hour* by Lillian Hellman, © 1934 by Lillian Hellman Kober, © 1942, 1953 by Lillian Hellman, renewed © 1961, 1981 by Lillian Hellman. All rights reserved.

Library of Congress Cataloging-in-Publication Data

Book, Stephen.
Book on acting : improvisation technique for the professional actor in film, theater, & television / by Stephen Book.
p. cm.
Includes bibliographical references and index.
1. Improvisation (Acting) I. Title.
PN2071.I5 B66 2002   792'.028—dc21   2002034514

ISBN: 1-879505-60-6

Cover design by Heidi Frieder
Frontcover photographs of Jacey Margolis
Backcover photograph by Kevin Langdon Ackerman

Printed in the United States of America

Silman-James Press
1181 Angelo Drive
Beverly Hills, CA 90210

Dedicated to the memory of Viola Spolin

CONTENTS

Introduction   *xi*

PART ONE
GETTING STARTED
   1. The Workshop   *3*

PART TWO
HOW TO IMPROVISE—BASIC TECHNIQUE OF IMPROVISATION
   2. Essential Starters   *19*
   3. Physical Doing   *49*
   4. Inner Doing   *107*
   5. Vocal Doing   *169*

PART THREE
**IMPROVISATION APPLICATIONS TO REHEARSALS FOR THEATER,
   FILM, AND TV**
   6. First Level Improvisations for Scripted Scenes   *217*

PART FOUR
IMPROVISING PROFESSIONAL ACTING SKILLS
   7. Character   *239*
   8. Camera and Stage Auditions: First Level Improvisation Applications   *313*
   9. Emotions   *329*
   10. Conflict   *403*
   11. Agreement   *475*

PART FIVE
ACTING THE SCRIPT WITH IMPROVISATION TECHNIQUE
   12. Purpose of Scene   *503*
   13. Monologues and Purpose of Scene   *541*
   14. Gaining More Finesse with Purpose of Scene   *565*

Conclusion   *605*
Appendix A   Sample Umbrella Arcs   *609*
Appendix B   Sample Emotion & Attitude Choices   *612*
Appendix C   Sample Character Arcs   *614*
Appendix D   Sample Attitude Lines   *615*
Appendix E   Suggested Workshop Formats   *617*
Appendix F   Traditional Children's Games   *621*
Notes   *623*
Index of Acting Focuses, Exercises & Processes   *627*
Acknowledgments   *629*

INTRODUCTION

"There's no rehearsal time."

"The director's an idiot."

"Help!"

Pressure? You don't know the half of it. Your first scene is opposite Marlon Brando. You're expected to cry on cue and keep the tears flowing until Jack Nicholson enters to rescue you. Forget about asking Marlon to do a repetition exercise with you first. Just hit your marks. We're losing the light. Action!

Welcome to the world of film and TV. With few exceptions, an actor must show up on the first day of work prepared to give an opening night performance. Most productions do not allow for sufficient rehearsal time, but even when they do, there is a price to pay. A sitcom rehearses for a week right up to taping, but actors are frequently fired for not being *immediately* good enough in the part. In fact, a high percentage of actors are fired at the end of the *first day* of rehearsal.

In this world, many directors are more concerned with their shot list than your performance. After a season starring in Steven Bochco's *Murder One*, Anthony LaPaglia said:

> TV's a producer-writer medium, not an actor-director medium, and I didn't find that out until too late. When you're shooting a one-hour series and you're in every shot, it's a sixteen-hour day. Also, you're shooting eight or nine pages a day, and they just don't have time for you to question anything. They want to make their day, and it's nobody's fault, but you get to the point you don't even know where you are or what you're doing. I like a little more time to prepare as an actor.[1]

Theater, on the other hand, does provide rehearsal time. However, the "visionary" director will spend it rhapsodizing his vision and leave you fumbling in the dark when he says, "Okay, let's run it."

An actor *must* be totally self-sufficient. He cannot blame a bad performance on the circumstances or the director. The art of acting demands competence with the tools of the craft. Sad to say, from my experience teaching, coaching, and directing professional and aspiring actors, far too many actors don't know what these tools are, much less how to use them skillfully. These actors are the ones who are seldom hired and when they are, are frequently fired and replaced.

Why are there so many unskilled actors? If you can't draw or paint something, you don't call yourself an artist. If you can't play a tune on an instrument, you don't call yourself a musician. But if you can walk and talk, you can call yourself an actor. Who's going to say no? Especially if you have an 8x10.

These "actors" are usually trained by inadequate teachers. In situations where the teacher does have ability, the student subscribes blindly, giving far too much authority to the teacher.

When Lee Strasberg died, Stella Adler told her acting class to stand and observe a minute of silence, "for a man of the theater has died." At the end of the minute she told them to sit down and she continued, "It will take a hundred years before the harm that man has done to the art of acting can be corrected."[2] She was probably referring to his overemphasis on emotional recall and underemphasis on characterization, style, script interpretation, voice, and diction. While Adler's teaching properly reversed this emphasis, she shared responsibility with Strasberg and others for fostering two of the most destructive aspects of American actor training: (1) Learning through listening and watching instead of doing. Acting is the only performing art in America where students spend most of their class time sitting and watching others work. (2) The "guru" teacher who pontificates or rants while the students spend still more time sitting and listening.

The actor, like a dancer, is an artist whose instrument is his *body*. Have you ever taken a dance class? If you're an actor, I'll bet you have. Come with me if you will to Graceful Jay's Dance Emporium. Jay's class begins with a warm-up. Everyone must warm up—so that they can then sit down. Two chosen students, Joe and Lisa, are permitted to dance for seven minutes. Then they will be judged and commented on by Jay and the other students. The commentary will be based on the seven-minute performance and the commentators' individual agendas. Fran, who recently separated from her husband, Roger, after she gave him the ten best years of her life, says that Joe's work was awkward, selfish, and downright cruel. A man his age should not be behaving that way! After twenty-five minutes of these comments and five minutes calming Fran down, Jay regains control of the class. He comments enthusiastically on Lisa's performance, "Notice the way Lisa's muscular thighs flowed from combination to combination. She seemed unaffected by the flapping of her large breasts. Lisa was focused. And so was I!" Jay concludes, "Great class! Next week is the beginning of the month. Don't forget your checks. See ya. Oh, Lisa, can I see you for a minute?"

Would a dancer put up with a class like Jay's? Of course not. Dancers spend most of their class time actually dancing. Actors and dancers have the same artistic instrument, the body. Both pursue training and, even after they are working professionals, continue classes to expand their instruments. But, actors tolerate classes similar to Jay's all the time. Rather than *doing*, actors spend most of their class time sitting and watching others act.

To learn how to use your body well—in acting, painting, sculpting, singing, carpentry, skiing, etc.—you have to *do* it! Academy Award-winning actor Richard Dreyfuss's response to a question from a student about the difficulty of a career in show business was, "Act your brains out. The more you act, the better you get. It's not a secret. It's true."[3] Taking an acting class where you don't "act your brains out" in every class is cheating youself. You didn't learn to ride a bike by watching others ride or by listening to a lecture on the theory of bike riding. You were out there on a bike with someone running alongside and *coaching* you. Whenever you learn something by doing it, you've learned it for life. Do you think anybody ever forgets how to ride a bike? It's called *kinesthetic memory*. The synapses in the brain that control physical movement have been altered; they hold those patterns forever.

Improvisation Technique

Improvisation Technique is a technique of acting that is learned experientially and equips the actor to be self-sufficient in the practice of his art and career. The self-sufficiency can start when the training does. Small or large groups of actors can get together for the training, following the guidelines presented here, *without an acting teacher*. Instead, the training requires a coach. The coach may be an actor who is a member of the group or the role of coach may rotate among some or all of the group members. In time, a permanent coach may emerge from the group.

Every part of the training is broken down into introductions or *setups*, *coaching* guides, *follow-up* questions not requiring criticism, and *summaries* that the actors can read at home for further understanding of what they are learning experientially in the workshop.

Improvisation Technique allows the actor to employ the tools of his craft so skillfully that he is able to *improvise his acting while speaking scripted lines.* Each performance, each take is improvisational, which means that every performance or take is spontaneous. True improvisation is always spontaneous.

Of all the facets of the actor's craft, *spontaneity is the most important.* One actor may have great emotional range but little spontaneity in his performances; another may have great chameleon-like dexterity in the range of his character portrayals but no spontaneity; a third may be limited in both his emotional range and the range of his character portrayals but give spontaneous performances. The third actor is the one with potential for a career.

Beyond spontaneity, Improvisation Technique offers magic—the magic of accessing the unknown, of rendering the invisible, visible. We all know what we know. Then there are the things that we don't know. Most of the time, we don't know what we don't know. Just because we don't, should we be denied access to those goodies? Imagination—a shaking up of our existing frames of reference—can be a limited process. If I say to you, "Imagine a blue cow," you go to your frame of reference for animals and come up with a cow, and then you go to your frame of reference for colors and come up with blue, and then you instantly put them together in an act of imagination. This process is vital, healthy, and important. But, it's also limited to the extent of the original frames of reference. Through Improvisation Technique, we can bypass our limited frames of reference and go to areas beyond our imagination. When I said, "Imagine a blue cow," did you consider a depressed cow?

Tony Award-winning actor Frank Langella, after completing the movie *Dave*, with Ivan Reitman directing, said:

> On *Dave*, whenever Ivan would yell, "Cut," my whole take on it would be, "Okay, he's printing it. He likes it. Let's see what else I can do," [and] not, as it used to be when I was a younger actor, "How can I reproduce it?" What I did is in the camera. The lens got it. It's there forever. If Ivan wants take six, Ivan is going to print it up and put it in the movie. But maybe on take nine, I might do something wildly, wonderfully different and free that he never thought of and I never thought of.[4]

Without depending on the whims of the god of acting, how do you get to these areas of playing that you never think of? Skillfully, through Improvisation Technique.

Why do I call it Improvisation Technique instead of just improvisation? For too many actors, improvisation just means making it up as you go along, or *ad-libbing*. Not true. Improvisation Technique is a specific body of work for creating skilled improvisational acting. It has its own rules, procedures, and applications.

Traditional Improvisation

Traditional improvisation is also a useful tool, however it is limited by a dependence on the actor's brain and his imagination, a process that takes place in the brain. There is nothing like the brain for killing spontaneity.

In order to understand how Improvisation Technique differs from traditional improvisation, let's look at the common forms of traditional improvisation.

In the most widely used form, there is a *change of the given circumstances*. If a scripted scene is primarily a wedding proposal, and the given circumstances include the fact that the man is in love with the woman, the scene is designed by the author to play in a certain way. Suppose in rehearsal the actor playing the man is performing in a low-key, not very compelling fashion and the scene plays like melatonin. An improv on that scene could start with the actor playing the man *changing the fact* that he is in love with the woman to a different fact, that he wants her money. The author's lines remain the same but the tone of the performance changes. The meaning of the scene changes from love to greed. This is probably not the way you want the scene played in performance, but for a rehearsal it just might up the stakes for the actor and get him in touch with a new level of intensity that can energize his performance. It will also force his scene partner to be more alert and present as she adjusts to his new way of playing the scene. After the improv, the actors return to the original given circumstances and the man will have a new appreciation for playing the scene, from love again, not greed, with higher stakes, increased focus, and more energy.

In another form of traditional improvisation, *the actors make up their own lines* while exploring the structure of the scene, or their characters' motivations, or the meaning of the scene. They stay in character and go through the events of the scene, but they substitute their own dialogue for the author's. This type of improv forces the actors to listen to each other and stay in the moment. It helps them to break bad habits, such as (1) waiting for cues rather than really listening, (2) giving stilted line readings, and (3) making assumptions about what is going on or about the meaning of their lines. Because this type of improv can be done before the actors are off book, it also helps the actors memorize their lines.

When I was participating in the directors unit and observing in the actors unit at the Actors Studio in the early seventies, Lee Strasberg's favorite version of traditional improvisation was to give actors real and personal intention-oriented tasks to do while rehearsing. In Jean Anouilh's *The Rehearsal*, the character of the Count is directing a play and is trying to get into the pants of the character Lucile, who is an actress in his play. Strasberg would not announce, "We're going to do an improv now." Instead, during a break from a traditional scene rehearsal, he would tell the actor privately to come on to the actress, to *really* make a pass at her. In other words, when the rehearsal resumes, the actor playing the part of a director who is making a pass at his actress, Lucile, should *really* make a pass at the actress playing Lucile. The actress will then *really* have to deal with that. Thus, the actors would get in touch with a higher-stakes level of authenticity. The actor might find himself discovering all kinds of opportunities for embracing the actress, or he might try to direct the rehearsal himself and get her to unbutton her blouse. Obviously, this heightens the drama inherent in the scripted scene. Strasberg would wait for subsequent rehearsals to see if the actors retained the goodies found in the improv. If they didn't, he would give them notes reminding them what discoveries they made during the improv and that they needed to retain them even though they were no longer employing those *real and personal* tasks. Strasberg defined improvisation as "behaving logically and believably in a situation that somewhat parallels the situation in the text."[5] He felt the improv problem must be real in order to arouse the actor's conviction.

Strasberg got it partially right when he switched the actors from improvising off of *imagined* changes in the given circumstances and onto *real* physical doing. However, he stopped short when he attached the doing to a task that the actor wants to accomplish, i.e., to get the woman in bed. In this form of improv the actor will inevitably pause, often repeatedly, and go into his head, considering, "What else can I do to [accomplish the task]?" Once the actor is in his head, spontaneity, which is crucial to an effective and truthful improvisation, vanishes. Also, he is now open to all kinds of troublesome thoughts—fear, or judgment of self or others, and the like. When that happens, forget the improv! The actor is no longer present.

While Strasberg's use of traditional improvisation, as well as the other common forms I mentioned, can be beneficial and even produce exciting results, the overall approach is quite limited and specifically in the Strasberg process, unnecessarily manipulative and intrusive with the potential for disastrous effect on the actors and the rehearsal process.

Improvisation Technique is Different!

Ever since Stanislavsky's groundbreaking work on the technique of physical actions, it has been commonly understood that *acting is doing*. The doing is a character focus on the application of physical and/or psychological energy to a task, cf., intention, objective, problem, or action. Improvisation Technique puts the doing *in the body, not in the "problem solving" head*. If there are any changes in the given circumstances, they are attached to a *body doing* improvisation that has no future goal: no task to be completed, no objective to be attained. Body doing, *physical doing*, without a future goal *takes place in the present, in the moment*. The body doing is accomplished through a technical craft device called the *acting focus*, a specific form of total body doing in the present.

Since body doing improvisations result in the actor's being in the moment, he doesn't wind up in his head imagining circumstances, leaving himself open to troublesome thoughts. He never experiences those moments of concern, frustration, or anxiety about "What do I do, or say, next?" This is true whether the improvisation involves improvised or memorized text. In Improvisation Technique, the head plays a supporting role for the whole body. It does not have to provide solutions. It simply provides the desire and will power to stay focused on what has been chosen for the body to do.

A way of describing the difference between Improvisation Technique and traditional improvisation is, in Improvisation Technique the head *is never concerned with the how of the doing*, i.e., how to reach the goal. Instead, the head is focused on what the body is doing right *now*. Since the doing is never attached to reaching a goal, which is in the *future*, Improvisation Technique eliminates the time-lag for thinking that is the enemy of spontaneity.

Spolin Theater Games

The training aspect of Improvisation Technique is based on a body of work commonly known as theater games, created by Viola Spolin and published in her seminal book, *Improvisation for the Theater*,[6] known deservedly as the bible of improvisational theater. Despite the fact that *Improvisation for the Theater* has been one of the top-selling books of all time on any subject in the performing arts, many actors have never heard of her. Those who have, often misunderstand the true nature of her work. My own life's work as an acting teacher/coach and as a director has been massively influenced by my exposure to her, first as her student in 1965, and then as her assistant, representative, and later, her partner, when she invited me to co-design with her and implement the Spolin Theater Game Center in Hollywood and to serve as its principal teacher and executive director, which I did from 1976 to 1979.

A theater game is an acting exercise in the form of a game. The playing of the game produces improvisational and spontaneous acting. When the game is played in front of an audience, instead of in a workshop/class situation, the exercise aspect is removed and the playing is viewed as improvisational theater. In the USA, improvisational theater as we know it emerged out of Spolin's workshops in Chicago in 1955 for her son, Paul Sills, and his friends and cohorts who had been producing their own theater company, Playwrights Theatre Club. This group evolved into the Compass Players (1956–58) and then into the Second City. Every improvisational theater in America can trace its roots to the Second City; its influence on American comedy is incalculable.

For an understanding of Improvisation Technique, it is important to know that theater games were not originally devised as tools for creating improvisational theater. Spolin was drama supervisor of the WPA Recreational Project in Chicago (1939–41) and then ran a children's theater in Hollywood (1946–55). During these years, she made two big discoveries working with children. In Chicago, the inner-city children, all from recently immigrated families, brought to the sessions their own fears and their families' prejudices about other ethnic groups. Spolin found it hard to get them to play or work together until she noticed that all their fears and prejudices disappeared the moment she led them into a traditional children's game like tag or red rover. They played happily together! The implication had a profound influence on her. All human beings, children and adults, are absolutely spontaneous when they are playing a physical game. It was probably here that she began her understanding of the difference between being *in the head*, where fear and prejudice dwell, and being *in the space*, where playing occurs.

The second discovery Spolin made had to do with the children acting in plays under her direction. When there was an acting problem, traditional adult directing approaches were sometimes inefficient and unsuccessful. She found that if she created an acting or theater game that addressed the problem, the playing experience would influence the children's acting in the problem area. For instance, a boy and girl playing Hansel and Gretel might be so deficient in relating to each other as brother and sister that if their relationship weren't revealed in the text, the audience would never guess they were siblings. Instead of giving a note about this and expecting the kids to fix it, she would invent a game:

> Let's play a game. You two are brother and sister, in the woods, setting up a campsite, and these are the rules of the game. Whenever you speak to each other, one part of your body must be physically contacting any one part of the other's body. Every time you speak, you must change to a new contact, a different body part. If you don't make contact, you may not speak.

There might be some initial awkwardness or embarrassment, but quickly enough the kids would get into the game. They'd discover all kinds of ways to contact each other when they wanted to talk and they'd have *fun*, the heightened energy that accompanies the joy of discovery, while playing the game. Then she would have them return to the scenes they were rehearsing, and there would be an immediate change in their behavior toward each other. Their scenes were full of sibling behavior, with embraces, horseplay, teasing, etc. The contact game experience increased the involvement *between* them, in the space where it could be seen, not in the head where it's invisible to all watching.

An advantage of working this way is that the children were never told there was a problem, so there was no need to introduce approval/disapproval issues or fear of failure to the creative process. So many acting teachers/coaches ignore the fact that when you tell an actor what his problems are, he frequently gets in his own way, prolonging the problems as he obsesses on solving them. As Spolin discovered, theater games fix the problem without wasting time talking about it or making it worse. With adult actors, there may be some value in a brief evaluation of the difference in the scene, but even here, only *after* the problem has been solved.

Theater Games and Improvisation Technique

Part One of the book introduces the workshop, describes the training process, and tells how to use this book as a guide.

Part Two includes essential theater games presented *not* as problem-solving exercises but as exercises for learning the skill of how to improvise. Given a specific curriculum of new and old theater games and other exercises, the skill expands into a technique.

The fundamental principle of the how-to-improvise technique is *Acting is doing and there is always more to do.* The actor experientially learns what to be doing, *always,* that will keep him in the improvisational state and not in his head. The sequencing of the games and exercises is emphasized so that the overall technique is more readily learned, experientially and intellectually. In addition, while neither Spolin nor the other writers on theater games or improvisation focused on camera acting, I do so here. This total how-to-improvise technique becomes the first level of Improvisation Technique for script acting.

Part Three shows the actor how to apply the first level of Improvisation Technique to rehearsals for any scripted project.

Part Four uses improvisations for learning the professional skills of character, conflict, agreement, and auditioning. It also includes a new and more facile approach to playing emotions.

The old and new theater games and exercises include evolutions from our work at the Spolin Theater Game Center (1976–79) and from the undergraduate and graduate courses I taught at The Juilliard School (1973–80), the University of Southern California (1977–91), and in my ongoing professional workshops in Hollywood (since 1985).

The training in Part Two, Three, and Four is ultimately an effective and sophisticated training in the entire craft of acting. Sophisticated, because it moves efficiently through all the different technical aspects of the craft, including the basics of spontaneity, authenticity, character, and emotions, as well as more particular tools like physical doing, inner doing, vocal doing, subtext, conflict, agreement, emotion arcs, switches, intensity changes, and more. Learning an entire technique of acting should include a wide range of exercises, each one structured to provide training in different aspects of the craft. Improvisation Technique is effective because the training covers so many different aspects of the craft and the learning of it is all experiential. Regardless of the number of participants in a workshop, everyone works, plays, improvises, and acts (!) a number of times in every session. *The experiential aspect of the training guarantees the learning of Improvisation Technique.*

If you do the training aspect of Improvisation Technique as presented in Part Two, Three, and four, you will not only learn and sharpen all the tools of the professional actor, you will also become adept and confident as an improviser of considerable skill. Never again will you fear being asked to do an improv; instead, you will be enthusiastic because you'll know how to do it. Your acting will be infused with spontaneity, confidence, and presence.

What can Improvisation Technique do for you?

Did you hear the one about the middle-aged actor who had a terrible day? He had eight auditions and not one callback. That evening, his wife said to him,

"What's the matter, dear? You look so depressed." He responded, "It's terrible. I'm finding out that I'm too old for the parts I used to be too short for."

Many actors who are dissatisfied with the level of their careers are slow to face the truth about the one thing they *can* do something about—*limited artistic self-sufficiency.*

Limited artistic self-sufficiency shows itself primarily in the area of preparation. For the professional actor, preparation is essentially twofold: (1) character and (2) choices. If you are satisfied with the level of your work, and if your booking average is fine by you, then put this book down and be secure in the knowledge that you are the first person to be happy and content in show business. If not, *your choices aren't good enough.*

Working toward a more practical and effective approach, one that would improve an actor's ability to make effective, successful choices and take advantage of the breakthrough technique of theater games, I began creating another way of working in 1987.

"What's the purpose of the scene?" —*Robert DeNiro*[7]

Part Five of Improvisation Technique creates a new emphasis on playing the *Purpose of Scene.* It shows the actor a new way to break down a script: discerning the purpose of the scene, finding where the choices must be made, interpreting what those choices might be, and determining which improv acting focus tools will best serve those choices and the script.

Making choices is no longer limited to the one basic traditional acting doctrine of playing objectives. Purpose of scene is very effective for those actors not confident with that approach. Actors who are skillful with playing objectives are encouraged to continue doing so as the jumping-off point when they begin rehearsing the part. *Then Improvisation Technique should be added to the process.* After you explore the use of Improvisation Technique a few times in preparing your parts, you will discover a curious phenomenon: traditional acting, the pursuit of an objective, is frequently limited in *serving the scene,* especially without rehearsal time or an effective director. When you approach the scene from the point of view of what your character wants, you see the scene from your character's point of view. You miss seeing the whole scene from the point of view of the author, who constructed the scene.

When you use purpose of scene, you get in touch with what your part of the whole scene is. Then it's easy to improvise appropriately with your Improvisation Technique tools. Purpose of scene is a methodology for directing your own improvised performance regardless of nonexistent rehearsal time or a clueless director.

It is possible for the experienced actor who would like to supplement his own training with this new approach to breaking down a script to go directly to part 5. Be fore-

warned, however, that learning this new way of making choices will eventually require the selection of the appropriate acting focus choice. At that point, without an appreciation and understanding of how to improvise the different acting focuses, the payoff will be minimal. *If you do go directly to Part Five, review the appropriate chapters for each acting focus.*

But will you get work?

My students and clients have found Improvisation Technique to be highly successful in improving their booking averages. The feedback they get indicates that their auditions, prepared or cold, are much more intelligent performances than are those of their competition; they look like the author directed them. That's because every choice made was based on a breakdown and interpretation of what the author was doing with the scene. Another common feedback note they receive is that they give the most spontaneous auditions too. Well, that's not surprising, considering that they are actually improvising the entire audition—and, without missing a word of text.

It's not hard to see that they have all increased their success ratio after employing Improvisation Technique. In the current TV season, at the time of writing, thirteen of my current and former students are employed as series regulars on prime-time TV, three of them in title roles. Many also appear as guest stars and co-stars, and in films and theater.

While artistic self-sufficiency has always been an important part of an actor's technique, in today's acting business it is an absolute necessity. Improvisation Technique is designed and has been effectively proven to be a means to that end. All of the film and television scenes used as examples in this book are from actual scripts of films and television shows in which the actors created their performances using Improvisation Technique. How do I know? I was their coach.

Getting Started

THE WORKSHOP

ORGANIZATION

All that's needed to get started are actors willing to show up regularly and participate, a space for them to play in, and enough chairs for everybody plus a few extra for the improvisations.

LOCATION

The space should be private and big enough for everybody in the group to run around freely at the same time. Many traditional acting class spaces—tiny theaters, fixed seating, small platform-type stages—are not conducive to a productive Improvisation Technique workshop. The kind of room suitable for a dance class is much better. If the group is small enough, a large living room with the furniture moved to the walls will suffice.

PARTICIPANTS

While the ideal size of the group is between twelve and twenty, the workshop could be conducted with as few as three. With three, they take turns: two actors participate in the exercise or improv and the third actor coaches. The group may be larger than twenty—my groups begin with thirty-five—but with larger groups there are special considerations. The space must be large enough to accommodate everyone playing at the same time. The larger the group the more time you will need for an individual session to be effective. Keep in mind too that larger groups mean more responsibilities for the coach. On the plus side, when you start a larger group, you anticipate attrition. For instance, my groups last about two years in length, meeting once a week for four hours. If I start thirty-five actors in a group, over the two years I will lose about fifteen of them for one reason or another, but as we head into the home stretch of our time together I will still have a healthy group number.

It is a distinct emphasis of the training that the learning is experiential and sequential. Accordingly, I greatly discourage the addition of new members once a group gets rolling because it is too difficult for them to catch up experientially. It is possible to add actors if you arrange catch-up sessions for them, but clearly, the earlier in a group's progress they are added, the easier it is to accomplish this satisfactorily.

THE ROLE OF THE COACH

Almost every aspect of the training requires a coach to select the format for the training session or workshop, provide the setup for the exercises and improvs, coach the actors as they participate, and conduct the brief follow-up discussions. Specific notes and instructions for doing this are included with every exercise/improv in the training.

In a group that forms without a designated leader, the role of coach should rotate so that all take turns coaching and playing. In time, a permanent coach may emerge. If it's a very small group, an exercise should be repeated a few times for practice' sake, affording an opportunity for a different coach each time. If it's a larger group, there may not be time to repeat an exercise. Frequently, such a group will divide into smaller teams with each team playing the exercise once; then there can be a different coach for each team. With a large group, you might consider a permanent nucleus of rotating coaches, who also take turns playing. Where there is an official teacher, she coaches the regular meetings of the class, and then the students may divide into smaller practice groups for additional sessions in which they coach themselves using this book as a coaching guide. This expands the out-of-class practice experience from periodic scene rehearsals to an ongoing regular schedule. Also, students coaching themselves will increase their self-awareness as improvisers. Whatever the situation, it is always helpful if the coaches have experience playing the exercises they are coaching.

SCHEDULE

The group should commit to meeting on a regular schedule. Groups that meet on a casual, catch-as-catch-can schedule tend to fall apart. The duration of a single session, of course, depends on the individuals' availability. However, the efficacy of a session depends on a time/size ratio. One-hour sessions are seldom fulfilling unless the group is fewer than six. With more than six, the actors are just getting up to speed and it's time to stop.

Here are some guidelines for ideal minimum times for single sessions:

Twenty to thirty actors	3 1/2 to 4 hours
Fourteen to twenty actors	3 hours
Ten to fourteen actors	2 1/2 to 3 hours
Fewer than ten actors	2 hours

These are speculative minimums. Keep in mind that regardless of the size of the group, the longer the session, the more you accomplish and the more quickly you complete the training. Meeting two or three times a week is far better than meeting once a week. Not only do you reduce the overall span of time for the training, but also you benefit from the increased momentum.

CURRICULUM

SEQUENTIAL PRESENTATION

Improvisation Technique training is a sequential curriculum. The subjects of the curriculum are particular technical acting skills. Proficiency in these skills is achieved by means of the exercises and exercise-structured improvisations presented *sequentially*, with *the sequence itself designed to facilitate the learning.* The exercises and improvs are structured in a way that is consistently familiar, accessible, and increasingly challenging. Following the sequence presented here will give the actor increased proficiency in the technical acting skills and will train the actor in the art and skill of improvisational acting with or without memorized text. Changing the sequence may work in some situations. However, the material in chapters 2 and 3 should always be presented first, and the exercises in these and other chapters should be done in the order presented in the chapter.

WORKSHOP FORMATS

Selection of the agenda for individual workshops is easy if you follow this book's presentation order and suggested workshop formats. See Appendix E for a complete list of sequential workshop formats. The formats presented are for four-hour classes, which is the average length for a professional class, with twenty-five to thirty actors. A group of ten will go through the training much faster. Unless the group is very small, fewer than six or eight, don't repeat exercises; move forward. Only groups with a great deal of extra time should repeat

6

an exercise more often than suggested by the formats. Otherwise, even when some actors feel an exercise is very challenging and they'd like another chance at it, it is more important to move forward. The next exercise in the curriculum usually provides further practice with the preceding exercise while building on it at the same time. *Moving forward* is directly related to one of the main principles of Improvisation Technique: *Acting is doing and there is always more to do.*

EXPERIENTIAL CURRICULUM VS. SCENE STUDY

Traditional acting classes rely to a great extent on *reactive* teaching. Work is prepared outside of class, then presented in class. The class and the teacher critique the work, and then the teacher redirects the work in order to improve the acting in the scene. I question this approach to actor training because very few really learn anything.

Two actors present a scene and the teacher sees that the scene is lacking in, let's say, the *subtext work* required for this particular scene. The teacher *reacts* to what he sees and makes subtext the subject of his criticism. He takes this happenstance opportunity to address the subject of subtext in the class. The class is informed about subtext as a subject, but because they are only watching the work, *they are not learning subtext as a performing skill.* If this were a dance class, would you be learning how to do kicks by watching someone else learning and practicing them? Of course not.

Consider too that while the actors on the floor are being redirected to include subtext, and therefore are learning about subtext experientially, what they are learning is very specifically attached to the scene they are working on. They are not learning the skill of doing subtext in a fashion that is applicable to all scenes requiring subtext. The very next day one of them may have a scene to perform on a TV drama series that also requires subtext work. If it doesn't greatly resemble the scene they were working on in class, they are likely to miss the necessity for the subtext work in their script analysis or be deficient in their performance of it. How effective was the class for them in learning subtext? The best that can be said about reactive teaching is that the actor gets practice in being directed.

In the training for Improvisation Technique, all learn the skill—in this case, for example, *subtext*—experientially and all at the same time, through their participation in the exercises and improvisations. By learning the skill through a series of improvisations designed and structured to experientially teach that skill, the actor learns it in such a way that it is not specifically attached to the one scene prepared for class presentation. This increases the actor's understanding of that skill and its application to all scripted scenes requiring subtext. Also, whenever the actor is watching others work, he is seeing how they attack the same problem he has either just been on the floor attacking or will be when he goes up next. The rest of the group is always involved with the actors working on the floor. The exercises themselves, not the teacher or coach, facilitate the learning. This increases the actor's dependence on himself, which is the object, and diminishes his dependence on the teacher.

In a traditional reactive class, actor breakthroughs to better work are limited because they require the teacher's input, through direction or coaching. In Improvisation Technique training, real and unlimited breakthroughs occur because the actor leads himself to the breakthrough. The coach's job is to facilitate the actor's journey.

ONE WORKSHOP RULE

There is only one workshop rule: *Everyone plays.* This means no selective, I-think-I'll-sit-this-one-out participation. This also means no outside auditors ever! Of course, if you are teaching a college class and your department chair wants to sit in on a class, the class will survive; but the no-observer rule should not be broken casually.

Professional actors live with judgment and rejection every day that they pursue their careers. When they choose to develop their abilities in a class or workshop, they should feel free to work, explore, and take risks in an environment that is uniquely *free of judgment or disapproval*. An observer in a class corrupts this environment. Regardless of the good intentions or kindheartedness of the observer, judgment is inherent in the act of observing. Is this work good? Is this a class I want to join? Is the teacher any good? How do I stack up against the students? These may be the observer's issues, and they may be overt or subtle, but they totally affect the regular group members, creating pressure and inauthenticity in response to judgment. "Uh-oh, we'd better be good tonight because Teacher has a guest watching; I'll make the safe choice in this exercise because I don't want to look like a fool to that handsome/pretty/important observer." No one gains from observers being present except the observers themselves. The actors, who have made the commitment of time, intention, struggle, emotions, and money, gain nothing but contamination of their space. Whenever I advise actors on choosing a new teacher, I tell them, "Try to audit all the classes you are considering, but be wary of any teacher who allows you to do so."

EXERCISES & IMPROVISATIONS

The exercises and improvisations are presented in the book with the components described below. The actors should be encouraged to do the exercises and improvisations first and to read the descriptions afterward, outside of class.

THE SETUP

Follow the setup for any exercise/improv just as it's written or paraphrase it in your own style but *avoid embellishing* on it. Embellishment creates problems in two areas. First, too much information puts the player into his head before he even starts playing. Second, any emphasis on *how to play* the exercise must be avoided because it leads to the perception that there is a correct way to play or solve the problem. Players who believe there is a correct way of playing will make safe choices, before they even begin playing, which they feel will allow them to play correctly. They limit themselves to one solution to the exercise problem, the *correct* one, according to the coach, when there may be other solutions that the coach never anticipated. This is harmful to the training and fosters a continued dependence on the coach. Every aspect of Improvisation Technique training should reinforce the actor's relying on his own resources.

When the coach gives the instructions for a setup, the actors will often ask questions, seeking specificity or clarity. Some of these the coach should avoid answering, saying instead, "I don't know," or commenting that the actors are seeking more information than is necessary, or saying, "If I answer that question I'll be telling you how to play. How you do it awaits your discovery." I often respond with a shrug and a smile. The coach must emphasize, *It is more important that you play than that you play correctly!*

Some exercises/improvs require the entire group participating at the same time. Others require one participant at a time. Most require small groups participating as teams. The selection of who is on which team must be left completely to chance. The best way to do it is counting off. If there are twenty group members and the exercise requires, or the coach desires, four participants at a time, then the group counts off in fives. All the ones work together, all the twos work together, and so on.

THE RULES

The rules succinctly reduce the setup to the essential structure for every exercise/improvisation. There is implicit group agreement that all will play by the rules.

THE ACTING FOCUS

The acting focus specifies the primary rule and challenge for the individual in each exercise/improvisation. In the sequential curriculum the acting focuses become increasingly challenging and sophisticated. How to focus is included in the early training in chapter 2, "Essential Starters."

THE COACHING

When an exercise/improv begins, the coach stays immediately outside the playing area and gives full attention to the actors, calling out succinct phrases or short sentences as needed. These are intended to: (1) keep the actors on the specified acting focus of the exercise/improv; and/or (2) raise the energy of the playing; and/or (3) assist the actors in finding the area in which they will discover their own solution to an acting problem that is inhibiting them.

Suggested and **essential [in bold type] coachings** are given with the exercises.

Coaching is basically conducted as needed. When it *is* needed, it is best that there be a continuous flow of coaching. This reassures and frees the actor to stay on the acting focus and maintain the structure of the improvisation, and it allows the coach to join the improvisation, as a facilitator and *not* as a judge. Coaches will undoubtedly improvise new and unique coaching in response to particular situations. Remember that such extemporaneous coaching should never tell the actor how to solve a particular problem, but should instead lead them to the area in which they will find their own solution.

If an actor does not respond to the coaching, then coach, "Respond to the coaching!" If there is still no response, assume that the actor doesn't understand the coaching. Rephrase it or try a different coaching to get the desired response. Do not use the actors' names when coaching. Even when you are coaching a particular actor, don't use that actor's name; direct the coaching to the entire group. If it's applicable to a particular actor, only he will respond; the others will ignore it. In this way, authoritarianism and its ill effects are eroded and the actors go further in their pursuit of self-dependence. Actors *responding to the coaching* should hear what has been coached and go with it without breaking stride. An actor should never stop playing or improvising in order to look to the coach for assistance or clarification of the coaching phrase. If an actor doesn't understand the coaching, he should ignore it. Baseball is a useful metaphor. During a play the player hears and heeds the coach's instructions. He doesn't stop running to seek clarification of the coaching, "Are you sure I need to slide into third base?" No hesitation; he slides.

If the coaching is not successful, try different coaching. Don't let an improvisation drag on if the actor is not committed to the acting focus.

The coach's primary responsibility is to run the sessions like a gym. The coach coaches and the actors work out. Session formats are designated ahead of time so you won't keep the group waiting while you figure out what to do next. It's the coach's job to keep the energy high. If a designated format doesn't do this, don't be a slave to it. Change the agenda in midstream. Depending on the length of your sessions and the intensity levels of the various exercises and improvs, *occasional short breaks* are appropriate.

Once a session begins, the coach's responsibilities are in five areas: (1) setting up an exercise/improv; (2) coaching the playing; (3) leading a brief follow-up discussion after individuals play; (4) leading a final follow-up discussion or summary after the entire group has participated; and (5) group integrity.

My comments and suggestions as to what the coach says in each of the above areas are presented with each exercise/improv.

THE FOLLOW-UP

When an exercise/improv ends, the participants' experience is not complete until there is a brief verbal follow-up acknowledgment of their playing. In a traditional acting class this process is called the critique. Critiques are infused with judgment and authoritarianism in both content and tone. The critic's words often carry a sense of frustration (anger) or patronization (disrespect) or admiration (love). If the criticism communicates anger or disrespect, the actor's body tenses up in an armoring posture. The actor becomes a closed system and is unable to benefit from the teacher's expertise (!). If the criticism communicates love, the actor feels relaxed and happy, and there's nothing wrong with that. However, with a critical teacher the class sees that sometimes they will be loved and sometimes, punched. The actors quickly ask themselves, "What do I have to do to get the love and not the punch?" That is the end of productive learning in the class. The actors enter an approval/disapproval relationship with the teacher and the only thing really learned is the dynamic of bribery. In the Improvisation Technique training, one of the coach's responsibilities is to make sure that critiques are avoided. No one is permitted to give an opinion or judgment of anyone's work, including the coach!

Verbal follow-up completes the experience and provides the participants with opportunities for increased self-awareness. Follow-up questions are provided with each exercise or improv. They are intended to be applied as needed. However, when following up the first team or actor to do the exercise or improv, I recommend asking every question listed in the follow-up sections. Actors who have not yet done the exercise will profit from hearing what is important or integral to what they are about to do. For the sake of time, with subsequent individuals or teams ask only the necessary or pertinent follow-up questions. To assist the coach, I have **indicated in bold type those questions that I feel are essential** for all the participants after every exercise or improv. Keep in mind, however, that playing time is more important than follow-up time. Any follow-up can be reduced to one or two questions, e.g., Were they/you on the acting focus?

If the coach sees a place for improvement or insight, he must not tell it to the participants. He should just ask the questions that, if answered truthfully, will allow the participant to arrive at the insight himself.

If no insight is necessary, then a simple question or two pertaining to the acting focus will suffice for acknowledgment and completion.

Coach	Joe, did you stay on the acting focus throughout the improv?
Joe	Yes.
Coach	Class, do you agree?
Class	Yes.
Coach	Next.

Here is an example of the questions and answers that would be appropriate where insight is necessary. Let's say the participants are doing an improv where the acting focus is on conflict. In the sequential, building-block exercises the actors have learned the dynamics of conflict through traditional rope-pulling tug-of-war games. Next, they learn how to substitute a conflict issue for the rope and how to apply the tug-of-war dynamics while they improvise a scene. The acting focus for the improv is to play a tug-of-war game with the conflict issue. When the improv is over:

Coach	Joe, did you stay on the acting focus?
Joe	Yes.
Coach	Class, do you agree?
Class	No.
Coach	Joe, what was the acting focus?
Joe	Pull the conflict.
Coach	Which means?
Joe	You always focus on pulling the rope [rope-as-conflict].
Coach	Did you do that?
Joe	Yes, I did, definitely. I was always pulling the rope, except when Lisa dropped the glass of milk and she started to cry. I was always pulling the rope!
Coach	Joe, are you sure you were *always* on the acting focus?

Joe I was, coach. Every moment, I was focused on pulling the rope, except when she was cry— I was . . . except . . . she was crying . . . No! I didn't pull the rope during the beat when she cried. I dropped the rope then. I wasn't always on the acting focus.

Coach Class, do you agree?

Class Yes.

Coach Thanks, Joe. Next.

The coach knew that Joe had dropped the rope, but instead of telling him (critique), the coach led Joe to the insight so that the insight would be Joe's and not the coach's. However simple or profound the insight may be, it is better taken and more meaningful if it comes from the actor himself.

This approach also assists the actor to trust his own resources and be less dependent on the teacher. Eventually the actor learns how to conduct his own nonjudgmental follow-up. How many times after an unsuccessful audition has an actor wasted an opportunity for learning? Which is more productive, to leave an audition saying to yourself, "Boy, did I louse that up," or to lead yourself through questions and answers to an insight which shows you where you went off? The coach should continuously remind the actors that the only time they "fail" at something is when they don't learn from it. Coaches should remember —and this is especially important for actor groups who are coaching themselves— that they are not expected to be insightful about each other's work. When you lead a question-and-answer follow-up, you don't have to know where the insight is. It's sufficient to know that something didn't feel right and then go through the provided questions and see where this leads you.

During a follow-up, the coach must monitor the group's responses to prevent anyone's crossing the line into critique. The moment a group member who is answering the coach's follow-up question begins to critique a participant, the coach stops the person with this reminder: "Answer the question I asked, not the question you think I asked." The coach then repeats the original question. After a few sessions, everyone learns the appropriate vocabulary for a follow-up.

In traditional classes employing critique, when the actor leaves the floor and returns to his seat, he has an opportunity to think about what has just happened. This period of reflection, which I call the post critique, can last any length of time. I've known actors who, six months after a critique, are *still thinking* about what happened in the class, or, if the critique was harsh, still *stewing* over it. After a harsh critique, most actors fall into one of two post-critique reaction patterns. In one, the actor returns to his seat thinking, "He's right. I'm no good. I'm a terrible actor. I should have listened to my mom and gone to dental school." In the other, the actor returns to his seat thinking,

"Screw him! Who does he think he is? I'm out of this class!" Is anybody learning anything? All that's going on is that their egos have been attacked and they are responding in their individual defensive styles. And they are paying money for this!

After the Improvisation Technique question-and-answer follow-up described earlier, Joe returns to his seat thinking, "Of course. I totally dropped the rope when I saw her cry. I got it!" His response is positive, appropriate, and productive. His ego hasn't been attacked, he's still open to learning, and while he may be a little disappointed that he dropped the rope, he is excited by the clarity of the insight and enthusiastic about trying it again. When Joe employs that particular acting focus again, either in class or career, he is not likely to drop the rope.

THE SUMMARY

After everyone in the group has participated in a round of a particular exercise or improv, a final follow-up or summary may be appropriate. This should be brief and to the point. If no point need be made, move on to the next exercise. Coaches must stay on focus to keep group discussions from becoming information sessions, which dampen energy, put everyone into the head, and take away from participation time where true experiential learning occurs. For every exercise and improvisation, I have provided summaries for the coach's consideration. In those classes at my studio that are taught by my assistant, she sometimes reads these summaries verbatim. Other times she simply uses them as a guide for what might be pertinent to her class. If the coach feels that my lengthier summaries are important, he can assign them for reviewing at home at the actors' leisure after the group has done the experiential work in class.

"TO THE COACH"

With most of the exercises and improvisations there is a section called *"To the coach."* This section is not intended for class discussion. It is only for the coach's edification and finesse in presenting and coaching, e.g., a suggested running time for that improv.

OTHER COMPONENTS

Occasionally, an exercise or improvisation may also have *Class Questions, Demonstrations, Selected Student Responses,* and/or special *Preparations.*

ENVIRONMENT

The environment is the responsibility of the entire group, coaches and players. I'm talking not about the physical plant, but about ambience and integrity. If you follow the procedures outlined above, you will find that the group goes about its work in a fun atmosphere. In too many traditional classes, cliques form. By maintaining the integrity of the original group and not adding new members once the group is underway, by insisting that everyone participate in all the exercises, and by having follow-ups instead of critiques, you quickly dispel the conditions that give rise to cliques and the feelings of exclusion that these create. Without critiques another undesirable characteristic of some traditional classes— i.e., the unequal relationship between the teacher/coach and different students/ actors—is eliminated as well: no more teacher's "pets" and "patsies."

Authenticity is crucial to group integrity. Lying—lies of commission and omission, conscious or unconscious—is not allowed. Dealing with this is a delicate issue. The follow-up is a helpful device for establishing the desired level of authenticity. If the coach has an uneasy feeling that he has been told a lie by a participant during a follow-up, rather than saying so, he should ask further questions, becoming increasingly specific until the participant's answers lead the participant to a more accurate response. At that time the coach may ask, "So, your earlier statement when you said [...] wasn't accurate or true?" After the participant acknowledges this to be so, the coach might address the entire group and remind them of the importance of being honest.

The more personally inauthentic an actor is, the more inauthentic his acting will be. Inauthenticity in acting calls attention to itself. It reminds an audience that the actor is aware of them and is giving a performance for them. Hence, the audience doesn't trust, believe, or learn anything about or from the characters.

If the follow-up doesn't lead to an answer that resolves the coach's uneasy feeling, then the coach should assume that there is no payoff here and move on. The uneasy feeling you experienced may be your problem and not the participant's. Keep an eye on that player and see if the feeling comes up again in subsequent follow-ups. If it does, it will eventually have to be addressed.

A common lie is not taking responsibility. In a follow-up, the questions and responses might be—

Coach	Were you on your acting focus?
Joe	I was, but when she spilled the milk and cried, I had to take care of her and that pulled me off focus.
Coach	So, it was her fault?
Joe	Well, no... I didn't say that.

Coach	Were you on your acting focus?
Joe	I . . . I . . . No.
Coach	Class, do you agree?

—and so on.

Other areas where inauthenticity can pollute a workshop include group discussions and conversations between an individual actor and the coach. Actors, like everyone else, often create personal dramas. These are a great breeding ground for inauthenticity. It is a wise coach who recognizes manipulation, avoidance, exaggeration, and false humility, all common acting-class behaviors, and avoids being drawn into the drama while assisting the actor to see things as they are and not as the actor thinks they are. The coach, while remaining supportive, should create a boundary which keeps him from being coddling, codependent, or manipulated.

THE JOURNAL

Finally, we come to a great and inexpensive tool that all the actors and coaches doing the Improvisation Technique training should be encouraged to employ, the *journal*. Keeping a personal journal increases self-awareness. The actor sees more clearly what is real and honest as opposed to what is imagined, inauthentic, or false about himself and his limitations. The journal assists actors and coaches to keep breaking through their own self-imposed limitations.

I encourage the actors in my groups to make journal entries after every session. They may write about their observations, discoveries, or conclusions related to the day's work. Specifically, they can write: (1) their reactions and resistances to the exercises/improvs; (2) discoveries about themselves; (3) observations of the work of others in the class; (4) discoveries about characters they play in improvs or in productions they are rehearsing or preparing; (5) reactions and observations made by the coach and other group members to their own playing. They may also *draw or sketch*. This might be an image for that day's work or for their feelings about the work or themselves.

The actor may make the journal entries an ongoing index of all the exercises/improvs worked on in class, i.e., the beginning of his own textbook of the training. Participants should be encouraged not to take notes during the sessions, which are best kept as a time for experience, in the body, and not information, in the head. The sessions are designed to access the child aspect of the actor, the purely uninhibited player. Once playing is achieved, it is a shame for the actor to lose this access, which is what happens when players stop playing to take notes. When the actor writes in his journal at home, he is already in a nonplaying experience and there is no loss of the playing aspect.

16

For those actors experiencing inauthenticity, there is a most effective journal tool. After completing a journal entry, the actor continues to write, starting with the question, "Where is the lie in what I just wrote?" This requires reading the journal entry with the express purpose of spotting any lies the actor may inadvertently have told himself in the writing. If any lies are found, and they will be, the actor has an opportunity to correct them, and then, to write about the lies. Frequent use of this tool greatly increases an actor's self-awareness and authenticity.

How to Improvise—
Basic Technique
of Improvisation

2

ESSENTIAL STARTERS

TRADITIONAL CHILDREN'S GAMES

Actors arrive at their workshop burdened with the day's stresses. A quick way to get everyone out of their heads and into their bodies is to start every session with a traditional children's game, an assortment of which is included in Appendix F.

The rules of the game place the player in a physical *crisis*, e.g., avoid being tagged or you're *it*! And if you're *it*, tag someone else! In response to physical crisis, people go quickly, deeply inside themselves, tapping reserves of energy to meet and resolve the crisis. It is from this pool of reserve energy that actors should be working.

Traditional children's games access this energy without the danger of real-life crises. All of the players accept and play by the same game rules in the same safe environment and in the same time, the present. Once playing begins, it is physically impossible not to be in the present. Outside distractions disappear, the energy rises for all, and all have fun.

ESSENTIAL STARTERS

In the first three classes, the opening game is followed by two or more *essential starters*. There are nine of these: *Making Changes, 40-Breath Process, First Focus Walk, Objects in the Space, Second Focus Walk, Space Ball/Motion, Third Focus Walk, Space Ball/Weight,* and *Unfocused/Focused.* They should be done in the first part of each of these three classes, followed by games and exercises from the physical doing chapter.

THE FIRST CLASS

The coach begins with a welcome greeting and then immediately asks if anyone is nervous. Regardless of the number of hands raised, *he responds*— So am I. So let's just start and see what happens.

TAG

The opening game is the traditional children's game, *tag*.

SETUP: The group counts off in twos. The coach selects either team to play first; the other team observes. Have the first playing team come out to the playing area and tell them the rules of the game.

RULES: Whoever is *it* must tag (touch) another player who then becomes *it*. Players who are not *it* avoid being tagged. No player may leave the playing area.

COACHING: After telling the players these rules, the coach immediately *calls out*— Not it! ◆ The players will follow suit. The last player to call out, "Not it," is the first one to be *it*. ◆ The coach *tells that player*— You're it. Go! ◆ While the players are running around playing, the coach walks among the observing team and *coaches them*— Watch the players' faces. ◆ After a few minutes of playing, the coach has the teams switch. He initiates the selection of the new playing team's *it* and commences the playing. To the new observing team, *he coaches*— Watch the players' faces. ◆ After a few minutes of playing, the coach ends the game and the players return to their seats.

FOLLOW-UP: What did you observe about the players' faces? ◆ The coach may acknowledge each answer by simply repeating it and avoid discussing the answer further. However, the first time a respondent answers the question and gives a reason for his answer, e.g., "All the players were having fun because they were like children again," *the coach immediately points out*— Whether or not that is true, it is an assumption that they were all having fun and a second assumption that it was because they were childlike. In our first session we should start paying attention to what is asked of us and not what we think is asked of us. The question was, *What did you observe about the players' faces?* The question was not, *What did the players' faces indicate and why?*

At this point, if the answer has not yet been provided, a respondent will answer, "All the players were smiling." *The coach may then respond*— Yes, we all saw the players begin to smile when the game began. That is factual and calls for no assumptions on our part.

How many of you were nervous or anxious while sitting there waiting for our first session to begin? Once we began, it was only a matter of minutes before you were playing *tag*. What did you notice about your nervous and anxious feelings? ✦ The group will respond that those feelings disappeared. *The coach concludes—* So, while you were focused on either tagging someone or avoiding being tagged, the negative feelings and thoughts disappeared. By the way, how did you feel while you were playing? ✦ The group will respond, "It was fun." *Coach—* Let's move on.

> **TO THE COACH:** The first class should provide the group with the continuous experience of playing and begin forming the individuals into a true group through the experience of playing together according to the same rules.

MAKING CHANGES[1]

The first essential starter, *Making Changes*, is presented only once in the curriculum, in the first class. The summary after the game draws upon the actors' experiences to introduce the entire training in Improvisation Technique.

> **SETUP:** The teams remain the same as for tag. All the ones come onto the floor and form a straight line. All the twos do the same, about five feet away from the ones. Both teams face each other. The person across from you is your partner. ✦ If there is an odd number, the coach gets on the shorter line and becomes a player/coach.

> **COACHING:** Introduce yourself to your partner. ✦ Now step back into your line and observe your partner. Look at how they are dressed. Look at the accessories: jewelry, hairpins, watches, etc. Notice whatever there is to notice. ✦ *After a minute—* Now, turn around. Make three distinct changes in your own appearance. They may be subtle or overt, but they must be visible. If we took a picture of you before and after you made the changes, we would see three changes in your appearance.
>
> While the players have their backs to their partners and are making the changes, *the coach continues—* When it feels like we have finished this game, do not change back to your original appearance. Everybody ready? Turn around and face your partner. Look them over and communicate to them what changes they made.
>
> Without leaving their lines the players interact with each other, pointing out and telling each other what changes the other made. When all are finished, coach one player at the end of either line to come down to the front of his line and all the others on that team to move down one spot, thereby creating new partners for everyone.

The coach continues— Introduce yourself to your new partner. ◆ Now step back into line and look them over. You now know what the game is about, so profit from that and look them over very carefully. ◆ *After a minute*— Turn around and make four brand new changes. These are in addition to the first three you've already made. They may be subtle or overt, but they must be visible. If we took another picture and compared it to the first, we would see seven changes. When you think the game is over, do not change back. ◆ Ready? Turn around. Face your partner. Look them over and communicate to them what changes they made.

Again without leaving their lines, the players interact as previously. Keep repeating this process, changing partners and adding one more change each time, until they are with their fifth partner and the coach is having them make seven new changes.

During the periods of actually making the changes, the players will comment to themselves, their line neighbors, and to the coach how difficult it is to come up with new changes. The players will ask the coach questions about the stringency of the rules, e.g., "Is the reversal of an original change considered a new change?" ◆ *Answer their questions with the following coaching*— Play the game! You know all you need to know. Make the new changes. Avoid cheating; it's not about getting away with anything. As long as you stay with the rules, anything goes! You may need to take a risk.

After the players have finished playing the last round of changes, instead of arranging for new partners, *coach*— Everybody back up into a large circle. Look around at your fellow players and observe whatever there is to observe. Observe yourself and take notice of how much or how little you have changed your appearance from when you started. Take notice of how much or how little your fellow players have changed. ◆ *After a minute*— Now is the opportunity to change back if you wish to do so.

FOLLOW-UP: Making changes is the beginning of Improvisation Technique training. Aside from it being fun to play and meeting some of your fellow group members, what relevance do you think it has to improvisation and acting?

The group discussion will provide the following answers: concentration; memory; awareness of how much we take for granted; importance of specificity and attention to details; consideration of choices; utilizing your resources in the service of creativity; really seeing each other and working together in our first class; learn a few names; have the experience of improvising new choices; anything goes within the rules; lessening our inhibitions, taking risks, and exploring our willingness to look silly or observe how we resist that. Among the reasons provided by the group, the most important is that *the nature of the game relies on the experience of improvising new choices when you think there is nothing more to do.*

SUMMARY:

When the group has finished providing their answers, the coach should introduce the entire training in Improvisation Technique by providing three additional reasons for beginning with making changes.

VOCABULARY

Our choice of vocabulary can further enhance what we're doing and provide additional learning opportunities. For example, every one of you could lead a group of friends in the playing of this game. Listen carefully to my version of the setup and coaching that you would probably provide, and see if you can spot a change in the vocabulary from what I originally said. Here is what you would probably do and say. You'd get everybody into two teams, line them up, and then you'd have them look each other over. You would tell them, "Look at where things are buttoned, where there's jewelry, where sleeves or cuffs are rolled up or down. Take a mental picture of your partner." After a while, you'd have them turn around and you'd say, "Make three changes in your appearance. Three changes. They may be subtle, they may be overt, but they must be technically visible. If you were to take a picture before the changes and then after the changes, you'd see three changes." Then, after you gave them time to do that, you'd have them turn around, face their partner, and have them guess what changes their partner made. Given that you would do, more or less, what I just said you would do, what in the vocabulary that I just used was very specifically, and in an important moment, different?

After the group's attempt at pointing out differences, if no one gets it, the coach should provide the answer.

In restating the setup and rules, I used the phrase, *Guess what changes your partner made.* However, I never used the word *guess* throughout the entire playing of the original game. What word did I use? Did anyone notice? I repeated it every round of the game. What I said was, *Communicate to your partner what changes they made.*

Why is this important? Where does guessing take place? In the head. It is an in-your-head, all-by-yourself process. Where does communicating take place? Between people, in the space between people. Communication travels through that space, from sender to receiver. When actors, acting, communicate to each other, they communicate *through the space* to each other, as well as through the space to the audience or the camera. Communication is an outside-of-your-head, in-the-space, sender-receiver process.

We are not wired together. I can't just think or say something and have it come up automatically inside of you. It has to travel through the space to get to you.

24

Simply using the word *communicate* begins taking you out of your head and into the space, which is open and available for all to see. What is in the head is hidden from the audience and from your fellow actors. What is in the space is not only visible, it is impossible to ignore. It is *there to be seen*. It is what the audience has bought their ticket to see.

When you use the word *communicate* rather than *guess*, your body actually increases its involvement in the act of communication instead of hanging out, the way it does when you are guessing and your mind alone is activated. Guessing has minimal value for an actor. Communication is essential.

The training takes responsibility for your success during the workshop sessions. In order to learn Improvisation Technique, all you have to do is show up and participate. You can maximize your learning, however, by paying attention to vocabulary. Over the course of the training, with the continuous use of carefully chosen words, there will be an impact on your work. You'll see the snowball effect that carries over into the work, into the process, into any changes that you will be going through as a result of doing this training. This will occur as you hear the vocabulary in setups, coaching, and follow-ups, and as you begin using it in the follow-ups and discussions. As Humpty Dumpty said, *When I use a word, it means precisely what I wish it to mean, neither more nor less.*

EXTENSION

How many of you, at some point during the game, entertained the thought, "There are not six more things I can change!" And did you then, in fact, find the six more things to change? Of course. That experience is why we play the game. Notice how quick our minds are to tell us what we can and cannot do. If your mind tells you, in the most innocent, safe, and innocuous game situation, that you cannot find six more changes, imagine how quickly it will tell you what you can't do when the stakes are higher. Why does your mind tell you that you can't come up with six more things, when you can?

During the group discussion someone will say, "Because we are afraid of failing." ◆ *The coach can expand on that*— When you were growing up, somewhere along the line you learned that it doesn't feel good to fail. We all have our own variations on that, depending on our own particular environments or families. Your mind has trained itself to be a watchdog, the protector of your being.

For example, your mind reads the signs it *thinks* it sees when you start dating someone to see if you are getting anywhere. Your mind provides your manipulative behavior when you go on an interview and *think* you know what they want to hear. Your mind provides your *rationalizations* when you hurt someone.

Your mind has trained itself to protect you from pain—in this case, the pain of failure, i.e., "No way! There are definitely not six more things I can change. If you insist on it, I'm going to fail and I don't want to fail because that makes me feel bad."

A very big problem with this safety-patrol feature is, it is a rote reaction with self-inhibiting limitations. The mind makes little or no distinction between telling you that you cannot jump off a cliff and telling you that you cannot come up with six more things to change. Your mind is geared to protect you from pain, but it will often err on the side of protection and so, keep you from discovering what you are capable of doing. Mark Twain observed that, *Once a cat sits on a hot stove, it will never do it again; however, it will also never sit on a cold stove.* The cat's mind keeps it from the stove, hot or cold. There may be a lot of goodies on the cold stove. Because this was only a game, you chose to continue playing after your minds said there were no more changes you could make and you discovered changes. Your mind was wrong. It will be wrong again.

Improvisation Technique training is a whole body training. Doing the training realigns the body-mind relationship. Right now, your mind is the boss running your body's whole show. Over the course of the training, your mind will become just another part of your whole body, *not* the boss. This is necessary for a free, unified instrument. You will find that you are capable of doing much more than you are presently aware of.

As we begin our work together, your mind will often tell you, "You can't do that. Don't do that!" It will tell it to you in many different variations, anything to keep you from going somewhere new or unknown. That's what the mind is afraid of. It could be dangerous. There might be a boogeyman there. I alert you to this so that you will observe your mind and begin to recognize when it is trying to put a wall between you and the unknown. Look for its latest variation on "There are not six more changes I can make," see it for what it is, and say, "Thank you, mind, for your comments. I choose to play anyway." An effective improviser goes beyond what he thinks he is capable of.

ACTING FOCUS

You will be provided with an *acting focus* for every exercise and improvisation. When you let your mind sabotage it, you deprive yourself of the experience the acting focus is designed to provide.

Let's return to your experience at the very beginning of the making changes game, before you knew the rules or what the game entailed. Here is a question not meant to be answered out loud; answer it for yourself. When you faced your first partner on the opposite line and I coached you to look them over, how many of you editorialized to yourself, i.e., "Oh, this person is angry" or "This person is a loser" or "He's a hunk." Editorializing is not healthy. Whether your assessment is negative or positive is not the point. The point is, you don't even know them and you are judging them, objectifying them due to your own prejudices. Notice that most of you did that in one form or another.

With subsequent partners, however, you did not do that at all. The editorializing disappeared. Why? With your first partner, you were not focused while looking at them because there were no game rules yet. After you played one round, you understood the game. From then on, when you were looking them over you were focused— "That sleeve is only rolled up three-quarters; there is an earring; he has a pen sticking out of his pocket." The editorializing disappears because it is replaced with *something to do*.

The premise of Improvisation Technique is *Acting is doing and there is always more to do*. The training includes all the things that there are to do. In the doing, in the focusing on what you are doing, the mind stops fragmenting and distorting your potential. Every exercise or improvisation that we do will have a designated acting focus and rules. You should never begin an exercise or improv without knowing what these are.

The acting focus and the rules keep you playing, which is the state you want to be in when you are acting. Playing frees you from the fear, prejudices, inauthenticity, and old frames of reference that keep you earthbound. Playing is your access to the magic zone, the unknown. You're too involved with your body doing and with the acting focus for your mind to hold you back with thoughts like "I don't normally do this" or "I don't want to play with him." Playing keeps you in a state of becoming. You never know what's going to happen next. Playing creates spontaneity.

> **TO THE COACH:** This lengthy summary in the first class is actually the introduction to the entire training. It introduces important themes in support of the training, as well as the key principles of vocabulary, acting focus, rules, and coaching. It also provides the first experience of safe group discussions free of criticism. The coach should guide the discussions, keeping them free of any criticism, either of self or others. It is best if the actors have not read the description and summary of the game prior to starting.

40-BREATH PROCESS

This next essential starter is the first of two excercises designed to give you the experience of what it means to focus

> **COACHING:** Stand still and we are going to do forty *big* and *quick* breaths. Pause after each set of ten. Inhale through the mouth into the middle of the chest, and exhale, with an emphasis on the inhale. Keep your eyes open. Stay here. After the forty, look around the room and make eye contact with everyone.

FIRST FOCUS WALK [2]

Go right into the third essential starter, the *First Focus Walk*.

SETUP: Everyone walks around the playing area responding to the coaching.

COACHING: The coaching will guide you where to place your focus while you walk. Your participation is nonverbal; simply respond to the coaching. If you do not understand something, let it go by. It will be clarified through subsequent coaching. Do not spend any time attempting to figure out any coaching that you don't understand. Make no attempts to communicate to the coach that you don't understand. Just keep playing. ◆ Walk around. Let's explore what it means to focus. Unless coached otherwise, everyone plays individually with no connection to the other actors. Just put your focus on what you are coached to do. ◆ —*Allow 2–5 seconds between coaching sentences.* ◆ As you walk around, focus on feeling the floor with your feet. Feel the floor with your feet as you walk normally with no exaggerated steps. ◆ Now change the focus and allow the floor to feel your feet. It's a new focus. Let the floor feel your feet. Keep walking normally with no exaggeration or sliding your feet. ◆ Go back to the first focus, feel the floor with your feet. ◆ Change the focus again and allow the floor to feel your feet. ◆ Here's a brand new focus, feel the floor with your feet and let the floor feel your feet at the same time. ◆ *Focusing means full body attention and the exclusion of any distractions.* Observe whether your head is talking to you and providing distractions. ◆ We talked earlier about communication traveling through the space between the actors and each other, the camera, and the audience. Put your focus on that space in front of you. While you are walking around the room in a normal fashion, focus on feeling the space through which you are walking. There is no right or wrong response, just focus on allowing your body to feel the space rather than taking it for granted. Feel the space against your whole body. ◆ Stay alert. There may be some mind comments coming in. Notice them, dismiss them by saying to yourself, "Thank you, I'm going to focus and see what happens." ◆ Feel the space against your body. Feel it with your forehead. With the tip of your nose. With your chest. Feel the space underneath your feet as you step and squash it out. Allow your arms to swing freely in the space and feel that space in which your arms are swinging freely, just the normal arm swing that accompanies walking. ◆ Everyone stand still. Take one hand and put it, palm to face, one inch from your face. One inch, not four inches, and not touching. Slowly move that hand over the entire surface area of your face, keeping your eyes open, and focus on feeling the intimate space between your face and your hand. Keep your eyes open. We never close our eyes in this workshop. Focus on the intimate space between your hand and your face as you slowly move your hand over that whole area. Go around by your ears, by your forehead. Focus on the feeling of the intimate space between your face and your hand. Now, continue doing that, and spread your fingers apart and gently wiggle them individually, and increase the feeling of the intimate space between your fingers as well as between your fingers and your face. Keep moving your hand all over your face. There is space there and you can feel it. It is so close to your face that it has an intimate quality to it. Focus on feeling that. Now, stop wiggling your fingers. ◆ When I give you the cue, move your hand slowly away from your face until your arm reaches its fullest extension away from your body. When you do that, feel your hand move through the space and focus on feeling the intimate space become the bulk space of the room. ◆ Do it now.

Slowly move your hand out from your body and focus on feeling the intimate space become the bulk space of the room. When your arm reaches its fullest extension, allow your body to walk, following it out into the space. Feel the space with your whole body. Increase your awareness of what it means to feel the space of the room with your body. You may lower your arm. You are free to move your arms in any way you wish. You are free to move them abstractly or to heighten the swing, but everything you do must be done while you focus on feeling the space of the room through which you are walking with your body. You are feeling the space with your chest; with your stomach; with your thighs; your knees; your feet, as you step down and squash it out. You are feeling the space between your arms and your body. ◆ You can back up into the space and feel it with the small of your back; you can feel it with the broad part of your back. Feel it with the backs of your thighs. You can move in any direction you wish, but whatever you do, you are focused on feeling the space with your body. Don't let your mind take you off of that. If you get off the focus, choose to get back on. We are exercising our focus abilities. ◆ Slightly pick up the pace of your walk, just slightly, and focus on your body moving through the space of the room. Feel that. Keep walking and change the focus right now and feel the space moving through you! Focus on feeling the space moving through you. This is a brand new focus. Don't think about it. Just do it. Your body understands. You are walking and you are focusing on feeling the space move through you. Change the focus again as you now focus on you moving through the space. Focus on moving through the space with your body. Change the focus again. Feel the space move through you. Feel the space moving through your forehead and wash away any thoughts similar to, "There are not six more changes to make." Now put it together—focus on moving through the space and feeling the space moving through you at the same time. That is a new focus. ✦ Keep doing that and let's add something new. While you are moving through the space and feeling the space moving through you at the same time, for the first time since you have started this walk, look out among each other. See that everyone around you has disappeared and the space through which you are walking is distinct and fully seen. Respond to the coaching and do the best you can. The space between you is revealed and available for viewing but the other actors cannot be seen. Take what you get; there is no wrong or right, success or failure. All that there is, is you responding to the coaching. Look out among each other and see that everyone around you has disappeared and the space through which you are walking is distinct and fully seen. See that as best you can. ✦ Now, change the focus. The space between you is unseen but all the actors are seen. The space between you has vanished but everyone is present, distinct, and seen. See that. Change the focus again. Now, everyone cannot be seen but the space between you is available for viewing. Change the focus again. The space between you is unseen but all the actors are seen. You can see each other and that is now the new acting focus, to see each other. Focus on that. See them. Focus on seeing them. —*Thirty seconds (30s)* ✦ Now change the acting focus to allowing yourself to be seen by everyone else. Focus on giving everyone the opportunity to see you. —*30s* ✦ Change the acting focus again as you look at them. Focus on observing them. See each other. Stay on your acting focus. See each other. —*30s* ✦ Now, let them observe you. Focus on letting everyone view you. Come out, come out, wherever you are! —*30s* ✦ New focus: observe, view, and see each other and, at the same time, be available to be seen in return. Look at each other and also allow yourself to be looked at. —*15s* ✦ When you feel you have really been seen by an actor, say your name to that actor. Don't just give it away, though. You must have an authentic feeling that someone has seen you, and when they have seen you, you can say your name to them. Take the time to hear their name. Hear the name. Let the name hear you. Stay on your acting focus. ✦ Return to your own walking. Move through the space and feel the space moving through you. —*15s* ✦ While you walk, select any object in this room, any object, and focus on observing it. Pick any object and look at it. Focus on examining it with only your sight. —*15s* ✦ Now, change the focus. Let the object observe you. All of you—head to toe, front and back, every part of you. Take what you get. There is no right or wrong, just focus on being seen by the object. Give the object the opportunity to observe you. Anything goes as long as you stay on the acting focus and follow the rules. —*30s* ✦ Now, you focus on looking at it. —*15s* ✦ Now focus on letting it observe you, all of you. —*15s* ✦ Put them together. View it and let it view you at the same time. Look at it and allow it to look at you at the same time. —*30s* ✦ Go over to another object, one that is within your grasp. Go over to that object and contact it. Focus on physically contacting the object. —*15s* ✦ Change the focus. Let it contact you. Focus on letting the object contact you. —*15s* ✦ Change the focus, you contact it. —*15s* ✦ Change the focus, let it contact you. —*15s* ✦ Now, put it to-gether—you contact it and let it contact you at the same time. —*15s* ✦ Keep doing that and add one more focus. See it. So, you are contacting it, letting it contact you, *and* you are seeing it. —*15s* ✦ While you are doing that, add one more focus. Give the object the opportunity to observe you. So, you are contacting it and letting it contact you, and observing it and letting it view you, all at the same time. —*30s* ✦ Now put that object down and go back out into the middle of the room and move through the space and feel the space moving through you, and see each other and allow yourself to be seen, all at the same time. While you do that, stay appropri-ate, and reach out and allow a part of your body to contact a part of your fellow actor's body as you walk by. Add to all the focusing you are doing the acting focus of feeling them and letting them feel you. Stay on the acting focus. See and feel each other and let everyone see and feel you. Notice if anything is coming up to distract you from the acting focus. Notice if you are just throwing in little touches without it being a part of the acting focus. Keep seeing each other and letting them see you, at the same time. You can feel their backs with your backs. It doesn't have to be all hands, shoulders, elbows. Just stay appropriate. See each other and let them see you. When you feel a fellow actor, let them feel you. —*30s* ✦ Now focus on moving through the space and allowing the space to move through you as you return to your chairs. Go through the space and allow the space to move through you. I'll tell you when the exercise is over. It is not over yet. Return to your chairs, moving through the space and allow-ing the space to move through you, seeing each other and letting each other see you, and as you sit in the chair, of course, focus on feeling the chair with your body and letting the chair feel you at the same time. The exercise is over. ✦ Cut.

FOLLOW-UP: Were you capable of focusing on feeling the space? Did you, if briefly, feel it? Were you capable of feeling the space with your body? Did you feel a different feeling when you felt the space move through you? Did you have a different feeling still when you moved through the space and felt the space move through you at the same time? Did you feel a different feeling when you felt the intimate space around your face? Did you feel that change as you felt the bulk space of the room? Did you experience different feelings when you changed your focus?

Could you feel a difference between just walking around and feeling the space versus focusing on seeing objects or each other? Did you feel the difference between seeing an object or another actor and letting the object or other actor see you? Could you feel a whole different feeling putting them together, seeing them *and* letting them see you? How did you feel when either a person or an object saw you? How did you feel when you were seeing and being seen, feeling and being felt, at the same time?

SUMMARY:

Notice all the different feelings you were able to have simply by changing your focus. Before adding the seeing and feeling elements, you simply walked around the room; but you had all of these distinctive different feelings that you just acknowledged, all through your power of focusing. In response to the coaching, you chose to focus on different specifics and got different results. This is the power of focusing.

You just spent time focusing on allowing yourself to be seen. How often, when you act, do you avoid allowing yourself to be seen? The nature of acting, for the actor, is to be seen. When you are acting with another actor, how often do you not only not let them see you, but you also don't see them? You've just had a rich experience of what it is to see each other and be seen in return. Do you have that experience of seeing and being seen when you are acting?

When you answered the follow-up questions, many of you talked about the warm feelings, feelings that accompany bonding and communion, that you experienced when you were seeing and being seen at the same time. Your mind chooses to focus and your body provides the feelings. If you don't have that rich experience in your acting, then maybe you are not using all of your powers yet. There is enormous focus potential, ability, energy, feeling, and power that you may not be tapping in your work.

This may be very true in business areas as well, at interviews and auditions. You go to an interview or an audition for one purpose only, to be seen. Are you doing that? Are you taking full advantage of your own instrument or are you limiting your potential?

> **TO THE COACH:** We are still laying a foundation for participating and for discussing the experiences. During the follow-up discussion, the actors may reveal that they are looking for the correct response to the acting focus or to the follow-up questions. They should be reminded that anything goes in Improvisation Technique training, as long as they are on the designated acting focus. There are no correct or incorrect responses to the designated acting focus. As long as they focus, they get what they get. It is individual and private.

Some specific guidance in the discussion will be necessary. When the actors answer the follow-up questions, some will give an answer followed by the word *because* and then give the reason that they think they had this or that experience. The coach should interrupt at the word *because* and immediately point out that in all discussions and follow-ups, the word *because* is to not be used. ◆ *The coach might say—* Let's get into vocabulary now. If I ask you for a response, give us the response, e.g., "I felt sad." That is a response. It is not necessary to analyze *why* you felt sad. When you use the word *because*, you only go deeper into your head, looking for a reason that is really nothing more than an assumption on your part anyway. The question was *What did you feel* and not *Why did you feel it*. Let's stay here and now. Answer the question I ask, not the question you think I'm asking. You can always say, "I don't know."

Another discussion or vocabulary issue to be addressed in this follow-up is the difference between concepts and feelings. Some actors will respond to the question, *What did you feel*, with concepts—e.g., intimate, vulnerable, passive, active. The coach should point this out and ask, *What did that feel like?* Keep asking this until the actors articulate what the specific feelings were.

Frequently, in the beginning, actors say *you* instead of *I*, generalizing their responses:

Coach How did it feel being seen by an object?

Actor When you first change from seeing it to it seeing you, it feels dramatically different, almost like feeling naked.

The coach should clean this up every time it happens:

Coach I didn't feel naked. I didn't let the object see me. I was coaching. Who felt naked?

Actor I did.

Actors generalizing like this rob themselves of acknowledging their own feelings and experiences and imply that these are the same as everyone else's.

UPSET

Upset is a workshop device for immediately infusing the group with energy after any lengthy follow-ups, summaries, or discussions, and/or to assure that the actors are not always teamed up with the same other actors. Just prior to the group counting off for new teams, the coach calls out, "Upset!" All the actors have to get up and reseat themselves in each other's chairs. After everyone is sitting in a new chair, proceed with counting off in teams for the next exercise. The first time upset is introduced, the actors will take about ten seconds to accomplish this. After that, coach that they only have three seconds. Then, coach upset again and everyone's energy will immediately escalate. Go right into the next exercise, improv, or game. Upset is usually employed two or more times in every class.

OBJECTS IN THE SPACE[3]

Most of Improvisation Technique requires use of space props. The fourth essential starter, *Objects in the Space*, is the introduction to handling space props.

SETUP: Two teams. One plays as the other watches. Then, they switch. If time is an issue, the whole group can play at same time.

ACTING FOCUS: Respond to the coaching.

COACHING: Focus on walking through the space and allowing the space to move through you. —*15s.* ◆ Stop walking and reach up into the space with both your hands and bring down a hunk of space between your hands. Focus on the hunk of space between your hands and begin to shape it. Move this hunk of space about and manipulate it in any way you wish, twisting it, turning it, elongating it, squashing it, moving it about. You are *playing* with this hunk of space. Stay focused on it as you play. If it turns into something you recognize, you can go with that. If not, fine. It can stay amorphous. You are focused on manipulating this hunk of space and the more you have your whole body involved in playing with it, the less your head will talk to you. Stay up on your feet with your whole body involved. It is not a wrist-to-fingers exercise only. Play with your whole body pouring its energy into it. If it wants to become an object, let it become an object. If it wants to change again, let it change. Allow the object, the hunk of space, a life of its own. Start to get out of your head deciding what to do with the space. Just let your arms, hands, and whole body work on their own as you focus on this hunk of space. You don't have to stay in one part of the stage. Let go of the control. Just twist it and turn it and let it change into something else and go for a ride with it. Let your body take a ride with it in any way it wants to but always stay focused on the space you are playing with. Allow it to expand or diminish if it wants, but keep playing with it. Let go of resistance. Let go of hesitation. Let go of caution. The object may have qualities that are yet to be revealed to you. You discover them as you play. If it becomes something recognizable, go with that. Focus on keeping that in the space. ◆ Now, take whatever object you have right now and hold onto it. Make eye contact with someone who is near you. Approach each other and fuse your two objects together. If there is an odd player, then three can play together. Play together with this new, fused hunk of space. Help each other. Keep twisting and turning the hunk of

34

space between you. Allow it to go wherever it wants to go. Let go of the control. Be aware of your fellow actor and let your fellow actor be aware of you as you both allow the object between you to turn into whatever it wants to turn into. It may be real, it may be amorphous, but allow it to have a life of its own as you work together. Keep going with it. Allow the object to dictate where it wants to go. Nobody knows where it's going. Everybody going together not knowing where we are going to. Keep playing with it. Keep pouring your combined bodies' energy into it. Go with it. One minute to play. There is no right or wrong. Let the object take on a life of its own and move the two of you. Play together with your partner. Together/together, not separate/together. Allow the object to have a life of its own. Let it take over. Let it do whatever it wants. Keep discovering the object's life. Keep the object connecting you and your partner. Censor nothing. Don't be afraid. Let the object go wherever it wants to go. Total body involvement. Not in your heads but in the space around you. ◆ Stop moving. Focus on the object right now as it exists between you and release it back up into the bulk space of the room. ◆ Cut.

FOLLOW-UP: Actors, did you find yourself playing with these space objects or did you find yourself thinking about them? A little of each? ◆ Audience, could you see when they were playing with the objects as opposed to when they were thinking about them? Could you see when they shifted back and forth from the space to the head? ◆ Actors, these objects that you were playing with, whether they were amorphous or identifiable, were they in the space, made out of the space, or were they in your heads, an idea? ◆ Audience, would you say the actors were on the acting focus as it was coached? ◆ Actors, do you feel that you were on the acting focus as it was coached? ◆ Change teams.

SUMMARY:

In all Improvisation Technique training, the acting focus is either provided through the coaching or designated as a rule prior to the start of playing. The acting focus provides the structure that frees you to go further in the realm of spontaneity. Letting go of the need to control the space object may be a first dunk in the pool of spontaneity. Letting go in pairs heightens the challenge and the experience. In time, an entire improvisational scene will replace the space object and, like the object, the scene will lead you where it wants to go. Staying on the acting focus—following the rules, responding to the coaching—in these early exercises and games prepares you to do that.

CONCLUDING THE FIRST CLASS

Continue the first class with *Activity Doing* from the beginning of chapter 3, "Physical Doing." If time allows, it is best to finish with a traditional children's game. Send them home happy, excited, and in their bodies.

◆　◆　◆

THE SECOND CLASS

The second class opens with a traditional children's game, followed by the next two essential starters, the *Second Focus Walk* and *Space Ball/Motion*.

SECOND FOCUS WALK [4]

SETUP: All do the 40-breath process, then walk around responding to the coaching.

COACHING: Walk around and shake it out. Respond to the coaching. The coaching will direct you where to put your focus. Your job is to stay on focus. Stay alert to your mind trying to take you off focus. Tell your mind, "I'm staying on focus to see what happens." Walk around and focus on moving through the space. Put your focus on feeling the space through which you are walking. Feel the space against your body. Feel it with your forehead. With the tip of your nose. Feel the space with your chest, stomach, pelvic area, knees. Feel the space beneath your feet as you step, squashing it out. Back up into the space. Feel it with the small of your back, with the broad part of your back. Keep your eyes open. Now move in any direction you wish, focusing on moving through the space. Your whole body is moving through the space. Focus on feeling that. Keep walking and change the focus and feel the space moving through you. Now focus on moving through the space. Now feel the space moving through you. Now put it together—move through the space and feel the space moving through you. Everyone is moving through the space and feeling the space move through you. ◆ Check in with yourself and feel if there is any tension within your body. Notice where it is. Chest? Forehead? Pelvis? Are any body parts tight? Notice where. Simply observe any parts of your body where you are feeling this tension or rigidity. Don't be concerned about it. Leave it alone and respond to the coaching to follow. ◆ Everybody is to take responsibility for firmly securing every part of your body. Keep it together; don't let go. Respond to the coaching and don't try to analyze it. Grip your arms to your shoulders. Do this deliberately, and do it from the inside. I do not mean put your hands to a body part and hold on. Grip your arms to your shoulders, tightly, from the inside. From the inside, secure your fingers tightly to your hands. Secure your head to your neck. Clench your face to your head. From the inside, secure your eyebrows tightly to your forehead. Just do this. Clutch your toes to your feet. Pull in all your body parts to your body as tightly as you can. Really tightly. Every part of your body is being held onto you from the inside. Respond to this coaching and do it. You can't do it too big. Now be very self-aware of what this feels like. Continue to walk as best you can; stay self-aware. Do not let go. Check in and notice what it feels like when you hold every part of your body onto you. In an exaggerated way, this is what it feels like when you are relying on yourself to control or hold everything together. ◆ Now, respond to the following coaching and we will gradually release these holds. We are going to replace them with a different control system, a *support system*. Instead of you holding yourself together, we are going to let the space hold you together. Gradually release the arms from the shoulders into the space, allowing the space to hold your arms onto your shoulders. Then release your fingers from your hand and let the space hold your fingers onto your hand. Release your legs from the trunk and let the space hold your legs onto your body. Release your toes and let the space hold your toes onto your feet. Release your eyebrows and let the space keep your eyebrows on your face. Release your face from your head and let the space support your face. If there are any body parts left where you feel tension, tightness, gripping, or clutching, release these parts, allowing the space to bolster them. Now walk around totally focused on letting the space sustain your entire body and all of its parts. Allow the space to uphold you so that you could almost lean on it and it would reinforce you. While you are doing this, use your self-awareness to take notice. Observe what the body feels like when you are not holding it all together and you are allowing the space to sustain, assist, and bolster you. Notice that. ◆ Now, when I give the cue, everybody is to forget about the space and go back to being your own control system, pulling in and gripping everything together from the inside out. Do that now! ◆ Tightly clench every body part onto the whole body. The lips onto the mouth, the eyebrows onto the face, the arms onto the shoulders; grip knees, toes, fingers. Don't let go. Again, observe what this feels like, and when I give you the cue, release every one of these holds and let the space, absolutely and entirely, nurture you. Go! ◆ Now relax and lean on the space. Move through the space and feel the space moving through you. Once more, when I give you the cue, become your own control system and hold everything in place. Now! ◆ Hold it all in place. Don't let go. Now when I give you the cue, let go of everything and focus on letting the space secure every part of you. Go! ◆ Now move through the space and feel the space moving through you. Walk around and check in. Remember when we started this, you were coached to go inside your body and discover, notice, or observe if there were any parts where you were feeling tension or rigidity. Check out those body parts now and notice if they are still tense, tight, or rigid.

FOLLOW-UP: None yet. Divide the group into two teams and proceed immediately, with one team playing and one team as audience, into the next essential starter.

SPACE BALL/MOTION[5]

COACHING: All of the ones return to your seats; the twos stay out here. ◆ Everyone is moving through the space and allowing the space to move through you. Stop walking. Reach up into the space, and form a space ball about the size of a volleyball. Bring it down in front of you and feel it all over with your hands as you look at it. Begin to play with the ball any way you wish and keep watching it. Throw it up and down. Bounce it off of a wall. You have the entire playing area available to you. No one is stuck in one place. As you play with the ball, I will give you an acting focus. This is what you must focus on while you play with the ball.

Focus on playing with a real space ball and not a pretend one. The ball is really there; it just happens to be made out of space. It is not imaginary. There is no pretending. Throw a real space ball and catch the same real space ball. When the ball leaves your hands, you must focus on it wherever it goes and however long it takes. Always see the ball wherever it is, especially when the ball leaves your hands. Give the ball its opportunity to travel where you send it. Respect that opportunity. Now heighten your playing by playing with every part of your body. You are in this workshop playground, playing with this ball. It is not a pretend ball. It is a real ball. It's not a ball from your memory. It's not the red ball you had when you were a child. It's a brand new ball. Instead of rubber, it is made out of space, but it is real and it is here right now and you have to see it every moment. Give the ball the time it needs when it's not in your hands. Make no assumptions about where the ball is and how long it takes to get there. Focus on playing with a real space ball and not a pretend one. We are working on how to keep it real and not imaginary. Play with all parts of your body. Avoid being precious. Run around, throw it, and catch it. How many new ways can you play with the ball? Can you bounce it off a different wall? Can you give it a kick? Can you use different body parts? Can you keep changing how you play with it? Take a risk by playing with it in different ways. Playing with it in the same way is playing safe. Use every part of your body to support playing with it in new ways. Avoid sameness. Keep going with it. Keep playing with the ball. The more you play with it, the more fun it is to play with. ◆ **SLOW MOTION.** Slow your playing to slow motion. When the ball leaves your hands, you must focus on it wherever it goes and however long it takes. Now it's all in slow motion. You and the ball are in slow motion. Always see the ball wherever it is, especially when the ball leaves your hands. ◆ **REGULAR SPEED.** Play with the ball at your normal speed. Play with it in different ways. Play with all parts of your body. Keep playing with it. Respect the size of the ball. Keep it the same size. Respect the time it takes for the ball to travel away from you. ◆ **TRIPLE SPEED.** The ball and you are moving at triple speed. When the ball leaves your hands it moves at triple speed and you must focus on it wherever it goes and however long it takes. Always see the ball wherever it is, especially when the ball leaves your hands. Never lose sight of the ball. Keep the ball really out there. No pretending! It is really there. Play with it. ◆ **REGULAR SPEED.** Play with the ball at your normal speed. Play with it in different ways. Play with all parts of your body. Keep playing with it. Respect the size of the ball. Keep it the same size. Respect the time it takes for the ball to travel away from you. Stay on focus. ◆ **SLOW MOTION.** Once more, slow your playing. When the ball leaves your hands, you must focus on it wherever it goes and for how long it takes. All in slow motion. ◆ **REGULAR SPEED.** Play at your normal speed. We are in the last minute of playing. Last minute to stay totally on focus as you play with every part of your body focused on the ball, never losing sight of it. ◆ **TRIPLE SPEED.** Throwing and catching, bouncing it different ways. Take nothing for granted. Still discovering new ways to play with the ball. Never losing sight of it. ◆ **REGULAR SPEED.** For the last thirty seconds of the game, stay absolutely on focus, never losing sight of it, your eyes following its path of travel. Respecting its size and feeling it when you catch it. ◆ Take the ball and throw it up into the large bulk space of the room. ◆ Cut.

FOLLOW-UP: Did you keep the ball real by focusing on it and respecting it as a space object or did you pretend to play with it? Do you know the difference between keeping it real and pretending? ◆ Audience, could you see the balls? Did you know when the actors were pretending? Did you pretend to see the balls? ◆ Change teams.

SUMMARY:

When you were focused earlier on walking through the space, could you feel the difference between having to hold your body together versus releasing those holds into the space? When first asked to find any tense body parts, did you find any?

At the end of the walk, prior to playing with the ball, you were asked to check in with those body parts, and what did you notice? The tension had disappeared.

When we started the exercise, you were not aware that you were carrying tension in specific body parts until you were coached to see if this was so. Most of you found that you had body parts that were tense, tight, or rigid, and by the end of the walk, they were less so. How many times do you go into an audition, or to work, and bring along these tensions that you are not even aware of? These tensions happen to any human being in the course of an average day. Someone cuts you off at a light; you get angry, and tension appears in your body. You wait for an important call to hear if you got the part; tension appears in your body. It happens every day and you may not even be aware of it. Even if whatever caused the tension is resolved or forgotten the tension remains in the body.

Your body is your acting instrument. Why limit your potential? How well can you play a violin that has knots in the strings? Instead of bringing these tensions with you, try this. *Coach yourself through the focus walk.*

Between parking the car or leaving the subway and walking into an audition or work, focus on moving through the space. Coach yourself to:

1. Move through the space.

2. Allow the space to move through you.

3. Put them together; move through the space and allow the space to move through you.

4. Hold every body part onto you, really tightly. Keep it together. Don't let go. Focus on that for twenty seconds, and then coach yourself to let go of all the holds.

5. Focus on the space taking over every place you were holding.

6. Then go back and forth between the self holding and the space taking over.

In the process of releasing the holds that you have deliberately put into your body, you will also release any tensions that you were unaware of. Coaching yourself through the focus walk gives your mind an active, healthy, and productive focus at the very time it is most susceptible to distractions and self-limitation. You are focused on active doing, in the present; there is no time or place left in your head for fear of not doing well (future) or self-blame for not preparing well enough (past). You will see a difference in your auditions and in your work when you arrive for them in the present; you're going to feel a lot better and you're going to do a lot better.

PLAYING WITH THE SPACE BALL

What is pretended, imaginary, or in the head is not available for communication. What is in the space is available for communication. When you were playing with the space ball, sometimes the ball was in the space and sometimes in your head. The ball was in your head if you were too lazy to focus; distracted by anything, including your own mind; visualizing a substitute ball; or looking at the space ball and waiting for it to transform magically into a vision of a real ball with a specific texture and color. A space ball is made out of space, and space has no color. If you were trying to visualize a particular ball, you were in your head. Perhaps you were remembering your favorite ball that you had when you were ten years old. That means that you were not all here in the now. Your body was here, but the rest of you was back there in the past. That is a fragmentation. Visualization is a head process. It can keep you out of the present and it creates pretending. Avoid it.

DEMONSTRATION

The coach should do the following with a space glass, space cabinet, and space sink: If I reach up into this space cabinet and I take out a glass, this glass is made out of space. I don't have to add something to the process and see a real, special glass in my mind—my New York Yankees glass at home. I don't have to do that. It is sufficient that I feel it in the space and it is here for me to do whatever I want to do with it—fill it with water, drink from it, whatever.

You need to see the space but you do not need to add another step, seeing your visualization of a real glass. In Improvisation Technique, we remove the visualization step. Visualization keeps you in the head and out of the present.

If you started with a visualization of a ball and that visualization eventually disappeared as you focused on the space ball, then the moment the ball moved—from your mental picture of it to a brand new space ball—is the moment it moved from your head and into the space.

GO WITH IT

What do you do when another actor walks through your space ball? It happens. Perhaps you don't even notice it. If you don't, it means the ball was in your head and not in the space. When you do notice it, you might have any number of reactions, like confusion, or anger. Noticing that someone has walked through or stepped on your space ball is an authentic moment. The improvisational actor doesn't get bogged down in confusion over the disruption. He goes with it. This is a fundamental rule of Improvisation Technique: *Go with it*.

What does it mean, to go with it? How do you go with it? If someone walks through or steps on your space ball, it only happens for a moment. Don't make a big deal about it and don't pretend it didn't happen. Resume focusing on the space ball, wherever it is. In time, space work will be a tool we use when we improvise on space sets and with space props. For now, you will experience your improv mates walking through walls, leaving drinks suspended in space, or handing you mysterious and amorphous hunks of space, expecting you to know what to do with them. This won't happen for very long, though. Soon we will be adept at using space props. Until that time, don't get bogged down in it and don't assume it didn't happen. That would be a lie, and actors don't lie. That's why we have agents. Just go with it. When you need to go with it, *let your body tell you how to handle the moment.* Go with your feelings within the rules and on the focus. The important thing is to keep playing instead of being concerned with playing correctly.

For some of you, it was easier to focus on playing with the space ball than it was to focus on walking through the space. When you are walking around during the space walk, the doing of that exercise is only focusing. When you played with the ball, that was real physical doing in addition to focus doing. *The more doing that is involved in the acting focus, the easier it is to focus.*

> **TO THE COACH:** Coach the speed changes in the speed desired, speaking slowly for slow motion, quickly for fast motion.

CONCLUDING THE SECOND CLASS

For the remainder of the second class, pick up where you left off in the first class with the exercises and games in the chapter on physical doing. If you finished *Activity Doing* and *Activity Doing/Avoiding Sameness*, go on to *Activity Doing/Checking Out*, *Sharing an Object*, and *Activity Doing/Helping*.

◆ ◆ ◆

THE THIRD CLASS

Begin the class with a traditional children's game. Then the group should all do the next essential starter, the *Third Focus Walk*.

THIRD FOCUS WALK [6]

SETUP: Everyone walks around responding to the coaching.

COACHING: Practice focusing, responding to the coaching and being alert to your mind telling you the equivalent of "There are not six more changes I can make." See that for what it is and say, "I'm staying on focus to see what happens." ◆ Stand still. Do the 40-breath process. Start walking. ◆ Everyone focus on feeling your body move through the space. Now feel the space moving through you. Now put it together. Feel your body moving through the space and feel the space moving through you. Everyone is moving through the space and feeling the space move through you. ◆ Put your focus on feeling your skeleton walking in the space. Feel your skeleton instead of seeing a picture of your skeleton in your mind's eye. Feel it. Avoid seeing it. Simply feel it with itself. ♦ Notice whether your mind is contributing to your being off focus. ♦ Focus on feeling your knees move as you walk. Focus on feeling your elbows moving. Your hips. Your ankles. Shoulders. Wrists. Toes. Whole legs. Pelvis. Whole arms. Spine. Neck. Head. Allow your head to be free. You don't have to hold it up. Let it do what it wants. Let it support itself. Whole body. Keep your eyes open. Notice or feel any obstructions to your free movement. Leave those obstructions alone, or not. Allow your body to align itself naturally. You stay out of it. Keep your mind out of it. Simply feel your skeleton's movement. Don't analyze or judge. ♦ Feel your head full of space. Feel your stomach full of space. Feel your face made out of space. Your elbows. Knees. Hips. Ankles. Shoulders. Wrists. Toes. Whole legs. Pelvis. Whole arms. Spine. Neck. Whole body. Keep feeling your skeleton walking in the space. Every bone is surrounded by space. ♦ Enlarge all of your body's movements. Let your skeleton move larger. Go with it. —*30s.* ♦ Allow your body to return to normal size. Feel your clothes against your body. Let your clothes feel you. Feel your clothes and let your clothes feel you at the same time. Feel your clothes and let your clothes feel you and feel the space in the room and allow the space to feel you.

FOLLOW-UP: None yet. Divide the group into two teams and proceed immediately, with one team playing and one team as audience, into the next essential starter, *Space Ball/Weight.*

SPACE BALL/WEIGHT [7]

COACHING: Start with the space ball/motion coaching to the point just prior to slow motion. Then, instead of coaching motion, *coach as follows*—**Lessen** the weight of the ball. Less. As little weight as you can make it. Give the ball the time it needs when it's not in your hands. Make no assumptions about where the ball is and how long it takes to get there. Focus on playing with a real space ball and not a pretend one. It just weighs less. Don't take your eyes off of it. ♦ **Change** the ball back to its original weight. Throwing, catching, bouncing. Give the ball the time it needs when it's not in your hands. Don't take your eyes off of it. ♦ **Increase** the weight of the ball. Heavier. Extremely heavy. You need the entire body to play with it. Focus on playing with a real space ball and not a pretend one. It just weighs more. Keep changing how you play with the ball. Give it a heave on one throw and see where it takes you, or bounce it off of a different part of the body or a different part of the wall. Don't take your eyes off of it. Play differently from time to time without stopping to think how you are going to play differently. Find the solution to the problem through the body and the focus. Keep throwing, catching, and bouncing with every part of your body. ◆ **Change** the ball back to its original weight. Throwing, catching, bouncing. Give the ball the time it needs when it's not in your hands. Don't take your eyes off of it. Play differently without thinking how to play differently. Just throw it off of something different. Twirl it. Give it a shake. Give it a kick. Full body involvement with the focus. ◆ **Lessen** the weight of the ball. [Repeat above *Lessen weight* coachings.] ◆ **Change** the ball back to its original weight. [Repeat above *Change to original weight* coachings.] ◆ **Increase** the weight of the ball. [Repeat above *Increase weight* coachings.] ◆ **Change** the ball back to its original weight. Throwing, catching, bouncing. Give the ball the time it needs when it's not in your hands. One minute until the end of the game. One minute to play with it at its original weight. Keep watching it while you play. Don't take your eyes off of it. Full body involvement. Continuously changing the way you play with the ball. ◆ Release the ball back into the bulk space. ◆ Cut.

FOLLOW-UP: Did you keep the ball real by focusing on it and respecting it as a space object or did you pretend to play with it? Did you respond to the coaching? Did you maintain your focus when changing the weight of the ball? ◆ Audience, could you see the balls? Did you know when the actors were pretending? Did you see the balls change from normal to heavy or light? Did you pretend to see the balls? ◆ Change teams. ◆ After the preceding follow-up for the second team, *ask the entire group*—

When you were focused on walking through the space, were you able to feel the different body parts and your whole body instead of visualizing them? Were there any obstructions to your movement? Did they clear themselves up? Did anyone employ a focus walk this week, in terms of going to auditions, interviews, or rehearsals? Did you discover anything?

SUMMARY:

We have already discussed the importance of a free and unfettered body as the instrument you bring to your acting. In addition, we have discussed how visualizing is a hindrance to spontaneity. When you are able to use your body freely and feel it in the present, without visualizing or thinking about it, you will have a whole body instrument that is ready to act. Whole body acting dispels any inclinations to tell instead of show and eliminates indicating, which is the result of partial body use. Improvement in these areas will consistently enhance your body's presence, which is essential to any successful acting career.

GROUP BLOCKING[8]

With this one exercise, actors learn how to improvise their own blocking within any improvisation.

SETUP: Depending on the group size, this is played in one or two teams. If the group is fewer than ten, one team; more, two teams. The coach marks out the boundaries of a playing area that is just slightly larger than will accommodate the playing team standing in a bunch, shoulder to shoulder and back to front.

COACHING: This designates the playing area. Even though it is crowded, walk around the playing area. Cover as much space as you can. *After 15s—* Stop! Don't move. When I say "group blocking," you're to move your bodies—without taking any steps—in such a way that at least one part of your body is visible to the entire audience. You are to help your fellow actors to have at least one part of their bodies be visible to the entire audience. That is your acting focus. **Group blocking.** Audience, can you see at least one part of everybody? Move around again. Cover a lot of space within your playing area. Stop! **Group blocking**.

If any actors are not responding, not moving their bodies at all and blocking other actors from being seen, *coach*— Audience, can you see actors who are ignoring the acting focus? ♦ Actors, are you all on focus? Some of you are still not responding. Your mission, your acting focus, is to have one part of your body be seen by everybody and to help your fellow actors have one part of their bodies be seen. ♦ Audience, can you now see everybody? ♦ Move around. Stop! **Group blocking**. Now move around again. Explore new ways of moving. Stop! **Group blocking**. ♦ This time when I call "group blocking," you only have one second to make all the movement adjustments. ♦ Walk around. Stop! **Group blocking**. Now move around again and we're going to leave out "stop!" I will simply call "group blocking," and you'll have one second to go into it. ♦ Move around. **Group blocking**. ♦ Audience, can you see everybody? ♦ Move around again. **Group blocking**. ♦ [The coach makes the playing area a little bit bigger.] ♦ This time, move in a constant, moving group blocking. That means that you're always following the group blocking rules while you move, and I'm simply going to call "stop!" to check you out. You stop where you are. There should be no adjusting necessary. You will already be in a group blocking. So move in a constant, moving group blocking. Stay alert to your fellow actors. Stay on the focus, always in movement. Frequently change your style of movement. Move high, move low, move in, move out. Use your arms. You are performers, not pedestrians. Stop! ♦ Audience, can you see everybody? ♦ Move around again in a moving group blocking. You are on focus every second and you are always fulfilling the group blocking rules. Stop! Okay, relax. ◆ [The coach makes the playing area a little bit bigger.] ◆ We're adding one final rule. Now you're going to move in a constant, moving group blocking, but from time to time, I will call out an actor's name. That actor is to become the moving center of a moving group blocking. ◆ Now, move with no center. One part of your body must be seen by everybody. Help your fellow actors to have one part of their bodies be seen by everybody. Keep playing, and [Liz] is the moving center. The moving center must keep moving all over the stage and all are moving around her, fulfilling the group blocking rules while making her the center of the group blocking. No one stops during this. You have to keep moving around, [Liz], if you want to be the center. If you stay in one spot, there is no challenge to the group. Use your whole playing area. Keep moving. Stop! ◆ Audience, is she the center of that group blocking? Does it need adjusting? ◆ Actors, who is not on the acting focus? Make that adjustment. Group, stay on your acting focus and move around without a center. Stay on your stage; don't go beyond the boundaries. Keep moving around, covering as much space as you can, and [Karl] is the moving center. Keep moving, [Karl]. Go wherever you want. Just keep moving all over the stage. Everyone is fulfilling the group blocking rules while keeping [Karl] the center of the group blocking. Stop! ◆ Audience, is he the center of that group blocking? ◆ Move around, everybody. No center. Now [Dan] is the moving center. Keep fulfilling the rules. Help your fellow actors to be seen. Everybody stop! ◆ Audience, is he the center of that group blocking? ◆ Change teams.

FOLLOW-UP: None.

SUMMARY:

Throughout the training, whenever you are doing an improvisation, you might be coached "group blocking." It doesn't mean that you stop improvising on the designated acting focus of the improv in order to begin playing like we just did. It means that you follow the rules of group blocking and take responsibility for knowing where you are on the stage. Are you visible to the audience? Are you helping your fellow actors in the improv to be visible to the audience? You don't stop what you're improvising. You just make an adjustment while improvising.

> **TO THE COACH:** If the group isn't large enough for two teams, the coach represents the audience and moves around the audience area during the coaching.

UNFOCUSED/FOCUSED[9]

The last of the essential starters is *Unfocused/Focused*.

SETUP: Regardless of the size of the group, this is played in two teams.

RULES and ACTING FOCUS: Respond to the coaching.

COACHING: First team, form a straight line on the stage. Now, don't do anything. That is the coaching. Just stand there. ✦ Audience, just watch them. Don't get in the way. Just observe them. ✦ Team on the floor, please don't do anything. Just stand there. We are going to observe you. You don't do anything and we watch you. ✦ Audience, watch them as a group. Watch them as individuals. ✦ Team on the floor, don't do anything. Don't take it upon yourself to improve the game. Respond to the coaching. Take what you get.

[The coach continues above coaching until he sees the actors exhibiting signs of unease, e.g., fidgeting, yawning, avoiding the audience, wearing a dazed/zombie look on their faces, etc.]

Then coach— Each of you, to yourself, silently name and remember all the colors you see in the audience's clothes. Respond to the coaching. ✦ Audience, keep observing them. ✦ Team on the floor, you only have to remember the names of the colors that appear at least once. Don't bother with duplications. You must finish with an exact list of all the colors you see in the audience. When you sit down, you will write your lists without comparing notes. ✦ *After a few minutes*— Return to your seats and write your lists. ✦ Other team, move onto the floor. While you are not doing anything, don't name colors. You will have a different assignment.

[The coach repeats the coaching for this team until it's time to have them name colors. Then, have them do so, adding—*I changed my mind.*]

FOLLOW-UP: Here are some questions for all of you. Please answer the question I ask, not the question you think I'm asking. What were you feeling when you were standing there and not doing anything?

If an actor's response is conceptual—e.g., "neutral" or "helpless"—point that out and *ask*— Specifically, what were you physically feeling? ✦ When the responses are along the lines of tired, rigid, itchy, fidgety, nauseous, numb, achy, swaying, difficulty breathing, *ask*— In what parts of your body were you feeling that?

If an actor has a hard time changing from a concept to a specific physical feeling, *ask*— How did that manifest physically? What did your *body* do that told you it was, e.g., embarrassed? For instance, were your arms folded up in front of you? Or, did you have the giggles? ✦ *When all have responded*— Do you see a similarity between all these very different physical manifestations? They are all negative feelings, feelings of unease or unpleasantness. Since your body is your acting instrument, that would be a significant thing to notice. Unless it were a choice for your character, you wouldn't want to feel that way while acting. None of you went up there purposely to feel these feelings. ◆ What did you observe about the actors' appearance on the other team when they were not doing anything? How did they appear to you?

[The group will respond with a list, e.g., glassy-eyed, stiff, angry, uncomfortable, sleepy, bored, confused.]

Would you say that all of those things fit on that list of negative feelings? So all of you, when doing nothing, felt that whole list of negative acting words and you looked it, too. ◆ Now, what were you feeling when you were standing there and naming the colors to yourself? Avoid conceptual answers. Just share with us how your body felt.

[Most responses will be along the lines of relaxed, focused, involved. To help them keep their responses nonconceptual, question those actors who previously expressed that they felt negative feelings.]

Were you still feeling rigid when you were naming the colors? No. Who felt fidgety? Did you still feel fidgety when you named the colors? No. Did you still feel sleepy while you were naming the colors? No. Was anybody aware of that negative physical feeling staying with you while you named the colors? No. ◆ What did you observe about the actors' appearance on the other team when they were naming colors?

[Most responses will be along the lines of relieved, awake, concerned, alert, relaxed, focused, involved.]

SUMMARY:

Notice that your responses to how you felt and how you appeared when you were naming colors are the extreme opposite of those negative feelings that you felt when you were not doing anything. These are positive feelings that are healthy for an actor's state of being, e.g., awake, alert, concerned, focused.

When acting, which means either rehearsing or performing in front of an audience or a camera, if you aren't doing anything, you are going to feel those same negative feelings that you experienced in this exercise. What's more, those feelings are seen by the audience and they will feel uncomfortable too. *If you are in front of an audience and you are doing nothing, you're in trouble.* The good news is, the solution is simple: be focused on doing something. If you are on an acting focus, your body is physiologically doing something and all those negative feelings disappear, from your body and from the audience. The more focused you are, the more comfortable the audience will be and the greater will be their involvement in what they are watching.

Every exercise and game we have played in these first three classes has provided you with an acting focus: avoid being tagged; observe, make, and communicate changes; feel the space; keep a space ball real; and, from the physical do-ing chapter, doing and showing your activity. *Acting is doing and there is always more to do.* You are learning, *experientially*, all the things available for doing so that you do them spontaneously and/or by design to serve particular script needs. This is the Improvisation Technique training.

> **TO THE COACH**: Unfocused/focused completes the essential starters. The underpinnings are now in place. Space work has been introduced, be-ginning an easy and gradual familiarity with space props. Preparation for, practice at, and importance of being on an acting focus has been emphasized.

CONCLUDING THE THIRD CLASS

For the remainder of the third class, pick up where you left off in the second class with the exercises and games in the chapter on physical doing. If you fin-ished *Activity Doing/Checking Out, Sharing an Object,* and *Activity Doing/Helping,* go on to *Activity Doing/Rhythm* and *Activity Doing/Job Title.* If time allows, it is best to finish with a traditional children's game.

◆   ◆   ◆

SUBSEQUENT CLASSES

For subsequent classes, which should always start and, if time allows, finish with a traditional children's game, the coach need only follow the training as it is presented in the book, picking up from *Activity Doing/Job Title* in the physical doing chapter. For further information, see Appendix E, "Suggested Workshop Formats."

3

PHYSICAL DOING

ACTING IS DOING AND THERE IS ALWAYS MORE TO DO

When performing, the actor should always be *doing* something. In traditional acting, the *doing*—what the character is doing in order to solve a problem—is always a verb requiring physical or psychological energy. By contrast, Improvisation Technique comprises many different types of doing available to the actor. The totality of them is the technique. Each of these doings is referred to as the *acting focus* and there are appropriate times for employing each acting focus. The actor learns and practices the required basic doings until kinesthetic memory kicks in and the doings become second nature. The actor's body initiates them on its own, without waiting for a cerebral message. When this occurs, the actor transcends technique—a prerequisite of great acting.

All of the skills learned in this chapter are essential building blocks to the conclusive physical doing skill, *Physical Doing Drill* (You're on your own/Player's choice, p. 94). Proficiency at this is the foundation of improvising acting.

All of the exercises/improvs in the training demand that whatever doing, or acting focus, the actor is involved in, he is also listening to and hearing any dialogue spoken by anyone in the scene, improv, or exercise. Should an actor be so immersed in his acting focus that he occludes his fellow actors, the coach will spot it *and coach accordingly*— Receive the communication.

ACTIVITY

The purest and most basic form of an acting doing is real physical doing of an activity, e.g., folding laundry, building a house, painting a picture, cooking a meal, fixing a car, etc. In Improvisation Technique, activity doing is called the *Activity*, and it *requires involvement with one or more objects*. A real-life activity without objects, e.g., dancing, posing, waiting, or watching, is not considered an activity in the early part of the training. It is an essential goal of the early training that doing an activity must become second nature without the actor having to remind himself to do so. The primary tool for achieving this is activity doing.

ACTIVITY DOING[1]

SETUP: 4–7 (ideally) per team; however, as few as two can play. (1) We play one team at a time. Any actor may start by coming out onto the floor and announcing his team number; then, only the actors on that team may play. (2) The *first actor* does an activity that is open to involving all team members. This might be building a house, preparing a picnic, etc., but it must employ objects. All objects must be made out of space. (3) When another actor on the team receives the communication as to the nature of the first actor's activity, the *second actor* chooses an activity—it *must* involve objects—that could be a part of the whole activity initiated by the first actor. The actor comes out onto the floor and joins the first actor, but does his own activity. Then a *third actor* receives the communication of the activity and joins the first two actors out on the floor, doing his own activity choice, which must also be considered a part of the whole activity. Continue, one by one, until *all of the actors* on the team are out on the floor doing their activities, all of which are parts of the whole activity initiated by the first actor.

RULES: Avoid speaking. No invisible people allowed. Every team member must play. All props must be made out of space. You may use real chairs as chairs; a few chairs as a bench or couch; or, as a bed, any set piece intended to support the body. You do not have to know ahead of time that you will need a chair. During the course of playing, if you want a chair, grab one from the audience.

ACTING FOCUS: While you are on the floor, your acting focus, what you focus on to the exclusion of everything else, is doing and showing your activity, which is a part of the whole team's activity.

COACHING (as needed): When more than one actor goes out onto the floor at the same time, *coach*— One at a time. Allow what's happening to happen before you join it. ◆ If a team member is staying in the audience and not getting up to play, *coach*— When you receive the communication of what the activity is, choose your own activity, go up, do it, and participate. Everyone on this team must play. Take advantage of the opportunity to play. That you play is more important than that you play correctly. Be brave.

This is the first time the actors are employing space objects and their space work will be somewhat sloppy. This is to be expected and not dwelled on. ◆ However, if their space work is extremely generalized, without even minimal attention paid to the handling of the objects, then *choose from*— **Respect your space objects. Feel them in your hands**. Look at what you are doing. Keep your objects in the space.

The actors are totally absorbed in their own activities and not very aware of each other while playing. This is appropriate to the acting focus; we are not yet looking for any real contact between the actors. ◆ Nevertheless, if an actor is oblivious, particularly with regard to trampling through the other actors' space objects, *coach*— **Be aware of your fellow actors**. Respect their space objects. ◆ If an actor begins to speak to another actor, *coach*— **Avoid speaking**. ◆ An actor may initiate a situation with another actor in which people would usually speak to each other. Although they avoid speaking, they substitute some form of nonverbal communication of dialogue. This will be exaggerated, with lots of hand gesturing, or facial grimaces, or even pantomime—their lips move but no sound comes out. ◆ In this case, *coach*— **Avoid** speaking or substituting for it! ◆ If an actor is standing around doing nothing, even if he is watching the others play, or if he has completed his own activity, *choose from*— Stay on your acting focus. Do your activity and focus on it. Focus on your own activity. **If you have finished your activity, do it again or select another activity that is also a part of the whole and do that. Avoid hanging out.** ◆ If an actor's activity includes no space props, *coach*— Choose an activity that requires using props. Choose an active activity, not a passive one. ◆ If an actor is minimally focused on his activity and is putting his energy into creating a character, it will usually be emphasized with cliché gestures and stereotyping; *coach*— Your acting focus is on what you are doing, not who you are being. ◆ If an actor should interact with an invisible person he has created, *coach*— **No invisible people**. Focus on **your** activity. ◆ Once all of the team members are on the floor, give the game no more than two additional minutes, *then coach*— Cut.

FOLLOW-UP (as needed): *Ask the audience*— What was everyone involved in doing? ◆ After the audience responds, e.g., "Medical operation," *ask the actors*— Is that correct? Were you each doing an activity that was a part of the whole group's medical operation? ◆ If any actors thought that the group's activity was different from what was intended, e.g., "Oh, it was a medical operation? I thought we were all stuffing a turkey." Simply point that out as a miscommunication. ◆ Then, *ask the audience*— What activity was each individual actor doing? What activity was [Ed] doing? ◆ [Ed], is that correct? No? What were you doing? Do you accept that that was not communicated to the audience?

After checking out the individual activities with each actor, *ask*— Audience, were all the actors on the acting focus? When weren't they on focus? When any actor was standing around watching the others instead of focusing on doing his activity, he was off focus. What other activities might also have been a part of the group's medical operation? Did the actors use space objects? ◆ If an actor used a real object, the coach can *ask that actor*— When you took off your watch to wash your hands, did you take off a real watch or a space watch? ◆ As to any speaking or almost speaking that may have occurred in the playing, *ask*— Audience, was there any speaking? Did they avoid speaking? What about the moment when Ed gestured to Amy and seemed to want to know if Amy needed help with her oxygen mask? Yes, they didn't speak; but did Ed *avoid* speaking or did Ed *invite* speaking, regardless of whether or not they then actually spoke? Ed, did you avoid or invite speaking?

SUMMARY:

Let's all stay alert to the difference between active and passive activities. An active activity requires the use of space props; a passive activity does not. Passive activities include wishing, waiting, wanting, hoping, longing, watching, etc. In the beginning of our training, only active activities are considered activities.

> **TO THE COACH:** The coach should know going into this game that what he wants to achieve is to have everybody focusing on doing the activity they selected in response to the first actor's choice. Some actors will attempt to turn the game into a scene with exaggerated, cliché characters and conflict or jokes. The coach should curtail this through the coaching and follow-up.
>
> Because this is a small team exercise/game of the type that most of the training follows, the first follow-up is fairly elaborate compared to the simplicity of the game itself. It is an extended opportunity for the coach to establish the format for the actors' receiving feedback on their work and to emphasize the specificity and authenticity that is expected of them. *Did you do what was asked of you or didn't you?* Remember that the follow-up is not only feedback for the actors who have just played, it is also information for all of the actors yet to play. Actors and audience see that no one is given the opportunity to comment generally on the caliber of

their work or to criticize, e.g., "I didn't believe that Lisa was really weeding." They see that nothing more is being asked of them than to be on the acting focus and to play by the rules. They are not being asked to make a scene happen or to be funny. We'll get to scenes. We go one step at a time.

ACTIVITY DOING / AVOIDING SAMENESS

For round two of activity doing, we add one new rule: avoiding sameness.

SETUP: The same as the basic activity doing.

RULES: The same as the basic activity doing, with the addition of—*avoid sameness.* An actor who joins his teammates on the floor should avoid choosing the same activity that another actor is already doing. If the group activity is yard work, for instance, and one actor is already weeding, an actor coming onto the floor should avoid the choice of weeding as his activity.

ACTING FOCUS: Doing and showing your activity, which is a part of the whole team's activity.

COACHING (as needed): The same as the basic activity doing. If any actors are still hanging out and not doing an active activity with space objects, *coach*— Avoid hanging out. Participate by doing your activity. Everything you need is available in the space. You must have an active activity. Reach out into the space and help yourself.

FOLLOW-UP (as needed): The same as the basic activity doing. When the coach gets to the section where the audience and the individual actors are identifying an actor's activity, refer to the actors in reverse order of appearance: last actor on the floor, first; next to last actor, second; and so on. The first actor on the floor is the last actor referred to. *Add this question about each actor*— Did [Ed] avoid sameness or was his activity the same as [Lisa's]? ◆ If any actor chose an activity that another actor was already doing, wait for the audience to point this out, and then *ask that actor*— Do you accept that you didn't avoid sameness? ◆ Potential for further follow-up is mentioned in "To the coach" below.

> **TO THE COACH:** This game is played for practice at doing activities and doing them with space props. It also extends the basic choice-making process. Each actor must choose an activity that is not only a part of the whole already on the floor, but also a part of the whole *not previously seen*, solely the contribution of the actor coming onto the floor. ◆ The coach may choose to point out in a summary that, from the audience's point of view, this round seemed to have a little more texture and interest in each scene than the previous round played without avoiding

sameness. ◆ The coach should assess whether or not it is time to point out the different available degrees of avoiding sameness. For instance, suppose one team of four did gym activities and each actor did a different activity—weight lifting, rowing machine, stationary bike, and stair master. In the follow-up, *the coach could ask*, Did they avoid sameness? When the audience responds, "Yes," the *coach continues*— Yes, they all did different activities, but they were all exercising. So on another level, they were all doing the same thing. What is another activity that could have also been a part of the whole but would have avoided sameness to a greater degree? As the group provides answers, the coach should point out anything that is still just another form of exercising. Some answers will be on the money: snacking at the juice bar, cleaning a machine, taking a shower, and changing clothes. With *space props*, actors feel free to remove *space clothes*, a necessary freedom in any acting class.

A coach might decide that it is too soon to go to this level. Perhaps the group has become hesitant in their playing; the actors are developing fears about breaking the rules. In these circumstances, discussing an advanced level of avoiding sameness will only add to their fears and contribute to putting them in their heads when we are actively working to get them out of there. This is a judgment call, and the coach should be honest with himself. Is it the right thing to do *for the group* or is it an opportunity *for the coach* to show off that he knows more than the group.

ACTIVITY DOING / CHECKING OUT

For round three of activity doing, we add one new rule: checking out.

SETUP: The same setup as the basic activity doing.

RULES: The same as the basic activity doing, with the addition of—*Check out your fellow actors*. This means that while you are playing, doing your activity, check out your fellow actors. See who they are, where they are, and what they are doing. You must integrate your checking out as a part of the whole doing of your own activity. To check out does not mean that you stop your own playing and hang out watching everyone else.

ACTING FOCUS: Checking out your fellow actors while doing and showing your activity, which is a part of the whole team's activity.

CLASS QUESTIONS: "Do we still avoid sameness?" Always. *Every time we add a new rule, the rule becomes a part of all future playing.* "Do we still avoid speaking?" Yes.

COACHING (as needed): The same as the basic activity doing with the addition of the following coachings, repeated frequently *as needed*— Check out your fellow actors. Are you aware that there are other actors on stage? Check them out. Check everyone out. **Integrate the checking out with what you are doing.** Keep it a part of the whole. See what's happening around you. ◆ People move and change their activities. You always want to know where they are and what they are doing. Is there someone behind you? What are they doing? ◆ Survey the stage. Make sure that there is not a spot with an actor in it that you have missed. Respond to the coaching. ◆ Is there someone behind your left shoulder? Do you know for sure? Take a look. Stay on focus! Keep doing. That's your focus. Avoid hanging out. Keep your activity active! ◆ Nothing comes from passivity. All potential is in action. Keep doing your activity and from time to time check out your fellow actors. Avoid hanging out.

FOLLOW-UP (as needed): The same as the basic activity doing, but by now, the third round, unless there are special problems with any particular actors, it can be done quickly. ◆ Audience, what was everyone involved in doing? What were the individual activities? Did the actors avoid sameness? Were the objects in the space? Did they check each other out? Did they integrate their checking out with their activity or did they turn their moments of checking out into periods of hanging out and doing nothing? ◆ Actors, did you check each other out? Did your checking out lead to any discoveries you then integrated into your activity doing? What did you discover and how did you go with it? Could you have done more checking out?

SUMMARY:

When we are on stage we are always checking out our fellow actors. We must see what's going on or how will we ever create the potential for coming together. There are many ways to check out your fellow actors without getting off your own focus. Sometimes what we see when checking out provides us with opportunities to take our own activity doing further.

THE WITNESS

With checking out, we begin to develop an aspect of the technique called the *witness.* This is a self-witness that is inside of you, supportive of you, witnessing what's going on and what you are doing. The witness eventually takes over the coach's role and helps you to coach yourself. As the training proceeds and with the experiential practice that you get, the time lapse between what the witness/coach observes, the self-coaching it provides, and your playing response diminishes until it all happens at once, spontaneously.

COMPLETING AN ACTIVITY

What do you want to avoid when you complete your activity? Watching someone else do an activity! Watching is passive. The acting focus is doing and showing

56

your activity. Watching another's activity is not the same as doing your own activity and frequently checking them out. If your activity is completed, you may (1) start a new activity that would also be a part of the whole, (2) redo the same activity and discover that there is always more to do, or (3) undo—*reverse*—the original activity.

The choice of what to do next should be made *when it is time to do it*, not planned ahead of time. If you complete the doing of your activity and then stand there thinking, "What should I do now," you get into your head and open the door for all kinds of problems to appear. Choose what to do next at the very moment you complete an activity.

TO THE COACH: If an actor doesn't check out his fellow actors and is not responding to the coaching, *add to the coaching*— Respond to the coaching. Check each other out. ◆ If the actor still doesn't respond, wait until all the actors on that team are on the floor playing. Immediately prior to calling "Cut," *coach*— Freeze. Don't move at all! ◆ Then, *ask the problem actor*— Ed, without turning your head, tell us who is on your right? What are they doing? ◆ Ed: "I don't know." ◆ Who is on your left, and what are they doing? ◆ Ed: "I don't know." ◆ Who is behind you? ◆ Ed: "I don't know." ◆ Everyone relax. Stop freezing. The game is over.

Ed, if you were going to play a scene and become involved with these fellow actors, do you think it would be helpful to know who and where they are and what parts of the whole scene they are playing? ◆ Ed: "Yes." ◆ If Ed should say, "No," *ask the audience*— Do you agree with Ed? ◆ They will answer, "No." ◆ However, if Ed is going to answer anything but yes, he will start his answer with an explanation. ◆ The coach should stop this explanation immediately by *interrupting*— Excuse me, Ed. It's a simple question, which, for your sake and ours, requires a simple yes, no, or I don't know. ◆ After Ed says, "Yes," *ask him*— Did you respond to the coaching? ◆ If he says, "Yes," a*sk the audience*— Do you agree? ◆ If he says, "I didn't hear the coaching," *ask his team members*— Did you hear the coaching? ◆ If they say, "No," the *coach should say*— I accept that. I didn't communicate to the actors.

If, earlier, Ed started to explain why he didn't check out his fellow actors and the coach didn't allow him to finish, then *conclude this section*— I know that you had a reason for not being on focus, and I wouldn't let you get that out. Actors are always going to find a reason to be off focus, so we have a rule. *There is never a reason to be off focus.* When you give yourself a reason to be off focus, you deprive yourself of the opportunity to go somewhere you did not anticipate, and that is the essence of spontaneity. Use the rules to springboard you into creativity you never imagined.

ACTIVITY DOING/RHYTHM

For round four of activity doing, we *subtract* some rules and *add* new coaching.

SETUP: This should be played with one, two, or three teams only. If the group is fewer than four, one team; four to twenty, two teams; more than twenty, three teams. The same setup as the basic activity doing, *except* don't be concerned with avoiding sameness or joining in one at a time. For this version of activity doing we have larger teams and we want to get everyone on the floor as quickly as possible. There will be new coaching and it can't start until all are on the floor.

RULES: The same as the basic activity doing, except as noted above.

ACTING FOCUS: Doing and showing your activity, which is a part of the whole team's activity, and responding to the coaching.

CLASS QUESTION: "Do we still check each other out?" Yes, if it feels appropriate with the new coaching.

COACHING: The coaching for this is not a response to what the coach sees the actors doing. It is meant to lead the actors and should be done in the order presented here. ♦ About thirty seconds after the last actor on the team starts doing his activity, and allowing about thirty seconds between coachings, *begin coaching*— Get on your acting focus. Do and show your activity. **Part 1.** Observe the rhythm that has emerged in the doing of this activity. Focus on the rhythm of your activity. Take a ride on the rhythm. Feel the rhythm in your body. Feel the rhythm with your skeleton. Heighten the rhythm. Respond to the coaching. ♦ Interrupt the rhythm and stay a part of the whole. Allow the rhythm to resume. ♦ Retard the rhythm of your activity. Allow the original rhythm to resume. ♦ Initiate any new rhythm for your activity. Focus on that rhythm. ♦ Interrupt this rhythm and make the interruption a part of the whole. [Pause] And out of that interruption, find a **new activity** that is also a part of the whole. **Part 2.** Repeat Part 1 coaching to [Pause], then continue with **Part 3. Return to the original activity** with its original rhythm. Focus on that rhythm. ♦ Cut.

FOLLOW-UP (as needed): Audience, did the actors respond to the coaching? Did they choose a second activity when coached to do so? Did they return to their first activity with its original rhythm when coached to do so? ♦ Actors, do you agree? Were you on the focus? ♦ Is there a difference between interrupting the rhythm and changing the rhythm? We'll have further follow-up after the last team has played.

SUMMARY:

Actors from all teams after the first team, how many of you preplanned your second activity? Do you accept that you deprived yourselves of the opportunity to come up with, or improvise, your choice of a second activity in the moment? Does interrupting the rhythm always mean changing the activity? No, of course not.

Other than the fact that you were coached to interrupt the rhythm, when you interrupted the rhythm, did a *reason* for the interruption appear as a part of the whole? If a reason appeared and you acted upon it *simultaneously with its appearance*, that was a true improvisational moment, maybe your first one since we started this training. If a reason appeared and you hesitated before acting upon it, then notice the fact that there was a time lag there. If you write about that moment in your journal, you will help yourself eliminate time-lag moments from future playing. If no reason for the interruption appeared and you still interrupted the rhythm, then you responded to the coaching. You might now want to consider if you included the interruption as a part of the whole. If you didn't, you could write about that in your journal.

At the end of the playing, when you were coached to return to the original activity, what did you discover? It was *easy*. You found that the original rhythm of the first activity was right there for you. It was natural, organic, and effortless; integrating it was spontaneous. Your body learned that rhythm as a result of all the focusing on it in the beginning of the game, and when you were coached to return to it, your body remembered it for you. That is called kinesthetic memory, and that is how we learn Improvisation Technique, in the body and not the head.

> **TO THE COACH:** When the actors interrupted the rhythm and spontaneously discovered and incorporated a reason for the interruption, it was an example of the *technique* rather than *story* orientation of Improvisation Technique. The actors were focused on doing an activity and responding to a coaching of "interrupt the rhythm." These are *technical devices* and can be applied to any situation, any scene, any story; hence, *technique* orientation.

SHARING AN OBJECT[2]

Before going on to round five of activity doing, actors should improvise on the exercise, *Sharing an Object*.

> **SETUP:** 2–6 per team. Each team huddles and selects one object and a simple activity centered on moving that object. The activity choice must require all of the actors to be physically involved with the object at the same time. There should be no discussion of *how* they are going to do the activity.
>
> **RULES:** The one object is made of space. No additional objects are allowed.
>
> **ACTING FOCUS:** Respecting the space object between you.

COACHING (as needed): Places. ◆ Action. ◆ Focus on the object's existence in the space between you all. Respect the space. *If actors laugh*— Use your laughter—it is energy—pour it into the acting focus. ◆ When you have completed the activity, call "Cut."

FOLLOW-UP (as needed): Audience, what was the object, and what did they do with it? Did the actors work with the object together and at the same time or did they all work individually on the object? Did the activity require the participation of all? Did they respect the space object between them or were some actors focused primarily on where they were going with it? Did they keep the object in the space between them or was it in their heads? Were they on their acting focus? ◆ Actors, do you agree?

SUMMARY:

Respecting something, whether it is a space object or a person, requires paying attention to it, him, or her. When more than one actor is respecting the same space object, their attention is paid to where the object exists in the space between them. Putting your attention only on where you are moving the object or paying attention to the object in the space only where it meets your hands negates the necessary mutual respect and isolates you and your version of the object from the other actors and the actual object in the space. This isolation means that the object is in your head and not in the space. Putting your attention and focus on the object out in the space between you generates group agreement on the object's existence in the space, where it counts, and not in the individual actors' heads, where it is useless and fosters pretending. In improvisational scenes employing space objects, as all of our improvs will do, this group agreement on the space object is fundamental. When sharing a space object with another actor, always *put your attention on the object where it exists in the space between you* and not just on your corner of the space object.

TO THE COACH: In this early exercise, the most common avoidance of the acting focus occurs when actors hold onto the space object but look in the direction they are headed with it. They are on their acting focus when each is focused on the object's existence *in the space between them*, glancing only occasionally in the direction they are heading.

Huddles

The *how* of any improv is what is improvised and not planned ahead of time in the huddles. Pointing out in the setup that there should be no discussion in the huddle of how the actors are going to do the activity allows for additional guidance on how to conduct huddles at this early stage of the training. There will be actors in every group who will try to dominate huddles and make sure everything is planned ahead of time so that there will be no mistakes. Without addressing these actors directly or correcting their behavior, the coach should continually stress that the actors never discuss anything in huddles pertaining to the forthcoming improv other than the specific choices they have been asked to make. Huddle choices throughout the entire training will always pertain only to what they need to be doing when action is called. Huddle discussions should never be about anything that is going to happen in the improvisation beyond the first seconds of it. Actors soon take responsibility for their own huddles and the huddle runners gradually relinquish their need to control.

ACTIVITY DOING/HELPING

For round five of activity doing, we add one new rule: helping.

SETUP: The same setup as the basic activity doing.

RULES: The same as the basic activity doing, with the addition of—*Help your fellow actor.* While doing your activity, and checking out your fellow actors, stay alert to opportunities for helping and then go with it and physically help each other. Your initial entrance should be focused on doing and showing us your activity, just as it has been in the previous rounds. Your initial activity should *not* carry an intention of helping another actor. Get established with your activity, check out, and then stay alert for helping.

ACTING FOCUS: Helping your fellow actors while doing and showing your activity, which is a part of the whole team's activity.

CLASS QUESTION: "Do we still avoid speaking?" Yes, unless you must speak.

COACHING (as needed): All the usual activity doing coaching, as needed. By this round, *probably all that will be needed is*— Focus on doing your activity and check each other out. ◆ In all versions of activity doing, a time may come when no one gets up to join the first actor because no one on the team receives the communication of the nature of the first actor's activity. All of the team members will still be in the audience, all with the same expression on their faces: "What's he doing?" ◆ When this happens, *coach the first actor*— The audience is not receiving the communication of your activity. What other aspects of your activity can you show us? ◆ If that doesn't solve the problem, *coach*— What other activities are also a part of this whole? Choose another activity to communicate the whole. ◆ **The new coaching is:** Stay open to seeing opportunities to help a fellow actor. Help your fellow actor. Stay open to creating opportunities for help. Stay open to receiving help. Go with it. Help your fellow actors accept help. When not helping, focus on your own activity and check each other out. People move. People change their activities. You always want to know where they are and what they are doing. Avoid hanging out. Nothing comes from passivity. All potential is in action. You can always return to your own activity. Your own activity will sustain you. Check each other out. Your checking out must be integrated with the doing of your own activity. ◆ When actors are helping each other and both are handling the same space object, *coach*— Focus on respecting the space object between you. ◆ When the actors stumble into situations that compel them to speak about what is happening but they are biting their tongues because of the rule about avoiding speaking, *coach*— Speak if you must! When the words demand to be said, say them! ◆ If the actors start speaking but their volume and vocal energy are low, don't hesitate to *coach*—Share your voices! If you must speak, share your voices! ◆ If actors take this new freedom to speak and abuse it by speaking unnecessarily, *coach*— Speak only if you have to! If you absolutely must speak, do so. Otherwise, avoid speaking. Speak only when you must! Avoid playwriting. ◆ Cut.

FOLLOW-UP (as needed): The same as for basic activity doing, *with the addition of*— Audience, did the actors help each other? What were some of the ways they helped each other? Did they keep the objects between them? Were there opportunities for helping that were not picked up on? Were there any other opportunities for helping? Were they on their acting focus? ◆ Actors, were you alert to opportunities for helping each other? Did you follow up on them? ◆ Lisa, when Ed handed you that space object and you didn't know what it was, how did you feel? Ed, did you hear her answer? Could you have taken more responsibility for communicating the nature of the object to her prior to handing it to her? Could you have done that without doing a pantomimed telling?

SUMMARY:

You are now coming together and involving yourselves with each other, around the helping, for little beats in the playing. You are no longer totally in control of your own playing. Working in tandem with another actor or actors, you begin to experience playing together with both the how of it and the outcome undecided. These little convergences with other actors create the beginnings of improvisational *beats*, which are physical as opposed to cerebral story building, not dependent on conflict, and which establish the potential for further improvisational development. Once actors come together, we have the opportunity for things to happen.

Whenever you hand a space prop to another actor, it is your responsibility to know whether you need to communicate what the prop is, and if you do, to communicate without having to do so in a pantomimed way.

SPEAKING

We now have some confusion as to when to speak. We are developing in the actors a sense of *dialogue vs. playwriting*. Improvisational *dialogue* is speaking that evolves out of what is happening on stage between the actors and that is open for the audience to see. *Playwriting* is information that has been made up in an actor's head and is then told to the other actors and the audience. When you learn that you only speak when you have to, everything that comes out is important. When you're given the license to speak whenever you like, you're going to get into lies, attempts at cleverness, going for laughs, talking your way out of acting challenges, and telling instead of showing. Unnecessary talking takes you off of the acting focus, out of your involvement with what is going on between you and your fellow actors, and puts you right into your head.

For instance, when an actor accidentally bumps into another actor and says spontaneously, "Excuse me," that is dialogue. The bump really happened; the audience saw it; and the bumper felt compelled to say, "Excuse me." However, if the bumpee then said, "Be careful! *I remember when you dropped that antique vase and we all got into trouble,*" the "Be careful!" was probably spontaneous and would be dialogue, but the "*I remember…*" line would be playwriting; it breaks the rules. The "Excuse me" and "Be careful" lines are examples of actors speaking when they must. But the vase breaking never happened and is just an idea in the actor's head rather than an expression he was compelled to make in the moment. Dialogue is truthful. Playwriting is always a lie and a breeding ground for inauthenticity.

> **TO THE COACH**: An actor should avoid negating or stopping another actor from performing his activity. Actors who tell another actor to "stop doing that" are not *going with it.* Usually these actors do not have an activity of their own and are inadvertently attempting to pull another actor off focus with them. They are sinking, and they want some company. They are also introducing conflict, which should be avoided at this stage of the training. ◆ Whenever an actor begins to negate another's activity, *coach*— Go with it! ◆ Coaches must be diligent in spotting playwriting. *Coach*— Avoid playwriting. Speak only when you must.

ACTIVITY REVIEW

Activity is the most important basic tool of the improvisational actor. More than simply doing an activity, it is the *focusing on the doing* of the activity that is important.

This *focusing* requires the brain's participation, which means the brain is not available for thinking about nonproductive issues or for provoking defensive or self-inhibiting feelings or egocentric behavior. Notice that these early rounds of activity exercises have all had an ensemble feeling in the playing. They were free of playing characterized by nervousness, showing off, competitions in cleverness, or hiding. This is because everyone had something to focus *on*, the doing of the activity. It is the focus that frees you and allows you to play, and the focus here is on doing. *Acting is doing and there is always more to do.*

In Improvisation Technique, you learn all of the different ways of doing available to you. When you act, you will always know what to do and how to focus on the doing of it. We are simply starting the work with the purest form of doing, i.e., real doing. Milking a cow, washing a car, and painting a wall are examples of pure doing, the real, physical doing of an *activity*. Passive activity is not as pure a doing as real, physical doing. For this reason, passive activity is never to be considered an activity.

When an actor is involved with, and focused on, doing an activity, there is no semblance of acting; he is *really doing* that activity. Despite, and because of, the fact that he is doing it with space props, he is *really* [focused on] *doing* it. Using space props as part of the activity requires hand/eye coordination. When the actor does an activity without space props, it doesn't require hand/eye coordination, and he will replace really doing something with acting, the very thing we are eliminating at this stage of the training. Space props and hand/eye coordination anchor the actor in focusing on the doing. Acting is doing, not acting. It is important that we now establish a rule for all improvisation scenes and games (as opposed to exercises): *No one is allowed on stage without an activity.*

We have also explored certain facets of activity:

1. *All activity choices must be a part of the whole group activity.* Choosing an activity that is a part of the whole group's activity narrows the range of possible choices. Too much freedom of choice is crippling. By employing the phrase *part of the whole*, we have some definition and we reduce the possible activity choices to a manageable number. Of those remaining choices, we have total freedom to pick anything we want. By subscribing to the *part-of-a-whole* concept, we also guarantee an actor's participation in the ensemble rather than his taking it over.

2. *Doing an activity is always integrated with checking out your fellow actors.* It is required that the actor not only be involved in his activity but also be aware of what's going on around him. The actor is not playing in an isolation tube.

3. *Through activity, we are able to seek and/or provide help.* Providing and seeking help brings actors together; this in turn creates the potential for things to happen.

4. *We can change rhythms of activities, as well as interrupt them.* Focusing on rhythm changes and interruptions takes the actors further into, and provides control of, the technique. As in music, the rhythm is the understanding.

5. *We can change activities.*

CHARACTER—WHO IS DOING THE ACTIVITY?

Up to this point, there has been no mention of playing character. Every time you entered an activity doing, you played as yourself. In your careers, no one is ever going to hire you to play you. They may take advantage of your physical characteristics and personality, but nobody has written a script with a character based on you that they're hiring you to play. Student actors often forget that the character is always someone other than yourself. *Always.* That doesn't mean you can't bring a lot of yourself to it, but it is still someone other than you. It is not your name on the script page.

In the next level of the training, we place some emphasis on character. This is a beginning approach. Later in the training, we will get deeply into playing a character. For now, all of our character work will be based on *relationships.*

Every character in a script has relationships to the other characters. There are two kinds of relationships between people, professional and personal. A professional relationship is any relationship based on an exchange of goods, services, or money. All relationships not based on such exchanges are personal. Sometimes a relationship is both personal and professional. The only exception is when a character is a stranger.

ACTIVITY DOING/JOB TITLE[3]

In order to explore how characters relate to each other, we will add some rules to our basic activity doing.

SETUP: 4–5 (ideally) per team; however, as few as two can play. (1) We play one team at a time. Any actor may start by coming out onto the floor and announcing his team number, and only the actors on that team may play. (2) The first actor selects a job title for himself, what his character does for a living. He doesn't tell his choice to anyone. He then begins the playing, doing an activity that is related to that job. The activity must employ objects. (3) When another actor on the team receives the communication as to the nature of the first actor's activity or job, the second actor chooses his own job title and job-related activity—it *must* involve objects—that could be part of, or professionally related to, the whole job activity initiated by the first actor. The actor comes out onto the floor and joins the first actor, but does his own activity. Then a third actor receives the communication of the job or professional activity or activities and chooses his job title and job-related activity, involving objects, which could be a part of, or professionally related to, the whole job activity initiated by the first actor. The actor comes out onto the floor, joins the first two actors, and does his own activity. Continue, one by one, until all the actors on that team are out on the floor doing their activities, which are all parts of the whole professional activity suggested by the first actor's choice.

RULES: The same as the basic activity doing. Every actor must choose what they do for a living and communicate this through their activity. Avoid speaking, but speak if you must. Every team member must play.

ACTING FOCUS: Doing, showing, and taking part in your professional activity, which is a part of the whole team's professional activity.

COACHING (as needed): The same as basic activity doing. ◆ **ADDITIONAL COACHING: Observe your fellow actors before joining. Avoid sameness. When you join, know what job you have.** You are a professional at it. **Check out fellow actors. See who they are. See what they are doing. Make it a habit to coach yourself to check out your fellow actors. Assume nothing. See what their relationship to you is.** How do you relate to that character? See what you actually see, not what you think you see. Avoid urgency. Stay alert to helping fellow characters. Stay available for helping. Stay open to needing help. **Checking out gives you the opportunity to see how things are evolving, and you may spot an opportunity to help fellow characters.** Maintain who you are when helping. Check out the new actor. Take a risk. Go with it. Keep an activity going. **Avoid hanging out. You are not allowed on stage without an activity.** When you complete an activity, discover a new activity that is also a part of the whole for your job title. There's always another activity that your job title does. Show us through your activity who you are. **Respect your space objects.** Feel the objects in your hands; they are really there. They are just made out of space. Follow the rules to solve any problem that comes up. **Speak if you must.** Avoid speaking. Avoid sameness. **Avoid questions.** ◆ Cut.

FOLLOW-UP (as needed): Audience, **what professional work was everyone involved in doing?** Tell us what you saw, not what you assume. ◆ Actors, was what you chose to do for a living a part of that whole? Did you stay alert to the possibility of helping each other? **Did you help each other?** ◆ Audience, **what activity was each individual actor doing and what was their job title? Did they communicate this through their activities in the space and how they related to each other or did they announce it?** What activity was Ed doing and who was he? ◆ Ed, is that correct? No? What were you doing? What was your job title? Do you accept that this wasn't communicated to the audience? ◆ After checking out the individual activities and job titles with each actor, *ask*— Audience, **were all the actors on focus?** Did they avoid sameness? Did they avoid sameness in their job choices? **What other jobs might have also been a part of the group's**

whole professional work? Was there any speaking? Did they avoid speaking? **Did they speak when they had to?** Did they avoid questions?

SUMMARY:

As actors stretch the boundaries of the whole through their job choices, we realize that the whole initiated by the first actor is limitless as long as the expansions are a part of the whole in some way. The *guideline* for determining whether or not an actor's choice of character or activity is a part of the whole initiated by the first actor *is —does the choice extend the whole or change it?*

The only thing we have added to the playing is the choice of what you do for a living and how that affects your behavior toward the other actors and what they do for a living. This is more than just choosing your job title; it's *becoming a person* who does that for a living. How do you do that in an improvisation? By showing us how you relate to the other job people. There are ways of behaving that accompany professional relationships. *How you behave toward each other is how you communicate a relationship.*

Here's some homework: observe professionals. When you are in places of business, observe the relationship behavior between the workers and the behavior between the workers and the customers or clients. Does the Sparkletts deliveryman behave differently toward the president of Sparkletts than he does to the foreman? Observe the dynamics of these relationships. Practice labeling them as if it were a class: he's the secretary, she's the executive, he's the doctor, she's the surgeon, she's the x-ray technician, etc. Label them and watch how they relate to each other.

In terms of script acting, you might want to work in your journals on the subject of how much attention have you been paying to the occupations of the characters you've been hired to play. Is there any carryover to the total character from what they do for a living, especially in scenes that have nothing to do with the job? Remember, except for strangers, every character in every script is in relationship to the other characters and there are only two kinds of relationships, professional and personal.

THROWN OFF THE ACTING FOCUS?

When you are playing, there will be times when you encounter problems, moments that you didn't anticipate, which throw you into your head. There are ways of handling these moments that allow you to return to the focus efficiently and productively:

- If you find yourself in your head, recognize that and don't judge yourself.

- Reduce all your head thoughts to one thought, articulating the problem—e.g., I'm dealing with an invisible person; I don't have an activity; I didn't pick a job title for myself; I don't know who my fellow actor is.

- Turn the problem into a question—e.g., What can I do to show what I do for a living, and without invisible people? Who can I be that might work with [fellow actor]? How can I stop talking and rambling?

- Focus on the question, keep playing by the rules, and trust that an answer will appear to you.

If, reading this, you are saying to yourself, "But all of that is so much in the head," remember that we are talking about a situation where you are *already* in the head and it is somewhat crippling your playing. This process organizes your thoughts, removes the self-victimization, and puts you on the path out of your head.

In our work, if you follow the rules you will develop an enormous sense of freedom within the rules. Always respond according to the rules instead of according to your sense of story. If you are about to play this game and a medical professional scene is evolving, get your flash, your first intuitive impulse, e.g., "I'll be a doctor," and ask yourself, "What is a doctor's activity?" Then enter and do that, playing by the rules.

EMERGING DIALOGUE

Now that dialogue is starting to creep into our scenes, stay alert to avoiding questions. I'm talking about anything more than simple questions requiring yes or no answers, or simple questions relating to the space objects, e.g., "Is there any more milk?" When you ask another actor a question, you hinder rather than help, because they have to get off their own focus in order to go into their heads to come up with an answer. To make matters worse, that answer will inevitably be playwriting. *When you have to answer a question, you are forced to playwrite.*

◆　◆　◆

ACTIVITY DOING/PERSONAL RELATIONSHIPS[4]

After a few rounds of activity doing/job title, go on to *activity doing/personal relationships*.

SETUP: No more than five on a team. A volunteer first actor from any team begins playing the basic activity doing without making a job title choice. The activity may be simple; it need not be one that is open for multiple actors to take part in. Other team members join the playing, one at a time, having individually chosen a personal relationship—pay no attention to job titles—which they have with the first actor. Each actor coming onto the floor does an activity, which is a part of the whole activity initiated by the first actor, and must communicate to the first actor—*through the activity*—what that relationship is. The first actor keeps playing—doing the activity, checking out the oncoming actors, going with whatever happens—until he receives the communication of the relationship. The first actor then *becomes* the other half of that relationship and integrates that as a part of the whole playing.

RULES: The same as the basic activity doing, with these differences: The first actor makes no character choices whatsoever. The second and subsequent actors select the personal relationships. A personal relationship is a relationship not based on the exchange of money, goods, or services. Avoid selecting "friend." *All communicating must be done through the activity.* No playwriting, and no *telling* of the relationship, e.g., "Hi, Mom." This is not about giving clues or dropping hints. It is about behavior. The first actor is neutral—no character—until he knows who he is. Then he becomes the character as chosen for him by each of the oncoming actors. He may not refuse any relationship choices. When he becomes the character, he must do it so that his fellow actors and the audience know who he feels he is.

CLASS QUESTIONS: "Can we speak?" Yes, if you need to. "Why can't we choose friends?" It's too easy. If you did nothing more than simply act naturally and relaxed with each other, you'd be acting like a friend. Where's the challenge? The exercise is about making a choice of a personal relationship and then having to *send that communication*. Being a friend lacks the element of sending. "If we can't choose friends, what other kind of personal relationships are there?" That is for you to discover. "Are all the oncoming actors defining the first actor, or can I choose to bring a personal relationship to the second or third actor?" Everyone is defining the first actor. In the course of doing that there may be auxiliary relationships to the other actors. These should be respected and played accordingly. But, you cannot come out onto the floor and communicate to another actor what the relationship between you and the first actor is. The first actor should receive direct communication of the relationship from each oncoming actor. "Does each actor bring a new activity on stage?" Avoid sameness and stay a part of the whole.

ACTING FOCUS: For the first actor: Being open to receive the character communication while doing an activity. For the other actors: Communicating the personal relationship while doing an activity that is a part of the whole.

COACHING (as needed): *When the first actor is on stage alone—* **Watch Actor #1. See what he is doing.** There is no character. **He is neutral and may become the other half of any personal relationship you want to provide.** ◆ *After the second actor enters—* **Actor #1, stay open to receiving communication.** Stay alert to all oncoming actors. Avoid assumptions. You can improvise with people and not know who they are. **Play neutral, stay open,** and avoid conflict. **Go with it.** ✦ **Oncoming actors, communicate the relationship while doing your activity. How else can you send the communication of your relationship through that activity? Include Actor #1 in what you are doing.** ✦ Actor #1, **stay open to what's being sent, rather than what you think is being sent. Speak if you need to.** Avoid questions. **Avoid telling.** Keep checking out your fellow actors. ✦ **If you speak, you must share your voices. There is no urgency. When you know who you are, share who you are with everyone by becoming it.** Show us who you are through your own activity. ✦ One at a time. Allow the previous player to communicate before you enter. ✦ Oncoming actors, if your communication has been received, join the other parts of the whole and allow another the opportunity to send his communication. **Your activity will sustain you through all problems.** ✦ If Actor #1 becomes someone other than who an oncoming actor intends them to be, *coach the oncoming actor who is being misidentified*— Maintain your own character. Do not change it. Find new ways of communicating the correct relationship. ✦ If an actor is reluctant to leave the audience and join his teammates on the floor, *coach*— Avoid being intimidated by the rules. It's more important that you play than that you play correctly.

FOLLOW-UP (as needed): Were they on their acting focus? Was Actor #1 open to receiving the communications or was he making assumptions? Were other actors open to receiving communication from each other? Did oncoming actors send the communication of their personal relationships? Did they send their communications through their activities? Is there a difference between choosing what the relationship will be and communicating it? Could actors have communicated more through their activities? ✦ **Actor #1, who was Actor #2 to you?** ✦ **Audience, who was Actor #2 to Actor #1?** ✦ **Actor #2, who were you to Actor #1?** ✦ **Audience, did Actor #2 send the communication? Did he communicate that through his activities in the space and how he related to Actor #1, or did he announce it?** ✦ **Actor #2, could you have used your activity more in sending the communication? Did Actor #1 become that character? Did he show that to you, or tell it?** ✦ **Actor #1, do you accept that?** ✦ Ask the previous questions for each oncoming actor's relationship to Actor #1. ✦ If Actor #1 mistakenly became someone other than the oncoming actor intended him to be, did the oncoming actor stay true to his choice, or did he change to the mistakenly identified character? Did the oncoming actor stay on the acting focus and then communicate in such a way that Actor #1 realized

70

the miscommunication and changed to the intended character choice? ◆ Did they avoid sameness? ◆ Were questions avoided? Was there any playwriting? ◆ How does one communicate a relationship? By how we behave with each other. It's not about depending on your activity choice to reveal your relationship. It's about how you send the communication of the relationship *while doing your activity.*

SUMMARY:

When you make an assumption about someone, you are not open to receiving his communication. As Actor #1, if you spent time figuring out who you were, or adding up clues, you were off focus. Figuring out is a process that takes place in the head. Staying open to receive the communication is more of a full body experience, a heightened form of checking out.

In becoming the character, you behave in a way that shows the oncoming actor, and the audience, that you received the communication. If you knew who you were, but didn't become it and show it, then your knowledge of who you were contributed little to your part of the whole. It wasn't communicated to your improv mates or the audience.

Sometimes Actor #1 will think he knows who he is and instead of showing us, he will tell us, e.g., "Thanks, Mom." The problem here is that he is labeling, or *tagging,* the oncoming actor as the mother when it's possible that this is not the case. If Actor #1 is not the son, but shows us that he thinks he is *without the tag*— without saying "Mom"—then the oncoming actor has the opportunity to correct Actor #1's incorrect assumption. Improvisation allows for remedying a miscommunication without anybody's reality being violated. As long as Actor #1 avoids the tag, an incorrect assumption can be made without anyone in the audience or on stage being thrown. So, speak only when you have to, and even then, avoid tagging people, because you never know when you're working on a miscommunication.

Sometimes an oncoming actor does not communicate his relationship choice. The actor enters and assumes that because he made the relationship choice in his head, e.g., "He's my brother," that the communication of the relationship is going to be sent. In fact, it is not. All that's being sent is the communication of the activity because that is the only thing being done in the space. The relationship is not available for being seen. The oncoming actor has to find a way of *sending* the relationship choice *through the activity.* There are no restrictions on how to do it, except that it must be done through the activity, and speaking is limited to necessity. The actor might ask the coach, "How do I do that?" ◆ *The response is—* That's for you to discover.

If oncoming actors ask questions of Actor #1, it sends Actor #1 into his head to figure out an answer when he doesn't even yet know who he is. Often the questioner is merely being clever, using the question to provide clues to Actor #1. Questions become a veiled way of telling.

If you were Actor #1, you experienced spontaneous playing when you had to *go with it* without yet knowing who you were. If you didn't go with it, especially if you precluded an oncoming actor's character choice for you, you denied yourself the opportunity of going somewhere new and unexpected, which is where all improvisational acting should take you. When you don't go with it, you are controlling the outcome.

PLAYWRITING VS. DIALOGUE

Unnecessary speaking often results in playwriting—dialogue made up in the head, almost always about fictitious past or future events. Real dialogue arises spontaneously from what is happening between the actors in the now. As dialogue is appearing more and more in our scenes, it is now a steadfast rule that *no playwriting is allowed.*

> **TO THE COACH:** After the first round of this game, the coach will notice that almost all the personal relationship choices were from the nuclear family: grandparents, parents, siblings, sons and daughters. For the second round, the coach should consider challenging the group to stretch beyond these to other personal relationship choices, e.g., lover, ex-lover, stepparent, neighbor, other woman, suitor, and so on. I recommend that the coach not provide these examples, but challenge the actors to find them.
>
> Examples of inappropriate personal relationship choices may be pointed out in a team's follow-up, e.g., *babysitter* is a professional relationship. ◆ If the coach gets an argument over whether a choice is personal or professional, *handle it this way*— If we take away that person's salary, are they still around? ◆ Student: "No." ◆ That's a professional relationship. ◆ If the student answers "Yes" to the salary question, *the coach continues*— In what capacity? ◆ Student: "The babysitter [physical trainer, personal assistant, etc.] is also a friend." ◆ *The coach points out*— Friends are excluded as a choice by the rules.
>
> Another common choice that is inappropriate is *enemy.* Designating someone as an enemy is not a personal relationship choice but an attitude choice. Your brother may be your enemy, but the personal relationship is still brother.
>
> Two or more rounds of this game are recommended, time permitting. Ideally, all the actors in the group get a chance to be Actor #1.
>
> In a small group, it is worthwhile to give everyone a chance to be Actor #1 in the following two-player version:

RECEIVING CHARACTER[5]

SETUP: Played essentially the same as the previous game, with these differences: Only two actors. Three chairs are placed next to each other, and Actor #1 sits with no activity as well as no character. *It's the second actor who enters and initiates the activity at the same time that he is using it as the channel through which he is communicating the personal relationship.*

RULES: The first actor is free to join the second actor's activity, or initiate his own activity as a part of the whole.

ACTING FOCUS, COACHING, and FOLLOW-UP: Essentially the same as previous game.

◆　◆　◆

EARLY CHARACTER REVIEW

At this point in the training, character is defined by relationships, personal and professional. Relationships are revealed by how the characters behave with each other. Different relationships accommodate different behaviors. Actors must find the time, within the playing, to behave with their fellow characters according to the nature of the relationship. It now becomes a rule of the technique that in every scene improv, *Every actor must choose what his character does for a living and whether or not he has any personal relationships with the other characters in the scene.* In other words, know what part (of the whole) you are playing.

In terms of script acting, you might work in your journals on the subject of how much attention have you been paying to the personal relationships of the characters you've been hired to play. Unless you are playing a stranger, every character in every script has relationships to other characters. Have you been bringing the behavior of those relationships to your work?

IMPROVISATION RULES NOW IN PLACE

- No one is allowed on stage without an activity.

- Every actor must choose what his character does for a living and whether or not he has any personal relationships with the other characters in the scene, and he must communicate it.

- There is never a reason for being off the selected acting focus.

> **TO THE COACH:** At this point, it is important to do one round of *Full Body Whisper*, the first vocal doing acting focus in chapter 5. In that summary, read *Acting Focus as Path to Improvisation*.

LOCATION

In Improvisation Technique, actors improvise in a bare space, yet no scene improvisation takes place in a void. The actors should know how to improvise the communication of the scene's location (other than stating it). Too many actors treat the location as no more than a picture, which they act in front of. The location or setting of any scripted scene or improvisation can be an important tool for the actor, offering potential for the development of the scene or improv. How can this potential be realized?

All locations are defined by the objects within them. Take a big room and fill it with tables and chairs, tablecloths, candles, serving stands, cutlery, glasses, and a counter with a cash register on it: you have a restaurant. Clear all the stuff out, bring in desks, a chalkboard, and books, and the same room is now a classroom.

PHYSICAL DISCOVERY OF LOCATION [6]

This is the first exercise in the location series.

SETUP: Teams of 8–10 each. If the group is fewer than ten, everyone is on the same team. In huddles, each team selects a location. Locations that are generally bare—dance studio, playground, etc.—should be avoided. If teams have more than five players, avoid small-capacity—private bathroom, tool shed, etc.—locations. After the huddles: (1) Everyone is coached to look out into the empty playing area and "see the empty space." (2) A volunteer first player announces his team number and enters the playing area. Playing is now restricted to this team only. (3) He "discovers" a furniture piece or fixture that is a part of the whole selected location and makes physical contact with it in the space. (4) He exits. (5) The next volunteer player from the same team enters the playing area and makes physical contact with the item the first player contacted. He then discovers a new furniture piece or fixture that is also a part of the same whole location. (6) He exits. (7) Each successive player on that team enters and plays one at a time. (8) Each player must physically contact all of the previous items discovered by the previous players and then must discover a new item by physically contacting it.

RULES: The playing area must be absolutely empty before a team begins. Prior to entering, avoid preselecting the item you will discover. The item you discover is a space item and must be a set piece or fixture. *For this one exercise only:* chairs, couches, benches, etc, are space items. No props allowed. You discover one set piece only and no props. You may only discover your item after you have physically made contact—in any order you wish—with every set piece previously discovered by your teammates. Set pieces are objects or items that are not portable hand props. They usually include furniture or fixtures that are a part of any location. For instance, a soda machine is a set piece while the money and the can of soda are props. A window is a set piece; the drapery and cords constitute another set piece. A sink is a set piece, and soap is a prop.

ACTING FOCUS: Relating to a location and everything in it.

COACHING (as needed): Everyone, look at the playing area. See the empty space. ✦ Action. **✦** *For the first player—* **Walk out into the location. Look all around you. See the whole location with everything in it. Something you haven't previously thought of will appear.** You may discover it. **Go and make physical contact with it.** Share your physical contact with the audience. Respect the space. **Exit. ✦** *For the second and following players—* Take a risk and avoid selecting your item until it's time to discover it. Avoid urgency. See the entire location in the space with all the set pieces in it. **Relate to everything in the location, including already discovered item(s). Make physical contact with everything already in the space in any way you want to.** In any order you wish. **Respect the space objects. Physically contact them in the space where they have been discovered.** Respect your teammates' discoveries. **Pay attention. Feel that in your hands. It's really there; it's just made out of space.** Share that physical contact with the audience. **When you have finished physically contacting everything already there, look around you and see the whole location.** Look out into the space, not within your head. Discoveries are available to you. **Explore the location with your eyes. See what there is to see and then see more. Something new to physically contact will appear to you. Discover it. Go and make physical contact with it.** If nothing is appearing to you, keep physically contacting what's already there as you keep looking around the location. Look behind, in front of, above, and next to previously placed set pieces. Look where there are no set pieces already. Allow something new to emerge. Keep looking; keep seeing. When you discover something new, go over and make physical contact. **As you make contact with your discovery, help your fellow actors who will follow you. Actors who have not yet played, keep seeing the entire location with everything in it and not a list of set pieces already placed. Everybody, stay on the acting focus: Relate to the whole location and everything in it, not just to individual set pieces. ✦** *After the last player exits—* Cut.

FOLLOW-UP (as needed): Everyone, look at the playing area. What location do you see? If the audience immediately calls out the name of the location, point out that before the exercise began they were all coached to see the empty playing area and now, with no "real" alterations to that empty area, they all see a specific location [name the location]. *The invisible has been made visible and that is magic.* If the audience is confused as to what the location is, point that out. ◆ Audience, **did the actors respect their own space items and each other's?** If they did, the location will be very visible and feel anchored to the playing area. If the location appears fuzzy, that is a sign that the space objects were not respected and were frequently in the actors' heads rather than truly in the space. If the same set piece was physically contacted in parts of the playing area different from where it was first discovered, then that item was more in the actors' heads then in the space. The same is true for items that were walked through. ◆ Did the actors follow the rules? **Did they physically contact all the prior discoveries before discovering their own contribution?** Did each actor only discover one set piece? Did anyone also discover props? Does everybody have to contact the items in the same way? Did the actors help their fellow actors? What about when John discovered his item and we couldn't see what he was doing because his back was in the way? ◆ **Players, how many of you made the choice of your discovery prior to entering the location? Do you accept that you deprived yourselves of the opportunity to make an authentic discovery? How many of you were focusing on the set pieces instead of the entire location?** ◆ *When the follow-up is completed—*

Magic Finger-Snap Location Disappearance

We have this [name the location] on the floor, and there is another team to go, so on the count of three, everyone snap your fingers at it. Watch it disappear and become the empty playing area again. **One. Two. Three.** ◆ All, including the coach, snap their fingers. ◆ Okay, next team.

SUMMARY:

In traditional acting classes, actors are frequently advised to "take more risks" and yet, they are seldom taught how to do that. The coach may point out that this exercise offered two opportunities for the actors to develop their risk-taking abilities: (1) To preplan vs. going up there and seeing what happens. (2) Volunteering to play early in the exercise vs. later. Playing later in the exercise was a greater risk. The coach might suggest that those who played early and/or preselected their object have an opportunity to write about that in their journal. In time, you may become more alert to opportunities to increase the challenge in your class and career work.

> **TO THE COACH:** Props are to be avoided because they too easily shift the emphasis from the location to activity. *The purpose of this exercise* is to expand the actors' physical doing prowess from doing activities to physically making contact with the location [set].

Beyond noting the more obvious disrespect of the space items—walking through items, inadvertently moving set pieces—the coach should observe the actor who changes an important detail of the object. For example, previous actors established a door with the hinge on the left, and he uses the same door, only now the hinge is on the right. This often suggests that the actor has been in the audience seeing his teammates' discoveries as items on a list he is memorizing to make his own playing by the rules easier. In such a case, the coach might point out that when watching teammates play, *the actor should be focused on the entire evolving location*, staying open to seeing it and relating to it instead of trying to manage it. To focus on something means to focus on it so totally that you exclude any outside thoughts, forces, problems, or considerations.

The coach should keep emphasizing the discovery of the set pieces because that discovery is the equivalent of *emergence*. Over time, as a deeper experience of emerging phenomena develops, it will carry over to emergence in activity, relationships, emotions, character, and dialogue.

End this session with another round of full body whisper.

◆　◆　◆

PHYSICAL CONTACT WITH THE LOCATION [7]

Having been introduced to location work, we now get into the meat and potatoes of it.

SETUP: Teams of 2–5 each. The coach, at a chalkboard, asks the group for the name of any location. He then asks for the names of set pieces found in this location and lists them on the left side of the chalkboard. Then he asks for the props found there, and lists them. The rest of the chalkboard is for drawing a floor plan, with all these set pieces and the props. The group calls out where they want each item placed in the floor plan; the coach draws them. ◆ Actors count off in teams and go to their huddles with a piece of a notebook-size paper and a pencil. In their huddles, the actors select a location. They list the set pieces and props on the left side of the page and then draw the floor plan. When they are finished, they call the coach over to their huddle. ◆ *Coach*— You have just drawn the location for your improvisation. Now, pick characters for yourselves. Each of you, choose a job title and decide what, if any, personal relationships you have between you. When you have done that, select a group activity in which all of you will participate. Once you begin the improvisation, you may all have different specific activities, but they would all be considered a part of the whole group activity that you are now selecting for the team. The choice of the activity is usually the reason a person is in a particular location. We are in a kitchen in order to eat or cook. We are in an office in order to work. Although this is not always the case—we may study in a kitchen, not a library—notice that the choice of an activity is frequently related to the location in which it is done. For this activity choice, avoid cleaning, searching, setting up, or closing down. Write your choices on top of the floor plan. ♦ The coach leaves the huddle and the actors make their final choices. When they have done this, the coach collects all the drawings. When a team gets up to improvise, the coach tapes the drawing to the upstage wall of the playing area.

RULES: Place real chairs in the playing area wherever they are drawn on the floor plan. Use real chairs for couches, benches, or beds, but nothing else. ♦ While improvising, you follow all previous activity rules—always doing an activity, checking out your fellow actors, helping each other, respecting the space items, behaving toward each other according to your character choices, etc. In addition, your primary acting focus is on *making physical contact with everything on your floor plan*. From time to time, you should consult the floor plan. It is not necessary to integrate this as a part of the whole scene. Just walk over to the floor plan and quietly check out what is left for you to physically contact, and where is it located. You will also be reminded of what is left to physically contact and where it is through checking out your fellow actors and noticing what they are physically contacting and where they are doing it. The exercise is over when all the actors have completed making physical contact with every item.

ACTING FOCUS: Physically contacting everything in the location as a part of your whole activity and character.

CLASS QUESTIONS: "What about speaking?" Speak if necessary and avoid playwriting. "Does the whole team together have to physically contact everything?" Each individual has to physically contact everything. "Do we have to physically contact every single prop?" You have to physically contact every single set piece and prop, except where there are multiple props of the same type, e.g., silverware. With those props, you must at least physically contact selective or representative props, rather than all of them. "Can we add props we didn't discuss in the huddle or draw?" It is always encouraged that you discover new items in the space. This means you need to check each other out in order to respect each other's discoveries, and to physically contact them.

COACHING (as needed): *Before starting the improvisation—* **Yes or no answers: Does everyone know the name of the location you are acting in? What your character's job title is? Whether or not you have any personal relationships with your teammates? What the overall**

78

general activity is that you are participating in? Avoid planning how you are going to accomplish the acting focus. Don't worry about playing correctly. You know the rules. Choose to stay on your acting focus. ◆ **Action.** ◆ *During the improv—* **Check out your improv mates.** See where they are making their contacts. No playing alone. Be a part of the whole team. Avoid telling what things are. Make physical contact with them. **Respect your space items. Each of you is responsible for physically contacting everything drawn for this location and respecting it in the space. See the whole location in the space. Relate to the location. No urgency.** Integrate your physical contact of the location with your activity. Avoid hanging out. When in doubt, return to your activity or **check out your drawing.** Respect your character. Respect the others' characters. **Stay alert. Stay open.** Make actual physical contact instead of announcing it. Avoid questions. Take responsibility for staying on your acting focus. **Is there anything you've left out?** Your acting focus is on the location, not the activity. Share your discoveries in the space. Avoid walking through set pieces. If you whisper, full body whisper! ◆ When it seems all have completed physically contacting everything, *call —* Cut.

FOLLOW-UP (as needed): **Audience, what was the location? Do you see it? Who were the characters: job titles? Did you see any personal relationships?** Were the characters available to be seen, or were they announced? **What was the overall activity?** What were the specific activities that were a part of that whole general activity? **Did the actors physically contact everything?** Who left what out? Did they frequently consult their floor plan? **Did they respect their space items?** Did they walk through set pieces? Did a set piece physically move around the stage by itself? Did they show us the items or announce [e.g., "I'll get the sugar. It's in the cabinet over the sink."] to us what they were? Did you hear the actors when they spoke? **Was there unnecessary speaking?** Did they integrate their physical contacting of the location with their activity and character? **Were they on their acting focus?** ◆ **Actors, do you agree?** ◆ *When the follow-up is completed, the group does the magic finger-snap location disappearance.*

SUMMARY:

As in physical discovery of location, the actors have transformed an empty playing area into a visible location, or set, for the improvisation to take place in. In addition, the actors have discovered that physically contacting the set pieces accomplishes a relationship between the actor and his surroundings so that the location is a great deal more than just a picture to act in front of. Also, with the physical contact of a location's set pieces, the actor extends his potential for more physical doing. *Every physical contact with the location creates a form of physical doing other than the initial activity.* Physically contacting the location creates a *miniactivity* around every physical contact, e.g., *opening* the cabinet door, *adjusting* the television set, *ringing up* the cash register, *fluffing up* the bed, *kicking* the tires, and so on. Miniactivities are activities of very short duration. Use of these gives the actors a variety of potential breaks from their ongoing activity without stopping physical doing. The miniactivities provide improvisational potential in addition to that provided by the main activity. We begin to see that there are opportunities for physical doing other than doing an activity. *Acting is doing and there is always more to do.*

TO THE COACH: The huddles usually take 20–30 minutes; each improv lasts about 10–14 minutes. ◆ Do not reveal the acting focus prior to the huddles. The first mention should occur just prior to the first team's playing the exercise, after they have placed the real chairs (if necessary) in the playing area. ◆ Dividing the huddles into two parts provides for uninhibited location choices and keeps the actors from playing safe. If they know what characters they are improvising and what they will be doing as they draw the floor plan, they will plan the improv and select set pieces and props to accommodate that. ◆ Teams are coached to avoid cleaning, searching, setting up, or closing down as general activity choices in order to maintain the challenge of the exercise.

Caution vs. Full Body Spirit

Some actors will play timidly, without verve. When this first occurs use the coaching to diminish their caution and heighten their energy. ◆ If the coaching is not successful, then in the follow-up, a*sk the players*— Did you play with full body energy? Did you feel you were in your heads figuring out what to do? Were you afraid? What does full body energy applied to an acting focus feel like? ◆ I always introduce physical contact with the location in a session that begins with the traditional children's game, *Red light Green light.* After the last question, I *ask the group*— Did you notice what everyone looked like playing Red light Green light? That is what it looks and feels like to be on an acting focus with full body—which includes mind and spirit—energy. In Red light Green light, when everyone was alert, ready, poised to spring into advancing forward without being seen by whoever is it, when everyone jumped into action without hesitation upon seeing the opportunity to do so, they were applying full body energy to a focus. You saw what they looked like. You know what you felt. You should approach every acting focus in the same way: no caution, no fear. There is no danger involved, except to your old frames of reference. You are encouraged to attack the acting focus. We want it to become second nature to make contact, unhesitatingly, with your location (active), rather than simply reside in it (passive). If you felt you played hesitatingly or fearfully, you might write about that in your journals.

Rules transcend assumptions

During a follow-up, what if a player protests that he was unable to physically contact a specific item because his character would never do so. For instance, when the character's activity is shopping and the location is a store, a player says, "My character's job title is a bank president. I'm a customer in this store, and I would never use their cash register!" The coach should acknowledge the logic of the issue *and then point out—* The customer must physically contact the cash register because *that is the rule of the exercise.*

It is logical that the customer doesn't go and use the cash register, but as Ionesco said, "Logic is the enemy of art." In our Improvisation Technique workshop, we are learning how to improvise acting. This is a theatrical and artistic process, not a pursuit of logic. If the rule is to make physical contact with the cash register, then go and make contact with it. Whatever problem this poses becomes part of the challenge of the exercise.

Use the rules as a springboard into the unknown. Following the rules, you can go to the cash register and *help a fellow actor.* Start helping the clerk ring up sales and the clerk will be challenged, *improvisationally*, to find a way of allowing you to do this because he too is following a rule, *go with it.* How you solve the problem is a big learning moment for you. While crossing to the cash register, you will find the answer, *and that will be an improvisational moment.*

The acting focus will take care of providing an artistic form to the scene rather than having general chaos with everyone just running around contacting everything. Remember, the acting focus requires that all the physical contacts be done as a *part of your whole activity and character.*

Improvisation Technique rules are designed to give you true freedom. Anything can happen, and you are free to follow any impulse, so long as you improvise by the rules.

LOCATION FOCUS [8]

For practice on location work, have the actors play a round or two of *Location Focus.*

SETUP: 2–5 per team. (1) We play one team at a time. Any actor may start by coming out on the floor. (2) The first actor privately selects a location and proceeds to make physical contact with the set pieces of that location while doing an activity, which is open to involving the teammates. Any set pieces or objects you use must be made out of space. (3) Once another actor on the team receives the communication as to the location and nature of the first player's activity, that actor chooses a character and activity that could be a part of the whole activity initiated by the first player. The second player comes out on the floor joining the first player and does his activity while *also physically contacting in the space those set pieces already discovered by the first player and discovering and physically contacting additional set pieces which are a part of the whole same location.* And so on, until all actors on that team are out on the floor doing their activities, physically contacting the location, and behaving according to their character choices.

RULES: When starting, announce your team number. All set pieces and props must be made out of space. You may use real chairs as any set piece that was intended to support the body. Grab one from the audience, as you need it. All previous activity and character rules apply. The first actor has no character; he just establishes the location and activity. Oncoming actors must make character (professional and/or personal relationships) choices. They may provide character for the first actor depending on their own character choices. If they do, they must communicate it to the first actor through their physically contacting the set pieces and activity. Speak if necessary. Every team member must play.

ACTING FOCUS: Making physical contact with the location while doing and showing your activity, which is a part of the whole team's activity.

CLASS QUESTIONS: "So we have to touch everything that everybody else touches?" Your acting focus is to make physical contact with the location, which means the set pieces. There will always be another set piece to get to and contact. "Are we allowed to use props?" Yes. "Do we have to contact everything?" It is not a rule like the previous exercise, which was a training exercise. However, making contact with everything is a challenge available to you. "Do we have to have a character?" It is recommended that you always make character choices and communicate them.

COACHING (as needed): Make contact with the location's set pieces or we won't know where you are. Integrate your activity with the physical contact of your location. **The activity never takes over from going to the location; it's always integrated.** See the location before you enter. Allow what's happening to happen, before you join it. Respect your set pieces and objects. Feel them in your hands. Keep your set pieces and objects in the space. **Check out your fellow players. They are adding set pieces that are suitable for you; they are making discoveries that are available to you.** ◆ Maintain your characters. Show us who you are. **Stay alert.** Stay open to receiving personal relationship communication. Relate to your fellow characters as necessary. ◆ **Keep contacting the location. Contact what others have discovered and discover your own set pieces. Respect their set pieces and objects. To look at a set piece is not enough; you must physically contact it.** Avoid hanging out while waiting to contact the location. Avoid walking through set pieces. **Add new set pieces.** Use the entire playing area for discovering new set pieces. **See what there is to see. Keep looking**

around, seeing the location, and going with it. **Keep checking each other out and you might see something for you to contact.** Exits and reentering are allowed. Avoid avoiding the challenge. Stay on your acting focus. **Everyone's free to add new set pieces and everyone must check each other out to know about previously placed set pieces. Trust your acting focus and let it solve your problems.** Apply more focus to the location. **Keep seeing the whole location and all the set pieces in it. Go to it.** Your primary acting focus is contacting the location; your secondary focus is activity and character. **The activity is to support your contacting the location.** Focus on the location while doing the activity. If you have finished your activity, do it again or select another activity that is also a part of the whole and do that. **Only looking at something equals hanging out. If you speak, share it with everybody.** Speak only when necessary. **Avoid announcing what you are contacting. Physically help your improv mates.** ◆ If the last team member is staying in the audience and not getting up to play, *coach*— Everyone on this team must play. Take advantage of the opportunity to play. It's more important that you play than that you play correctly. Discover your bravery. ◆ After all the team members are on the floor, the game needs less than three more minutes. For the final minute, *the coach might say*— One minute! One minute to heighten your acting focus and contact those items you haven't previously contacted and/or discover another set piece. ◆ *The coach ends it*— Cut.

FOLLOW-UP (as needed): Audience, what was the location? Do you see it? Was it the same location for all the actors? ◆ **Who were the characters:** job titles? **Did you see any personal relationships?** Which actors? Were the characters available to be seen by us or were they announced? ◆ **What was the overall activity for the team?** What were the specific activities that were a part of that whole general activity? ◆ Did the actors physically contact each other's set pieces? Did they discover and contact new set pieces? Did they physically contact them in a way that allowed fellow actors the opportunity to know what they were? ◆ Did they respect their space items? Did they walk through set pieces? Did a set piece physically move around the stage? ◆ Did they show us the items or announce to us what they were? Did you hear the actors when they spoke? **Was there unnecessary speaking?** When they spoke, was it dialogue of necessity, or playwriting, or announcements of what they were physically contacting? ◆ **Did they integrate their physical contacting of the location with their activity and character?** Were they open to receiving personal relationships? Did they bring on personal relationships? ◆ Did they avoid sameness in their activity choices? Did they avoid sameness in their character choices? ◆ How can you avoid sameness in the location choices? By discovering different kinds of set pieces, yes, but what about when all have to contact the same set piece? By physically contacting them in different ways. ◆ Did they use the whole playing area for their location? ◆ **Were they on their acting focus?** When weren't they on their acting focus? When any player was standing around watching the others or just doing their activity for a lengthy period of time without physically contacting the location, he was off focus. ◆ Actors, do you agree with the class's observations? Did you choose any personal relationships we didn't see? Did you discover any set pieces, or only contact others' discoveries? Did you feel you were on the acting focus? ◆ *When the follow-up is completed, the group does the magic finger-snap location disappearance.*

SUMMARY:

Hopefully, you can now all distinguish between physically doing an activity and physically contacting the location. You see that they are done concurrently and can support each other. When an improvisation is short in either area, you have the ability now to make up the difference and provide what is missing or necessary.

CONTACT VS. TOUCH

It should be noted that when I was asked the question about touching the set pieces, I answered without using the word *touch*, but with the stated vocabulary—*physical contact*. The moment you start using the word touch you limit your physicality capabilities to fingers and hands. You have your entire body to use as an instrument to make contact with things. Why limit yourself through your vocabulary choices?

LOCATION FILLS WAITING

Frequently in these improvisations, there is a moment or beat when one of the actors is waiting to make contact with a set piece. For instance, it is a gym location and he is waiting to use the stair master while someone else is on it. From our activity work, we know that waiting is a passive activity to be avoided. So, while the actor's basic activity during this beat is waiting, he has an opportunity to fill that passivity by contacting another item in the location. He can go to the water fountain, contact it, and have a drink of water. This gives him a *miniactivity* during the passivity of waiting. The exciting part of this is that he won't have to come up with the choice of drinking from his head. All he has to do is follow the rule, physically contact the location, and in going to contact the fountain, the drinking part will happen spontaneously. Miniactivities emerge out of the physical contacts with the location. Whenever you find yourself hanging out on stage, or involved with a passive activity, *physically contact the location*. All those activities forbidden you during the activity part of our training—waiting, looking, wishing, wanting, seeing, etc.—are now available to you as long as you support them with the physical doing which accompanies *physically contacting the location*. The other side of the coin is that if your activity is already an active one, you can enhance and heighten it, also by *physically contacting the location*.

LINEAR FOCUS VS. LATERAL FOCUS

The way an actor relates to contacting the location is different from the way he relates to doing an activity. Doing an activity is a linear process. Contacting the location is a lateral process. With an activity one follows a natural order—beginning, middle, and end—in a linear fashion. Contacting the location does not have a beginning, middle, and end. It's all middle. In doing an activity, the actor sort of looks up and down at what he is doing. In contacting a location, the actor sort of looks sideways at what he can next contact or discover. When he is making the contact, the moment of the miniactivity, he is back to looking up and down, but then he has to go on to looking sideways for the next set piece. This is a lateral relationship between the actor and the location.

For instance, in an improvisation set in a parlor (location): As soon as the actor establishes she is knitting (activity), she's up and away from the chair, moving laterally, following the horizon. What's over there? Ah, the stereo! She makes contact with it and then she's away from that, following the horizon. What's over there? Ah, the coffee table! In contacting the location, the actors are going all over the place and the location just emerges into existence.

> **TO THE COACH:** Many great moments in acting are the moments of *emergence*. For example, that moment when you look at your scene partner and something spontaneously emerges about your relationship that you never knew before that moment. Improvisation Technique training is designed to put the actor in a constant state of allowing things to emerge. Whenever an actor takes the opportunity to discover rather than preplan something, he strengthens his instrument in the emergence mode. We begin developing this facility in basic space work like contacting the location, establishing emergence experientially as a part of the improvisational process. We'll see the carryover in the more sophisticated aspects of improvisational acting, without or with memorized lines.
>
> The coach should be aware that he is introducing multiple focuses. He is asking the actors to be on more than one acting focus at the same time: contacting the location, doing the activity, and communicating character. I don't recommend pointing this out to the actors prior to playing this exercise; they have enough going on just to participate.

❖   ❖   ❖

LOCATION REVIEW

Physical doing now includes making physical contact with the set pieces and props that are found in the particular location in which an improvisation takes place. *In future improvisations, prior to starting, teams set up their location by locating essential space set pieces according to team agreement.* They also discover additional set pieces as they improvise. Making physical contact with the location provides the actors with their set and turns this set into an area of opportunity for further physical doing. New activities may emerge from the actors' use of the location. Miniactivities also emerge around each of the physical contacts with the location's set pieces and props. While the actor employing Improvisation Technique would never be concerned with asking himself what any particular improvisation needs in terms of story development, he is in a position to see whether or not the location or set is contributing to the whole improvisation. Employing physical contact of the location is the means for immediately and spontaneously responding to this need.

TO THE COACH: Should the coach feel that the actors are not appreciating the distinction between activity and location, there is a little *demonstration* I do which might be beneficial.

I tell the group I'm going to do *two brief improvisations*, each one with a different acting focus. I place a chair center stage before I begin.

For the first, I enter the playing area carrying a space briefcase, cross to the chair, sit, and place the briefcase on the floor next to me, open it, remove my space book, notebook, and pen, place them on space table in front of me, look in notebook, open the book, leaf through the pages until I find the correct page, read from book, and take notes in notebook. ♦ Cut.

The whole thing takes less than two minutes. *I ask the group*— What was my acting focus? They respond, "Activity, studying." I announce that for demonstration purposes, I'm going to do the same improv again and it will truly be an improv because I'll have a different acting focus. I go off stage to the same spot I entered from for the first improv.

For the second, As I enter, carrying a space briefcase, I push through a space turnstile, cross to the chair, sit and place the briefcase on the floor next to me, open it, remove a space book, notebook, and pen, place them on space table in front of me, get up and cross stage right, take a drink from space water fountain, return to the chair and sit, look in the notebook, get up and cross downstage center, make contact with space card-catalogue drawers, finger down and across different drawers until I find correct one, open it , thumb through cards until I find the correct one, keep one finger on the correct card while the other hand slides out a writing surface, take a slip of paper off the top of the card-catalogue set piece, find a pencil on a string attached to the set piece, write down the Dewey decimal number from the card, push the writing surface back into the set piece, close the drawer, cross upstage center, my back to the audience, look on space shelves for a required book, don't find it, find a

86

different book that seems interesting, remove it from the shelf, look at it, replace it on the shelf, look at the slip of paper again, cross around shelves, face the audience now, continue looking on the shelves, making contact with various books, checking the slip of paper in my hand against books on the shelves, find the required book, cross to the chair, open the book, leaf through the pages until finding the correct page, read from the book and take notes in the notebook, decide there is too much material to take notes on, get up with the book and cross stage left to the space xerox machine, operate the machine, make a copy of a page from the book, return to the chair, and resume studying. ◆ Cut.

I ask the group— What was my acting focus? They respond, "Location, library." Am I still doing my activity, studying? "Yes." They now get the distinction between activity and location, and they appreciate how much more there is to do when employing both. When I do this demonstration—between rounds of physical contact with the location and location focus—I do it because I see the teams not contacting the location with gusto.

IMPROVISATION RULES NOW IN PLACE

- No one is allowed on stage without an activity.

- Every actor must choose what his character does for a living and whether or not he has any personal relationships with the other actors in the scene, and communicate it.

- Every actor must frequently make physical contact with the location.

- There is never a reason for being off the selected acting focus.

STATIONARY DOING

The final part of physical doing training deals with the discovery and use of objects *when the actor is limited in his mobility* for any reason, e.g., seated, must stay in place or on his mark, in a crowd, and so on. The introductory exercise is *Eating and Drinking while Listening and Speaking*.

EATING AND DRINKING WHILE LISTENING AND SPEAKING[9]

SETUP: 2–8 per team. Each team huddles and selects a topic for a conversation that they all feel comfortable participating in. The only topic to be avoided is food or food related. No character choices are made: all participate in the exercise as themselves. No activity or location choices are made. The improv starts with all sitting in the playing area in a semi circle around a space table. Prior to starting, they all agree on the height of the table by placing their palms on the space table surface and adjusting their palms until all are at the same height about the height of a real table. When the exercise starts, the actors begin, for the first time in the training, a *double acting focus:* Each actor is to *eat and drink* an entire large meal, from start to finish, using space objects *and simultaneously,* each actor is to *participate equally* in the verbal discussion.

RULES: Avoid selecting what you will eat and drink prior to playing. You may never leave your chair. Each of you is responsible for doing *two things* at the same time: *continuously eating and drinking* an entire space meal *and participating equally* in the verbal conversation.

ACTING FOCUS: Continuously eating and drinking while listening and speaking.

CLASS QUESTION: "Do we take turns speaking or all talk at the same time?" You will have to solve that for yourselves. Always use the rules you have learned to solve any problems that come up. For instance, *help your fellow actor* to participate equally in the conversation.

COACHING (as needed): *Prior to improvising—* Continuously eating, drinking, listening, and talking does not mean alternating between them. You talk or listen *while* eating or drinking. This is a double acting focus. No matter how interesting the conversation may become, you keep eating or drinking. ◆ Set the height of your table. ◆ Action. ◆ *While improvising—* **Respect your space props.** Feel your utensils in your hands. Take your time. Continuously, not urgently. **Really chew. Really swallow.** No pretend eating. Really taste the food and the beverages. While you're doing this, you are also carrying on the conversation. **Avoid stopping to listen. No matter how interesting the conversation, keep eating or drinking. Reach out and discover the food on the table.** What you need is out there; just reach and discover. Taste what you are drinking. What's the temperature of that beverage? Smell the smells. **Participate in the conversation.** Allow your improv mates to share the conversation. **Allow your meal to proceed.** Stay on the double acting focus. Find a way to participate in the discussion. Avoid hanging out. The food and drink are discovered on the table. Keep up your involvement in the discussion. **Share the conversation. Speak if you have something to say. Share that thought. Two things at once.** ◆ Cut.

FOLLOW-UP (as needed): Audience, did the actors eat, drink, and converse simultaneously? Were they all on the double acting focus or did they alternate between the two? Did you notice actors stopping their eating and drinking because they were interested in the conversation? If the conversation is really interesting, do you have to heighten or lessen your focus on the eating and drinking? Did they participate equally in the conversation? Did some actors limit their verbal participation to telling stories? **What were they eating and drinking? Were their props in the space or in their heads?** ◆ Actors, do you agree? Were you aware of times when you were not on the double acting focus? Those of you who were on the double acting focus and didn't alternate them, did you find that the improvisational aspect of the verbal conversation was difficult or easy? ***Did you find yourself making discoveries in the space of what you were eating or drinking?* Did you discover anything else in the space? What were some of these discoveries?**

SUMMARY:

When actors begin applying a multiple focus they increase their capabilities for doing many things at once. The more you do at the same time, the more your abilities as an actor extend. This also increases your presence.

Those of you who were able to improvise on the double acting focus, instead of alternating between them, discovered that it was easy, verbally, to go with the conversation. The more you are physically involved in the doing, in this case, eating and drinking, the easier it is to improvise verbally with authenticity and no pretense or inhibitions. Everyone was free to say what he had to say and everyone had something to say. If you stopped the eating and drinking, you found it difficult to participate in the verbal aspect of the improv. You became stifled by a need to be clever or funny, or you were worried about what to say next. At these times, some of you further impeded your spontaneity by telling a story. Storytelling deprives you of the opportunity to improvise dialogue. For instance, "That reminds me of something that happened last week. My husband and I went shopping and when we got there . . . [rest of story]" is storytelling. It keeps you out of the improvisational state and anchored in the past because the story has its beginning, middle, and end, which you already know. Improvisation is about the unknown! When you are improvising dialogue, always avoid telling stories.

The name of the acting focus is *Eating and Drinking while Listening and Speaking*. You can substitute any activity for eating and drinking while retaining the second acting focus, listening and speaking. Speaking may now be more accessible than we have previously allowed. No longer do you only have permission to speak when you must.

As long as it's integrated with the physical doing aspect of the improvisation and you do not playwrite, *you may speak when you have something to say*. You now have the opportunity to be double focusing on the conversation in which you are involved as well as on the continuous physical doing of any activity and contacting the location. However, at this early stage in the training, you don't stop your physical doing just because you want to speak. The minute you stop physically doing in order to speak, you are going to start playwriting, telling stories. Focusing on the activity (eating and drinking) pulls your attention away from self-absorption, self-limitations, and self-consciousness and makes the verbal part of your scene easy, free, and authentic.

> **TO THE COACH:** Actors on this focus begin to employ their senses of taste and smell experientially without emphasizing memory of the past, the way a traditional sense memory exercise does. The tastes and smells are here *in the present*, accompanying the space food. *Every moment of remembering is an obstacle to spontaneous acting.* Even when memory is employed in an exercise and is not intended for use in performance, it fosters process not grounded in the moment (present).
>
> While the summary highlights the dialogue aspect of the exercise and its relationship to the activity, the coach should be aware that the primary acting muscle being exercised here is *the development of the actor's ability to reach out into the space from a stationary position and discover space objects.* We expand on that with the next exercise.

❖   ❖   ❖

DISCOVERING OBJECTS NEAR YOU[10]

SETUP: 2–6 per team. Each team huddles and selects a topic for a meeting they will all participate in, e.g., PTA meeting to raise funds, merchants' association meeting to plan security, students planning a dance. No activity or location choices are made. The first team to improvise sits in the playing area in a semicircle around a space table. When the exercise begins the actors commence a *double acting focus:* (1) each actor continuously discovers, with physical contact, numerous (space) objects during the meeting and (2) each actor participates equally in the verbal discussion.

RULES: Avoid selecting what you will discover prior to playing. You may never leave your chair. Each of you is responsible for doing two things at the same time: *continuously* discovering objects throughout the meeting and participating equally in the verbal conversation. The objects, made out of space, are available for discovery in three or more areas: on the table, on the floor within your reach, on or about your body and clothes, or anywhere I haven't mentioned, as long as you don't leave your chair. Avoid overuse of any object you discover. In other words, don't change the acting focus from continuously discovering new objects to doing an ongoing activity with one of your discoveries, e.g., discovering a sandwich and then eating it throughout the meeting to the exclusion of discovering anything else. All objects are discovered and disposed of as a part of the whole meeting.

ACTING FOCUS: Discovering objects near you while listening and speaking.

COACHING (as needed): *Prior to playing—* **This is a double acting focus. Keep up your part of the discussion while continuously discovering with physical contact numerous objects on the table, the floor, your body, or anywhere you can reach without getting up. No matter how interesting the conversation may be, keep discovering more objects. Set the height of your table.** ◆ Action. ◆ *While playing—* **Respect your space props.** Feel them in your hands. They are really there; they are just made out of space. **Keep up the discussion.** Participate in the discussion. **Reach out and discover an object.** Use it a little bit, then put it down and discover something else. **Avoid overusing any one object.** Avoid stopping to listen or speak. Keep discovering. **Avoid urgency.** Stay on the double acting focus. Avoid hanging out. Discover the next object. **Share the discussion.** Share your voices. **Share that thought. Say what you have to say.** Avoid hanging out with one object. Share the object with us. Avoid announcing it. Stay alert to your fellow actors. Share the object with your fellow actors. It is your responsibility to communicate it without telling. **Discover things not previously discovered.** The moment you find yourself totally immersed in the conversation is the moment for your next discovery. **Reach and discover.** Help your fellow actors to participate in the discussion. ◆ Avoid discovering all of your objects in the same area. Reach out on the table and discover. Reach down to the floor and discover. Reach into a pocket and discover. Avoid talking about the object; make physical contact with it. Take a risk. Discover your bravery. ◆ Cut.

FOLLOW-UP (as needed): **Audience, were the actors capable of conversing and discovering objects simultaneously? Were they all on the double acting focus, or did they alternate between the two?** Did you notice actors stopping their discovering objects because they were interested in the conversation? If the conversation is really interesting, do you have to heighten or lessen your focus on discovering objects? Did they participate equally in the conversation? Did some actors limit their verbal participation to telling stories? What were some of the objects discovered? Did they discover objects in all three areas available to them or did they limit their discoveries to only one area? Did anyone find a new area to discover an object in? **Were the objects discovered and disposed of as a part of the whole meeting?** Were their props in the space or in their heads? Did they announce their discoveries or show them? Did they share the conversation with the audience? ◆ **Actors, do you agree?** Were you aware of times when you were not on the double acting focus? Those of you who were on the double acting focus and didn't alternate them, did you find that the improvisational aspect of the verbal conversation was difficult or easy? Did you limit your discoveries to items you needed? These are discoveries through association—e.g., you are smoking a cigarette and you need an ashtray, so you discover one. Or **were you open to appearances and surprises? What were some of these surprising discoveries?** Did you see your fellow actors' discoveries? Did you contact any of them?

SUMMARY:

To reach into the unknown not knowing what is out there is scary, and it is the essence of the improvisational challenge. Trusting the acting focus further gives you experiential knowledge that there is always something to discover. Your fear turns into excitement, which results in energy and presence.

For those of you who had limited appearances of objects, do you think there is a relationship between that and an *unwillingness to reach out* for the discovery? Discoveries do not come to you; they are available to you when you commit to reaching out for them. The more you reach without knowing what you are reaching for, the better off you are. Very quickly, you begin to trust that you can just reach out and an object will appear.

Developing the ability and willingness to reach out and discover, just when the discussion is most interesting either for a listener or a speaker, increases your acting technique and availability for doing more. Anyone can be very involved in a discussion, but *an actor should be able to be very involved in a discussion and do something else as well.* In time, that something else may be more sophisticated than discovering space objects. It might be climbing a preselected emotional arc or exploring subtext. We are training your instrument to do multiple things.

Occasionally, the following question arises: "If I thought of an object, one that I didn't need, not an association, and then I discovered it in the space, is that an appearance?"

When you think up an object first, it is an *invention*. The difference between an invention and an appearance is spontaneity. When you invent something in the head, the amount of time it takes, from the idea in the head to actually physically discovering it in the space, is out of the present tense. On the other hand, if you look out on the table, reach out without knowing what you are reaching for, grasp and discover what it is at the same time, that is an appearance. That is spontaneity. The key to achieving appearances is to stay on the double focus, trust it, and before you know it, appearances start to happen.

> **TO THE COACH:** Each improv lasts about ten minutes. ◆ If the actors are all talking at the same time, *coach—* Slow motion! Keep playing in slow motion. *After 30 seconds, when things have calmed down, coach—* Regular speed.
>
> When actors announce their objects, they are off the acting focus and in their heads. For example, while discovering cigarettes and a lighter, an actor says, "I just have to have a cigarette. Have you seen my lighter? Oh,

here it is." The coach should be alert to the possibility that what they are really saying is, "See how good I am. Look at what I am discovering." This is often an appeal for approval. It is still early in the training, and some actors haven't yet made the leap to a nonjudgmental workshop experience. Through the follow-up or journal assignments, the coach might lead this actor to the insight that since *there are no judgmental critiques in the training*, neither approval nor disapproval will be forthcoming.

For further practice discovering objects near you, play a round of *Ad Agency*. The coach should familiarize himself with the summary beforehand.

AD AGENCY

SETUP: 2–6 per team. In huddles, the actors pick specific advertising agency job titles for themselves, e.g., account exec, designer, media rep, accountant, talent coordinator, agency president, etc. They seat themselves around a space table. The audience selects a nonsense name of a product. The name must not suggest the product's function. Examples of appropriate choices: Top-Tids, Zamalo, Drildrens, Formula 22. Examples of inappropriate choices: Stickers (suggests adhesive product), Crunchies (suggests cereal product). When the improv begins, the players are on the double acting focus of *participating equally* in the verbal discussion of planning an advertising campaign for the product and discovering objects near you.

RULES: Same as discovering objects near you, with the addition of: All the actors are to participate in the discussion as if they know the purpose of the product. No one should ever reveal what the purpose of the product is.

ACTING FOCUS: Discovering objects near you while listening and speaking.

COACHING (as needed): Use the same coaching as in discovering objects near you. ♦ If the players laugh but drop character or their acting focus, *coach*— Use that laugh. Go with it. Stay on your acting focus every moment. **Keep up the double focus; don't alternate them.** Everything is a part of the whole. One minute.

FOLLOW-UP (as needed): Start with the same follow-up as in discovering objects near you. ♦ *Then*— Did you go further in your reaching without knowing what you were going to discover than you previously did in discovering objects near you? What were some of these discoveries? When you were laughing, did you stay on your acting focus?

SUMMARY:

Were you more capable of staying on the double acting focus than when we first played discovering objects near you? How did it feel? ◆ You must always use your laughter. Laughter is a spontaneous creation of energy and that energy is available for integration into the improvising or the acting focus. ◆ Did you have more appearances? Appearances are the height of spontaneity. When you reach without knowing what you will discover, you *will* yourself beyond your present limitations and out of the head. If you reach out without your brain's involvement, you break through your limitations. This has a profound effect on your acting. You become looser and more spontaneous. Trust the acting focus and let it work for you. Trust that when you reach out you will discover an object. You do have to reach, though, because the objects will only appear in your hand if your hand meets them halfway. The more the hand gets into reaching, the more it will start discovering, and the more it will bypass the brain's need to know what it's going to find. That's how you train yourself to go deeper and deeper into physical spontaneity, which is the cradle of all spontaneity.

> **TO THE COACH:** Make sure the actors do not get the name of the product until the moment before they start playing. This prevents their discussing what the product does. In setting up the exercise, if the actors are confused about how to plan a campaign without knowing a product's purpose, use scotch tape as an example. Would the ad agency planning the marketing for it have to discuss its purpose? The assumption is that all know what the product is. Each improv lasts 8–10 minutes.

STATIONARY DOING REVIEW

Discovering objects is a form of physical doing. Every time you discover an object and do a little something with it (miniactivity) you are physically doing something. It can be as active as doing an activity or contacting the location. Discovering objects near you differs from activity or location in that it is done without any walking. Contacting a location usually requires walking; doing an activity frequently involves walking; discovering objects near you never involves walking. Should the circumstances of any particular improvisation or any particular moment in an improvisation preclude the possibility of walking, discovering objects near you is the acting focus that will provide you with physical doing.

COMBINED PHYSICAL DOING

Regardless of how many of the previous exercises the group has done, this final exercise should be done as it will require, and further instill, the basic skills that are the purpose of this entire first part of the training. It will also provide a deeper appreciation of physical doing and its components, and it will reveal whether or not the group needs to return to any of the previous exercises for further practice.

PHYSICAL DOING DRILL

SETUP: Divide entire group into two teams unless the playing area isn't big enough to accommodate half the group doing an improv in a location with lots of set pieces. The group will be provided with a location by the coach, required to select their own characters, and then coached in exploring the acting focuses comprising physical doing. The team not playing will have the opportunity to observe the different acting focuses in action and the different qualities that each provides. ◆ The coach designates that the first team's location is a train station and arranges a number [half as many as there are actors on the team] of chairs to be seats in the train station. I usually make two benches next to each other, a little downstage of center, facing downstage with an aisle between them. ◆ The first team to play comes into the playing area. The coach informs them that when the improv starts they are all on stage waiting for a train, at 8:30 A.M., and when the train arrives it will arrive downstage left of them crossing to stage right. There is no discussion of location set pieces other than the coach pointing out the seats. ◆ The coach instructs the actors to privately make character choices. Remind them that at this point in the training, no attention to personality, attitude, or intentions is to be considered. The only character choices available to them are their job titles and any personal relationships they may desire. For this exercise, these would be primary personal relationships with characters off stage; e.g., I'm a plumber and I have a wife and daughter at home. They have no personal relationships with the other actors, as they are all strangers. Give them thirty seconds to do this. ◆ The coach then points out that they now know all the basic circumstances necessary to improvise: character—they just picked it; location—train station; and activity—waiting for a train. ◆ *Then coach*— Except for knowing your acting focus, which hasn't been revealed to you yet, you know everything you need to know to improvise, *or do you?* Whenever you hear that your activity is waiting—whether assigned to you, or self-selected—an alarm bell should go off warning you that another choice should be made. Waiting is an activity of *passive doing*. You need to turn that to *active doing*. How? By privately and quickly selecting an active doing *activity which is a part of the whole* character, location, and activity (in this case, waiting). What is an active activity that your character might be doing *while waiting* in this train station? When the improv starts, you want to be doing something while waiting for the train. Select that now. ◆ Give them thirty seconds to make these choices for themselves. Avoid giving them examples. They are not to tell anyone their choices. Hopefully, they will come up with: reading a newspaper, eating and drinking a snack, playing a guitar, knitting, doing homework, etc. ◆ We're just about ready to start. Each of you, go to places anywhere in the playing area you wish. When I call "Action," each of you is to focus on doing your activity, which is part of the larger activity called waiting. As the improv progresses, from time to time, I will coach an acting focus change for you. When you hear it, you retain your character, stay in the same location, and simply change your acting focus immediately to the one I call out. ◆ *To the audience—* This drill is as much for you as for them. Avoid watching this as a scene; watch this as a technical exercise and watch the difference that each of the acting focuses makes in the texture of what you see. Observe the changes that changing the acting focus brings about.

RULES: This is a drill. Play by yourself within the larger whole group. Dialogue is not allowed, unless it's absolutely necessary. Immediately respond to the coaching.

ACTING FOCUS: *At the start—* Doing and showing your activity which is a part of the whole team's activity (waiting).

COACHING (as needed): Action. ◆ **Focus on doing your activity.** ◆ If some actors are not doing active activities, *coach—* If your activity is not active and requires no space props, change it. Do an activity, which requires space props and is a part of the whole character, waiting in this train station. ◆ Integrate your activity into the larger activity: waiting for a train. **You are doing this activity while waiting for a train. Respect your space items.** Feel them in your hands. From time to time, check out your fellow actors. Avoid urgency. Avoid dialogue. Focus on doing your activity. ◆ *After a few minutes—* **CHANGE YOUR ACTING FOCUS. PHYSICALLY CONTACT THE LOCATION.** Contact the location. **Go and make physical contact with the set pieces in this location.** Discover them in the space. Everything you need is there in the space. Your acting focus is now to make physical contact with the location set pieces. Keep making contact with the location as a part of your whole character, waiting for a train in this train station. See the location all around you, and go and make contact with it. **There is always another set piece to get to.** Contact your own discoveries. **Check out your fellow actors; you will see set pieces revealed to you.** Contact your teammates' discoveries. **Respect the set pieces in the space.** Stay alert. Stay open. Contacting the location is a never-ending process. There's always another set piece to discover. **The location is not something to be looked at. It's some-**

thing to be used. **Explore the location.** Avoid urgency. ◆ *After a few minutes*— Stop walking. Stay where you are. No more steps. **CHANGE YOUR ACTING FOCUS. DISCOVER OBJECTS NEAR YOU.** Stay right where you are and focus on discovering objects near you. **You may move your body any way you wish but you may not take any more steps. Discover objects on your costume. Discover objects on set pieces within your reach. Discover objects on the floor. Discover objects in the space.** Respect your space objects. **Always integrate your discoveries as a part of the whole character, waiting in this train station.** The focus now is not doing an activity, not going to the location, but discovering numerous objects, one after another. A continuous stream of objects to be discovered. Avoid urgency. When you discover something, avoid settling on the use of that one object only. The continued use of any one object changes the focus from discovering objects, to doing an activity, and the focus you are now on is discovering objects, not doing an activity. Reach and discover. **Discover an object, give it a little usage, and then move on to the next discovery.** There's always another object to discover. Discoveries are in the space and not in your head. **If you are spending all your time discovering objects on your costume, challenge yourself to discover some somewhere else.** Stay in the process of discovery. ◆ *After a few minutes*— **CHANGE YOUR ACTING FOCUS. YOU'RE ON YOUR OWN.** The final acting focus is an alternating focus and it is **PLAYER'S CHOICE.** Practice alternating on your own between the three acting focuses we have just used. Do your activity. Contact the location. Discover objects near you. Your choices. **You have the opportunity to practice alternating between the three or combining them.** There are no restrictions as long as **you're always on one of these acting focuses, fulfilling the overall activity of the scene— waiting for the train.** Take responsibility for the exercise. Do not settle. Challenge yourself. **Avoid hanging out with just one focus. Integrate and combine all three acting focuses:** doing the activity, contacting the location, and discovering objects near you. Observe your own playing. **Always know which acting focus you are employing.** Notice if you are only doing one acting focus. You've already shown the ability to do all three. **Take responsibility for your improvising, and for the exercise, and shift from one to another, to another.** Avoid hanging out in any one focus. Combine them as well. Stay out of your heads. The only thing going on in your head, if anything, is self-coaching: Contact the location, do the activity, discover objects. You're on your own. Acting is doing and there's always more to do. ◆ *After about 5 minutes*— Stay on the alternating focus as you hear or see the train approaching from a distance. **You're on your**

alternating/combined focus until I call "Cut." The train is getting closer. Integrate what you are doing with the approaching train. **It's pulling up in front of you. Stay on your focus. It stops. The doors open. Get on.** There are no seats available. Stay on your focus. Thirty seconds to go. The train is leaving the station. ◆ *To the audience*— **Notice actors who have dropped their acting focus.** ◆ *To the actors*— Last chance to accept the challenge. You're in a new location. Your activity may have changed. **Can you still stay on the acting focus until I call "Cut"?** Observe yourself. Notice if you have been avoiding any one focus. If you have, that's the one you want to get to. Are you afraid of it? Last chance to discover your bravery. Avoid hanging out. Reach and discover. ◆ Cut.

FOLLOW-UP (as needed): *If there is another team waiting to play*— Actors, return to your seats and consider what has just happened. Review the problems and/or discoveries that came up for you. We will discuss it after the last team has played. ◆ *The group does the magic finger-snap location disappearance.* ◆ For the next team, change the location to a bus station and rearrange the chairs. ◆ After the last team has played, *to the whole class*— Did you respect your space items? Did you respond to the coaching? Did you discover anything? How did you respond or how did you feel when you were on your own, during player's choice? Did you experience any self-coaching? When you were watching the other team(s) play, what happened when they got on board the train (bus)? Did they stay on the acting focus? What were they doing? Was there more they could have done?

SELECTED STUDENT RESPONSES

—It's the first time I understood self-coaching. In the past, I judged myself when I self-coached. This time, when I went up into my head, I played by the rules and said, "Okay, focus on the location," and I started to see things that would be in the location and I went over and used them. The more I did, the more other things started to happen.

—I went to look for things and I didn't let myself even have a glimmer of what was going to be there. Things just kept appearing. I felt like I was letting go of control.

—At first, I just stood there saying to myself, "What can I find?" I couldn't think of anything and I felt nervous. Then you coached us to discover objects near us, so I just bent over and I found a ladybug and it crawled on my finger, and then I . . . [Class shouts: "You killed it!"]

—When I was off focus, I became very aware of my bad habits as an actor: my inner dialogue as an actor, not the character; lots of tension in my body; and inability to make a choice. When I went back to the focus and began something active, it all stopped and I felt great.

—When we couldn't move from where we were, I was sitting and all of a sudden I started stealing from people's briefcases; I erased a guy's hard drive; I ate someone's sandwich. I saw all those props earlier when I was checking everybody out.

—I was discovering all kinds of interesting things in my pockets and then I actually saw hardwood floors and I found change in between the creases, which was something that I just…I mean, it just happened.

—I discovered stuff about my relationships. I used the phone and since we had to avoid speaking, my mom wasn't there when I called; she's always gone. Damn it! I hung up the phone, looked at the phone booth, and discovered that my girlfriend had carved her name in with another guy!

SUMMARY:

GETTING ON THE TRAIN/BUS

When the other team got on the train/bus, did the actors stay on the acting focus? How could you tell if they were off focus? They were just waiting and not doing anything, maybe carrying a briefcase, maybe holding on to a strap, but just waiting. What acting focuses are available to you in that situation? All three of them. Say you're holding on to a strap, or just leaning there, or even holding a cup of coffee. You can still reach and discover all over the place—on your costume; on the train seats, poles, straps; on the floor; on another actor's costume. You have a whole new environment to reach out into and discover. You may possibly still do your activity from the train station. Maybe it's a new activity. Maybe you're finally in place on the train, you're hanging on, and you reach into your purse or your back pocket, pull out a palm pilot, and start computing. Bingo! You have a new activity. And you can still go to the location. You're in a brand new location, somewhat limited, somewhat crowded, but just getting from one end of the train to the other end and making contact with a strap or a pole keeps you on focus. Just because the environment or location changes is no reason to be off the acting focus. Who were the most interesting people to watch standing on the bus or the train? The ones who were still doing. The others were just hanging out.

CHOOSING INITIAL ACTIVITY

When you choose an activity, to serve you well, it must have active physical doing with space objects. When you are involved in doing something with a space object, you don't have to act; you don't need to act; you don't want to act. It takes enough of your energy and attention just to focus on eating that sandwich, or knitting, or whatever it is. An activity such as dancing, exercising, or posing that doesn't include space object(s) requires acting and inventing in your head. "What am I going to do next? Which exercise? Which ballet step? Which pose?" One purpose of an activity is to keep you *physically doing* with space props so you don't go to your head and ask these questions.

EXPERIENTIAL LEARNING

Do you see how much more you are capable of doing than you might have thought six or seven classes ago when we began the training? Suppose I had said to you on the first day, *You're going to do an improv. You are in a train station, waiting for a train. Go!* I doubt you would have had all these discoveries and physicality. You probably would have been uptight, frightened, and would have *acted* a scene full of playwriting information. And yet, what we are doing here is real acting. There are no real props, there is no real train station, and you are not really these characters. This is all acting.

Is there anybody who didn't discover objects? Anybody who didn't contact the location? Anybody who didn't involve themselves with activity? You just did it. This part of the training is over. This is physical doing. The train station drill could be the character, activity, and location of any scripted scene you might be working on. There is no difference. Whether the scene takes place in a kitchen or a public room like this one, realize how much more is available to you than you have previously assumed.

It's obvious that most of you felt pretty good doing this drill. As it went on you discovered more and more confidence. You enjoyed the exercise of reaching and discovering. Stay alert to the idea that this is what can energize a scene, simply being in the process of discovering your physicality. You were very busy out on the floor and yet, you were in control. The drill started with me declaring the acting focus but then with players' choice, you took it away from me. You were in control. And out of that control of doing, many of you had many discoveries accompanied by excitement and significance.

From doing comes more doing. And it's only in the process of doing that real discoveries happen. Discoveries are always spontaneous. True spontaneity always accompanies real doing.

> **TO THE COACH:** The actors are experientially learning the basics of Improvisation Technique. This exercise reveals to them that they have the capabilities to improvise. They are discovering and creating in a spontaneous mode with no dependence on thinking or planning. They now have skills and have greatly diminished or eliminated their fears. They know what to do and are prepared to do it. That is technique.

◆　◆　◆

PHYSICAL DOING DRILL RETURN

At the start of the next class, or in subsequent classes, it may be valuable to do this short exercise to extend the experiential review of the physical doing acting focuses. Repeat the physical doing drill with different locations. You can even do this with smaller locations, e.g., office, living room, if you have each actor improvise in their own individual and smaller part of the playing area at the same time as the other actors. If more than one team is playing, change all the locations for each team.

SETUP, RULES, ACTING FOCUS, and COACHING: The same as physical doing drill.

FINAL PHYSICAL DOING REVIEW

Acting is Doing and There's Always More to Do

You have now learned the basics of Improvisation Technique. In order to improvise you must always be in a state of doing. Your bodies now know to be always in the process of doing an activity, contacting the location, and being open to discovering objects around you. This puts you into the improvisational state of being where anything can happen (emergence), and you are prepared to go with it on a journey whose destination is unknown to you. Beyond going with whatever emerges, your bodies-as-instruments are now taking responsibility for participating in the creation of the emergence. With this comes a complete loss of fear about the prospect of improvising.

The work has all been technical. There has been no emphasis on character other than communicating relationships (professional and personal) and no exploration of motivations, intentions, or objectives—all standard tools of traditional acting. No attention has been paid to improvising story. Our time has been spent getting your body to do things spontaneously. Each exercise led you to the next. Each class led you to the next. Proficiency at being on your own/player's choice with physical doing is the foundation of improvisational acting upon which everything else will now be built. We will place every new acting focus on top of these skills.

Evolution of Dialogue

Your ability to improvise authentic dialogue has grown through your response to a specific evolution of rules: (1) Avoid dialogue, which led you to (2) Speak when you must, which led you to (3) Speak when you have something to say. You have discovered that if you follow and improvise within the rules, you are continually surprised at how you exceed your expectations.

> **TO THE COACH:** For the rest of the training, should the coach feel the need to stimulate dialogue in any improvisation where the actors are reticent to speak, wait until the actor clearly has a new thought about anything, *then coach*— Share that thought. If you have something to say, say it! Share your voices.

How do you improvise?

You start by choosing or knowing who you are; that is, what you do for a living and whether or not you have any personal relationships with your improv mates. You choose or know the location of the improv. You select a physical activity, i.e., What am I doing in this location when the curtain goes up or action is called? You commence the improvisation by doing your activity, contacting the location, and behaving toward each other according to your character choices. It has to be physical. It is not about making up a story in the head.

IMPROVISATION RULES NOW IN PLACE

- No one is allowed on stage without an activity.
- Every actor must choose what his character does for a living and whether he has any personal relationships with the other actors in the scene, and communicate it.
- Every actor must frequently make physical contact with the location.
- Every actor must be open to discovering objects nearby.
- There is never a reason for being off the selected acting focus.

EARLIEST APPLICATIONS TO SCRIPTS

Physical doing may be applied to improvisations with scripted scenes. Compared to the complete Improvisation Technique this is the equivalent of testing the water with your toes before jumping in for a swim.

To begin, reduce the scene to character, activity, and location choices.

Look at the character: (1) What is your job title? Many actors playing characters whose occupation is not germane to the scene don't bother to look at the occupation for background or influence on their physicality. They avoid considering, "How does my occupation affect how I relate to the other characters?" Does a cook treat people differently than a salesman? How? (2) Articulate what personal relationships your character has with other characters in the scene. Are you behaving according to those relationships and communicating it?

Look at the activity. Does the script provide it? Is it active with the usage of props? If not, make no choice yet.

The script always provides the location choice.

After articulating the character, activity, and location of any scene, you are ready to improvise.

Memorization

The first thing you must know about improvising with scripted lines is that the lines must be memorized. Otherwise, you cannot improvise. When you are on book or struggling to remember lines, you are too busy to be able to focus on the improvisation.

Begin with traditional work, or not.

First things first. Take advantage of what you already know—Stanislavsky, Michael Chekhov, Strasberg, Meisner, or whatever traditional technique you usually employ. Do it and get everything you can from it. If you start improvising before you've done your basic traditional work, you bypass a basic grounding in the scene and potential discoveries.

When you reach a point where you've done the scene with your traditional approach and you think you've got it, that's the time to ask, "What else is there that I haven't explored yet?" *The purpose of improvisation is to go beyond what you already know how to do.*

The only time you should start your process with Improvisation Technique is if you lack confidence with traditional technique or there is a time factor.

Choosing the Acting Focus

Location Improvisation

In a rehearsal, you're either working on the actual set or you're in a rehearsal room with tape on the floor and a couple of tables and chairs. In a rehearsal room, you usually limit your business to whatever is there, the tables and chairs and a couple of key props that the director and stage manager have provided. Other than that, you seldom relate to the set. Your first improv, *relating to the location*, will address this limitation and it will provide you with the biggest form of physical doing as it will take you all around the set.

Say to yourself, "I'm going to do an improv during the next run-through of this scene and my acting focus is going to be on relating to the location." In that run-through, you say all the dialogue in the scene, on cue. You don't make up a single word. However, you focus on relating to the location. **In order to improvise, you must be willing to throw out everything that you have rehearsed up to that point and go into that scene with the improvisational acting focus of relating to the location.** You will make contact with all the space set pieces in that location, whether pictured in the sketch, or in the model, or discovered by you. When the rehearsal begins, you are totally focused on making physical contact with the set pieces, listening to the other actors, and saying your lines on cue. **Make no attempt to retain moments, intentions, line readings, or any previous discoveries you were working on.** Be willing to leave the earlier work. Your body will take care of retaining previous discoveries of value.

If you let go of your previous work and stay on your improvisational acting focus, you will discover whole new moments, business, blocking, feelings, thoughts, and line readings. Some of these discoveries you can return to later and work into the evolution of the scene with the director. This location improv should be done prior to freezing the blocking.

For film and TV, this application is much more limited. You should arrive on the set, for a rehearsal or shooting, having done your traditional work at home. If there is any running of the scene prior to blocking, you can approach the work with the same location focus improvisation and see what happens. On the actual set, of course, you don't deal with space set pieces. The set is there. Make contact with it. Use it. See what you discover.

One of my students, Valerie Mahaffey, told me she did this in a cowboy movie where the scene was set outdoors next to a covered wagon.

> I knew I was limited to staying in one place, so I reached out to the only set piece available to me, the covered wagon. On the side of it was a water barrel. It was intended as set dressing, but in the improv, I made contact with it. I found myself turning the spigot, and putting my hands underneath to catch some water to dampen my face. I planned none of this, only the fact that during the scene I was going to improvise by making physical contact with the location. When I opened the spigot, I discovered that there was no water in the barrel. Why would there be? There was no indication in the script or from the director that anyone would use the barrel. I went with it, adding tension and upping the stakes of the scene, because my character was faced with a new circumstance: we were out of water! The director loved it and they built the whole scene around it, all without changing one line of the script.

Activity Improvisation

For another rehearsal of the same or different scene, choose a different acting focus, *activity doing*. If the script or director provides the activity (active with props), that is your first choice, especially if it hasn't been employed in rehearsals. It may be that your character has not been given an activity by the author or the director. The way the scene has been unfolding, you have just been standing there, hanging out. So, for this improv, you select an activity. (The selection can be done on the spot or as homework in preparation for this improv. Necessary props can be real or space.) What guides your selection? The activity you choose should be an appropriate part of the whole. Juliet could be doing needlepoint by the moonlight or candlelight on the balcony, but she wouldn't be washing a car. In this run-through, your acting focus is on doing the activity. But you've got to commit to doing it *as an acting focus*, not as a piece of business. What's the difference? If you do it as a piece of business, you're going to say the lines and act just the way you rehearsed it. That's not an improv. But if you totally focus on doing the activity, listening, speaking on cue, letting everything else that's been rehearsed disappear for the sake of this rehearsal improv—after all, it's a rehearsal, and rehearsals are for experimenting and discovering—you will discover whole new moments, feelings, thoughts, and line readings. Lots of discoveries will reveal themselves to you in the improvising, which you can subsequently retain and integrate into the evolving rehearsals of that scene.

For film and TV, the application is the same. If you have selected a few activities in your homework, bring the necessary props to work or ask the prop person to have them available for you. Sometimes by looking around the set, you will discover a potential activity. If nothing is available and you are still in the rehearsal mode, use space props. One of my students, Christopher Titus, was in the cast of *The Damon Wayans Show* on TV. He relates how he employed an activity acting focus improv on the set.

> I was in a scene where I played a train porter and all I really had to do was sling luggage onto a loading platform. After we worked on the scene once, Damon came up to me and said, "Chris, they've written us a flat scene. See if you can come up with something." So we ran the scene again and as I was slinging the luggage, I focused on the rhythm of the activity (the slinging), and then I just coached myself to *interrupt the rhythm*. What came up was, I accidentally slung one suitcase into the platform post and it fell back and popped open. I went with it, and immediately started to gather up all the belongings, using space props. Damon went with it by making it *his* suitcase and belongings. We had this great moment where he was pissed at me, and I was the stumblebum, and we built a whole comic scene around the suitcase, all from my interrupting the rhythm. It was great. Of course, for the taping, they filled the suitcase with real clothes.

Discovering Objects Improvisation

For another rehearsal of the same or different scene, choose a different acting focus. If the scene has been blocked and your character must stay on one spot, you can still do an activity acting focus. You can also improvise one run-through with *discovering objects near you*. Listen, speak on cue, and focus on discovering the objects. If you do it at home first, use space props. You may make some discoveries that you like and you can then bring the real props into the rehearsal. If you do the improvisation at the rehearsal, use space props. For any discoveries that the director and you want to keep, the real props can be obtained. My student, Malcolm-Jamal Warner, relates:

> When we are rehearsing scenes for my show, *Malcolm & Eddie*, I'm always improvising activity and discovering objects and at the end of the rehearsal, the prop people ask me what props I want. I think about what I used (in

space) that I liked and then I tell them those. And they get them for the next rehearsal or shooting.

Mix and Match

Ideally, there is enough rehearsal time and a supportive director. In that case, after doing location and activity improvs, do another one where your acting focus is *player's choice—you're on your own.* In this improv, you will alternate and combine location, activity, and discovering objects near you, just as in the physical doing drill.

Fear of Improvising at Rehearsal

As you read this process, you are concerned. "Do I have to use space props?" The answer is, you should. Props are your tools. Why should you limit yourself to what was selected by others in preproduction? *It's your discovery process.* The director may say, "Holy cow, when you improvised putting the keys back on your key ring, it captured the whole meaning of the scene! Props, key ring!" The director *and your work* inform the prop person what to get. It's not important if any specific props or business remain in the final production or shot. Their value was found in the rehearsal process. And, frequently, the discovered business is retained. It's a win/win situation.

Think how you've limited yourselves. You never relate to your set in rehearsals because it's not there, when in fact it is, it's just in the space, right there and available for discoveries. And if the actual set *is* there, how often has it been no more than a picture that you perform in front of? Why limit yourself? What do you think, you're going to be bad because you're using a space prop or a space set piece? Somebody's going to holler at you? You are coming from a victim stance when you think that way. If you're not confident with your space work, then maybe you're not ready to do this. Aside from not knowing your lines, nothing will screw up an improv more than sloppy space work.

Some of you will not have the courage to do what I am suggesting. Don't get down on yourself. We are still at the beginning of our training. You might work in your journal about being frightened of this process. In truth, what's the worst that could happen? The director could say, "Excuse me, don't do all of that." That's it. That's the worst. If you are frightened of a director's saying that to you, then you have a lot of work to do on yourself and your career. It will be very hard for you to be very good at what you do if before you attempt anything, you shut yourself down in anticipation of what a director might say to you.

Improvising before Rehearsal or Shooting

While working in rehearsal with the other actors is preferable, you can also do these improvs at home, in private rehearsals. Have someone else feed you the lines while you explore the three basic improvisations. If there is no else one available, you could put the other characters' lines on a tape recorder, leaving space for your lines.

What about the other actors?

Doing these improvisations in rehearsal requires nothing other than the normal rehearsal participation from the other actors in the scene. When you work with another actor(s) who is somewhat rigid in his approach and doesn't like surprises, even in rehearsal, you would be wise to be sensitive to this. Prior to employing an improv, merely tell them (privately), "In this run-through, I'm going to be experimenting a little."

What about the director?

Another fear you may be experiencing as you imagine this improvisation process is, "What will the director say?" Try it and find out. The worst that can happen is he will tell you to stop. After your **LOCATION** improv he may say, "Excuse me, Tom, you're really all over the place. I appreciate the fact that you're so creative and you're using the set. There are a few things that I really liked, and maybe we'll use them. But it's a little too much for the eye, so could you please not do that?" Okay, fine. Because of the director's comments, your second improv will need to be smaller, with less walking around the set. What's smaller than going to the location? Doing your **ACTIVITY** becomes the acting focus. Afterward, the director says, "Tom, it's good. You didn't go all over the place; I like that. Even though you stayed in that one area, it's still too active for me. I'm afraid that because you're so involved in cleaning, filling, and smoking that pipe, the audience will only watch you. Could you please not do all that?" So, you reduce the size of your doing for your third improv. Go to one spot on the stage that's germane to the blocking and focus on **DISCOVERING OBJECTS NEAR YOU.** You're no longer going to the whole location or doing a whole activity. You're playing the scene while you focus on discovering a few objects within your reach, listening, and speaking on cue.

After this improv, the director may say, "Okay, Tom, enough is enough. You took Book's class, I can tell, but I really don't want you doing anything during this beat. No moving, no props, nothing. Just stand there and listen and speak." Then, how do you improvise? You move the doing from outside of you to inside of you. How? That's the next part of Improvisation Technique training—*Inner Doing.*

4

INNER DOING

Given the emphasis thus far on the importance of physical doing, what can the actor do when the situation—perhaps the blocking, or the size of the shot—does not allow for physical movement? There is another form of doing that is initiated and pursued within the actor instead of outside him in space with objects (real or space).

Inner Doing is active doing in the form of character thinking and feelings. Improvising a character's thoughts and being open to their impact on the character's feelings, behavior, and dialogue is the crux of inner doing training.

The work is divided into two forms of inner doing. *Traveling* is totally expansive and leads to discoveries in many areas, especially character. *Off stage* is attached to physicality; it is no less powerful, and more closely related to the text and story of the script.

Both forms are built on the idea that people generally, and characters specifically, are almost always thinking. In Improvisation Technique, we don't want the actor thinking when he is acting. Just because the actor shouldn't think, however, doesn't mean the *character* shouldn't think. A character who doesn't think is neither interesting nor real. There is a difference between being in the actor's head and being in the character's head. If an actor makes an activity of pursuing his character's thoughts, he is not open to the problems he would face if he pursued his own thoughts, and he provides himself with a doing for those times when physical doing is not an option.

TRAVELING

We begin this part of the training with an exercise.

ACTIVE & STILL #1[1]

SETUP: 4 or 6 per team. They huddle and divide into two subteams of 2 or 3. Each subteam huddles. They choose their characters (personal relationships and/or job titles) and an issue to be discussed that is important to the characters. There is no limitation on what the issue is. It may be simple, complex, or even flamboyant; the higher the stakes, the more interesting it is to play (and watch). It makes no difference if the characters have purely professional relationships or personal relationships, although personal relationships and the accompanying issues tend to have higher stakes for all the characters. E.g., husband and wife: one reveals he/she wants a divorce. Or siblings: what to do with elderly parent. The location is an outdoor cafe. The characters have just ordered or completed a meal. The meal itself will not be a part of the improvisation.

After the first team to improvise has been selected, each subteam sits around its own space table, center left and center right, about 6–8' apart, at the outdoor cafe. The coach chalks an A on the floor in front of one space table and a B in front of the other.

The coach begins the **introduction.** The name of this acting focus is *Active & Still*. Active & still has to do with spontaneously directing the audience's attention between different, and simultaneous, scenes. We are going to have two separate scenes improvising simultaneously at this cafe and we want to avoid the chaos of having the audience try to watch two scenes at once and not hear either scene because both scenes are speaking at the same time.

In this improv, the actors focus on directing the audience's attention to one scene at a time by being either active or still. While the characters at one table are active, the characters at the other table will be still, and the audience will spontaneously direct their attention to the active table. Being active is accomplished in two ways, through speaking and/or movement. If a character speaks or moves, he is active and the audience will watch him. If you want to direct the audience's attention to the other table, you have to stop speaking and stop moving, which we call being still.

Beyond practicing when to go active or still, the exercise is about what one does during a still. *What do you do when you are not allowed to move or speak?* What is the *doing?* That is what I am going to coach you to do, privately, while you are up here.

When your table is active, you improvise the scene, behaving according to your character choices and the issue you have selected to discuss. For the first time since we began the training, there are no rules about the dialogue, such as avoiding playwriting. You can say anything. You must stay at your table. There is no ongoing activity other than occasionally discovering objects near you. You can reach and have wine, smoke a cigarette, eat a peanut, etc. The meal itself has been completed or has yet to arrive. Any objects you discover must be in space.

TO AUDIENCE: Your natural inclination will be to watch the active table. That's where all the action and fun will be, where all the soap operas will play out. The real action, though, is at the still table. That's where the learning, what to do when the director stops you from doing, will go on.

RULES: How do you know when to be active and when to be still? I will coach A or B. The letter of the table I call will be the table that is active. When we start, both tables will be active so that they can both get up to speed in their improvisations. After a minute or so, I will coach either A or B. That table keeps going, keeps being active. The other table stops, midsentence, midword. No matter what you are saying, you stop. It is a stillness, not a freeze. I'll show you the difference. Everyone on stage and in the audience, move around a little bit. Freeze! Do you feel your toes clawing the ground? Tension all through your body? In a freeze, there is tension. Now hold the pose you are in, but take all the tension out. Just be still. Got it? That is a stillness. So, when you go into a still, you just stop what you are doing and saying. I will come to your table and coach you privately.

When I call "Action," both teams begin improvising your scenes. You will be out here a long time, so if there is some big denouement or revelation in your scene you may not want that to be the first line of your scene. Build to it. Explore who you are and let it go the way it wants to go. When you are active, you may not leave your table, and you should occasionally discover an object near you. When you return to being active, after you have been still, your scene should be further along than where you left off when you were previously active.

ACTING FOCUS: Responding to the coaching while being active or still.

COACHING: Action. ◆ *Two minutes after both tables begin improvising their separate scenes—* A! A, stay active! B, go still. ◆ The coach approaches the B table and coaches the whole table, in a low voice so that only they hear him. I usually pull up a chair and sit right in front of them.

OPTION 1—QUESTION & ANSWER RAILROAD TRACKS

Stay still. Don't move. Don't look at me. Look right where you were looking. Let's explore what to do when the director or the circumstances will not let you move or do anything physically. Let's discover how your characters think and how to improvise that thinking. Every character is different. Every character has a brain, which operates just like your brain. It thinks about things. Right now, your character may be thinking something that you are choosing not to share with the other characters. Characters have hidden agendas. They plot, plan, and scheme. They try to figure out what is going on. At this moment in the scene, based on whatever you know about what's going on in it, there is a question available to your character. It has something to do with this scene, but it's private and you don't ask it out loud. It's a hidden question. It might be "What the hell am I doing here" or, "What does she want from me" or, "What do I want from him?"

So now, each of you pick *any* hidden question that your character might be considering privately at this moment in the scene, some inner question you might have that you are not asking out loud. It should be something basic, like "Why did she just say that to me?" or "Where is this leading?" When you have the question, nod your head. There is no such thing as a bad question. Whatever you choose is a good choice. ♦ *After they all nod—* Now, make up an answer to that question. What do you think the answer might be? Consider it. There is no such thing as a wrong answer. Whatever you think your character might have for an answer is a good choice. Just remember who you are in the scene so far and make up an answer. For example, if my question was, "What does she want from me," I might answer, "My money." When you have an answer, nod your head. ♦ *After they all nod—* Now, take the answer and turn it into a second question. For example, if my answer was, "My money," I turn that into a second question, "Do I want to give it to her?" Let the first answer lead you to a second question, and when you have it nod your head. ♦ *After they all nod—* Now, take the second question and come up with an answer. Anything goes. Whatever you think. ♦ What does she want from me? My money. Do I want to give it to her? No. ♦ When you have the answer, nod your head. ♦ *After they all nod—* Now take the second answer and turn it into a third question. ♦ "What does she want from me?" "My money." "Do I want to give it to her?" "No." "How is she going to feel about that?" ♦ Every answer will point you to another question. Once you have your third question, answer it, then let the answer point you to a fourth question, and so on. Pause for a moment and listen to me.

This is called *Question & Answer Railroad Tracks* because it provides the means for *traveling* further through the scene and through the character's thoughts and it is like going along the ties of a railroad track. The first question is the first tie. It leads you to the first answer, which is the next tie. That leads you to the second question, which is the next tie, which leads you to the second answer, which leads you to the third question, which leads you to the third answer, which leads you to the fourth question, and so on. Before you know it, you are traveling through these questions and answers. You just keep going.

Look at how much more you know about how your character thinks and what they are considering with only three questions and answers. When you are in stillness, this will occupy you. It's a very active process, which keeps you busy doing, keeps you in the scene, and informs you about who you are and how you think. It is an *inner doing*. You are in stillness, you are not directing the audience's attention to you, but inside you are doing something, improvising your character's thinking, and learning a great deal about who you are and how you think.

When I call your letter, B, you have to go active and the audience will come back to you. Real time has passed, so your scene has to be further along than where it was when you were last speaking out loud. You will have gone through all these questions and answers, and you will have traveled (down these railroad tracks) further into your scene. It's from that place that you continue the scene.

Whether or not you choose to talk about anything that you discovered on these railroad tracks is your choice, just like in real life. You draw from it, refer to it, or keep it a secret. It is up to you.

When you get to a question and answer that you feel completes the railroad track, get off the train, and get on a new one. If you first started with, "What does he want from me," and you went all the way down that track until there were no more questions, then start now with a brand new question, "What do I want from him?" Any question will start the train, and you will probably never run out of the railroad tracks.

This is what you practice doing when you are in a still. When I come back later, I'll show you more to do. I am going to leave you now. Resume your railroad track with your fourth question, or start a new track with a brand new first question, and practice this.

- While coaching the above, occasionally look over at the other table, which is active, and, if needed, *coach them loudly*— Share your voices. Discover an object near you.

- After the coach leaves table B, allow another two minutes, and *coach*— B! B is active. A, go still. [Then do the above coaching for table A.]

- After table A has been coached in question and answer railroad tracks and allowed an additional two minutes, the coach watches table B for a moment when there is a heated dialogue exchange between any two actors at that table, and immediately *coaches the switch*— A! A is active. B, go still.

- The coach immediately returns to table B for private coaching, and addresses the last actor spoken to in the dialogue, e.g., Ira.

OPTION 2—SILENTLY CONTINUING DIALOGUE

Answer him, Ira, with your eyes. Continue the dialogue that I interrupted with the coaching, but say what you have to say to Al *with your eyes*. Al, receive his communication. Assume whatever he is telling you—your assumption is always right—and answer him back *with your eyes*. Say what you have to say with your eyes. Ira, you receive his communication, hear him—whatever you think he is telling you, you're right—and respond back to him. Keep the dialogue going, just as if you were speaking lines from a script or improvising, only don't let the audience hear it. Don't move your lips. Say it with your eyes. *As needed*— Go with each other. Go with that. Let your eyes dance with each other.

This is a second option for inner doing, different from question and answer railroad tracks. If the still starts when you are in the middle of a heated exchange, your voice goes silent, but you keep the improvised dialogue going with your eyes.

If you are a third character at the table, like Lili is, you have been left out of this silent continuing dialogue between Ira and Al, so you use option one, question and answer railroad tracks. You are set up for it perfectly. "Why aren't they talking to me? Why are they ignoring me? What has just happened?" Choose your question, answer it, and set off down those railroad tracks. However, stay alert because at any moment one of the actors involved in the silent continuing dialogue might choose to bring the dialogue to you. Then you have to switch into the silent continuing dialogue. Practice this until each of you has had the chance to be the left-out third character. *Allow one minute.*

This alternative to question and answer railroad tracks is called *Silently Continuing Dialogue*. It requires at least two people, whereas railroad tracks are always done solo.

You now have two options for inner doing, or what you do when you are still. Sometimes you are going down railroad tracks by yourself and sometimes you are continuing the dialogue with another player. You are free to alternate between these two options. It is a player's choice; you are on your own.

When you go active again, your scene has traveled to someplace new. Just bring voice into it and you are right there. Practice this now and I will be back soon with the third and final option.

- While coaching the above, occasionally look over at the other table, the active one. If needed, *coach them loudly*— Share your voices! Discover an object near you.

- After the coach leaves table B, allow another two minutes, then *coach*— B! B is active. A, go still. [Then do the above coaching for table A.]

- After table A has been coached in silently continuing dialogue, and allowed an additional two minutes, *coach*— A! A is active. B, go still.

OPTION 3—PICKING UP

The coach returns to the B table for private coaching. *He coaches*— Now we will explore the last of the three options, *Picking Up*. Let your eyes roam over each other. Look at how your fellow actors are dressed. Look at jewelry, clothes, makeup, and hair. You are free to look around, but keep your head movements small. Maintain your sense of stillness. Remember that it is your character who is looking at the other characters—not you the actor, but you the character.

While you are looking, you are free to use the other actors' clothes and appearance to serve your needs. I may notice that cross around Lili's neck. If I was mad at her at this moment in this scene—the attitude is up to you; it depends on what is going on at the moment you go into the still—I might say to myself, "God, she is such a hypocrite. She is the most unspiritual person I have ever met and yet she goes around waving this big cross." Or, perhaps at this moment in the scene I am spontaneously feeling warmth toward her and would respond differently. I would say to myself, "Look at that beautiful cross she is wearing. I love that about Lili, she is so religious and spiritual."

There are things to see, things to *pick up* on and develop from your character's point of view. Notice Al's tank-top shirt. What can you do with that? If you are upset with him at this moment, it might be, "Who comes to a fancy restaurant in his underwear?" The attitude is totally improvisational in nature. It is up to you, based on what happens at the moment that you choose to do the pick up. Is anybody not wearing a wedding ring that should be? Where did that jewelry come from? What is that nose ring all about? When did that hair turn that color? When did that hairline start to recede? Why is she wearing so much makeup? [The coach should adapt these examples to the appearances of the actors at the table that he is coaching.]

In other words, be in your character and observe. See all of these things on or about the other characters. Pick up on what is really there on the actor, but respond *as your character* about the other character. Pick up from what you actually see in the space on each other and then develop it inside as another form of inner doing for your character to be thinking about. When you go active again, whether or not you ever talk about what you pick up on is up to you, just like everything else in a still. Nod your head if you understand this option of picking up.

This is the last time I am coming around to you. When I walk away now, practice picking up. Soon I will only coach, active & still. On those switchovers, you are on your own, player's choice. Practice alternating among the three options: question & answer railroad tracks, silently continuing dialogue, and picking up. Alternate and combine them, so you are always doing on the inside.

- After the coach leaves table B, allow another two minutes, *then coach—* B! B is active. A, go still. [Then do the above coaching for table A.]

- After about two minutes, begin alternating which table is active through frequent coaching. Vary the time between switches from ten seconds to two minutes, to continually surprise the actors. A, B, A, B, etc. ◆ Cut.

FOLLOW-UP: Audience, were they active & still? ◆ Actors, do you understand these options available to you when you are in the stillness? ◆ *To the rest of the group—* How a team gets to where they are in the scene when they go active again has a lot to do with what they do in the still. Notice that real time has passed during their still and they are further along in their scene when they go active again. They are just doing it in a way that doesn't direct the audience's attention to them while they are doing it, in a stillness. On the other hand, if they were to go active and just pick up the conversation where they last left it, they would deny that passage of real time. Notice that it's just like playing a script. You are traveling through succeeding pages silently, while the other team is active. When you are active again, you are on a later page. Next team.

SUMMARY:

This is only the introduction to inner doing, what you can be doing on the inside when the circumstances don't allow for physical doing on the outside. Improvising and exploring how your character thinks fills your silent stillness with improvisational doing. Discovering your character's thoughts allows you to make discoveries about your character, which may pay off immediately, later in the scene, or in other scenes.

The three options you have just learned are called *traveling*. They allow you to travel further into the scene without dialogue or business.

Option 1 is *question & answer railroad tracks*. Notice that while you were doing it, you were always ready to become active as soon as you were coached to do so. That is the equivalent of picking up a cue in a text scene where the dialogue isn't improvised. While pursuing what is going on in the character's brain, you must never be so out of it that you miss what is going on between you and the other characters. As we develop inner doing in future classes, you will have the opportunity to practice this.

Option 2 is *continuing the dialogue silently*. This is an option that is especially pertinent should you have to go into the stillness in the middle of a heated dialogue exchange with another actor. Then the two of you can improvise the continuing dialogue scene. What might these two characters be saying if the author chose to give them text where he hasn't? That can take you right up to your next cue. It gives you preparation building blocks for where you are going, or for what you are going to say next.

Option 3 is *picking up*. You can pick up at any time and on anything. Picking up doesn't have to be limited to costume, hygiene, and jewelry on the other character. It can include features on your own character, e.g., "Ooh, my nails are dirty. When did I become a slob?" It can also include picking up from the props, the set, and other characters on the set that you may not be involved with, e.g., at another table in this cafe. You can even pick up on another character's attitude or facial expression. There's a whole wealth of material to be discovered: on the real set you're working on, the space set you are improvising or rehearsing on, the actors, the costumes, the rehearsal clothes, whatever. Anything you see can become a springboard for traveling.

Traveling opens subtextual doors you did not previously consider. It is beneath the text because it is unspoken. Unlike traditional subtext, which is always related to the text, this is *character subtext* because everything about it is informing your character. For example, you are discovering that you are suspicious and jealous of your girlfriend or you're discovering that you appreciate your sister more than you thought you did. These are more character-driven than text-driven issues.

Do you see how active it is, how much you can do in stillness, and yet you don't move your body for one moment? It is the inner equivalent of what we have been training to do with physical doing. Ideally and ultimately, you do both. While you are doing the physical doing, you can also be doing the inner doing when it's necessary.

Acting is doing and there is always more to do. You always have to be in the state of doing more, of wanting to do more. We will get to a point where your body is doing so much that it will take over and demand that you always be in this process of doing more. Then you are working the whole instrument. The more you do that, the more you are where you belong, in the transformational state— never knowing what is going to happen next, what you are going to become, think, or feel next. That is spontaneous experience.

> **TO THE COACH:** Allowing playwriting will create soap operas, and that's all right in this exercise because the emphasis is on the still team, which is not speaking. Soap opera and playwriting will also introduce new information for the characters to use as springboards for practicing traveling in the still moments. Also, freed of playwriting rules for the first time, the actors will experience a different level of freedom to ad-lib and make jokes which ordinarily contribute nothing to good acting but here will make the active scenes fun to do and watch.

Should the coach notice that the actors are just sitting and talking at the active tables, with no involvement at all with an occasionally discovered space object, he may choose to do a demonstration on the value of discovering space objects in support of inner doing discoveries.

Wine Glass Demonstration

Picking up doesn't have to be relegated to just other people. Notice how actors deprived themselves by not occasionally discovering a space prop here and there. I'm going to pick up a space glass of wine, bring it to my lips and then, someone coach, "Still." ◆ The coach does this and when the group calls, "Still," he goes still with the glass at his lips. He looks at the glass, and travels along the following track, *silently* to himself. ◆ *This glass is filthy. Leave it to her to bring me to a bar like this. We never go anywhere fancy. Only she would pick a hole like this. Oh my god, I almost drank this. Holy cow, I've been on the wagon for seven weeks. And I'm so caught up with her and her problems that I'm going to be drinking in about two seconds. How can I get out of here?*

Now, let's repeat that and this time, I'll share my traveling with you for the purpose of this demonstration. ◆ Repeat the glass-to-lips gesture, and this time, while in the still, *think the previous traveling out loud.*

When finished— And there's the first question for question and answer railroad tracks. I discovered the glass and then I picked up from it that it was dirty. You can also pick up from the location. You could be sitting here with your partner, and you could look out over her shoulder, see the other subteam at their table, and pick up on, "Wow, who's the blonde over there? What am I doing here? I should be over there." And you set off down your railroad tracks.

If there are two coaches in the group, the second coach monitors the active table to insure that they have traveled from the point they were at when they were previously active. Other coachings that they might employ, *if needed*— Share your voices. When you are active, be active! Share the active. Share the responsibility for being active.

◆　◆　◆

ACTIVE & STILL #2[2]

PART A

SETUP: Same as active & still #1. The coach begins the **introduction.** In an interview with Bob Hoskins, he said, "When the lens is that close to your face, it can see you *think*, the camera can see you think." [So what you do is think like hell?] "Yeah. You've got this volcano inside you. The lens is close and you've got this volcano inside trying to get out."[3] The whole point of the still is exploring how your character thinks. There is a difference between being in the character's head and being in the actor's head. Being in the actor's head means that you, the person, are usually commenting to yourself about what is happening to you as an actor, not the character, and it is almost always in negative terms: self-judgment, fear, put-downs, comparisons, etc. You never want to be in the actor's head, but as Hoskins says, there are times when you must be in the character's head.

We have been practicing being in the character's head and thinking like the character. There are three options that serve as springboards for this and you learned them in the last exercise: question and answer railroad tracks, silently continuing dialogue, and picking up. The ultimate still is mixing and matching, or player's choice, where you are on your own. On that level, you alternate and/or combine the options, choosing spontaneously, in the moment, what you will employ and when.
The three options serve as jumping-off points, sending you on your own journeys. As you become more familiar with employing these three, you will discover other options of your own devising.

In the first part of this exercise, we practice what we learned in the last exercise. When you are not participating in the improv, please take a more involved role in watching the improv. It will increase your awareness of the importance of, and the necessity for, traveling. You should monitor the still tables for traveling, to make sure that when they go active again, their scene picks up at a point further along than where it was when they were last active. Audience left should monitor the table stage right; audience right should monitor the table stage left.

RULES: Same as active & still #1. Whatever letter that I call keeps going, keeps being active. The other table stops, midsentence, midword. No matter what you are saying, you stop, go still, and practice traveling. Here we go. Ready, set, action.

ACTING FOCUS: Active or still.

COACHING (as needed): Both tables begin improvising their separate scenes. *After two minutes—* A! A, stay active! B, go still. ◆ [Switch back and forth frequently but not at regular time intervals.] ◆ *After about five minutes—* Cut.

FOLLOW-UP: Audience, were they on their acting focus? Did they play active & still? When they became active again, were their scenes further along? **When they were active, did they occasionally discover an object?** ◆ Actors, do you agree? **Were you busy, doing (traveling) in your stills?**

Keep the actors at their tables and go right into:

PART B

SETUP: At this level, we remove the coach from the process. Instead of your being coached to go active or still, *the table that is active initiates going still,* whenever they like. The other table responds immediately by going active. Let's say that Table B is active and Table A is still. Table B, spontaneously, with no discussion, initiates going into a still. The other table must respond immediately, coming out of their still and going active. Now Table A is active and Table B is still, and at some spontaneous moment Table A, as a team, will initiate going from active into a still, at which time Table B must respond in kind by changing their still to active. While you are in your own still you will have to stay somewhat alert to the other table, which you did not have to do in the last exercise, in order to know when they have gone into a still. Also, you have to be alert to your own team-mates when you are active because if one of your teammates at your table initiates for the team that you are going into a still, the teammates need to see that and go with it. Anyone at the active table may initiate the still.

RULES: *When you are active, you are focused on choosing to go to a still rather than on what you are saying.* Don't get caught up in your little soap opera and only initiate going still at the end of each beat or the completion of a monologue. Go still frequently and at odd moments. *When the active table initiates a still, the still table must go active right at that moment.* We don't want any time to transpire with two tables still at the same time. *Only go active when the other table goes still first.* We don't want any time to transpire with two tables active at the same time.

ACTING FOCUS: Initiating stills while playing active & still.

COACHING (as needed): To get started, the subteam that was just active when we ended the last round will continue being active, from right where you were. The other subteam will return to your still and be alert to the other table going still. ◆ Action. ◆ Don't go active until the other table has first gone still. When the other table goes still, you go active immediately. No two tables still at the same time. ◆ **Active table, stay on your acting focus. Choose to go still!** Surprise the other table. Vary your stills. ◆ **Stay alert to your table mates. If someone at your table initiates a still, go with it.** When you go still, commit to it. ◆ Don't be so caught up in your soap opera. Choose to go still. Avoid being polite. ◆ When you are active, your acting focus is to select moments to go still. When you are still, your acting focus is to travel and stay alert to the other table. ◆ Cut.

FOLLOW-UP (as needed): Did you see players initiate their team into a still? Did their table mates go with it? **Were they on their acting focus when active or were they more concerned with their soap opera?** Did the tables fall into a regular rhythm of how much time they were active prior to going still, or did they go still at varied times? **When they were active, did they discover objects? ◆ Actors, did you travel in your stills?** Did you have trouble knowing when your table mates were choosing to go into a still? ◆ Now we go on to the next part of the exercise. [The coach immediately introduces Part C of the exercise with the same teams still in place at their tables.]

> **TO THE COACH:** Allow 5–8 minutes for Part B. Actors not on the acting focus are the ones so caught up in their active soap opera that they forget they are supposed to be choosing to go still. They will only go still when their table mates find a way of demanding it. Coaching must get these actors onto the acting focus. If that fails, stop the exercise, ask follow-up questions, and then resume from the point it was stopped.

PART C

SETUP: In the last round, you were focusing on going still without being coached to do so. Now we work on developing the opposite acting focus, *initiating active*. In this round, both tables are active simultaneously. There is no going still whatsoever in this round. Active has been defined for you as speaking and movement, anything that directs the audience's attention to your table. In this round, you want to focus on being active in such a way that the audience is always directed to watch your table only. This is a competition for the audience's attention. Anything goes, short of physical violence. You are continuously focusing on what more you can *do* to get the audience to keep watching you. If you hear me coaching in some strange way, go with it. Don't let it stop you. Resume your scenes from the point you were at when we ended Part B.

RULES: All are active. No one is ever still. Anything goes.

ACTING FOCUS: Heightening being active.

COACHING (as needed): Ready, set, action. ◆ [Coach with increasing volume to spur them on to more heightened active, so that the tables are not only competing with each other's rising volume, but also with the coach's.] ◆ Active. More active. More active! More Active! Heighten it! Anything goes! Keep the audience at your table!

FOLLOW-UP (as needed): Audience, were they on their acting focus? **Were they afraid to be more active?** Could they have been still more active? Were there other ways they could have been more active? [Look for a yes answer, but avoid letting the audience say *how* they could have been more active.] ◆ **Actors, do you agree? Could you have done more?** ◆ [Proceed immediately to Part D, the final part of the exercise.]

TO THE COACH: Allow 3–5 minutes for Part C. ◆ The actors will probably stand at some point. If the two subteams begin to merge, keep them apart through the *coaching, for example*— Separate scenes! Avoid combining! ◆ While anger may emerge at either table, it is all right as long as there is no physical contact between the angry actors. *If needed, coach*— No touching in anger! If angry contact is attempted, stop the improv and *discuss it*— It is against the law of acting ever to touch another actor in anger. The only exception to this law is if it has been planned, rehearsed, and choreographed. If another actor ever touches you in anger, when it has not been planned, immediately walk off the set. Don't get caught up in it. ◆ Should any actors complain, "Why do we have to yell," the coach should avoid getting into a discussion on this point and *respond*— You don't. However, your acting focus is to get the audience to watch only your table.

PART D

SETUP: This is the last part of the exercise, where we put it all together. It is total active & still, player's choice. Only one table can be active at any time. Any table may go active whenever it chooses. Any table may go still whenever it chooses. If one table initiates going active, the other table must go still. If one table initiates going still, the other table must go active. This will be complete active & still and the audience will never be asked to look at two tables simultaneously active or simultaneously still. Improvisationally, you will direct the audience's attention back and forth from one table to the other. For the sake of your exercising, I encourage you to practice initiating both of the options. Initiate going still and initiate going active. Within those options, you need to be alert to go with what your table mates may be initiating. Resume your scenes from the point you were at when we stopped.

RULES: Only one table may be active at a time. Either table may initiate going active or still.

ACTING FOCUS: Active & still.

COACHING (as needed): Ready, set, action. ◆ If you are going active, do it! No false starts. Initiate active or still whenever you want. Avoid politeness. ◆ Be still immediately when they go active. ◆ When the other table goes still, you go active immediately. ◆ No two tables still at the same time. ◆ Surprise the other table. ◆ Stay alert to your table mates. If someone at your table initiates a still, go with it. When you go still, commit to it. ◆ Don't be so caught up in your soap opera. Choose to go still. ◆ When you are active, your acting focus is to select moments to go still. ◆ When you are still, travel or go active. No two tables active at the same time.

FOLLOW-UP (as needed): Audience, were they on their acting focus? Did they initiate and exercise both their options? Was there always one table active and one table still or were there two tables being active or still at the same time? Did you see actors not recognizing their table mates initiating a still for the table? **When active, did they occasionally discover objects? When still, did they travel?** ◆ Actors, did it feel like you were on your acting focus? **When still, did you keep doing (traveling) or did you freeze?**

SUMMARY:

Did anyone experience a heightened willingness to go active? Did you find that if you were willing to go active when the other table was active, you had the ability to do so and let them know it so they would go still? Did you find new areas to pick up from? Did anyone pick up from the other table, the location, or from yourself? Did anyone experience a sense of going active & still within your own table scene?

Acting is doing, not pretending. Doing the exercise, you were really pursuing the different thought patterns. When you really do that, the camera catches it. When circumstances deprive you of physical doing, your doing moves to the inside of you. You must never stop acting, or doing, even when you are still or silent. The engine must never be turned off. Keep it revving.

The thoughts you improvise during one scripted scene may show you the path to the end of the scene or to the setup or the solution to a problem in another scene.

The three options for being in a still are not the only options, but they are there for you to spring off from. What matters is that you are practicing inner doing and traveling, which puts you in the character's head, not the actor's head.

Inner doing is allowing thoughts and feelings to happen spontaneously with the control of a craftsman. Applying form to spontaneity creates your improvisation technique.

What about your hearing abilities? It became easier to listen with less effort. You could play your scene and still keep a part of your consciousness listening to the other table. We're starting to work on a level that exceeds your average listening level. Actors, like athletes, have to use their instruments in a heightened fashion.

An actor has two levels of consciousness. One belongs to the character; the other, to the actor. In performance, neither level should shut down. The actor's consciousness is the craftsman level of heightened awareness, an unobtrusive witness waiting in readiness should the need for self-coaching arise, e.g., "If they are active, I go still."

In the past, whenever we had a scene on the floor with more than four actors in it, it would sometimes break up into miniscenes going on simultaneously and the whole scene would turn toward chaos. That need never happen again because you now know to go automatically into active & still.

> **TO THE COACH:** Allow 5–10 minutes for Part D. ◆ If the coach notices any actor(s) who never initiated going active and deprived themselves of practicing that option, they were probably the same actors who displayed fear of heightening their active in Part C of the exercise. They were also the ones who probably complained, "Acting shouldn't have to be about screaming and yelling."
>
> The coach may *point out this connection*— In the active/active round (Part C), the setup required that you: (1) compete for the audience's attention and (2) anything goes. You were coached— keep heightening your active, *as big as you can.* Why? So that your body, including your voice, has an experience of how big it *could* get should it ever *need* to. No one is expecting you to work at the top of your voices, but now that you have had a body experience of how big you *can* get, you are more likely to call upon that when it is needed. Parts A, B, and C were training rounds for Part D.

PARTY UPSET[4]

Now we get the actors up on their feet, away from their tables, and bring back aspects of physical doing.

> **SETUP:** 4–10 (ideally, 8) per team. In the huddles, the team subdivides into pairs. If there is an odd number, one subteam may have three actors. Each subteam huddles by itself and makes character choices (occupations and personal relationships). The location and activity are the same for all subteams: large living room, partying. Each subteam is attending the party together; they do not know the characters in the other subteams.
>
> After the huddles, the coach sets up the location: three chairs placed together forming a couch, center stage right; two chairs facing each other, center stage left. Everything else is in space: a buffet table, down center; help-yourself bar, stage left; fireplace, up center; doors leading to a terrace (which is considered on stage), up right; stereo system, stage right. The walls are covered with paintings and books on bookshelves.
>
> The first team to play takes the stage. The subteams are coached to go each to a different acting area. When the coach calls action, all the subteams will simultaneously go active, beginning the improv. Actors relate to only their subteammates, according to their character choices. *They are free to move about the location* as they see fit. Of course, when they are active, they are encouraged to contact the location, discover objects near them, or do activities that are a part of the whole party scene. All

subteams will be active for a minute or two so that all the subteam scenes can improvise up to speed. Then the coach calls out "active & still," and from that point on, the subteams are to focus on playing active & still. When any subteam is active, the other subteams are still.

RULES: Same as active & still. Only one subteam may go active at a time. All other subteams must go still. Any subteam may go active whenever it wishes. Going active means to talk or move. When you are still, you may not talk or move and you are expected to travel. *Unlike the previous exercise, you do not have the option of initiating a still.* You only go still if another subteam goes active. Subteams are not to merge with each other unless coached to do so.

ACTING FOCUS: Active & still, with traveling.

COACHING (as needed): Action. ✦ All are active. Explore the location. Discover objects. ✦ *After 1–2 minutes—* **Active & still! Go still when they go active.** If you want to be active, go active. Keep the subteams separate. Explore and contact the location. Once you are active, you must stay active until others go active, then go still immediately. **When you are in a still, practice traveling.** Integrate that still. Active & still! When you go active, go active! When you go still, do it immediately. ✦ *After about eight minutes (After ca. 8m)—* **Upset! All teams go active simultaneously and merge into one group. Right now! Mingle. Meet each other.** ✦ *After ca. 30s—* **Now, find a brand new partner. Break up your subteam and form a new one.** Head out into the location. Stay with your new partner. You are now in a new subteam. ✦ *After 30–60s—* **Active & still.** (Same coaching as above.) ✦ *After 5–8m—* Upset! Mingle as a group. ✦ Find a brand new partner. Go to a different part of the location. ✦ *After 30–60s—* Active & still. ✦ *After ca. 5m—* One more minute to practice traveling and to stay on your acting focus. ✦ Cut.

FOLLOW-UP (as needed): **Audience, were they active & still? Were they on their acting focus?** Were there times when more than one team was active at the same time? Did they maintain their characters when they had new partners? Did they respect their space objects? ✦ **Actors, did you travel when you were still?** Did you practice all the options? When you were active, did you contact the location and discover objects?

SUMMARY:

When you were traveling, did you discover any new personalized traveling options that emerged spontaneously? ✦ Did anybody discover anything new about picking up? Picking up means noticing what is around you, seeing or hearing it as a jumping-off point for inner doing or traveling.

In some cases, you were involved with your space objects when you had to go still and you picked up from them or you picked up from a scene mate's space objects. There were times when you picked up upon spotting a character in another subteam. Some of you paid that pick up off when you managed to mingle with that character during the upset and then made him/her your new partner.

Did anyone pick up from the location, seeing something in the location that served as a springboard for new traveling? It could have been from the buffet, the bar, the bookshelves, or the fireplace. Did anyone discover a pick up based on the still posture you found yourself standing in when another subteam went active? For instance, if you had to go still while you were bending over, you could commence your railroad tracks from that posture: "Why am I bent over like this? Oh, my back is stuck. Damn! Why does my back have to go out now in the middle of this party? It is because I was drinking." Your own body becomes the source of a potential pick up.

Did anyone, while you were in a still, pick up from overhearing another subteam's dialogue? Keep your ears open while traveling. There may be dialogue from another subteam that relates to your own inner doing and serves as a diving board to further your own traveling. Hearing others while traveling is very important, especially when you are traveling in script acting. *If your scene mate is talking to you and the shot includes you listening, you must still listen to them as you travel.* If you do that, you will have action in your reaction.

You now have the opportunity to expand the scope of picking up to other characters' dialogue, the set, props, or yourself. You will continue to find more available to you.

> **TO THE COACH:** The actors may initially experience difficulty going active due to the increase in subteams from the original active & still. *Coach, if necessary*— Share the active & still. Help your fellow actors. Be a part of the whole.

ACTIVE & STILL REFRESHER [5]

To start the workshop, this is a physical warm-up for further work on inner doing.

> **SETUP:** All the actors form a circle, standing. For very large groups, divide in two and form two circles. One actor in the circle initiates a movement (goes active) and at any time thereafter, another actor initiates a different movement. As soon as the second actor begins his movement, the first actor must immediately go still regardless of the pose he is in. A third actor begins a movement at any time, and the second actor goes still. And so on, until all the actors are freely initiating movements and then going still when the next actor initiates movement. Actors will initiate movements

multiple times and do not have to wait for all the actors to have initiated once before they initiate again. ◆ When an actor is still, there is no inner doing of the traveling type. In their stills, the actors are focused on holding their poses, without freezing or tension, in readiness for going active again.

RULES: Only one actor is active at a time. Anyone may go active whenever they wish. When you go still, it must be immediately.

ACTING FOCUS: Waiting in readiness to go active.

COACHING (as needed): Don't go still until someone goes active. When someone goes active, you go still. Immediately still! Take turns going active. Avoid being precious. Play the game! **Anyone can go active at any time.** Avoid freezing. It's stillness. Remove the tension. **When you are still, you are waiting in readiness to go active again.** Only one can be active a time. ◆ *After 5m*— **Double speed!** ◆ **Heighten your movements!** ◆ *After 3m*— **Add sound!** ◆ *After 2m*— **Everyone go active at the same time!** No stills! ◆ *After 30s*— Cut.

FOLLOW-UP: Not necessary.

SUMMARY:

Not necessary.

> **TO THE COACH:** If the size of the group requires two circles playing simultaneously, coach the two circles into one prior to coaching them to add sound.

TURNS

INNER TURNS FOR THE CAMERA

INTRODUCTION TO GROUP:

> One of the most crucial jobs you'll have as an actor will be to know what you're thinking when you're not talking. . . . The film actor knows how to reduce a performance physically but not mentally. In fact, oddly enough, your mind should work even *harder* in a close-up than it does during other shots because in the close-up, the performance is all in your eyes; you can't use the rest of your body to express yourself. —Michael Caine[6]

Traveling is thinking in character. Having learned to do this in stillness prepares you for what to do in the close-up shot when you do not have any lines. We will now work on how to bring more dynamics and presence to traveling, especially for camera acting.

Audiences have changed over the years as a result of television and the impact of special effects in action movies. By time the average person reaches adulthood, they've seen maybe 350,000 commercials, very short, quick films with fast cutting. A current shoe commercial has eight edits per second! Even in a non-action movie, directors provide action by keeping the camera constantly moving. Today's audience is used to movement and action. Their attention span is geared to things changing all the time. Today's actor should be prepared to bring the equivalent of a car chase into his acting, not speed or explosions, but *movement*. Movement in acting heightens the audience's attention. The question for us is, how do we infuse more movement and so, more action into our traveling.

When an actor is on camera, hanging out in one mood, or one thought, he is on a plateau, not going anywhere. The editor will cut away immediately. Your job as an actor is to give the editor/director reason to stay on you even when you don't have the lines. If the other actor has the lines and the director/editor chooses to stay on you because it's better for the film, it's because you gave them *more action in your reaction* than the actor with the lines gave them.

Action in your reaction is defined as doing more, or traveling further, or traveling more interestingly. This is accomplished through an acting focus called *Turns*. Turning means that you're traveling on a railroad track, and you decide to extend the tracks off into a new direction, so you *turn*. E.g., you are traveling north and you decide the tracks should turn to the right; and now you're traveling east. Every time you take a turn, the camera (and the audience) stays on you. *They want to know what just happened.* Where are you going now? What happened to cause you to change direction? Without turns, the audience gets used to the direction you are going in. The editor knows that this feeling is his enemy and he will cut away from you and look for the action somewhere else. The more turns you make, the more interesting the trip will be for you and for the audience.

How and when you make these changes of direction is what we will work on now.

SETUP: Identical to party upset. However, during play, the coach will go out in the location and coach subteams privately when they are still.

RULES: Same as party upset. However, if the coach is working with you while you are still, do not go active until he leaves you; then you may go active whenever you wish.

ACTING FOCUS: Taking turns in your traveling as you play active & still.

CLASS QUESTION: "What are the qualities of a turn?" A change of attitude or emotion, or a change of subject if it creates a new insight, attitude, or emotion. However, these changes or insights can only come after discovering the turn. You cannot plan them.

COACHING: Action. ◆ After a minute of all subteams being active, *coach*— Active & still. ◆ After a minute, the coach approaches any subteam in a still. In a very low voice so that only that actor hears him, the *coach asks one of the actors*— What are you thinking? ◆ The actor, coached to lower his voice if necessary, answers the coach. The coach immediately repeats the question to the other actor on that subteam and receives the answer. The coach stays by these actors but says nothing more to them for about thirty seconds; then he returns to first actor *and asks*— Now, what are you thinking? ◆ The actor responds. ◆ If his answer is on the same railroad track as his first response, the coach *points this out*— Notice that your first answer to me was on the track of your partner's good looks and your second answer is still on that same track. Now, get off that track and pick up on something else to become the next track. It can come from your character's brain. Or you can look out into the location and pick up something you see in the location—objects or people. Or you can pick up on something you overhear in other subteams' dialogue, or [if the track he was on didn't relate to his partner] from something you think or feel pertaining to your partner. When you have something, tell me your first question on the new track. ◆ If the next question is still on the original track, point that out and have him do it again until he provides a question that is on another track. ◆ Okay, now you are on another track. Proceed with your questions and answers, traveling down that track. ◆ The coach turns to the second actor and repeats the process, *starting with*— What are you thinking now? ◆ If an actor's second answer was already on another track, *acknowledge it*— Notice that you are now on a different track than you were when you answered my first question. That's on the acting focus. Continue.

Return to first actor *and ask*— What are you thinking now? ◆ If the actor is on the same track as he was when you last checked in with him, point this out and *remind him*— Your acting focus is to turn from one track to another. Once you get on a track, you must not stay there beyond three questions and answers. You may turn earlier than that, but you must practice turning by the third answer. If you go more than three questions and answers, you missed the turn. Keep picking up on something else to become the next track. Reach and discover. Now go with that. I'm going to leave you now. Stay on focus and practice making turns whenever you are in a still. As soon as I leave you and your partner, you may return to going active & still whenever you wish.

Return to the second actor and repeat this process. ◆ Proceed to each individual subteam with the above coaching process.

When all the subteams have been coached privately, the coach returns to each subteam with the framing device, an empty picture frame about 1.5' x 2'. Hold the frame up in front of an actor's face (during a still) approximating the close-up ratio of face to movie screen. Hold the frame so that the audience

128

can see the face as well. The coach watches the framed actor and *acknowledges the actor's turns*— I saw that turn. ◆ If the actor doesn't seem to be turning, *after ca. 30s*— Have you turned since I've been framing you? ◆ If actor says, "Yes," *ask*— What track were you on before the turn? What track did you turn onto? ◆ The chances are the actor will describe the same track. The coach can point this out and coach accordingly until actor is turning while being framed.

While being framed, each actor should be *coached (as needed)*— Remember, in a close-up it is not necessary to put any extra energy into making sure the camera sees the turn. If you are doing anything extra, you're *muscling* it and that's too much. Make a real, authentic turn and the camera will see it. ◆ Don't go out of your way to hide the turn. Allow your face to be free and elastic. Don't censor anything. Don't censor the elasticity of your face. If you feel anything, let your face feel it, too, in the cheeks, in the lips, in the eyebrows. ◆ When you go into a still, it must start immediately, but it needn't start abruptly. Explore all options for a source of new traveling, new tracks, and new turns: from yourself, your location, your partner, other characters, your body posture. ◆ The coach may take advantage of a subteam's positioning in a still and frame both their faces at the same time, *coaching*— You are in a two shot. Work off each other. Use each other to stimulate a turn.

After all the preceding steps have been accomplished, *the coach calls out to the whole team*— Upset! All subteams go active and mingle together. ◆ When everyone is in one grouping, *coach*— Change partners. Meet someone new. Maintain your own character. ◆ When everyone has paired off with new partners, *coach*— You are now in new pairs. Each pair, head off to a different part of the location. ◆ When the new couples are spread out around the location, *wait ca. 1m, and then coach*— Active & still. ◆ The coach resumes framing individuals when they are in stills and coaching as needed. *Additional private coaching might include*— Stay alert. Be aware of what you are doing so that you will know when you've been doing one thing for too long. Look out the window of the train you have been on. Spot another train going in a different direction and get on it. ◆ *After ca. 5m*— Cut.

FOLLOW-UP: After each team has played, *ask*— Were you on your acting focus? Do you feel you understand what it is to make turns? Was your brain in overdrive? Save your questions and comments until after the last team has played.

SUMMARY:

You see now how the mind has to work harder, thinking every moment, because the camera looks into your mind. You will never have a reaction shot that lasts as long as what you've just practiced. It will always be easier than what you just did.

In a reaction shot on you, you need to take a turn so the camera sees something new. A turn may be a new subject to think about, a change in the intensity or importance of what you are thinking about, or a change in attitude toward what you are thinking about.

E.g., my girlfriend and I are at a party and she has a monologue that builds to her breaking up with me. I'm listening to her and inside I'm traveling on a railroad track: *Is she going to leave me?* Yes. *Why?* She's found someone else. *How do I feel about this?* I need a drink. *Do I want to deal with that crowd at the bar?* At this point, the turn has been completed. This turn is very related to the track I've just turned from. It doesn't *have* to be related. It is improvisational and everyone and every situation is different. Your character, the dialogue, and the given circumstances will guide you and keep you within the parameters of the scene.

If there is no movement in her monologue—we will get to providing movement in monologues in chapter 13—and there is movement in my traveling, the editor will be encouraged to stay more on my reaction. In the ideal situation, both actors are providing movement and the cutters have potential for editing the sequence for maximum effect.

On *What Dreams May Come*, starring Robin Williams and Cuba Gooding Jr., I was creative consultant to the director, Vincent Ward. In the editing room, I saw that in the reaction shots, everything that wasn't a turn was thrown out. If an actor stayed in the same reaction, they cut away. But every time the actor had just a slight change, they went to that. *They didn't even bother to discuss what the change represented.* The turn hooks the audience's attention; they want to know why you turned. The editors and directors keep it in because that is where the movement is. The turn is the action in the reaction.

When you start to feel comfortable with the railroad track you are on, *take that as a cue* to get off and get on another track.

There is a very common actor's tool called *the secret*. You make up some secret for yourself that you are not going to tell anybody and you work off that in a scene. Well, these railroad tracks are your secrets, but you are methodically improvising in and around the secret by turning it into questions and answers rather than into an inner monologue, which lacks spontaneity and pizzazz. When you do questions and answers, you truly don't anticipate the questions, or the answers. They are discoveries, and there is a spontaneous burst of energy that accompanies each one.

> **TO THE COACH:** Good acting compels an audience to watch. It's easy to say they are compelled because an actor has presence, but if an actor has presence, it's because *his acting is compelling.* Turns create movement in the traveling, action in the reaction. They are technical devices that compel an audience to watch the actor in a reaction close-up.

The more an actor turns, the more he puts explosions and car crashes into his reaction close-up. Although the actor on a job may not make the far-reaching turns encouraged in this exercise, the exercise is training the actor to go as far as he is able. *All Improvisation Technique training should push the actor further than he may ever need to go on the job.* That way, the job is always within his grasp and is attacked with confidence.

When coaching the subteams privately, stay alert to the actor's responses to your questions and notice if their railroad tracks are inner monologues. If so, *coach them to transform the monologue into a question & answer railroad track—* Make a question out of it. Answer it. Inner monologues seldom take you anywhere new. Question and answers always do. The question itself will be new knowledge. You discover what it is that you are concerned about.

When responding to what the actors are thinking, if they give you a declarative sentence, coach them to put it into a question.

When first coaching the actors privately, I keep a pen and paper with me in order to jot down the name of the track they are on, so I don't have to remember it.

ACTIVE, STILL, & DISCOVER

Now that everyone can travel and make turns, let's remove the complete body stillness from the process and combine traveling with doing more physically.

> **SETUP:** 2–5 per team; 4 or 5 is best. The location for every team is a waiting room, and the activity for all is waiting. Teams huddle and select the type of waiting room and their characters. All characters have their job titles and must have personal relationships with at least one other character. ◆ Prior to playing, each team sets up their location, placing real chairs and essential space set pieces. ◆ When playing begins, each actor will play active & still. There is to be no dialogue, so to be active, one must have movement. If one actor is active, the other actors will be still and practice traveling. ◆ However, when an actor goes into a still, he must then discover an object (p. 89), or more than one, near him. The actor stays involved with his discovery while he travels and turns. He may go active whenever he wishes. *Actors in stillness may move to accommodate their involvement with their discoveries,* but they may not take any steps. This movement should be physically less than the movement accompanying going active. The audience should always have their attention pulled to the actor who is going active by the larger size of his movement.
>
> **RULES:** All start in a still (without objects). Only one actor may go active at a time, whenever he wishes. Going active is accomplished solely by move-

ment. After going active, you must continue being active until someone else goes active, and then you go still and discover an object near you. All actors in a still must travel. Avoid dialogue.

ACTING FOCUS: Discovering objects near you and taking turns in your traveling as you play active & still.

COACHING (as needed): Places. ◆ **Travel in your stills when "Action" is called.** Don't go active until "active & still" is called. ◆ Action. ◆ *After 30s*— **Active & still. Don't discover an object until you've been active once. When you are active, stay active until someone else goes active. Let everyone know you are active. Avoid dialogue. Make your active more active.** ◆ When in a still, pursue your traveling, and **make a discovery. When you go still, don't become a statue. Reach and discover an object near you. Integrate your discoveries as a part of the whole character, waiting. Reach and discover something new. Always know when you are being active or in a still/discovery.** Fill the still with discovery doing. Fill the active with active doing. **Show us you are active.** ◆ **Distinguish the quality of your movement in a still/discovery from the quality of your movement when active. The discovery movement must not direct the audience's attention to it.** The active movement must demand the audience's attention to it. Heighten your active. Diminish your still/discovery. ◆ *To the audience*— **All the actors are on their acting focus when only one of them has your attention, yet if you choose to look around, no one is a statue.** ◆ After about five minutes of the actors doing the physical requirements of the exercise, *remind them about traveling*— **ADD YOUR TRAVELING. Continue your inner doing, railroad tracks, questions and answers, picking up. Make turns. Avoid hanging out on the inside. There's always more to do. Can you make turns that take you to new places and make you feel different? Go there. Heighten that feeling. Stimulate a turn with a pick up.** ◆ **Become involved with your discoveries.** Don't muscle the discovery. **Always know who's active.** ◆ **Go active frequently. Catch the others off guard.** ◆ *Can you mark a turn with making a discovery at the same time?* **At the moment of your discovery, turn onto a track about the discovery. Can you use the discovery to show a turn? Your traveling may have something to do with your discovery, or it may not.** ◆ **Check out your fellow characters; you know some of them. Pick up tracks or turns from them. Only one actor active at a time. When you go active, do it sharply. Someone else has gone active; go into a still and discover an object. When you go still, do it immediately.** ◆ **Coach yourself to travel on the inside on subjects, feelings, thoughts, attitudes that do not relate to your discovery, even while**

you involve with the object. **If your inner doing relates only to what you are discovering, then there's more to do. Mix it up.** ◆ **Stay on your focus. Active, still, & discover. Stay alert. Know when you are active and know when you are still. Show us the difference. No statues. Every still is a still/discovery.** ◆ [If the coach feels it is appropriate, use the picture frame and frame individual actors as in close-ups.] ◆ Avoid muscling the discoveries. Know what you are thinking and feeling and choose to change it frequently. Is it possible to be on a set of railroad tracks that have nothing to do with the object you discover and make a turn while involved with that object? Make those turns. Explore how your discoveries can enrich turns. Explore combining your turns with your discoveries. Check out the others. Pick up the beginnings of new tracks or turns. **Make a turn that takes you to a whole other feeling or attitude and make it a part of the whole. Feel the moment to make the turn.** ◆ **One minute**. Will yourselves to make turns. Travel and discover. Use your instrument. ◆ Cut.

FOLLOW-UP (as needed): Audience, what type of waiting room was it? Who were the characters? Were they on their acting focus? When they went active, did they stay active until someone else went active? What is the importance of staying active until another actor goes active? It forces you to keep improvising because you can never initiate the conclusion of your physical doing. **When they went still, did they discover objects near them?** Did they do this without confusing us as to who was the active one? Were the discoveries a part of the whole character, location, and activity? **Were they traveling in their stills?** Did we lose the statues from the stills? Did they go active whenever they wanted, or did they wait politely until the previous actor finished doing something? Politely waiting hinders the exercise and reduces the improvisational challenge for all the actors. ◆ **Actors, were you on your acting focus? Did you travel in your stills? Did you make turns? Did you make discoveries?** What can you do if you feel you have completed your involvement with a discovery? You have at least three options: (1) discover more involvement with that discovery; (2) discover another object near you; (3) go active.

SUMMARY:

When you add physical doing to the inner doing of the still, you're doing more and your instrument is experiencing how much it is capable of doing simultaneously. Your instrument improvises all of this with no opportunity for planning any of it because you are so busy. If you are on camera for ten seconds, you can simply listen; or, you can listen and do inner traveling; or, you can listen, do inner traveling, and make turns; or, you can listen, do inner traveling, make turns, and use an object; or, you can listen, do inner traveling, make turns, use an object, and discover another object. There is no stopping until some cop—the director, the prerequisites of the script, or the staging—stops you. If a cop stops you, fine. If not, don't stop yourself. It's easy to come up with reasons for not doing something. Too often, you will sell yourself short. Just make sure you are a part of the whole and keep going for more until the shot is in the can.

Do this and everything changes for you. You will quadruple both your potential for inspiration and your presence in front of the camera.

If there is rehearsal time, use space object discoveries to help you discover turns. Your body discovers opportunities for discovering, and in front of the camera, where you can't discover space objects, the body seizes that opportunity and fills it with a turn, or an inner discovery.

A discovery doesn't have to be an object. It can be a moment of relationship discovery or a detail that you focus on in the scene after discovering it in the moment. You can discover somebody looking at you or a tear on your scene partner's face. You can discover *anything*. While you are listening, you won't be a product of Acting 101 where they taught you to be a real good listener! Instead, you will be a real character concerned with what your character is really thinking and feeling while listening, revealing it to the camera in a dynamic fashion, and your body knows enough to keep it a part of the whole.

It is pertinent as well to being in a crowd scene. One night in the editing room on *What Dreams May Come*, I pointed out to Vincent Ward, the director and my client, that a lot of the day's footage wasn't useful *because of the background extras*. The scene was a large one where Robin Williams enters heaven and walks through these pockets of extras who, unfortunately, looked not at all like heaven's inhabitants, but tourists who were all smiling for the camera. From preproduction, I knew that Vincent's concept of heaven was not some storybook place where everyone just walked around smiling. Vincent scowled and said, "You're right. Before each shot, the A.D. (assistant director, in charge of directing the extras) calls through the bullhorn to the extras, 'Smile, everybody. You're in heaven!' I've been too busy with the principals and the special effects people to fix it. Damn!" When I arrived on the set the next day, they were shooting more coverage of the same scene. Vincent called me over and said, "Fix the extras." He smoothed things over with the A.D., who looked very relieved, and I spent the day providing the extras with relationships, activities, and subjects and attitudes for railroad tracks. I told each extra what he was concerned with and how to do question & answer railroad tracks and some other character tools that we will get to in the character chapter. They were very happy to get direction from me, something other than "Smile," and they proceeded to play their parts with individuality and excitement.

Just because the A.D. says, "Smile," does that mean that you smile and hit your marks like a puppet? Or do you find out why your character is smiling, or what he is smiling at? Every part in a script is a character. Every character is different and individual. When you are given little or no direction, it is your job to fill in the gaps.

> **TO THE COACH:** At the end of the setup, if the actors are confused as to what a still/discovery is, *have them walk around the stage, and coach*— The **character** for each of you is actor. The **location** is acting workshop. The **activity** is walking and warming up. Walk around. Keep walking. ◆ *After 10s*— Go still. Stop moving. ◆ *After 10s*— Active. Move. ◆ *After 10s*— Still. ◆ *After 1s*— Immediately discover an object near you. No steps allowed. ◆ *After 20s*— Active. Move around. Respect that space object. What are you doing with it? It can't just disappear. You can do anything with it as long as you respect its existence. ◆ *After 10s*— Still. Discover an object near you. Involve with it. ◆ *After 10s*— Cut. ◆ That's it. Every time you go into a still, you immediately reach out and discover an object near you, involve with it until you choose to go active again or choose to discover another object near you.

MULTISCENE ONE ACTS[7]

In the area of dialogue, the training so far has jumped from minimalism, speaking only when it is necessary, to soap opera (during the active periods in the active & still series), the pinnacle of excessive information. Ultimately, improvisational dialogue falls somewhere between these two extremes. In the next exercise we explore and practice this middle ground. *Multiscene one acts* brings all the previous training into play as the actors improvise complete multiscene one-act plays with the freedom to speak at will, as in active & still, while building on the dialogue rules learned in the physical doing series.

> **SETUP:** 4 (minimum) to 6 (maximum) per team. In the huddles, the team divides evenly into two subteams, called A and B. If there are five on a team, the subteams subdivide into three and two. Both subteams huddle together. Each subteam selects a location, activity, and characters. Both scenes will take place at the same time. The first choice to be made in the huddle is what the group relationship between the subteams is. *The characters of subteam A's scene must have a group personal relationship with the characters of subteam B's scene.* That is, the characters of each subteam know and have some investment in the characters of the other subteam. ◆ [The coach should read the "To the coach" notes on this point.] ◆ There may also be specific personal relationships between characters from subteam A and characters from subteam B. Within a subteam, the characters should have personal and/or professional relationships. The locations of each subteam should not be confined, e.g., in a car, and they must be out of

sight and hearing of each other. The activity for each subteam must comprise active physical doing. Subteam members know the location, character, and activity choices for the other subteam. The *characters* of one subteam may or may not know that the other subteam's scene is taking place, or what the location is, or who's there, or what they are doing. The choices are up to the team in their huddles. The exercise works just as well whether the characters in both scenes do or do not know that the other scene is taking place.

When the huddles are completed, the first team to play divides the acting area into two equal, adjacent areas; each subteam claims one area. Each subteam sets up their location, placing real chairs and essential space set pieces. ◆ When the improvisation begins, both subteams will be in an active state employing their physical doing tools of improvisation: (1) relating to each other according to their character relationships; (2) doing their activity; (3) contacting the location; and (4) discovering objects near them. After about two minutes, when the coach calls out "active & still," the two subteams focus on playing active & still with each other. When A goes active, B must go still, and vice versa. Or, one subteam may go still first, and the other subteam must go active.

When you are active, you have total freedom of movement within your own acting area and *you may speak whenever you wish*. If you speak, *you must avoid playwriting*, i.e., introducing off stage information.

When you are still, you are traveling with the tools of (1) question & answer railroad tracks, (2) turns, (3) silently continuing dialogue, and (4) picking up. You have freedom of movement to reach and discover objects near you and to involve with them, but you may not take any steps. The quality of your movement in a still/discovery must not pull the audience's attention from the other subteam while that team is active. Stay alert to the continuous possibility that some discoveries do not have to be objects, but may be turns or inner discoveries. If that occurs, stay fluid and avoid becoming a statue in your still.

You have learned and practiced everything described so far in previous improvisations. Now we add something new: *picking up from the other subteam*. While you are in your stills, practicing your traveling and discoveries, keep your ears open to what is going on in the other subteam during their active. You may hear something in the other scene that provides you with a whole new railroad track or discovery. Then you can explore it further in that still or when you go active again.

For instance, suppose I'm a father on team A. My daughter is on team B, and during her active, she reveals she's feeling horny and frustrated. Upon hearing and picking up on this comment, many different railroad tracks open up for me. I might turn onto a track about my daughter's blossoming sexuality, and when my team goes active again, I might develop that further with dialogue to my wife, e.g., "Don't you think it's time we had a talk with Louise, you know...about things?" The result will be an initiation of a whole new beat that comes out of what is happening—my daughter's comment— on stage. The beat includes no off stage information and is therefore not playwriting. While this example stimulated a character's concerns, another example will deal with stimulating primary character development.

For instance, perhaps in the same scene the daughter reveals that she can't talk to her father about sex because she feels that he is intimidated by the subject. When the father picks up on this comment during his still, he might turn onto a new set of tracks and discover that he is in fact cowardly about everything. Then when the father goes active again, he may never bring up the daughter's sex issues but proceed to play his character as a coward and a victim in whatever direction his subteam's scene develops. Or, he could go in the opposite direction when his subteam goes active and make his daughter's expressed feelings about him a lie. He could do this by developing his character as a brave and considerate person who would be totally available to his daughter. Or, he could develop his character as a bully, full of aggressive behavior. Either way, the daughter in a subsequent still, picking up on what he is doing, would realize that she had lied, commence railroad tracks off that insight, and develop her character accordingly—e.g., Why is she lying about her father? What else does she lie about?

Picking up is getting something from over there, bringing it back over here, and allowing it to stimulate and initiate new railroad tracks for you, which you may then draw from in exploring and heightening your character and/or scene. What you do with it is totally up to you and is improvised in the moment.

The one form of picking up that is of little value is *echoing*, in which the pick up is used simply as reiteration. For example, Louise, the daughter on Team B, says while active, "I don't like sushi." When team A goes active, if Mom says, "Let's take Louise to dinner, but not sushi because she doesn't like it," it's an *echo* because it adds nothing. It simply reiterates what Louise has already revealed. However, if her mother says, "Let's take Louise out for sushi tonight." This is a *true pick up* because it reveals that Mom doesn't know what her own daughter likes.

Really strong pick ups are often camouflaged. While the sushi example is totally *un*camouflaged, a camouflaged pick up might look like this. After sushi is mentioned in team B, the father might pick up on it and say to his wife, "Let's go to Japan for our next vacation." He could even skip Japan and just say, "Let's take a vacation." It's sufficient that he heard his daughter on the other subteam mention sushi and that sparked in him "sushi-Japan-travel-vacation." The example of the father developing cowardly traits in his character without ever talking about sex is another example of a camouflaged pick up.

Pick ups may even be trivial. For example, Dad, upon hearing the sushi line, refers to someone else later as Susie. *Sushi*-Susie, get it? It doesn't matter if it's funny, or important, or even if the audience gets it. What matters is that the actor doing the pick up does something with what he picks up. Picking up is discovering food for thought. You don't have to do it on every single scene exchange. Do it when you want to. You may be selective as long as you remain brave and open to exploring pick ups.

Picking up does not cancel the playwriting rule: *no information allowed which was not developed on stage*. Actors may initiate dialogue about their thoughts, feelings, and desires, but they may not introduce facts about the past or future of their own or any one else's character. Present tense information is considered dialogue because it is developed in front of the audience and is fair game for picking up usage by either team.

RULES: Both subteams start active until coached to begin active & still. From then on, only one subteam may be active at a time. The other subteam must be still. Either subteam may go active or still whenever it wishes. Going active is accomplished by movement and/or dialogue. All stills must be filled with traveling, turns, discoveries, silently continuing dialogue, and picking up.

ACTING FOCUS: Traveling, turning, discovering, and picking up while playing active & still.

COACHING (as needed): Action. ◆ *After a minute*— **Active & still ◆ Avoid statues in the still.** You are in a still/discovery state. **Reach and discover an object when you go to the still.** Stay involved with your discovery while you **keep your ears open to what's going on over there. You are not a statue.** In a still, don't pull the audience to you. No walking in a still. ◆ When you go active, let the other team know it. Share your voices. Share that thought. Active team, **avoid hanging out.** Stay physically involved. **Go to the location and contact it.** Do your activity. ◆ **Avoid playwriting.** Keep the dialogue in the present. No off stage information. Avoid questions requiring information. ◆ Pick up from the other team. You can build on anything the other team says or does. You don't have to take what you hear at face value. Characters sometimes lie, sometimes tell the truth. Go with it. Explore that pick up. Extend that pick up. Help your fellow actor to pick up. Keep one ear on the other team, so you can pick up. ◆ Five minutes. ◆ One minute. ◆ Cut.

FOLLOW-UP (as needed): To the audience, about each subteam: **Who were the characters? What were their locations? What were their activities?** Was everyone involved in the physical doing? Did they employ all the aspects of physical doing available to them? ◆ Were both subteams' characters related to each other in a significant way? ◆ **Did the subteams play active & still?** ◆ **Did you see pick ups? Did the pick ups take the scenes further or simply echo what the other team said?** Did the actors allow picking up to heighten and expand their own scenes or limit them (to one or two issues)? **Were any pick ups carried through or were all dropped after a single pick up usage?** Carrying through over multiple actives can up the stakes of the pick up and the scene. Single usage pick ups tend to keep the scene in a treading-water mode with little benefit. Did the actors profit from their pick ups? Did you see pick ups that develop character? ◆ **Do you feel they traveled during their stills?** ◆ **Actors, did you travel? Did you pick up? What were some of your discoveries about your character or the scene that you developed from your pick ups? How did you develop them,** or did you drop them after a single usage? ◆ Was there any playwriting? Examples? ◆ Is dialogue pertaining to the other subteam playwriting? Only if it doesn't pertain to what's been developed on stage in either scene.

SUMMARY:

TRAVELING AND PICKING UP

In scripted acting, you *know* what the other character is going to say. But if you focus on traveling and picking up while he says it, you will hear it spontaneously, from a new angle. In each take, you can give yourself an acting focus of picking up on something new. This guarantees spontaneity while the camera is on you because in every take you are doing something new while listening. You may also pick up something about your character or the scene that pays off two speeches or two scenes later. *The pick up is not about you initiating ad-libbed dialogue based on the other's lines.* It is about you discovering a new way to hear what's being said and a new way for you to understand and realize, spontaneously, what you are going to say next, your memorized lines, in this or a later scene.

On the set, it will be easier than it was in these improvs. Why not show a response to what you have just picked up on, something that you never thought about when you previously read the script or rehearsed it? The editor may discover a little moment in your traveling and picking up that is interesting to cut away to, even briefly. You are not being a ham. You are giving them two options instead of one.

TECHNIQUE

Everybody improvised multiscene one-act plays lasting about a half-hour each. Notice how *not nervous* you were. You were not winging it or ad-libbing. You were improvising with technique.

You were doing: activities, relating to the location, discovering objects, playing character relationships, traveling, turning, picking up, discovering, exploring, and directing the audience's attention back and forth between simultaneous scenes in two different locations. That's a lot of technique. Do you know what that produces? Presence. Presence is what is necessary if you want to be a great actor.

> **TO THE COACH:** I usually allow about a half-hour for each team but the exercise duration is totally flexible. ◆ The coach should monitor the huddles, checking on each team's choices. Subteams may fail to provide themselves with an activity for their scene or will not realize that what they have chosen is some form of waiting. Make sure the subteams select activities that have an ongoing physical doing aspect. They are going to be up there for a half-hour. They need a home-base activity to sustain them, not an activity that lasts five minutes from start to finish.
>
> **Character choice confusion in huddles:** Sometimes there is confusion about the relationships between the characters of one subteam and the other. Group relationships between subteams should be encouraged. How does one subteam know the other *as a group?* For example, subteam A, engaged couple, subteam B, her parents; A, football team, B, cheerleaders. Within these groups, there may also be more individualized relationships between the subteams, e.g., A, football team includes an ex-sweetheart of someone in the B, cheerleaders. However, it is not sufficient that there be a specific personal relationship between an individual from one subteam and an individual from the other and another specific personal relationship between a second individual from one subteam and a second individual from the other. There must be some group relationship between the subteams.
>
> While monitoring the huddles, the coach should encourage the actors to raise the stakes of their choices. For example, A, boyfriend and girlfriend, and B, her parents, can be changed to A, *engaged couple.*
>
> The coach should also nip in the bud any attempts at playwriting, actors choosing some past event pertaining to their characters prior to their actual scene. Huddles select only what the audience sees when the curtain goes up, character, activity, and location.
>
> When the actors are transitioning from active to still, the coach should stay alert to them pulling away from each other to make private discoveries or to be totally available for picking up. If something important is

happening to them in their relationship to each other, especially in dialogue or emotions, those actors should be coached to stay with what's happening between them as they enter the still, developing it as silently continuing dialogue or improvisational railroad tracks.

The coach should remember that no tool is the only tool. The active & still series prepares the actor experientially for the improvisational doing available to him when the director or circumstances restrict him from physical doing.

EARLIEST APPLICATIONS TO SCRIPTS AND CAREER

When do you use traveling in memorized script acting? Not all the time, but explore it whenever you are deprived of physical doing. When the other character has the lines, you can travel. For example, suppose you are Happy in the Biff and Happy scene from *Death of a Salesman*, and Biff starts his lines about being out west and how Happy should join him there. You might start a railroad track with "What does Biff really want from me?" or "What's wrong with Biff?" Maybe the question is, "Why am I listening?" Whatever the question, whatever the railroad track, it's pure discovery for you into your character.

Or, say you are in rehearsal for the same scene and you look up and see what Biff is wearing. You are coming from the mind of the character you're playing and all of a sudden, you pick up that Biff has a hole in his sock. Maybe the question is "Who's going to give a job to a man with a hole in his sock?" However that track goes your heart and feelings are going to follow the thoughts with no extra effort or consciousness on your part. Traveling allows you to access what's going on in the moment for the character, and lets you do it spontaneously. Why not do it when someone else has got the lines, instead of standing there, hanging out and waiting for your cue?

Observing Another Scene

Here's another way to employ traveling. Let's say you're playing Willy Loman and you're not in the scene between Biff and Happy in their bedroom. You stay off stage, take as a given circumstance that you can over hear the boys in their bedroom, and play active & still and travel off of what you hear. Whatever you find, you are maximizing a moment that doesn't even exist for your character in the script and what you discover during your traveling can have tremendous payoff three scenes down the road.

SUBTEXT (OFF STAGE)

The next form of inner doing is intended to accompany physical doing and is best employed as an improvisation on subtext. In script acting, the subtext is suggested by the given circumstances of the script. In the scene improvisation exercises, the actors select the subtext and their character (professional and personal relationships), activity, and location.

As preparation for the subtext work, it is necessary that the actors acquire an important tool of Improvisation Technique, *Reflection*.

BASIC REFLECTION [8]

SETUP: All pair up, then divide into ones and twos for coaching purposes. In pairs, the ones face the twos with about 4' between them and maximum space around them.

RULES: Depending on the coaching, one actor, mirror-like, *reflects* the other actor.

ACTING FOCUS: For the reflector, reflecting what you see; for the nonreflector, initiating movement.

COACHING (as needed): In each pair, one player will initiate movements. The other player will reflect what you see as you see it. ◆ Start with ones initiating and twos reflecting, and switch according to the coaching. Respond to the coaching. ◆ Action. Initiators begin movement without taking steps. Any kind of movement. The initiator can make facial expressions, can move the body abstractly, can use space props and do a little activity, anything you wish. Initiators, help your fellow player to reflect you. Respond to the coaching. This is not about tricking your partner. The two of you are working together as a team. **Initiators, never come to a stop. One movement flows into the next.** ◆ Reflectors, focus on complete and total reflection. Facial expressions reflect facial expressions, feet reflect feet, stomachs reflect stomachs. Complete and total reflection of the whole body. Reflect everything you see, not what you think you see, or what you want to see, or what you anticipate seeing. ◆ *After ca. 1m—* **SWITCH. Let the movement continue. Simply exchange roles. Don't come to a stop. Make the switch in the middle of whatever movement is occurring.** The new initiator takes it wherever he wants. ◆ Keep the movement fluid. **Avoid coming to a stop.** Initiate anything you wish. Initiators, explore new kinds of movement. Reflect everything that you see, nothing that you think you see. Total reflection: lips, eyes, knees, etc. **Always know if you're initiating or reflecting.** Complete and total reflection. ◆ Work together. Initiators, never come to a stop. Keep the reflection silent. ◆ **SWITCH.** Without any hesitation or stopping, change roles. The ones become the initiators; the twos, reflectors. Head-to-toe reflection. Everything that you see. Nothing that you think you see. All are working together to create an effective mirror with no time-lag. Stay on focus. ◆ **SWITCH.** Eyes reflect eyes. Initiators, keep the movement fluid. Let each movement transform in to the next. ◆ **SWITCH.** Keep it on the feet. Don't sit or kneel. ◆ [Repeat switches at varied intervals. Entire playing time, about seven minutes.] ◆ Cut.

FOLLOW-UP (as needed): Were you on the acting focus? Did you respond to the coaching? Did you reflect what you saw as you saw it, or did you reflect what you anticipated seeing? When you were initiating, did you come to stop points, or keep the movement flowing?

SUMMARY:

This is the first exercise in a body of work that will become increasingly more sophisticated. Every time we practice it and add new rules, it is important that you stay on the acting focus, respond to the coaching, and not take it for granted that you know what's coming.

TO THE COACH: The coach should walk among the couples as he coaches. ◆ Reflection may seem like a simple exercise and it *is* relatively easy to play; however, its importance cannot be overestimated. It is the primary tool of all the work that follows in *Off Stage*.

REFLECTION WALK

SETUP, RULES, and ACTING FOCUS: The same as basic reflection.

COACHING: Coach the actors to play about three minutes of basic reflection, *then continue*— Without any hesitation, everybody walk around the room. You are all mirrors reflecting anyone else. Just do it. Walk around the room and reflect someone new. You're no longer working with one partner. Focus on reflecting the other players. No one is initiating. Keep walking. You choose whom to reflect, any of the other players. You don't have to let them know. They can be anywhere in the room. Frequently change the person you are reflecting. All are walking and all are reflecting whomever you wish. There's no wrong way to do it as long as you are reflecting. Reflect everything that you see. Reflect nothing that you *think* you see. You are walking around and on your own, you are selecting whom to reflect. Use the whole stage. ◆ Continue walking, continue reflecting, and without hesitation, begin to *reflect the room you are walking in*. You're no longer reflecting other players. Reflect all the features of this room. Respond to the coaching. Don't try to figure it out. Keep walking. Avoid reconstructing the room. Avoid abstract interpretations of the room. See the room. Reflect it. See features of the room. Reflect them. Reflect textures. You are walking in a normal fashion. No abstract, interpretive gestures. An outsider watching us would only see a group walking around. See that wall of photos over there. Do you get a feeling from it? Reflect that feeling. See the concrete wall over there. Do you get a different feeling from it? Reflect that different feeling. Can you reflect it with your back, without looking at it? Your body might be feeling different, reflecting the audience chairs or reflecting the flats. Focus on reflecting this room. Make your own choices. There is no wrong way of doing it as long as you commit to the focus of actively reflecting the room. If you have different feelings reflecting different parts of the room or the whole room, and you are reflecting those different feelings, you are on your acting focus. See something, some area of the room, or the whole room. Let your body respond to it spontaneously with feelings, and reflect those feelings.

Now continue walking and see your own living room at home. See it in your mind's eye. Without thinking about it, allow your body to reflect it. See the large furniture pieces in your living room; reflect them. See the colors; allow your body to reflect them. See the objects in the living room; reflect them with your whole body—knees, chest, face, back, toes. See the lighting there; reflect it. See the entire room with all of its features and reflect it with all of your body.

Keep walking. Go neutral. Stop reflecting. Keep breathing. Keep walking. Observe what your body feels like when it's not reflecting.

Now we're going to change the room in your mind's eye. Everybody see the last office you were in, whenever that was. See it clearly in your mind's eye and keep your eyes open. Continue walking and reflect the last office you were in. You are not in the office. You are here in our space, using your mind's eye to see that office, and using your body to reflect it. See all the large furniture pieces and reflect them. See the colors; allow your body to reflect them. See the objects in that office; reflect them with your whole body—knees, chest, face, back, toes. See the lighting there; reflect it. See the entire office with all of its features and reflect it with all of your body. See it one hundred times clearer, and reflect it with your body while just walking. If you're swinging your arms exaggeratedly, *don't*. Just walk and stay in the process of reflecting that last office you were in. Actively focus on the office and reflecting it. ◆ Keep walking. Go neutral. Stop reflecting. Keep breathing. You should be feeling a shift in your body from what it was doing to what it's doing now. It's important to observe your body feeling now so you feel the difference between your body reflecting and not reflecting.

Keep walking. Now choose any room that we haven't done yet, any room that's real, that you can see in your mind's eye, and reflect it. There's no wrong way; just focus on reflecting that room with a regular walk. See all the large furniture pieces; reflect them. See the colors; allow your body to reflect them. See the objects in that room; reflect them with your whole body—knees, chest, face, back, toes. See the lighting there; reflect it. See the entire room with all of its features and reflect it with all of your body.

Keep walking and immediately shift your acting focus to reflecting your fellow actors again. Reflect anyone you wish. They don't have to know you are reflecting them. They could be across the room. • Now reflect any sounds you hear. Any sounds at all. Heighten it. Heighten your reflection. • Cut.

FOLLOW-UP: Were you on the acting focus of reflection? Do you know what it means to reflect? Did you feel the difference between reflecting people, reflecting rooms, and not reflecting at all?

SUMMARY:

Reflection is done with the body. It is a form of doing. Reflecting things other than people is not about abstract theatrical and interpretive gestures; it is done with the body in normal positions. Whatever you feel can be reflected by the body. If you feel differently, the body reflects differently. The reflecting body puts the feeling in the space where it is observable by an audience or camera. Reflection is always instantaneous and spontaneous, a process that doesn't allow for editing, commentary, or judgment. You simply reflect what you see and as long as you are in that process there is no right or wrong, no railroad tracks, no sense memory, just immediate and total body response in the moment. Every time you select something different to reflect, you will have a different body feeling. Sometimes it's slightly different; other times, very much so. Reflection is always about what is, not about what you want to be. When you select something to reflect in the mind's eye, it is still a body process. The head is seeing what you have selected. The body does the reflecting immediately.

TO THE COACH: Ending with sound reflections provides a burst of energy at the end of the walk. • If it looks to the coach as if the actors are confused by the introduction to reflecting the room, coach the group to look at one specific area of the room and reflect it. Then have them look at another part of the room that has a very different look to it, e.g., a cold brick wall vs. a warm lounge area, and reflect that. *Then coach*— Raise your hand if you don't have a different body feeling for each of these two areas. • If actors raise their hands, stop the group's walking around and have them join you in facing a specific part of the room. *Coach*— Let's all see that area. Now let your body respond with a reflection of what you see.

[The coach reflects alongside the group.] See that grey concrete wall. The body should be shifting around until it feels like it is capturing a reflection of the cold, grey wall. There is no right or wrong. Your body (you) will know when you feel that you are reflecting that color and texture. How does your chest feel? Is it tight or loose? Do your legs feel secure and planted or stretched up high? Reflect it. Your reflections are responses to what you see. The wall feels cold. Let your body respond to that. The body should be shifting around until it is a reflection of that coldness. Now, let's all look and see that oriental rug and the couch on the other side of the room in the lounge area. It feels brighter with lots of colors. Let your body shift around until it's reflecting that brighter and more colorful feeling. The texture of the rug feels much warmer than the concrete wall. Reflect that. Doesn't that body feeling feel different from the body feeling you had reflecting the wall? Return to walking. ◆ If this moment occurs and it is light outside, it's a great tool to lead the actors outside. ◆ We're going outside. Keep reflecting everything you see. Feel the body shifting as it changes its reflection feeling from inside to outside.

◆   ◆   ◆

The *Off Stage Reflection Walks* introduce past and future time as areas in which a great deal of subtext may be found.

OFF STAGE REFLECTION WALK #1[9]

SETUP: A solo exercise. Stand off stage and select any real room, not an imaginary one. The room you choose will be the room you are leaving when you enter on stage. There should be no one else in the room when you leave it, and there should be no attention paid to having done something in the room you are leaving. Stand off stage and I will coach you to reflect that room with your body. When you feel that you are reflecting it, enter, and simply walk across the stage until you exit the other side of the stage. The entire time that you're walking across the stage you are totally focusing on reflecting the room that you have just left. Reflecting it with your body. The on stage area is to be thought of as nothing more than a neutral hallway through which you are walking. When we see you on stage, your body should be doing nothing more than walking and reflecting. *During the walk, there should be no gestures or business indicating where you have come from.* Audience, stay open to receiving spontaneous flashes of communication about what room the actor has left. If there is no flash of communication, or the flash suggests a different room, that's fine. In this exercise, there is no goal of communicating what room you've come from.

It's all about what you go through during the walk, the process the actor goes through when his acting focus is reflecting. Who's first?

RULES: Stand off stage. Pick a room to exit from. Respond to the coaching. Walk across the stage and exit.

ACTING FOCUS: Reflecting the room you have left off stage.

COACHING: Stand off stage. Pick a room that you will be coming from, any room at all, other than this room.

BASIC OFF STAGE REFLECTION PREPARATION COACHING

See the location that you've chosen in your mind's eye. Keep your eyes open. Let your body reflect it. See all of the large set pieces and furniture in that location and include that in your reflection. Every time we add a detail, you should feel your body shift slightly as you accommodate that in your reflection. Now see all the colors, and include that in your reflection. See the objects, and include that in your reflection. See the whole location a hundred times more clearly as you allow your body to reflect it. See it all. Reflect it all. Reflect everything you see in your mind's eye.

Then coach— Enter when you feel you are on your acting focus. Keep reflecting it, as you walk across the stage. ◆ After the entrance and as they walk, coaching will probably not be needed, *other than*— **Keep focusing and reflecting the room you have just left.** ◆ If the actor begins indicating with gestures or clues, e.g., he enters zipping up his fly, *then coach*— You're not to do anything but walk your walk and keep reflecting. No business at all. No clues. As you walk, you have an acting focus, reflecting the room you've just left, so just keep reflecting it, and walk across the stage. ◆ Audience, stay open to receiving any flashes of where he's come from. ◆ Actor, keep reflecting the room as you walk and exit.

FOLLOW-UP: What room did the actor come from? Any flashes of communication? ◆ Actor, what room did you come from?

SUMMARY:

Every entrance in a play, TV show, or movie is an entrance *from somewhere else.* Always consider where are you coming from, how it is a part of the whole scene you are entering, and how can it be useful to you.

Reflection requires the whole body's participation. The mind is involved to the extent that it selects and focuses on what to reflect and then the body responds and does the reflection. As we watched these walks, we could see that no actor walked casually or indifferently. They were all focused on doing something, in this case reflecting.

TO THE COACH: *Note to the audience.* If you sit there trying to *figure out* where they're coming from, by looking at this or that part of the body, their attitude, and whatever else, then you're not on focus. Figuring it out is the audience version of telling instead of showing. Instead, just sit back and receive a flash. The first thing that pops into your mind is your flash. Stay open to flashes, avoid figuring out, and see what happens. Receive the communication instead of guessing.

If the audience has trouble letting go of their need to figure out the off stage room, the coach can *coach them at the same time he is coaching the actor*— Audience, feet flat on the floor. Sit up straight. Observe your breathing. Focus on observing your own breathing. Audience, increase your breathing just a tad to help you focus on it. Keep your eyes open and focus totally on your breathing. Nothing else. Audience, look at the stage between the two wings and when he enters, just observe him. Focus on him. ◆ Alternate between the actor's reflection coaching and this audience coaching, prefacing each coaching with either the actor's name or "Audience."

If there are time constraints, have a few actors do the exercise, one at a time, then have up to four actors do it simultaneously, coming from four different entrances and going to the same or different exits. All four will respond to the same single coaching, and the coach can stagger their entrances so the audience gets to watch one at a time.

Off Stage Reflection Walk #2 [10]

SETUP: A solo exercise. Stand off stage and select a room. The room you choose will be the room you are *going to* after you enter and exit the stage. Also choose an event you will participate in when you get to that room. Avoid making a choice that includes urgency. Do not change your age. Stand off stage and I will coach you to reflect that room and the event with your body. When you feel that you are reflecting it, enter, and simply walk across the stage until you exit the other side of the stage. The entire time that you're walking across the stage you are totally focusing on reflecting the room that you are going to and what you will do there. Reflecting it with your body. The on stage area is to be thought of as nothing more than a neutral hallway through which you are walking on your way to the selected room. When we see you on stage, your body should be doing nothing more than walking and reflecting. There is to be no business in which you indicate to us what room you're going to or what you will do there. There is no goal of communicating what room you're going to and what's going to happen there. It's all about the process the actor goes through when his acting focus is reflecting.

RULES: Stand off stage. Pick a room and an event you are going to. Respond to the coaching. Walk across the stage and exit.

148

CLASS QUESTIONS: "Can there be people in the room?" Definitely. "Do we choose something from our own lives that's going on now?" Choose anything you want or make it up. "Are we supposed to choose where we are coming from as well?" No.

ACTING FOCUS: Reflecting where you're going and what you're going to do there.

COACHING: Stand off stage and pick a room and an event that you will participate in when you get there. ◆ Do *Basic Off Stage Reflection Preparation Coaching.* ◆ **NEW:** See all of the people there, or the lack of people there, and include that in your reflection. See yourself there, participating in whatever you're going to do there, and keep reflecting with your whole body. See how you feel about being there and participating. Keep reflecting. Stay on this acting focus. Enter when you feel you are on your acting focus. As you cross the stage, keep reflecting where you are going and what's going to happen there. When you're ready, enter. ◆ After the entrance and as they walk, coaching will probably not be needed, *other than—* **Keep focusing and reflecting.** ◆ If the actor begins indicating with gestures or clues, *then coach—* You're not to do anything but walk your walk and keep reflecting. No business at all. No clues.

FOLLOW-UP: What room did he go to? Any flashes? What was going to happen there? We are only interested in flashes. ◆ Actor, what room did you go to? What were you going to do there?

SUMMARY:

Every exit in a play, TV show, or movie is an exit *to* somewhere else. When you have an exit, consider where you're going and what may happen there, and rehearse accordingly to see if somehow that affects the scene you're exiting.

Our vocabulary—and the name of the acting focus—for these kinds of choices about what is happening that the audience doesn't get to see is *off stage.* What's off stage that pertains to the scene on stage? The walking across the floor is on stage, in front of the audience's eyes. The room and the event you've left, the room and the event you're going to, these are off stage but they can greatly influence what is happening on stage.

> **TO THE COACH:** The coach has an opportunity to introduce the subject of raising the stakes. If an actor has chosen an insignificant event, e.g., washing the car, studying at the library with a friend, buying a pack of cigarettes, etc., the coach can ask if a more important event might engage the actor more fruitfully and be a more exciting choice. Mightn't there be more engagement and challenge if the choice were, e.g., buying the car, arguing with a friend, buying drugs, etc.

◆ ◆ ◆

We are ready for subtext improvisations. The primary acting focus is called *Off Stage*.

OFF STAGE/PRESENT[11]

SETUP: 2–5 per team. In huddles, select character, activity, and location. In addition, they select an off stage event that is occurring at the same time as their scene is unfolding. None of the characters can be present at this off stage event since they are all present in their on stage scene, yet all the characters know that the off stage event is occurring. The off stage event must be one that concerns and affects all of the characters on stage. The off stage event cannot be seen or heard by the characters on stage. • Avoid choosing waiting for an activity. Avoid choosing an activity requiring urgency. Avoid choosing a confined location.

In addition, the choices of the character, activity, and location must have *distance* from the choice of the off stage event. This means that if the audience were to know the identity of the characters, their location, and activity, they would not automatically assume the nature of the off stage event. For example, characters, husband and wife, who are also business partners; location, kitchen; activity, preparing and eating dinner; off stage, an arsonist hired by the couple is burning down their business (for the insurance money). An example of choices with no distance would be: characters, husband and wife; location, hospital waiting room; activity, waiting; off stage, their child is being operated on. The kind of on stage choices that usually diminish the distance are (1) *activities* that are somehow related to the nature of the off stage event, or (2) *locations* that are unique and point the audience to a probable off stage event. Waiting is always a bad choice for an activity. Not only does it not provide an ongoing physical activity, but also it always removes the distance. The off stage event is what everyone is waiting to hear about. After a team huddles, they should double-check their choices to make sure that there is distance so that the off stage choice is not inherently revealed.

RULES: While employing physical doing tools, all of the actors must continuously reflect what is taking place off stage. No one may discuss or refer to the off stage event in their dialogue. No one is allowed to bring the off stage event on stage through their physical doing choices, e.g., in the arson example, taking out the insurance policy and reading it. You may speak when you wish, according to our no playwriting rules.

ACTING FOCUS: Reflecting what is off stage.

COACHING: After chairs and location space set pieces have been placed and prior to starting, *coach*— Your bodies are going to contact the location.

You're going to do the activity. You're going to relate to each other according to the character choices. Everyone to places now. ◆ *Reflection warm-up*— Everybody see, in your mind's eye, the location where the off stage event is happening. Begin reflecting it with your body. Move your body about until the reflection feels right. See all the large set pieces there. Reflect that. See any furniture. Continue reflecting it with your body. See the colors. Add that to your reflection. See all the people there. Include that in your reflection. See what they are doing. Allow your body to reflect that. See how you feel about what they are doing and reflect that. This is what it feels like to be on this acting focus. Stay on the acting focus you're on right now. Add the location, activity, and character doing while reflecting what is happening somewhere else. Never bring the off stage event on stage with dialogue or activity. ◆ Action. ◆ **Coach (as needed): Avoid rushing to dialogue.** Avoid questions. Share your voices. **Avoid hanging out.** Do your activity. Stay on your acting focus no matter how involved you are with your activity. Keep what's off stage, off stage. Reflect the off stage with your knees, your fingers, your face. Contact the location. Stay on your reflection focus no matter how involved you are with the location. **Keep reflecting what's off stage.** Reflect what's off stage with your back. ◆ **Check out your fellow actors. Stay on your focus every moment. When you see another character, see them with the off stage event between you.** The actual off stage event is off stage, but its presence is here, on stage, in the space between you and your fellow characters. **See each other with the off stage between you.** Feel it between you and another character. **You share knowledge of what's off stage.** Keep what's off stage, off stage as well as in the space between you. *Respond to the coaching: See the off stage event right now in your mind's eye and make actual eye contact with another character. The off stage event is now between you—connect through it.* Share the off stage reflection with another character. Explore the sharing of the off stage. Find another character you haven't shared the off stage with yet and share it with them. ◆ Share your voices. Stay on your acting focus. Keep reflecting with your body what you see in your mind's eye. Open to being seen with the off stage moments between you. ◆ **Every time you contact another character physically, you are contacting the off stage event.** Feel it. Let the off stage between you thicken. Heighten the off stage between you. ◆ As long as you don't discuss or refer to the off stage event, censor nothing. Anything goes. ◆ **One minute to heighten your reflection of off stage and keep it between you and the other characters.** Check out your fellow characters with the off stage between you here and now. Feel the tip of your nose touching the off stage and your fellow character's nose touching the same off stage. ◆ Cut.

FOLLOW-UP (as needed): Audience, who were their characters? Activity? Location? Were they on the acting focus? Did they respond to most if not all of the coaching? Did they keep what was off stage between them as well as off stage? Did they share their voices? ◆ Actors, do you agree? Did you have a feeling that you let the acting focus work for you? Did you make any discoveries as a result of being on your acting focus? Did you make any discoveries as a result of responding to the coaching? ◆ Audience, did you flash on the off stage event? What is it? ◆ Actors, what is it? ◆ Audience, did you see the off stage event affect the characters on stage? Did the actors bring the off stage event on stage?

SUMMARY:

This is all about playing *subtext*. Often the sign of a good scene is when it's about something other than what it's about. William Goldman, a top screenwriter, advises writers: "If all that's going on in your scenes is what's going on in your scenes, think about it a long time."[12] Writers make a scene about something other than what it's about by using subtext. The text of the scene is about one thing and the subtext, or unspoken acting, is about something else.

It's an important skill for actors to be able to play the subtext and play it well. In the improvisations we just did, the off stage event was the subtext of the improvisational scene. When you're working on a scripted scene, you have to determine whether it employs subtext and what the subtext is. Does the scene have an off stage event that informs the scene but is not spoken about? The off stage event may be in the present, as we just did, or it may be in the past or future, like the walking exercises we did earlier. Think about the scripts you're working on in your career right now and consider how many things happen off stage that influence you on stage? You have to relate your inner doing to the appropriate influence. What's the event your character knows is going to happen in scene 3 that is never mentioned in scene 2, yet totally influences how your character behaves in scene 2? In the next class, we'll be working on scenes with past and future subtext.

The subtext is what the character is focused on, *regardless of what he is saying*. For the scene to be about the subtext and not the text, the character has to focus on what the subtext is. Then all the text comes out of that focusing (reflecting) on what is off stage. It is not important that we (audience) actually get what the subtextual event is. What is important is that you are reflecting it. If you are on that focus, then the audience gets the feeling that there is something else going on. That's what hooks them. They want to know what's going on and they pay attention. The audience comes to see the mystery. Even in comedy, it's a mystery. What's going to happen when Oscar comes home late and Felix's roast is burned but Felix *says nothing about it?*

Acting is doing and there's always more to do. Look at how much you do when you improvise on the subtext. You're playing the character, activity, and location of a scene on stage and simultaneously, you're reflecting another scene occurring off stage.

The subtext is one area that you can improvise on in every different take or performance. You're free to go wherever you want in your reflections and considerations of that event. You also have the freedom to change the author's suggested subtext, which is your interpretation of what the script suggests, as long as it has the same values as the author's. In other words, if the author's subtext has to do with somebody dying, you don't want to change it to winning an Oscar, but you could change it to some other sad event. And you could change it on each different take, thereby guaranteeing spontaneity.

In the improvs we just did, if you had started talking about the off stage event, the subtext would have disappeared. It would have become text. The one thing you do easily in your acting right now is play the text, and it's the one thing you shouldn't be doing. It's not good acting. Good acting is when there's something going on under, above, around, and through the text that is other than what the text is saying. If your text line is "The floor looks great," you should be communicating something to the audience other than that the floor looks great. Maybe the subtext you're playing is "Damn, I hope I don't have to mop this floor again for another thirty years." Your frustration is not in the text, but that's what the audience sees and hears. You get two for one.

One for one is playing the text. Two for one is the text plus the feeling or thought derived from the subtext. You say to an actress playing in *Romeo and Juliet*, "I love you," and all you're acting is love for the girl. Boring. Why not get two values for the three words of stage time? Value one is the sentiment and revelation of the line "I love you." Value two could be anything else, e.g., "Boy, are we going to be in trouble when our families find out about this." Two for one. The more you do, the better the acting.

When you lose the subtext or elevate the subtext into the text, you go from two for one to one for one. The moment you bring it on stage it has no power any more. That's why you weren't allowed to bring it on stage in any of your improvised scenes. As long as you keep it submerged and reflect it, in an off stage focus, you're getting two for one every step you take, every word you say, because no line is just what the words mean. It's totally filled with the impact of the subtext or, in this case, the off stage event. The power comes from not talking about it. It's all that concerns you but you won't talk about it.

Off stage events are one way of playing subtext, but subtext is sometimes created through other devices. Traveling during a still often gives this 2-for-1 value, giving the sense that something else is going on. The difference is that traveling is character-inspired inner doing while off stage is script-inspired inner doing.

In active & still, when you're in a still you have total freedom to travel on anything you come up with. With off stage, you're totally restricted to travel in one area, the event off stage and its implications for you. If all the characters in a scene are aware of the off stage event, it heightens the drama because all the characters are in that same area. When you're traveling in a still, you're seldom in the same area as the other characters, who may also be traveling. With off stage, from start to finish, you're all on the same event as the subject of your inner doing. This is crucial because most scripted scenes relying on a subtextual event require the character(s) to be restricted to that event.

Most of our work in active & still was spent in showing you all of the different places you could choose to let your traveling lead you. On the other hand, off stage demands that you don't get off the subject. You don't have the freedom to go wherever you want. You've got to play the scene reflecting, for example, that your mom is in the hospital being operated on. The script demands that; if you don't do it, you're not doing your job because that's the way the author wrote the scene. That's the effect that he wants this scene to have.

Not all scenes demand subtext work. Some scenes have to be about what they're about. A conflict scene has to be about the conflict. Still, in some conflict scenes the textual conflict is *based* on another subtextual conflict.

> **TO THE COACH:** The duration of each improv should be about ten minutes. ◆ Distance is meant to keep the character, activity, and location choices from pointing to the off stage event. When your activity points you right to the off stage event, you are bringing the subtext on stage so it's no longer serving the function that the author intended it to serve. Even though the characters may not be discussing what's off stage, by the nature of their activity, the scene on stage is all about what the scene is all about. You want any communication about what's off stage to be revealed through the characters' behavior, not through their activity choice.
>
> Making sure, through the coaching, that the actors keep the off stage event between them, as well as off stage, is to get it (the subtext) out there in the space between one character and another character(s). This connects the two of them, rather than separating them. Separating means that an actor may be focusing on reflecting what's off stage, but when he turns to another character and sees him and talks, the subtext is staying up in his head and in his body. It is not being sent out into the space where it has the improvisational potential to converge with the other actor doing the same thing.
>
> During the warm-up reflection between places and action, the coach should monitor the actors to make sure their visualizing process (seeing in the mind's eye) is translated into physical body reflection. Many actors will respond to the coaching by solely visualizing and neglect to

move their bodies around as they seek out the reflection aspect. What they see in their mind's eye must be manifested in the body or the exercise is almost worthless. The acting focus of off stage is not to play the scene thinking about the off stage event but to play the scene *physically reflecting* what they are thinking about. Watch and see if their bodies are shifting around in response to the coaching. If the actor is absolutely still throughout the coaching, he is visualizing without physicalizing. On occasion, I have interrupted the exercise to deal with this by demonstrating what my body looks like doing this reflection warm-up. I quickly select an off stage event and have the actors coach me through the reflection warm-up. They get to see my body shifting around in response to the coaching. Then I start their warm-up again.

In the follow-up, if a team reveals that their off stage event was a general condition, e.g., a member of the family is missing, and not a specific event taking place in a specific location, this should be pointed out as not fulfilling the setup conditions of off stage. ◆ Sometimes an off stage event choice will create heavy and down feelings. An actor may be totally on his acting focus, but there will be no energy or volume in his dialogue. He must be coached to share his voice. Responding to this coaching will provide presence to his performance and further enhance his acting focus. Regardless of the exercise the actors are working on, they must always be coached to energize the work through complete body physicalization, *as in*— You don't have to speak, but if you do, you must share your voices. ◆ There are no specially indicated coachings or follow-up questions because I usually use all of them.

◆ ◆ ◆

REFLECTION EXERCISE

We finish the off stage preparatory training with a reflection exercise that introduces an acting focus of great importance to the entire training.

PART I

REFLECT THE REFLECTOR[13]

SETUP, RULES, and ACTING FOCUS: The same as basic reflection.

COACHING: Coach the actors to play about four minutes of basic reflection. ◆ *After 4–6 switches at varied intervals, continue*— Initiators, larger-size initiations. Use your whole body to initiate. ◆ [Begin to call switches at shorter and shorter intervals.] Continue coaching the initiators toward full body size initiations and the reflectors to stay on their acting focus of reflecting what they see right now. When the switch intervals are back to back with no time between them, *coach*— Switch. Switch. Switch. Switch. Reflect the reflector. Don't initiate. Only reflect. Reflect everything there is to reflect. Nobody initiate! Everyone is a reflector. Right now. And, right now. And, right now. Keep renewing the reflection! Everybody is reflecting what you see right now. Assume nothing about the next moment to come. Stay focused on reflecting head to toe what you are seeing right now, and right now, and right now, and right now. There is always a brand new right now to completely renew the reflection with. Never assume what you are going to see in the next right now. As you arrive in the next right now, reflect what you see. Stay focused. Reflect the reflector. ◆ *After 1–2 minutes*— Cut.

FOLLOW-UP: [Keep everyone on the floor and do a quick follow-up prior to proceeding to Part 2, which is *Reflection Walk Return.*] When we were in reflect the reflector, what did you experience? Did you really feel you were on the acting focus? Were you truly reflecting, or were you sometimes initiating? When in reflect the reflector, you must take responsibility for not initiating movement and only reflect what you see your partner doing. You must not make any assumptions about where the movement may or may not lead. Renew your reflection every moment instead of assuming that nothing will change since no one may initiate. That is an assumption, which may or may not be true. Now, everyone Upset! [Change partners.]

PART 2

REFLECTION WALK RETURN

COACHING: Repeat part 1, allowing only 2–3 minutes. ◆ After the actors are in reflect the reflector for thirty seconds, coach them through a reflection walk (p. 142) in which they first reflect each other and then reflect the workshop room. ◆ Then continue with the **NEW COACHING:** Now continue walking and see in your mind's eye any room that you will be in later tonight. Keep your eyes open. See that room and allow your body to reflect it. Actively reflect it. Feel your body shifting as you respond to the coaching. See the large set pieces in that room. Reflect them. Feel your body shifting around to take that in. See the colors; allow your body to reflect them. See the objects in that room; reflect them with your whole body: knees, chest, face, back, toes. Again, you should feel your body shifting a little bit. A shoulder drops, a knee bends a little bit, an elbow bends, or your face changes somewhat. Every time you select—in this case I am selecting it for you—a different aspect of what you are reflecting, it should have a slightly different body feeling. See the lighting there, reflect it. See the entire room with all of its features and reflect it with all of your body.

Go neutral. Stop reflecting. Keep walking. Keep breathing. Observe what your body feels like when it's not reflecting.

Select any person in your life who is close to you. See them in a particular room they might be in right now, while you are here in class. Choose somebody important to you. Place them in a location that they might be in right now. Select what they are probably doing there. See that location and begin reflecting it with your body. Feel free to move your body about until the reflection feels right. Now allow your body to start reflecting this scene that is off stage, that is not here, that is somewhere else right now. You have a location off stage. You have a person in it, and they are doing something. You are seeing that in your mind's eye and allowing your body to reflect it. See all the large set pieces there. Reflect that. See the furniture. Continue reflecting it with your body. See the colors. Add that to your reflection. See whoever is there. Include that in your reflection. See what they are doing. Allow your body to reflect that. Notice how you feel about what they are doing and reflect that. Put it all together and see that whole off stage scene with whoever is in it a hundred times more clearly. Reflect that with your entire body as you walk around. ◆ Now staying on this focus totally, you are going to return to your seats in the audience. Stay on focus. The exercise is not over. I will let you know when the exercise is over. Even after you are sitting, you are still going to be doing this reflection. Keep reflecting. Keep breathing. Keep reflecting what you are seeing in your mind's eye. Add to this that you are going to take a nice, long breath. Inhale through the nose and exhale through the mouth. Take three or four of these breaths. With each successive inhale and exhale, let the vision in your mind's eye fade. Allow your body's reflection of that to fade as well, simultaneously. One more breath. ◆ Cut.

FOLLOW-UP: Did you find it easier to reflect these off stage locations than the last time we did it? Did you more fully use your body to reflect? Did any feelings emerge?

CLASS QUESTIONS: "What is the difference between reflecting a person in the mind's eye and feeling something about them?" As a result of the reflection, spontaneous feelings may come up and then they are reflected as well. "Is it wrong to bring the room here?" Yes. It will cause confusion regarding where you are, in the on stage room or the off stage room. You are always in the on stage room, even if your focus is in the off stage room.

SUMMARY:

None needed.

TO THE COACH: Reflect the reflector is the basic tool for developing the skill of *going with it.* We will evolve it as an acting focus in much of the work ahead. Bottom line: practice reflect the reflector.

◆ ◆ ◆

An opportunity to practice what we have done so far and to warm up for the final and most sophisticated level of off stage training is provided in the next single-player walk.

OFF STAGE KITCHEN (PAST OR FUTURE)

SETUP: A solo exercise. Stand off stage and make a choice to be coming from or going to a particular event in a particular location. Your choice is a past or future event and location. Everything on stage is in the present. When you enter, you are coming on stage into a kitchen. In this kitchen, [coach demonstrates the business]: *Enter, cross downstage center to space cabinet next to space sink, take space glass out of the cabinet, fill it with water, drink it, put the glass down, exit.* Now the entire time that we see you—enter, do the business, exit—in the present tense, you are to focus on reflecting the past or future event and the location that you have chosen. There is to be no business done beyond your assigned business. This is not about you giving us clues to where you're going or coming from. There is no goal of communicating the off stage event. It's all about the process the actor goes through when his acting focus is reflecting and he has business at the same time. ◆ While you are sitting in the audience waiting for your turn, I suggest that you practice reflecting off stage events by piggybacking on the coaching for whomever is in the wings preparing for their entrance. Choose different events, past and present, and do the reflection preparation in response to the coaching. Stop when the preparation coaching is finished and watch the actor on stage. When it's your turn, make sure you choose a new event, one that you didn't practice with. Also, pay special attention to letting your body shift around as it responds to reflecting the different details of the off stage event.

RULES: Stand off stage. Pick a location and an event you are going to or coming from. Respond to the coaching. Enter the kitchen and do the business while on your acting focus. Exit.

ACTING FOCUS: Reflecting the off stage event.

CLASS QUESTIONS: "Should we stay our own age?" Yes. "Is it all right if we pick an event/location that we have never really done or been to in our own lives?" Absolutely. Your acting choices should never be limited to your experience. You can play Macbeth without having murdered anyone.

COACHING: Go and stand in the wings and respond to the coaching. **Make a choice.** Decide whether you are going to do a past or future event. Choose where you are coming from or going. Choose what has happened there or will happen there. **Now consider the possibility of raising the stakes of your choice. Avoid making a choice that includes urgency.** ◆ *When the actor has made the choices—* Do *Basic Off Stage Reflection Preparation Coaching.* ◆ **NEW:** See all the people there, or lack of people there, and include that in your reflection. See yourself there participating in whatever you're going to be doing there, or have done there, and keep reflecting with your whole body. See how you feel about being there and participating. Keep reflecting. Stay on this acting focus. Enter the kitchen when you are ready and keep reflecting the off stage the entire time you are on stage. ◆ *Coach as needed—* Keep reflecting. Fill the glass. See and reflect everything that's off stage. See yourself there. Taste the temperature of the water. Reflect with your tongue. Keep reflecting. Really swallow, and keep focusing on the event off stage and how you feel about it. Reflect that with your neck. Keep reflecting what's off stage every moment. You don't have to communicate anything to us; just stay on your acting focus. You don't need to muscle it; just reflect it. Exit. ◆ Cut.

FOLLOW-UP (as needed): Audience, was he on his acting focus? Does it make any difference whether we know what the off stage event was? Whatever it was, did it affect how he did the business? **Any flashes? Past or future? Specific flash?** ◆ Actor, were you on your acting focus? **What was off stage?** ◆ Audience, did you practice reflecting by piggybacking on the preparation coaching?

SUMMARY:

If you stay on an acting focus you're not acting, you're doing, and it never looks like you're acting. Stay on the focus and let the focus do the acting.

It is no big deal to be able to stand in front of a camera or an audience and think about the subtext or off stage event. What *is* a big deal is to be able to focus on reflecting the subtext or the off stage event *while your body is doing something else.*

How does subtext get communicated to an audience? In every kitchen walk there was a sense of emotional tone underlying the business and that must be present in subtext work. A person who comes from witnessing a hit-and-run accident takes a glass of water with her body behaving differently from a person who is going to her wedding. The body is the reflection of what's going on inside. Everybody did the same business differently and with different emotional tonality because the differences in the choices of the off stage event affected the way they moved their bodies. The actor's body communicates the subtext to the audience. How you move your body and how you handle objects is what the audience sees and understands. So, subtext work must always be combined with physicality. It's a necessary skill, the ability to go through a whole scene with dialogue and business and be totally focused on something else.

Do you now feel that you can coach yourselves in reflecting the off stage? When you do, I recommend that you go through all the steps. No shortcuts. When you reflect the different aspects of the off stage, it keeps you in process and in the moment. If you jump to a complete reflection, you often jump to a reflection of your assumption *about* the off stage event instead of an evolving response to *what is*. This will become clearer later.

> **TO THE COACH:** In this exercise, the actors are doing their first improvisation on non-improvisational material (the business and blocking), not unlike improvising on the job with a script. ◆ If there is confusion about raising the stakes, point out that in this exercise the stakes are best raised in the off stage event, not in the character (yourself).

OFF STAGE/PAST[14]

SETUP: Same as off stage/present, **except** they select an off stage event *in which they have all participated.* The off stage event must be significant (high stakes) to all of the characters and one they were all involved in *within the past 24 hours.*

RULES: Same as off stage/present, **except:** While employing physical doing tools, all of the actors must continuously reflect the off stage past event.

ACTING FOCUS: Reflecting the off stage past event.

COACHING: After a team's location has been set up, and prior to starting, *coach—* Your bodies are going to contact the location. You're going to do the activity. You're going to relate to each other according to the character choices. Everyone is in places now. ◆ Everybody see, in your mind's eye, the location where the off stage event took place. See the location where it happened and begin reflecting it with your body. Do the *Basic Off Stage Reflection Preparation Coaching,* and **then coach—**See all the people there. Include that in your reflection. See what they are doing. Allow your body to reflect that. See yourself there, doing whatever you did, and reflect that. Reflect how you feel about what you were doing there. From here on in, you're going to stay on the acting focus you're on right now. While you go through the character, activity, and location, you are always reflecting what took place off stage earlier. Never bring the off stage event on stage with dialogue or activity. **Stay alert for new coaching.** ✦ **Action.** ✦ *Coach as needed*— **Avoid rushing to dialogue. Avoid hanging out.** Do your activity. Stay on your acting focus no matter how involved you are with your activity. Keep what's off stage, off stage. Reflect the off stage with your knees, fingers, face. Contact the location. **Keep reflecting what's off stage.** Reflect what's off stage with your back. ✦ **Check out your fellow actors. Stay on your acting focus every moment. When you see another character, see them with the off stage event between you.** What's off stage is not only off stage, it's between you as characters right here and now. It's in the space between you and your fellow characters. **See each other with the off stage between you.** You share knowledge of what's off stage. ✦ Share your voices. Avoid questions. Avoid playwriting. ✦ See your fellow actors at the off stage event and reflect what they were doing. Look around your off stage event, explore it, and reflect that. Reflect whatever you discover there.

NEW: **Go somewhere new in the off stage event and reflect that, even as you stay involved in your on stage activity. Choose to go somewhere new in the past event and reflect that. Choose to reflect something new from the off stage event, something you haven't previously reflected,** and stay involved here in the on stage activity.

NEW: **Take what happened in your off stage past event and relocate it to a new location, explore it there and reflect it here,** all while you stay involved in your on stage activity. Move the event to a whole other location and explore it there, and reflect whatever you discover. You have the opportunity to contact and reflect the off stage event in a whole new way. **Avoid hanging out in the past event. Go somewhere new there.** Avoid hanging out here and in the off stage event. **Take turns in your off stage reflection. Then take more turns. Go somewhere new in the past event and keep reflecting what you discover.** Travel through the past event, turning, going to parts of it you haven't previously reflected. *Stay alert to discovering what you haven't previously seen, and reflect it.* Take a trip through your off stage event, exploring it, and reflecting what you find. Choose to reflect something new derived from the past event. ✦ Check out the other characters. Stay open to sharing what's off stage between you. Keep reflecting with your body what you see in your mind's eye. Be open to extending the off stage moments between you. ✦ **One minute. Last opportunities to go someplace in the off stage event you haven't been before and reflect it.** Let the acting focus work for you. Let the acting focus solve all your problems. ✦ One minute to heighten your reflection of off stage and keep it between you and the other characters. Check out your fellow characters with the off stage between you here and now. Feel the tip of your nose touching the off stage and your fellow character's nose touching the same off stage. ✦ Cut.

FOLLOW-UP (as needed): Same as off stage/present.

SUMMARY:

What were some of the discoveries you made in response to the coaching? Did you notice whether or not emotional changes accompanied the discoveries? What emotion were you in prior to the discovery, and what emotion where you in after the discovery? Were your discoveries germane to being a part of the whole? What was different in this round of improvs from the previous round, off stage/ present?

Responding to the coaching in this round revealed something new, the aspect of traveling and turning through the off stage event. You discovered thoughts and feelings that you hadn't previously considered, discoveries you hadn't anticipated. For instance, a frequently employed off stage/past improv in class is that all the characters had just had an orgy together. That scene usually starts with everybody being happy, playful, and bawdy. As they explore in response to the new coaching, some of them discover that maybe having that orgy wasn't such a great thing. Jealousy might come up for one of the characters, e.g., "Has she been making love to my husband before last night's orgy? I'm starting to feel abandoned whenever he smiles at her." Someone else comes up with an AIDS issue, e.g., "Did he use protection? I really don't know him that well." No one anticipates this as they come out of their huddle. All they anticipate is the fun and bawdiness of their secret. The drama of the situation evolves out of their spontaneously discovering the dark side. There are lots of unanticipated thoughts and feelings surrounding subtext. When you are working on off stage, explore it and be open to discovering what you hadn't thought, felt, or anticipated before.

I guided you in that direction when I coached you to put the off stage/past in another location. Putting it in a new location didn't change what you did, but it forced you to see it differently. Changing the orgy location to the xerox room at your office might lead you to issues of appropriateness and fear of getting caught. The coaching was designed to propel you to take turns, to consider all kinds of new thoughts and feelings, and to integrate these discoveries into the subtext of your scene.

Every time you discover something new and reflect that, you create a turn. When you create a turn, you hook the audience. What about the effect it might have on your fellow actors in the scene? It might just demand of them a heightened organic presence in the scene. They start thinking to themselves, "Why did he just change his mood?" Before you know it, you have some real spontaneous acting going on between everybody. Everyone is working off each other, initiated by you working off of yourself in the off stage.

It's too easy, predictable, and limiting to dwell in the obvious and anticipated response to the subtext. If your subtext is an off stage of winning the lottery, you have an immediate response, an immediate *assumption* that you are going to feel great and this is going to be one very happy scene. But somebody might discover that with money comes responsibilities, and with those responsibilities, who knows what happens? When actors make spontaneous new discoveries about an off stage event and immediately reflect them, they add new layers to the on stage scene and to their characters.

You should always be open to, and desirous of, ongoing emotional changes during the course of a scene or else you are treading water and hanging out. When you create changes during a scene, you create a hook that keeps the audience attentive, caring about what happens to you. They feel that they are on a trip with you to uncharted areas.

It's all about change. The Unitarians say it well—*That which does not change is not true.* Characters go through changes in the course of a script or a scene. It's called the character's arc. I am suggesting to you that every character has the potential for change *within every moment* of every scene, and *that is where the goodies are.*

Every aspect of the work, of the acting or the scene, has the potential for change, which is the antidote to hanging out. Your job as good actors is to meet that potential and develop it. If it's possible to change, and you must *always assume it is possible*, use your technique to improvise and discover the potential for the change.

> **TO THE COACH:** The coach should always stress that there's nothing wrong with not being able to imagine something. What is wrong is limiting your instrument so that it can't access anywhere beyond your imagination.

OFF STAGE/FUTURE[15]

SETUP: Same as off stage/past, **except:** they select an off stage event *in which they will all participate within the next 24 hours.* The off stage event must be significant (high stakes) to all the characters.

RULES: Same as off stage/past, **except:** While employing physical doing tools, all of the actors must continuously reflect the off stage *future* event.

ACTING FOCUS: Reflecting the off stage future event.

COACHING (as needed): Same as off stage/past, but modified to refer to the off stage future event rather than the off stage past event. Be sure the coaching includes placing the event in a new location and taking turns in the off stage reflection.

FOLLOW-UP (as needed): Same as off stage/past.

SUMMARY:

What were some of the discoveries you made in response to the coaching? Having explored making discoveries with off stage/past, was it easier to travel and make discoveries this time with off stage/future?

In scripted acting, not every scene has an off stage event or subtext. It is your job as an actor to determine that, based on your interpretation of the scene in collaboration with the director. Once you do, it's your job to know what the subtext is, and to play it. Off stage, an effective tool for this purpose, requires that it be an event: past, present, or future. And it must be specific. The result of reflecting generalities or incomplete events is drifting, not exploring. If you decide that a scene has subtext, choose the issue, select an event that captures the crux of the issue, and do an off stage improv when in rehearsal or shooting a take.

When you are on the off stage focus, exploring, you discover other aspects than your first response. Avail yourself of them! Exploring the subtext improvisationally doesn't mean that in performance you need to play every discovery. It's a process of discovering *what serves you best.* Be selective.

Don't let the subtext dominate you so much that you exclude physical doing. Without some physical doing, you sit there and think about the off stage event. That brings it on stage, making the scene totally about the subtext. *You must be doing two things at once.* The first thing is the text—the dialogue and the blocking—which in our improvisations would be the character, activity, location, and dialogue. The second thing is the subtext (reflecting the off stage event).

In a scene with subtext, and with circumstances that don't allow physical doing, travel (active & still) with the off stage event as the railroad yard in which you find all your railroad tracks.

Frequently, you will make character discoveries as a result of employing off stage. You may discover that your character always sees the dark side of an event. This alerts you to the possibility that your character is pessimistic, depressed, or angry. You then bring that discovery to your total character work, or it opens a door for a new approach to another scene elsewhere in the script.

> **TO THE COACH:** During the off stage training, it is recommended that every workshop begin with a reflection exercise. Reflection is a major acting process for staying in the present. Mirrors have no past or future. You look in a mirror and it only reflects what is there right now. That's a very healthy and necessary state for an actor to be in. If the actor thinks about the off stage and doesn't reflect it, his acting will be from the neck up. If he only *thinks* about the hit-and-run accident he caused, he communicates fear or sadness *from the neck up.* If you look at his body, the fear or sadness isn't there. This creates indicating and is a lie in his performance. Reflecting demands a complete body process.

By using the vocabulary word, *reflection*, and participating in that process, the actor doesn't even have to remind himself to use his whole body. It is automatically involved, from head to toe.

When the teams reveal their off stage choices in the follow-up, the coach, upon hearing that a team's choice was witnessing an event, should comment on the difference between witnessing an event—a lower-stakes choice—and *participating in it*. A future event that requires participation brings up the higher-stakes issue of perhaps not going through with it. The exception to this is if the script demands that the choice be witnessing, as in witness-to-crime dramas.

EARLIEST APPLICATIONS TO SCRIPT AND CAREER

I'm reminded of an acting lesson I learned years ago. You always have to walk on stage with a secret, something the audience doesn't know about. It's a great thing, because it magnifies you. It makes you more in*teresting, even if they never figure out what the secret really is.* —Emma Thompson[16]

What is the subtext?

How do you use off stage in a script? How do you know what the subtext of a scene is? You must look at what has happened to your character prior to the scene you're working on, or what will happen after it, or what is happening during it (with other characters elsewhere). The given circumstances usually provide you with the information, which you turn into an off stage selection. If any major event occurs in the script, you look at the scenes after that event, and ask yourself, "Is that something I'd be concerned with while I'm playing this scene?"— off stage/past. And, look at the scenes before that event and ask yourself if parts of these scenes are played with an anticipation of that event—off stage/future.

If the subtext of a scene is important, frequently the writer will bring it on stage late in the scene. All you do is spot the important issue in the scene, the one the characters have been avoiding talking about but finally get around to. Reread the scene up to that point and determine if that is what was on their minds all along. If so, you have found—and it's your interpretive decision—your subtext for the scene. Use the off stage from the beginning of the beat or scene to where they start talking about it, at which time you simply allow it to rise into the text.

When you have selected the off stage, making sure it has been reduced to an event, you focus on reflecting it while playing the on stage scene's lines and business. And you keep exploring and reflecting it from different angles so you don't hang out with one cliché or obvious feeling.

Sometimes, the off stage scene hasn't been written and then you have to invent it. For example, an audition situation and you only have one scene. You don't know the past, future, or anything else about the rest of the script. Look at that scene and while you're making choices, consider, "Would this scene work better if I played it focused on and reflecting that I just got fired? Or, would this scene work better if I focused on the fact that someone who is referred to in the scene is doing something right now somewhere else that concerns me?"

Heightening the Writing

It's perfectly legitimate to heighten a scene by choosing your own off stage that's not in the given circumstances. However, in choosing to do this, you must remember to make choices that are a part of the whole scene and not simple impositions for the sake of making your part bigger.

For instance, suppose the scene is about a card game. The given circumstances are that four guys playing cards at a hideaway in scene 4 will rob a bank in scene 5. We've seen this scene in many gangster movies. Now, in playing scene 4, the robbery is clearly an off stage/future. However, discussion of the robbery is in the text of the card-playing scene, so it's of limited value as an off stage/future. What can the actors do on their own that's not in the script?

Let's say that Actor #1 adds to the scene that he doesn't trust Actor #2. It's not written, but he chooses to do it, making the scene about more than it's about. Actor #1 uses an off stage/past that he and Actor #2 were on a previous heist and Actor #2 betrayed him. If he focuses on that off stage/past, the resulting effect, without the audience knowing he's reflecting an imaginary event, is distrust from #1 to #2. Actor #2 could choose to add to the scene that he wants Actor #3's girlfriend. He could choose an off stage/future—making love with the guy's girlfriend. Actor #4 could choose to add to the scene that he's very frightened about the whole situation. He chooses an off stage/present. His mother is dying right now in the hospital.

Can you imagine what that scene's going to look like compared to the scene without these choices? Which is better? Which is more? They don't add one speck of time to the script time. They don't change one word of dialogue, but they're all doing more and it's all spontaneously improvised in front of the camera. None of it came out of the given circumstances. It just came out of their smart acting and the opportunity to do more than there is in the scene.

You must develop an intelligence about the scripts you're working with and be aware of their limitations. If the scene is only about what it's about, you can help it by making it about more than it's about. This is especially valuable for you in TV drama series acting. TV scripts tend to be about what they're about. A good film script is usually about more than what it's about. A good play is almost always about more than what it's about.

Working with the Director

Whether or not you discuss your intention to add subtext to a scene with the director depends on the size of your role, what's important in the scene, the amount of rehearsal time, and your assessment of the director's abilities. Usually it's not necessary. Go for it, and when the director says something, adjust.

Totally Subtext

Whole scenes are seldom based entirely on subtext. You might have one beat, two beats, or a page-and-a-half of subtext. The subtext is inserted by the writer to create that mysterious feeling in the audience, i.e., "Something's going on. What is it?" Then the writer changes that feeling by changing the construction of the scene. It's no longer about subtext. It's about conflict, story development, or something else.

The first scene in *Dominick and Eugene*, a film about two brothers who live together, is an example of a whole scene based on subtext. One brother is a doctor; the other is retarded and works as a garbage man. The doctor has just been offered the perfect job at Stanford Medical Center, which will require moving upstate. He comes home and has to deal with what he is going to do with the retarded brother. Can he take him to Stanford or not? From the moment he walks into the first scene with the brother, the dialogue is as simple as, "Let's have breakfast. Did you pack your lunch," etc. It's a neutral breakfast: characters, activity, and location. However, you see clearly that the doctor is totally focused on the off stage/future—having to deal with the brother, having to tell him that he has to leave him. The actor, Ray Liotta, is clearly on that acting focus. It colors everything he says and does in the scene.

Harold Pinter writes many scenes *and entire plays* based on one subtextual event, e.g., *The Birthday Party*. The secret to playing Pinter is that the actors and the director have to sit down in rehearsal and all agree on what the off stage event is. Although they never talk about it in the text, all of the actors agree on exactly what happened in the past and focus on that in the subtext. It places the mystery in the audience where it belongs.

Superior Position

Writers also employ subtext in order to give the audience a feeling of being in a superior position to some of the characters. The story will unfold in such a way that the audience knows what's on your mind as you play your part of the scene on the subtext, but the other characters don't know what's going on and have no subtext. This gives the audience a feeling that they are in on your secret and the other characters aren't. Superior position is a writer's device to increase audience involvement and enjoyment. When a writer uses it, it is the actor's job to know it, since it may mean playing the subtext.

For example, in a movie, a couple hires thugs to burn down their business. We see the scene establishing the couple's reasons—the insurance money—for doing it; we see the scene where they hire the thugs; and then we see a scene in a restaurant with the couple and their dinner guests—establishing their alibi. Regardless of how skillfully they deceive their guests, the actors playing the couple absolutely have to know that the only thing they could be thinking about at that time is that their business is burning. Throughout the restaurant scene, the couple play the subtext of the fire occurring right now (off stage/present). The audience knows what their subtext is because of the previous scenes and, therefore, they have superior position to the couple's guests, who don't know about the fire.

Subtext Substitutions

You don't need to limit your off stage choices to things that come from the script. You might find that in using an off stage event, the characters and situation from the script don't inspire you. Let's say the subtext of a scene is that you are going to make love at the end of the scene. Pick anyone you're going to do it with in your own life, and focus and reflect that. It's your choice to explore a substitution. Nobody needs to know about it but you. All you're concerned about is the effect it has on you. This is your inner doing. The trick is to self-monitor the stakes. Look at how high or low the stakes are of the subtext built into the script. Then make sure that your personal choices are going to create that same level of higher or lower stakes.

Multiple Takes

In camera acting, once you have decided on your subtext issue and reduced it to an off stage event/ past, present, or future, you can consider alternate choices to have available for multiple takes. Each of these preselected choices would be chosen for their ability to put you in the same area of the desired response that you (and the director) are looking for. Let's say you had a subtext scene in a film and it was appropriate to use an off stage/future. You would preplan, let's say, three off stage/futures for the scene. Take one, off stage/future: "I'm going to make love." Take two, off stage/future: "I'm going to get the Oscar." Take three, off stage/future: "I'm presenting my parents with a gift, a beautiful house at the beach." Notice how all three of those choices are happy future events. When they shoot the scene, each take is totally focused and improvised. The dialogue and blocking remain the same for each take and all three takes will come out with a happy undertone. But you are newly improvising each take and that creates, by necessity, true spontaneity. You are always doing it for the first time even though it is the third take. And no one needs to know what you are doing. All the director sees is someone who is so spontaneous that there are subtle differences in each take.

Small Parts

In *Hamlet*, Fortinbras enters one minute before the end of the play in order to wind things up. He sees the bodies, says he's going to look into taking over the kingdom, praises Hamlet as a good guy, and tells the soldiers to clean up the mess. That's his text. The chances are, he will be directed to act and say it decisively, in contrast to Hamlet. When the actor hears the direction, he should ask himself, "Is there a subtext opportunity?" He might discover an off stage/future: his coronation as king. He still does everything the director is asking him to do, says the same lines, but now his character displays a hint of ego, maybe even the slightest touch of pleasure at his good fortune. Subtext adds dimension to the smallest part.

Part of the Whole

Subtext allows you to explore what else is going on. What else can you bring to the text while still serving the author and still being a part of the whole text, instead of taking it over? Always remember that your choices must serve being a part of the whole, the whole script and the whole production.

IMPROVISATION RULES NOW IN PLACE

- No one is allowed on stage without an activity.
- Every actor must choose what his character does for a living and whether he has any personal relationships with the other actors in the scene, and communicate it.
- Every actor must frequently make physical contact with the location.
- Every actor must be open to discovering objects nearby.
- When the actor is deprived of the opportunity for physical doing, he should be traveling on the inside, or reflecting what concerns him off stage.
- There is never a reason for being off the selected acting focus.

5

VOCAL DOING

Many actors' voices are isolated from the rest of their instrument. The goal of this part of the training—*vocal doing*—is the complete, experiential integration of the actor's body and vocal mechanism. The result is a more expressive and efficient voice, heightened communication, an expanded energy source for the other components of the actor's instrument, and a tremendous increase in the actor's presence.

After the challenging work of inner doing, vocal doing improvisations offer a respite from the emphasis on focused thinking. They serve an important role in repositioning the inner doing as something the actor accesses through spontaneous selection. They are also fun to perform and further enhance the actor's confidence as he develops additional technique as an improviser.

The exercises in this chapter can be done in the order presented or, after sufficient exposure to physical doing, mixed in with exercises from the previous two chapters. A suggested presentation order can be found in Appendix E.

Except for warm-ups and preparations, or where noted, each scene improvisation lasts about ten minutes.

By now, it is understood that in each exercise selecting characters in huddles means choosing occupation and or personal relationships.

❖   ❖   ❖

The first vocal doing acting focus teaches a technical acting skill that's a necessity for stage acting with memorized lines and is also beneficial to any form of improvisation.

FULL BODY WHISPER[1]

SETUP: 2–6 per team. In huddles, they select characters, activity, and location. The choices should be such that whenever these characters speak to one another, they must whisper. High-stakes choices—it is important that the characters are not heard by off stage characters—are better choices. Examples would be burglars; breaking, entering, stealing; office, house, museum. Or, young couple; illicit date; her bedroom next to parents' bedroom. A low-stakes choice would be students, studying, library.

RULES: While improvising (doing the physical doing associated with) your character, activity, and location, all dialogue is to be spoken with full body whispering.

ACTING FOCUS: Whenever you speak: whispering in full volume with a fully open and relaxed throat, supported by your whole body.

COACHING: Introduction. ◆ Turn to somebody next to you and whisper a quick little chitchat conversation. Use a regular and normal whisper. Notice what part of the body provides the breath for the whispering. Observe that in yourself as you do a regular whisper. ◆ Volunteer first team, set up your location.

After location is set up— **Preparation:** Form a circle around the stage. Breathe through the mouth. Observe your own breathing. Keep your eyes open. Focus on gently opening your throat a little further, allowing the breath in, then out, from a little further down the throat. Keep the body relaxed. You're going to have to open your mouth at some point. Draw the breath in and out from a place further than you observed it coming from normally. Gently exhale. Now open your throat into your chest and bring the breath to and from there. It's okay to push this a little bit. It's like panting. Pant and help yourself. Panting automatically activates the breathing mechanism to deeper places. You don't have to do it on every breath. Always take care of yourself. When you feel that you've got it to the chest, go lower. Go to the diaphragm. Always focus on opening the throat. Add voice and help the breath travel further down in and out of you with a vocalization of any sounds. Keep going further. You are now feeling your breathing mechanism working from the center of your body. Get it down into your thighs. Notice your body start to become involved in it. You don't have to do it on every breath. If you get dizzy, stop and then pick it up again. Keep going until you feel your feet involved in pushing the breath up. Right now everybody pant, pant with a full open throat. Feel your legs involved. Send the breath deeper down. Open the throat. Open the throat to the floor. ◆ Stop the panting and continue to keep the throat open that much. Keep that body feeling of the panting, without actually panting, and with that open throat we're going to send our breath into a theatrical stage whisper where the voice and breath come and go all the way down to the feet. Everyone is going to do a 2-4-6-8 cheer together, with your focus on full body whispering with a full open throat. ◆ *The coach demonstrates full body whispering*— Notice my legs as I do this. Notice how involved they have to be in order to open the throat all the way through the body so that I can fully vocalize with that *whisperish* quality. If your throat is fully open and your body is involved and supporting the whisper, you can do it for long periods of time without strain. It requires a full open throat to the floor. On cue, everyone do a 2-4-6-8 cheer for me. Ready? Full body whisper. ◆ *Now*— 2-4-6-8, who do we appreciate? Stephen, Stephen, Stephen, yeah! ◆ [*Still demonstrating*] Without saying another word, go to places. When action is called, allow your bodies to do your activity, contact the location, and behave according to your character choices. In addition, your primary acting focus is that whenever you speak, you must use a full body whisper. Stay consistently alert to the circumstances that necessitate whispering.

Action. ◆ *As needed*— Speak only when necessary. Share that thought. If you speak, you must full body whisper! Avoid hanging out. **Do your activity.** Discover objects. Contact the location. Stay alert to active & still. Stay on focus for every word. Keep full body whispering until the end of your sentences. Keep effort out. All words are full body whispered to the person you are speaking to. **Full body whisper with a full, open, and relaxed throat. Let your body help send the communication to the one you are speaking to,** even if you have to stop doing your activity briefly. **Get your legs into it!** Stay on your acting focus. **Stay alert to the circumstances requiring the whispering.** Communicate! ◆ One minute. ◆ Cut.

FOLLOW-UP (as needed): Audience, **location? Character occupations? Personal relationships?** Activity? Did they whisper in a normal fashion or **did they full body whisper?** Could you tell the difference? Profit from that when it's your turn to play. Did they substitute talking in a low volume for full body whispering? **Were they on their acting focus?** Did their circumstances demand that they whisper when speaking? Did they stay alert to those circumstances? Did they participate in doing their activity? Could they have physically done more? Examples? More contacting the location? More activity doing? More discovering objects? Did they respond to the coaching? **Was there any playwriting?** What was it? ◆ Actors, do you accept that? Did you hang out without activity? Could you have physically done more? Were you totally committed to the acting focus? **Do you feel that you let your acting focus lead you through the improv? Were any of you nervous prior to the improv? As actors, not characters, were any of you nervous while you were improvising?**

SUMMARY:

FULL BODY WHISPER AND THE BREATH

Full body whispering requires that the breath come from a different part of your body than usual. If the breath comes from your mouth only, then the whisper will be tiny and will not be communicated to the audience. Make the breath come from the toes. That means a full, open passageway through the throat and the entire body. You have to open the throat deeper, deeper, and deeper so that the whole body is involved in the whisper. Even though the breath actually does not flow below the diaphragm, feeling that it does will create the open throat and body support necessary for a full body vocalization.

ACTING FOCUS AS PATH TO IMPROVISATION

Note: This part of the summary should be communicated early in the training, at the time that full body whisper is first learned. Once the actors have completed physical doing and inner doing, they already know this information.

Activity + Acting Focus = Out of the Head + Fun + Spontaneity

Each acting focus is at once a specific technical acting skill like full body whispering, which can be used anytime it is necessary, and a part of the whole learning of how to improvise acting. We've just done our first round of complete improvisations. They are called *complete* because the entire team knew before the improv began what characters they were playing, where the scene took place, and what they were all doing. In addition, there was minimal restriction on dialogue. In fact, for the first time dialogue was encouraged, as long as it was full body whispered. For the most part, no one was nervous while improvising and everybody had fun. As a bonus, every improv was fun to watch.

Did anyone experience or observe anything about the improvising you want to share with us? It was easier for you than usual. And it's no mere coincidence that this happened for everybody. This is a direct result of your playing by certain rules that your bodies have learned up to this point. (1) Doing activities. Acting is doing and doing an activity is the purest form of doing. When you are involved in an activity, everything becomes easier. There's no time to think, which is where your troubles come from, because your brain is focused on the doing of the activity. (2) You are starting to stretch your instrument and are now able to do three things at once: the physical doing of the activity; relating to each other according to your character choices; and the doing of the acting focus, in this case, full body whisper. When you are occupied with all of these doings, you free up and release your instrument to its potential. That's when it starts to become fun and easy. That's when you're not censoring yourself.

Those of you who felt nervous during the improv, notice that you are the ones who stopped doing your activity during the improv. The minute you stop doing the activity, you go right into the head, and experience nervousness, anxiety, and fear—not knowing what to say or do next, not getting approval from your peers or the coach or from yourself. If you didn't stop doing the activity but you stopped doing the acting focus, you'd also have felt nervous. In a complete improvisation, when you are only doing the activity and not the acting focus, you will have the anxiety of feeling you are not a part of the whole scene and you will feel lame. At the least, you will not work at your potential.

Each acting focus becomes a rule and all the rules together are the building blocks of Improvisation Technique. Because the rules have been learned by your body, it automatically improvises accordingly. You don't have to remember the rules *mentally*. There's a reason the training requires so many early rounds of the activity game. It was over the course of those rounds that your body learned *kinesthetically* to be doing, always doing, and more doing. Now it does its doing automatically and you are free to put all your attention on the acting focus, which is the real doing of acting. With your body taking care of the physical doing, and you paying attention to and focusing on the designated acting focus, you have total freedom within the rules of the improvisation to do whatever you want, whatever comes up.

Through the doing of the activity and the doing of the acting focus, you get rid of any anxiety, have fun, and use your instrument to the maximum potential. Committing to the primary acting focus while letting your body take care of the physical doing of the activity will prepare you for what is ahead of us when we deal with what to do when the director or the circumstances keep you from doing physical activity.

Ensemble Acting

A noticeable characteristic of each of the improvs was equality between the actors. In none of the improvs did we see a ham actor attempting to be the center of the improv, nor did we see any actors hiding in the corners. The rules—everyone's respect for them and the fact that they are the same rules for everyone—create this equality. All played their parts of the whole; no one attempted to be the whole all by himself; and no one attempted to run from playing his part of the whole. In addition, the underlying rule we have adopted of helping your fellow actors adds to this feeling of one for all and all for one. Along with a complete absence of competition, there is an inherent feeling while improvising that if you get in trouble, a fellow actor will come to your rescue. That feeling heightens your own confidence and your respect for each other, which enhances the feeling of equality. This state of equality is an early example of the ensemble acting that Improvisation Technique creates. The fact that you are already at this stage in improvisations after only a handful of classes should be dramatic to you.

Dialogue

You should also notice that each of these improvs contained a great deal of dialogue compared to what we are used to. Look how easy it was to include dialogue in your improvising. In our previous classes, you've been trained to avoid dialogue unless it is absolutely necessary. Now that your bodies have learned that kinesthetically, they are prepared to avoid storytelling, playwriting, unnecessary questions, and jokes whenever you choose to speak.

Ad-lib vs. Improvisation

There is a difference between ad-libbing and improvising. It's the writer's job to create the jokes, not the actor's. Actors who make jokes while improvising are breaking the rule, speak only *when you have to*. Joke comments are speaking *when you want to*. They come from the head, and they are an avoidance of an acting focus that is challenging you. Your ability to be clever and make jokes is not a muscle you need when acting scripted lines. A muscle you do need is the ability to stay in character and on an acting focus. Many of our improvisations will be extremely funny, but not because of individuals *inauthenticating* the situation by making jokes.

Spontaneous use of Full Body Whisper when not the Primary Acting Focus

You have learned how to do an effective stage whisper. Let's say that two weeks from now we're improvising on another acting focus and during the course of the improv, your character feels the need to whisper to another character. At that moment, your body should automatically go into full body whisper for the duration of the whispered dialogue. Then you come right out of it and back onto the designated acting focus that you're working on. Every new acting focus is a tool to be plucked spontaneously from your actor's tool bag and used when necessary.

> TO THE COACH: It is highly recommended that full body whisper be done early on, while the training is centered in physical doing. This adds variety to the training process and provides the actors with a taste of what's to come, when all improvisations are complete improvisations with a primary acting focus other than physical doing. It also initiates the vocal doing training, which is deliberately spread out over the training in order to achieve the continuous impact of the physiological involvement of the body in the voice, eventually leading to its use when speaking normally during acting.
>
> There are several reasons for starting vocal warm-ups with, "Observe your own breathing." It centers the actor and relaxes the body; it makes the actor aware of and focused on the body's vocal apparatus and mechanics—throat, diaphragm, breathing, etc.; and it sets up a basis for

self-comparison when the actors are coached to pant and open the throat in preparation for vocal doing acting focuses.

Panting is about inhaling and exhaling the air from deeper parts of the body than just the mouth. Mouth leads to throat, leads to chest, diaphragm, gut, legs, and toes. Even if the breathing mechanism doesn't actually extend to the toes, for any full body vocal doing focus, the whole body from the top of the head to the toes are involved. The full, open throat is what you fill with the voice.

For a more thorough and individual introduction, engage each actor in an individual full-body-whisper conversation similar to the introduction for the next acting focus.

Actors may not know the meaning of the question, *Do you feel that you let your acting focus lead you through the improv?* If they do, they usually have an instantaneous response. If they don't understand the question, leave it alone. They will get it later. When an actor lets the acting focus lead him through the improv, he and everyone in the audience know it.

During the follow-up, if any actor says he was nervous while improvising, ask him if he did his activity. Then ask if he thinks there is a connection between not doing his activity and his being nervous.

FULL BODY CALLING[2]

SETUP: 2–6 per team. In huddles, they select characters, activity, and location. The choices must include significant physical distance between the characters so that whenever they speak to one another they will have to call out over that distance to be heard. The distance challenge may not be replaced with a character choice of deafness or a smaller location choice with a great deal of noise. Examples: ground crew, working, football stadium; archeologists, exploring, large ancient caves; family members, lost and searching for each other or a way out, dense forest.

RULES: While improvising (doing the physical doing associated with) your character, activity, and location, all dialogue is to be spoken with full body calling. No telephones or amplification devices allowed.

ACTING FOCUS: Whenever you speak: calling to the one you are speaking to, who is far away from you, with a fully open and relaxed throat, supported by your whole body.

COACHING: Volunteer first team, set up your location. ◆ *After location is set up*— **Preparation:** Form a circle around the stage. Observe your breathing. Keep your eyes open. Do gentle panting to open your throat in a relaxed way, relaxing your throat a little more with each breath. Keep it gentle. Observe your throat opening in a relaxed way. The air from your breathing is going in and out to deeper places in your throat. It goes into a deeper place and you exhale from a deeper place. Go to the top of your chest. Now the bottom of your chest. Your midsection. Keep taking it deeper with successive breaths, opening your throat more and more. There is no urgency. This should be relaxing for your body and especially for the throat as you open it further and further. Eventually, you want a feeling of an open throat all the way down to the toes. Now keeping this full open throat, let's practice the new acting focus called *Full Body Calling*.

The coach demonstrates:

> FULL BODY CALLING IS PLAYED LIKE THIS. KEEP- ING YOUR THROAT OPEN, YOU ARE SIMPLY CALL- ING TO SOMEONE WHO IS VERY FAR AWAY FROM YOU. ASSUME THAT THEY ARE FIFTY YARDS FROM YOU. YOU HAVE TO USE YOUR WHOLE BODY TO SUPPORT THE CALLING. NO SHOUTING OR YELLING. SHOUTING AND YELLING USE ONLY THE VOICE, NOT THE REST OF THE BODY, AND THEY PUT TREMENDOUS STRAIN ON THE VOICE. FULL BODY CALLING CREATES NO STRAIN ON THE VOICE. IT IS LOWER IN VOLUME THAN SHOUTING OR YELLING. USE YOUR WHOLE BODY TO SUPPORT YOUR CALLING, SLOWING THE WORDS AND SENDING THEM TO THE ONE YOU ARE TALKING TO. SEND THE COMMUNICATION THROUGH CALLING OVER A L - O - N - G D - I - S - T - A - N - C - E.

The coach has a brief dialogue with each actor in the circle, using full body calling. He stands at the farthest part of the room from the actors. He should still be able to see them. He uses this dialogue to coach each actor individually.

COACH: Are you out there? ACTOR: Yes. COACH: Can you get your body more involved in supporting the full body calling? ACTOR: Yes, I can. COACH: Why don't you experiment with it? If I am farther and farther away, what else can you do? Can you get your body to help support sending the communication? If you get your body behind what you are doing, you will energize it much more. ACTOR: I can get my body more involved by pointing it in the direction of your voice. COACH: All right. Now, everybody in class, there is more than one way to do full body calling. Everybody finds his own way. ◆ *To another actor—* Are you out there? ACTOR: Yes, I am. COACH: Where are you? (Remember, the coach and the actors can actually see each other.) ACTOR: I am way over here in the back. COACH: Can you get your eyes more involved in calling to me? Doesn't it help if you look in the direction of my voice? ♦ *To another actor*— Who else is out there? ACTOR: Hello. COACH: I can't hear you. ACTOR: I am over here. COACH: Still can't hear you. Trust your impulse. You started to help yourself briefly, then you stopped it. What did you just do physically with your body? ACTOR: I don't know. COACH: You took your hands out of your pocket and you started to put them somewhere and you never completed that and then you brought them back to your chest. ♦ (The actor brings her hands up to her mouth and forms a megaphone with them.) ACTOR: How's this? COACH: There you go.

ADDITIONAL COACHING (as needed): Can you support your calling with your legs? How about aiming your body in my direction? Is your body swaying like that supporting a direct communication or distracting from it? Can you use your pronunciation to call more, *extending the sounds of the words* instead of cutting them short? Speak slowly so that the voice has time to carry over the presumed distance between you.

Without saying another word, everyone go to places. When I call "Action," allow your bodies to practice all the physical doing we have been working on—contacting the location, discovering objects near you, doing your activity, communicating to each other according to your character choices (relationships and occupations), and employing active & still. Your new and primary acting focus is, whenever you speak, focus on calling to the one you are speaking to, who is far away from you, with full body calling with a fully open and relaxed throat. You must keep the distance between you in order to speak. No yelling or shouting. ♦ Action. ♦ **If there is no distance between you, avoid dialogue of any kind.** Keep the distance between you that necessitates full body calling. **Avoid hanging out.** Do your activity. Discover objects. Contact the location. Stay alert to active & still. Stay on focus for every word. **Keep calling until the end of your sentences.** Keep effort out. All words are s-t-r-e-t-c-h-i-n-g like a rubber band to the person you are speaking to. Extend your communication. Call over the long distance with a full, open, and relaxed throat. Let your body help send the communication to the one you are speaking to. Find a way to let your body help send the communication, even if you have to briefly stop doing your activity.

FOLLOW-UP (as needed): Audience, location? Character occupations? Personal relationships? Activity? Did they use their whole bodies to call over long distances or did they shout, yell, or simply talk loudly? Could you tell the difference? Profit from that when it's your turn to play. **Were they on their acting focus?** Was there distance present in their setup? Did they call to each other at the same time or did they employ active & still? Could they have done more physically? Did they respond to the coaching? ◆ Actors, could you have done more? How? More contacting the location? More activity doing? More discovering objects? Were any of you nervous while you were playing? **Were you on the acting focus and totally committed to it? Did you allow the acting focus to lead you through the improvisation?**

SUMMARY:

VOICE & BODY

How is full body calling similar to full body whisper? Both (1) are examples of vocal doing that use the voice in specific and extratheatrical ways; (2) require an open and relaxed throat; (3) use the whole body more than usual, heightening the body's energy and involvement in the verbal communication; (4) create more challenge in communicating; (5) increase the feeling of being connected to the one you are talking to; and (6) dispel casualness, as everyone seems highly focused on what they are doing and saying.

Full body calling and full body whispering create *a physiological involvement of your bodies with your voices* and this heightens vocal communication and authenticity. An actor who is acting up an emotional storm with his face and voice, but whose body is clearly not experiencing the same feelings, is simply not present and is working only from the neck up. For an authentic and dynamic performance, the whole body's physicality must support the verbal communication. It is physiologically impossible for this not to happen with full body whisper or calling. You must bring your body along when you communicate. It's like bringing a 500-watt amplifier (body) to the sound rather than a 10-watt amplifier (head).

As we do more of the vocal doing acting focuses, your body will open up and have a kinesthetic understanding of what it means to speak with full body involvement. In time, without the aid of an extratheatrical full body vocal doing acting focus, your body will demand of you that you include it in verbal communication.

When you use a full body vocal doing acting focus, the process creates a bridge between the speaker and the listener. Communication travels on this bridge through the space. The connection is efficient, effortless, and effective. Maximizing communication gives you more control over it, in much the same way that you have far greater control and fine-tuning ability with a $10,000 stereo sound system than you have with a $20 kiddy disc player. With the high-end system, you have individual controls for treble, bass, separation, phasing, muting, and so on, whereas with a little kiddy disc player, you have a little volume control, nothing more. The more full body energy you are bringing into the communication, the more control you ultimately have over it. As we advance in the training you will discover and explore your abilities for using these controls.

TO THE COACH: Stay alert for shouting. Coach the actors out of it and into full body calling. Shouting creates strain in their improvising and pain in their throats.

NONSENSE LANGUAGE

One of the most important improvisational tools, widely used with dramatic results, is *Nonsense Language*. It is presented here in a series of different exercises, beginning with an experiential presentation.

Nonsense Language Presentation Party[3]

SETUP: The coach should become proficient in speaking nonsense language, *mixing up sounds and words of nonsense to replace real language*, prior to presenting it to the class. A sentence in nonsense language might be, "Gazhooby, mix plot nik frefloby la la rillaroan." Although he should have an idea of what he is trying to communicate—the above sentence might mean, "All right, I want you to pay attention,"—*the speaker should not take the time to think of what he wants to say first* and then come up with a literal nonsense language translation. That would kill the spontaneity and defeat the whole purpose of this acting focus. *It is enough that he desires to communicate and to receive communication.* In the early stages of practicing nonsense language there will be times when the speaker is speaking fluently and has no idea what he is attempting to communicate but will, nevertheless, be caught up in the *process* of communicating. As he moves through the series of exercises and improvs, the speaker will lessen the number of times he speaks without knowing what he is attempting to communicate. In the following presentation, wherever I suggest what the coach should say in nonsense language, it is a given that *there will always be spontaneous body gesturing supporting the communication*.

Part 1: The presentation begins without an introduction in English. The class should be surprised when the coach starts talking to them in this strange language. ◆ It may help the coach to have an idea that what he is saying substitutes for "All right, I want you to pay attention. We are now beginning a new body of work and it requires your total attention. Also, you will be asked to participate in a process totally new and alien to you." ◆ From this point on, continue improvising in nonsense language on the theme of "Don't worry, you will all get it, etc." ◆ *After ca. 30s*— Direct your attention to one actor in the group and, in nonsense language, ask him anything, like "How are you doing today?" If the actor looks totally bewildered and frightened, try again. In nonsense language, ask him another question or make a statement, like "It's all right, you can talk to me." [Everything that I suggest the coach say is to be spoken in nonsense language.] If the actor still doesn't respond, move on to another actor and ask or say something.

When you get a nonsense language response from an actor you are addressing, immediately *understand* what the actor has said back to you (even if you don't) and respond in turn, commencing a brief conversation with that actor. Then turn to another actor and get a brief conversation going with him. After the coach has conversed briefly with four or five actors, he should show surprise at something an actor says to him, then turn to another actor and ask him what he thinks about what the previous actor just said. By now, there will be occasional unsolicited outbursts of nonsense language from different actors talking to the coach and to each other. The coach should *work the room* until all have spoken briefly in nonsense language. ◆ A reticent actor should not be pressured to speak. When an actor doesn't participate in a brief conversation with the coach, the coach should shrug it off, as no big deal. But always return to that actor and afford him another opportunity. Sometimes the coach may elicit help from another actor. ◆ For example, if Actor #1 is the reticent one, turn to Actor #2 *and say*— What do you think, #1 doesn't want to play? ◆ Actor #2 will know what you are saying and may turn to Actor #1 and attempt a conversation between them. Eventually, all will participate and the spirit in the room will be a fun one, accompanied by lots of laughs.

Part 2: After all have spoken briefly, address one actor in particular. [Everybody is now speaking only in nonsense language.] Tell him to stand up, bring his chair out on the floor, place it up stage left, and sit down. When he gets the communication and is sitting up stage left, turn to another actor and tell him to bring his chair to up stage right and sit. Then, another actor with his chair, down stage left and another, down stage right. Go through the whole group dividing them up by sending each individual to one of the four areas. [The choice of four different areas is arbitrary, based on having 4–8 per grouping. If there are only fifteen actors in the class, use three areas.] The actors don't know this but the coach chooses who goes where based on combining the ones who spoke with ease in part 1 with those who had some difficulty.

Part 3: Approach each group and communicate to them to form their chairs into circles and converse with each other. They will get it and respond immediately. Leave them alone for three minutes. The coach will observe the four groups having conversations with different degrees of enthusiasm.

Part 4: The coach approaches one group at a time, wheeling a space bar up to them, getting their attention, taking a space bottle of booze off the bar, unscrewing the top, pouring the booze into space glasses on a space tray and handing one to each actor, saving the last glass for himself. The coach holds up his glass to make a toast and tells the group to be careful, as this booze is powerful stuff. Of course, all of this is in nonsense language and the communication about the powerful booze should be done with great flair. The coach makes the toast and all drink. The coach indicates the bar right next to them, holds up different types of booze bottles, and tells them to help themselves. The coach walks away.

Part 5: We now have four separate parties going on and all are participating with enthusiasm, speaking fluent nonsense language to each other. After about five minutes, the coach goes to an empty part of the stage and gets the attention of some or all of the actors. He establishes a space buffet table with lots of space food and invites the players to come join him. When a few of them begin filling up plates of food and eating, the coach goes around the room making sure that everyone knows about the food and that it's fine to combine the four parties into one big one. The party now begins to go full blast and the coach has the option of participating at the same level of everyone else or fading off to the side and observing. It is important that the coach now give up all leadership position and let the party evolve. On the other hand, the coach should stay absolutely alert and ready to step into any part of the party to avert any negative drunken behavior. Sometimes, after about fifteen minutes, I add recorded instrumental rock and roll music. The whole party should last 20–30 minutes.

RULES and ACTING FOCUS: None mentioned.

COACHING (as needed): Only those suggested in the setup.

FOLLOW-UP (as needed): Did you feel festive? Did you really feel like you were partying? Did you speak and understand the nonsense language? Did you get better at it as the party progressed? Was it because of the liquor? But, the liquor was made out of space. How were you able to act the party with such a high level of intensity?

SUMMARY:

We just acted a party and somebody said it was better than most parties they go to. But do not be fooled. We acted it. There was no booze. There was no food. It was all made out of space. I never instructed you to have a party. What you felt during the party, the ability to be so involved in what you were doing, is the result of being on the acting focus. We used space props and we focused on communicating spontaneously in this made-up *nonsense language*. That's the name of our new acting focus. Nonsense language is the substitution of any nonsense language for a real language, replacing real words of any real language with any nonsense words or accumulation of vocal sounds. No real languages of any kind are permitted in nonsense language. There were no English instructions whatsoever—e.g., Everybody, act a party and have a good time—but through this acting focus you got there. Most of you felt happy. For some of you, there were moments of anger and sadness. There were moments of people feeling drunk. There were moments of affection and love. The point is, you always *felt* it. For those of you who think acting is about reaching a point where you really feel the feelings, then you certainly were acting. But the important thing is, where did it come from? It came from *doing*. You *did* the party. You did the acting focus, communicating in a nonsense language. Unlike our previous training, I didn't tell you what your acting focus was, nor did I tell you what the setup or rules were. My invitation to you to participate was communicated in nonsense language. You accepted the invitation, the space props, the convention of a nonsense language, and the acting focus of *communicating* to each other. You went with it. You stayed on the focus of the nonsense language and you got to that state of really doing the party. All acting has to be done with that level of experiential involvement and commitment. The way you get there, which is important to this technique of acting, is by committing to the acting focus with everything you have, not splitting off from it.

> **TO THE COACH:** Should any actors choose to respond to the liquor by developing negative symptoms, e.g. headaches, nausea, anger, then the coach becomes a healer. He goes over to the actor, puts a hand on his head, smiles at him, and in nonsense language lets him know he is going to make the actor feel better. In that way, the coach helps the actor turn the corner from the choice of feeling and behaving in a down state to choices that are more festive and fun. The coach should smile and communicate that he is going to replace any symptoms in the actor's belly, head, or facial expression through some kind of gesture, maybe a light tap on the hand or forehead, and the actor will respond with feeling good. There should then be a final communication from the coach in nonsense language that it is the actor's choice to have a good time or a bad time, and that he should go with the good time.
>
> If lifestyle considerations preclude using liquor, omit that part of the party. On the other hand, if the group is made up of actors, it's a perfect opportunity for nondrinkers to participate because the booze is made out of space. After all, what happens if they get cast in a part that requires drinking?
>
> It is recommended that the group go immediately into the next exercise as soon as any summary is completed.

NONSENSE LANGUAGE COMMERCIALS [4]

SETUP: One by one, each demonstrates and sells a product to the group. Create a brand new commercial for any product, either for the camera or live for a trade show. Your props must be space props.

RULES: Speak in nonsense language. No real languages. Explore different sounds, syllables, and words, discovering diversity and variety for your nonsense language. This shouldn't be any longer than a couple of minutes.

ACTING FOCUS: Using nonsense language to communicate.

COACHING (as needed): Communicate to the camera. Communicate to the group. Include us. Heighten your communication. Keep your props in the space. Explore your nonsense language. Use different sounds, letters, syllables, words. Go somewhere new in your nonsense language.

FOLLOW-UP (as needed): What was he selling? Did he communicate in nonsense language? Did he share his voice? **Did he explore his nonsense language?** Was he using more sounds, different syllables, new words as the sales pitch went on? That's exploring. **Could he have done that more?** If the nonsense language had a specific accent, could he have explored other accents? Were his objects in the space?

SUMMARY:

Nonsense language resembles full body whisper and full body calling because nonsense language also results in bringing your body into your voice. In all three, it is impossible to leave your body out of the vocal process. Take the opportunity with every nonsense language improv to further your dexterity. Extend the language with new sounds, syllables, words, or accents.

> **TO THE COACH:** If the actor makes his sales pitch with low energy, have him repeat it, selling the same product in a different setting. The new setting is a trade show or a carnival where people are wandering around and he has to attract his crowd and keep them there until he makes his sale. ♦ *Coach*— Heighten it! Heighten the communication! You're losing the crowd! Keep them there! Make the sale!

NONSENSE LANGUAGE / TEACHING AND LEARNING [5]

SETUP: 2–6 per team. In huddles, select characters and location for a teaching/learning situation. Select what is being taught and who plays the teacher.

RULES: While employing physical doing tools of Improvisation Technique for activity, location, relationships, and occupation, actors must communicate to each other in nonsense language. No real languages allowed.

ACTING FOCUS: Using nonsense language to communicate with each other.

COACHING (as needed): Set up the location. ◆ Places. ◆ Action. ◆ Share your voices. Share that thought. Communicate with the teacher. Communicate with each other. **Active & still.** Communicate in nonsense language with each other. Contact the location. Respect your space props. **Go with it.** ◆ **Group blocking!** One minute. ◆ Cut.

FOLLOW-UP (as needed): What was being taught and learned? Did the actors send and receive communication in nonsense language? Did they understand each other? Were they on their acting focus? ◆ Actors, did you understand each other? Did you allow the acting focus to lead you through the improv?

SUMMARY:

PRESENCE

What did you notice about the acting? There was more freedom, energy, alertness, checking out improv mates, sharing of voices, and risk taking—in a word, more presence. Since we began playing with nonsense language, everyone's presence has been markedly increased. What is it about this acting focus that allows your presence to come out?

Your body's involvement in your acting is heightened. While all of our training since the first class has been body oriented, and previous vocal doing acting focuses have brought the body into the voice, nonsense language is the first vocal doing focus to deprive you of English words. This shows that the power of vocal doing is not in what you say, the words, but in the body's full involvement in the verbal communication. Without the physiological involvement of the body in the voice, there is no presence. You can have talent and technique, but without presence, you will not have a career.

In class when you are coached to share your voices, you know that you are not bringing your body along. With continued experiential exposure to different vocal doing acting focuses what will eventually happen is that your body will relish this heightened communication and it will bring itself along in all the verbal aspects of your acting.

> **TO THE COACH: Checking huddles:** If you are following the order of presentation as it is in this book, this is an excellent time to walk around and listen in on the huddles prior to these improvs. If necessary, the following may be appropriate after the summary or just prior to the next set of huddles.
>
> Stay alert to playwriting, picking things way beyond naming the character, activity, and location, e.g., past developments or back story, future points in the story, or ramifications of what will happen. Discussions of

"If we do this, then that can happen" must be avoided. ◆ *Coach the actors*— You are just there to name the character, activity, and location that the audience sees when action is called.

Another self-limiting huddle characteristic is bossism. Stay alert to certain people trying to take over huddles, attempting to force their choices through. ◆ *Coach the actors*— You must be alert to that happening. If that is happening, everyone is free to reject any choice. Huddles are meant to be group agreement and if somebody says, "I do not want to do that," then that should be it. There should be no salesmanship. No trying to sell an idea to someone else. All have to take responsibility in the huddle for saying, "That is playwriting and we should not be talking about this." Or saying, "No, let's not do that. Let's go someplace else." You have to avoid having the huddle turn into any one, two, or three people having an idea of what is going to happen. Stay sensitive to each other. Stay alert. It is a group thing. If you sense that people are not excited by an idea that you volunteer, spot that. Then pull back. See what someone else has to offer. It has to be group agreement going toward character, activity, and location choices only.

NONSENSE / ENGLISH[6]

This is a conversation-only improvisation introduced with a demonstration.

DEMONSTRATION

SETUP: Two volunteer actors sit on chairs facing each other with the coach between and behind them. The actors pick a topic for a conversation.

COACHING: Begin your conversation on the subject in English and respond to any coaching to follow. ◆ Share your voices. Share the conversation. ◆ After the conversation begins to flow easily, *coach*— Nonsense language. Switch to nonsense language without stopping. Keep the conversation going. ◆ *After ca. 30s*— English. ◆ Then coach them back and forth between nonsense language and English at surprising moments in the conversation, i.e., midword. The whole conversation should last 3–5 minutes.

FOLLOW-UP: Did the conversation move forward and progress throughout? Did the actors communicate to each other in both English and nonsense language? ◆ Actors, did you understand each other and respond to each other?

IMPROVISATION

ACTING FOCUS: Communicating in either English or nonsense language.

SETUP, COACHING, and FOLLOW-UPS for entire group: Group counts off, 3 per team. They get chairs and spread out around the floor, each team forming a triangle. ◆ Each triangle is going to play three rounds of this game. In the first round, any two of you have a conversation on any topic you wish. The third member of the group is the coach, coaching the conversation back and forth between English and nonsense language. You will play for a while, and then I will stop everybody. We will do a quick follow-up with each other and then we will start round two with a new player in each group being the coach. Then, in the third round, the third player will be the coach. This way everyone gets to be the coach. Each round, the two players choose a brand new topic. ✦ When you are coaching, have them start in English, let the conversation begin to flow, and then coach the switches whenever you want. Stay alert to surprising the players with your coaching. The coaching is intended for both actors, and we never have one actor speaking English while the other is speaking nonsense language. ✦ Actors, respond in the moment to whatever is coached, moving the conversation forward with no backing up. Let your conversations be conversations and avoid storytelling or lengthy monologues. Designate who is going to be the coach, pick a topic, then go ahead and get started. ✦ Allow about seven minutes for each round. ✦ Cut. ✦ Use the same follow-up questions as above, in the demon-stration. ✦ Select a new coach, a new topic, and start whenever you are ready. Remember, the conversation must start in English. Coaches would be well advised to let the conversation build momentum before the first switch to nonsense language. ✦ Do the follow-up and commence the third round.

SUMMARY:

What did you discover while coaching? ✦ Typical responses include— When they spoke in nonsense language, their body language was much more height-ened, there was much more connection between them, their voices rung out more, their eyes came alive and sparkled, and they were much freer. ✦ As the conversation progressed, these qualities started to carry over into the English part of the conversation until it was just as heightened as the nonsense language parts. Like any vocal doing acting focus, nonsense language creates a height-ened involvement of the body in the voice, and by the end of the conversation, the body continued to stay in the voice during the English sections. Your bodies are starting to enjoy the empowerment they feel when they join in the process of verbal communication.

Did anybody notice anything about when to coach the switch from English to nonsense language? It was most effective when you caught them off guard. The least effective time is the moment when they conclude a paragraph or en-tire beat.

> **TO THE COACH:** Make sure all rounds begin with a preselected topic. The actors shouldn't search for a topic while playing. ✦ Walk around and monitor all of the trios but don't get involved unless it's to solve a prob-

lem. ◆ If the actors are improvising their conversations as characters, e.g., an engaged couple discussing where to have their wedding, remind them that they should be themselves discussing a topic between them. ◆ If any actor is exhibiting fear while speaking nonsense language, it might be suggested they write in their journals about it.

NONSENSE SPEECH TRANSLATION [7]

Prior to these improvs, the entire group should warm up with reflect the reflector.

SETUP: 2 per team. Actor #1 is from a foreign country and improvises a speech on any subject in nonsense language. We in the audience are Americans and do not understand a word she says. Therefore, we have hired an interpreter for her, Actor #2. Actor #1 stands center stage, facing the audience. Actor #2 stands stage right, facing Actor #1.

Both actors must play *reflect the reflector* with each other. You learned reflect the reflector as a part of a traditional reflection game; however, this is not a traditional reflection exercise. You are not to literally reflect each other's body movements. Actor #2 is going to give *full body attention* to Actor #1, just as you would do in playing the reflection game. ◆ Actor #1 starts the speech in nonsense language and introduces the topic she is going to be speaking on. Before the speech begins, Actor #2 has no idea what the topic will be.

After a few sentences, Actor #1 stops to allow the translator to translate what she has said. ◆ The moment she stops, Actor #2 must turn to the audience and without the slightest hesitation translate into English whatever communication he received from focusing on Actor #1 during her nonsense language speech. ◆ While Actor #2 is translating, Actor #1 faces him with *full body attention*, just like in a reflection game. As soon as the translator finishes his translation, he turns back to facing the speaker. That is her cue to face the audience and resume the speech from that point. After an appropriate period of time, decided by the speaker, she pauses again for the translator to translate, and faces him. The translator faces the audience and immediately provides the translation of what has just been said by the speaker. They continue in this fashion, back and forth, until the speaker concludes the speech and the conclusion has been translated.

While this is not a direct reflection of body movements, it should feel just as physically involving, from head to toes, as playing reflect the reflector. When playing reflect the reflector, you always go with it. If you stop going with it, it means that you are initiating, and there is no initiating in reflect the reflector. Both actors must go with what they get. Whatever communication the translator receives from focusing on the speaker, he must translate it that way. Whatever translation is provided, the speaker must proceed from that. Should the translator change the topic, then the speaker must go with the new topic, because that will be what she has received from the translator. If the translator changes the speaker's original topic, it will not be because he *intentionally* changed it but because that is what he received. Reflect the reflector means that both actors are following each other, wherever it leads. While nonsense speech translation is not a traditional reflection game, the essence and feeling of reflect the reflector is the acting focus.

After one couple has done the improv and the follow-up, proceed with the rest of the group, two at a time. After all have done it once, do another round with everyone who was a speaker in the first round now taking on the translator role and vice versa. It is recommended they all do the second round with different partners.

RULES: The speaker is to lecture and not do a demonstration with space props. ◆ The only initiation is the first time the speaker speaks. ◆ The speaker must pause frequently to allow for translations into English. ◆ The moment you get the cue, either to translate or to resume the speech, you must begin speaking immediately. There should be no time-lag after the cue. ◆ The translator is not to *deliberately* change the topic or any part of the speech in his translation. If the translation does change any of the speaker's original intent, it must be because it is what the translator received from focusing on the speaker. ◆ Once the translator translates, the speaker must accept that that is what she originally said and proceed from that point when she resumes speaking.

ACTING FOCUS: Reflect the reflector.

COACHING (as needed): As soon as the speaker stops speaking, the **translator starts immediately. No time-lag** for thinking. Immediately, say what you know. Whatever you know is what you say, even if it's sparse. Your body knows before your heads knows. Say it. Avoid deliberate or intentional changes. Avoid assumptions. Take what you get. ◆ As soon as the translator stops speaking, the speaker starts. Continue the speech. The moment you get the translation cue, you speak. Say what you know. You will find that you know more than you think you know. Don't pause for the translation after every sentence. **Vary the pauses for translation.** ◆ Reflect the reflector. **Reflection requires full body attention.** Go with it. Use your laughter. Communicate. Receive the communication. ◆ **Avoid demonstrating. It's a lecture!**

FOLLOW-UP (as needed): Speaker, *after* **the topic introduction was translated, was the translation accurate?** Were you surprised? ◆ **Actors, were you reflecting the reflector?** Could you have reflected the reflector more? ◆ **Audience, were they on their acting focus** or did either impose their ideas of how the speech should go? Did the speaker make a speech, or give a demonstration with space props? Could the translator have begun his translation quicker? ◆ Actors, were you open to finding out where the speech would go, or did you have an idea of where it should go?

SUMMARY:

REFLECT THE REFLECTOR = PRESENT-TENSE ACTING

This is the first time we have focused on reflecting the reflector without the reflection of body movements. Reflect the reflector is an acting focus guaranteed to place the actor in the present tense. It is hard enough to be in the present tense by ourselves. Reflect the reflector puts two or more actors there at the same time.

Being in the present tense is the opposite of being split off. When you are in the present tense, you are totally present. That is what we strive for in our acting. Progressing through Improvisation Technique training will result in increasing the amount of time that all are capable of being present in the present tense.

Being present, in the present tense, with another person is a very special occasion. For some it is mystical; for others it is called communion. The philosopher, Martin Buber, calls it the *I-Thou* experience. When actors can do it in performance with each other and a camera or audience watching, it is very exciting because the audience is witnessing a truly spontaneous event despite the fact that it was actually prewritten and rehearsed. Being present in the present tense allows you to let go of control and trust the acting focus as it leads you through the scene. Anyone watching can't help but see and feel *viscerally* that there is something very special going on. We have all seen great acting scenes where two people are so in touch with each other that every little ripple in the air between them affects them both. Reflect the reflector is one of the tools that gives us more and more experience of what that feels like and heightens body familiarity with the process.

In follow-ups, you have frequently been asked if you allowed the acting focus to lead you through the scene. The purpose of that question is to keep drawing your attention to the experience of trusting the acting focus and letting it do the work for you, resulting in spontaneous solving of the acting challenges or problems you may be faced with.

Reflect the reflector requires full body attention to each other. Only then can you achieve the state of traveling together into the unknown. The unknown is a synonym for the present tense because it is a state where anything can happen due to the lack of a controlling element (frequently supplied by the actors). It feels like you are walking on a tightrope or the edge of a cliff and you have no idea what is going to happen next, but you are ready for it, whatever it may be. That is what acting should feel like.

When you are open to going with whatever is going to happen, you are ready to go with the wind, however the wind takes you. The wind just might take you to a place you've never been before. If it does, real growth is possible. When you act in areas you have never experienced, drawing from resources previously unknown or untapped, you expand your abilities, technique, and presence.

This was the genius of Viola Spolin's contribution, placing acting exercises in a game format so that as in all physical games, the players or actors participate with full body attention and alertness.

In order to have presence, in order to act from an unknown and exalted place, you must be giving full body attention to someone or something. Without doing that, you are too capable of being split off. When you are split off, you are not present. The full body is not integrated, much less applying itself toward the other actor or the scene. Presence requires *being there*. If you are not in class, you are not present. Of course, it is possible to be in class with your body, but without you. At that time, you are still not present, even though your body is there. It is also possible to be acting and not be there. You are not present.

It is only a small step from the *present* to *presence*. To create a state of presence, which is the higher state that you must have to be a successful actor, you must have total body involvement with the space, your scene mates, the scene, and your acting focus. You have to be there in such a way that you have absolute fluidity in the moment to go in whatever direction, no matter what happens in the scene. You can do that while playing preselected choices. I am not talking about anarchy.

Reflect the reflector brings you together with others and nonsense language puts you in your body. It is impossible to talk in nonsense language, full body whisper, or full body calling without filling the voice with your whole body. For actors, that should be a necessity. Without it, you are acting from the neck up. You have a thin voice that is totally attached to your brain and whatever your brain can think up, bypassing authentic feelings, instead of having a full voice that is an integral part of your whole body and that has responses to stimuli that affect the whole body. A stimulus could be something as extreme as somebody hitting or betraying you, or as subtle as a ripple in the space between you.

When you can feel those ripples in the space, you have a highly tuned instrument. When you can feel them in such a way that you have a total body response to it, which includes the voice, then you are present and you will have presence. How do you get present and have presence? By being in the body. How do you do that? By staying on your acting focus and trusting it. Every acting focus produces full body involvement. Your job is to be on the acting focus and then let the acting focus do the work for you as it creates the performance.

TO THE COACH: If either actor looks at the audience while the other is speaking, he is not on focus. He is not playing reflect the reflector because he is not giving full body attention to the translator. He is listening with his head for what the other says. This is cerebral attention—coming from the head rather than their body. Playing reflect the reflector requires giving full body attention to the other actor, the one whom they are following. Then there is full body involvement in the focus. ◆ There should be no communication between the two actors prior to the actual start of the speech. ◆ The coach may decide to end the speech by initiating audience applause after any translation section. ◆ Coach actors away from demonstrating their topics with space props. The use of props is a *tell* and a manifestation of the speaker's attempting to play safe by guaranteeing that the translator understands what the speaker is saying.

FEAR DISCUSSION

Since many actors will experience fear prior to playing nonsense speech translation and also prior to the next acting focus, *Full Body Singing*, I take advantage of this by having a discussion about fear between the two exercises.

When we were playing nonsense speech translation, how many of you experienced fear in anticipation of playing or while playing? What do you do about fear in your career?

[The actors share their experiences and approaches to dealing with fear.]

Fear is frequently a manifestation of personal issues, but these are more appropriately dealt with elsewhere. There are meditations, relaxations, and calm-down processes, which you can also address elsewhere.

What can you do right now to help yourself? Become *honest.*

Fear and nervousness are feelings. In the moment that you are experiencing these feelings of fear, be honest. Observe that you *are* experiencing and feeling them. Do not attempt to diminish the feelings through lying, rationalizing, explaining, or denying. Your body is the source of the feelings; it will know that you are lying. When the body knows that you are lying to it, it will exacerbate the very feelings you are trying to dissipate. All you need to do is notice that you are nervous or frightened and *acknowledge it*—"I'm nervous. I'm scared. I'm frightened."

If you are being honest, you must avoid the self put-down: "Oh, I am such a jerk. I always get frightened at these moments and it is no help at all to the actual audition. Why do I do that? I'll never be a good actor. I'm so dumb." This is self-destructive and dishonest. Instead of dealing with the problem, you are caught up in blame. You don't like it when someone else avoids solving a problem by focusing on who is to blame for the problem. Why do it to yourself?

Learn to self-observe without adding to the problem: "Oh, I'm scared right now. I'm nervous right now. I'm shaking. I'm sweating." Just see it and name it. Be a witness, not a judge. "Just the facts, Ma'am, just the facts."

After acknowledging the fear, make sure that you are very clear what the job asks of you. *What is the acting focus* of what you are about to be doing? If you are doing an audition and you have the sides, then you have made some choices. You have an idea what you are going to do. Remind yourself what that is. Remind yourself what the acting focus is, because chances are, if you are frightened, you have lost your focus.

If the situation arises in class, you can say to yourself, "Oh, I am nervous. Now, what is the acting focus? The focus is to reflect the reflector when I'm translating. That's what I have to do." Then you walk out on the floor and you stay on your acting focus, even if it's for one moment. Then you stay on it for the next moment, and the next, and so on.

Dorothy Stickney fought a lifelong battle with stage fright. "When panic overtook me and I felt absolutely unable to go on, I would tell myself, 'You don't have to do the whole play—you don't even have to play the next scene—all you have to do is say the next line.'"[8] While she may never have totally eliminated her fear problem, she always managed to say the next line, and she became a legend in the American theater.

Fear can be fear and you can still do the job by *choosing to focus* on what you have to do. You can take care of business or you can dwell on the fear. It's your choice. If you can stay honest, you will see what there is to see, "I'm nervous," rather than what you think you see, "I'm all upset because all the other actors are distracting me and I can't concentrate. I'm not a professional because I let them get to me." See what there is to see and then choose to focus on your assignment, either with the sides, the scene choices, or the acting focus. Then when you're in places, you just say to yourself that it is now time to be on that focus. That will help guide you through it.

There is one more thing that you can be doing right now to help yourself. Any time you get nervous or frightened, at the very first opportunity, write about it in your journal. Do a little exploration in your journal, again without lies or self put-down. You can ask yourself questions like "When did it start? What was happening when it started? Did it change at all? Did it multiply? Did it diminish? If it got worse, what happened when it got worse? How do I feel about it?" Just write about it honestly. If you want to change your behavior, you have to be aware of it. Writing honestly about it increases self-awareness. You have to start to *know* it. Your journal is the best place to get started.

Fear can serve a purpose. It is there for you to face and overcome. It can provide the juice. Without the fear, the work just might be too easy. Let fear be an opportunity for exploration.

Those of you who have your own personalized processes, if they work, keep doing them. If they don't work, you now have a work program outlined for you. Acknowledge your feelings honestly. Articulate what the job is, i.e., the acting focus. Choose to be on the focus. Work in your journals.

FULL BODY SINGING[9]

SETUP: 2–5 per team. In huddles, select characters, activity, and location.

RULES: While employing physical doing tools of Improvisation Technique for activity, location, relationships, and occupation, actors must sing all their dialogue.

ACTING FOCUS: Singing out all dialogue with full body support of the voice.

COACHING (as needed): Set up the location. ◆ Places. ◆ Action. ◆ **Sing out with your full body.** Total body commitment to your singing. **Enlarge your singing. Sing it out!** Enjoy your singing. Share your singing with everybody. Explore your singing. Extend your singing into new areas. Take the singing into new directions. **Explore that discovery.** Keep discovering new areas for the music, for the singing! **Avoid old melodies and explore new melodies.** ◆ Duet! Sing together. Explore singing together. ◆ New duet! **Go with it! Avoid hanging out.** Stay on your acting focus. One minute to stay on focus. ◆ Cut.

FOLLOW-UP (as needed): Characters? Activity? Location? Did they avoid their physical doing tools (contacting the location, doing their activities, discovering objects near them)? **Were they on the acting focus? Did they discover new directions for their singing or did all of the singing sound similar?** Could they have further explored other directions to take the singing? Was there any playwriting? ◆ Actors, did you sing all your dialogue? **Did you feel like you were on the acting focus? Did you allow the acting focus to lead you through the improv?** Do you accept that there were still more directions you might have taken the singing? When new melodies, tempos, styles, or groupings (duets, trios, and quartets) emerged, did you go with it? Were you alert to, and did you go with, all opportunities presented to you?

SUMMARY:

What effect did this acting focus have on your body? It enlivened it, opened it up, affected its rhythms, and made it more free and expressive. What other acting focus is this similar to? Full body whisper, full body calling, nonsense language, and full body singing automatically bring your body into your voice.

This acting focus will present you with many opportunities for taking your singing in new and unanticipated directions. Going with these provides you with paths into the unknown. Time spent in the unknown strengthens your abilities in the realm of spontaneity. Declining the challenge of going with it keeps you in the realm of playing safe, where no growth occurs.

194

TO THE COACH: Those actors who grew up believing that they have no singing abilities will experience fear upon hearing the setup. Discussing fear between the presentations of nonsense speech translation and full body singing will touch upon the fear they may have experienced with the first and provide an immediate and accessible challenge with the second. They have an immediate opportunity to profit from the fear discussion. ✦ Coach actors out of real, i.e., previously known, songs or melodies.

STRETCHING SPEECH[10]

This acting focus requires a preparation prior to each team's improvisation.

SETUP: 2–6 per team. In huddles, select characters, activity, and location. *After location is setup*— Begin a *stretching speech* preparation. The team divides into two lines, facing each other, with about 8' between them. Actors opposite each other are partners. All the couples (partners) do the preparation at the same time.

Preparation coaching: Send a sound to each other. One [partner to the other partner] at a time. Any sound. Back and forth. Keep changing sounds. ✦ *After 30s, stop them.* ✦ Continue the same thing and add an acting focus. When you send the sound, see the sound arrive (at your partner). ✦ Begin. ✦ While they are playing, *coach (if needed)*— See the sound arrive. Focus on the sound arriving. See it arrive at your partner. ✦ *After 30s, stop them.* ✦ Now, the same acting focus, only instead of a sound, send a word to your partner, and focus on seeing it arrive. ✦ Begin. ✦ While they are playing, *coach (if needed)*— See the word arrive. Focus on the word arriving. See it arrive at your partner. Back and forth. Don't repeat the same word. ✦ *After 30s, stop them.*

Now continue what you are doing, and add to your acting focus— stretching the sounds of the word through the space between you. Discover how to occupy the space between you and your partner with the word, up to its arrival. ✦ While they are playing, *coach (if needed)*— Extend the word through the space to your partner and see it arrive. Stretch the word to your partner. Stretch the word between you and your partner. Avoid muscling it. Remove the effort. No need for extratheatrical gesturing. Simply stretch the sound on every letter of the word. ✦ E-e-e-k-k-k-s-s-s-t-e-e-e-n-n-n-d the word. ✦ Stretch the sound of the word so you are filling the space between you, from the moment the word begins to leave you until the word arrives at your partner. Let the word extend through the space between you. See it arrive.

After 30s, without stopping them, coach— Continue this acting focus with short, complete sentences. Extend every word of these sentences. ◆ While they are playing, *coach (if needed, to individuals only)—* Avoid muscling it. Pull the effort out. See the words arrive. Stretch the sound on every word of the sentence. Avoid being selective. Extend all the sounds of all the words, not just some of them. A continuous flow of stretching words throughout the sentence. Stretch the sounds more. ◆ *After 2–3m, or until all are doing it, coach—* Stop. Don't say another word. Go to places for your improv.

ACTING FOCUS: [It helps if the coach says the following in stretching speech, addressing parts of each sentence to a different actor.] Your acting focus, while doing the physical doing associated with your character, activity, and location, is to stretch your speech through the space to the person you are talking to and see it arrive.

RULES: There is to be no mentioning or commenting on the unique way you are all speaking. Avoid being selective. Every syllable of every word must be in stretching speech.

COACHING (as needed): Action. ◆ See the sentence arrive at the actor you are talking to. Extend the middles of words. Send the stretching words to the one you are talking to. Extend the sounds through the space. Watch the sounds travel and arrive. Stay on your acting focus with every word. **Every syllable is stretching, not just some of them. Avoid hanging out.** ◆ Cut.

FOLLOW-UP (as needed): Characters? Activity? Location? Did they extend the sounds of the words in the space between them? Did the speaking actors see the sounds arrive? ◆ **Actors, were you on focus? Did you allow the acting focus to lead you through the improv?**

SUMMARY:

What did you notice watching or participating? Usual answers to this question are: more aware of fellow actors; intensity between actors was extremely heightened; feelings were heightened; active & still was easier; bodies much more involved in the speaking; communication was heightened; more focused than usual; easier to stay on the acting focus; the space between the actors seemed filled; everyone was more energized.

Is that desirable? Absolutely. What causes this? The body's involvement with the voice, which is unavoidable when on this acting focus, creates a heightened presence. You are taking ordinary, skinny little words and enlarging them by putting your whole body *into each word*. That is a real commitment to communication. The enlarged words create a bridge between the actors. The actor's body may be absolutely still when speaking, but by extending the words through the space and watching them arrive, the body fills out every word, forming a bridge, which it then crosses over. The actor being spoken to feels the heightened impact of every word as it arrives at her because a whole body is coming across that bridge, and not just ordinary, skinny little words. This bridge of communication connecting the actors is in the space and is seen by the audience. Communication is heightened between the actors and between the actors and the audience or camera.

Did anyone notice anything about line readings? They were to the point and lacked excessiveness. They also had clarity, ease, and spontaneity. There was no effort to them and they felt spontaneous to say. Did you notice how you never felt rushed? You felt as if everything was taking the time that it should take.

Something special was happening with time. On stage time was heightened and expanded, moment to moment. You had the feeling that you were doing more in any one real second of time than you normally do. It's as if you stopped the clock for each second and heightened and expanded that second. This is a result of the relationship between the words and the space they travel through on their way to the listener. This acting focus forces the sound to occupy the space as it travels through it, heightening and expanding the theatrical experience. Don't assume that the moment you utter sound it travels and arrives all by itself, or that when you say your lines they are going to fill the space between you and your scene partners. It requires full body participation with the words. Sound is like a thought with wings. If you can put a full body focus in your sounded thought, you can actually reach another, timeless world of spontaneity and authenticity.

As with the other vocal doing acting focuses, your body learns what it feels like when it is physiologically involved in verbal communication. Over time, it will begin to do this on its own without the necessity of these extratheatrical acting focuses, which you could not use in performance. However, you could use them in rehearsal.

> **TO THE COACH:** The coach should practice speaking stretching speech prior to presenting it to the group. ◆ With an uneven team, use an actor from another team for the preparation, or the coach participates. The preparation takes about seven minutes; the improv, twelve.

PARTS OF SPEECH[11]

SETUP: Ideally, 14 per team; as few as 2 can play. There must be an even number of actors on each team. The team forms a circle with each actor pairing up with the actor across from him. **Introduction:** Step out of your circle and pick a topic for a conversation with your partner. Then, return to your original position in the circle.

Every couple has their conversation simultaneously. During the conversations, whenever you are speaking, you will focus, depending on the coaching, on either the vowel sounds or the consonant sounds within the words you say. You should literally pay attention and connect with the vowel or consonant sounds within the words you are saying to your partner, not your partner's response. This focusing on the sounds has nothing to do with what you are talking about. It simply occurs at the same time, regardless of the topic. You are to have heightened awareness of only the vowels or the consonants.

This is a new type of vocal doing acting focus in that it is not vocalized and does not create another way of speaking. When responding to coaching of "vowels," you are not emphasizing the vowel sounds *vocally*. The sentence will sound normal. However, you are involved in focusing on the vowel sounds as they come out of your mouth. When the coaching is "consonants," you do the same thing with the consonants.

Unlike full body whispering or calling, nonsense language, or stretching speech, the focus is invisible to someone watching and listening. There is no extratheatrical sound, rhythm, or speech pattern. With an unsounded acting focus like this, it is very easy for you to get so caught up in the conversation that you forget to do your acting focus. Choose to remain on the acting focus.

When we start playing, everyone speaks at a fairly low volume, just loud enough to be heard by your partner. From time to time, you will be coached to lower the volume further. Respond to the coaching and go with it.

In order to start, we must make your circle as small as possible. Slowly walk in until there is only a few inches of space between you and the actors next to you. We are going to start at a very low volume. Ignore everyone but your partner across from you. There is no focus until you hear me coach vowels or consonants.

RULES: Have a conversation with your partner. Ignore the other conversations. When on your acting focus, focus on those coached parts of speech that come out of your own mouth, not your partner's. Keep your volume low. Respond to all coaching.

ACTING FOCUS: On the designated parts of speech within your conversation.

COACHING (as needed): Begin your conversations. Lower your volume. Take one step backward and lower your volume. Vowels. Focus on the vowels. Take the time to do it. Don't avoid the focus. ◆ Everybody stop. Most of you are totally off focus and it is simply because you are not choosing to do it. You might be telling yourself that you don't know what the heck he is talking about with this vowel stuff, but that is not the truth. You are just not choosing to attempt it. When I coached you to start focusing on the vowels, you all just kept jabbering away. This is a major acting focus and you will not realize how much you are missing until you see the second team do it. They will profit from watching you. So, take advantage of my stopping you to get you to be on the acting focus. While you are talking, focus on looking at and paying attention to the vowel sounds. Feel them and connect to them. See them as they come out of your mouth and travel across the space to the one you are talking to. Get honest with yourself and choose to be on the acting focus. ✦ **Resume your conversations without the acting focus.** ✦ **Continue to speak normally and put your attention on the consonants as they come out of your mouth.** Speak at a normal rate of speed. Feel those consonants. Touch them. Make contact with them. Allow the consonants to contact you. ✦ **Switch to vowels. Focus on the vowel sounds. Stay on focus.** ✦ **Take a giant step backward and lower your volume. Consonants.** ✦ **Vowels.** Focus on the vowel sounds as they come out of your mouth. Pay attention to them. ✦ **Giant step backward. Lower your voice. Vowels.** Consonants. Lower your volume. Talk at a normal speed without emphasizing the vowels or consonants. Stay on focus and lower your volume. Vowel sounds. Focus on the vowels. **Consonants.** Feel the consonants. Make contact with them. Take a ride on your consonant sounds. ✦ **Giant step backward. Keep the conversation going. Keep focusing on consonants. Vowels.** Stay on focus. ✦ **Without any hesitation, close your eyes and continue. Vowels.** Keep going. Consonants. **Stay on focus. Commit to the focus. Allow the focus to solve your problems.** Just choose to stay on it. Play the game. Vowels. ✦ **Open your eyes. Vowels. Lower your volume. Vowels.** ✦ **Back up as far as you can. Vowels. Without any hesitation, close your eyes and continue. Trust the focus.** Avoid muscling the focus. Just stay on it and trust it. **Consonants. Vowels.** ✦ **Open your eyes. Consonants. Take a step forward and lower your volume more. Vowels. Consonants.** Stay on focus. **Take a step in. Lower your volume. Vowels.** Lower your volume. ✦ **Take two steps backward. Consonants.** One minute to complete the conversations. ✦ **Without raising volume, walk in extremely slowly toward original circle size. Don't raise your volume.** Continue your conversation. **Vowels.** Last opportunity to stay on your focus. Thirty seconds. ✦ Cut.

FOLLOW-UP (as needed): Actors, did you feel you were on the acting focus? Those of you who were not on the acting focus, you deprived yourself of an experience. The team to follow, you have to choose to play this. Choose to be on the acting focus and see what happens. We won't discuss it until the other team plays. Change teams.

SUMMARY:

Were you capable of communicating with each other through most of the conversation? Were you surprised how much communication was maintained when you were speaking across such a big distance at such a low volume? When your eyes were closed, were you somewhat able to continue communicating? When you were able to maintain some of the conversation with your eyes closed, you had a body experience proving to yourself that it wasn't about reading lips. When you were on the acting focus, did you have a physical response to the words you were saying? Did you feel your body was connecting to the words? Were you surprised how much communication was maintained with all those conversations going on simultaneously?

What were some experiences, if any, that seemed unique or new that you are willing to share? This is only relevant from those of you who participated on the acting focus.

What did you observe when watching the other team play? By the end, everyone is all around the room, and there are many conversations going on simultaneously with 25' of space between the partners within each conversation, and yet anybody watching could not hear any of the conversations, because they had so little volume. That is a lot of communication going on at an incredibly low volume.

How is this possible? It occurs because the same process is going on that we have been experiencing in the other vocal doing acting focuses. The result of your staying on this acting focus is that your body comes along into the verbal process of communication. You bring your body up and out and into each word.

When we learned stretching speech, we saw that sound occupies space. Picture each word represented by a short line in the space between the actors. A sentence is a string of these short lines. When your body comes up and climbs into each word, each line becomes thicker and bigger, taking up more space. You impregnate each word with all of your body. The lines are thicker and bigger. We actually need less volume to communicate because the word is making a larger impression *in the space* as it travels to the listener. If it makes a larger impression in the space, it will make a larger impression when it arrives at the one you're talking to, and it will be easier to receive. Pregnancies are all about potential. A pregnant word carries more potential than an empty word.

If both partners are doing this, what happens to the space between the players? The space gets smaller because the words fill that space with density. The more that that happens, the more these short lines resemble a bridge between the actors. When employing this acting focus, both actors are climbing up onto that bridge and meeting in the space between them. The space between actors is where all the action takes place. What happens between actors is much more important than what they are saying.

Did you ever act with someone when there was no connection at all? That is an example of a complete absence of filling the space between you. Focusing on the parts of the speech does just the opposite. It fills the space between you, impressing the words into the space and creating a bridge between you and the other actor. You make the space between you fuller and more available for the audience to see. It's great when you feel the connection between you and a scene partner, and greater still when the audience sees that connection. When there is no actual physical contact between actors, nothing connects them better than a bridge. You affect the size of the bridge by making a larger commitment to what you're saying. The commitment I am talking about is the willingness to put your body into the words being spoken. That's what *connecting with another actor* is all about.

Parts of speech can be employed at any time in rehearsal or performance, stage or camera, as an unsounded vocal doing acting focus.

> **TO THE COACH:** When coaching this, you may hear a tiny emphasis on the vowels or consonants without the actors being aware that they are doing it. If the emphasis is such that you suspect the actors *are* aware they are putting the emphasis there, then they are muscling and are not on focus.
>
> Coach while walking around the outside of the circle. In a low voice, privately coach individual actors, as needed, to lower their volume. When the circle is at its largest, the levels of all the conversations should be so low that no one in the audience can hear them.
>
> Coach the switches between vowels and consonants arbitrarily, continuously varying the amounts of time, from 30–90 seconds, that the actors spend with each part of speech.
>
> If time or group size dictates only one team will play, when the circle is at its largest size and actors are barely audible, privately coach one couple at a time to stop their conversations and observe the rest of the group for thirty seconds. Then have them resume their conversations and coach the next couple to do the same.

SOUNDLESS STRETCHING SPEECH[12]

This acting focus requires a preparation prior to each team's improvisation.

> **SETUP:** Same as stretching speech.
>
> **Preparation coaching:** We are going to start off in a similar fashion to stretching speech but it is going to change. Send a sound to your partner. Back and forth. New sounds. —*30s.* ◆ Focus on seeing the sound arrive. —

30s. ◆ Send a word to each other. Back and forth. New words. —*30s.* ◆ Focus on seeing the word arrive. —*30s.* ◆ Pause and listen to the coaching. When you complete saying and sending a word, gently throw a softball-sized space ball to your partner. Say a word and throw the ball to your partner at the end of the word. It's an overhand throw, a lob, releasing it from near your ear. Don't rush the throw. It is better if the ball takes more time to travel. Gentle lob. No high arc. Don't throw it at the beginning or the middle of the word. Release the ball when you finish saying the word, when you complete the vocalization of the last letter of the word. Partners, catch the ball right in front of your face. Then throw it back when you finish saying your word. Catch the ball, say your word, throw the ball. Resume sending your words accompanied with the ball throw. —*30s.* ◆ Continue what you are doing and add this: When you throw the ball you must focus on watching the ball travel through the space to your partner until they catch it. Say a word, throw the ball at the end of the word, and your eyes watch the ball travel through the space until it is caught. **Watch the ball. Keep your eyes on the ball. Keep the ball in the space. It is a space ball, not make believe. Throw the ball so it arrives at your partner's shoulders or head area,** no lower than the shoulder. —*60s.* ◆ Now, **say short, complete sentences to each other and continue to throw the ball at the end of each word. You do not go on to the next word in the sentence until the ball has arrived and been caught.** At this level, you do not wait for your partner to throw the ball back to you. You throw a different ball for each word. It is like an automatic pitching machine at a ballpark. There is always another ball there for the next word. Your eyes must travel with the ball, watching the ball travel through the space and arriving before you go onto the next word. Watch the ball. The person being spoken to doesn't catch the balls. Let the balls arrive right in the face. They are made out of space and there will be no damage. Don't act out the ball hitting your face. —*90s.* ◆

Keep playing and respond to the private coaching that is going to begin right now. ◆ The coach now coaches each actor individually, from right next to him. Until the coach approaches an actor, actors continue with the previous level. ◆ **Put your hand down and continue without throwing the ball. Say the words. Watch the end of the word travel and not the ball. Keep your body involved. Don't rush it. Say the word normally. Each word has a tail attached to it, like a kite tail. There's no ball now, so watch the tail. When the tail gets to your partner's face, you go on to the next word.** Stay focused on the soundless extension at the end of the word, the kite tail. Watch the soundless extension of the word travel and arrive. **Watch the kite tail, not the**

word. ✦ As soon as the word has been said, the coach moves his hand from near the speaker's mouth, shaking his fingers, across the space to the partner's face. ✦ My hand represents the kite tail. Watch my hand travel and arrive. Say a word and watch my hand. My hand is a kite tail tied to the last letter of the word. Watch the end of the kite tail. Now say the next word in the sentence. ✦ The coach rushes back to the speaker and repeats the hand business. ✦ Watch my hand. Keep your eyes on it and watch it reach your partner's face. Continue without me. After every word, watch the end of the word traveling and arriving. Say another word. Don't stretch the word. Just watch it travel. You are watching the last letter of the word travel. Watch the silent tail of the word without my hand. When it arrives, that is when you go on to the next word. ✦ 3–4 minutes for three couples. If they are doing it correctly, each word will have a normal pronunciation; however, there will be a pause between each word. ✦ **Stop. Don't say another word. Walk to PLACES.** ✦ Now, look at me. ✦ *In soundless stretching speech, addressing each word to a different actor—* Your— acting— focus— while— doing— the— physical— activity— associated— with— the— character,— activity,— and— location— is— on— this— soundless— extension— of— the— word. Watching— the— tail— behind— the— word— travel— through— the— space— and— arrive— at— the— one— you—are— talking— to. ✦ Your eyes get on the back of the word and watch it travel through the space to the one you are speaking to, and arrive. Avoid being selective. **All the words are followed by these silent tails. It is not about just speaking slowly. It is about watching the silent tail of the word travel through the space and seeing it arrive.** That is your acting focus.

ACTING FOCUS: While doing the physical doing associated with your character, activity, and location, focus on the soundless extension of each word of dialogue. See it travel through the space and arrive at the one you are talking to.

RULES: There is to be no mentioning or commenting on the unique way you are all speaking. Avoid being selective. Every word is spoken in soundless stretching speech.

COACHING (as needed): **Action.** ✦ **Share your voices.** Active & still. Avoid commenting on the way you are speaking. Avoid hanging out. **See the soundless stretched speech travel and arrive before going on.** It is not just speaking slowly, it's the whole process of watching the silent extension of the word travel and arrive. Say the word normally and then watch the tail of the word travel across the space to the one you are talking to. **Watch it**

arrive. Stay on your acting focus and don't take it for granted. The one being spoken to is free to stay involved in their physical activity and should feel free to do so. Speaker, keep your eyes on the tail of the word, not the word itself. One minute. Watch the silence behind the word travel and arrive, not just the word. Watch the silent tail travel and arrive. ◆ Cut.

FOLLOW-UP (as needed): Audience, character? Activity? Location? Did they keep the silent extensions of the words in the space between them? **Did they watch the silences arrive?** Did you notice them physically extending the silences? **Were they on the acting focus or did they just talk slowly?** Do you understand the difference between just talking slowly and this acting focus, which also results in a slowly spoken speech? ◆ **Actors, did you feel you were on the acting focus?** Can you tell the difference between the acting focus and just talking slowly? **Were you aware of physically extending the soundless extension? Did you have a body feeling accompanying that?**

SUMMARY:

What did you experience improvising with this acting focus? Usual answers to this question are: relationships immediately present and full of life; felt the power of dialogue and that it was heard; spontaneous speech—starting sentences not knowing how they would end and trusting they would end all right, like discovering objects near you, only it was discovering words; the words became so important that you couldn't waste one of them.

With this acting focus, there is a silent moment, or a silence, after every word and you are participating in that silence with the one you are talking to. The result of the earlier exercise, stretching speech, was filling the words between you with your body. In this exercise, you are filling the silences between the words with your body. Silences, like words, can fill the space between actors. Even when a sentence is completed, you are still participating in that communication. This heightens your commitment to what you are saying by filling the space between you with your presence. When you fill the empty space with your body's presence, you can actually feel where the space ends and your scene mate begins. If your scene mate says or does anything, it will reverberate in the space and you will feel it where the space ends and you begin. This results in your being more highly attuned to being in the moment.

This is another way to enlarge and heighten your presence throughout the whole process of verbal communication. You are, in fact, sending your body across the space to the other actor. You extend *you* out into the space. If the other player is doing the same thing, the essences of both meet in the space between you and embrace. This is seen and felt by the audience or captured on camera in a two shot.

When your acting is only within yourself, it is masturbatory. When you are acting in the space between you and the other actors, you create presence. You are available to be seen by the audience. The ability and willingness to be essentially naked to an audience, to show what others conceal, is the act of bravery that actors always display when they work. Soundless stretching speech allows you to feel the experience of coming out from behind your self-protection boundaries and filling the space with your bodies.

DIALOGUE

Soundless stretching speech creates a heightened connection between your body and what you say, to the extent that your body won't settle for playwriting because it feels so inauthentic. Bringing your body along into the verbal communication benefits you with authentic dialogue, improvised or scripted. Your presence is greater, your dialogue more important. In addition, as with any vocal doing acting focus, it is impossible to give a preselected line reading. All line readings are totally spontaneous because you are in the moment of the word a*s it is said* and not even thinking about the next word, much less the next sentence, until you come to it.

> **TO THE COACH:** If the actors are not getting it, they will speak in slow motion, without any focusing. Draw a diagram on the board of a word coming out of a mouth. Draw a kite tail coming out of the last letter and ask them to follow the kite tail. When they are playing, as each person finishes saying a word, *coach*— Now follow it. See it arrive. It's there! ◆ When the next word leaves their mouth, *coach*— Now, follow it. ◆ The preparation takes about twelve minutes; the improv, fifteen.

PHYSICAL CONTACT SPEECH[13]

SETUP: *2–5 per team.* In huddles, select characters, activity, and location.

RULES: You must have one part of your body contacting one part of the body of the person you are talking to for the entire time you are talking to them. Every time you speak, you must initiate and maintain physical contact. If you can't make physical contact, you are not allowed to speak. If what you are saying goes on beyond a sentence or two, the equivalent of a short monologue, then every time there is a new thought involved, you have to change your physical contact. If you are talking to a group, you vary your physical contact between them. The operative words are *physical contact*, not mere touching. A part of your body must be physically contacting any part of the other player's body that you are speaking to. Only the actor talking has to make the physical contact.

ACTING FOCUS: While doing the physical doing associated with your character, activity, and location, should you speak, focus on physically contacting anyone you are talking to.

COACHING (as needed): *After the location is set up—* Places. ◆ Action. ◆ Avoid rushing to dialogue. **Share your voices. Avoid hanging out. Active & still. No speaking without physical contact. You must contact the one you are speaking to; you can't get by on their contact of you. Discover new ways of making contact. Integrate different body contacts. Employ different body parts in your contacts. Explore using the whole body. Can you contact without just touching? Keep exploring** new aspects of physical contact. If you whisper, full body whisper! No dialogue without contact, even if you are speaking to someone who is already contacting you. **Avoid playwriting. Censor nothing. One minute to explore different ways of making contact.** No contact in anger! New thoughts get new contacts. Mix up your physical contacts. Change them midstream. Solve the problem without your hands. Discover how to make new and more varied contacts. Go with it. ◆ Cut.

FOLLOW-UP (as needed): Audience, location? Characters? Activity? Were they on their acting focus? Was all the dialogue spoken during physical contacts between the actors? Did they discover new ways of making physical contact, or were all the physical contacts redundant or repetitious? Were the physical contacts limited to the same body parts? Do characters have to speak all the time? No. **Did they find ways of integrating their physical contacts as parts of the whole scene? Did they employ active & still when needed? What did you notice about the involvement between characters resulting from the acting focus?** Physical contact created a heightened involvement between the characters. ◆ **Actors, were you on your acting focus? Did you limit your physical contacts to only using your hands? Did you allow the acting focus to lead you through the improvisation, or were you more concerned with improvising cautiously or successfully?**

SUMMARY:

Here is another approach to physiologically involving the body in verbal communication. The challenge of how to make the physical contact created a crisis to which your bodies responded with heightened and focused energy. Your bodies went ahead and made the contacts and then your acting followed what your bodies initiated.

What the body does, the mind follows. This is a major truth that many actors don't know about. The converse, however, is not necessarily true. What the mind does, the body does not necessarily follow. Your mind and emotions could choose to do one thing, and the body another. That's fragmentation, an unhealthy and inauthentic state for an actor. But when the body leads, *everything else follows in a unified and organic way.*

> **TO THE COACH:** Monitor all class discussion, from the introduction to the summary, and continuously correct the actors every time they use the word *touch* as a replacement for *physical contact*. When the vocabulary word becomes touch, the implication is that the contact is always hand related. Physical contact, rather than touch, opens it up to full body usage. As is the case with all vocal doing acting focuses, we are interested in the carry-over from the extratheatrical, in this case, the mandatory physical contact when speaking, to normal speaking. *Contact* has far greater potential for involvement between characters than does *touch*.

REFLECTION LISTENING[14]

In the final acting focus of this chapter, we turn the tables and experience the physiological involvement of the body in the *listening* process.

> **SETUP:** The group pairs up into couples. All couples sit on the floor facing each other.

Introduction: When we start the exercise, each couple will have a conversation. Take a minute to select a topic for that conversation. Avoid trivial topics. Select one that has some importance, something that you both know about or have feelings about, something that will form the basis for a real conversation. ◆ Allow one minute.

PART I

Here are some conversation guidelines. See if you can avoid asking questions. Also avoid using the word *I*.

Notice that in both guidelines, you are asked to *avoid* questions or the word *I*. You are not being told *don't* use questions or the word *I*. If you use the word *I* or if you ask a question, the other actor should not point it out. Just see if you can be self-aware of it and do not put yourself down. Do not make a drama out of it. Just notice it and attempt to avoid using *I* and asking questions for the rest of the conversation.

Let's now address what the acting focus will be. While I am talking to you right now, I want every one of you to reflect my lips with your lips. In other words, your lips should be moving without sound, forming the same words that I am saying as close as possible to the same time that I am saying them. You are reflecting my mouth. In order to do this, *you must hear my words and watch my lips.* You are looking at my mouth and that is helping you to silently reflect my lip movements. Your mouth is reflecting the words that I am saying at as close to the same time as possible. In Part 1, all you are to do is have a spontaneous conversation with your partner. You have your topic, and the conversation may take off in any direction it wants to. However it evolves is fine. When your partner is doing the speaking, you are to focus on *reflecting your partner's lips*, like you are doing with me right now. Whenever the speaking role spontaneously switches, so does the listening/reflecting role. There are to be no comments about the acting focus itself. One person is always speaking. One person is always reflecting the speaker's lips. In order to create the reflection, you have to be looking at the lips. You are not reflecting the face; you are reflecting the lips. *Do not change the rules of the exercise for any reason.* Look at the lips and hear the words. Put those two things together and reflect the other's lips at as close as possible to the moment they are saying it. You want the briefest possible time-lag between the speaker and the reflection. Share the conversation so you both get to speak and listen equally. This is going to be a two-part exercise. I will stop you all at the end of Part 1. Begin your conversations.

Allow 5–10 minutes. The coach walks around and unobtrusively monitors that the listeners' lips are moving and that both actors in each pair are sharing the conversation.

PART 2

Everyone stop. We will continue these conversations in a minute. Let's review what is going on here. If you are sitting still and not talking, you create no energy. But when you start talking, you do create energy. When your partner reflects you, he is taking in this energy in two ways. First, he is listening to your words and so he is hearing. The energy is traveling from the speaker's mouth to the listener's ears. Second, the listener's eyes are on the speaker's mouth, in order to reflect the words, so there is a second path of energy that is going from the speaker's mouth into the listener's eyes. The listener, who is creating no energy, is receiving two paths of energy, through the ears and through the eyes. These two paths of energy merge inside the listener and are then sent back out into the space through the listener's lips moving. With the listener's lips moving, he is now creating more energy than he would be if he were just listening normally, without reflecting. That is what you just did.

Everybody do the acting focus with me right now. While I am talking to you, you have your eyes on my lips. You have your ears on my words. You are taking these two paths of energy into you. The paths of energy are merging inside of you and are then expressed back out into the space through your own lips moving, reflecting my lips. Keep doing this. In Part 2, you play almost the same way. You keep your ears on my words like they are right now. You keep your eyes on my lips like they are right now. You receive the two paths of energy from my mouth and words. Let those energy paths merge inside you, and right at the moment when that energy is about to be expressed back out into the space through your own lips moving, *stop moving your lips.*

So, as I keep talking now, nobody's lips should be moving but you are playing the same exact process. Nobody's lips should be moving but mine. Your eyes are on my lips in order to reflect them. You are hearing the words I am saying in order to reflect them. Your body should feel the exact same way it felt when your lips were moving; but just at the moment you would normally move your lips in a reflection response, don't move your lips. It is essentially the same process, only you leave out the very last step of your lips moving. This acting focus is called *Reflection Listening*. Keep doing it until I finish.

This is the acting focus now for Part 2. Commit to the focus. *Do not come up with any reason whatsoever to improve on it.* Don't change the rule. Keep your eyes glued to the lips of the speaker. Keep your ears glued to the words of the speaker. When we resume, pick up your conversations where you left off. Avoid using *I* and asking questions. Don't move your lips. ◆ While you are playing, I will come around and tap you on the shoulder. When I do, stop playing, stand up as a couple, and watch the whole group while I chat with you. ◆ *Go right back into your conversations and stay on this acting focus.*

Allow about ten minutes for the rest of the conversations. After about two minutes, the coach begins selecting couples for watching the rest of the group. All couples must ultimately have this opportunity for watching before the coach ends all the conversations.

Single couple private coaching: The coach goes to each couple one at a time, taps them on the shoulder, stands them up, tells them to look at the group. Then the coach whispers the following in their ears—Look around the room. Just hear me as you watch everybody. I am going to ask you some hypothetical questions. Answer them to yourself, not out loud. Imagine that you are a stranger coming into the room and you see all these couples having conversations. You didn't hear any of the introductions, nothing about reflecting. All you see is twelve couples sitting and having conversations. Now, if you were this person watching and didn't know anything about what was going on, *what would be glaringly obvious to you about all of these conversations?* Something very significant is going on in each conversation that a casual observer would have to notice. What would that be? Answer that for yourself. Let your eyes wander around. Look at [actors whose faces are visible to the observing couple]. Look at [actors whose backs are to the observing couple]. Look at [couples where both partners are seen in profile]. Just answer to yourself what I am asking you. If you were this stranger, *what would you have to notice that is unique and consistent in every conversation?* ✦ Also, notice that if you were a stranger walking in now, *it would never occur to you that anyone is looking at anybody's lips.* Do you see that? ✦ Now, return to sitting and continue your conversation. Go back to your topic with your acting focus, and do not discuss any of what you just observed. Stay on your acting focus. ✦ The coach moves on to next couple.

RULES: As coached in introduction.

ACTING FOCUS: Part 1, reflecting partner's lips; part 2, reflecting partner's lips without moving your own.

COACHING (as needed to individual couples): *Part 1*— Keep the reflections silent. Share the conversation. Stay on your acting focus. ✦ *Part 2*— Reflect their lips and don't move your own. Share the conversation. Stay on your acting focus.

FOLLOW-UP: Were you able to maintain communication? [The group will answer, "Yes."] What did you observe when watching the other couples?

SELECTED STUDENT RESPONSES

—Everyone seemed so caught up with whatever they were talking about. I wanted to go over to each couple to see what the subject was—it looked like the most important subject in the world.

—The connection between everyone was amazing. Everybody was incredibly interested and involved in what everyone was talking about.

—Everybody was totally present. They were totally there.

—People were tilted toward each other; they fit together like puzzle pieces, like two parts of a whole. It was amazing to see so many people similar in their behavior, smiling and nodding; everyone seemed joyous.

Was the *quality* of your conversation the same, less, or more, than your usual everyday conversations?

—Incredibly more. It seemed the walls we all put up as people were down.

—The articulation of thoughts and ideas seemed clearer.

—I wasn't so focused on myself.

What was different about these conversations from how you usually feel when conversing?

—The intellectual level was higher.

—I was not self-conscious at all; it felt extremely intimate.

—I felt I could be honest because I felt I was being listened to.

—My mind didn't wander while my partner was speaking.

—I was more truthful; I didn't censor myself.

—Every single word of that conversation was important to me.

What did you notice about your own bodies during these conversations, your physicality?

—My body was more open and available; I felt ready for anything.

—My body leaned into my partner's; I felt drawn into what she was saying.

—My bad ankle did not hurt when I was on the focus.

—I was invigorated.

Does anybody want to say anything else?

SUMMARY:

Everyone has agreed on two responses to this acting focus. First, the quality of your own conversations was greater than normal. Second, everyone looked like they were intensely involved with each other, talking about something so interesting that the observer really wanted to be there listening and involved with them.

A scene without physical doing, inner doing, or conflict will be based on authentic communication. You want the audience to have a feeling that the dialogue and what's going on between you is so damned interesting that that they want to be there with you. The only way you can get that interest from an audience is, if what's going on between the characters is as interesting as you found while doing reflection listening. An audience watching these conversations will be drawn as if you were a zillion-pound magnet. When you are communicating on this level, you won't allow them to go anywhere else. This is listening at the optimum level. This is total physical body involvement in the act of listening.

You all noticed your bodies *leaning in.* Throughout full body whisper, full body calling, nonsense language, stretching speech, soundless stretching speech, and physical contact speech, you explored bringing the body into the words *you're saying.* With reflection listening, you put your body into the words the *other person is saying.* You involve your body physiologically in the *listening* process. That's what the leaning in was all about. If the person saying the lines is putting his body into the words being said and the listener is putting his body into those same words at the same time, they will experience what you felt. They will be totally involved in the present tense with each other.

IN THE NOW

The body feeling you experienced while playing this exercise is the body feeling that comes with being in the moment, focused on the here and now. You didn't run an inner monologue commenting on, or judging, the other person while they spoke. You didn't finish anybody else's sentences the way you frequently do in normal conversation. You allowed them to finish their own sentences. You didn't plan your own sentences ahead of time, nor did you feel the need to do so. You were on every word as it was said to you. That's called being *in the now*, or in the moment. It's spontaneous listening and speaking, totally authentic. Both parties are in the same present-tense moment at the same time, almost in communion, and almost in a reflect-the-reflector relationship. You are totally ready to go wherever the conversation between you goes. You are in a state of waiting in readiness, which is an essential feature of being in the now.

RESPECT

There is a word that captures every comment you made about your experiences playing reflection listening and watching the others play it, *respect*. Every moment that you're playing reflection listening is a moment of incredibly heightened respect for the other person. You are giving them your whole body in attention, without judgment, without editorializing, without commentary, and without inauthenticity. Utter respect.

REFLECTING LIPS VS. LOOKING AT EYES

In reflection listening, you have to be looking at the speaker's lips in order to reflect the words. For some of you, this creates a dilemma because you feel that it's important to look in the other person's *eyes*. We all agreed that it was not apparent that people were looking at lips rather than eyes, so there should be no concern that an audience will think you are looking at lips rather than eyes. Besides, you are still free to look in their eyes when you are speaking.

As to the actual experience of reflecting lips vs. looking at eyes, you were brought up to believe that looking into the speaker's eyes is good manners. It shows respect. I suggest that very often when you choose to look into the speaker's eyes, you are adding to the communication process a hidden agenda that is a breeding ground of inauthenticity. The hidden agenda is, letting that person know what a sincere and respectful person you are. You are selling *you* instead of being in the experience of authentic, spontaneous communication. The inauthenticity deepens as you go into your head and have private thoughts—comments similar to active & still traveling—about the other person. You impose your story about them onto them. That can be adventurous, fun, and romantic or it can be judgmental, dangerous, and objectifying, but it has nothing to do with the topic of conversation or the process of authentic communication.

The Greek philosopher Galen said, "It's not the eyes that mirror the soul, it's the voice." Reflection listening takes your focus to the speaker's voice and, as you have just experienced, enhances and heightens sincerity and respect, while totally eliminating distraction and inauthenticity.

What you found with reflection listening is that the other's lips are so active compared to their eyes that your involvement in reflecting the activity of their lips takes you off of yourself and your hidden agendas, inner monologues, judgments, and future-tense thinking and planning. You're so busy *doing* something that you get out of your own way. The result is *authentic communication* between you.

BACK TO ACTING

Reflection listening is not an appropriate acting focus when scenes are about a lack of communication, e.g., fights, preoccupations, subtext, emotional displays, etc. It is appropriate when any aspect of the scene requires authentic communication and demands that the characters, at minimum, respect each other. It's always important to improvise scenes about lovers with this acting focus. This focus can also be helpful in career interviews where you might tend to be nervous, inauthentic, or bored. It will transcend those conditions and make you present. Reflection listening is a perfect acting focus for rehearsal or performance with stage or camera acting, as it requires no extratheatrical doing.

> **TO THE COACH:** In Part 1, after the acting focus has been introduced and the actors are reflecting the coach during his introduction, the coach should monitor the actors to make sure their lips are moving.
>
> During the follow-up, if the actors replace *reflection listening* with the phrase *looking at their lips*, then there is confusion about the difference between reflection speech and simply looking at the speaker's lips. This must be corrected immediately. If the whole process of reflection listening is reduced to simply looking at the other's lips, there is no process, no focus, and no benefit. To clarify this, lead the group through the following—

Demonstration

> There is a difference between the phrase *looking at their lips* and the focus called reflection listening. ◆ Right now, everybody play reflection listening with me. Don't move your lips. So, I'm talking to you and the point I'm trying to make is that it is a focus of active doing. What you are doing right now is very active. It's called reflection listening and it is different from what I'd like you to try next, so that you can *see* the difference.
>
> Everybody stop reflecting my words. Get off the acting focus. Instead, look at my lips while I talk. Don't play reflection listening. Just look at my lips. Respond to my coaching. ◆ While I'm talking right now you should be feeling something very different from what you just felt in reflection listening. Do you see how you've just kind of gone away into your own thing? Your mind is wandering. You're not with me anymore. All you're doing is superficial attentiveness.

That is *not* the acting focus of reflection listening. Looking at people's lips is *not* what we have been practicing.

Now, everyone return to playing reflection listening with me. Right now. Do you feel the difference? When you are just looking at the lips, the mind wanders, and you become distracted and self-conscious. If you are truly playing reflection listening, your mind *can't* wander. You are too busy to be distracted or self-conscious.

Should there be any confusion about the difference between playing reflection listening vs. *looking in the other's eyes*, do the above demonstration and, for "lips" substitute "eyes."

Everyone has a great deal to say in the follow-up and it is suggested that, at first, the coach limit the group's responses to answering only the specific follow-up questions. *Coach*— Answer the question I ask and not the one you think I am asking. When we are through with the questions and answers, we will hear anything else you want to say.

The suggestion that the actors avoid using the word *I* and avoid asking questions has nothing to do with the acting focus. They are conversational guidelines that help things along. When you use the word *I*, you tend to tell stories you already know, e.g., "Last night *I* did this, *I* did that." There is no adventure, no spontaneity. When you don't use the word *I*, you are more open to having an adventure, going somewhere new, and discovering what is going on between you. Questions should be avoided because they interrupt the evolving flow of the conversation. Most of the group will still use *I*, and will still ask questions, but maybe a little less often.

Warm up for reflection listening with a few minutes of basic reflection.

VOCAL DOING REVIEW

When you are on a vocal doing acting focus, the body becomes more involved in the verbal communication thereby *heightening the verbal communication*. You want a *total body involvement* with everything you do and say. All of the acting focuses in this chapter are designed to produce the experience of bringing your body into the spoken word. With practice, there will be a natural crossover. You will start doing it automatically, without having to employ the acting focus. The more you have the experience of what it feels like, the more your body will demand it of you. You will start to know when your body is absent and you will know that you can fix this by employing one or more of the vocal doing acting focuses in a rehearsal.

An additional exercise available for increasing the experience of full body speaking and listening is to coach the actors to switch to normal speech in the middle of any vocal doing acting focus improvisation. After 15–60 seconds, switch the actors back to the designated acting focus. A vocal doing switch can be employed frequently during any improvisation.

To explore expanding the nonverbal component of verbal communication, vocal doing acting focuses can be combined with reflection listening, e.g., a speaking actor is focusing on stretching speech and the one being spoken to is focusing on reflection listening.

The important thing is to get used to knowing that there is a whole instrument there and if your toes are not in your words, you are not working with the whole instrument. If you were a guitar player, would you want to play with only three strings, or all six?

PART THREE

Improvisation Applications to Rehearsals for Theater, Film, and TV

6

FIRST LEVEL IMPROVISATIONS FOR SCRIPTED SCENES

First level improvisations are an introductory use of Improvisation Technique with scripted lines. They use only the acting focuses we've covered in chapters two through five, they require no script analysis or breakdown of any kind, and they are a valuable addition to the actor's rehearsal technique.

ASSIGNMENT

Over the course of a few weeks, the actors pair up and select a five-minute, two-character, modern scene, which they *memorize and rehearse in any traditional manner* they are used to. In the designated class, they perform the scene and then learn how to apply Improvisation Technique to it. All scenes must be from published plays. The scene should be rehearsed to performance level. No underrehearsed scenes allowed. Actors may use real or space props.

> **TO THE COACH:** In my classes, I emphasize the importance of selecting well-written scenes. Look for scenes from whole scripts, not scenes written for a scene-compilation book. Avoid scenes that are heavy with monologues, as these are dealt with later on in the training. The actors should select five consecutive minutes of a scene *as it was written*.

Don't allow the actors to make their own cuts within the scene or patch together parts of the same or different scenes. They may start a scene later than it really begins or end it earlier than it really ends.

Avoid scenes where the characters are drunk or stoned. Avoid accents, unless they can do the accent easily and without thinking about it. Avoid highly stylized pieces by such writers as Samuel Beckett, Eugene Ionesco, and Bertolt Brecht. The style should be realistic. It may be from a comedy or drama. I encourage the actors to select scenes from the works of Anton Chekhov, Henrik Ibsen, August Strindberg, Eugene O'Neill, Tennessee Williams, Arthur Miller, Lillian Hellman, Tom Stoppard, Noel Coward, Edward Albee, George S. Kaufman and Moss Hart, Neil Simon, Sam Shepard, Wendy Wasserstein, David Mamet, John Guare, etc.

THE EXERCISE

When the scenes are presented in the designated class, work one scene at a time.

Setup

The first scene is presented with a minimal introduction from the coach, *along the lines of*— They present the scene then I will get up and take it from there. For now, everybody just watch the scene. Let's go to the theater. ◆ The scene is performed. ◆ *Coach*— In order to begin, we establish the convention that we are in a rehearsal now. We close the curtain so there is no audience at the rehearsal. [The coach pulls a space curtain across the stage separating the class from the performers.] This is now a private rehearsal for the actors who are about to do an improvisation. Actors, here is how you do a first level improvisation on a scripted scene. *Like any improvisation we do—*

1. Select your character, activity, and location.

Who is your *character?* It is the same choice as when you are doing a nonscripted improvisation. Just choose what your character's occupation is (if provided in the script) and what the personal relationship between the two characters is. No dealing with personalities, back stories, reasons, and explanations, other than your occupation and naming the personal relationship. Does the script provide an *activity* for you? Choosing the activity is the same as our regular improvisations. It must be an ongoing physical doing activity with space props. If the script provides one, then that is the activity we will select. If the script doesn't provide an activity, the actors may choose any activity or activities that might be a part of the whole scene. If the given circumstances demand that there be no activity, do not select one. Where does the scene take place? The script always specifies the *location*.

2. Introduction to the improvisation

We have just completed the equivalent of a huddle prior to a nonscripted improvisation. You are almost ready to improvise. You know what you do for a living. You know what your personal relationship is, and you are going to behave toward each other according to that. You know your activity, what you are physically doing during the improvisation. If we have not selected an activity, then you are free to improvise any activity or activities that might be a part of the whole scene. You are also free to supplement the lack of an activity choice by improvising other physical doing through contacting the location or discovering objects near you. You know your location and that entire location is available for contacting during the improvisation.

When we do an improvisation, we always have a primary acting focus on top of our character, activity, and location doing. You always commit to that primary acting focus and let it lead you through the improvisation. We will select that primary acting focus in a moment. In this improvisation, *the only thing that is going to be different from our nonscripted improvisation approach is that when you choose to speak, you are going to say memorized lines.* Since this is going to be an improvisation, it is very important that you *avoid attempting to re-create what you rehearsed.* You have to be willing to let go of line readings, blocking, prepared moments, preselected emotion choices, pauses, etc. Just commit to being on the acting focus.

Whether or not you used real props in the scene you brought in, for this improv, you must use space props.

3. The coach selects an acting focus from the list below.

The actors will be familiar with the acting focus, from the training in physical, inner, and vocal doing. If, for any reason, the actor did not learn a particular acting focus, do not select that one.

FIRST LEVEL IMPROVISATION ACTING FOCUSES

Group I (Physical Doing)	Group II (Vocal Doing)	Group III (Inner Doing)	Group IV (Special)
Activity doing	Full body whisper	Active & still	Reflect the reflector
Location focus	Full body calling	Active, still, & discover	Space ball
Discovering objects near you	Full body singing		
	Stretching speech	Off stage/present	
Sharing an object	Soundless stretching speech	Off stage/future	
Eating and drinking while listening and speaking	Parts of speech	Off stage/past	
Physical doing drill	Nonsense language		
	Nonsense/English		
	Physical contact speech		
	Reflection listening		

GUIDELINES FOR SELECTION

To select the acting focus:

- Select a different acting focus for each scene.

- Comedy scene—Avoid Group III.

When the actors perform the scene the first time:

- If their energy level is low, choose from Group I or II.

- If their dialogue lacks clarity or sufficient volume, choose from Group II.

- If their energy is sufficient and their dialogue is clear but they employ little or no physical business, choose from Group I or III.

- If their performances are isolated from each other, lacking connection, choose from Groups II or IV.

It is very important that the coach realize that *he may choose any acting focus from the list and he will not make a mistake*, even if he doesn't follow the previous guidelines.

The coach should not discuss any reasons for the acting focus selection with the actors. Once the coach selects the acting focus, he provides any extra setup from the notes on each acting focus near the end of this chapter.

4. The actors do the first improvisation with the designated acting focus.

After the actors hear their designated acting focus, any special setup for it, or adjustments to the given circumstances (required for that particular acting focus), *remind them of the rules immediately prior to beginning the improv*— Approach this as you always approach your improvisations. Do your physical doing—activity, location, discovering objects near you—and stay totally on your designated acting focus. If the given circumstances or the nature of the designated acting focus preclude doing an activity, you are still capable of reaching and discovering an object near you or occasionally contacting the location. Stay very open to exploring any physical doing. *Commit to the improvisation acting focus and say your lines on cue. Your job is to stay on the acting focus and let the acting focus take care of the acting.* There is very likely to be new blocking and new line readings resulting from the acting focus and any new physical doing. Take whatever you get. That is all you have to do. Don't get in the way of the improvisation by attempting to hold on to the way you rehearsed it. Assume this is a private rehearsal and nobody is watching.

During the improvisation, if necessary, *the primary coaching is*— Stay on the acting focus. ♦ Or, use any coachings specific to the acting focus as presented in this book.

FOLLOW-UP: After the improvisation, there is only one question. ◆ Class, were the actors on their acting focus? ◆ If the class, the coach, and the actors feel the actors were not on the acting focus, then the actors do another improvisation with the same designated acting focus, before going on to the next step. ◆ If the actors were on their acting focus—

5. The coach sets up the second improvisation.

Now you are going to run the scene for a third and final time. In this run-through, there is no specific acting focus other than to *go with it*.

You are not to deliberately run it the way you rehearsed it at home, nor are you to deliberately re-create the way you did it in the first improvisation. If part of the scene ends up coming out that way, fine, but what you are to do is simply *allow your body to play the scene* however it wants to. Your body will know what to do.

During the previous improv, your body learned some important things about the scene. Your brain is not aware of what your body has learned. So, you have to *keep your brain out of it*. You are not to coach yourself while you are playing. Don't let your mind run the scene by attempting to set up particular moments or beats or by delivering lines in a preselected favorite way. Just play the scene as it unfolds and take a ride on your own body. *Stay out of your body's way. Let it follow its own impulses.* Trust that it knows how to play the scene.

If your body wants to come up with brand new and surprising business, feelings, or line readings, let it. If it wants to build on something you rehearsed or did in the previous improv, let it. If it wants to play a moment that it discovered during the previous improv, let it. If you don't let your body do what it wants, and you tell it what to do based on the way you rehearsed the scene and brought it in, or based on the previous improvisation, then there will be no room for a further payoff.

Do not attempt to deliberately initiate impulses from the mind for anything brand new. Don't tell yourself to "Go to the location" or "Do an activity." Just play the scene and get out of your body's way. Your acting focus is to go with it (your body). ◆ Go to places. It is probably better to *give yourself a new blocking position for the top of the scene to encourage the scene's unfolding afresh*. Do you understand your assignment? *Play the scene, enjoy it, and go with whatever happens.* Do not censor yourself. Whatever your body feels like doing, go with it. Keep using space props as needed.

The coach opens the space curtain. ◆ Audience, in this run-through the curtain is open for you to watch. You are looking at this run-through in comparison to the way they brought it in. Forget about the previous improvisation. That was a private rehearsal. Watch and notice for yourselves any differences between the first and the third versions.

6. The actors do the second improvisation with no designated acting focus, other than to go with it.

There should be no coaching.

FOLLOW-UP: Audience, did you see a difference between the first version and the third version? ◆ Actors, could you feel a difference between the first and the third? What was different? Did you like doing the third version? Did you make any discoveries? What were they? ◆ Audience, any improvement between the first and the third? What were the improvements? Can you be specific? ◆ [Optional] Here are some of the changes I saw . . . [describe improvements]. ◆ Before going on to the next scene, notice that the improv produced all these improvements. How much time did we take to get those improvements? Ten minutes. We simply ran the scene twice more, the first as an acting focus improv and the second as a *go with it* run-through. There was no critique, and no notes were given after the first run-through. The actors discovered all of these improvements *on their own*. We were just observers. ◆ Next scene.

TO THE COACH:

BENEFITS OF FIRST LEVEL IMPROVISATIONS

The differences in the scenes between the first and third run-throughs will be significant and numerous. During my many years of conducting these workshops, the follow-up discussions invariably reveal that the *third run-through results in a host of new goodies.*

Typical comments experienced from the *actors'* perspective include: total physical freedom and spontaneity; lack of self-consciousness; the experience of doing without thinking; more going on between actors; actors more in touch with the scene; much easier; emotions bursting forth; new relationship discoveries; more physical interaction between actors; more focused; exciting discoveries relating to character and emotions; more concrete, interesting relationships; more connected and spontaneous; more humor; more fun; stronger needs, hurts, and other emotions; higher stakes and more energy; clarification of author's intent; more physically and vocally powerful; total self-trust; discovery of new levels without effort; the experience of being totally in the moment; and the absence of preconceived notions about scene, character, relationship, and movement.

Improvements in spontaneity, character, relationship history, emotions, blocking, line readings and the overall scene will also be observed from the *audience's* perspective.

Summary of First Level Improvisations

The coach lists the name of each scene and the acting focus that was employed with it on a chalkboard in front of the class. ◆ We saw that every scene profited and improved with the introduction of a first level improvisation. After each presentation of the rehearsed scene at performance level, there were no critiques, notes, or direction. All the coach provided was the name of the acting focus, and you can provide that for yourselves. In each scene, *the discoveries and improvements were made solely by the actors.* These discoveries would now be available for further exploration, heightening or polishing in subsequent rehearsals. The third run-through is not meant to be a finished and polished scene. The improvs simply opened doors to previously unexplored levels of the work.

One of these doors led to discoveries about parts of the scene that you had not even previously considered. We usually know what we know about a scene; however, we seldom know what we don't know. Simply because you did not imagine or think of some aspect of the scene, should you be denied the opportunity to work in that area? First level improvisations are tools that allow you to go beyond the limitations of your thinking, imagination, and preparation and give you *access to the unknown.*

A second door opened by the improv leads to the realm of spontaneity. It's impossible to do a first level improv and not infuse the scene with a massive dose of spontaneity.

A third door leads to the filtering out of inauthentic acting. You may not even have known in the first run-through that some of your acting wasn't working; it was inauthentic. By the time you finished the third run-through, any acting that didn't work was replaced by authentic acting. Often, this allowed you to discover the true meaning or significance in the scene, especially if it had eluded you in your preparation.

The use of first level improvs requires extremely little time in proportion to the quantity and quality of the discoveries to be made. When you are rehearsing, just pick an acting focus, run the scene with it, and run it once afterward. How difficult is that?

Do you have any comments or questions?

Selected Student Responses

—I'm amazed and excited. We did a lot of rehearsing and I thought we had gotten to a high level; then, within three minutes of the improv, it went to a whole different level.

—I felt like I had stepped outside my body, and it just roamed and played. It was like a spiritual experience.

—There was no effort in the third run-through. It felt like I was at an amusement park having a blast. All these rides were happening and I could go on any of them and have a great time without any effort. A whole new, different world opened up.

224

—The physical experience was overwhelming. It took me over and pushed me in directions I would never have thought of. We rehearsed that scene as many different ways as we could think of. What we did here in the final run-through was nothing like anything we rehearsed. It was totally new.

—There have been some nights when I have left here saying, "Oh, this is cool. I learned something new in this class." Other nights I have left saying, "What the hell are we learning this for? What was the point?" From my experience of my scene, and after seeing all the scenes, I realized, "Oh my god, that is why we were learning that. This is what it has all been building up to."

—After doing the improvs, every single actor demanded our attention more. We were compelled to watch them. It was like everyone's charisma was multiplied by a thousand. I always thought charisma was more of a personal quality; certain people have it, and certain people don't. But it occurred to me in this exercise that everybody has charisma; it's just a little bit different for each person, and it's released by the improv.

—Everybody here surprised themselves—every single person here.

THE SECRET!

The one question on everyone's mind will always be the first question asked.

How do you choose the acting focus?

There is no method to it at all. Different acting focuses may address different aspects of the work, but unless you are a director there is no need for you to get caught up in what each acting focus might accomplish. *Any acting focus will do the job.* This is proven by the fact that we used a different acting focus for every scene. (The coach should review *Don't tell guidelines* in to the coach on page 234.)

How do you do this with an actor in the cast who doesn't know Improvisation Technique?

If you use an acting focus that is not extratheatrical, there is no need to tell anyone you are improvising. Say, "Let's run the scene again," and you go on your acting focus.

Extratheatrical acting focuses are those that would be inappropriate for a performance. With these, communicate with your scene partner prior to beginning the improv. Say, "Let's run that beat again. I find it valuable to play with the words, and I am going to sing all my lines, okay?" Don't be a know-it-all when you do it, e.g., "I have this great acting focus that always works and we have to do it. We sing our lines to each other!" Customize it so they know what is going to happen and give them the opportunity to say no. Use vocabulary they will understand; instead of, "I'm going to speak in *stretching speech,*" say "in *slow motion.*" You might add, "If you have something you want to do, that's great. If you want to go along with what I'm doing, that's great too; whatever you'd like. I just want to let you know that I will be trying some different things so you won't feel like you're being thrown a curve."

Use the approach that carries the most respect for your fellow actor. Be casual, supportive, unthreatening, and as simple as you can be. If it takes you more than thirty seconds to enroll them in participating, then you are putting too much into it and you are going to scare them off. Usually, most professional actors will say, "Great. Go for it." Some will even say, "I'll try that too," or, "I have something I like to do too, so after we do it your way, let's try my way."

Suppose rehearsal circumstances, or a pain-in-the-ass star, or a stubborn director don't allow for improvising? E.g., they block the scene in the first rehearsal and want every subsequent rehearsal to follow that blocking?

The circumstances may add challenge to how you improvise, but you can still do it. For example, if you must stick to specific blocking and can't employ an extratheatrical acting focus because it will upset the star and/or director, you can improvise with parts of speech, reflection listening, active & still, or off stage. It is not as effective as a full-blown improv without restrictions, but it will still serve you.

Also, you may be assuming that circumstances preclude your improvising. Keep improvising and doing more until somebody else puts handcuffs on you.

How do you do this when rehearsing on your own at home?

Most of my students tend to network with each other: "I have an audition. Can we get together and you read the other lines for me while I do my improvs?" Or, ask a friend. All you need is for them to feed you lines like a stage manager. If you have no one, put the other lines on a tape recorder, leaving blank time for your lines. There are a few focuses that you won't be able to do with a tape recorder, e.g., reflect the reflector. If you have to focus on your lines arriving at the other character, let them arrive at the tape recorder, which you should place in the middle of your rehearsal space.

If we were to work further on the scene after doing the first level improv, would our discoveries be retained?

Absolutely. The improv puts all the beneficial discoveries into the body, which will always retain what is authentic—until you show it something even better, which would happen through another improv. If you start doing traditional work after the improv, or if you don't pay attention to what you discovered, then you can get in your own way.

When you finish doing your first level improv, sit with your journal, your fellow actor, or director and review: What did I just discover? Articulate it as best you can and then commence your next rehearsal—if there is time for another—on that scene by paying attention to what you discovered. Stay alert to *exploring* it. At the same time, don't get caught up in trying to remember any moments or discoveries. "Trying to remember" is a head process, which will take over from your improvisational process and kill spontaneity.

Staying alert to your discoveries will also allow you to spot missed opportunities. Once your body makes an experiential discovery, it knows when it bypasses exploring it in a subsequent run-through. At that time, a simple follow-up for yourself will solve the problem: My body is telling me that I missed an opportunity to explore something. What did I discover in the improv that I didn't explore in this run-through? *Was I allowing my body to* go with it, *or was I trying to do something different?*

Trying to do something is different from doing something. Trying to do something is attached to a goal. *When you work with improvisation, there is no room for goals.* They are antithetical to being in the present and frequently create inauthenticity. Authentic transformation is more readily available when you are not striving.

On the other hand, when reviewing a subsequent run-through, you may notice that you missed an emotional moment that you found in the improv. Make a note that on the next pass of that beat you are going to explore that moment. It's important to use conducive vocabulary, i.e., *explore* that moment, instead of *re-create* the moment. *Trying to re-create anything when doing an improv defeats the purpose of the improv.* Change your vocabulary and you will change your approach.

Should we be concerned that we might lose good stuff from the preimprovisation rehearsals?

No. Acknowledge to yourself that this is now improv time, a time for adventure and experimenting. You are not negating your previous work; you're setting it aside to shake things up and see what survives the shakeup. What does, is good, worthy work; what doesn't, was inauthentic. Notice that when you did the third run-throughs, they weren't 100 percent different. They retained some of what you brought in. That means it was good, solid *stuff.* The stuff that didn't survive was limited; the improv replaced it with better stuff.

When is the best time in the rehearsal process to do first level improvs?

Complete your traditional technique first. Improvisation Technique is designed as either a supplement to or a substitute for what you already do. If you have no traditional technique, memorize, and then commence first level improvs.

How much material should we apply to a single first level improv?

Keep it under ten minutes of material. Also, you don't have to work in a run-through format. You can apply a fist level improv to a single beat if you wish, rather than a whole scene. The process is open to personalization.

In a rehearsal, should you keep doing it over and over with a different acting focus each time?

I would do one focus and run it again, just *going with it*. Then go on, rehearse something else, and bring that up to the same level. Then if there is time, and you want to, go to the first scene again. Do it with another focus. Don't do a train of focuses, one right after another, on the same material. You will wash the whole thing out.

When you employ first level improvs on a regular basis from job to job, you will discover your personal favorites and probably use them accordingly. However, stay open to employing those acting focuses that might seem personally difficult for you. The acting focus you fear, e.g., nonsense language, may be the one that ultimately leads you to the biggest breakthrough.

What about bad writing?

Any material will be improved. The better the writing, the more significant the improvement. The worse the writing, the more necessary the improvement.

Do first level improvs ever not work?

No. They always work. They always take you out of the head, infuse the work with spontaneity, fix inauthentic acting, and open doors for discoveries. And, they do this without the necessity of somebody giving you notes. After an improv, you may on occasion realize that a discovery is not pertinent. When you articulate your discoveries, you have to be selective: Let's explore this. Let's avoid that. If you have a director watching you improvise, he will participate in the "editing." Tell him as little as possible, if anything at all, about your improvisation process. It should be sufficient to say, "I'm going to try something. Tell me what you think." This is your technique. Your technique doesn't include explaining your technique to the director.

Remember, this cannot be done with material that is not memorized.

SPECIAL SETUP INSTRUCTIONS FOR EACH ACTING FOCUS

If necessary, in order to remind the actors what the acting focus entails, the coach should review the original presentation of the particular acting focus in chapters 2–5. If the coach isn't thoroughly familiar with each acting focus, this can be done with the actors right at the time the coach is assigning the acting focus for the improvisation.

Group I

ACTIVITY DOING   Prior to starting the improv, the actors—if necessary, with the class and coach's assistance—select an activity or activities that would fulfill being a part of the whole character/activity/location of the scene, i.e., "What might the characters be doing during this scene?" The activity selected must fulfill Improvisation Technique's definition of an activity, i.e., needs space props.

LOCATION FOCUS   Remind actors that during the improv, they are focused on contacting the location's set pieces and respecting them in the space.

DISCOVERING OBJECTS NEAR YOU   Remind the actors that whenever they are not moving, i.e., taking steps, they are focused on discovering objects within their reach.

SHARING AN OBJECT   Prior to starting the improv, the actors—if necessary, with the class and coach's assistance—select an activity and an object necessary for this acting focus. There are two available options: The activity and the object choice must be something that would be a part of the whole scene; or, the original location of the scene may be discarded and any object/activity appropriate to the acting focus employed.

EATING AND DRINKING WHILE LISTENING AND SPEAKING   Remind actors that they must stay at the table, making the meal last as long as the scene.

PHYSICAL DOING DRILL   After making sure the actors have reduced the scene to their character/activity/location choices, there are two options: If actors are skilled at their physical doing, start the improv *at the level of*— You're on your own. If the coach feels it is necessary, do the whole acting focus as originally presented in chapter 3 (p. 94). During the progression of the improv, *coach*— Focus on your activity. Contact the location. Discover objects near you. You're on your own.

Group II

FULL BODY SINGING   No special setup necessary.

STRETCHING SPEECH   No special setup necessary. It does require extra time. A five-minute scene in stretching speech can take up to thirty minutes, but it's worth it!

SOUNDLESS STRETCHING SPEECH   Same as stretching speech.

PHYSICAL CONTACT SPEECH   No special setup necessary *other than*— You are encouraged, when you are not speaking, to move, to go to different parts of the location, so you are helping your scene mate to improvise new and varied contacts. If the two of you just sit next to each other for the whole scene, you will dissipate the potential of the acting focus.

PARTS OF SPEECH   No special setup necessary. It does require the coach's participation throughout the improv, coaching the switches between vowels and consonants.

NONSENSE LANGUAGE   No special setup necessary. It is wise to have someone sit on book and allow the actors to call for line if they get lost. Obviously, the one on book will have to be very alert to where the actors are at any time in the scene and if he provides a line, he does so in English.

NONSENSE LANGUAGE/ENGLISH   Same as above. In addition, it does require the coach's participation throughout the improv, coaching the switches between nonsense language and English.

FULL BODY WHISPER   The coach creates new given circumstances that require the characters to whisper the entire scene. Stay as close to the original given circumstances as possible, but change one or more of the activity/location choices and/or add a given circumstance not in the original scene. For example, a scene in Clifford Odets's *Golden Boy*, where the prizefighter professes his love to his manager's secretary/girl friend, is moved from the original park setting to the anteroom of the manager's office. Both characters know that the manager is on the other side of a very thin wall in his office, and the door between the anteroom and the office is open! The **setup**, by the coach, for the improv sounds *like this*— ◆ Set up a new location. Go to new places and treat it as an improv: *Going to the new location, doing new activities, discovering new objects near you, and focusing totally on all dialogue must be full body whispered with a full open throat, never losing sight of why you must not be heard.* If her boyfriend hears you, you will both be in big trouble. This improv will change everything, so be totally willing to let go of how you rehearsed the scene. ◆ Action.

FULL BODY CALLING   Same as above, but the changes require the characters to call over a long distance to each other. ◆ For example, place the characters on opposite sides of a lake with no other people around, if the dialogue wouldn't be spoken in public. Or, place them on balconies with a giant courtyard between them, with or without other people around, depending on how private the dialogue needs to be. Other than a new location, there usually is no need to change the given circumstances. The **setup**, by the coach, for the improv sounds *like this*—

We are going to relocate the scene to two apartment-house balconies. Between and below them is a courtyard loaded with kids screaming and yelling, and the distance from one balcony over the courtyard to the other balcony is about forty times the size of this stage distance between you on your separate balconies, stage left and right. ◆ For your improvisation, you have to be willing to let go of everything you have rehearsed and commit to doing the acting focus. ◆ Behave toward each other in accordance with your character choices. The location is your balcony. There is no activity, however you are still capable of reaching and discovering objects near you while you are improvising. ◆ Your primary acting focus is full body calling. That is the one thing you must commit to. ◆ Places. ◆ Action.

REFLECTION LISTENING   No special setup necessary. Actors should be reminded that they are responsible for improvising new blocking that allows them to see and reflect the other character's mouth whenever the other character speaks. The **setup**, by the coach, for the improv sounds *like this*— ◆ Your acting focus is to improvise reflection listening with each other. Practice with me while I am talking to you. Your eyes are on my lips. Your ears are on my words. Whatever I say, you are reflecting my lips with your lips like you are doing right now. ◆ This is a preparation step. ◆ When you play the scene, you are going to start at the higher level, which we will practice right now. ◆ Keep doing what you are doing right now, only stop moving your lips. ◆ You are doing the exact same process that you were doing in order to move your lips in reflection, only you are nipping it right at the tail end of the process and *not* moving your lips. ◆ This means that you are really going to have to change the blocking because you are going to have to take responsibility for yourself to be in position to do this to the other player. ◆ The one who has to take responsibility for being able to do it is the one who doesn't have the lines. ◆ The one who *has* the lines is free to go wherever he wants and to do whatever he wants. ◆ The other person is going to have to take care of herself in the blocking in order to stay on the acting focus. ◆ Places. ◆ Action.

Group III

ACTIVE & STILL   No special setup necessary. Actors should be reminded of the rules of active & still as presented in chapter 4, i.e., when one speaks or moves the other goes still. The options available for traveling in a still are question & answer railroad tracks, silently continuing dialogue, and picking up. The actors should be told not to bother with the need to make turns.

In addition, there is one potential pitfall that will occur when an actor applies active & still to a script. When we do an unscripted improv, you never know who is going to go active or when. In a script, you know that when you finish your line, the other person speaks. In order to maintain the improvisational aspect of the dialogue, and to eliminate these predictability and anticipation factors, you have to deliberately let go of that tendency to know ahead of time that, when you get to the end of your line, your partner is going to speak. If you don't, what will happen is you will get to the end of a line and you will automatically go into a still before the other person goes active. So, you can *help each other by going active nonverbally through movement at odd times, instead of only when you speak*. If your scene mate has a two-line speech, then anywhere during her first or second line, you might deliberately go active through movement, forcing her to go still before she finishes her speech. Then, in order to complete the speech, she would have to go active again, forcing you to go still. This will help you keep each other on your toes and require checking each other out continuously. It will defeat the problem of knowing ahead of time when every one of your stills begins.

Another way of dealing with this is to assume that *you are not allowed to go still until the other actor goes active.* Don't say the last word of your lines and automatically go still. After you say the last word, keep staying active, nonverbally, until you see or hear the other actor go active; then you go still. Look at it this way. The *actors* know when the words end and the other person speaks, but the *characters* do not know this. They don't know that the other character is going to respond, or when. So, when you finish your lines continue being active, with movement, until the other actor *surprises* you with speaking or movement. Remember that you will also help each other if you deliberately go active at unexpected times, e.g., in the middle of the other's lines.

ACTIVE, STILL, & DISCOVER Same as above.

OFF STAGE/PRESENT, OFF STAGE/PAST, OR OFF STAGE /FUTURE These require the coach to lead the actors, prior to improvising, to a choice of the off stage event. There are three options. (1) The off stage event is provided in the given circumstances. The actors just need to have it selected for the acting focus, e.g., almost any scene in act 4 of Chekhov's *Three Sisters* is provided with an off stage future or present— the duel between Tusenbach and Solyony. (2) The coach provides a fictional off stage event that is not present in the given circumstances. (3) The coach may provide a different off stage event to each actor. With any option, the off stage event must not be referred to in the scripted dialogue. If it is, you have selected the wrong event for the acting focus.

The **setup**, by the coach, for the improv sounds *like this*— ◆ [Bill and Ben are doing a scene from Miller's *All My Sons*. The coach separates the actors so the introduction is private.] ◆ Bill, your acting focus is going to be off stage/future. Start to prepare when I talk to Ben. You are going to see the location in your mind's eye and you are going to reflect it with your body. You are going to see all the colors and reflect that. You are going to see all the people there and reflect that. You are going to see yourself there and how you feel about being there and reflect that. You are going to keep reflecting with your body the off stage event in the future, focusing on that for every moment of the scene and just saying your lines on cue. You have to let go of everything you have rehearsed, say your lines on cue, and commit to the acting focus. That means that every single moment of the scene you are exploring the off stage event, taking turns in the off stage event, going somewhere new in it. If that changes the blocking, then it changes the blocking. If it changes line readings, then it changes line readings. ◆ You are not to deliberately re-create one moment from how you rehearsed it. If there are sections that come out the same, so be it. If your body wants to do that, fine, but you are not to direct the scene that way. You will deprive yourself of the experience that everyone is getting from this assignment if you try to hold on to anything. Your off stage event in the future is your wife's funeral. ◆ Ben, your acting focus is going to be off stage/future. ◆ *Then*— Use the same coaching as above. ◆ Your off stage event in the future is your wedding in a small town in Alaska, where you don't know a person. Start preparing. ◆ Ben and Bill, commit to the acting focus. Take whatever you get. Don't concern yourselves with re-creating anything you have rehearsed. Take whatever comes up new. Ready? ◆ Places. ◆ Action. ◆ *The primary coaching is*— **Stay on focus.**

Group IV

SPACE BALL   The actors discard any location and activity doing. They simply play catch across the stage with a space ball. The coach may, if necessary, coach weight changes for the ball from time to time.

REFLECT THE REFLECTOR   The first improv requires three run-throughs. The actors discard any location and activity doing. They simply stand, facing each other, and play a full body reflection acting focus with specific rules.

Part 1. The character saying lines is the initiator of movement and the other is the reflector. The role of initiator and reflector switches as the speaker changes. The actors are to commit to the reflection acting focus, allowing their lines to be said spontaneously and not attempting to re-create line readings discovered in rehearsal. ◆ The coach reminds the actors of the rules and coaching of the reflection acting focus (chapter 4), i.e., the initiator does not intend to trick the other person but, simply to contribute to both parties being two parts of the whole mirror with as minimal a time-lag as possible. ◆ The initiator never comes to a stop. One movement always flows into the next. Movements can be abstract or they can be specific with space props. ◆ When you do the switchovers, when the speaker changes to the other character, the new initiator continues from the movement he had been reflecting instead of stopping it and abruptly initiating a whole new style of movement. ◆ It's not necessary to do reflection listening, just a complete full body reflection—except for reflecting the lips. You certainly want the faces to reflect each other, expression-wise and movements, but you don't have to reflect the words. ◆ *Coaching includes*—Don't cross the mirror line. Leave space for the mirror. Tell him/her your lines! Share your voice. Hear each other. Don't come to stop when you finish your line, keep the initiation of movement going until your partner starts speaking then just switch from initiator to follower. Help each other.

Part 2. After they have improvised the scene on the previous acting focus, they do it again with a new rule—in this improv, *the initiator is the person who doesn't have the lines*. So when one is speaking, the other is the initiator. The speaker is the reflector.

Part 3. After they have improvised the scene on the previous acting focus, they do it again with a new rule—in this improv, *the initiator is designated by the coach*. The coach calls the actors' names, switching them back and forth, so for periods of time, they are initiating (or reflecting) while speaking and listening. The coach gradually reduces the time between coaching switches until the switches are fast and multiple within any one line of dialogue. *Then he coaches*— Reflect the reflector. ◆ Reflect what there is to see, not what you think you see. Reflect everything. Reflect every part of the body. Reflect the reflector. Share your voices. Keep reflecting, totally, everything you see. Don't come to a stop. Avoid initiating. Everything you see is available for reflection. Reflect facial expression. Reflect breathing. Stay alert to everything. Renew your reflection. Reflect the reflector. ✦ The coach should get the actors to the reflect the reflector section about halfway through the scene and keep them there until the end of the scene. If the movements come to a stop, he can restart them immediately from the stop point by coaching an initiator by name, coaching switches, and getting them back up to reflect the reflector. This run-through is followed by the standard second improv—the *go-with-it* run-through.

TO THE COACH:

Assignment

The exercise will also work with classical scenes.

Performance level

If the actors don't bring in the scenes at an advanced stage of rehearsal, they waste the exercise, as their focusing ability is diverted to playing catch up or trying to remember lines.

When to choose acting focus

The coach should make his selection of the acting focus by the time the first run-through is finished so he can go from the introduction to the improvisation to doing the first improv with the designated acting focus without any hesitation.

Each scene/different acting focus

For the sake of the assignment and to make sure the actors understand that any of the acting focuses will do the job, make sure you choose a different acting focus for each scene.

Don't tell guidelines

Not revealing to the actors that certain guidelines may have been used in selecting the acting focus is important. If the actors finish this project thinking they have to follow guidelines, as simple as they are, then that would lead to self-critique of their work. The emphasis built in to this project is that first level improvisations require no critique whatsoever, can be employed with minimal time commitment, and that any acting focus will do the job, which is true. Any self-awareness about the scenes is focused on positive self-discoveries, and not on *fixing* things. ✦ If any actors reveal a reluctance to believe that any acting focus will do the job, *ask that actor and the group*— What did you see that was consistent for all the scenes, regardless of the acting focus choice, in terms of improvements. ✦ The group will answer, "Increased freedom, more authenticity, more connection between the actors, more full body connection to the dialogue, replacement of preconceived ideas with a massive infusion of spontaneity, which led to multiple discoveries, etc." ✦ The coach may then remind them that these improvements were consistent with every scene regardless of the acting focus choice, *telling them*— ◆ It would be foolish to denigrate all these improvements and cripple yourself with the need to know the particular acting focus that might lead to an additional improvement. ◆ Groups of actors conducting their own workshops can discuss the guidelines at the end of the project, after they have all received the training with the emphasis that any acting focus will do the job.

During the follow-up discussions, if the class asks why the coach chose a particular acting focus, *say*— ◆ Save your questions until all the scenes have been performed and everyone has done the exercise.

Vocal warm-ups

With the vocal doing acting focuses, the coach should have the actors chat with each other, employing the acting focus, prior to starting the improv so that they can practice and refresh their memory of what it means to be on this acting focus. *Remind them*— ◆ Your acting focus is going to be *soundless stretching speech*. This is the one where you say a line to each other and at the end of every word you watch the silent trail of the word as if there were a kite tail tied to the last letter. You watch it travel across and arrive. It is very important that you see it arrive at the face of the player you are talking to. Chitchat now in soundless stretching speech for practice before we start the improv. ◆ *After 60s*— All dialogue must be spoken in soundless stretching speech, like you just did. The speaker's job is to see it arrive. So, the speaker must find the listener. Whether you are speaking or not, you are free to go to the location, do an activity, and discover objects near you.

Off stage

When choosing off stage as the designated acting focus, it's the coach's choice whether or not to reveal it to the rest of the class prior to the improv. I don't tell them, just for variety's sake. It keeps the class on their toes as they watch the improv and figure out what acting focus is being employed. In the follow-up, it is revealed.

Number of scenes per class

With all the setup instructions and class discussion about the differences between the prepared scene and the third run-through, it takes about forty-five minutes per scene. Extended speech, soundless sound, and reflection take longer.

Scenes in subsequent classes

If the exercise is spread over more than one class, encourage the actors scheduled to perform in subsequent classes not to employ the first level improvisations as a part of their remaining rehearsals. ◆ *Tell them*— The learning experience is heightened if you have the same experience as the actors who performed in the first class of presented scenes. Just work your traditional way, the way you have always worked, bring it in at performance level, and get the experience of your first scripted improvisation in class. Once we complete the exercise with everyone, we can start to include that in your outside preparation for professional work.

Improvising Professional Acting Skills

7

CHARACTER

Find yourself in the character, a traditional acting catch phrase, has sent many an actor on a misdirected search for the similarities between himself and the character. This reduces the character to the actor's personal frames of reference. The author creates the character, not the actor. An actor who works only from what he knows about himself too easily misses creating the part as written.

In Improvisation Technique, the search for the character avoids any self-examination and focuses on the character as written. We look for the differences, not the similarities. The actor brings his own individuality and persona, but he applies these, organically and spontaneously, to playing those differences, creating a character who is *not* the actor.

There are two main components of doing the character. The first is creating the character's physical *body*. Wardrobe or costume and makeup devices aside, that means posture and movement. How does the character carry himself? The second component is personality or *attitude*. Attitude is a lifelong feeling embedded in the body's muscles, which informs and manifests itself in the personality and the body. Certain emotions first experienced and dealt with in childhood become fixed and held, forming the personality style. This is true for all humans and even truer for fictional characters. The Improvisation Technique vocabulary word *attitude* is different from the vocabulary word *emotion*. Emotions refer to transitory feelings. Attitudes refer to feelings held over longer time spans, i.e., the length of a scene, or a lifetime.

Except for warm-ups and preperations, or where noted, each scene improvisation lasts about six to eleven minutes.

REFORMED BODIES IN SPACE[1]

The work begins with discovering experientially what it is like to be in a different body. This exercise is done in the first character class and repeated, along with Part 2, in the next class.

SETUP: If there is sufficient stage space, everyone participates at the same time; or, the group may be divided in two.

RULES: Respond to the coaching.

ACTING FOCUS: As designated through the coaching.

COACHING: Unless otherwise indicated, allow a few seconds between each coaching.

PART I

Do the 40-breath process. ◆ Start walking around. Focus on feeling the floor with your feet as you walk normally with no exaggerated steps. Change your focus now and allow the floor to feel your feet. Keep your eyes open. ◆ Now, another focus change. Feel the floor with your feet and let the floor feel your feet at the same time. Feel your toes with your toes. Keep your head out of it. Focus on feeling the arches of your feet move. Focus on feeling your knees move. Focus on feeling your hips move. Focus on feeling your chest. Shoulders. Elbows. Wrists. Fingers. Whole arms. Spine. Neck. Head. Whole body. Feel your skeleton's movement instead of visualizing it. ◆ Feel your clothes against your body. Let the clothes feel you. Feel your forehead and allow your forehead to be free of censoring you. Can you feel the expression on your own face from the inside? Feel the hair on your head. Let your head feel the hair. Focus on feeling your body move through the space. Now, feel the space moving through you. Put it together. Feel your body moving through the space and feel the space moving through you.

Stop and take a step out into the space in front of you, and then step back out of it, leaving your body impression in the space in front of you. Take a step forward. Make your body's impression in the space and then step back out of it, leaving the impression there in front of you. ◆ Now, look at your body impression in the space. See it in the space as you walk around it. See it in the space, not in your head. See it there. —*Allow 30s.* ◆ Now feel your space body. Feel it all over. Avoid commenting on it. Just feel what there is with no comments on it. —*Allow 90s.* ◆ Now, continue feeling it, but with no hands. Feel it with your real body against your space body. Avoid hanging out with one part of your real body or one part of your space body. Use different parts of your real body to feel different parts of your space body. —*Allow 30s.*

Now, pick up your space body and carry it around the room. Stay focused on the space body as you carry it. It is made out of space; it is not heavy. As you carry it, keep the space body in motion. In other words, keep adjusting the *carry* so that you carry different parts of the space body as you walk around in any direction. Can you carry it in other ways, other than with your hands or holding it out in front of you? Can you use other parts of your real body to help you carry it? Keep changing the carry. Stay focused on what you are carrying. —*Allow 30s.* ◆ Now take the space body and set it down on its feet in front of you. Walk around it, seeing your space body. Focus on seeing all of it with all of you. ◆ Now reach out, and without hesitation, reshape this space body, keeping it human and the same sex as you. You can reshape the body any way you wish. Don't change its age. Don't change its sex. Other than that, any way you wish. Now is your chance. Would you like to alter your own body any way you wish? Reshape it? Stay focused on the body that you are reshaping. —*Allow 2m.* ◆ One minute. —*Allow 1m.* ◆ Thirty seconds to finish the reshaping. —*Allow 30s.* ◆ Now finish the reshaping. Walk around it and see the new body. Feel it all over. Feel the new, reshaped body all over. See it clearly. Walk around it and see all of it with all of you. —*Allow 30s.* ◆ When you finish walking all around it and seeing it, stand behind it, looking at its back.

Step into the new body and allow your body to reform itself to the new space body that you step into. Do it. Don't think about it. Feel your own body changing as it adjusts to the new body that it has just stepped into. From the inside, feel the new shoulders. Keep your eyes open. From the inside, feel the new neck that you are wearing. Feel the new stomach. Feel the new facial features. Don't freeze into it. Stand there, taking it on. If your new body is in a weird pose, you are free to lower an arm or adjust so you are standing comfortably in the new body. Feel the new head that you are wearing. Feel the shoulders with your shoulders. Keep your eyes open and keep breathing. Feel the new elbows. New hips. Legs. Chest. Feel your new, reformed body. If you need to, add breathing for a better fit. If there are any new parts of the body that don't fit well, breathe into those parts and the fit will take care of itself.

Now, *focus on retaining this new, reformed body* and walk around the room, retaining this new, reformed body shape, not letting go of this new body. Censor nothing. Take what you get. Stay on focus. You are now holding this new body on you. Allow whatever comes up to come up. If you are feeling tight or uncomfortable in the new body, breathe into it, deep breaths. Don't muscle the breathing, but breathe your body into the new body. Maybe it isn't meant to be comfortable in certain parts of this body. Leave those parts uncomfortable, or not. ◆ Keep walking in the new, reformed body allowing whatever comes up to come up. Don't think about it. Just do it. Your focus is retaining the new body. You have to hold this new body. Don't let go. ◆ Now, if you turn to your left, you will find a clothes rack with clothes on it in the space. Reach out, not letting go of the new body, and find the clothes that go with this new body. Don't think about it. Just do it. Reach and discover in the space. Put on the first costume that comes off of that rack. It's possible, as you put on the clothes, that they will reveal themselves to you. Discover clothes on the rack and put them on, accessories too. Maybe there's a hat or jacket that goes with that body. While doing this, *stay on your acting focus of retaining the new body*, not letting go of it. Don't let go. —*Allow 30–60s.*

When you are all dressed, keep walking around the room, staying on the acting focus, retaining the new body. Staying on the focus, see what it is like to sit down with this body. Walk up and down some space stairs. Write a letter. Perhaps there is some space business that you can do. Pour yourself a drink at a space bar. Select any activity. ◆ Throughout these activities, you have an acting focus. Always hold onto this new body. Retain it. Don't let go. ◆ Avoid hanging out. Explore the space. Discover how this body does things. How does it shop in a supermarket? Keep trying other things, but whatever you do, you have an acting focus, retaining the new body. —*Allow 2m.*

Keep walking around, retaining the new body, and now, discover each other. See the other actors and let them see you in your new body. Allow yourself to mingle. Allow yourself to talk, and take whatever voice comes out of the body. Don't try to invent anything. Don't try to censor anything. Just take what you get. Mingle and chitchat. Stay on your acting focus throughout the chitchat, retaining the new body. Meet new people. — *Allow 2–3m.* ◆ Stay on the acting focus. Keep retaining the new body. One minute to complete the conversations. Always retain the new body. ◆ Return to walking around by yourself and retaining the new body.

In the first class, proceed with the following shake-out process.

In the second class, go to Part 2 at this point.

SHAKE-OUT

Everybody spread out. Release the new body. Let go of the holds. Let the space support your body. Release your limbs from your body and let the space support them. Release your face and let it feel where the face ends and the space begins. Release all the holds and allow the space to support your real, actual, authentic body so that you are not holding onto or retaining the other body. Shake it out. Do the 40-breath process.

In the first class, go to Follow-up (Part 1).

PART 2

Stay on focus, retaining the new body, and just walk around. Avoid dialogue and respond to the coaching. ◆ You are outside on a clear day, two blocks from your new body's home, and you are walking. ◆ Stay focused on retaining the new body and make some choices. Take the first thing that comes into your mind. ◆ Who is going to be home when you get there, in relation to this new body? This new body is your character. Who is going to be home in relation to the character? Does the character have any relationships? ◆ Just make a choice and keep retaining the new body. ◆ Decide what are you going to do with this person or persons when you get home. Or, is there no one at home? What is going to happen with you and this person or persons when you get home? Your choice. Now, with your new body, your *character*, how do you feel about what is going to happen when you get home? Reflect that with your new body. It is a **double focus.** *Focus* on the off stage event in the future, which means seeing it and reflecting it, including how you feel about what you are going to be doing, and *focus* on reflecting it with the new body that you are holding onto. Practice the double focus, reflecting the off stage future with this new body that you are retaining. Keep walking. — *Allow 30s.* As you continue walking, you are going to change the off stage event as you remember something, the first thing that comes to mind, that happened earlier today involving your character, the new body. See it and focus on it as an off stage past. Take whatever you get. It is a double focus. You are *focusing* on what happened in the past earlier today and reflecting it with your new body, which you are also *focusing* on retaining. —*Allow 30s.*

Now, stay on this double acting focus, retaining the new body and reflecting the off stage past with it, as we move on to a **triple focus.** On top of what you are already doing, *chitchat with each other.* Do not refer to the past event, but that is all that is on your mind as you chitchat. Reflect the off stage event with your new body while you chitchat. Stay on the triple acting focus: off stage past, retaining the new body, and dialogue. No playwriting. —*Allow 1m.*

Avoid dialogue. Stay on focus and listen to me. I suspect that you were not on the triple focus just then. I suspect that you just went to chitchatting with the reformed body. I will give you the same coaching again. This time stay on it. You are retaining the new body, and every moment during any chitchatting, you are focused on reflecting the off stage past. *Don't drop that.* Every single moment of the chitchat, all that you are thinking about is the off stage past, what happened earlier today, and reflecting it with your new body while you chitchat on any subject *other* than the off stage past.

Resume chitchatting and stay on the triple acting focus. —*Allow 1m.* ◆ Stay on the triple acting focus. Avoid avoiding people. Meet and greet. Walk around. —*Allow 2m.*

Walk around and avoid dialogue. Respond to the coaching. Retain the body. Don't let go. Walk around in a park. Enjoy the park. Look around you. Drop the off stage focus. You are back to a **single focus** of retaining the new body. See all these other people in the park. Let them see you as you hold onto the new body. You see them and let them see you. Now you are going to meet and greet people you haven't seen before, only this time, there is no off stage. Chitchat with new people who you haven't spoken with before. Stay on the focus of retaining the body. —*Allow 2m.* ◆ Everyone return to walking around the room. Last opportunity to focus on retaining the new body. Just walk around and avoid dialogue. Focus on the new body.

Very shortly, I am going to give you a cue that will be your exit. The park is actually a stage setting, and when I give you a cue, you will have reached the wings. Stay on focus. The exercise will not be over when you think it is, so stay alert until I have coached you that we are through. Okay, everybody is in the wings. You are off stage.

At this point in the second class, do the shake-out process from the end of Part 1. The exercise is not over; continue to respond to the coaching. Everybody start heading back to your chairs, which are in your dressing room. Avoid talking to anybody. You are off stage and you don't have to come back on for another half-hour. *Wait a minute!* The stage manager runs up to you and reminds you that they added another scene for you this afternoon. You have another entrance right now. Return to your new body character, take it on immediately, and enter. Focus on the new body. Same character. Chitchat with the first person you encounter. Play your new scene. Improvise chitchat. —*Allow 30s.* ◆ Now we are over. Do a stretch and some nonsense language.

FOLLOW-UP (as needed): Part 1: Were you capable of staying on the acting focus? When you stepped into the new body, were you open to letting the new body effect changes in your body? Did you feel those changes? Did you observe if your real body actually changed? Were your voices different in any way? Did you discover that or did you select that? Discovered it. Did you notice if the rhythms of your own body changed? Did you discover anything else? ◆ *If no one volunteers the following, ask* — **Did you discover the emergence of an attitude or new personality?** What kind of attitude emerged? Did the new body have a different attitude than your own body has?

SUMMARY:

Part 1: Let's review the facts we have observed: (1) Everyone experienced some changes in their bodies. These changes showed up in your posture and the way you walked. (2) Everyone's voices were affected. (3) Everyone's rhythms were affected. (4) Everyone discovered the emergence of an attitude.

Notice that none of the changes were coached. The coaching was directed at simply reshaping your body. Yet with that reshaping, all these changes emerged.

It is important to notice that you began this exercise walking around in a focus walk and ended up embodying, or creating, a character other than yourself. This character had a different body, voice, and personality. This character's body, voice, and personality all fit together like parts of the same whole. Most of you were totally surprised by the emergence of the new personality or attitude, or by voice changes. You didn't anticipate or expect that. When you mingled with each other, you were also surprised by what you said and by what you noticed about each other. You looked at each other differently. You were surprised by how it felt to be overweight, or beautiful, or taller. You only changed your body. You weren't expecting a change in your perspective as well. You thought thoughts that you don't usually think. You were surprised by how much more quickly, or more slowly, your emotions engaged. Anything that happens in your acting that you didn't expect, anything surprising, is *spontaneous*. When you are spontaneous, you are always out of the head and authentic. When you're in the head, you never surprise yourself. When you are out of the head, lots of surprises happen.

As we go further in this chapter, we will always be dealing with the creation of a character. You will be exposed to different acting focuses and you should stay alert to what is consistent from acting focus to acting focus. The consistent features let you know what is necessary in the creation of a character.

> **TO THE COACH: Part 1:** The types of attitudes that will emerge include, to a greater or lesser extent, self-esteem, vulnerability, confidence, beauty, fat, skinny, mischievous, cocky, daring, adventurous, sad, funny, scared, angry. ◆ Some actors will feel relief upon returning to their own body. In each case, the actor probably discovered an emergence in the reformed body of a negative attitude, e.g., despair, helplessness, or fear. ◆ If an actor experienced little change in his attitude or perspective, the coach should ask him if the alterations he made with his space body were minor or minimal. The smaller the changes in his physicality, the smaller the other changes will be.

FOLLOW-UP (as needed): Part 2: *Use the Part 1 follow-up, plus the following.* ◆ **Did you alter your space body in different ways from the last time we did this? Were the attitudes different?** Describe the difference between this new attitude and the attitude that emerged in the reformed body in the last class.

Everybody experienced changes in their bodies. Voices were affected. Rhythms were affected. Everyone discovered the emergence of an attitude. When the off stage component was added, were you able to remain on the double acting focus? **What did you notice after you brought the new body with its new attitude to the off stage event and reflected that?** Did your character change as a result of your focusing on the off stage event or did you just discover new aspects of the character? For instance, did your character not change, but, experience new or different emotions? Did your attitude influence your response to the off stage event? How? ♦ Did you notice a difference in your dialogue when you were coached to stay on the off stage focus? Were you capable of staying on the triple acting focus? If you were, you were improvising character, dialogue, and subtext. The subtext, the off stage event, influenced what you said. Did you feel the difference in that chitchat from all the other chitchat segments? ♦ **When you came back from the false exit, did you have any difficulty getting back to the character?** (The class will respond, "No.")

SUMMARY:

Part 2: Returning to the character was easy, effortless, and immediate. The earlier work in reforming your body and retaining it pays total physical attention to your new body. You had an *experiential* relationship with that reformed body while it was in the space, making it more tangible when you put it on. Then, when you stepped into the new body, physicalized it, and improvised while focusing on retaining it, your body created a muscle memory of it. Once it has muscle memory, your body knows what to do. It can go back to it at a moment's notice. It's like riding a bike. Once you've learned something experientially, you'll have it for life. Your body knows what to do. This is very important in film work where you are shooting snippets of scenes over a long period of time with lots of down time in between.

Paying physical attention is different from paying mental attention. When you create a character from mental preparation only, the body has no knowledge of what to do. Also, if you only learn it in the head, e.g., writing a character biography without turning it into a physical experience, it doesn't stay with you. When you physicalize something, your body knows what to do and can create it over and over for a very long time.

The secret to character work is the body. Once you are physically in the character's body, the character starts to build on different levels. The body provides you with the emergence of an attitude. You all discovered that an attitude came up today just like the last time we did this, but it was a different attitude each time. A different body creates a different attitude.

By reforming the body in the space prior to stepping into it, we avoid any visualizing, which takes place in the head and takes us out of the present tense. On the other hand, visualization enters the process when we apply an off stage event, or subtext. Whenever there is subtext, the character is not supposed to be totally present. There is something on his mind. There may be a hidden agenda. The scene is not about what it appears to be about. We bring our subtextual off stage into the present as much as possible by attaching our visualization of it to a very present-tense process, reflection of it with the body. In this case, our reflection instrument is the character's body.

For some of you, the addition of the off stage focus added to the creation of your character. Off stage is always a worthwhile improvisational acting focus when working on a scripted scene. Every scene can have an off stage event. The author may or may not have provided it in the given circumstances. If he hasn't, then you select it. Take a walk around the room in your character's body and focus on reflecting it. See what doors open. Every open door has the possibility of a discovery on the other side of it. That discovery may feed what you're doing. Explore!

ANIMALS[2]

The second acting focus for exposing the actors to the components of creating a character is *Animals*.

SETUP: 2–5 per team. In huddles, select character (occupation and/or personal relationships), activity, and location. First team sets up its location. If there is sufficient stage space, the entire group walks around the stage to learn the animal acting focus. Otherwise, team by team.

Introduction coaching: Let's do a **group preparation** to learn the acting focus. At the end, everybody will sit down except the first team. Their location has been set up and they will go to places and begin their improvisation. We'll do a **miniprep** for each successive team. ◆ Do the 40-breath process. ◆ Everyone walk. Focus on your body moving through the space. Focus on feeling the space moving through you. Now, move through the space and feel the space moving through you at the same time.

Group preparation: Everybody select an animal. Just select it. Don't do anything with it. Respond to the coaching as we go further. ◆ Focus on changing your **forehead** to take on the exact physical characteristics of the animal you have selected. Move your forehead around. Sculpt your forehead. You can move your forehead with muscle control from within or you can use your hands on the forehead, or both. Your choice. There should be a real physical moving of the forehead. You are changing your forehead to take on the characteristics of the animal's forehead. It requires some contortion. It is not an idea. It is not a concept. It is truly a muscle control issue. You want to move that forehead around, eventually taking your hands away if you were using them, and holding the new forehead through muscle control. From here on in, don't let go of this. Hold it in place through muscle control.

Without letting go of the new forehead, do the same thing with your **nose.** Take on the characteristics of your animal's nose or beak or whatever the equivalent would be. Move it about. When you have the nose, don't let go of the forehead. Feel the joining of forehead and nose. Through muscle control, you are holding onto and not letting go of a new kind of nose and a new kind of forehead. You must feel that you are using muscle control to hold everything in place, otherwise you are off the acting focus. Don't let go from here on in. ◆ Now, take on the animal's **jaw,** or the equivalent of a jaw. Make sure that there is a **mouth** in there with some sort of **lips.** Make sure that it feels like a part of the face that you have already constructed two-thirds of: the forehead, the nose, and this is the final third. ◆ You now have a whole new face, which you are holding onto through muscle control. If your face feels like it always feels, you are not on the acting focus. Keep holding it on. Don't let go of it.

Now, we are going to reshape your **spine.** If your animal walks on all fours, then get on the ground and walk on all fours. The focus now, while not letting go of the face, is taking on the spine of this animal. ◆ So now, through muscle control, you have a reshaped face and a reshaped spine. Don't let go of it. ◆ How does the **tail** affect this animal? Feel the tail in place and feel how it works. Feel how it affects the spine. ◆ Focus on taking on the characteristics of the **back legs** or the equivalent of them. What is at the end of those legs, paws? Claws? Include that in your physical transformation. ◆ Don't let go of those body parts that we have already physicalized. ◆ Now, focus on the **front legs.** What is on the end of the front legs? The front legs might be wings. Let your hands and arms take on the physical characteristics of that animal. ◆ Don't let go of any body parts that we have already paid attention to. We are adding to what we have done. We are reforming the body to take on the characteristics of this chosen animal.

Don't let go of anything you have discovered. Retain it and focus on the **rhythm.** How does this animal move? Include that as a part of your whole animal, reshaping what you are doing. Retain everything you have found. Don't let go. ◆ How does this animal **see?** Avoid getting involved with your fellow actors, but focus on seeing them. Add that to what you are doing. Don't let go. Does seeing them affect the physicalization of your animal in any way? Now focus on how your animal allows other animals to see it. Again, don't get involved with the other actors, but in your physicalization include an awareness of how your animal allows other animals to see it. Does it allow other animals to see it? Don't let go of anything we have already done. ◆ Now, without any hesitation, add the **sounds** of your animal. Let's hear the sounds.

Coach to individual players (as needed): Make a sound, even if you don't know what that animal sounds like. Just go for it immediately and see what sounds come out. It doesn't have to be the correct sound. There is no right or wrong. Take what you get. Heighten that sound. Come up with one and heighten it. Let me hear the sound. Explore the sound. Take a risk. Don't let go. Keep holding it on the face and in the body.

Coach to the group: Everybody, lose the sound. Keep holding onto the face and body but lose the sound. ◆ Now, without any hesitation, keep maintaining the animal's characteristics but **evolve your animal.** Your animal now walks on two legs. Keep holding it on the face. Keep the rhythms and all the physical characteristics. Bring the essence of everything that you did as a four-legged animal into a two-legged version. That's it. Keep retaining it on the face. Everything is the same as it was; it is just that this animal walks on two legs. Be aware of your fellow actors as you hold onto your own physicalization. ◆ Now, bring your actual animal sounds to this new two-legged version, the same animal sounds. Heighten that sound. ◆ Everybody, lose the sounds. When I give you the next cue, you are going to take everything that you are doing right now and you are going to evolve one step further into a human being, but you must retain most of what you have going, the face, the body, the rhythms. The pitfall is, you can lose too much. It's important at this stage to retain as much as you can of what you have created. ◆ Now, with the slightest adjustment, be a human being who moves like this, whose face is held like this, whose rhythms are like this. Don't lose the physical characteristics. You are humans, but don't lose these characteristics. Dare to be big! Have that face. Retain that face. That is the one thing that you don't need to lose at all. ◆ Now, while you are doing this, add the full animal sound. Retaining these animal sounds, now make the slightest adjustment into saying words. Do any familiar monologue, or the Gettysburg Address, or any speech, and bring that animal's sound into the voice. ◆ Now, everybody but the first team drop the holds of the animals and walk through the space back to the audience. ◆ First team, stay right with what you are doing. Keep the sounds and words going. Retain what you have created.

Coach to individual actors on the first team: How do those arms move? What is your name? Can you get more of your animal's sound into your voice? Say some words with that sound. Okay, [Shelly], keep holding it on the face and in the body and make the sounds. Don't let go. Over here is a table (in space) and it is full of food. Make yourself a sandwich while focusing on retaining your animal's characteristics. ◆ Hi. What is your name? Hi, [Sally]. (Shake hands.) That is how your hands work? Is your hand that strong? What feels right? Remember, you are not an animal. You are a woman with these characteristics. Over here is a closet (in space) full of clothes. Why don't you open it and see if you like anything. Stay on your acting focus and retain the characteristics of the animal on the face and in the body. Try something on. ◆ *The coach returns to each actor*— Hi, [Shelly]. Are you having a good time? What did you find to eat? Good. Now, retain the animal's characteristics in the face and in the body. ◆ Everybody, go to places. Remember that your character is not finished and polished. You are on an active and continuous acting focus of retaining these animal characteristics. ◆ Action.

RULES: Employ physical doing tools of Improvisation Technique for activity, location, relationships, and occupation.

ACTING FOCUS: Retaining the animal's characteristics in your face, body, and voice.

COACHING (as needed): Check out your fellow actors. Stay on your acting focus. Retain this animal's characteristics in the face, body, and voice. Don't let go. Use your muscle control to retain all of the characteristics. Keep it on the face and in the body. Keep it in the voice. Retain the animal's vocal qualities. Share your voices. Put words to that sound. **Avoid hanging out.** Get involved with the physical doing. Do an activity. Go to the location. Discover objects. Avoid conflict. Active & still. Stay alert to each other. **Stay open and available to converging with or helping another character.** Stay open to meeting each other. **Censor nothing. One minute to stay on you acting focus, censor nothing and avoid conflict.** ◆ Cut.

FOLLOW-UP (as needed): Character? Activity? Location? **Were the actors on the acting focus? Did they consistently hold onto the animal characteristics throughout?** Were their bodies different? Were they open to transforming their own bodies? **Did they reveal character qualities or characteristics that we have not seen from them before in class?** Were their voice qualities different, their rhythms different? Do you feel that they were afraid to let go? ◆ Actors, do you agree? **Did you discover the emergence of an attitude? What attitude came up for you? Did that attitude stay consistent and remain with you throughout the improv?** ◆ **Audience, did you see that attitude?** ◆ Actors, did your voices change?

Did emotions come up? It's not important that we know which animal but, for the fun of it, which animal did each actor use?

Miniprep: *After they set up their location—* Walk around and focus on your body moving through the space. Focus on feeling the space moving through you. Move through the space and feel the space moving through you at the same time. ◆ Let's return to the animal you worked with earlier. Reshape your forehead. Same animal. Don't get ahead of the coaching. Hold onto it. Retain it. Don't let go. ◆ Now reshape your nose. Attach it to the forehead using muscle control. Reshape your jaw. Add that to the face. You have to hold on the animal's face. You have returned to it and you are retaining it. ◆ Now, unless your animal walks on only two legs, get on all fours and focus on the spine. Don't let go of the face. Focus on the spine. Include the tail. How does the tail affect the movement of the animal? Legs! Feet! Paws! Claws! Wings! ◆ Focus on the rhythm. Don't let go of any body parts we have already addressed. Add your ability to see other animals. Don't get involved with them, but see your fellow animals and allow them to see you. ◆ Add the sounds. Keep the sounds going. Heighten the sounds. Now, do the two-legged animal version. You are still the animal with those sounds. Keep the sounds going. Heighten that sound. ◆ Go to the next level. Go one more evolution to the human version. You are retaining most of what you have discovered but it's the human version. You have the same face, same body configurations, same rhythms, but there is a human element to it now. Keep the animal sounds going. ◆ Now, go immediately into words and let the sounds inform the voice. Go into dialogue. Say lines, lyrics, a monologue, anything.

Coach to the individual players (as needed): Same as above. ◆ Places. You are going to do all your physical doing, and your acting focus throughout the scene is retaining these animal characteristics. Don't let go of them. It is better to be too big than too small. This is your workshop. ◆ Action

SUMMARY:

With our first character acting focus, reformed body in space, we only improvised some brief chitchatting. Now, with animals as our character catalyst, we have gone further by improvising scenes as we held onto the character as influenced by the animals. This is still the beginning of character work. You should not equate character with either of these acting focuses. Instead, notice what is similar and consistent about these and the character acting focuses to come. Allow each to reveal certain truths about what it takes to create a character. Use your journals during this period to assist you in making your observations.

TO THE COACH: Before the huddles, *advise the actors*— Avoid outrageous choices. Your character, activity, and location choices should be fairly down to earth. Don't be frogmen searching Atlantis for your transvestite uncle. Avoid astronauts on the moon and vampires from hell. In all of the character work huddles, outrageous choices deflect us from our purpose of learning how to create characters for script acting.

When coaching individuals and asking for their names, if necessary, coach the actors to retain their own names and not change them. Changed names are not familiar to improv mates and frequently give a lie to their relationships.

If the actors have difficulty retaining the animal-influenced character, here is an extra section for the preparation part:

When the actors are most fully retaining the animal's characteristics in a human form, coach— While holding onto your animal's characteristics, step out into the space and then step backward, leaving your character's impression in the space in front of you. Walk around it. See it. Feel it. Get to know it. This is not a reshaping. You are already in character and your space impression is simply a duplication of what you already are doing. Feel it and get to know your facial expression, height, weight, and posture. Talk to it. Retain the animal's characteristics in your voice. Walk around it, retaining the animal's rhythm. Look at it. It should be similar to looking in a mirror. Let the space body reflect you. You reflect it. Step into it again. Walk around and retain your animal's characteristics.

If the actors lose their animal characteristics during the improv, coach— Everyone immediately become your animal again! Get on all fours! Make the sounds. Heighten it! Now, right back to the evolved human with these characteristics. Resume the improv.

❖ ❖ ❖

BODY CENTER[3]

SETUP: 2–5 per team. In huddles, select character (occupation and/or personal relationships), activity, and location. The first team sets up its location. If there is sufficient stage space, the entire group walks around the stage to learn the body center acting focus. Otherwise, team by team.

Introduction coaching: Let's do a **group preparation** to learn the acting focus. At the end, everybody will sit down except the first team. Their location has been set up and they will go to places and begin their improvisation. We'll do a **miniprep** for each successive team. ◆ Do the 40-

breath process. ◆ Everyone walk. Focus on your body moving through the space. Focus on feeling the space moving through you. Now, move through the space and feel the space moving through you at the same time.

Group preparation: Observe how much energy you are using. Keep your eyes open. Whatever level of energy you are using is fine. Be aware that the energy must come from somewhere. ◆ For the sake of the exercise, I am going to suggest where the energy is coming from. It is as if you have an energy source inside your body, a power plant, in the same way that electrical energy has a source, a generator or power plant. ◆ *Your body's power plant is located at the base of your spine.* ◆ Focus on feeling a center in your body at the base of your spine. Whatever energy you are using to walk around right now is coming from this body center. As you walk now, feel the energy source at the base of your spine. Focus on that as the source of your energy.

Now let's track the energy that comes from that body center to energize the body. Everybody focus on a *path of energy* that begins at this center at the base of your spine. It is unbroken path of energy running from this center down your **left leg** to your toes and returning to the center. Focus on that path, on the energy, the *current* that allows your left leg to move. The energy goes all the way down your left leg to your toes and then back to the center. Feel the path of that energy in your leg. The energy never stops. If it did, you would not be able to move your left leg. ◆ Keep focusing on that and add another path of energy. Remember, we are adding, not replacing. Add a *second path of energy* running from your center at the base of your spine down your **right leg** to your toes and back to the center. ◆ Now focus on the body center, the power plant, sending energy along those two paths. The energy runs from the base of your spine, down both legs, and returns to the base. Focus on it. Feel the paths of energy within your legs. Avoid seeing them. Feel them with your legs. Feel the two paths of energy. The lower half of your body probably feels more energized than the upper half. ◆ Now let's add a *third path of energy.* It runs from the center, up the left side of your body, through the shoulder, down the **left arm** to the fingers, and back along the same route to the center at the base of your spine. Focus on that path of energy. Feel the energy coming from your center from the base of your spine. That is what energizes your left arm. ◆ Now let's add a *fourth path of energy.* It runs from the center, up the right side of your body, through the shoulder, down the **right arm** to the fingers, and back along the same route to the center at the base of your spine. You are now focusing on feeling the source of your energy at the base of your spine, sending energy out along the four paths of energy. These four unbroken currents are allowing you to walk and be alive and have feelings. The energy moving along these four paths is what operates the limbs. Focus on all four paths and feel the empowerment that it gives you. ◆ Let's add a final *fifth path of energy*, which runs from the base of your spine all the way up the spine to the **head.** Feel the energy traveling up the spine, through the neck, your tongue, right to the brain, and back again.

These are the five main paths of energy in your body, all coming from the power plant at the base of your spine. So, you are in fact now sending energy from the base of your spine to your head, your arms and hands, your legs and feet. Focus on feeling it, all of this energy. Feel the flow of energy to all parts of your body. No holding up the flow. Keep breathing. Feel the flow of energy in all of your joints. Feel the flow in your arms. The flow of energy arises from your center at the base of your spine. Wave your arms around and focus on the flow of energy that is allowing you to move your arms. Reach out and find some objects in the space. Focus on the paths of energy as you do that. If these paths of energy were broken, the current interrupted, you would not be able to do any of this. ◆ Stop walking and do an activity while focusing on all five paths of energy. It is like a double acting focus. The first focus is all the paths of energy, which allows you to do the second focus, which is an activity. Feel the energy that allows you to do this activity. Now, return to walking and stay on focus.

The focus is the energy that flows from the body center. All five paths of energy arise from and return to the body center, which is at the base of your spine.

Keep your eyes open and keep responding to the coaching. ◆ While you are walking, *increase the size of your body center* at the base of your spine and allow your body to respond. Observe whether or not the energy flows in an increased fashion. Feel that increase. Don't see it. Feel it at the base of your spine. Feel the body center with the body center. If the center was an inch in diameter, make it three inches. If it was six inches, make it ten. You just bought a bigger generator. There is more energy coming from it. Feel that. —*Allow 30s.* ◆ Okay, now return it to the size you had when we started. Feel the change in the currents through your body. Stay on focus. ◆ Now decrease the size of your power plant or body center. Make the center smaller. If the center was an inch, maybe it's an eighth-inch. Feel the changes. Stay aware of your five paths of energy. —*Allow 30s.* ◆ Now return the center to its original size. The original size chose you and you chose the original size. Whatever it is, it is fine. There is no right or wrong. ◆ Keep walking.

Everybody choose any specific location in the body. Pick any part of your body: the right elbow, the left knee, the right eyebrow, the top of the head, the stomach, etc. Make a choice. Pick any one body part. Know specifically and exactly where it is in your body. Don't do anything with it yet; just name it to yourself. ◆ Now, without any hesitation, *move your body center* from the base of your spine to the location that you have just selected. ◆ Move it there. Walk around feeling that body center, that energy generator. Feel it relocated to its new location. *If there is any shifting in your body's posture or demeanor as a result, allow it.* Don't look for it and don't muscle it. I will help you get there through the coaching. If anything comes up right away, allow it to happen.

You are focusing on this new body center in its new location. ◆ Focus on the path of uninterrupted energy flowing from this location to your left leg, to the toes, and back to the new center. Notice, observe, experience, and focus on the rerouting it has had to take. It is no longer traveling the same exact route as from the base of your spine. It is now traveling through more or less of the body in different locations because of where you moved the center to. Feel that flow of energy to the left leg and toes. Allow your left leg and toes to respond if there is a response. Focus on feeling this and let your body respond. ◆ Keeping this, add a path of energy from the new body center to the right leg, to the toes, and back. Feel that. It may not be the same distance that it was originally from the base of the spine to both legs. The route from the new body center to one leg and back might be shorter than the route to the other leg and back. ◆ Keep these two paths. Don't let go. Add a path of uninterrupted energy from the new body center location to the left shoulder, down the left arm, through the elbow to the fingers, and back. It is a whole new route. Allow your body to adjust. Don't let go of the bottom half of your body while you do this. ◆ Now add a path of energy from this new center to the right shoulder, down the right arm, through the elbow to the fingers, and back. ◆ You now have a body center, located somewhere other than the base of your spine, and four paths of energy to your four limbs. Don't let go. Take what you get. ◆ Let's add the fifth path from the new body center into the spine, up or down through the throat, the mouth, to the head, the brain, and back again. It may be a shorter path than the original one. Keep your eyes open. It may be a longer path. It may have to go through different routes.

Focus on feeling this new center of your body and the five paths of energy from it. Notice, observe, and allow your whole body to realign itself according to this new body center. Stay on this focus. Commit to it totally. Don't let go. ◆ Let's practice some moves. Stop and make a space sandwich or a drink. Sit down and get up. Walk up and down some space stairs. Try the different things that a body does in life, but stay focused on the realigned body. Your original body center was the base of your spine. This character's body center is where you have placed it. The new body

256

center has, to some degree or other, realigned your body. So, you are practicing the moves that your character might make. Stay on focus through every single moment. The focus is on the new body center, and the five new paths of energy, and the resulting realignment of the body. Avoid hanging out. Try new movements. —*Allow 1m.*

Everyone return to walking. Allow the body center to return to the base of your spine. Feel the resulting shift. Feel the disappearance of the character and the reemergence of you. Stay focused on your body center. This is your body center, the base of your spine, and the five paths of energy. ◆ Now, we are going to move the body center from the base of your spine to another part of the body, which I will select. You are going to have a new body center that will be tiny, hard, and powerful. Put it at the tip of your nose. All the energy for your entire body is now created at the tip of your nose. Feel that. ◆ Focus on the path of energy to and from your left leg. It has to go down the whole left side of your body all the way to your toes. It travels a whole different route now. Focus on it and feel what that different route does to you. ◆ Add the path going to the right leg, down the right side and going all the way to the toes. Focus on these paths of energy coming from your nose instead of the base of your spine. Allow your body to respond to these new paths of energy. Take whatever you get. Now add a path from the new center to the left shoulder, down the left arm to the fingers, and back. Now add the right shoulder, down the right arm to the fingers, and back. Focus on the center at the tip of your nose, the rerouting of the energy paths as a result, and how your body responds to that. Does it change? Add the fifth path from the tip of your nose to the head, the brain, and returning. This is obviously a much shorter route than the one from the base of your spine. Feel what it does to you. Take whatever you get and focus on the center of the body being at the tip of your nose for all of the energy paths in your body. Focus on the new body center and the realignment that results.

Now, as you walk around, discover each other. Stay on focus, retain your new body, and discover each other. See the other actors and let them see you. Allow yourself to mingle. Allow yourself to talk and take whatever voice comes out of the body. Don't try to invent anything. Don't try to censor anything. Just take what you get. Mingle and chitchat. Stay on your acting focus throughout the chitchat, retaining the new body. —*Allow 1m.* ◆ Okay, avoid dialogue. Stay on focus. Keep walking. ◆ Move the body center from the tip of your nose back to the base of your spine. Allow your body to realign totally. Feel the disappearance of the character and the reemergence of you. Focus on the currents from the normal center at the base of your spine going out to all of the limbs and up to the brain and back. —*Allow 30s.*

Now, we are going to move the center one more time. The new center is big. It is heavy. It is dull. It is sloppy. It is at the seat of your pants. Focus on the center being there. Focus on and feel that new center. ◆ Now feel the path of energy going from that center down your left leg to your toes and back. Add a second path of energy from the center down your right leg to your toes and back. Focus on that. See how your legs realign to the new paths of energy. ◆ Now add the third path of energy up the left side to the left arm and fingers, and back. Feel that new path and how it affects you. Now, add the fourth path of energy up the right side to the right arm and fingers, and back to the center. Focus on these four new paths and how this changes your body. ◆ Now add the fifth path up to the head, the brain, and back. ◆ Does the body center affect the size of the paths, affect the amount of energy that travels up and down these paths? Feel that for yourself. Discover that answer for yourself. Again, stop and chitchat with your neighbors and take whatever comes out of your mouth. —*Allow 30s.* ◆ Avoid dialogue. Keep walking. Stay on focus. ◆ Now shift the center back to the base of the spine one more time, allowing the character to disappear. Focus on your body center and your paths of energy.

For the final part of the exercise, everybody, on your own, is going to choose a new location, a part of the body that we have not already employed as a body center. Instead of all doing the same one, you are all free to decide where the next one is going to be and what characteristics it has. Choose a new location and give it whatever characteristics you want to give it: small, hard, tough, medium, anything at all. These are not the qualities of the character, just of the body center, the power plant. For example: small and hard in the left elbow; big and floppy in the right knee; very tiny in the abdomen. Do not concern yourself with the results it will have.

Now that you have made the choice, let's go through the process. Focus on moving the body center to the location you have chosen. Don't worry about the paths yet. Feel all the energy in your body coming from this new center. Feel how much energy it produces. If your body has an immediate realignment, go with it. ◆ Now focus on the new path of energy going from the new center to the left leg, to the toes, and back to the center. Feel what that does to your body. Now add the right leg path. Take whatever you get. Now add the upper left path. Add the upper right path. Add the fifth path from this new body center to whatever part of the spine is available to it, to the mouth, the head, the brain, and back to the new center. Focus on feeling this new center of your body and the five new paths of energy from it. Notice, observe, and allow your whole body to realign itself to this new body center as you are now doing and feeling. Stay on this focus. Commit to it totally. *This is your acting focus.* Don't let go.

Now let's practice some moves with it. Stop and make a space sandwich. Have a drink. See how the legs and arms move. Go sit down. Get up. Walk upstairs, downstairs. Try the different things a body does in life, but stay focused on the realigned body as a result of your new body center. This is your character's body center. You are practicing the movements that your character might have to go through. Stay on focus every single moment. *The focus is on the body center, the new five paths, and the resulting realignment of the body.* Feel how this character's body center empowers this character's body. —*Allow 1m.* ◆ Stay on focus and hold onto some space props. Mingle with the other characters. Chitchat and see what voice comes out. Go with it. —*Allow 2m.*

Everybody avoid dialogue and return to walking. Stay on the same focus. Everybody *except the first team*, return your body centers to the base of your spine. Allow the character to disappear. Allow yourself to return. Everybody *except the first team*, return to your seats. ◆ First team, go to places. Stay on your acting focus while you do the character, activity, and location doing. Retain this new, realigned body that results from the new body center. ◆ Action.

RULES: Employ physical doing tools of Improvisation Technique for activity, location, relationships, and occupation.

ACTING FOCUS: Retaining the chosen body center and the resulting realigned body.

COACHING (as needed): Check out your fellow actors. Stay focused on the realigned body and the five paths of energy. Censor nothing. Take whatever you get. **Avoid hanging out.** Avoid isolation. Stay open to helping a fellow actor. **Stay open to needing help.** Go with it. **Share your voices.** Avoid questions. Avoid playwriting. Active & still. Turn up the energy at the power plant of the body center by twenty percent. **Stay on focus. Don't let go. Feel your body center energizing the whole body through the five paths. One minute to stay on focus.** Last chance to feel your body center energizing the body. **Retain the realigned body.** ◆ Cut.

FOLLOW-UP (as needed): Character? Activity? Location? **Did you feel that the actors were on the acting focus?** Were they open to realigning their bodies? **Did they hold onto their realigned bodies? Did you feel that their realigned bodies were somewhat different from their own bodies?** Were rhythms different? Were voices different? **Did you see the actors reveal any character qualities or characteristics that we don't usually see from them?** ◆ Actors, do you agree? **Were you open to realigning your body? Did you hold onto it? Did you feel like you let the acting focus lead you through the improvisation? Did you dis-**

cover the emergence of an attitude with this body? What was the attitude? What was your body center?

Miniprep: *After they set up their location—* Walk around. Shake it out. Focus on your own body center at the base of your spine and the five paths of energy that come from that body center. —*Allow 10s.* ◆ This is your body, the actor's body.—*Allow 10s.* ◆ Move your body center to the last location you did in the group preparation. Return to that body center; allow your body to realign.—*Allow 10s.* ◆ Focus on the five paths of energy that come from that body center. Focus on the totally new, realigned body. Your acting focus throughout the improv is on this new body center and the resulting realigned body for your character. Go to places. Don't let go. ◆ Action.

SUMMARY:

What is consistent with the three character acting focuses that we have done so far, the reformed body in space, the animals, and the body center? What, in your opinion, is necessary to creating a character?

> **TO THE COACH:** During the improvs, due to the emergence of a shy or introverted attitude an actor may become caught up in improvising by himself in a corner of the stage. Coaching should guide that actor back to improvising with his improv mates and away from isolation. ◆ In the miniprep, if necessary, remind the subsequent teams to go through the process again, rather than jumping right into the character they created in the introduction walk. The character may come out the same or slightly different.
>
> If there is time at the end of class, summary questions and answers should be included as part of the following discussion. If not, assign the questions as a journal assignment. In the next class, start with another round of body center improvs, condense the coaching, and then conduct the following discussion with summary questions and answers.

MIDREHEARSAL APPLICATION OF CHARACTER BODY WORK

Character as Part of the Whole

What *part* are you playing? Characters are referred to as *parts* because each character is a different part of the whole. The writer has created each character to serve his part of the whole script. If a production is highly conceptualized, then the director becomes a partner with the author in the design of a character's part of the whole.

It doesn't do the script or the production any good if an actor creates a different part than was intended. All of his scenes will be distorted as they rub against the grain of the script. The whole production will be distorted by the impact of those scenes.

Actor's Individuality

When the author creates a character, it is only about seventy-five percent created. The other twenty-five percent allows for the individual actor's persona and interpretation of the part. For that twenty-five percent to work, it must be attached to the seventy-five percent that is the author's invention. For that seventy-five percent to work, it must be enlivened by the actor's individuality.

Many acting teachers urge actors to *find the part within yourself*. While accurate, this can be misinterpreted to exclude the character as written and you will just play you. The part wasn't written to be *you*. In Improvisation Technique, you *bring yourself to the character* you create. In creating what the author had in mind, you automatically bring yourself to the part. It's impossible not to do so.

Creating a Character

There are two main aspects of creating a character. First, you must find the **body** of the character. When Sir Laurence Olivier said he never felt he had his character down until he found the right nose, he was talking about the work you have been doing in the last three classes.

Demonstration

Each of you, form a space nose that is very round and bulbous. Put it on your real nose and let your face respond as it feels its new nose. See how your face goes into a realignment, just as we have been doing. Now take that off and go back to your own nose. Now form and put on a long, angular, pointed nose. Let your face respond. Do you feel that?

Olivier, through makeup, found a nose, a putty nose, and that was his equivalent of what we have been doing. The nose was a catalyst through which he shifted his body.

Have you ever been in a play, usually a period play, and, when you put on your costume for the first dress rehearsal, looked in the mirror and said, "Oh, I get it!" Then you started standing and walking differently. Unfortunately, those who wait for the costume to do the job for them waste too much rehearsal time out of character. Imagine the confidence, finesse, nuance, and attention to detail that could have been found had the actor been in character throughout the rehearsal period.

Instead of putty noses or real costumes, we have been using animals, body centers, and reformed bodies as catalysts to do the same body shifting. These character doing improvisations can be done at any time in the rehearsal process.

In creating a character, you must also find the character's personality or **attitude.** Every one of us has a distinct personality, a distinct attitude. The same is true for every character, but to a much greater degree. Dramatic characters must hold an audience's attention. They must be larger than life. To accomplish this, authors deliberately highlight the character's attitude because that is what makes a character compelling. Think of Lucy Ricardo, Stanley Kowalski, Blanche DuBois, Iago, Tartuffe, Willy Loman, Antigone, Ratso Rizzo, Indiana Jones, and Seinfeld's friends.

What is your character's attitude about her life? Without knowing and embodying that attitude, you'll always be playing the text, which is what you *never* want to play. When your character has a life attitude, e.g., Blanche's "I'm entitled," that she brings to everything she does, the character's main ingredient is present regardless of the subjects of her text.

In our character work thus far, we have discovered that with every character's body we create, an attitude automatically and spontaneously emerges. In the next part of our character work, we will explore creating the character by starting with an informed choice of what the attitude is and then creating the body that accompanies that attitude.

Finding the Character

How do you find the character? Ask yourself some questions about the character and the script, starting with what is the difference between you and the character presented in the script. With this question, you focus immediately on how the character is *not you.* What is the character's mind like? How does it occupy itself? What does it think about? Does the character think more or less rapidly than I do? Is his understanding of the way things are clearer or cloudier than mine is? Does he access his emotions more often than I do? Is he more or less of a victim than I am? Is his personality lighter and sunnier or darker and more somber than mine is? Does he have a stronger idea of how things should be? Is he more persistent and unyielding than I am? When he doesn't get what he wants, what does he do? Does he have an attitude or defensive armor that is not mine? What is his psychological baggage? Does he have any *physical characteristics* baggage? How is his baggage different from mine?

Animals

As you work this way, you begin to get a sense of the character. If you were looking to benefit from the acting focuses we've been doing, you could begin using your ideas this way: What if this whole script was a jungle world and all the characters were animals? What animal or part of this particular animal kingdom of the script would my character be? You do not just pick willy-nilly. You pick as a result of dealing with these types of questions and answers. Is he the King of the Jungle and everything has to happen his way? Do all of the other characters (animals) fear him? It's starting to sound like my character may be like a lion. Sometimes, it can be as simple as discovering that your character is extremely inauthentic and is always deliberately (for whatever reason) making trouble for others. You feel he can be categorized as *slimy*, a snake. What animal has the same characteristics as or behaves in a similar fashion to your character?

What does the author say about this character? Gee, the author refers to her as "Maggie the Cat." What do other characters say about your character: "God, you are just a big baboon, the way you climb around the house." List the things your character is, and is not, concerned about. These are places to start.

Body Centers

In your daily lives, you might see a person who embodies the same characteristics as your character. Notice that person and observe where their body center seems to be and what kind of characteristics it might possess.

Let's talk about body centers. Suppose you are doing Molière. You are playing Harpagon, the title role in *The Miser*. Where would you start looking for a body center? Hands? Why? Money grabbing. That is one approach. How about the tip of the nose, because this guy can smell money a mile away? You get to be creative in the interpretive process. There is no right or wrong; there is only experimentation. All that matters is that something makes sense to you. You need the catalyst, so you need to make particular choices about the catalyst instead of just some arbitrary body response. For instance, suppose you are playing a very wise and generous man, where might you start looking to put the body center? In the head, and it should be large and glowing. Suppose you are playing a bigot, someone who is mean, small-minded, and obsessed? I would put a tiny, rigid center between my eyes.

Reformed Body in Space

If no animal or body center is apparent to you, you might benefit from the reformed body in space. Suppose, as a result of your delineating the differences between you and the character, you find that your character has an inflated sense of their physical attractiveness. Reshape your own body in space to have more attractive features than you think you possess, e.g., thinner, bigger muscles, straighter nose, bigger chest, etc. Then, step into it and allow your body to re-align, as we did in the exercise. The result will be that you have the same physical characteristics as before, but you will carry yourself as if you felt more attractive. You will carry yourself *as the character.* If you interpret that your character goes through life carrying a burden, reform your space body to add thirty pounds of weight, step into it, and discover what it's like to carry extra weight that you feel but that the audience doesn't see.

Animals, body centers, and reformed bodies are important because they are catalysts for body change. Your job is to read a script and interpret it so that your choice of the catalyst makes sense. Choose, and then ask yourself, are these values and characteristics that the author emphasizes or are they my personal inclinations or favorites?

> **TO THE COACH:** Give the Script-Influenced Animal or Body Center homework assignment.
>
> ASSIGNMENT: Actors are to select a well-known character from a play and to work on the script as if preparing to create that character. Specifically, they are to come into class having picked an animal to base the character on and a body center with characteristics to base the character on.

◆   ◆   ◆

EXTENSION BUMPS [4]

This exercise introduces the concept of boundaries.

SETUP: Everyone walks around the stage responding to the coaching.

COACHING: Do the 40-breath process. ◆ Walk around and focus on your body moving through the space. Focus on feeling the space moving through you. Move through the space and feel the space moving through you at the same time. ◆ See your fellow actors. ◆ Let them see you. ◆ See them and let them see you. ◆ Feel yourself at the center of your own space as you walk. You are at the center of your own space, and your own personal space extends out from you in all directions. It travels with you wherever you go. Get a feeling of how much your space extends out from you in all directions. Stay in the center of your own space and take all you need. There is enough room for everyone to have their own extensions of space without anyone else being in it. Your space is your own and no one can come into it unless you invite them in. Feel that. There is no right or wrong amount of space available to you. It is what you feel comfortable with. ◆ As you walk, see your fellow actors and avoid their extensions of space around them. Instead of thinking about this, go with what you see. Sense or see the space around others and feel the space around you. Avoid each other's space extensions. Feel your own space extension, low and

264

high. Let your head rest on its own pedestal. Keep feeling your own space. It moves with you wherever you go. Get the experience of your own space. Be aware that every actor is at the center of his own space. See the extensions of everyone else and their own space. Avoid bumping into another player's space with your space.

When I clap my hands, *bump* space extensions. Not bodies, just space extensions. Keep your body quiet at the center of your own space. Only your *space* is bumping into the others' space. Let the space extensions bump and collide. ◆ [Clap.] ◆ Only your space is colliding, not you or your body. Stay open to any feeling that comes up. ◆ [Clap three or four times with about ten seconds between claps.] ◆ Feel the space around you. Be aware of the space around others and know your own space. ◆ [Clap.] ◆ Avoid acting out the bumping. Your body doesn't need to do anything, except be open to feelings; it's the space that's bumping. Your body is quiet in the middle of your own space feeling whatever it feels. Just do the bumping and allow the body to respond however it wants without you pushing it. ◆ [Clap.] ◆ Avoid telling your body what to do when it collides with another's space. Let it experience whatever it experiences. Stay out of it and take what you get. On your own, keep bumping or colliding space extensions as you pass each other. Stay open to feeling something. Don't act out the bumping. Don't control. Stay open to feeling anything when somebody else's space contacts your space. Allow your body its own alignment, movement, and feelings. —*Allow 1m.* ◆ Stop bumping and continue walking. ◆ Let go of your own space extensions. Go through the space of the room and let the space go through you. ◆ Cut.

FOLLOW-UP: Did you feel your own space extensions? Did you know where they ended? How did it feel being at the center of your own space? When your extension bumped into another's, did you feel it? What did you feel? Were you capable of feeling that without acting it out, without performing the feeling?

SUMMARY:

In your own personal lives, you experience these space extensions without being conscious of them. They are called *boundaries*. When somebody comes into your space, they cross your boundary. How does that feel? How did you feel when that happened during the space extension bumps? Irritated. Aggressive. Claustrophobic. Sad. Threatened. What else? These are all negative feelings. This is what happens when somebody crosses your boundary. Another word for what you feel is *inundation*. You feel inundated when they come in on you. It is your space. If you focus on your own boundaries and establish what they are, you will be respected and you will feel safe.

Why shouldn't your characters have boundaries? You do. It may only be a half-inch around you. For another person, it could be four feet. Whatever it is, whenever someone crosses your boundary, you want to step back. You have a feeling of violation that manifests in many different ways.

You may not have ever thought about your boundaries before, but you certainly felt when you were inundated. Think of some stranger coming up to you in a bar or on the street and getting just a little too close. Remember how you felt when your mother went through your dresser drawer when you were a child or teenager? How about when a teacher or employer got in your face? Sometimes, comments that certain people say to you are just a little too personal, and that feels like an inundation. When you feel inundated, your body responds. In your personal life, you can have an authentic response to an inundation, which is healthy, or you can act out your response to an inundation, which is inauthentic and not healthy. How does your character respond at these times?

WHERE ARE YOUR CHARACTER'S BOUNDARIES?

Characters also have responses to feeling inundated. How does your character feel when his boundaries are crossed? How does your character feel when inundated? How healthy is the character? How self-aware is the character? Does the character you are playing act out? What form does it take? Fear? Tears? Volatile anger? Silent treatment? Have you ever asked yourself these questions, much less taken the time to integrate your answers into your performance? These are important questions when you are playing a character. Every character has boundaries and they are different for every character. They come into play during interaction with other characters and with events. What are the boundaries of the character? When are those boundaries violated? Does the story, blocking, and the business ever involve your character's boundaries being violated? What are the ramifications? What does that feel like for the character, and how does he respond to it? If your answer is that it feels the same way it does when your own personal boundaries are violated, then you are wrong. You are not the character. The author did not have you in mind when he wrote the character. So you must distinguish between you and the character, between how you would react and how the character would react.

Generally, characters are much-higher-stakes drama queens than you are. That is why they are in the script. Whether it's Stanley Kowalski, who is totally inundated by Blanche, or some punk in the Mafia gang, or an anal-retentive clerk in a sitcom, there may be moments in the script where your character is inundated. Your job is to play your responses to that, consistent with the character you have created. You can be sure that writers are writing scenes that are layered with inundations because that is frequently where the drama is.

SCRIPT-INFLUENCED ANIMAL OR BODY CENTER

Go right into the next exercise and improv. In a previous class, actors were given an assignment to select a well-known character from a play and to work on the script as if preparing to create that character. They are to come into class having picked an animal to base the character on and a body center location and characteristics to base the character on.

SETUP: Divide group into two subgroups, those who prefer to work on their character from an animal catalyst and those who prefer to work on their character from a body center catalyst. Within each subgroup, form teams of 3–4 each. Teams huddle and select location, activity, and characters (occupation and personal relationships). If possible, given the choices of location and activity, each actor's choice of occupation should be the same or similar to their script character's occupation. Attempting a further parallel through the personal relationships in the team may be difficult, but if it can be done, actors are encouraged to do so. When each team sets up its location, the coach privately inquires of each actor what script character he will be working on (I jot it down on an index card, so I don't have to remember). **First team to improvise sets up its location and is then led through (1) the preparation, then (2) the character boundary walk, and right into (3) the improvisation.**

CLASS QUESTIONS: "What if your script character doesn't have an occupation?" Are you sure your script character doesn't have an occupation? How about housewife, student, heir, homeless person? "Should the location parallel the script character's location?" Only if you can find one that's suitable for all the characters in the improvisation. "Should we tell our improv mates what character we are doing?" No.

RULES: (1) In the preparation, employ the animal or body center catalyst you selected doing the homework assignment. **(2)** Respond to the coaching. **(3)** During the improvisation, while employing physical doing tools of Improvisation Technique for activity, location, relationships, and occupation, the actors must retain the realigned body resulting from their chosen body center or animal.

ACTING FOCUS: (1) Same as animal or body center acting focus. **(2)** Retaining the character's body and responding to the coaching. **(3)** Retaining the character's body.

COACHING (as needed): (1) Preparation: Do the 40-breath process. ◆ Walk around and focus on your body moving through the space. Now focus on feeling the space moving through you. Now move through the space and feel the space moving through you at the same time. ◆ [Depending on whether this is an animal team or a body center team, the coach takes them through the steps of the appropriate acting focus from earlier in this chapter.]

For **body center teams**, start them with the coaching for the body center at the base of the spine and the five paths of energy, and then coach them through a switch to the new, preselected body center for the script character. For **animal teams,** start them with the basic group coaching from animal forehead through human evolution.

After the group coaching— I am going to come around and work with you one by one privately. Until I get there, continue to walk around with your focus being either the new body center and the resulting realignment of your body or retaining the animal's characteristics in your face, body, and voice. ◆ The coach then walks with each [actor], privately coaching to further refine the character.

SAMPLE BODY CENTER HUMANIZING COACHING

[Javier], walk with me. You are George from *Of Mice and Men*. Stay focused throughout on the body center. Does this walk feel like his walk? Is it possibly too big? Stay alert and consider it. Does he bounce that much? What can you do that would affect the bounce and bring it down just a bit? Shake hands with me. Does that handshake feel authentic? Stay on focus throughout the scene. Can you say some lines for me from anything? Now stay focused on retaining this new body as a result of the body center.

SAMPLE ANIMAL HUMANIZING COACHING

[Tom], humanize him some more. Shake hands with me. How do his fingers work? Show me, don't tell me. Do his elbows extend up that high? It is the essence of that, rather than the exaggeration of that. ◆ [Danica], this is a human who has all of these characteristics, so integrate what you are doing with your shoulders and arms into a natural arm swing. Do you carry your hands like that or is there an adjustment that needs to be made? There you go. That seems natural. ◆ [Liz], start to put words with that voice, retaining the sound quality in the words. Does she always scream that loud? How can you retain the animal's vocal characteristics in a human voice? There you go. The scream has become a laugh. How does that laugh affect the rest of the body? Remember, you are human. [Sue], is this the rhythm she always walks at? Is she capable of walking faster if she needs to? How does this character stand when she's not walking? Is she that big in the hips? Don't think about it; just respond with the body immediately. ◆ [Dan], does he make that growling sound between all his words? Retain the characteristics, but he is human and you don't have to be that extreme. Why don't you go to that space table and make yourself a space sandwich? Focus on holding on to the character.

COACHING: (2) Character boundary walk: *The actors are now walking around in character.* ✦ Now, everybody focus on holding this character. Hold it in the body. Put down any space props and focus on retaining the character's body and characteristics as you walk among each other. See your fellow players while you do it. Let them see you. ✦ See them and let them see you as you retain the character's body. ✦ *Feel yourself at the center of your character's space as you walk.* You are at the center of your character's space, and it extends out from you in all directions. It travels with you wherever you go. Get a feeling of how far your space extends out from you in all directions. It is what you feel comfortable with. Retain your character's body. ✦ Sense or see the space around others and feel the space around you. Retain your character's body. Feel your own space extension, low and high. Let your head rest on its own pedestal. Retain your character's body. When I clap my hands, bump space extensions. Not bodies, just space extensions. ✦ [Clap.] ✦ Keep your body quiet at the center of your own space. Only your space is bumping into the others' space. Let the space extensions bump and collide. ✦ [Clap.] ✦ Only your space is being hit, not you or your body. Stay open to feeling any feeling that comes up. Retain your character's body. Go where you have to go in order to bump. ✦ [Clap three or four times with about ten seconds between claps.] ✦ Avoid acting out the bumping. Your body doesn't need to do anything except be open to feelings. It's the space that's bumping. Keep bumping. Your body is quiet in the middle of your own space, feeling whatever it feels. Just do the bumping and allow the body to respond however it wants without you pushing it. Avoid telling your body what to do when it collides with another's space. Let it experience whatever it experiences. Stay out of it and take what you get. ✦ Stop bumping and walk around, focusing on retaining your character's body. ✦

COACHING: (3) Improv: Places. ✦ When I call "Action," do location and activity physical doing and stay on your acting focus, retaining the character's body. ✦ Action. ✦ *Animal.* **Keep focusing on retaining the character's body. Feel the tail affecting your body. Hold onto the face. Feel the rhythm.** Retain the vocal quality. ✦ *Body Center.* **Focus on your body center realigning your body.** Increase (or decrease) the power from the body center generator by twenty percent. ✦ *Animal/Body Center.* **Avoid hanging out. Check each other out. Stay on your acting focus.** Retain the body. **Stay alert to anyone coming into your space and what**

happens. **Feel where your space ends and others come into it.** Stay alert to what you do. Seek opportunities to converge. Can you help someone? Can you be helped? Share your voices. Avoid playwriting. Keep it here and now. No stories from the past. Active & still. **Retain your character's body. Censor nothing.** Allow your acting focus to solve any problems. One minute. ◆ Cut.

FOLLOW-UP (as needed): Audience, did you feel that they were on their acting focus? Did you see them allow their bodies to realign into the characters' bodies? Did they retain the body? ◆ **Actors, do you agree?** ◆ **Audience, tell us what you know about each character.** Despite the fact that it could be any character from any script, **did anybody flash on a specific character** for [name each actor]? ◆ **Actors, did an attitude emerge? What was it?** Did it stay with you throughout the scene? **What character were you working on? Did you discover anything about your character that you didn't previously consider when preparing with the script or from any previous knowledge of the character? What was your animal or body center? What in the script informed you or led you to that choice? Did you notice or have any response to experiencing what his boundaries are?**

SELECTED STUDENT RESPONSES

—Ben (Gentleman Caller/*The Glass Menagerie*): When I was considering it alone at home, I thought how self-absorbed he was and how he wanted to be the center of attention among these people. In the improv, I felt his need to make everyone else happy override that need to make himself the center of attention. In the scene with her, he is always talking about himself but I discovered that is just done to make her feel good. *Boundaries?* I got agitated when she wanted to get so close and flirt. I felt out of control. *Animal?* A peacock. In the scene with Laura he is preening the whole time. Preening took me to peacock.

—Helena (Maggie/*Cat on a Hot Tin Roof*): I discovered that she needs all men to love her, not only her husband. *Boundaries?* Any time a woman came near me, my boundaries went up. Whenever there was a man around me, I had none. When I was inundated, I got very hot. *Animal?* A cat. It wasn't just that in the script she says, "I feel like a cat on a hot tin roof." It was that she is very manipulative and knifing. When she wants something, she is very kind and sweet. Like a cat.

—Bill (Shelly Levine/*Glengarry Glen Ross*): I found out how endlessly inventive he could be when faced with obstacles. He would keep coming up with something and he was shameless about it, a *super* salesman. *Boundaries?* I didn't mind touching them, but I didn't like it when they touched me. It made me angry. Who the hell does he think he is? *Animal?* A velociraptor. He is a "pack" animal. They run in pairs, and the main thing they have is a hypnotic thing that they do. While they are doing that, they get someone else to come in from the side.

—Javier (George/*Of Mice and Men*): I discovered he is very suspicious of people. I had thought of that before, but not in the way it presented itself with the body center and the boundaries. ***Boundaries?*** Any time someone got close I would get suspicious. ***Body center?*** A heavy, dull generator with a short on the back of my shoulders because of the way he would go off and get angry a lot and then calm down and be gentle with Lenny. He would also let people in once he got to know them, so it was off balance.

—Liz (Harper/*Angels in America*): ***Boundaries?*** They were very wide spread. They stretched out far. When someone came in, I was very scared but ready to fight. ***Body center?*** The back of my head, an orange throbbing light. In the script she is so inside herself and she hallucinates all the time. She knows the truth in the back of her head, in the back of her brain. She knows what is going on but she denies it.

—Elise (Hedda/*Hedda Gabler*): I discovered that I was often surprised by what other people would say to me. ***Boundaries?*** I liked having people in my boundaries. ***Body center?*** A real sharp, vertical center right behind my eyes. I felt she was watching every move everyone made and she would also process that immediately in her brain, so there was a lot of information going into her eyes to her brain.

SUMMARY:

Notice that all of the improvisations were consistently stronger than our usual improvs. Many resembled little one-act plays. This has to do with the fact that all of these improvs contained stronger characters than our usual ones, which are based only on occupation and personal relationships. When you are playing a fully realized and physical character, everything becomes heightened, stronger, and much more interesting.

WHEN TO CREATE CHARACTER

Most of you had some knowledge of your character prior to this assignment. In addition to that, your specific assignment was to work on the script, finding clues to your catalyst choice. When you work professionally, unless you are doing a revival in the theater, you will not have prior knowledge of the character. This suggests that any work on the creation of your character would be limited if you jumped into it right at the start of rehearsals. Regardless of how much rehearsal time there is or whether you get to rehearse at all with the company, *you should not begin your rehearsal period or preparation process with specific emphasis on creating your character.* This is the time in the preparation process when you know the *least* about your character. The early stages of rehearsal are the time when you enter the world of the script and do your traditional work, e.g., breaking down scenes and discovering your problems, obstacles, and actions; doing first level improvisations and discovering what else there is. Once you have done that work, and you know a great deal more about your character, that is the time to choose a character catalyst and develop the physicalization of your character.

However long you have to prepare and rehearse, by the time you get to the halfway mark you should start specifically looking to create the character's physicalization. You now have some knowledge of the script and you know what's expected of your character. You know how the character thinks. You know what the character's problems are. You now have all of that behavioral information available to you as well as the information about the character derived from the text. You can now add it all up and make your interpretive choices for character catalysts. If a choice doesn't work, throw it out and profit from what you learned as you make another choice.

You can do the early stages of creating the character from a catalyst by yourself. The homework leading to the catalyst choice and the first physicalizations of it can be done by yourself. Working by yourself is an opportunity for experimenting. You must stay honest as you consider your discoveries. Do not evaluate or judge your work while you are creating the physicalization. Use your journals to evaluate them after the fact. What did you like? Not like? What alterations should you make? Keep writing about it, and what is important will emerge to you. Improvising with that character can be done with or without cast mates. You can do the improvs with any actor friends. Do not bring your character work to the set too early. When you have your humanized and proportionately sized character, bring it to rehearsal or the set. Now the director's involved and hopefully there's a give and take between you. He can say, "Too big." He can say, "Too little." Whatever. However it goes, it's generally a good rule not to tell anyone about your character catalyst. Use the word *character* and not the words *animal, reformed body in space*, or *body center*. The minute you use those words, some directors might freak out, e.g., "I don't want to see a monkey on the stage." Whereas if you never mention *animal*, maybe he'll say, "Yeah, that's good, but why are you doing all of that arm swinging?" Then you know you've got to humanize the arms a little more, but everything else worked. If you are using a body center and you get a note that your character is too big, just reduce the size of the body center.

Now you're at the last stage of creating the character, when a lot of interesting things start to happen. When you are pretty much finished with the humanizing, regardless of the catalyst, you may discover that previous choices made in earlier rehearsals, like actions, motivations, blocking, etc., don't work as well. Maybe you defined a problem and an action in a scene as, "I come into the bar and I want to get everybody out of the bar, so I'll intimidate them." That was your problem and action. However, in a later rehearsal, after physicalizing your character, you find that doesn't feel right. Instead of trying to jam old choices into your new physicalized character stay focused on retaining the character and do the scene as a first level improvisation. You want to stay open. That's why we improvise, to stay open to things that we didn't think of. In the first level improv on retaining the character, you discover experientially that you don't want everyone to leave the bar. You get that what the scene is really about is your wanting everyone in the bar to be impressed with you. You've made a rediscovery about the internal structure of the script as a result of doing it now in character. When you start working with the fully realized character, all the loose ends start to come together and you discover how to handle every moment.

Stay open to feeling an alteration of your character's attitude in different scenes. If the entire basic attitude changes, however, you weren't on your acting focus. Basic attitudes don't change; they just go through some alteration due to different given circumstances.

ARE YOU THE CHARACTER?

Sometimes you think you are cast in a part because of how you look. That's silly. You may have been seen for the part because of your *look*. There were others called back who also had the *right look*, but you got the part, and you are going to discover that some transformation is required. The character is not you. The character is someone else. You have to find out who she is and physically manifest that. The transformation may not be as drastic or extreme as the ones we have done in these improvisations; however, there is some transformation. It frees you to discover behavior that goes beyond your natural inclinations. Without the transformation, you will only rediscover what you already know. The character's frames of reference will be yours. She will do what you would do. How limiting is *that?* How could you possibly reduce Juliet, Princess Leia, or the girls on *Dawson's Creek* to you? Is your life as dramatic as their lives?

Academy Award-winning screenwriter Alan Ball is also a TV series writer, creator, and executive producer (*Six Feet Under*). He says, "When you write something and then an actor says to you, 'Well, I would *never* say that,' it's infuriating. You just want to go, 'Yeah, well you know what? This isn't about you! This is about this *character* and your job is to portray this character.' Real actors can look at a character and see a character doing things they would never do, and go, Oh boy! This is going to be *fun.*" He was on the set of *American Beauty* every day during filming and talks about the leads, Kevin Spacey and Annette Bening: "Well, they're both *actors*. They come out of the theater. They're used to portraying people who are not themselves, and even though they've both become stars, they've retained that. They just love acting. They don't necessarily want to be themselves every time they're on screen, and I think that, to me, is the definition of a true actor, and that's really the only kind of person I want to work with." [5]

If you do reduce the character to you, it is going to come in conflict with the way the part is written even though the character's physical description is exactly the same as yours. At the very least, there will be a difference in the character's basic attitude. She has a different personality and concerns. Authors write characters *around* attitude. Hamlet's got an attitude; he's been wronged and he doesn't know what the hell to do. Blanche DuBois has an attitude; she feels she's entitled to whatever she wants. If you don't play your character's attitude, you are polluting the chemistry of the scene. Even if the change in your body is minimal, you must find the character's attitude. How do they live outside of the script, the way we explored in these improvisations? If you don't do a transformation from you to the character, you are not creating the character. You're also not playing your part of the whole.

You might discover your character's attitude as an intellectual exercise, but you must physicalize it in order to bring the attitude to every part of your being so that you can live that character's life spontaneously. What you do on stage or in front of the camera should be an expression of the life attitude that your character has. This is especially so when the script is about how a character changes.

Stanley Kowalski has an attitude about life regardless of his dialogue. He could be playing poker and his lines could be nothing more than, "I'll raise you two. Pass. Whose got the aces?" A well-played portrayal of him will communicate his life's attitude. Unless you spiritually embody that attitude in your whole being, which must start with the body, you won't capture it in those lines that are seemingly off the subject of the attitude.

Animals, body centers, and reformed body in space are all catalysts for working from the outside to the inside. Next, we will look at a catalyst for creating the character from the inside to the outside starting with the attitude the author intended.

ATTITUDES

What is an attitude? When you realigned your body, you discovered an attitude. What were some of the attitudes that emerged? Some of you discovered that you were angry. Some of you discovered that you were very precise, or happy, or impatient, or lonely, or adventurous, or bossy, or were caretakers, or had low self-esteem, and so on.

You all know someone who goes through life manifesting in their personality that no one loves them, or that they are superior to everyone else, or who has a sunny disposition, or they are very wise, or very macho, or they flirt with every person of the opposite sex. What would their *attitude* be?

ASSIGNMENT: For the next class, bring in a list of five attitudes. State each attitude in a personal expression, worded as succinctly and directly as possible. Avoid being clever. Articulate it in three words or less. In each attitude, there should be only one idea expressed, so avoid *because*. (Any attitude with the word *because* will automatically contain at least two ideas.) Examples would be: I'm sweet; I'm lonely; I'm angry; I'm the best; Nobody loves me; I love life; I'm pretty; I'm the smartest; Screw you; I'm very happy; I'll try anything; I'm impatient; My way! List your attitude lines on a notebook-size page with your name on it.

ATTITUDE LINES [6]

SETUP: 2–6 (ideally, 4) per team. Instead of huddles, prior to each team's improvising, they give their lists of *attitude lines* to the coach and he selects one attitude line for each actor by placing a check mark next to it. ◆ [See "To the coach" for how to select the line.] ◆ The coach retains the lists. The volunteer first team takes the stage with chairs and sits in a straight line across the stage down center. ◆ *The coach tells the players—* After I conclude these brief notes, I will give back your page to each of you on the first team and you will find that one attitude line is checked. That will be the line you will be working with. Memorize that line, that one line, exactly as it is written. In many cases, you will find that I've done a bit of a rewrite on it. Frequently, "I am" has gone to "I'm." In other cases I have cut or added a word. Be very clear on what the line is as I have doctored it. That is the line that you memorize. Then you put the page away. You won't need it again until next class.

We are going to do a group preparation for each team before their improvisation. During the preparation, you will be led to being on the acting focus. You will know what it means to be on this acting focus. Then, I will call out your character, activity, and location for your improvisation. You will immediately, under my coaching, go into that improvisation. The first thing that you do, and you do this very quickly, will be to move your chairs around to approximate the location. There is to be none of the discussion you would normally have when you set up a location. You just move your chairs around into a new configuration appropriate to the designated location. It should take no longer than ten seconds. Then you are ready to improvise. When that improv is finished, I will coach you to stop. Then I will give you new circumstances and you will immediately rearrange your chairs and go right into the second improvisation. Each team will be on the floor for about a half-hour, doing a series of improvisations. I announce the character and location immediately before you start each improv. You have five to ten seconds to rearrange the location. There is no group huddling about the rearrangement of the location. You do it immediately, and go with it.

RULES: Explained in the setup.

ACTING FOCUS: Revealed during the preparation.

PREPARATION COACHING: Do the 40-breath process. ◆ Now, sit up straight and breathe normally, calmly, gently. Observe your own breathing. — *Allow 15s.* ◆ Now, begin to repeat your selected attitude line silently to yourself over and over *to the exclusion of all other thought.* Without urgency, repeat it over and over and over. Keep your eyes open. Allow the line to tell you how it wishes to be said. Keep repeating it throughout the exercise. ◆ Respond to the following coaching as you continue repeating the line to yourself. [*For subsequent teams, add*— Don't get ahead of the coaching.] The line will always tell you how it wants to be said. ◆ Send the line as a message to your **feet.** Move your feet around in a response to that attitude line. Keep your eyes open. Move your feet around until you feel them adopting the attitude. If we lowered a curtain in front of you to just above your ankles, we would want to see the feet of someone who feels and has this attitude. Physically explore for an expression of that attitude line with your feet. Move your feet around until you find the position that best reflects that attitude. Your toes, arches, heels, and ankles are expressing that attitude. Now, don't let go of that. ◆ Let's add the **legs.** Allow your legs to be totally impacted by that attitude. Move them around until you find the expression in your legs. Let your knees reflect that attitude. Don't let go of the feet. Attach the feet to the legs. Don't let go of the feet and legs. ◆ Go up to the **midsection:** stomach, abdomen, pelvis, genitalia. Send the attitude as a message to the midsection of your body. Move that part of your body around until it is an expression of that attitude. Allow the midsection of your body to be totally affected by the attitude and when you find it, adopt it, hold onto it, and don't let go. Attach it to the legs and the feet and don't let go. Check in and make sure that you haven't let go of the feet and legs. The whole lower half of your body is now an expression of that attitude. You feel that attitude with every part of your lower body. Don't let go of it. You can keep moving the body parts around, but don't let go of the attitude. Keep repeating the line to yourself. ◆ Now, let's add the **chest.** Move your chest around until your chest is an expression of that attitude. Move your chest around until it receives the message of the attitude and reflects it. Show us the chest of someone who has that attitude. Don't let go of that. ◆ Now, go to the **shoulders.** Each shoulder is an expression of that attitude. Feel the attitude sitting on each shoulder. Move each shoulder around within that attitude. Express the attitude with each shoulder. Don't let go. ◆ Go to the **elbows.** Express the attitude with each elbow. Move your elbows around within the attitude until you find the expression of the attitude with the elbows. ◆ Now your **hands:** wrists and fingers. Each hand is affected by the attitude. Each hand is an expression of the attitude. These are the hands of someone who has this attitude. Move your fingers around until they best position themselves in that attitude. If there was a spotlight on your hands alone, we would want to know what this person's attitude was by looking at his hands. Don't let go. • Feel the attitude going up and down your **spine.** Feel it sitting on each vertebra point. Move your spine around until it is a complete expression of that attitude. How does a person sit who has that attitude? That is what your spine should be showing us. Don't let go. • Now, your **neck.** Let your neck be totally impacted by that attitude. Don't let go of any parts of the body that we have already visited. • Go to the top of your **head.** Feel the attitude sitting on the top of your head. Keep your eyes open. The attitude is sitting on the top of your head. How much does it weigh? Don't intellectualize it, just feel it. Whatever that attitude weighs, that is what it feels like on the top of your head. Allow it to sit there and allow your head to react. Move your head around until it captures the attitude. Don't let go of your body and what we have done so far. • Come over the top of your head and let your **eyebrows** reflect this attitude. Express the attitude with your eyebrows. There is no right or wrong. It is just what you feel. Move your eyebrows around until you feel the right setting. Then hold them in place and don't let go. • Go down to the tip of your **nose.** How does your nose feel when you have this attitude sitting on the tip of your nose? Let your nose express the attitude. Don't let go. • Now, your **lower lip.** Feel your lower lip manifesting this attitude. Move your lower lip around until you have it. Add your **tongue.** Let your **whole mouth** express the attitude. • *Smile* with this attitude. *Frown. Scowl.* • Breathe with this attitude. Allow your attitude to affect your breathing. • Now, *increase the volume of your inner line readings and send it as a message to all parts of the body at the same time.* Allow your body to respond. When you find the total positioning that best reflects this attitude, hold onto it. Don't let go. Focus on not letting go of this physical expression of the attitude. Keep it in the body and don't let go. **Retain this.** • One at a time, each of you *say your line out loud.* • *Before you do—* • *Audience, there is to be no response* from the audience whatsoever, no matter what happens, until the improv starts. Then you are on your own to respond spontaneously as a traditional audience. • *Actors, one at a time, say your line out loud.* • Now, tell each other your lines. You may overlap. Don't let go of your bodies while expressing the attitude. Keep telling each other. Now, immediately get up and *start walking* around upstage of the chairs. Keep expressing the attitude with your body and keep telling each other your lines. Stay up there. Spread out up there and keep holding the attitude in the body. Your focus is to not let go of holding the attitude in the body and on the face. ◆ From up there, tell the audience out loud. *Tell the audience your lines.* Big. Bigger. Bigger! ◆ Tell us! Big! Bigger! Stop speaking! ◆ Don't let go. Don't move. ◆ *Hold that attitude on your face and in your body! Feel the expression on your face. Feel the way your body muscles are holding themselves in place. This is what you must not let go of throughout the entire range of scenes.* ◆ In a moment, you will start the first improv scene. As soon as you hear what it is, quickly set up the chairs and go right into it. Throughout the improv, your *acting focus*, in addition to all of the improv doing skills that you have learned so far, is *to not let go of this attitude in the body or in the face.* There is also a *rule. You may never again say your attitude line out loud.* You should *say your attitude line to yourself frequently* in order to help you retain this body alignment and facial expression, but never out loud, unless I specifically coach you to do so. ◆ Feel the way your muscles are working together right now. Feel your body stance. Your focus is to not let go of that. Feel the expression on your face. It is like a mask. Your focus is to keep it on, to not let go of it. Through all of the scenes, you must retain this muscle composition, this facial expression, and never let go of it. It is a *physical* acting focus.

FIRST IMPROV: You are five years old in kindergarten. ◆ Action.

COACHING FOR THE IMPROVS (as needed): [Each improv is about seven minutes.] Stay on your acting focus. Share your voices. Avoid hanging out. Share your voices and practice all the skills you have learned so far. Discover an activity. Go to the location. Do an activity. Discover objects. **Stay on your acting focus of not letting go of the attitude. Silently, repeat your line to yourself frequently. Avoid talking about each other's attitudes.** Group blocking. Fix your group blocking. Respond to the coaching. Help your fellow actors to solve a problem. Stay on focus. Active & still. **Don't let go of your attitude. Keep it in the body and on the face.** Integrate your laughter with your attitude line. Don't let go. Don't let your particular attitude keep you from involving with the others. Find a way, for the sake of the improvisation, to involve with the other actors. Show us; don't tell us. Use your space objects. Acting is doing. ◆ After coaching all through it, the coach *ends the improv*— Everybody go still. One at a time, say your attitude lines out loud. ◆

As soon as the last actor says his line, the coach calls out the circumstances for the next improv.

SECOND IMPROV: You're now fourteen years old at McDonald's. Don't let go of your attitudes. Keep them in the body and on the face. Move your chairs around quickly. You may repeat the line to yourself as often as you wish, whenever you want, but you cannot say it out loud. You must keep it in the body and on the face. ♦ Action. ♦ Coach (as needed) from first improv.

The coach *ends*— Everybody go still. One at a time, say your lines out loud.

THIRD IMPROV: You are twenty-one years old, in two cars on lovers' lane. ♦ Action. ♦ **New:** Stay in the cars. Stay on focus. Keep expressing your attitude with your body and your face. Play active & still. Discover objects near you. **Keep the attitude on your face and in your body.** Active & still. **Let the other team know you are gong active and they will go still.** Stay on your acting focus and say the line to yourself as often as you wish, but keep it in the body and on the face. ♦ The coach *ends the improv*— Everybody go still. Say your lines out loud, one at a time.

FOURTH IMPROV: You are forty years old at the office Christmas party. ♦ Action. ♦ The coach *ends the improv*— Everybody go still. Say your lines out loud, one at a time.

FIFTH IMPROV: You are sixty-five years old at the country club. ♦ Action. ♦ The coach *ends the improv*— Everybody go still. Say your lines out loud, one at a time.

SIXTH IMPROV: You are ninety years old at a senior citizens' home. Move your chairs around. Break the setting. ♦ You are in a new scene now. It is twenty-five years later. ♦ Action. ♦ Don't let go. Keep the attitude on your face and in your body. Stay on the acting focus. Don't let go of the attitude. Say it to yourself as often as you wish. Stay on the acting focus. ♦ *Allow ca. 4m, then coach*— **Avoid dialogue, momentarily. Keep playing; just avoid dialogue. You are in the last minute of the scene. During this minute, you are going to find a place to integrate your actual attitude line as a line of dialogue. However, it will be the last thing your character says, for you will immediately die after saying it. You indicate the death by simply lowering your head, and the others will then simply ignore you.** ♦ **Continue the action.** ♦ *After all have lowered their heads*— Cut. ♦ Everyone, do a shake-out (p. 242).

FOLLOW-UP (as needed): Audience, **did they create characters from their attitude lines? Did the attitudes affect, change, or realign their bodies? Did they retain the attitudes in their faces and bodies throughout the scenes?** Is it possible for an attitude to be retained and still be slightly altered over time? What's the difference between an attitude altering and dropping an attitude? It's the difference between being on focus and being off focus. **How were characters' relationships influenced by their attitudes? Was the characters' dialogue influenced by their attitudes? Was their behavior related to their attitudes?** Did any actors change their attitude line, even slightly, over the course of the scenes? When beginning a new scene, did they change their locations and make physical contact with them? Did they employ active & still? Did they find new activities and discover objects in each new scene? Did they avoid questions? Did they avoid commenting on each other's attitudes? Was there any playwriting? ◆ Actors, do you agree? **Were you on your acting focus? When you found yourself thinking, did you think as the characters or for the characters?**

SUMMARY:

Did you feel your character affected by his attitude through his whole life? Extreme attitudes can make for a life of freedom or enslavement.

CHARACTER ARMOR

In real life, attitudes are formed in early childhood and become a conditioned response to dealing with the world. They form a personality style that is physically embedded in a person's muscles, which is the reason we walk the way we walk, talk the way we talk, and respond to stimuli the way we do. Some people's attitudes are healthy and expansive; others' attitudes are self-limiting. We developed our basic attitudes as an individual defensive style to the way our parents and the environment treated us in early childhood. As we grow, the body aligns itself to go with that attitude. That body alignment then becomes a part of the physical being and forms what the psychologist, Wilhelm Reich, called *character armor.* We all go through life wearing our own armor, our character armor. It's interesting to note that psychologists use the word *character* in phrases that describe this phenomenon, like character armor or character style. They don't use the word *personal,* as in personal armor. Why a theatrical word? In the real and personal world, the taking on of this attitude and the accompanying armor is not authentic to the child. It is a *role* the child learns to play in order to deal with the environment. Actors can profit from this by realizing that when they create a character, they have to take on the attitude and the armor that goes with the role.

When you play a character, you are putting on another's armor. This can be clunky and inauthentic unless you remove your own armor first. We began this improvisation with the 40-breath process because that is the quickest and fastest, even if temporary, way to remove your own armor. Forty big explosive breaths oxygenate the blood and put an electrical charge into your body. Sometimes you will feel dizzy immediately following the breaths. If you immediately focus on something you can *see,* whether it is making eye contact with the other actors, or looking around the room and naming the colors you see, e.g., yellow shirt, blue sweater, orange jacket, the dizziness goes away. Then, you focus on your own natural breathing to begin the process of focusing on the character's attitude and realigning your body accordingly.

In our earlier character work with reformed bodies, animals, and body centers, the catalyst realigned the body and we then discovered what attitude emerged. In our work now, with attitude lines, we start with an articulation of the character's attitude, and then realign the body from that catalyst. With this work, it must be remembered that choosing an attitude alone, without allowing it to affect the body, is worthless. It must affect the body in order for it to be ingrained and become the character's armor.

THE SCRIPTED CHARACTER

The most important thing about character work is living in the character's body and possessing his attitude. When you can do that, you will also spontaneously think and feel as the character.

While every character has an attitude, it may alter over the length of a script. This is usually called the *character's arc*. It can alter in the way that it altered over the life span of your characters in the improvisations. You felt and said your attitude line at age fourteen very differently from the way you felt and said it at age ninety, but the attitude line stayed the same. Let's say that your basic attitude line is "Nobody loves me." At age fourteen, "Nobody loves me" means "I feel like killing myself." At age ninety, it might mean "Nobody loves me and that's the way it is. That's life. What else is new?"

As different story points, character involvements, and episodes of the script occur and impact upon your character, your attitude line may alter, but it remains the same basic attitude line. If not, you are wrenching or changing the character. A character's basic attitude does not change. It becomes unreal if you change it.

If you have a character who is presented as a timid and somewhat fearful person through most of the script and in the climax, he does some very brave act, he has not changed his basic attitude. Chances are he approaches the climax and does his heroic act with an accompanying fear. The alteration is that he has found just enough courage to perform the deed. That would be authentic. If he approaches the climax and does his heroic act with no fear at all, his attitude has totally changed. That would be inauthentic.

The character's attitude affects everything you say and do. It impacts on how you hold your body, walk, pick up something, think, and relate to other characters. During the improvisation, you discovered that the attitude spontaneously influenced every single acting impulse and choice. It colored all your improvisational dialogue and affected when you spoke, what you spoke about, and how you spoke. This will also be true with memorized dialogue. Even though the author has chosen what you say and when you say it, the attitude will totally affect *how* you say the lines.

While the author of a script probably did not employ a specific attitude line in creating his characters, he certainly imagined, visualized, and created a specific and different personality for each character. The foundation of that personality is the character's attitude. The author of a script has very knowingly paired and combined your character with other characters in the scenes you are in, based on attitude differences. In our improvs, you saw how a victim attitude character frequently combined with an anger attitude character and created a very dramatic dynamic. If we replaced the victim character in the scene with another anger character, it's a whole different scene. It's just two characters fighting. Authors know this. They're very careful about who they are combining in scenes.

An attitude line is another catalytic tool for creating a character and in some ways it's easier to use than the other character acting focuses. This is because it is frequently easier to derive the character's attitude from the text than to interpret what animal or body center to use. Many times, the character will say his attitude line in the script. Sometimes, he will repeat it. That is the author making sure you (and the audience) get it.

Your job is to find your character in the script where the author designed and created it. If you ignore this and turn the character into you, you rob all your scenes of their intended dynamics. Turning your character into you also requires great and unnecessary effort, as you will always feel like you are going against the tide, which you are.

ARTICULATING THE ATTITUDE LINE

An attitude line is effectively articulated when your body easily and immediately responds to it. If the line is too intellectual, you will not get an immediate response. There is a delay while you *think* about the meaning. A line isn't intellectual just because it includes an intellectual word. There is nothing wrong with "I'm conservative" if your body responds to it. Your body might respond to *conservative* just as immediately and easily as it would to an emotional word, e.g., *happy*. An ineffectual attitude line would probably be, "I tend to be conservative." It has too many words, too many beats, too many issues, and it waters down what's important. Get to the point and you will find that "I'm conservative" or "I'm a conservative" is much better. This, for example, was the attitude for Michael J. Fox on *Family Ties*.

If you have an attitude line that you like, but suspect that it is ineffectively articulated, you can rewrite it. Let's take "I don't want to get involved" as an example. What's wrong with "I don't want to get involved"? Too long. Too wordy. Two beats or ideas instead of one. (First beat, "I don't want." Second beat, "to get involved.") Also, it is built around a negative, "I don't," instead of any variation on "I am." There are some attitude lines that are effective and are built around a negative, but in general, this is a warning sign that the line needs a rewrite. Look at the opposite way of saying the same thing. What's the opposite of "I don't want to get involved"? "Stay away," or "I'm aloof," or "I'm detached," or "I like safety."

Always personalize the attitude line. Don't just write the key word, e.g., "angry." Make it, "I'm angry."

Be careful of lines that use the pronoun *you* as the subject, e.g., "You don't love me." This line is about someone else. Rewrite it so that it's about your character, e.g., "I'm unloved." On the other hand, lines that start with *nobody* or *everybody* frequently work well, as in, "Nobody loves me" or "Everybody understands me."

Avoid cerebral ideas. When you think that as long as you can understand the line, it's fine, you miss the opportunity to improve the articulation of the line. You've got to word it in such a way that your body has an easy, immediate, visceral, and total body response. When you send the attitude to the different body parts, the response must be immediate. You can then spend time exploring the most effective body part response.

Any time your line includes the words "I am," reduce it to "I'm." The shorter the line is, the more singular a feeling it has, the more impact it will have on the body, and the more effective the body response will be. The best attitude lines have only two or three words, sometimes as many as five; more, and it needs rewriting.

The attitude line should not be ambiguous. There is nothing ambiguous about "I'm happy." But how about "I need to be happy"? No good. You've got the issue of *need* and the issue of *happy*. There's a duality there and the body's response will be confused. So, rewrite it. Instead of describing what I need to feel, I'd describe what I *do* feel. If you need to be happy, you are what? Sad, depressed, angry, scared? You decide. Put an "I'm" in front of your choice and you have an effective attitude line. You could even go with "I'm unhappy," if your body responds to it. The test is you. Can you do the process and get as strong an impact response as you've gotten with other lines you know to be effective? If not, something is wrong. Try it on before going through the whole process.

ATTITUDE LINE TEST

I'll give you an example right now. Let's take the line, "I need to be happy." Repeat the line to yourself, "I need to be happy, I need to be happy." Don't improve the line. Let your whole body immediately and totally respond to that attitude. Do you notice how hard it is? Do you feel that? It's vague. Now let's take the same idea and do "I'm sad." Let your whole body be immediately and totally affected. Can you respond to it? Notice how specific it is. That's all we're talking about. Even though we all clearly understand and know what "I need to be happy" means, it just does not create an immediate and totally physicalized body response. "I need to be happy" first creates a body feeling of sadness around the phrase "I need," and then a body feeling of happiness around "happy." You got both of these signals, the duality, and they canceled each other out, creating a body feeling of vagueness. It's got to be a singular feeling without ambiguity.

You can do this test on any attitude line. After you have selected the line and reduced it to the fewest words, do the test. See if you have a complete body response to it in one second. You will know immediately if the line is a good one. If your body is wishy-washy and can't get a hold of it, the line failed the test. Rewrite it.

When rewriting an attitude line, keep asking yourself, "What do I really mean?" or "What do I mean by that?" Say your first draft of a line is, "You can't always get what you want." You're suspicious of the line's efficacy because of the number of words, "can't" is negative, and the subject of the line is "you." Ask yourself, "What did you mean by you can't always get what you want?" Your answer might be, "The reality of what has taken place has not met my expectations." Then ask yourself, "What does that mean?" "I'm disappointed." Now you have an effective attitude line that means what you originally intended. If it doesn't mean what you originally intended, go back to your original line. Ask the question about what does that mean, and come up with different answers. Keep bringing it down to the one thought, the one feeling, the one expression.

Characters don't know their attitude lines. A character's attitude line may be "I'm stupid." That doesn't mean he thinks he is stupid. It's the actor creating the character who knows the attitude line. It's just like all the previous character catalysts. A character doesn't know that he is evolved from a particular animal or has a particular body center. If you do have an intuitive, negative response about the attitude line articulation, consider it. For instance, you might substitute "I don't know" for "I'm stupid."

ASSIGNMENT: For the next class, profit from this discussion and make a new list of five attitude lines. Add this list to the page with the first list you have already done.

> **TO THE COACH:** Doing the 40-breath process at the beginning of the attitude line process is important because it removes the actor's personal character armor while retaining his individual authenticity. This is necessary to allow room for the character's armor to fit onto the actor's individuality. The coach should make sure that the breaths are deep and quick, and not slow, meditation-style breaths. Doing the character shakeout is important for removing the character's armor, allowing the actor to let go of the attitude physiologically.
>
> When selecting the attitude line from the actor's list, put a check mark on the selected line. Remind the actors to not lose this page. There will be future assignments that need to be done on the same page. Selecting the actor's attitude line should be done at the same time as the coach is selecting the lines for all of the actors in the same scene. The coach should be matching the actors' attitude lines to make potentially interesting relationships, just as an author would. In other words, avoid hav-

284

ing five "Nobody loves me" lines in the same scene. For a four-actor improv, I usually look for two positive and two negative attitude lines. The coach might also take into account whether an actor's list includes an attitude line quite unlike the attitude that particular actor normally shows in his improvisations or personality. Choosing that attitude line can present an opportunity for the coach to provide a stretch and a challenge for the individual actor. Of course, this reason for the selection of the line should not be shared with the actor.

After counting off teams, the coach should monitor the male/female ratio in each team and do some rearranging in an attempt at a fairly equal ratio.

Prior to the actors saying their attitude lines out loud for the first time, it is important to coach the audience not to respond vocally, because laughs at that moment may create self-consciousness at a vulnerable time, i.e., "What am I doing that's funny?"

The coach should provide different setups for each successive team's improv:

Age 5—birthday party	Nursery school playground	Day care center	1st grade class/ teacher is late	First day of kindergarten
Age 14— McDonalds	Jr. High School planning school newspaper	Jr. High School bio lab	Jr. High School waiting for graduation ceremony	Record store
Age 21—setting up campsite	Card party	Wedding reception	Miniature golf	Lovers' lane
Age 40—office Christmas party	Paris restaurant	Hotel restaurant	*Parents without Partners* meeting	Community theater rehearsal
Age 65— country club	History museum	Art museum	Beijing restaurant	Rome restaurant
Age 90—senior citizens home	Cruise ship	Church bingo night	Arts & crafts class	Friend's funeral

◆ ◆ ◆

ATTITUDE LINE / CHARACTER, ACTIVITY, LOCATION [7]

For practice creating characters from attitude lines:

SETUP: 2–4 per team. In huddles, actors select activity, location, character (occupation and personal relationships) while the coach selects attitude lines from their lists. The first volunteer team then sets up its location. The coach gives back the lists, and each sees the attitude line he will be employing. The coach takes them through the attitude line preparation from the previous exercise and the actors begin the improvisation.

RULES: In the preparation, respond to the coaching. During the improvisation, employ physical doing tools of Improvisation Technique for activity, location, relationships, and occupation.

ACTING FOCUS: Retaining the attitude on the face and in the body.

COACHING: Do the preparation from the previous exercise. ◆ Now, stay on the acting focus as you rearrange the chairs back to where they were in your floor plan. ◆ Places. ◆ While you are employing all of the improv skills that you have learned so far, your primary acting focus is retaining this attitude on the face and in the body. **Say your attitude line to yourself frequently** in order to help you retain this body alignment and facial expression, but never out loud. ◆ Action. ◆ **Coaching for improv (as needed): Stay on your acting focus.** Don't let go of the attitude. **Keep it on the face and in the body. Say your line to yourself but not out loud.** ◆ **Find a way of involving in the scene regardless of your attitude and stay true to your attitude. Avoid hanging out. Make it a habit to check out your fellow players.** Stay open to helping anyone. Stay open to needing help. Respect your space objects. **Censor nothing** while sticking to your attitude line. Share your voices. Active & still. ◆ Audience, observe the group as a whole as well as individuals. One minute to heighten your acting focus. Cut. ◆ Do a shake-out.

FOLLOW-UP (as needed):: Location? Activity? Occupations? **Relationships?** Were the actors open to realigning their bodies? **Did they create characters from their attitude lines?** Did they let go of their characters? Did the character's attitudes affect their relationships? Did the actors reveal characteristics we don't usually see from these actors? **Did they stay on their acting focus?** ◆ **Actors, do you agree? Did you hold onto your character's attitude?**

SUMMARY:

Do you recognize some of these characters' characteristics in people you know? In yourselves? Do you recognize that the attitude lines lead you to play characters we never see you play? Regardless of who you are, through attitude lines you have the capability to play any character ever written. This is also true for any of the character catalysts we have already learned.

When improvising with an attitude line, or any character catalyst, remember the importance of your physical doing improvisation technique. If you go through the whole preparation process, creating the character, and then sit or stand doing nothing through the whole scene, your character will not be shared with the audience. Dialogue, behavior, and physical characteristics are how an audience gets to know a character. Doing nothing deprives them of everything but the dialogue. Communicating behavior and physical characteristics require action. Doing provides action. It's in the doing that the character manifestations are revealed. How does someone with an angry attitude make coffee? How does someone with a happy attitude make coffee? It's in the making of the coffee, or whatever the physical doing is, that the attitude is revealed.

It is important that when you create a character from an attitude line, you not get ahead of the coaching during the preparation process, the coach's or your own self-coaching. When you do, you go into the head and jump to an *imagined* concept of the character based on the attitude line, and this will frequently lead to a cliché character. When you allow the attitude line to affect you one body part at a time, you create a brand new character. It is important when you create a character that you not know who it is from the beginning. You should discover who it is after you create it.

Another self-defeating behavior during the preparation process is closing your eyes. If you close your eyes when you are first observing your breathing or repeating the attitude line over and over, you go into a meditation and that works against the acting focus. A meditation is all about relaxation and centering, which is exactly what we don't want. We want you to be off kilter. The attitude and its manifestation is the degree to which you are off kilter. If you're relaxed within that attitude, in a meditative way and not in an actor's way, you're only going to water it down and get mellow. You can have any attitude and find its mellow version but it won't serve the purpose of creating or playing the character.

> **TO THE COACH:** All of the assignment lists of attitude lines should be on the same page. This allows the coach to insure that each actor experiences a wide range in the lines they use to create characters in the class improvisations, and it facilitates selecting the team's attitude lines with an eye for potentially interesting relationships. Avoid showing the actors the selected attitude line until they are seated for the preparation process so that they won't think about or imagine their character during the other actors' improvisations.

Party Mingle Attitude Lines

SETUP: Same as party upset (p. 122). *However, this time we will do it with it attitude lines as a character catalyst.*

We will do a group preparation and you will create your characters and then go to places. From that point on, you must retain the character through the attitude line. ◆ Each of you go to your assignment lists and select your own single attitude line. It must be one you have not used before. All the ones you have used have check marks next to them. After you have selected it, put a check mark next to it. Then put your list away and go back out on the floor. I have put out five extra chairs. Each of you go to a chair for the preparation process. *When we get to the part of the process where I tell you to say your lines out loud, you are to silently mouth the line.* I will coach you in the same way by saying, "Say it," but you should only mouth it. You must mouth the words but not say them. We don't want the audience or your improv mates to know what they are. This will also be true when you are coached to get bigger and bigger.

RULES: Same as active & still. Only one subteam may go active at a time. All the other subteams must go still. Any subteam may go active whenever it wishes. Going active means to talk or move. When you are still, you may not talk or move and you are expected to retain your attitude on your face and in your body while you do your inner doing, i.e., traveling. You do not have the option of initiating a still. You only go still if another subteam goes active. Subteams are not to merge with each other unless coached to do so.

ACTING FOCUS: Retaining the character's attitude while playing active & still.

COACHING: Preparation from basic attitude line exercise. ◆ When the actors get to the point where they say their lines out loud, *coach*— Silently mouth your attitude line to each other. Say the line without volume. Get up and walk around upstage. Keep silently saying the line to each other upstage. Now, tell us. Silently tell us. Tell the audience. Big. Bigger. Bigger! Stop speaking! Don't let go. Don't move. Hold that attitude on your face and in your body! Feel the expression on your face. Feel the way your body muscles are holding themselves in place. That is what you have to retain physically throughout the scene. Don't let go of it. ◆ Find your partner and go to places. Choose an acting area for the two of you in the location. Say your attitude line to yourself frequently in order to help you retain this body alignment and facial expression, but never out loud. **Coaching for improv (as needed):** Action. ◆ All teams are active. ◆ *After 1m—* Active & still. Any team can go active whenever they want, but they must keep going active until another team goes active. If you go active, go active! Let everyone know you are going active. There is no walking around when you are in a still. You can have movement by discovering an object near you. Share your voices. Stay on your acting focus. Retain the character's attitude. Don't let go. Let the attitude line inform your inner doing. Don't merge the teams. ✦ *After ca. 8m—* **Upset! All teams go active simultaneously and merge into one group. Right now, merge into one group! Mingle. Meet each other.** ✦ *About 30s after they are all in one group—* **Now, find a brand new partner. Form a new subteam.** Head out into the location. Retain your character. Stay with your new partner. You are now in a new subteam. ✦ *After 30–60s—* Active & still. ✦ Audience, keep track of the different actors and their characters. ✦ Actors, retain your character's attitude. Don't let go. ✦ *After ca. 5–8m—* Upset! Mingle as a group. ✦ Find a brand new partner. Go to a different part of the location. ✦ *After 30–60s—* Active & still. ✦ *After ca. 5m—* One more minute to stay on your acting focus. ✦ Cut.

> **FOLLOW-UP (as needed): Did the actors create characters from their attitude lines? Did they retain them throughout the improvisation, especially after they changed partners? Describe each actor's character.** ✦ **Actors, is that accurate? What is your attitude line? Did you stay on your acting focus during your still periods? Did you feel the influence of your attitude line on your inner doing?** When you were thinking in the still periods, did you think as the character or for the character? Which is preferable? As the character. **Did you allow the acting focus to lead you through the periods of active & still?**

SUMMARY:

Until this improvisation, I have selected your attitude line from the lists you created. This time, you selected your own. Did you discover anything from making your own choice? Did you find your choice to be effective? If you didn't, what are the characteristics of an ineffective attitude line? There is less presence, energy, and a low impact on you. An ineffective attitude line will put you into your head rather than your body and not activate any feelings. Can a low-energy attitude, e.g., shyness, be formulated in an effective attitude line? Absolutely, if you word the line according to the standards we've discussed, e.g., I'm shy. The most common mistakes in forming an effective attitude line are not personalizing expressions, too clever, too many words, and/or negative words, i.e., what you *are not* instead of what you *are*.

If you felt your attitude line was less effective than you would have liked, before you blame it on the articulated line, evaluate for yourself: Did you do the preparation process thoroughly or superficially. Did you get ahead of the process?

TO THE COACH: This improvisation comes in handy when time is running short in class because of the number of actors on each team. If the coach has planned an improv that would require five teams (with five preparation processes), but time won't allow it, he can switch to this improv, which employs up to ten actors per team.

The coaching of the attitude line preparation process may be reduced with successive exposures to this acting focus. This is a shortened version that I use when an actor is about to do his third improv with an attitude line:

PREPARATION COACHING: Do the 40-breath process. Make eye contact. Now, observe your own natural breathing. Repeat your line to yourself over and over, without urgency, allowing the line to tell you how it wishes to be read. Keep saying the line to yourself over and over again, throughout the preparation process. *I will be using fewer words in this preparation because you know what I mean.* I will be primarily naming the body parts. You allow the body parts to respond to the attitude and find the positioning that best reflects that attitude. Send this attitude to your feet. Don't let go of the feet and go up to the legs. Don't let go. The midsection. Chest. You're moving the body part around until it is completely expressing the attitude. Shoulders. Elbows. Wrists and fingers. Spine. Neck. Top of head. Eyebrows. Tip of nose. Lips. Smile. Frown. Increase the volume of your inner line reading, and send it as a message to all body parts at the same time. Don't let go. Now, all at the same time silently say your lines. Mouth the words. Say them to each other. Retaining the attitude in the body, get up and walk around upstage. Continue saying the line silently to each other. Now, tell the audience silently. Use your whole body. Tell us. Big. Bigger. Bigger! Stop speaking! Don't let go. Don't move. Feel the look on your face. That is the expression you must physically retain on your face throughout the entire improvisation. Feel the way that your body is holding itself together. That is the way you have to hold your body together throughout the entire improv. Now, staying on your acting focus, find your partner and go to places. Choose an acting area for the two of you in the location. You may never say your line out loud.

The actors should be given the opportunity to do an attitude line improv *where they coach themselves in the preparation process.* It can be done with a repeat round of attitude line/character, activity, location improvs, or with the first or a repeat round of party mingle.

After setting up their location and selecting the attitude line, *coach—* Now we are going to play the way we did last class, where you simply create and retain your character from the attitude line as you go through the improv. What is important now is that this is the first time that you all coach yourself through the preparation process. So, find a seat, and I will tell you when to start. Everybody begin your preparation process now.

They do the whole process without any coaching. At the end, the coach calls "Places."

◆　◆　◆

MIDREHEARSAL APPLICATION OF CHARACTER INSPIRED BY ATTITUDE LINE

The majority of the actors I work with prefer creating the character from an attitude line, rather than the *body-first* acting focuses. The main reason for this is that it is less of a guessing game. While there may be specific hints in a script as to what the animal or body center might be, it is usually a very interpretive and highly intuitive selection process. With attitude lines, it is much less so. Very frequently, the attitude line is spoken as a part of the dialogue in the script and doesn't even need modification. Your character has a line that jumps off the page as an expression of a lifelong attitude. Sometimes, the author has the character repeat the line more than once. When that happens, you can be sure that the author is telling you that is the attitude line. Sometimes the line will appear in the script as a perfectly articulated attitude line; other times you are going to have to play with the phraseology and whittle it down to an effective attitude line articulation. Sometimes other characters will talk about your character and describe your character's attitude, e.g., "Oh, he is so vicious!" Your attitude line could be, "I'm vicious." Regardless of the acting focus you use for your catalyst, a reformed body in space, an animal, a body center, or an attitude line, the resulting character will be fully formed.

Creating the Attitude Line from the Script

If you select an attitude line from your character's dialogue, you should back it up with an analysis of the character. If an attitude line does not appear in your character's dialogue, you can form one from the same type of analysis.

You start by simply writing about attitude issues of your character. The character seems to be a snob. He has a superior attitude. He seems to behave as if he is better than everyone else. Then you list certain lines of dialogue that bear this out. There will be a *consistency of attitude* throughout your character's part in the script. Once you have done that, you are in the ball park. Then you create a short, effective attitude line that will be the equivalent of the attitude. In other words, a line that will create that type of attitude in your behavior. So, if your character has the attitude characteristics listed above, effective attitude lines would be "I'm the best," "I know it all," "I'm better," or "I'm superior." Then you have to play with it. You try it on. You work with it. You create the character, using the attitude line preparation approach. Create the body from the line you have selected and see if it gives you what you want. If it doesn't, you make an adjustment. Suppose you are doing "I'm superior." You may discover that the character comes out a little too upper class. What if your character is a blue-collar person? In trying it out and improvising, you realize, "Oh, this is not a blue-collar person. I feel good about the attitude, but this is working against the creation of a blue-collar person." With this new information, you select another attitude line from your list or create a new attitude line that is appropriate to the list. Instead of "I'm superior," try "I'm the best." Play with it. It takes practice and finesse. You're not going to get it right off the bat.

When dealing with descriptions of your character from other characters, you have to stay alert. Is the description about you echoed by more than one character? If not, is the character describing you accurately or are they coming from their own agenda? Are they lying? What if another character says about your character, "She's such a bitch"? If you decide that description is accurate, it would be your job to figure out how or why you come across as a bitch. It could be the result of your superior attitude, as in "I'm the best." Remember, the way you feel on the inside and the way you come across to others aren't always the same.

An important place to look for hints to an attitude line besides script dialogue is any descriptions in the script provided by the author.

Audition casting breakdowns frequently include descriptions with hints to the attitude line. These should be considered but not necessarily taken as accurate. Who knows who wrote the descriptions? When it comes to casting directors, there is no quality control.

Theme

A really thorough actor considers the theme of the script when contemplating the creation of a character. The author created your character as a part of the whole script and your part has to serve a function in the whole script. Creating your character without knowing its function is working with blinders on. My student, Gloria Loring, played the lead in the premiere of a new play, *Queen of the Soaps*. The theme of the play is "dishonesty kills the self." Based on how the play was written, we knew that the character's arc went from dishonest to honest. The play has a happy ending, and the character emerges from the play's climax a more honest person. It was Gloria's job, after the climax, for her character to stop being dishonest and become a true, authentic person in front of the audience's eyes. In that way, she served the whole play's theme and her function was to reveal the theme to the audience. We chose two attitude lines, one for before the climax and one for after. The first one was "I'm a liar," and the second, "I'm honest."

Let's look at Chekhov's *Three Sisters*. If the theme of the play is "In the conflict between culture and vulgarity, vulgarity will win," the actor has to decide which side of that conflict Chekhov meant for him to be on. If he is on the vulgarity side, then his character must appear to have some form of vulgar characteristics. For example, Natasha's character might be created from an attitude line of "I want it now!" On the cultured side, Irina's attitude line might be "I have wonderful thoughts!" Of course, these attitude lines will be altered over the course of the play as the conflict unfolds and the victors and losers begin emerging. It's similar to the first attitude line improvisations we did, in which the attitude lines altered over a lifetime. Think of Irina, radiant and glowing in the beginning of the play, as her body expresses "I have wonderful thoughts." Then think of her at the end when her spirit has been extinguished and her body sadly expresses "I have wonderful thoughts."

Knowing the theme of the script and what function your character has to serve assists you in the creation of that character.

When playing an important supporting character, you will find yourself in scenes with the lead(s) where they have the central position in the scene with most of the dialogue. If the director deprives you of business or movement, and the script deprives you of lines, then your attitude line becomes an important acting focus. You can use inner doing or simply focus on physicalizing your attitude line. You will be absolutely in character and spontaneously doing within the confines of the direction and blocking.

You can see this in operation if you view some of my students' film performances I have coached. Watch George Carlin as Barbra Streisand's upstairs neighbor in *The Prince of Tides*. His attitude line is "I'm lonely." In the film *Memphis Belle*, Tate Donovan's attitude line, "I can do it," got him through many scenes where he just sits in the co-pilot's seat playing second banana to star Matthew Modine.

Television Sitcoms

Sitcom writers have spent a great deal of time on the attitude of the character. That is how sitcoms are written. Attitude-inspired characters prevail. Think of every sitcom you've ever seen. In *The Mary Tyler Moore Show*, Ted has got his attitude, Mary's got her attitude, and Murray's got his attitude. In *I Love Lucy*, Lucy's attitude line was "I'll try anything!" Take *Seinfeld*. Jerry's attitude line is frequently "I'm suspicious." When it comes to his girlfriends, he is suspicious of a different aspect concerning the girlfriend: She always wears the same dress. Is he on her speed dial? Why won't she give him a massage? With George or Kramer, he is suspicious of their schemes. For the other characters, Kramer's attitude line is "I'm outrageous." Elaine's, "My way." George's, "I'm pissed off." And for Newman, "I know everything."

From Auditions to Looping

In dealing with auditions, especially for supporting roles, the sides often indicate very little about your character. So the great pitfall is that you don't do anything with the character. You do it as blandly as it's written, and that's why you don't get the part. The part goes to the actor who creates a whole character with those same few lines.

How do you go about picking the character in that situation? Look carefully, and you'll find that in whatever lines you have, there will be hints. The hint might take you in the direction of an attitude line, an animal, or a body center. Also, when you understand the purpose of the scene itself, you can then design your character to serve that purpose. This is discussed thoroughly in chapter 12.

If there are no hints in the lines, and until we get to chapter 12, you have the opportunity to be very creative in formulating an attitude line. My student, Haynes Brooke, had an audition for a small, recurring role on the TV show *Home Improvement*. The role was the bandleader on Tim Allen's character's cable TV show. The lines for the audition revealed nothing about the character other than his function as a straight man to Tim Allen. Prior to the audition, Haynes decided to watch the bandleaders on the real late-night talk shows to glean any hints. He observed that bandleader Paul Shaffer was always bemused by everything David Letterman said or did. Haynes chose an attitude line of "I'm bemused" to build his character on. Since Haynes looks nothing like Paul Shaffer, he wasn't worried about it coming off like an imitation. He got the part.

There are occasionally auditions without any sides or script. They are just casting types. My student, William Schallert, tells this story: "Many years ago, I used to go out on auditions where there would be three of four of us who would be trotted out onto a set when they had stopped shooting, and the director would take a look at us to decide if we were going to be in the picture, no lines or anything. We just stood there with two or three other guys and everybody was always very pleasant, and it occurred to me that maybe a way to distinguish myself and make them remember me was to be unpleasant. My attitude line was 'This shit sucks. Go fuck yourself.' That worked four times out of five. Then one time, I went on an audition over at Paramount for a good director, George Marshall, and he picked up on what I was doing and he said, 'What the hell is that?' It put an end to it, but it was a way to distinguish yourself, even without the script, and it was pure attitude and nothing else."

Sometimes crafting the attitude line in a specific vernacular can do the trick. For example, if the description indicates that the character is a country bumpkin and the lines themselves offer no further hints, a worthy attitude line might be

"Yee-hah!" A character created from that line will have a country tone and not be very bright, a country bumpkin.

Frequently, small roles that are not defined well in the sides are bad guys, henchmen to the lead bad guy. These parts are usually cast with actors who look mean or tough at the audition. If that is not your natural look, then adopt that demeanor for the audition through an attitude line, e.g., "I'm mean," "I'm tough," "I'm a killer." This approach is effective if the dialogue lines are neutral, e.g., "Yes, boss. I'll do it. What time should I be there?" Another approach can be much more effective, but it is only usable if the lines are appropriate. If the lines include nasty things like, "I'll cut his guts out and send them to his wife," you might go in the opposite direction with attitude lines that, on the surface, are innocent, e.g., "I'm kind," "I'm sweet," or "I love life." That kind of attitude combined with nasty dialogue will create a sinister character. One of the great modern villains in literature and film is Nurse Ratched in *One Flew Over the Cuckoo's Nest.* Her attitude line is something like "I'm cooperative" or "I'm on your side." She doesn't say nasty things, but her dialogue and actions always put her in conflict with the hero, which accomplishes the same thing.

Regardless of whether you find hints in the sides or script or have to create from whole cloth, the less specifically the part is written, the more important it is that you create the character.

If you are employing an attitude line during an audition, and the casting director asks you to do it again, "But this time do it more (or less) —," it's easy to adjust your attitude line based on the note. For example, if your line was "I'm angry" and the note is that you were too angry, change your line to "I'm irritated." Attitude lines allow you to know exactly what you are doing, and provide a specific reference point for adjustment.

Whether you are at an audition or on the set shooting, there is always that anxious moment when you are on your mark and waiting for "Action!" Focusing on retaining your character's attitude line during those moments will simultaneously deflect nervousness and increase your preparation for the scene.

Sometimes, weeks or months after shooting has been completed, you have to return to your character in order to loop some lines. If you used an attitude line in the creation of your character, when it comes time for the looping, it is easy to return to the character by re-creating it through the same attitude line.

A list of sample attitude lines is provided in Appendix D.

ASSIGNMENT: For the next class, bring in a list of five pairs of attitude lines. A pair is two opposite lines linked together, e.g., "I'm sad / I'm happy," "I'm brave / I'm scared," "I'm alone / Let's party!" Add this list to the other lists you have already done.

◆ ◆ ◆

ATTITUDE LINE SWITCH[8]

Attitude lines may be used to reveal attitude changes in a scene or movement on the character's arc.

SETUP: 2–4 per team. In huddles, select character, activity, and a location that places the characters in an emotional situation. The coach selects an attitude line pair from the actors' lists and assigns them to the actors just prior to the preparation process. Actors memorize their selected pair of attitude lines and are coached in the preparation process to retain attitude line #1 only. When the improv begins, the actors are open to discovering a turning point when they will immediately switch to retaining attitude line #2 (with no preparation process). Until the switch, all are totally alert to fellow actors and themselves in order to see and hear an opportunity for switching attitude lines. The opportunity, or turning point, can come from anywhere in the improv as long as it's spontaneous and not preplanned or set up ahead of time. It may come from another actor's dialogue, a development in the evolving action of the improv, or from the actor himself.

The opportunity to switch may be thought of as an invitation. When he spots the opportunity, the actor unhesitatingly and totally switches to attitude line #2, dropping attitude line #1. The actors individually choose their own turning points.

It is not necessary to switch just because another actor switches. After each actor switches, he focuses on retaining attitude line #2 until the improv ends. The amount of attention previously applied to spotting the opportunity to switch is now applied to furthering the impact of line #2 in the body. No attention is paid to attitude line #2 until the moment of the turning point. Each actor is totally responsible for finding his own opportunity to switch and is encouraged to avoid switching early or late in the improv. The switch should occur somewhere in the middle section of the improv.

RULES: While employing physical doing tools of Improvisation Technique for activity, location, relationships, and occupation, the actors retain attitude line #1 in the body and discover the turning point for switching to attitude line #2. Turning points are not preplanned. Attitude lines may never be spoken out loud.

ACTING FOCUS: Retain attitude line #1 and stay alert for the opportunity to switch to attitude line #2; then retain attitude line #2.

COACHING (as needed): Coach the usual preparation process for an attitude line. ◆ *Then, coach—* Your acting focus is retaining attitude line #1 and never letting go of it throughout the first part of the scene. You should repeat the line to yourself frequently but not say it out loud. While you are doing this, stay open and alert to spotting an opportunity to switch to the second attitude line. When you spot a switching moment or turning point, switch immediately and totally. Your acting focus is then to retain the second attitude in your face and your body, deeper and deeper. You may never say either line out loud during the scene. Staying on focus, move your chairs to places. ◆ Action. ◆ **Improv coaching (as needed):** Don't let the nature of your attitude line prevent you from playing as a part of the whole and using all the previously learned improvisational tools with your fellow actors. **Avoid hanging out.** ◆ **Stay on your acting focus; keep retaining #1 while staying open and alert for an opportunity to switch. Stay alert for spotting a turning point.** Stay open to a turning point revealing itself to you. ◆ **After you switch, retain #2. Keep reinforcing your attitude line in the body.** Keep heightening the attitude in your body. Take every opportunity to put it further into your body. ◆ Share your voice. Censor nothing. One minute. ◆ Cut. ◆ Do a shake-out.

FOLLOW-UP (as needed): Audience, what was the location? Activity? Occupations? Relationships? **Did each actor find a turning point and switch? Were the switches accomplished and integrated as a part of the whole scene? Did they stay on their acting focus? Describe each actor's character before and after their turning point.** ◆ **Actors, were you on your acting focus? What were your attitude lines?** ◆ **Audience, what were the turning points?** ◆ Actor, is that correct? Did anyone plan their turning point?

SUMMARY:

Attitude line switch creates an arc for the character within a single scene. The character goes through a sudden transformation during the scene, rather than the gradual transformation over the course of an entire script, which is commonly referred to as the character's arc.

If your character already has a deep body retaining of animal, body center, or attitude line characteristics, then doing an attitude line switch would be clunky and inappropriate. In such a case, a more suitable acting focus is emotion switch (chapter 9), which will accomplish the same effect.

SCRIPT

It is imperative to look at the character's arc over the course of a script. Frequently, unless it's a lead role, there is no transformation. However, any character can change in one scene, or have the potential to do so. If the character is a lead who does change over the course of an entire script, it doesn't usually happen at a single turning point. It's a gradual change, if it's well written. Then there will be some catalytic moment or scene that is the turning point for the final part of the transformation, completing the arc.

If you're working on a scripted scene, determine if it is important that your character go through a change. Is that what the writer had in mind? If it is, attitude line switch is a suitable acting focus. Decide what is the essential attitude prior to the change, and what is the essential attitude after the change. Reduce these to attitude lines. Start the scene retaining attitude line #1 and finish the scene retaining attitude line #2. Switch from the first to the second at a turning point, just as you did in this improvisation.

WHERE IS THE TURNING POINT?

In many scripts, the turning point will be very clearly written: a discovery, the finding of a dead body; an event, reuniting with someone you love; a betrayal, your wife having sex with the whole Polish army. These moments are called story points, and prior to them you are retaining attitude #1. As the moment occurs, you switch to retaining attitude #2. The moment itself is the turning point. The scene is written that way, and this turning point is usually the meaning of the scene. In these cases, you must follow the script's dictates and make that moment the turning point.

Sometimes, it's not so clearly written. What might be clear in the script is that the character goes through a change, but it's not so definite what the turning point is. When that is the case, you can either preplan the turning point as an interpretive, homework-type of choice or you can approach it as an improv where you discover it in a different place each time you rehearse or shoot it.

Approach it like a first level improv. Don't preplan the turning point. All you know is that you're going to do an attitude line switch. You're going to say the lines of the script, play the scene, and you're on an acting focus of "Staying alert for the turning point and switching attitude lines." As you play the scene with the memorized lines and with the blocking, you're open to letting a turning point reveal itself to you. You can seize on any moment that addresses your desire to switch, and switch attitudes. You can do the scene three or four times and, each time, give yourself a rule not to use the same turning point. You will find you can turn on almost anything. All you have to do is stay alert to it.

The improvisational approach forces you into the present tense, guaranteeing spontaneity. There is always a feeling of, "Should I switch *now?* Should I switch *now?* Should I switch *now?* Oh, here it is. I'll switch *now.*" When you preplan the turning point, all those *nows* are lost and it becomes, "I'm going to switch *then.*" While it may still be spontaneous because until the turning point you are improvising on retaining line #1, it is not in the realm of maximum spontaneity. Being in the present and not knowing when you are going to switch infuses your acting with vitality. This is because you are walking on a tightrope not knowing what will happen next. This is a form of artistic crisis to which your body responds by providing you with the extra spontaneous energy necessary for encountering a crisis. This will only heighten the presence in your performance and draw the audience or the camera to you.

There are some turning points that are not caused by something that occurs in the improvisation or something another character says. These are self-initiated. In a way, all turning points are self-initiated because you are choosing when to turn and switch attitude lines. However, the turning points that are created or set up *by you, in order to give yourself an opportunity to switch attitude lines,* are the totally self-initiated turning points. This type of turning point should be avoided. It has no connection to other characters or what's going on in the scene. It's almost as if the other characters don't need to be there. This type of self-initiated turning point is neither very vivid nor in the spirit of always being a part of the whole scene. Should you find yourself choosing to set up a self-initiated turning point, you have the opportunity to reject it. When improvising, you sometimes find you're going along on line #1 and an opportunity to switch presents itself to you and you choose to reject it and wait for another one. In that same way, you can choose to reject a totally self-initiated switch in the hope of having one come out of the scene. When it comes out of the scene, it's more a part of the whole scene and less isolated. The audience will see it more.

RETAINING ATTITUDE LINE #2

When you did this improvisation, you found it easy to switch to attitude line #2. However, it was not as ingrained in your body as attitude line #1 because you didn't go through the preparation process for #2. If you didn't take advantage of the post-turning point part of the scene to further the impact of line #2 on the body, you found that it gradually diminished because it was primarily in your head and not in the body. After you have made the switch, continue to coach yourself throughout the rest of the improv to get the attitude line to affect all your body parts. In other words, do your preparation process for attitude line #2 *while you are improvising* after the turning point. From that point on, take every opportunity to heighten it into the feet, chest, face, etc.

When you are going to employ attitude line switch on a scripted scene, do a separate preparation process on attitude line #2 at some time prior to the scene rehearsal or take. That way, when you do the switch, your body will benefit from kinesthetic memory and execute a thorough body response to attitude line #2. If you decide to use a preplanned turning point, you may rehearse it up to the turning point as a standard basic attitude line scene using a thorough preparation process. The scene ends at the preplanned turning point. Then, rehearse it from the turning point to the end of the scene as if that were a separate scene with its own attitude line (#2), again using a thorough preparation process. Then, run the two parts together. Because your body has been impacted with attitude line #2 with as much attention as you usually give #1, it will be in the body in a much more thorough way when you do a run-through, or take.

IMPROVING WRITING WITH ACTING

If you decide that your scene has very little happening for your character, look at how your character might change during the scene. You have to be smart because you can do this well or you can do it poorly. An example of doing it poorly would be to impose on what is a nebulous scene for your character an extreme polarity change, e.g., going from sad to happy, frightened to brave, etc. It will jump out, be inappropriate and not serve your part of the whole.

Instead, ask yourself how your character changes throughout the length of the entire script. This is something you should always be doing in every script anyway. Once you have articulated this, think of it as your character's arc for the whole script. Then, look at where this scene occurs in the script. Near the beginning? Near the end? In the middle? If the scene is in the beginning of a script, you can't switch to an attitude line that is more appropriate to the end of the whole script arc. For example, Hamlet goes from feeling hurt, uncertainty, and indecision to complete conviction. That's his character's arc. If you are playing Hamlet and working on a scene near the beginning of the script, you don't want to impose an attitude line switch that's going to take you to conviction because you still have most of the script in front of you where you are undecided, indecisive, and scared.

So you look at where your scene occurs in the script and ask yourself, "All right, what more might I do? What changes on the big arc might be occurring in this scene?" And here's the key thing. An attitude line switch or a character's arc in any one scene does not have to have the polarity that you had doing this improvisation. It can have gradations. It can go from "I'm suspicious" to "I'm nervous," or from "I'm nervous" to "I'm scared." In any one scene, you can arc a few small steps that are appropriate to where you should be on your overall arc for the whole script.

Sometimes a scene needs improvement because it's an exposition scene and the writer couldn't figure out a better way of getting important information out. You can add your arc to his information and improve the scene by making it be about more than it's about. The audience is going to watch what you're doing while they hear the information. The point of them watching you, instead of staying home and reading the script, is to see what you interpret, what you do with the text. You improve the scene by giving yourself something to do. For example, the doing here might be "This is a scene where my character changes from being nervous to being scared" or "This is a scene where my character changes from being alert to being cautious." If you approach it like a first level improvisation, you can do the switch on any text, expositional or not. A competent actor could do it with the telephone book. That's an example of what the doing in acting is. What are you *doing* with the lines?

It's never about what you say. When making these choices, especially if you're improving the text, always look to see that the choices you make are as far away as possible from, while being appropriate to, what the text is saying. Put distance between the text and your doing choice. If your character has a line where he says, "I'm jealous," one of your attitude lines should *not* be "I'm jealous." Instead, it could be "I'm scared," "I'm nervous," or "I'm angry." *Never play the text.* Playing the text is redundant, a twice-told tale. No matter what the acting focus is, no matter what you're doing, make it a cardinal rule that you never play the text.

I'm not telling you to go out and go to a really extreme choice like "I'm happy" when the text is "I'm jealous." But, you don't have to play jealousy *on the button.* You could play "I'm bitter" switching to "I'm sad." Both are perfectly suitable, authentic attitudes or emotions that often accompany jealousy. You can improve bad writing.

Remember that you can go either way in these arcs. It's just as valid to go from positive to negative as it is to go the other way, and is frequently more interesting, e.g., bravery to cowardice. I use the word *positive* to indicate an attitude that is open and expansive and the word *negative* to mean one that is limited and closes a person to life. Let's put that into perspective. If you go from a limited attitude to an expansive attitude, then your scene would be about growth, e.g., "My character finds some truth." If you go the other way, your scene is going to be about diminishment, e.g., "My character loses self-respect." If your scene is near the end of the script, you're probably going to go from negative to positive, or if you're a villain, from negative to more negative. Think of your scene arc as a part of the whole script arc for your character.

Assume that the author chose your arc until you are convinced that he didn't. Look carefully for what he gave you to change from, and to, in the scene. Consider what the character's attitude might be in the beginning of the scene and what might it be at the end. Use the dialogue and the given circumstances as indicators. When you're absolutely sure that the author didn't write an arc for you, then say, "Well, what would be a good arc that he should have written?"

When you start a job, determine your character's arc and draw a schematic of how your character changes during the course of this script. Draw a big arc and divide it into the number of scenes you have in the script. Then label the scenes as well as you can. It may mean that in the beginning you're only labeling scene one, *the nerd*, and the last scene, *most popular kid in school*. As you work, fill in the labels for the rest of the arc. Choreograph your part in the film in which you go from A (nerd) to Z (popular). Your second scene is B, your third scene, C, etc. In each scene, you are to travel to the next scene. After you have done that, you have the opportunity to travel within each scene. That's when you're doing all over the place and the audience can't stop looking at you.

Here is an example of a character arc schematic. It was used for Tate Donovan's preparation for *Memphis Belle*.

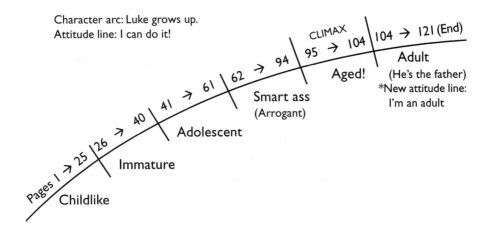

Character arc: Luke grows up.
Attitude line: I can do it!

As you watch movies for entertainment, start watching fellow actors. Label the first scene of the lead character. "Oh, Meryl is doing this. And Bob is doing this. I got it. He's a nerd." Watch for changes in each scene. Make sure you label what they're doing at the end of the movie. Start to see the arcs that good actors use. Notice turning points. You'll start to realize where the author writes a turning point and how good actors introduce turning points where the author didn't write one. It's a good way to watch movies. For sample character arcs see Appendix C.

You can be an extra without dialogue and still do an attitude line switch. Suppose the scene is a delicatessen. Robert DeNiro and Meryl Streep are standing at the counter discussing whether to buy salami or bologna. You're another customer. Your part is to come into the store, walk behind them, and then disappear down an aisle. A professional extra would most likely decide what he is shopping for and focus on looking for it as he does the blocking. I suggest that the extra could do more. Assuming appropriate part-of-the-whole choices for attitude lines, he could do an attitude line switch during the time he is seen on camera. For instance, he could enter the store retaining the attitude line "I'm sad" (that once more I have to cook dinner for myself and eat alone). At the beginning of the aisle, he spots a particular food item (the turning point), which appeals to him for dinner. He switches to "I'm pleased." It makes the background very real and textured, and it might highlight what's going on with the principals in the foreground. If the extra's choice is inappropriate because it steals focus from the principals, it's the director's, or the assistant director's, job to give him a note not to do that and just shop for what he is looking for.

An attitude line switch with any size part adds to the script because you're doing more. Yes, it's about having some taste and discretion as to what's appropriate to your part and what's going on in the script at that time. Always look for what you can be doing that will serve your part of the whole scene better. Use every tool or acting focus in the service of making your part as bright, significant, and well defined as it can be.

> **TO THE COACH:** After hearing the setup, if actors ask for definition of "an emotional situation," give examples: packing up a home in preparation for impending hurricane; cooks preparing a meal at a cooking contest; co-workers preparing a store for opening day, or going out of business.
> • If the coach suspects an actor's turning point was preplanned, even by five seconds, *ask that actor in the follow-up—* When did you know that would be your turning point? Was that against the rules? • Preplanned turning points are usually self-initiated.
>
> Although most script usage of attitude line switch pertains to switches in gradation of attitudes, it's a more effective learning of the acting focus if the two attitude lines are extremely different, like polar opposites.
>
> In the follow-up, if an actor doesn't remember what his turning point was, ask him if he remembers selecting a turning point. That might jog his memory.
>
> By now, the actors have practiced a number of attitude line improvisations. Some may notice a discrepancy between the attitudes they are doing and what is coming across. Encourage them to write about this in their journals.
>
> If the coach selects the attitude lines from the actors' lists, keep a separate list of who is doing what. Then you will be sure when an actor has completed his switch.

◆   ◆   ◆

PHYSICAL CATALYST + ATTITUDE LINE

SETUP: Divide the group into three subgroups based on the choice of acting focus: animals, body centers, or reformed body in space. Within each group, count off teams of two to five actors. All teams give their attitude line lists to the coach, and then huddle and select their activity, location, and character (occupations and personal relationships). During the huddles, the coach selects the attitude line to be given subsequently to each actor. • Each team sets up their location. The coach coaches them through the preparation process according to their team choice of acting focus. When the coach has finished the final part of the preparation process, any necessary whittling (humanizing) of an actor's character, the team sits in their location, retaining the character's body. ♦ The coach returns their attitude line lists to them with the selected attitude line and then coaches them through the attitude line preparation process so that they take on the attitude line on top of the character's body they are already retaining. ♦ The actors begin the improvisation.

RULES: Employ physical doing tools of Improvisation Technique for activity, location, relationships, and occupation. Actors may never say their attitude line out loud.

ACTING FOCUS: Retain the attitude line in the realigned body.

COACHING: Coach the appropriate physical catalyst preparation from animal, body center, or reformed body in space. ♦ Privately coach individual actors, if necessary, in whittling (further humanizing) the size of the character's realigned body. Usually this step is only necessary with the animals. ♦ *Then coach the group*— Retain your realigned body and sit down. Keep focused on not letting go of this realigned body. Cross your legs; uncross them. Discover and use some space props in your lap. Read, knit, whatever. Practice the movements of the activity with the objects while maintaining this realigned body. Don't let go. Get used to retaining this body. Stay focused on the realigned body. Get rid of the objects. ♦ [The coach gives them their attitude line list with the selected line.] ♦ Just memorize the line. Don't do anything physical with it yet. Stay on focus. Keep retaining this realigned body. ♦ Coach the attitude line preparation process *with following adjustments for the already realigned body*— Now, throughout this entire process, retain this new body alignment for your body. Repeat the attitude line to yourself over and over again. Let *this body* tell you how it wants to say the line. Throughout this entire process, retain the attitude line in *this* body! Let *these* feet express this attitude. Send the attitude to *these* legs. Hold onto it and don't let go. Let *this midsection* reflect the attitude. ♦ Continue in this manner through all the usual body parts, although by now you only need to name the body part, ending with smiles and frowns. ♦ *When finished, coach*— Increase the volume of your inner line readings and send it as a message to all parts of *this* body. Get up. Walk around, retaining the attitude in *this* body. Silently, say your lines to each other while retaining this body. Silently, tell the audience. Bigger. Bigger. Bigger! Retain that! Feel it on your face. Feel it in your body. Feel the way your body is realigned and is now reacting to the attitude. That is what you must retain, the way your body is holding yourself together. Retain the attitude in the realigned body and never say the attitude line out loud. Staying on this acting focus, go to places. ◆ Action! ◆ **Coaching for improv (as needed):** Focus on retaining the realigned body from the catalyst and the attitude. Check out your fellow players. Share your voices. Censor nothing. **Stay on your acting focus.** Don't let go of the attitude. **Avoid hanging out.** Keep retaining the body influenced by the [animal, body center, or reformed body in space]. Don't let go of the body. **Retain the attitude. Retain the body.** Active & still. One minute to stay on focus. ◆ Cut. ◆ Do a shake-out.

> **FOLLOW-UP (as needed):** Audience, what was the location? Activity? Occupations? Relationships? ◆ Were the actors open to realigning their bodies? **Did they create characters from the combination of a physical body catalyst and their attitude lines? Did they retain them throughout the improvisation or did they let go of them?** ◆ Actors, do you agree? **Did you discover an emerging attitude from the original character catalyst? Could you change it to the attitude line's attitude and still retain the previous realigned body?** ◆ **Audience, describe each actor's character.** ◆ Actors, what was your attitude line (and animal, if applicable)?

SUMMARY:

Combining a physical character catalyst with an attitude line can take you to unique characterizations. If you respond to your scripted character with an idea for a physical catalyst like an animal or a body center, and in creating the character the emerging attitude is not appropriate, experiment with retaining the body and applying an appropriate attitude line as you did in these improvisations.

Tom Hanks won an Oscar for his Forrest Gump and presented a perfect illustration of what it takes to create a character. His characterization was noticeable for two primary features. His realigned body and costuming had to contribute to a feeling of slowness, the emerging attitude. And then, on top of that, he retained the attitude (line) of "Do the right thing," which had been instilled in him by his mom. The combination of the two created drama for his character and for the audience as he consistently struggled, due to his slowness, to figure out what the right thing was.

> **TO THE COACH:** In the physical catalyst part of the preparation, only the animals will require a vocal component. That should be kept to a minimum or they will begin to cement the emerging attitude into the realigned body. Let the actors discover the emerging vocal characteristics, then move them on to the next step. Ultimately, in this exercise, we want the characters to have the attitude of their attitude lines, not the emerging attitude that first comes with the realigned body.

MULTIPLE REFLECTION

This is a final experiential jolt of how characters' bodies are different from our own.

> **SETUP:** The entire group lines up at one end of the largest available empty space. If the space is too small for the entire group, do it twice with two teams. One actor goes to the other end of the space and faces the group. This actor walks toward the group and the group walks toward the actor. When they meet in the middle of the space, the actor walks through the group's line and turns around. At the same time, the group turns around. All continue walking backward until they reach the opposite end of the space they started from. The group and the actor are still facing each other. Everybody repeats the same walk, and then once more, for a total of three walks across the floor. *During each walk, everyone reflects the solo actor.* The solo actor simply walks normally and observes the group's reflection of him.
>
> **RULES:** Solo actor walks normally and does not change his walk upon seeing how he is reflected. Group reflects the single actor.
>
> **ACTING FOCUS:** Single actor, walk normally and see what there is to see; group, reflect the single actor.
>
> **COACHING (as needed):** *For the single actor—* Begin! Walk the way you always walk. Avoid changing your walk. Watch everyone. Take what you get. See what there is to see. Walk normally. Don't rush it. ◆ *For the group—* Reflect the actor. Reflect his body. Reflect his walk. Avoid imitating. Avoid commenting. Simply reflect. Reflect all his body parts: legs, arms, face, hips. Reflect head to toe. ◆ When you cross each other, turn and walk backward to the wall.
>
> **FOLLOW-UP (as needed):** *After all have walked as solo actor—* What did you observe and experience? Did you notice that every single actor has a different walk? Did you notice that you had to realign your bodies in order to reflect their walk? Would you say that no two walks were the same? As you were reflecting another's walk, did you ever get a sense of experiencing the tensions or holds in their different body parts? The relaxations? Their attitude? Did you get a sense of what it's like to be in another's body?

SUMMARY:

You just had an experience of how everyone walks and carries themselves differently. When you were the solo actor walking and watching everyone reflect you, you got a sense of what you would look like if you were a character. Look at how twenty actors required twenty physical transformations in order to reflect each other. Aside from the fact that we are actors, which may make us crazier, we are basically average people and not extraordinary human beings. On the other hand, characters are more extraordinary than average people or they wouldn't be worthy of the attention that the writers, actors, or audiences give them. Characters should be considered a little bit larger than real people. If, as you just experienced in the multiple reflection, everyday average people have different body alignments and walk differently, then shouldn't characters, who are larger, have their own physical carriage? Every single character has a different body alignment and carries himself differently.

You agreed that while playing multiple reflection, you had moments of feeling what it was like to be in another person's body. That is the feeling an actor should have while being in a character's body. The inner life of a character resides in the character's body. This is true from the smallest walk-on part to a leading role. You've got to change your body to the character's body and that's what we have been exploring.

> **TO THE COACH:** The coach should participate in this exercise. If there is confusion over the difference between reflection and imitation, it may be pointed out that imitation requires the imitator to go into his head and select one aspect of the solo walker's body or walk to exaggerate. Imitation requires comment and judgment. Reflection does not.

IMPROV PROCESS FOR CREATING THE SCRIPT CHARACTER

1. **Catalyst choices**—Select the character acting focus and the specific catalyst choice.

2. **Body realignment**—Create a character using the selected acting focus and catalyst choice. Do the *physical work*, which results in the realigned body, physicalization of the attitude, boundary identification, and the ultimate emergence of the character. You can't really create the body of the character until you first exaggerate the body using a catalyst, as in animals, body centers, reformed bodies, and attitude lines. It gives the body size. What is discovered is so large that it becomes totally visible and visceral; you see and feel it. Once you know what your core is, you can whittle it to an appropriate size.

3. **Whittling**—Experiment with heightening the acting focus or with heightening or diminishing some of the physical characteristics to bring the character to an appropriate size. If retaining an animal's characteristics was your acting focus, diminishing the gesture size would be considered a further humanizing.

4. **Improvise with character, activity, and location**—If you have other actors to do an improv with (whether in the production or not), pick a location and activity, either similar or tangential to the script. Your improv character's occupation is the same as the script

character's, and you have the same personal relationships with the other improv characters as you have with other script characters. Do the improvisation. Your acting focus is the particular character acting focus you are employing, e.g., retaining the character's body. During the improv, you may discover the need for further whittling (humanizing). Once you are happy with the way your character is developing, and it may take a few improvs, *you are ready to bring it to the production.*

5. **Improv with script**—Select a rehearsal to introduce what you have been working on. In addition to rehearsing whatever the director has selected, choose to add a *first level improvisation.* In other words, while rehearsing with the memorized text from the script, employ an acting focus of retaining the character that you created in the previous improvisations. You need no extra involvement from the other actors in the production other than what they normally bring to rehearsal. To them, and to the director, it will just look like you are developing your character. The director may or may not give you feedback. If he does, discuss it and make appropriate adjustments. In subsequent rehearsals, stay alert for discovering new insights as to why your character carries himself, moves, or speaks that way.

At any time during the preceding process, if you decide that your choice is leading you in the wrong direction, discontinue the process and evaluate what isn't working for you. Then allow that information to influence another catalyst choice and begin the process again. Approach this whole process as an experiment in your personal acting laboratory.

CHAPTER SUMMARY

Essentials

Transforming your body's alignment and adopting an attitude are the essentials of creating a character. You can come in either way, body to attitude or attitude to body. If you find the appropriate body, you don't have to preplan the appropriate attitude because the body will always carry the attitude with it. If you find it easier to choose the attitude before creating the body, do so. Articulate it effectively as an attitude line, and then create the body that goes with that attitude. Either way, the final result is the same: the realignment of your own body and the adoption of a highlighted attitude at the core of your character's personality.

If you play a character and use your own body's alignment, you create a discrepancy that is inauthentic. The only body you have is your body. You do not have the body of Tartuffe. Don't make the character become you. You become the character. You will never have any range as an actor if you don't do that. Your bodies carry your life experience, the joys and pains, physical and psychic, that you are aware of and those you are not aware of. They carry your generation's civilization and culture. Your bodies are the products of your lives. Tartuffe did not have your life. He had a very different life, and he's got a body that's the product of his life. Jack Nicholson said that when he prepares a role, "What I have always done is not necessarily have to act but become the physicality of the person."[9]

Acting is Doing

Having a character and knowing his attitude can be the doing that gets you through many unscripted moments in a most productive way. In the improvisations you did during this character period, there were so many times where you weren't the central focus of the scene and you didn't have dialogue. The focus of the scene was stage left and you were stage right, doing very small things. You were either listening to someone else or doing a little activity, and yet you were totally busy inside. That's when you know you're in character: if the scene's not about you, the pressure is off, and you totally feel like you are the character as you spontaneously respond to everything you hear and see from your character's point of view. Dustin Hoffman said he knew he had internalized Raymond in *Rain Man* when he could improvise as the character. "That is always the signal to me," he said.[10]

Private Actor's Lab

The creation of a character usually begins in your own private, experimental workshop. Think of it as your home laboratory where you solve problems in the creation of a part. When you go into this lab, you're not going to nail the character the first time out. It's a process of trial and elimination. Sometimes, it's a lot of juggling. You may find the body that works, but the attitude isn't quite right, so you retain the body and try different attitude lines. You may feel lost trying to discern the body center, but you have a hint as to an animal choice. You have the tools. Experiment. Develop your own personal approach. It's your lab.

You may begin to see that different characters cry out for different catalysts. If a script refers to your character with consistent imagery, take the hint. A script might say your character is a cluck-in-hand with her mother, a turtledove with her boyfriend, and a sparrow hawk with her employees. This character cries out for experimenting with an animal acting focus. One character strongly suggests a body center focus; another clearly demands an attitude line approach. You must develop your own finesse in working.

The real question is *how do you develop that finesse*. The answer, to this and many other questions, is *by doing it and practicing*. You have to find the discipline and courage to do the work.

Take a Risk

The risk is to do the work. That is what *take a risk* means. To do the work. Instead of watching an hour of television, take some script off the shelf that you're not even up for, and make up your own exercise. Maybe there is a character that you want to play someday. Work on that script and find the animal, body center, and attitude line choices. Go into your lab and work on creating the character. The more you take responsibility for the work, the more accessible it becomes to you and the more potential there is for payoff when you actually choose to do it for a real audition or a real job. Just think how many parts you have let get by you because you didn't do the character work. Perhaps you have been fooling yourself about creating a character. Perhaps you thought that all it took was sitting down, writing a bio for your character, and you were finished. You can sit and write character bios from now until next Christmas, but unless those bios lead you to catalytic choices, a particular body center, animal, or attitude line, they are practically useless. If you only have a limited number of hours or minutes to focus on building your character, what percentage of that time do you want to devote to writing and what percentage to experiential work?

Actor's Individuality

Do not be concerned about losing your individuality in this process. How you fulfill the attitude line or other catalyst is different from how another actor fulfills the same line or catalyst. It is still *your version* of that attitude. If you think you are being cast for your look, you are not going to sabotage that. On the physical level, you are not changing that much. You're not changing your hair color; you're not going to the plastic surgeon and losing five years; you're not adding one hundred pounds. You're you. You are just adding the attitude of the character that you find in the script or shifting your body carriage a bit. They still have the person they cast and you are still playing the character, not yourself.

Scripts

You must realize that a writer understands that a character is fictionalized. He writes the character with a more highlighted attitude than our everyday, average attitudes. Hamlet, Blanche, Indiana Jones, Ratso Rizzo, Scarlett O'Hara, and the cops in *Lethal Weapon* are all heightened. Everyone is heightened in the world of dramatics. The stories in which they are involved are heightened because a story has to be compressed into a two-hour presentation. Everything is compressed and everything is heightened.

310

The creation of a character is not the be all and end all of acting. It is one part of it. You still have to play the purpose and structure of your scenes, and do so in spontaneity. But the character has got to be there through it all. When your character is poorly written, you can strengthen it. If English actors are often held up as being better than American actors are, it's because they understand this and are more prepared to do it.

Theater Rehearsal Framework

If you are working on a play, and not a camera job, you shouldn't bring your character to beginning rehearsals. Take advantage of early rehearsals to find out about your character and bring what you glean from these rehearsals to your decision-making process about the catalyst choices. In the early rehearsals, work in a traditional manner (whatever basic Stanislavsky-derived approach you have always used prior to learning Improvisation Technique) while following the director's game plan.

When you have exploited that approach and received its goodies, then do first level improvisations to reinfuse that work with spontaneity and to discover what else there is that you hadn't previously seen. Then focus on creating your character. You will now know a great deal about the character and be in a knowledgeable position to make your catalyst choices. If you do not employ a traditional approach at the early stages because you are not confident with one, start with first level improvisations.

Working with the Director

It is hard to be specific about how to work with a director on creating your character because there is such a disparity of abilities among directors. If your director initiates discussion with you about your character prior to actual rehearsals, hear him and evaluate his comments. Anything specific and helpful should be integrated into your catalytic choices during your personal preparation process (the lab). Frequently, there will be minimal or no discussion until he sees what you bring in. That is all right because the work we have done here will allow you to prepare and bring in a character by yourself.

In a camera production, you don't have the luxury of rehearsal time. Start your character work the moment the contract is signed and bring it in on the first day of work.

When you bring your character to rehearsals and your director stops you and says it should be changed, don't defend what you are doing. Instead, be grateful that you are getting feedback on you choices. If he is specific, make the changes. If he isn't specific (very common), say, "Okay. Can you tell me what it is that I'm doing that you think is wrong and then can you tell what it is you think I should be doing? Can you talk to me about the character?"

There are many directors who don't know beans about character work. Just accept that. Then there are directors who are very clear about characters, but they assume you know your job and you're going to do it. All directors are different. The bottom line is, if necessary, start a dialogue. "What is it that's not working? Am I too smarmy? Am I too slutty? Am I too sensitive?" Get him talking. "What do you think? Oh, you think I should be more confident?" Then take and use that information to adjust what you have been doing.

If you were using "Nobody loves me" for an attitude line and the director says to you, "I don't think she's so shy. I don't think she hides all of the time. I think she's more outspoken," you say, "Okay. Give me a minute." Go off stage, choose another attitude line, and go from there. In times like this, employ an attitude line rather than an animal, reformed body in space, or body center. It's quicker when you need to bring in an immediate change.

An advantage of using Improvisation Technique's catalysts is that when you get a director who can look at what you are doing and say, "Stop! It's too this or it's not enough that," you have a frame of reference to address his issue from, because you know exactly what the catalyst was that you were using. If you are using a body center in the head, and he says it is too cerebral, you have to move that center out of the head. With Improvisation Technique, you always know exactly where and what the source was that created the work that you are doing.

In any dialogue you have with the director about your character, you don't need to tell him about the catalyst or acting focus you are employing. It'll scare him. If you need his help, you can be clever about it.

Suppose you are doing an animal for your source choice and he says, "It's not working. I think your character is going in a weird direction." You can start this dialogue, "What's weird about it? What would you like?" If you feel it is appropriate at some point, you could say, "Hey, what about this. Let's say what you just saw me doing was a giraffe, but you don't like a giraffe. What animal would you pick?" Then he says, "Well, I see the character as more snakelike." Bingo! He has given you another choice and you try that.

The same approach could be used with an attitude line. He tells you there's something wrong with your character. You can say, "I understand what you mean. I saw the character as being very sensual and horny. It's almost like what you saw me do today was someone who was expressing 'I'm horny'. What do you think she should be expressing? If it's not horniness, what do you think should be the dominant value?"

Guide him in helping you toward an attitude. Don't expect him to come up with an attitude line, but he'll get you into the ball park and then you take that information and whittle it down into an attitude line. That's all process.

Some young movie directors are afraid of an actor's creating a character. They

312

know the actor is creating a character so they *assume* the audience will think it is phony. When you bring a character to one of these directors, he will direct, "Just be yourself." Ask for a minute to prepare, then drop your character acting focus and the body and attitude realignments and focus on a new attitude line, "I am." That will reinforce your own natural personality.

Casting

The application of this character work to casting is that you will extend and stretch the range of types of characters you might be cast as. Prior to this work, when you went to an audition, maybe you went and auditioned as you, saying the lines, feeling the emotions, playing the intentions, or whatever approach to auditions you used. Now you have the opportunity, if you do the work, to bring in the character. That will stretch your availability. Why limit your casting potential to you, your body and personality? You already know to dress for the part, but if you are only doing you in another's clothes, how far have you gone toward creating the character? If you now include in your homework and preparation the transformation of your body and personality into the character's body and personality, you increase the odds of getting that part.

Finale: Pinocchio Becomes a Real Boy

We have been working on creating the character armor, or the *dummy*, that the author wrote, designed, and intended. In doing this through Improvisation Technique catalysts and process, the individuality of the actor will come through and bring the dummy to life.

8
CAMERA AND STAGE AUDITIONS

FIRST LEVEL IMPROVISATION APPLICATIONS

Any actor who has reached this point in Improvisation Technique training has the ability to improve his auditions immediately.

While the individual actor can easily do this process at home and alone, it is learned most effectively in the class setting. Two weeks prior to the designated class, I request anyone in the group who has had an ineffective audition to call me. I ask them what happened and why they think it didn't go well. If the reasons have to do with circumstances beyond their control, e.g., the casting director switched the scene on them at the last minute, then their situation is not suitable for this exercise. If they had the sides early enough to prepare and they still didn't do well, then their situation is suitable. I select three or four actors from the ones that call me.

I have them bring in copies of the sides, including cover sheets from the casting director or agent, so that everyone in class has the material. I ask them to prepare for the class in a very specific way: (1) Memorize the lines, whether or not they were memorized for the actual audition. (2) Go over the audition in their mind and rehearse, if necessary, so that they can re-create the ineffective audition in class. They are not to rehearse it in order to improve it. We need as close as possible an approximation of the actual audition.

314

In the designated class, the actors select other actors to serve as casting director and read with them. We give the selected casting directors time to go over their lines so they won't stumble.

The first actor establishes the size of the room he auditioned in and tells the group what the audition was for and who was present. He positions the casting director and gives him any special instructions about how the casting director read the lines. They then re-create the audition to the best of their ability.

Following the re-created audition, the actor hands out the sides to the rest of the class and informs them of any additional information he gleaned prior to the audition.

THE PROCESS

Coach's Introduction

What we are about to do is not about me playing the role of a director/critic and showing you what you did wrong or how to fix it. That would be of minimal value to you when it comes time for your next audition. It is more important that when you leave class tonight, you have a methodology that you can apply on your own.

This process does not have to be your entire preparation for an audition. Think of it as a tool to be added to whatever else you like to do. A real benefit is that you already know how to do it. Tonight, I'm simply going to package it for you in an audition context.

I. Memorize the lines.

In this highly competitive business, the best performance gets the final callback and you cannot give your best performance while you are reading. Casting is frequently based on considerations other than skills. However, if you are reading the sides at the auditions, you're not even placing yourself in the running. If you want to carry the script with you because you're nervous, that's something else. But *if you go into an audition without memorizing the lines, you are not professionally competitive.*

2. Do traditional technique (optional).

If you are not confident with any traditional approach, skip this step. Otherwise, work on the sides employing whatever traditional Stanislavsky-based approach you favor. When you have exploited this approach and received its goodies, move on to the next step.

3. Reduce to character, activity, and location.

From the sides, designate who the character is. Does the script provide the information as to your character's occupation and any personal relationships between your character and the other characters in the scene? If it doesn't, make choices that would seem to fit as a part of the whole scene.

Designate what the activity of the scene is. If the script doesn't provide one, select an activity that could be a part of the whole scene.

Designate the location of the scene. This is almost always provided in the script. If it isn't, don't concern yourself with this yet.

After everyone has had time to work on the provided sides and make their own selections, the coach and the class discuss the selection, beginning with whichever selections are clearly provided in the sides.

Usually, the **location** will be clearly provided. If it isn't, select one that might be appropriate to what is going on in the scene and would work as a part of the whole scene.

The **character's relationships** to other characters in the scene will probably be found if not in the sides themselves, then in the information on the cover sheet provided with the sides. If the *personal* relationships are not clear in the scene or from any other source, then make a choice based on what is going on in the scene according to the given circumstances or on being a part of the whole. Stay open to the possibility that there are no personal relationships between the characters in the scene. In this case, don't invent one. Go with the knowledge that the relationship(s) are *professional*. The **character's occupation** may be found easily if the scene relates to it or on the cover sheet. If the occupation is not available, consider what it might be, based on what goes on in the scene. The final choice must be one that in no way conflicts with what is going on in the scene, seems appropriate to the given circumstances, and could easily be a part of the whole scene.

Although the **activity** choice may be provided in the sides, in which case that is the selection, it is the one choice that is most often missing. Given what is going on in the scene, what might the character be doing for an activity? What would be a suitable part-of-the-whole-scene activity? Consider the location as well. Why is the character in this location? The reason a person is in any location is usually to do a particular activity, e.g., kitchen/cooking, office/paperwork, store/shopping. Make a list of choices. Then, select your first choice from that list based on the one that provides for the most physical doing and requires space objects.

The coach should list (chalkboard suggested) the various class choices. The coach then leads a discussion of which activities on the list would be best: (1) Which ones are a part of the whole, i.e., would the character do the activity at this time of day and in this location? Which ones are appropriate to what the scene is about, e.g., would the character be doing this activity when the scene is about her telling her mother that her father has been killed in an accident? (2) Does the activity provide maximum potential for physical doing with space props? (3) Is this activity really an activity in Improvisation Technique? Activity is supposed to keep you focused on doing something. For instance, smoking, despite the use of space props, is not an activity. It is a habit. Habitual doing is not an activity if it doesn't require attention or concentration. The actor working alone and not in a class uses the same criteria in choosing the ultimate selection.

At the end of the discussion, the class, or the auditioning actor, agrees on a designated activity. By now, the actor has his character, activity, and location. Write these choices on the top of the sides. It's time to improvise.

4. Do activity improvisation.

You're at home, you've got the sides, you've memorized the lines, and you have designated the character, activity, and location. Get somebody to read the other characters' lines. The other person does not have to be an actor. He just has to read all the other lines on cue. If you don't have somebody else available, put the other characters' lines on a tape recorder. Leave empty recording time for your lines.

Commence a first level improvisation with your acting focus on physically doing the activity as a part of the whole (character, activity, location) scene. Avoid holding onto any previous line readings or business from the traditional work. All your attention is placed on physically doing the activity and saying your lines on cue.

> **FOLLOW-UP:** *[For all follow-ups in this process, the actor working by himself must put these questions to himself.]* ◆ Audience, did actor stay on his acting focus? Did he respect his space objects? If he completed the activity prior to the end of the scene, did he discover another activity? Was it a part of the whole? ◆ Actor, did you stay focused on doing your activity throughout? If the answer to any of these questions is no, do the improv again and stay on the acting focus. Before beginning the improv for the second time, there may be some profit from the first unfocused improv. Do you see another way of doing the same activity that might be beneficial? For instance, are there better prop choices for the same activity or better body positioning?

5. Do location improvisation.

There are **three options**. In my experience, most actors do the second or third. The first option requires more time, but it is especially valuable when actors discover that they are making assumptions about what may or may not be available in the location.

Option 1: Total preparation of floor plan. Prepare a floor plan (as in physical contact with the location) of the designated location. Place real chairs on the stage where you have drawn them in the floor plan. Tape the floor plan to a wall or chair. You may consult your floor plan while you improvise so the improv doesn't become about having to remember everything on the floor plan.

Option 2: Totally improvised floor plan. Without preparing a floor plan, you are improvising what is in the floor plan as you make physical contact with it.

Option 3: Partial preparation of floor plan. Prepare a floor plan of the designated location without drawing it on paper. Take a minute to designate for yourself what the key set pieces are and where they are located in the space. Place real chairs where you want them. This option is similar to actors setting up their location prior to doing any improv.

For all options: Commence a first level improvisation with your acting focus on making physical contact with the location as a part of the whole scene. Avoid holding onto any previous line readings or business from the traditional work or the previous activity improvisation. All your attention is placed on contacting the location and saying your lines on cue.

> **FOLLOW-UP:** Audience, did the actor make physical contact with many of the set pieces and props within the location? Did he do so as a part of the whole or in an arbitrary fashion? Did he respect his space objects? ◆ Actor, did you stay focused on contacting the location throughout? If the answer is no, do the improv again and stay on the acting focus, or consider repeating the improv with a different option.

6. Do combined activity and location improvisation.

Place real chairs where you want them. Commence a first level improvisation with your acting focus on doing your activity and physically contacting the location as a part of your whole activity and character. You may choose to change your activity to another appropriate choice; however, if you do, retain the same location. If you consulted the floor plan during the previous improvisation, do not do so during this improvisation. Avoid holding onto any previous line readings or business from the traditional work or the previous improvisations. All your attention is placed on doing the activity, contacting the location, and saying your lines on cue.

> **FOLLOW-UP:** Audience, did the actor sustain his activity while making physical contact with many of the set pieces and props within the location? Did he do so as a part of the whole or in an arbitrary fashion? Did he respect his space objects? ◆ Actor, did you stay focused on doing your activity and contacting the location throughout?

7. Do vocal doing improvisation.

Select any acting focus from the vocal doing chapter. If you are not improvising with an actor, avoid reflection listening and physical contact speech. Make any necessary changes in the given circumstances to accommodate your acting focus selection. For instance, if you choose full body whisper, add a circumstance that requires your character to whisper the scene. If your choice is full body calling, add a circumstance that requires calling from far away. On the other hand, if you do nonsense language, stretching speech, soundless stretching speech, or full body singing, no additional given circumstances are needed.

Do the improvisation with your acting focus on the vocal doing choice. You may change the activity or the location, or not. You should respect the relationships and integrate your activity and location doing as parts of the whole improvisation. However, all your attention is on the acting focus and saying your lines on cue. Avoid holding onto any previous line readings or business from the traditional work or previous improvisations. It is not necessary for your improvisation partner, whether actual or tape recorder voice, to employ the acting focus. If your improvisation partner is an actor and will play the scene with you, you may find some value in selecting reflection listening or physical contact speech. However, you will get all the mileage you need from one of the other vocal doing focuses.

> **FOLLOW-UP:** Audience, did the actor stay on his acting focus? Did you see full body involvement with his voice? Did the actor support his primary acting focus with physical doing? Did he respect his space objects? ◆ Actor, do you agree?

8. *Go with it* run-through.

Now we do the scene to check the progress we've made so far. There is no acting focus other than *going with it*. This time you don't set out to repeat the scene exactly the way you rehearsed it in the traditional approach. You are not going to go out of your way to retain anything you liked in the preceding improvisations, nor are you to go out of your way to make up new stuff. Your body learned something about the scene during the improvisations. Now you have to get out of the body's way and let it tell you how it wants to play the scene. It knows how to do that, and your brain is not meant to know what that is. It may choose to retain some things from the way you rehearsed it originally or something from the improvisations. There will probably be new stuff. It is up to your body to determine what it wants to do. Let your body play the scene and you go for the ride and see what happens. Don't censor. Don't plan ahead. *Go with it.*

> **FOLLOW-UP:** Audience, how does this compare to the audition the actor brought in? What are the differences? ◆ Actor, do you agree? Does it feel

different? ◆ Everyone, notice that these improvements were made by the actor without direction from the coach.

9. Do full character improvisation.

Based on your personal preferences for character catalysts and your reading of the sides to see if they point you in the direction of a catalyst choice, select a character acting focus. Due to the short time available for preparing an audition, I suggest that an attitude line is most serviceable. Also, when working from sides instead of an entire script, there is less information available to you for making the catalyst choice, and an attitude line will be more accessible than choices for animals, body centers, or reformed body in space. Follow the process outlined in the previous chapter for articulating the attitude line you select for your character.

In class, everyone has the sides, and the coach should allow five minutes or so for everyone to come up with attitude line choices. List (chalkboard suggested) the various class choices for the attitude line. The coach may lead a discussion of the choices, point out necessary changes in the articulation of a line, and discuss any strengths or weaknesses. The class, or the auditioning actor, selects the attitude line to be employed.

The actor does the attitude line preparation process leading to retaining the attitude in the body. Then, do a *first level improv* with your acting focus on retaining the attitude. Let go of any prepared line readings or business you may already have arrived at in the traditional work or previous improvisations. Put your acting focus on retaining the attitude and say your lines on cue. Pay no attention to how you say your lines. All your attention goes to retaining the attitude in your body. Allow your body to do as much physical doing as it wants. Respect the relationships between your character and whomever you are speaking with. Don't miss any cues.

If you are not happy with the result, select another attitude line and do another improv. Profit from knowing what you didn't like about the previous attitude line in making your new selection.

> **FOLLOW-UP:** Audience, did the actor retain his character's attitude throughout the scene? Did the character emerge? How did that effect the audition? ◆ Actor, do you agree? Do we need to select another attitude line? How does the audition compare to the one you brought in? How do you feel about that? ◆ Everyone, notice that these improvements were made by the actor without direction from the coach.

10. Play the scene with reduced (office audition) space.

You now need to evaluate how much physical business with space props is ultimately appropriate for the audition. How do you do that?

First of all, if the sides designate an activity for the scene, it is appropriate to do that activity with space props or minimal actual props during the audition. If the sides do not indicate an activity, but your character is at his job during the scene, that too is an appropriate opportunity to do a job-related activity. After my client, Dan Gunther, was cast as the recurring bartender on *Melrose Place*, the casting director told him that of all the actors auditioning for the role, he was the only one who sliced lemons and rinsed glasses (all space props) during his audition. The sides didn't designate that, but the scene took place while he was working—and the producers loved it.

If the above circumstances aren't present, be cautious about doing an activity throughout the audition. If you feel that it is important to you and your performance, go for it. The worst that can happen is that they will tell you to do it again without all the business. If it's not that important, then avoid doing it. This doesn't mean don't do it in the preceding steps of this process. *Doing the previous improvisations with physical doing has put it in your body and the benefit will still be present even if you don't do the physical doing at the actual audition.* After the improvisation process, the body understands and responds at the appropriate energy level regardless of whether you are still doing the physical doing business.

To prove this to you, and for practice, we now do a run-through of the audition in a smaller acting area to approximate a casting director's office. Your acting focus is to retain the attitude and to improvise only the physical doing—if any at all—that you feel either meets the above requirements or is absolutely necessary.

> **FOLLOW-UP**: Audience, was this run-through comparable? Did he retain the attitude? Is any physical doing that is still being done *necessary?* Is any unnecessary? ◆ Actor, do you agree?

11. Play the scene seated.

If the audition scene requires that your character be seated, the above comments about physical doing still pertain. Sometimes your audition will be put on tape and they will request that you stand on a mark or sit. For further practice and preparation, we now do a run-through of the audition with the actor seated. Your acting focus is to retain the attitude and, while seated, only improvise physical doing that you feel either meets the above requirements or is absolutely necessary.

> **FOLLOW-UP**: Audience, was this run-through comparable? Is the physical doing that is still being done necessary? ◆ Actor, do you agree?

◆   ◆   ◆

The audition is ready. It is now a complete performance that is prepared, spontaneous, and professionally competitive. Whether or not this is the characterization the casting director is looking for, it is the one you arrived at. If it's not what they are looking for, what is important is that you made a choice and executed it. That will be received with respect. If they feel it should be different, they will give you notes and ask you to do it again. *If you come in without having made a character choice, without having done the preparation, they will not respect your work or ask you to do it again.*

GENERAL COACHING FOR THE IMPROVS

The primary function of the coaching for the improvisations is to keep the actor on the designated acting focus and off of any inclination to hold onto any previous line readings or business at the expense of being on the designated acting focus. Most of any necessary coaching should get the actor to let the acting focus inform everything.

No coaching should be needed when the actor is doing run-throughs without a designated acting focus (steps 8, 10, and 11). If the actor's body rediscovers any previous line readings or business, that is all right. The body will desire and retain that which is authentic, works, and is best. The actor will not consciously attempt to retain this or that *bit*. During the improvs (steps 4–7, and 9), if the actor is on his acting focus, there will usually be no room for the retention of something that worked before. When that retention occurs during an improv, it is usually an indicator that the actor is not on his acting focus.

General coaching for steps 4–7, and 9 (as needed): Focus on [*designated acting focus*, e.g., contacting the set pieces, communicating in nonsense language, retaining your attitude line]. Commit to it. Say your lines as they come out, not as you rehearsed them. Respect your cues. Trust your acting focus. It will take care of everything.

Specific coaching for final run-through: Whichever improv is going to be the final one in the process (probably steps 9, 10, or 11), the actor should be given *a directorial note*— Remove all pauses. Don't say your lines any faster. Just pick up your cues. Cut any pause between your cue and saying your line.

MORE ABOUT THE PROCESS

The following are among the many benefits of this process:

- With each step, the actor becomes more familiar with the material, and this builds confidence.
- The material is put into the body, deeper and deeper, through the multiple improvisation acting focuses. After four or five improvisations, it is definitely *in there*.

- The more the material is in the body, and the more the actor understands experientially what it means to go with it, the more he increases his presence. Increased presence means increased impact on the audition space and everybody in it.

- The process gets the actor off of fixed line readings. In his traditional preparation, the actor may discover a great line reading. In subsequent rehearsals or at the audition, he is so overly concerned with re-creating it that spontaneity goes out the window and he often fails to make further discoveries about that particular moment or other parts of the scene. It is much healthier and more productive to trust that however you say a particular line it will be just fine because your body knows what to do. *This will only be true if you have gone through the improvisation process.*

  A common mistake about this point is experienced by students of faulty Meisner teaching, who think that if you are just *organic* and truly hear and respond to the other's lines, it will come out spontaneous and okay. The problem with that approach is, not only is the contribution to the emergence of a character minimal, but also, while the line readings may be authentic and spontaneous, the actor is not exploiting what is going on in the scene or what the writer has set in motion. Besides, how can anyone be authentically organic with a casting director or assistant who frequently reads the lines as not much more than cues, with little or no emotion?

  The improvisation approach breaks previously held patterns that may have become labored and reinfuses spontaneity into the scene while setting up maximum potential for further discoveries.

- This improvisation process prepares the actor to give an opening night performance for his auditions. There is so much competition for the same role and so much pressure on the casting director that the actors who get the callbacks are the actors who blow them away, not the ones whose auditions suggest that with some work there is promise. This is most emphatically true of TV casting. A major Hollywood casting director, Debi Manwiller, says:

  > Generally, I have maybe three or four days to cast an episode that may have fifteen or twenty people in it. . . . TV producers tend to be looking more for performance, more for a result, and if you can't produce it in the room, they're less likely to hire you than film producers. In episodic television, they shoot eight pages a day, and they're looking for something pretty close to what they're going to get on the set, because they don't have time for anything less. There is no real rehearsal.

You hit your mark, you shoot. You're lucky if you get to say hello to the director again. They need to know, *in the audition*, that you can get to that place or pretty close to it, whether you're directed or not. Sometimes you get a director who doesn't work with people in auditions for that reason. They just want to see you do it. The director knows that there isn't going to be time to rehearse or explain, and casts accordingly. Some directors will work with people and they'll be able to see through the nerves of an audition or know that it isn't at performance level. But I find, more often than not, that they tend toward the people who don't require too much of their time. It's just easier.

She continues, on the subject of preparation:

I think actors need to take more responsibility for their careers. . . . Taking responsibility means coming to auditions prepared and ready to work. Until you have a job, your work is getting the job. And it always surprises me how many people will come in who, it seems, haven't really read it carefully. The lack of basic preparation sometimes just amazes me. Of course, it's not everybody, but it happens more often than I would like.[1]

Try this approach for a few months and see if your batting average for callbacks or bookings improves. Another way of measuring success will be how you consistently feel immediately following your auditions compared to how you consistently feel now. Try it and see what happens. What have you got to lose? Take a risk.

Q & A

Why would I want to try this new audition approach?

If you are not pleased with your callback batting average, you have an opportunity to try something new. If you continue your present way of preparing for auditions, you would be foolish to think your batting average will improve. Why should it?

How really important is it to memorize lines?

If you don't have time to memorize, you can't do this process. You must be off book completely to focus on the improvisation's acting focus. Don't fool yourself into thinking you can do the improvs and read your lines at the same time. You need your attention and energy to go to an acting focus, not to reading. Also, you're hired to be an actor, not a reader. Some of you may be skilled at reading lines, and it may be a good indication of your acting, but as long as you are reading, *you are not acting*. Finally, the physiological process of reading takes a certain amount of time and when you are acting you don't have that time because spontaneity happens in the present tense. Reading takes maybe a split second for those who read fast, a whole second for those who don't. In that second, split or whole, your spontaneity goes out the window.

When others are going in and giving a Broadway opening night performance, and you are reading, you are not making a good-faith effort to get the part. Your audition goal is to make the callback list and you simply are not competitive when reading.

What if I can't get the sides ahead of time?

Sometimes, logistics prevent you from getting the sides early enough to memorize. At this stage of the training, you will not be able to do this process.

On the other hand, can you influence when you get the sides? Is it truly necessary that you receive sides with only a little bit of notice? I have found that many actors play the victim instead of taking care of themselves. Why not go to the casting office and pick them up instead of waiting for your agent to forward them to you? Some professionals, who would really love that job, would say to the agent, "I want the sides now. Where's the office? Just give me the address." Boom! You get in your car, drive over, walk in, schmooze the secretary, and you get the sides. If your agent tells you, "Be at the casting office at 2:00 P.M. They'll have the sides there." Do you go earlier? Why not?

My student, William Schallert, adds:

> When I was president of the guild [SAG] in 1980, one of the things we accomplished was to provide that a full script must be available for every actor who is going to audition. They don't have to send it to you, but they have to provide you with it if you go to where they are, so long as they've got it. If they say, "All we have is sides," and you see pages 52, 53, 54 and pages 18 and 19, you say, "Where did these come from? You have a script and I am entitled to the script." Demand it and don't worry about it. It is your right as a professional actor.

Of course, there are times when you can't get the sides early enough, but fewer than you think. Why jeopardize your potential for getting the job by limiting yourself to their rules, which they've set up totally out of their need for efficiency and frequently, out of ignorance of what an actor needs in order to do quality work? Why victimize yourself? You're an actor. You know how to prepare. You know how to walk in. You know how to do a job. If they want to hire you, great. If they don't, fine, but you did your job. Take responsibility for your career.

Here's a more extreme example that I support very much:

Agent   You have to be at CBS at 4:00 p.m. for a new pilot.

Actor   Do you have the sides?

Agent   No, they'll give them to you there.

Actor   Pass. I'm not available. I can do it tomorrow or the next day. Rebook me.

Agent   But they want to see you.

Actor   I'm sorry I do not give unprepared auditions anymore. Rebook me.

Remember, your agent is your employee not your employer. You pay him.

If you find that you often receive sides too late, you have an opportunity to work in your journals on this issue. Make sure you use the journal tool, "Where is the lie?" [Cf., chapter 1, final paragraph.]

How important is it to do the traditional approach first?

If you don't have confidence in your traditional technique, make Improvisation Technique your technique. If you do have confidence in your traditional technique, do it first and do it thoroughly. All the benefits that usually accrue with that approach will still pay off. Then if you want to try something new, add this. It will reinfuse your work with spontaneity and may reveal discoveries that didn't appear with your traditional approach.

Should we select the attitude line when we are picking the character, activity, and location?

No. Whether working alone or during the class's discussion of the character (step 3), restrict all discussion to occupation and naming the relationships between the characters in the scene. You will learn a great deal about the character during the improvisations and that will enrich your pool of information from which you select the attitude line.

When doing the first improvisation, what do you do if you complete the activity before the end of the scene?

Start another activity that's a part of the whole scene; or, undo the original activity, e.g., dressing/undressing; or, do the improv again and do the same activity but make it last until the end of the scene; or, do the improv again with another, longer-lasting activity.

How do you reconcile some casting directors advising actors not to use space props?

When casting directors advise against space props, it is because they see actors using them sloppily and looking silly, e.g., an actor takes a drink and brings the glass to his nose. If you have done the training to this point, you know how to use them. You have more experience with space props than most actors. Make sure that you respect the space props and communicate what you are doing. During the preparation process use space props, and if the space prop issue still concerns you at audition time, substitute real props. You're a professional. Go in and do a professional's work and you'll be respected. If your audition is solid and they don't like the space props or activity, they will ask you to do it again without the business. You'll be prepared for that. So, what have you lost?

On the other hand, when you use space props and activity, your audition is a co mplete theatrical performance that commands their attention. You look like a creative and inventive actor doing something with the material. It will definitely highlight you from everyone else who auditions just standing and talking.

If an actor reading this book wants to try this process but hasn't done the previous training, I would suggest not doing it, because there is no experiential familiarity or confidence with space props.

How do we know if we are doing the process correctly when we are working by ourselves?

Ask yourself the follow-up questions, the most basic and important of which is always, "Was I on the acting focus?" For this to be of value, you must answer honestly. If you have been doing the journal work throughout the training and employing the tool, "Where is the lie," that work will pay off when you answer the questions.

If the audition includes more than one scene, how do we handle that?

Do the whole process for each scene.

During the process, is it best to work with other actors, or a non-pro friend, or use a tape recorder?

It's always good to work with other actors because they will play with you and they will appreciate and have respect for the seriousness of your preparation. It's even better to work with your fellow Improvisation Technique group members because they will more freely participate in your improvisations, even employing the same acting focus. They will also be especially helpful during the follow-up. In my groups, the actors are always calling each other to get together and help during an audition preparation. However, if you must rely on a non-pro friend or use a tape recorder, the process will still work. All the other person has to have is a patient, respectful attitude and the ability to read the other lines on cue. I do *not* recommend you asking the non-pro friend for criticism. If they keep wanting to put in their two cents, work with a tape recorder.

If you do the process the night before the audition, what do you do the next day?

All you need is a brushup. This process puts it in the body. Once it's in the body, it's there. Just do a run-through.

Do you arrive at the casting office in character?

There are no rules about this. There are people who believe that you should arrive in character. There are other people who believe that it is equally impressive, if not more so, to come in as yourself, neutral and pleasant, and then show them you are an actor by transforming into the role.

There is an approach that combines the two. When you enter the casting office and during any preaudition chitchat, be yourself *at the character's energy level.* That increases the casting director's receptivity to you as the character without typecasting you for future roles, and you still get to show them that you are an actor by completing the transformation into the character for the actual audition. Different auditions require different approaches. You've got to choose what works best for you.

Should we hold the script at the audition?

If you know that you are not going to do any physical activity, then it's all right to carry the script; but don't read it. It disrupts your rhythm to pause and look down.

Never pause during an audition, for any reason, unless it is planned and filled with acting choreography. If you do pause and the pause is empty of some striking new element, whatever level of involvement you have earned from the casting people is out the window. They start thinking about lunch and you now have to re-earn their attention.

Warning: Don't get clever and hold the script, pretending to read it. If you do, you are adding inauthenticity to your performance.

Do you use the attitude line as an acting focus during the actual audition?

You have to learn about your own instrument before you know whether or not to do this. Test yourself. Try it without the attitude line focus. If you find the character's attitude fading, then employ the acting focus.

Suppose the casting director or stage manager delivers his lines flatly?

By forcing yourselves to do all of these improvs at home as a part of the preparation process, you are becoming further and further physically indoctrinated into the scene and are less likely to be dependent on the reader. All you need are the cues anyway. If they give you more, it's gravy.

Is this the Improvisation Technique approach to auditions?

Absolutely not! This is only a process based on what you've learned so far. Even though we haven't reached the end of the training, why not profit from what you already know how to do?

A really complete audition preparation includes a script breakdown leading to choices and their improvisational execution. This is still to come in the training. Until then, this process will improve your batting average.

> **TO THE COACH:** Have all the actors do step 3 for each of the sides they are provided. If the original audition was on a stage or set, it is not necessary to go past step 9.

9

EMOTIONS

INTRODUCTION TO PHYSICALIZATION

In Improvisation Technique training there are three aspects of the actor's use of emotions: (1) Learning how to open and use the body so emotions arise spontaneously while performing. (2) Discovering and expanding the ability to create a preselected emotion on cue. (3) Learning the skill of playing emotions with a dexterity similar to that required when playing musical instruments, i.e., playing the scales of an emotion and changing emotions on cue. All of the skills learned in this chapter are essential building blocks to the conclusive emotion doing skills: immediate physicalization of emotions, emotion switches, and emotion arcs.

For most actors, *this is an entirely new approach to emotions.* As we begin the work, I have a few suggestions. Stay open to a brand new approach and avoid using previously learned tools from your traditional technique to solve whatever challenges are presented to you in this part of the training. Upon completion of this work, you will have a whole additional way of approaching emotions.

Acting emotions with Improvisation Technique breaks the most oft taught rule of traditional acting: Never play an emotion or attitude; play your objective. Playing an objective was Stanislavsky's antidote to the histrionic and declamatory style of nineteenth-century acting. Because we now know a technique of physicalizing emotions, the old rule should be changed. If you know how to physicalize emotions, you may play the emotion choice; if you do not know how to physicalize emotions, limit yourself to playing an objective (problem and action).

330

In professional acting, frequently a director will say, "Get angry/happy/sad/ etc.," and then the actor will complain (silently or vocally) that this is a "result" direction and he needs an "action" direction—a verb or an objective. Instead of complaining about the form of direction or suggesting that the director sit in on an acting class, he should see the "result" as a "choice" and know how to play it immediately and spontaneously. Improvisation Technique's method of physicalizing emotion prepares the actor for fulfilling an emotion direction without a context of verbs, actions, problems, objectives, or tasks. In the new millennium, actors, directors, and teachers should be open to new approaches.

EXTEND, INTENSIFY, AND ENLARGE[1]

SETUP: 2–4 per team. In huddles, select character, activity, and location.

RULES: While improvising your character, activity, and location, you will be presented with opportunities to extend, intensify, and enlarge different aspects of the improvisational acting. In order for you to respond to the coaching, to your fellow actors, and to whatever direction the improv takes, you must be attentive and *open* to going with whatever is happening, including the coaching. At a certain point in the improv, you will be given an opportunity to proceed on your acting focus without the coaching.

ACTING FOCUS: Parts (1) and (2), go with the coaching! Part (3), go with it on your own!

COACHING (as needed): Set up the location. ◆ Places. ◆ Action. ◆ **Check out your fellow actors.** Share your voices. Avoid hanging out.

PART 1: SOUNDS, MOVEMENTS, POSTURES:

Enlarge that movement. Extend that style of movement. Go with the coaching. **Intensify that gesture.** Enlarge and extend it more! **Enlarge that rhythm.** Enlarge the movement physically. Enlarge that posture. Go with it. Enlarge it more. Bigger! Assist your fellow actors. **Enlarge those sounds you are making. Extend those sounds.** More! Bigger! Extend that movement. Go with it. Extend it more. **Extend that posture. Enlarge that face.** ◆ **Stay open.** Stay alert to each other. **Go with it.** Censor nothing. Show us; don't tell us. Respect your space. **Avoid hanging out.** Avoid questions. Integrate what you are doing as a part of the whole.

PART 2: FEELINGS, EMOTIONS, ATTITUDES

Go with that impulse. Intensify that impulse. **Intensify that feeling.** Intensify that mood. Enlarge that mood. Enlarge that emotion. Intensify that emotion. Amplify that emotion. More. More! Show us; don't tell us. Enlarge that new feeling. Intensify that new feeling. **Extend that feeling throughout the body and intensify it.** More. More! Enlarge that attitude.

Extend that attitude throughout the body and intensify it. **Extend that attitude.** Use the whole body. ◆ Avoid censoring your fellow players. Avoid hanging out. Nothing comes from nothing. ◆ Extend that silence. Enlarge that silence. Intensify that silence.

PART 3: YOU'RE ON YOUR OWN

You're on your own. Stay alert to what you're feeling and be available to extending, intensifying, or enlarging it. Go with it! Stay on your acting focus. One minute to take advantage of the acting focus. ◆ Cut.

FOLLOW-UP (as needed): Characters? Activity? Location? ◆ **Were they on their acting focus?** Did they respond to the coaching? Did they extend, intensify, and enlarge? **Were they open to going with it,** or were they guarded and closed? Examples of being guarded and closed would be not responding to the coaching or negating opportunities to go somewhere new, regardless of the reason. Did some actors interfere with other actors going with it? Did some actors interfere with themselves going with it? When they responded to the coaching, what happened? **Was the coaching arbitrary and not a part of the whole, or was it a response to what was already taking place in the improv?** When they were on their own, did they make their own discoveries and go with it? ◆ *Only for teams that follow the first team—* Prior to going on their own, did they anticipate the coaching and rush to enlarging the emotions? ◆ **Actors, were you on your acting focus? Did you allow it to lead you through the improvisation?** Did your bodies feel different when you were on the acting focus from how they normally feel? Can you describe the difference in body feelings between feeling open or closed?

SUMMARY:

The actors and coach are in a reflect-the-reflector relationship. The coach responds to what he sees the actors doing, the actors respond to the coaching, the coach responds again, and so on. When the actors are on their own, without the coach, they've removed the middleman. They stay open, go with it, and discover that any moment of acting, including the feeling of emotions, can be the jumping-off point for extended, substantial, and unanticipated beats of the scene. *They discover a willingness to intensify what is already happening.*

When you are not open to going with it, your head dictates what you will or will not do. It has an idea of how things should be, and anything that doesn't subscribe to that agenda is declined. This robs you of your true potentiality and keeps you chained to the ground when you have the capability of real flight into the unknown. In being open to going with it, you have the experience of being out of your head.

It takes courage and a willingness to let go of what you think should happen. Most student actors take direction and simply execute it, feeling that they have done their job well. A professional actor takes direction and goes somewhere new with it. They make the direction their jumping-off point.

Once you found the groove of being open and going with it, notice how easily you escalated the initial feelings into full-blown emotions. A slight feeling of pleasure was intensified to absolute hilarity by *intensifying it more and more in your body*. An emerging attitude of caution was escalated to feelings of fear and then further, to absolute terror. You didn't have to stop the scene to prepare yourself with corresponding emotional memories or to seek motivations, select intentions, or pursue actions.

> **TO THE COACH:** At first, the actors will more easily understand and effectively respond to extending, intensifying, and enlarging *sounds, movements, and postures*. The coaching must take the actors to responses that are beyond what they would normally do. The actors must reach extratheatricality and have an experiential feeling that breaks their individual ideas of how things should be. As they become accustomed to responding to the coaching in these areas, the coach guides them into the same type of responses with their *feelings, emotions, and attitudes*. When the actors are responding in these areas with natural and integrated elevations of feelings that are a part of the whole scene, and they spontaneously arrive at a moment of silence, the coach applies the silence coaching as a segue into *You're on your own!* Allow about five minutes for each part.
>
> When working with the actors to enlarge, extend, or intensify a sound, the sounds are usually laughs, coughs, grunts, whistles, etc. ◆ Any conflict that arises between the characters in the improvs should alert the coach that the actors are not on their acting focus. Conflict almost never occurs on this particular acting focus because conflict is an example of people holding onto their ideas of the way things should be. ◆ If the actors' responses to the coaching create ritualized group transformational dances, it means that they are limiting their responses to reflecting each other. This is a healthy, albeit limited, response to both the acting focus and the coaching. ◆ *To move them on from this, coach*— Find your own unique and original part of the whole.

This is always a fun exercise to play and to observe. Without discussion or breaking down the process of physicalization, the actors get an experiential dose of how easy it is to change intensities of emotions through physicalization.

◆　　◆　　◆

While the actors may have spontaneously intensified their feelings, they will not have explored the complete *range* of feeling intensification available to them. Also, the previous improv exposed them to only those feelings that happened to come up spontaneously during the improv. A complete range of intensification and control over a previously selected emotion choice based on script breakdown, or director's note, is less easily arrived at. The real work on physicalization and emotions begins now.

EMOTION WALK #1

SETUP: Actors place their audience chairs in a semicircle at one end of the room. All walk around the room responding to the coaching.

RULES: None.

ACTING FOCUS: Respond to the coaching.

COACHING:

1. Stand still. Do the 40-breath process. ♦ *[Allow 10–15s between sentences.]* ♦ Walk around. Everyone focus on feeling your body move through the space. Feel the space moving through you. Put it together—move through the space and feel the space moving through you. ♦ Focus on feeling your skeleton walking in the space. Feel your skeleton instead of seeing a picture of your skeleton in your mind's eye. Feel it and avoid seeing it. Keep away from any visualizing. Feel your skeleton walking in the space. ♦ Respond to the coaching instead of thinking about it. ♦ Focus on feeling your knees move as you walk. Focus on feeling your elbows moving. Your hips. Your ankles. Shoulders. Wrists. Toes. Whole legs. Pelvis. Whole arms. Spine. Neck. Head. Allow your head to be free. You don't have to hold it up. Let it do what it wants. Let it support itself. Keep your eyes open. Feel any self-obstructions to your free movement. Leave those obstructions alone, or not. Allow your body to align itself naturally. Simply feel your skeleton's movement. Don't analyze or judge. Observe what is or isn't. ♦ Feel your head full of space. Feel your stomach full of space. Feel your face made out of space. Your elbows. Knees. Hips. Ankles. Shoulders. Wrists. Toes. Whole legs. Pelvis. Whole arms. Spine. Neck. Whole body. Keep feeling your skeleton walking in the space. Every bone is surrounded by space. ♦ Enlarge all of your body's movements. Go with it. —*Allow 30s.* ♦ Allow your body to return to normal size. Feel your clothes against your body. Let your clothes feel you. Feel your clothes and let your clothes feel you at the same time. Feel your clothes and let your clothes feel you and feel the space in the room and allow the space to feel you. Take note and observe your own breathing right now. No need to do anything with it; simply observe your breathing. ♦ Keep walking.

2. Everyone select an **emotion**. Don't do anything with it, just name it. Now, focus on feeling that emotion with your toes. Physicalize that emotion with your toes. If you chose *happy*, have happy toes. If you chose *angry*, have angry toes. Keep physicalizing it with your toes and add your ankles. How do happy ankles feel? How do angry ankles feel? Physicalize that. Keep your eyes open throughout the entire process. Now physicalize your whole feet with that emotion. Choose to have your feet have that emotion. Keep doing that, and go up to your knees. Physicalize the emotion with your knees. Keep doing that, and add the pelvic area. Feel that emotion with your pelvis. Physicalize it. The whole lower half of your body is now physicalizing the chosen emotion. If it helps you to feel it more, heighten the physicalization of the different body parts. Now, go up to your chest. You are now physicalizing the emotion with your chest. Keep physicalizing it, and add your shoulders, elbows. If your emotion is *sad*, choose to have sad elbows. Move your shoulders around in that emotion. Now, add the wrists, fingers, whole hands. Physicalize the emotion with your spine. Feel the emotion with your spine. Go up the neck. Move your neck around in that emotion. The top of your head. Eyebrows. Tongue. Lower lip. Using your whole body now, have a complete total body physicalization of that selected emotion. If you want to feel the emotion more, heighten it. Check if there are any parts of your body where you are not feeling or physicalizing the emotion. While you are physicalizing the emotion, observe your breathing. Keep physicalizing the emotion and heighten it with an exaggerated body. Now bring the body exaggeration down a little bit but keep sustaining the physicalization of the emotion. Everybody stay on this focus of physicalizing the emotion and return to your seat. Stay on focus. Keep physicalizing the emotion while sitting. Let's check in. Are you exaggerating with your body? Do we still see the remnants of the body heightening physicalization? You do not need to do that. Bring down any large-sized movements and keep physicalizing the emotion in the body. Stay on your *current focus* of physicalizing the emotion. Check in with yourself and notice that you are feeling the emotion. Observe that. Now, keep physicalizing and feeling the emotion and look around at each other. Allow your eyes to look around the room. Stay alert. Notice the responses and emotions. Notice if you see any different emotions. Keep breathing. If you feel the emotion slipping, heighten the physicalization. See what there is to see. Allow your fellow actors to see you. Now, everybody return to the floor. Spread out, and now we are going to do a step-out.

3. Do the **step-out.**

STEP-OUT[2]

Pick a spot at eye level on a wall across the room. Look at that one spot and take five slow, long breaths, inhaling through the nose and exhaling through the mouth. Five counts to inhale. Five counts to exhale. Don't strain yourself. If you can't do five counts, do three or four. Look at that spot and do five inhales and five exhales. —*Allow 1m.* ◆ When you finish the breaths, do some full body stretching and speak nonsense language out loud. Loudly. —*Allow 1m.* ◆ Take your fingertips and gently pat all over your face with the individual fingertips as if each tap is an expression of you loving you. ◆ Now say to yourself in a very soothing voice, "Hello, I love you. I love you. How is my old friend? Here we are together again. There are my lips. This is my nose. Here is my forehead. Hello." —*Allow 30s.* ◆ Now, bend over and pat your knees with your palms and your fingers. —*Allow 10s.* ◆ Is everybody back? Are you all here?

FOLLOW-UP: Did you feel your selected emotion? Twice you were coached to observe your breathing. Did you notice a difference? When you were sitting and observing each other, did you see different emotions being felt by the rest of the group? What emotions could you identify? Did they seem authentic? Did you use any uncoached tools to help you feel the emotion, e.g., attitude lines, memory recalls, *as if*, images, etc.? If so, were you encouraged not to do that? Do you agree that you deprived yourself of the opportunity to experience a new process?

SUMMARY:

You have just had an introductory taste of one of the two main steps in the process known as *physicalizing an emotion.* You took a preselected emotion, physicalized it, and arrived at feeling the emotion. You did this without employing any previously learned traditional or privately developed tools. **We are beginning to develop a new tool for feeling emotions that requires only your choosing to feel it.** With practice and exploration, we will decrease the amount of time between the moment you select the emotion and the complete feeling of the emotion. Do you think it is possible to do it instantaneously? We shall see.

If your response to the physicalization wasn't strong enough for you in terms of feeling the emotion, you just have to heighten the physicalization.

Don't respond to the coaching with an attitude line. Throughout this period of working on emotions, avoid making the emotion choice into an attitude line. You know how to do that. Let's learn something new.

Should a thought about the past or an image come up in your head when you are physicalizing an emotion, that's all right. It arose spontaneously with the onset of the emotional feeling. However, avoid seizing on it and using it. Cer-

tainly, avoid going out of your way to create it. If it drifts in, allow it. Then allow
it to drift out.

> **TO THE COACH:** It is important to begin emotion work immediately with
> very little discussion. In my experience, actors have made commitments
> to how they do their emotional work and jump freely into debates about
> one approach vs. another. To begin with one of these debates is coun-
> terproductive and sets defensive mechanisms in play at precisely the time
> the actors need to be open to experiencing a new approach. ◆ *For all
> emotion walks*— When the coaching sentences address the same body
> part, it is not necessary to pause between sentences.

PARALYSIS / ALONE [3]

SETUP: A solo exercise. Each actor chooses a character, location, and circumstances that provide for his character to be paralyzed and faced with impending physical threat. The threat must be high stakes and beyond the
character's control. The paralysis must be physical and may be necessitated
by the circumstances of the threat or may be a medical condition. E.g.,
woman tied to a chair (no possibility of escape) as men approach to rape her;
paralyzed person in bed as room he is in is being consumed by flames.

RULES: Respond to the coaching.

ACTING FOCUS: On being paralyzed.

SPECIAL GROUP VOCAL WARM-UP: After the actors have had about five minutes
to make their choices, bring the whole group out on the floor for a vocal
warm-up. ◆ **Part 1:** Everyone, find a spot against a wall. You are going to
be leaning with your back against the wall, so it has to be something that
supports you. [If there is not enough room for all actors against a wall,
players can lean back-to-back.] Everybody lean back against the wall
slightly, so that your feet are about a foot away from the wall. Your stomachs should be out a little. We are going to breathe from our diaphragm,
so let's just practice taking a deep breath in. When you breathe in, the
diaphragm and the stomach go out. When you exhale, they come in. So,
everybody breathe in. Breathe out. Keep your eyes open. If you want to
check that you are doing it correctly, put your hand on your belly and feel
it going out on the inhale and back in on the exhale. On an exhale, we are
all going to say the word *I*. Look at a spot on the wall opposite you and
focus on extending the word and sending it to the wall opposite you. Keep
breathing from your diaphragm. The word lasts as long as the exhale. Let's
all do it together. Inhale. Go. ◆ The next step is, we are going to say two
words, *I want*. You have to split the exhale in half. The first half of the
exhale goes to the *I*, sending it to the far wall. The second half of the

exhale goes to the *want*, sending it also to the far wall. Let's all inhale. Go. ◆ Now, let's do three words during the single exhale. *I want to.* Inhale. Go. ◆ Let's add another word. *I want to go.* We are going to send it to the far wall. Stretch the four words over the length of the single exhale. Inhale. Go. ◆ Your voices are warmed up now. ◆ Return to your seats. ◆ **Part 2:**[4] Feet flat on the floor. We are going to shout in silence. Just follow the coaching. We don't want to hear anything. ◆ *[Allow five seconds between sentences.]* ◆ Shout with your ankles. Shout with your knees. Shout with your pelvis. Shout with your chest. With your shoulders. Shout with your arms, all the way to the fingers. Shout. Can you shout more with your arms and fingers? Shout to the maximum. Include your shoulders. Now, shout with your face. Now, shout with your whole body. Add sound! — *Allow 3s.* ◆ Silence! Breathe in through the nose and out through the mouth. Five long breaths.

COACHING: Actor, go to places. Take five big and quick breaths. Inhale through the mouth; take the breath to the center of the chest. Exhale through the mouth. Put more emphasis on the inhale than the exhale. ◆ Follow the coaching and don't get ahead of it. ◆ Don't move. Look out and see what there is to see in your location from your position. ◆ See all the larger structures, set pieces, natural phenomena. ◆ See all the colors. ◆ See any tiny details or props that you can see. Keep breathing naturally. ◆ Now get on your acting focus of paralysis. Focus on the fact that you are too paralyzed to move. Keep your eyes open. ◆ *[10s pause.]* ◆ Now, be aware of the presence of the danger and stay on the focus of your paralysis. *[5s pause.]* ◆ **Action!** The danger is here and you are paralyzed. Focus on your paralysis. ◆ There's a feeling coming up for you right now. Take that feeling and spread it throughout the body by choosing to physicalize that feeling all over the body. ◆ *[3s pause.]* ◆ Keep focusing on being paralyzed and simultaneously physicalizing that feeling that has come up. That feeling chose you. Now you choose it by physicalizing it throughout the body. Begin to heighten the physicalization of that feeling throughout the whole body. ◆ [The coach's voice should begin boosting **urgency.**] ◆ Physicalize it in your neck, feet, spine, in your eyelids, in your tongue, your teeth, your fingers, pelvic area, chest, stomach. Keep heightening the physicalization. The danger is heightening. ◆ [The coach's voice should begin boosting **volume.**] ◆ Higher. Physicalize it more. More. Keep physicalizing it more. Keep heightening the physicalization as you focus on your paralysis. Heighten it. Keep heightening it. Go! Heighten it! Keep heightening it! More! Go with it! Go with it! Go! Go! More! You're on your own! Stay on your focus! Go with it! ◆ Cut.

Take your time. There is no urgency. Catch your breath. No urgency. Just hang out. The exercise is over. When you can control one breath, then go for two breaths, then three, and so on, until you are back in charge of your breathing. There is no urgency. Come down at your leisure. When you feel like it, we are going to do a step-out. ◆ [Take the actor through the step-out.]

FOLLOW-UP (as needed): Did you see the actor escalating the intensity of emotion? Did you see the actor traveling emotionally? **Can you name the stages of that traveling,** e.g., apprehension to fear to terror? **Did you feel that the emotions that you were watching were authentic?** ◆ **Actor, did you escalate the intensity of emotion? Did you feel that the emotions were authentic? Did you feel a stoppage of further escalation? Were you aware of reaching points where the escalation would not continue and you either plateaued at the highest level achieved or started to decrease the intensity?** Notice that that occurred. Observe it. It's called a cork or a ceiling. ◆ **Class, did you see any corks or ceilings preventing further escalation of the emotion?**

SUMMARY:

The traveling of the emotion is called the emotional arc. When first doing this exercise, most actors will reach a ceiling or corking point, where the emotion will not intensify further. Our job in working on the instrument is to remove the corks and continually raise our ceilings until they disappear. We will do that through the exercises and improvisations. It is the actor's job to be able to play all intensities of an emotion without limitation.

With Improvisation Technique, there is no need to dwell on the reasons for the corks, the psychology of the individual actor, or the psychology of emotions. Stanislavsky discovered in his later work with physical actions that the most reliable route to the emotions is through the muscles and not through the mind. Spolin went further when she introduced the process of physicalizing emotions. Another approach to the physicalization process is a technique of adding appropriate breathing patterns to the body's physicalization of emotions. Developed by neuroscientist Susana Bloch, this breath work technique is called Alba Emoting. The step-out employed here, while fairly similar to breath therapy in the healing process and slightly changed by me, was created by Bloch as the component of Alba Emoting that returns the body to emotional neutrality. I learned it when I studied Alba Emoting with Bloch in Cachagua, Chile, in 1993. Except for the step-out, any breath work we have been employing is not a part of Alba Emoting but eastern-influenced traditional breathing exercises designed to oxygenate the blood, release body holds, and make the actor more present.

TO THE COACH: The usual running time from "Action" to "Cut" is about four to five minutes. This is an intense exercise. Except for one variation on it, repeated in the next class, no other exercise in Improvisation Technique is so intense. The coach might point this out to the actors at the end of the session.

Do not skip the vocal warm-up. Many actors will scream during this exercise. If their vocal apparatus is not warmed up, that can be harmful. The coach should make no mention at all of the reason for the warm-up. If he does, the actors will assume that the *right* way to play the exercise is to scream.

If the group is large and time is a problem, after two or three actors have done the exercise individually, you can divide the acting area into as many as five subareas and do five actors at a time. Coach all simultaneously. Warn the actors to ignore the other actors on the floor. Another timesaver is to have the actors do their step-out outside the workshop immediately after their follow-up. *If you do this, the following notes are very important.*

It might be wise to inform the actors that if they leave class and feel any emotional residue later, they should do another step-out on their own, at that time. I usually bring everyone back on the floor at the end of the class for a final, whole-class step-out, immediately followed by dancing to an up-tempo rock 'n' roll tune.

During the come down period, between "Cut" and the beginning of the step-out, the coach might make simple physical contact with the actor. Touch a shoulder, top of head, an ankle, etc., to help ground the actor with a supportive gesture.

◆　◆　◆

EMOTION WALK #2

The second class on emotions begins with our second emotion walk.

SETUP: All walk around the room responding to the coaching.

RULES: None.

ACTING FOCUS: Respond to the coaching.

COACHING: Part 1. Walk around and shake it out. Breathe in through the nose and out through the mouth. Take long, extended breaths. Four counts to the inhale. Four counts to the exhale. Breathe normally. ◆ *[Allow seven seconds between sentences.]* ◆ Focus on feeling your chest moving through the space. Feel your chest with your chest. Feel your thighs moving through the space. Feel your thighs with your thighs. Feel the space underneath your feet as you step down and squash it out. Let the floor feel your feet, and let your feet feel the floor. Feel the tip of your nose moving through the space. Feel the tip of your nose with the tip of your nose. Feel your toes with your toes. Feel your knees with your knees. Move your pelvis around in the space, and as you do it, feel your pelvis with your pelvis. Feel your shoulders with your shoulders. Feel your elbows with your elbows. Move your wrists around in the space and feel your wrists with your wrists. Keep your eyes open. Keep breathing. Move your neck around in the space, and feel your neck with your neck. Feel the space inside your head, and let the space inside your head feel your head. Go inside your body and locate any parts of your body where you feel dead. Observe and locate them, and then put space there.

Part 2. *[Each ◆ represents 15s.]* Select an **emotion,** a different one from the last class. Just select it. ◆ Now, feel that emotion with your toes. Choose for your toes to feel this emotion. Move your toes around in that emotion. Physicalize that emotion with your toes. ◆ Once you feel it there, keep it there as you then physicalize that emotion with the rest of your foot, your ankles, the arch. Move your feet around in that emotion. What do happy feet feel like? What do sad feet feel like? Allow your feet to feel that by physicalizing that emotion with your feet. ◆ Keep it there and go up to the knees. Move your knees around in that emotion. Physicalize that emotion with your knees. *Heighten the movement if that helps you to feel it.* It's up to you. You are physicalizing that chosen emotion with your feet and your knees. ◆ Move your pelvis around in that emotion, with that emotion. Happy pelvis. Sad pelvis. Angry pelvis. Whatever it is, make it happen. Just do it. ◆ Now the whole lower half of your body is physicalizing the emotion. Go to the chest. Don't lose the lower half of your body. Physicalize that emotion with your chest. ◆ Add the shoulders. Move your shoulders around in that emotion. How do happy shoulders feel? How do sad shoulders feel? Allow your body to respond. ◆ Physicalize the emotion with your elbows, wrists, and fingers. ◆ Observe your spine physicalizing that emotion. If it isn't, then physicalize it with your spine. ◆ Physicalize that emotion with your neck. There is lots of spine in the neck to physicalize the emotion. ◆ Now, physicalize that emotion with your whole face. What do happy eyebrows do? What do sad lips do? Your body will know what to do. You just send the message and your body will do it. You choose to do it, and your body will respond. ◆ Allow your whole body to be in complete physicalization of this emotion. Keep physicalizing the emotion.

Part 3. Keep the physicalization going, and at the same time bring down any large body movements to normal size. In other words, *take out the* *heightening of the body movements without decreasing the physicalization of the emotion.* Let's say we are shooting a movie right now, and you are all in the crowd scene. The set is a mall, and you are all walking around the mall. Your job as an actor is to feel this emotion by physicalizing it, but the size of your body movements must be appropriate to someone walking in a mall. ◆ Check in with your breathing and observe it. Don't do anything about it. Don't *not* do anything about it, but observe your breathing right now. ◆ Everyone's focus is on walking and physicalizing the emotion. Check in with yourself right now and observe if you are in fact feeling some degree of this particular emotion. Keep physicalizing it. There is a door at the far end of the mall and it leads into a giant train station. Everybody make your way through that door and into the train station. Keep physicalizing the emotion as you do it, and when you come into the train station, stay on the single focus of physicalizing this emotion and add a second focus of going to the location or maybe discovering some objects. In other words, do some physical doing while you maintain your physicalization of this emotion. Move about through the train station. Find different location set pieces to contact. Find different objects to discover in the space or on your body. You are on a double focus now. Keep breathing. —*Allow 1m.* Now, look at your watch. It is time to go to the train in any corner of the room. Go out into the train area, into the four corners or the room. There is a door in each corner. When you go through the door, you are off stage. ◆ Cut.

Part 4. Everybody, walk back out into the playing area. ◆ [Do step-out.] ◆ Okay, we are all stepped out. Everyone is out of the emotion. Just walk around the room now, not a space walk, just a walk. While you are walking, observe your breathing. Observe it in comparison to the last time I asked you to observe your breathing, which was during the physicalization of the emotion. ◆ Cut. ◆ Return to your seats.

FOLLOW-UP (as needed): By the end of the physicalization process, were you feeling the emotion? Are you avoiding previously learned acting tools to help you feel the emotion? Twice you were coached to observe your breathing. Did you notice a difference? Are you aware of a further difference between your breathing in this emotion from breathing in the emotion last class? Do you think that different emotions have different patterns of breathing? Would you consider breathing a part of the physicalization process? When you went into the mall, were you able to sustain the emotional physicalization with physical doing?

SUMMARY:

A good way to check on your own physicalization process is to notice your breathing. If it hasn't changed from the preemotion state to the fully physicalized emotion state, you are probably not doing the physicalization. For now, just keep breathing and take whatever breathing patterns emerge.

As in learning character work, avoid making assumptions about the totality of this work until we get further along in the process. Your concept of what physicalization is and how to do it will broaden as we get further into the work.

Here is what the great English actor, Sir Alec Guinness, writes about emotion work in his autobiography, *Blessings in Disguise:*

> From the moment I first saw Edith Evans, I became her ardent admirer and rarely missed a new performance. For me, she was the greatest high comedian in, and probably the finest actress in the English-speaking world. I never saw Laurette Taylor. When finally I was in a production with her, playing the tiny part of the Apothecary in Gielgud's *Romeo and Juliet*, I had the fortune of watching her Nurse each night, but never a word was spoken to me. I would hold open doors and not even get a nod, let alone a "thank you." It didn't worry me. I was proud enough to be ushering onto the stage her tall, emperious presence. She did speak to me once, though. For the first time, during a night rehearsal of *The Seagull* that Komisarjevsky was directing. That was at the New Theater in 1936. I was understudying Stephen Haggert as Constantin and also appearing as the workman (wordless) who operates the curtain to the little outdoor stage in Act I. In this particular night, during a rehearsal of the last act, I was sitting in the darkened seats, a few rows behind Edith. Peggy Ashcroft and Stephen appeared to have gotten into emotional difficulties with the scene, and Comis was being belligerently unhelpful. I could see the back of his bald head twitching. Edith decided she had spotted the trouble. Wanting to voice her opinion without interfering with the rehearsal and straying from side to side seeking an audience, she spotted an unknown face in the darkness, mine, and said, "You see young man, it is all a great big glass tube and you blow down it." She redirected her vision to the stage while satisfied with her perspicacity, but leaving me totally in the dark. Later I worked out what she was getting at. That emotion must be channeled through some invisible technical achievement which would direct it, shape it, and lend it force. At least I think that is what she meant.[5]

PARALYSIS / GROUP[6]

SETUP: 2–5 per team. In huddles, select character, location, and circumstances that provide for all of the characters to be paralyzed and faced with impending physical threat. The threat must be high stakes and beyond the character's control. The paralysis must be physical and necessitated by the circumstances of the threat. E.g., Anne Frank's family keeping still on the occasion of the Nazis searching the house; a group stuck in a bus, which is hanging precariously off a cliff.

RULES: Respond to the coaching.

ACTING FOCUS: On being paralyzed.

SPECIAL GROUP VOCAL WARM-UP: Same as in paralysis/alone.

COACHING (as needed): Before the improvs, coach the audience to watch the improv through a slightly open fist, like a film director, and choose what they would focus on if they were editing the scene. ◆ Select your shots. Open your fist wider for whole group shots. Slightly close your fist for close ups on the face. Switch back and forth between actors as you see fit. ◆ Actors, go to places. Take five big and quick breaths in through the mouth, to the center of the chest. Exhale through the mouth. Put more emphasis on the inhale than the exhale. ◆ Follow the coaching and don't get ahead of it. ◆ Don't move. Look out and see what there is to see in your location from your position. ◆ See all the larger structures, set pieces, natural phenomena. ◆ See all the colors. ◆ See any tiny details or props that you can see. Keep breathing naturally. ◆ *[5s pause.]* ◆ Now, be aware of the presence of the danger. ◆ Now get on your acting focus of paralysis. Focus on the fact that you are too paralyzed to move. Focus on that, now, and stay on the focus of your paralysis. ◆ *[5s pause.]* ◆ **Action!** ◆ [The remainder of the coaching is the same as in paralysis/alone. Finish with the standard step-out.]

FOLLOW-UP (as needed): Same as in paralysis/alone. *Then—* ◆ Audience, what did you observe or notice from being cameras and selecting shots? What determined when you cut away from someone? What determined whom you cut to? Who was the actor you found yourself covering the most? ◆ The responses to the camera questions will include: (1) the more visible the intensity changes, the more the camera stayed on that person; (2) if an intensity stayed on one level, the camera cut away; (3) physical changes like sweating and flushed faces held the camera; (4) actors who internalized, keeping their feelings inside, seldom had the camera on them.

SUMMARY:

You have now done this exercise twice, once as an individual and once as part of a group. From your own experience and from watching the others do it, you are becoming aware of the potential movement within an emotion. This movement, or traveling, is called an *emotion arc.* As long as you are traveling on this arc, you bring the audience with you. When you stop traveling and plateau on one level of intensity, you lose the audience because they quickly get used to what you are doing and there is no *promise of change.* Without that, they get bored and are not compelled to watch you.

344

Our work is now beginning to be about not only creating emotional feelings through physicalization, but also developing the self-awareness and the facility to intensify these feelings, with control, in order to travel on the emotion's arc. Ultimately, you will be able to choose the entry level from which you will commence the arc, take your arcs higher than you can now, and have the control to play a three-intensity-level arc or even a ten-intensity-level arc.

It is this technical facility that will influence the director's and editor's decisions when to cut away from you. As long as you are traveling, your footage remains. When you tread water or plateau, it will all be cut. Your job is to give the cutters the most opportunities for cutting the sequence, and not to limit them.

As Edith Evans said, "It's all a great big glass tube." What's the primary feature of any tube? It's hollow and there are no obstacles. "It's a big glass tube and you've got to blow down it." Every time you put a cork in, you plug up part of the tube and impede the flow of energy. With this exercise, we are becoming aware of that.

What does it feel like to blow down the tube, which in a way is the heightening of the physicalization? In this case, the feeling was initiated by your acting focus, the paralysis, and the presence of the threat. As you improvise, notice that the more you blow down the tube, the more your emotions travel, and the more things happen to you. You are in control. You're the one who's choosing to blow or not to blow and how hard to blow. Is the tube unimpeded? You could blow very hard down the tube, but if it's stuffed up, nothing comes out. There are two issues: blowing, and keeping the tube open.

You may be confused about how to blow down the tube. Your experiences with physicalizing the emotion are based on emotion walks and paralysis. Your body's process during both may be completely different. This confusion will clear up as we continue. Just stay alert and open to having a clear tube, unimpeded by obstacles.

As you become more aware of your ceilings or corks, you may want to write about them in your journals. A cork is anything that keeps you from traveling further. We may have corks in our real lives, but as actors, we don't want limits. Stay alert to your tricky mind, which has many ways of introducing limitations. It will provide you with all kinds of reasons for not doing something. Your mind will tell you, "I can't go anywhere else." That's only an idea and it comes from fear, yours, not the character's. It may have arisen out of your discomfort at some point in the exercise when you said to yourself, "What's going to happen to me if I keep going like this? I don't want to do this. I don't want to go through this." There are many ideas that can create corks.

For some, the idea to go no further is a rebellion. "The coach wants me to do more traveling and I'm not going to do it because nobody can tell me what to do!" Notice that some actors, upon hearing "Cut," uncontrollably climb multiple levels of intensity, even crying, immediately after the coach ends the exercise. Why didn't they achieve those higher levels of intensity prior to the cut? For some actors to go further, they need the pressure to be turned off. They have to be let *off the hook*. For them, something happens in the body the moment that there's no more pressure. They say to themselves, "Oh, the scene's over. I don't *have* to do that anymore. I can relax." Then all of a sudden, there is this giant release of feelings. The pressure to go further was a cork inside the tube, an impediment to the free flow of energy. Pull out the cork, and the energy flows freely. The body feels that and the physicalization jumps much higher.

> **TO THE COACH:** Traveling is the opposite of hanging out or treading water in one level of emotional intensity.
>
> Notice that prior to "Action," the coaching reverses the order of focusing on the paralysis and then the danger from the order in paralysis/alone.
>
> During the step-out, make sure the actors are not stretching in any form of anger. The stretches should be neutral and fluid in order to loosen residual tension. Stretching in anger adds tension to the body.
>
> From beginning to end, "Places" to "Cut," the coaching usually lasts between four and five minutes.
>
> Having the audience watch parts of the improvs through their fists, as movie cameras, heightens their watching experience and increases their awareness of the importance of traveling through the emotion rather than treading water in one level of intensity. They discover this when they instinctively cut away from someone who is treading water to someone who is traveling.
>
> When the audience responds to the follow-up question, "Who was the actor you found yourself covering the most," avoid any discussion of their reasons.

SILENCE

We now explore the body's emotional physicalization from a different angle.

> **SETUP:** The entire group pairs off in twos. Each couple brings their chairs on stage and sits facing each other, with about three feet between them. Use the entire stage so there is maximum space from couple to couple.
>
> **RULES:** Respond to the coaching.
>
> **ACTING FOCUS:** Communal silence.
>
> **COACHING:** *[Each ◆ represents ca. 15s.]* In a soft voice, loud enough to be heard, but no louder, *coach*— Keep your eyes open. Send silence to your partner ◆ Receive silence from your partner. ◆ Enter the silence between you. ◆ Meet your partner in that silence. ◆ Feel where the silence ends and

346

you begin. ◆ Feel where the silence ends and your partner begins. ◆ Allow the silence between you to thicken. *[Each ◆ now represents ca. 25s.]* ◆ Be in that silence with your silence. ◆ Keep yourself silent. ◆ Be with your partner in that silence. ◆ Silence surrounds you. ◆ Keep your silence, silent. ◆ Go with the silence. ◆ Be there in the silence with your partner. ◆ Feeling that silence. ◆ Feeling that silence more. ◆ Censoring nothing in the silence. ◆ Going with the silence ◆ Wherever it leads. ◆ End it when it's ended and take all the time you need. ◆ [Wait for all couples to finish, *usually 2–3m.*] ◆ Cut. ◆ Step out.

FOLLOW-UP (as needed): What did you experience? Did any feelings come up? What were they? Did those feelings change to other feelings?

SUMMARY:

Other than responding to the coaching, there is no correct response to the exercise. You take whatever you get. Despite the fact that there was no mention of emotions in the coaching, many of you experienced a lot of emotions during the exercise. Entering the communal silence allowed you access to your emotions. Silence can be a space through which emotions travel, like through a tunnel. Remember, there was no acting going on here. No character, activity, or location to help stimulate you, as in paralysis. It was about as minimal as you can get. Two people sat and faced each other and through the power of the focus, things started to happen. The question we will continually face with emotion work is, *if we can make the beginnings of feelings happen easily, what do we then do with the feelings?*

TO THE COACH: If possible, dim the lights somewhat for the exercise. The exercise usually takes about 11–13 minutes.

SCENE SILENCE[7]

Immediately following the silence exercise, the actors get to explore the same experience in an improvisation.

SETUP: 2–6 per team, but best with even numbers per team. In huddles, select characters, activity, and location. Any activity choices should be minimal and not require lots of physical doing. The character, activity, and location choices must add up to a situation wherein the characters are enshrouded in a tension that precludes dialogue. E.g., family in a hospital waiting room during father's major surgery; office workers who have all just been fired.

RULES: No dialogue.

ACTING FOCUS: Communal silence.

COACHING (as needed): The audience should watch parts of the improv like a film director, as they did with paralysis/group. ◆ Action.

GETTING THE ACTORS ON THE ACTING FOCUS

See your fellow actors. See the silence **between** you. Continue seeing the silence **between** you. Locate where **between** you is. **Between you isn't inside you, it's out there. Find where between you is and meet your fellow actors there.** If there is no one in your communal silence with you, find someone. Open to all silences extended to you. **Out of your head and into the silence. Avoid imposing on the silence.** Your acting focus is more important than an intention.

MAINTAINING THE ACTING FOCUS

Stay on your acting focus at all times, even if you are doing an activity or contacting the location. The silence is in the space **between** you. Being patient in that silence. Keep the silence silent **between** you. Open yourself to the silence **between** you. Entering further into the silence **between** you. Willing to open to the silence **between** you. **Stay on the acting focus every moment. The communal silence between the characters.** Seeing where the silence ends and your fellow actors begin.

TROUBLESHOOTING

Avoid being alone in the communal silence. Opening to your fellow actors in your silence. Avoid avoiding the silence **between** everyone. Discovering more silence **between** everyone. **Enter an available silence.** Searching for the silence in the communal silence. Staying with the search. Getting back on the focus of the communal silence. The communal silence is not yours alone, it's everyone's. **You are a part of the whole communal silence. Traveling together in the communal silence.** Help a fellow actor into the communal silence **between** you. Reflect the reflector in the communal silence. Taking whatever you get and putting it back into the communal silence. Allowing the silence to go where it wants to go, with you in it. **Out of the head and into the communal silence.** Hearing nothing in the silence **between** you. Being brave in the communal silence. Avoid avoiding the communal silence. The silence is out there. Avoid hiding from the communal silence. **Avoid being an observer of the silence; enter it with a fellow actor.** Embark on a trip into the communal silence. Bring your body with you on your trip. **Allow your body to go where it wants to go. The silence is bigger than you. Let the silence take you where it wants to take you, not where you want to go.** Traveling together into the communal silence.

HEIGHTENING THE ACTING FOCUS

Let the communal silence thicken. *Keep breathing in the communal silence.* Feeling the other's presence in the communal silence. Letting your fellow actor help you go further into the communal silence. Releasing your body into the silence. Opening further to the communal silence. Opening your whole body to the communal silence. Censoring nothing in the silence. **Feel the silence come out of you and into the space between you. Come out, come out, wherever you are.** Fearing nothing in the communal silence. **The silence is a place for what you don't know about. Open to letting the silence take you someplace new.** Open to the unknown in the communal silence. **Willing to explore the unknown in the silence between you.** Going to the unknown parts of the silence. Taking a risk in the silence between you. Always choosing to enter the difficulty in the silence. **Censoring nothing in the silence between you.** Trusting yourself into the silence **between** you. Give it up to the communal silence. Staying in the silence. Committing further to the communal silence. **Avoid running from the communal silence.** Relate to it. Heading toward the furthest parts of the communal silence. ◆ One minute to heighten your focus on the communal silence. **Opening to those parts of the silence that are still unknown.** Go further into the communal silence. Going further into the silence **between** you. Staying with it. Letting the silence **between** you thicken. Being with your fellow actors in that communal silence. Wherever it takes you, go with it. ◆ Cut.

FOLLOW-UP (as needed): Audience, character? Activity? Location? Did you receive a flash of the special circumstances that set up the tension? ◆ **Actors, what was it?** ◆ Did the actors use any physical doing to avoid the communal silence, or did they integrate it with the acting focus? **Did they leave the communal silence and pursue their own thoughts?** Where is the communal silence? In the space between them. **Were the actors with their fellow actors in the communal silence, or were they by themselves?** Did they travel emotionally? ◆ **Actors, were you on your acting focus? Did emotions come up for you? Did their intensities change? Did the emotions change to other emotions? Did you leave the communal silence and pursue your own thoughts?** Was there communication between you in the communal silence? Did anybody feel that you put more attention into communicating a feeling, than allowing the silence to move you and your fellow actors? **Did you discover any corks or ceilings?**

SUMMARY:

Communal silence means being *in* the silence *between* you and the other actor(s). Being there provokes emotions from deeper sources. You know when you are on the acting focus because it creates body feelings. You could feel things happening to you, to others, and between you and the others. The acting focus of the communal silence is not the destination; it's the springboard.

CAMERA ACTING

Ultimately, you may not even need another actor at the other end of the silence. In camera acting, you frequently have setups requiring you to work alone without lines. Instead of going inside for inner doing, you have the opportunity to *enter the communal silence between you and the camera.* This type of setup is frequently used in soap operas at the end of an act, just prior to the commercial. The actor is left alone after something has happened to him or he has learned something. While most of those moments are handled by the actors with inner doing, it might be much more effective and spontaneous if they entered the silence between them and the camera.

Whether the communal silence exists between the actor and the camera or the actor and other actors, you must *enter* it. Improvising railroad tracks alone can never have the power of entering the communal silence between you. It is the coming together in this unknown silent area that propels your total instrument into the zone of unknownness. Facing this unknownness, in tandem with the camera or with the other actors, creates absolutely vivid, spontaneous behavior and moves your emotions around. Being in the communal silence is outer-directed.

Notice the difference between the outer-directed acting focus of communal silence and the inner-directed acting focus of still (cf., active & still). With still, you pursue thoughts stemming from what's happening in the present tense. You learned still to make sure that you were always doing something even when denied physical movement. But now we are in the realm of emotions and emotional life happens spontaneously, especially working in tandem with another. It's like taking a person's hand and going into a totally dark room when you have no idea what is on the other side of the door. Every single step in that room will be physiologically spontaneous for both of you. When you employ communal silence as your acting focus, you avoid thoughts and allow your body to travel through feelings on its own, with no selectivity from your head. It will be much more emotionally active and powerful than your inner doing railroad tracks. If they shoot you in close-up, *that footage will not be cut.*

Not every tool is suitable for every occasion. Sometimes railroad tracks are much more suitable. If it's a soap opera scene where you are dealing with lots of scheming and hidden agendas, well, that's railroad tracks.

But suppose you are one of two leads playing lovers in a film and you have a break-up scene. They may hold the camera on you after the last line. You could commence railroad tracks, thinking, "Oh, my God. What's life going to be like? I'm going to be so depressed. Will I ever find another woman as good as her?" Or, "Thank God, I'm free. Can I just walk away now? Sure, it's best." These types of railroad tracks are very available to you and the attitude will be influenced by your character and the given circumstances. However, imagine the emotional power if the lovers enter the communal silence after the last line of their break-up scene. The director may not have planned much more after the last line, but if you enter the silence between you without railroad tracking, they're not turning that camera off. It's one of those moments when directors dance cartwheels thinking that they are brilliant because the actor is coming up with all of this stuff the director didn't anticipate and *the camera is running!*

Thoughts are in the head. Emotions are in the body. You cannot count on spontaneous *thinking*, like railroad tracks, to create emotions. When you go up into the head, it doesn't necessarily mean that the rest of the body will have feelings. Sometimes it happens, but there's no guarantee. When you focus on what's between you, like the communal silence, you are with someone in a state of communion. In that communion is authenticity, and in that authenticity is feeling.

AUTHENTICITY AND EMOTIONS

When we are inauthentic, dishonest with ourselves, we avoid many feelings. Have you ever been in denial with yourself? Something is going on with you and your lover, or your mother, or whomever, and it is very emotional, but you're lying to yourself, denying what's really happening. Denial frequently pertains to other people. Someone in your family is an alcoholic or an abuser and everyone is denying it. There is a rhinoceros in the living room and we pretend it isn't there. When you're in denial, you are not honest. You are not real. You are not here. *You have no presence.* You are inauthentic. Inauthenticity hampers the emotions. It is a barrier to keep feelings out. *Authenticity is married to feeling feelings.* What's in the heart, what you feel when you're authentically in touch with someone, when you're in the silence together, is true authenticity happening between you. That's why it stirs things up. The glass tube opens wider. And pretty soon, we are going to start really blowing down it like it was a clarinet with keys to play, different breaths to blow, and heightened musicality for solos, duets, or ensembles.

EMOTION CORKS

During the improvs, when you traveled emotionally to the unknown in the silence, some of you were surprised by feelings that came up. You were experiencing the removal of corks and feeling what is on the other side of them. Pulling the cork out will always take you to an unknown place where you will be continuously surprised. If you are open to the surprise and your instrument is trained to operate in that realm, you are maximizing spontaneity. The work we are doing now is in opening to that realm and, at the same time, training for operating within that realm. If the scene's a page-and-a-half long and it needs the emotion throughout, you can't afford to have it die halfway there. You have to have the ability to play it longer, higher, smaller, to arc it, to change it, whatever.

During these improvs, the emotions came and chose you. They came and they went. With Improvisation Technique, as emotions come up, you can control them and play them further and do it spontaneously. Being in control of your "out-of-control" is technique applied to spontaneity. As Martha Graham said, "The aim of technique is to free the spirit."

On the other hand, if you found yourself within the communal silence and experiencing feelings *and then your head took over,* putting you on a thought train, or railroad track, that was an example of a cork being put in. Your head got frightened of the unknown and said, "Let's get the hell out of here." You left the unknown and went to the known, the control of thoughts that railroad tracking provided.

It's a natural impulse to put the cork in. What's more, due to your abilities as actors, you will do something fancy to cover up the cork. Examples include *ending the beat* of silence you are in and initiating a whole new beat with someone else or *pulling out of the silence* between you and another actor and going into a personal and private silence filled with railroad tracks. These are cover-ups for the corks.

If you did put a cork in during this exercise but responded to the coaching and went right back to the acting focus, kicking the cork out, you were brave. Every time you felt the onset of a cork, but rejected it and stayed on the acting focus, you were brave. On each of these occasions, you experientially practiced a response to the coaching, "Okay, I'm not going to put the cork in. I'm going to stay with it." That's part of your physical growth toward ultimately removing all the corks. As you become more aware of the corks, you will take more responsibility, becoming braver and braver and expanding the scope of your instrument. Eventually you eliminate the need for coaching.

Another cork looks like this—*the anticipation* that if you stay on your acting focus, there will be a sudden release of built-up emotional outpouring. When there isn't, the resulting frustration takes you off of the acting focus. Anticipation is having an idea of what's supposed to happen. *The cork's supposed to fly out. And you are waiting for it!* When you anticipate, you're doomed. Did you ever have a girlfriend? Did you have an idea of what she should have been like? She never was that, though, was she? And you ended up missing who she was. Let go of your ideas of things. Just go with it. Reflect the reflector. Let go of "what's supposed to happen" and more corks will disappear.

Part of our work is noticing the various kinds of corks and getting rid of them. You can't change what you are not aware of. When a cork appears, you can deal with it after the fact through journal work. The writing makes you self-aware. With self-awareness comes the opportunity for change.

TO THE COACH: Communal silence doesn't mean a central point in the space between all the actors at the same time. The communal silence

352

may change from a point between two actors looking at each other to a point between three or more actors looking at each other. There can be communal silence between different pairs of actors at the same time.

The actors should minimize their physical doing. *If the actors leave the communal silence to focus on their physical doing, coach immediately*— Avoid that activity and return to the communal silence. ◆ The coaching should always emphasize connecting the actors to each other in the communal silence between them with or without physical doing.

When an actor begins this improv with a strong attitude and maintains it for more than half a minute, he is not open to being in the communal silence. He is closed to it and he is busy filling the silence with a preselected attitude. An actor pulling away from the silence to be alone is another example of a cork.

Each improv lasts about 10–15 minutes. If any improv is particularly intense, have the actors do the step-out at the end.

◆　◆　◆

EMOTION WALK #3

SETUP: All walk around the room responding to the coaching.

RULES: None.

ACTING FOCUS: Respond to the coaching.

COACHING: Do the coaching from part 2 of emotion walk #2, *followed by*— Last chance to heighten it in any single part of the body that you wish, in order to feel it more. Keep physicalizing it like this. If your heightening has created an exaggerated-size walking, maintain the same physicalization while you lose the exaggerated-size walking. If you were in a background shot, the size of your walking should not call attention to itself. However, keep physicalizing the feeling. From here on in, no matter what else you are coached to do, keep physicalizing that feeling. ◆ We're going into a **DOUBLE ACTING FOCUS**. Until I say the exercise is over, keep physicalizing this emotion. At the same time, add the second acting focus: reach up into the space, find a space ball about the size of a basketball, and feel it all over. Establish it in the space for yourself, not in the head. Keep it out there in the space by feeling it and looking at it. Now begin to play with the ball. Use the whole room to play with the ball any way you wish. *You are simultaneously physicalizing your chosen emotion and keeping the ball in the space as you play with it.* ◆ Stay on the double acting focus, even if you would never play with a ball while feeling your chosen emotion. Keep physicalizing the emotion while you play and don't change the emotion. Extend your physicalization to the ball. Keep physicalizing and pour it into the ball, especially in the arms and the legs or any part of the body that comes in contact with the ball. You must physicalize the emotion into those parts of the body. Out of the head. Into the body and space. Keep the ball in space. Keep your eyes on the ball. Follow the ball in space with your eyes, taking all the time it needs. Keep physicalizing that emotion. Every time you catch, throw, or kick you are simultaneously physicalizing that emotion, especially with those body parts making contact with the ball. All of your handling of the ball must be with the physicalization of your emotion. How you handle the ball is also helping you to feel the emotion more. Don't change the emotion. ✦ One minute to play. One minute to heighten the double acting focus of physicalizing that same emotion and playing with the ball in space. ✦ Throw the ball back into the space. Walk around. Keep physicalizing the emotion. Observe your feelings. Notice if you have maintained, heightened, or lessened your feeling of the emotion from before you began playing with the ball. ✦ Cut. ✦ Step out.

FOLLOW-UP (as needed): By the end of the physicalization process, but before you played with the ball, were you feeling the emotion? Compared to last class, was it the same, more, or less? Notice that the time we took for that process was shortened from previous classes. Were you able to keep the ball in the space, and not in your head, while physicalizing the emotion? Were you able to extend your physicalization into the playing with the ball? When you got rid of the ball, was your feeling of the emotion maintained, heightened, or lessened?

SUMMARY:

Some of you had to really stretch when coached to play ball with emotions that you probably never felt in real life while playing with a ball, e.g., sadness, fear, or anger. If you had an unusual emotion choice for ball playing, you had the more challenging exercise. It's pretty easy to physicalize happy while playing ball, but how do you play sadly or with fear? The exercise is designed for your bodies to discover that.

Our emotion exercises so far are about stretching particular muscles in the body and getting you to be aware of those muscles and how they can be used in an emotional way. When you focus on physicalizing a particular emotion, and then actually feel that emotion, you're learning about the potential of your instrument. You are learning that the muscles in the body feel the emotions and that they're the key to acting the emotions. If you want to play an instrument, you must know where the keys are.

TO THE COACH: This exercise has an additional significance that need not be mentioned to the actors. It is actually an experiential introduction to the handling of objects, which is the second component of physicalizing emotions.

OBJECT STRUGGLE[8]

SETUP: A solo exercise. Actor struggles with a single small object or clothes item that isn't working right. Avoid any objects having to do with the eyes. Examples: tight pants won't zip up; ring won't come off finger.

RULES: Struggle must be with one object or clothes item. Objects or clothes items must be made of space. No real props.

ACTING FOCUS: Struggling with the object.

COACHING (as needed): Respect the space object. Detail the object. Show, don't tell. ◆ **Focus on the struggle. Heighten the physicalization of the struggle.** Enlarge the struggle. ◆ **Extend what you are feeling into the object. Heighten what you're feeling in the whole body.** Stay focused on the struggle. Feel the struggle throughout the whole body. Feel the struggle with your neck, your toes, your elbows. ◆ **Take what you are feeling and spread it throughout the whole body.** Enlarge the struggle and heighten the feeling. Spread that feeling throughout the body and physicalize it more. Heighten the physicalization of the feeling throughout the whole body. Regardless of the business, heighten the physicalization of the feeling. **Heighten that feeling** as you heighten the struggle! **Censor nothing! Keep heightening it!** More physicalization! Go with it!

FOLLOW-UP (as needed): Audience, what was the struggle? Was the object in the space? **Was the actor on the acting focus?** ◆ Actor, did you stay on the acting focus, the struggle? **Did you** respond to the coaching and **heighten the physicalization of your feelings? Could you have gone further?** ◆ Audience, do you agree? ◆ **Actor, did you feel any corks?**

SUMMARY:

Why were most of these solo improvs compelling to watch? What was consistent for everyone was that they were having a total body experience in physicalizing the struggle and feeling frustration. As you heightened the physicalization, the frustration became more intense and changed to anger. The more you continued the heightening, the angrier you got. We, the audience, were caught up in that emotional trip. The trip was an *anger arc*, beginning with frustration and climbing through anger to fury. Everyone ended the improv in a different emotional state than the one they began in. You played this arc with your whole body. Acting emotionally requires the whole body's participation in the physicalization.

Did you ever see a poorly acted scene based on anger? In the close-ups, the characters are very angry with each other. Then they do a master shot and from the chest to the feet, you see a body that could almost be reclining in a lounge chair at the pool. The anger is displayed from the neck up. The rest of the body gives the lie to the performance.

These exercises are designed to give you the experience of full body emotional acting. Your bodies must become accustomed to full body acting so that it becomes second nature. Only then will the body start to act from that place. When you are shooting a close-up and you know you can cheat below the neck, how will you ever think of integrating your body from the neck down if you aren't used to it? If your body does not demand it of you? When you are working with the whole instrument, from the head to the toes, guess where it is going to show up most of all? *In the close-up.*

In hindsight, if you feel you could have become angrier, consider the possibility of a cork. Whatever the cork is, it impedes your ability to travel further emotionally. Sometimes you will need to travel to the top of an arc. You want to be able to do so. Other times, you won't have to travel all the way, but the choice should be yours and not the dictate of a faulty instrument.

What we are working on here is preparing your instrument for knowing what to do with a preselected emotion and waiting in readiness for the appearance of spontaneous emotion. As emotion spontaneously appears, you have the opportunity to run with it intuitively and with great skill. It is not sufficient to feel emotions authentically. You must have the skill to express the emotion in the space for the audience to see. You are not paid to have an experience. You are paid to provide an experience for the audience.

> **TO THE COACH:** The acting focus of object struggle always provokes an initial emotional feeling in the actor. The coaching should guide the actor to take that feeling from wherever it first appears in the body and spread it throughout the entire body. In doing that, the actor will start to heighten the feeling. Subsequent coaching to continue heightening or enlarging the physicalization with the whole body will further heighten the feeling, propelling the actor up the arc. Should the emotion change, e.g., anger turns to sadness, the coaching begins again on the new emotion right from the moment of change.
>
> Doing this exercise heightens the actor's awareness of the emotion *while feeling it.* With subsequent exercises, this awareness expands into the will and control necessary to playing with an emotion, e.g., emotion arcs and switches. Increasing the awareness of the emotion also increases awareness of the corks.
>
> Each improv lasts about three minutes. After all have played, do a group step-out.

Emotions & Objects #1[9]

Now we begin exploring the second half of the physicalization process.

SETUP: 2–5 per team. In huddles, select character, activity, and location. The activity should be elaborate and must have a beginning, middle, and end and must pertain to an emotional situation. The characters should have strong feelings about doing this activity in this location at this time, so pick an event that you assume would carry a feeling with it. Urgency should be avoided. Examples: family preparing house for wedding reception; team dressing in locker room for championship game. ◆ In the huddles, each actor also privately selects one emotion for their character to feel during this activity. ◆ As the characters near the conclusion of the activity, there is a turning point and the characters must undo the activity. Examples: wedding called off, house returned to normal; game canceled, athletes change back to street clothes. ◆ Unlike all previous improvisations, which do not allow for planning anything beyond the character, activity, and location choices, in the huddles for this improv one actor is selected to provide the turning point. It is his responsibility to create the turning point near the conclusion of the original activity. He should not share what the turning point will be with the rest of the team. During the improv, he creates the turning point with a minimum of dialogue and time. Example: answers a phone, receives a quick message, and tells the family, "The wedding is off. The groom left town." ◆ The only dialogue in the scene, if there is any, must relate to the turning point moment. ◆ Each team sets up their floor plan prior to improvising.

RULES: Avoid dialogue. ◆ Do your preselected emotion until the turning point. ◆ Actors are not to preselect any emotion choices beyond the turning point. ◆ After the turning point, undo the original activity. ◆ All props, as usual, are in space.

ACTING FOCUS: Physicalize your emotion and communicate it by how you handle the props.

COACHING: Actors, set up the location. ◆ Audience, observe the individual actors. You will be asked what their emotion choices are. ◆ Before "Action," the team walks around the stage for one minute. ◆ *[Allow ca. 10–20s between coaching sentences.]* Physicalize your emotion choice with your feet. Knees. Pelvis. Chest. Shoulders. Arms. Hands. Face. Whole body. ◆ Places. ◆ Action. ◆ **Coach (as needed):** It's as if you were wearing a mask, dressed in black to the elbows. **All the audience can see is your arms, hands, and props. You want them to know how you feel.** Feel what you are feeling and **explore handling your props with that feeling.** Extend that feeling into the props themselves. Heighten the physicalization in your arms, elbows, and hands. Extend that heightened feeling into the exploration of the props. ◆ Avoid dialogue. Avoid urgency. **Stay on your acting focus and check out your fellow actors.** ◆ Every gesture with your hands and props is an opportunity to show us how you feel. **Express with your hands and props what is on your face. Every contact with a prop is an opportunity to show us how you feel, through that contact. Stay alert and take responsibility for every gesture.** Every finger is an expression of that emotion: how you hold the prop, how you carry it, how you maneuver it, how you pull it, how you push it, how you adjust it. Keep making contact with the props. ◆ **Pour that emotion into your use of the props. How else can you handle those props to show us that consistent feeling?** Feel a burst of that feeling going from your hands into that object. **Every moment, be very aware of what your hands and arms are doing with the objects** and showing us how they feel. ◆ Your hands and props are the canvas on which you are painting the emotion. ◆ **Stay on your acting focus.** ◆ *If the actor responsible for the turning point is waiting too long to create it, then coach—* Approaching turning point. Turning point should be near. Take responsibility for creating the turning point. ◆ **AS SOON AS THE TURNING POINT IS COMMUNICATED: No urgency. Allow your body to feel whatever it is feeling. If it's feeling lots of feelings, notice which one becomes prominent. Select that feeling as the feeling you will play with for the second half of the scene. Physicalize that feeling throughout the whole body. Spread it throughout the body. It chose you, now you choose it by physicalizing it throughout the whole body. Now, get on your acting focus and communicate it by how you handle the props as you undo the original activity.** ◆ Avoid hanging out. **Explore your use of the props with this new feeling.** Avoid relying on your face. Assume the audience can only see you from the elbows down. Anyone can show with their face, the actor uses his whole body. ◆ [Use coaching from before the turning point as needed.] ◆ **One minute to heighten your acting focus and make sure the audience receives the communication of how you feel.** When you look at what you are doing, check it out for yourself. Is what you are doing showing us that feeling? ◆ Cut.

FOLLOW-UP (as needed): Audience, characters? Activity? Location? **Were they on their acting focus? Did all the actors have some emotional response to the turning point?** ◆ **Actors, were you on the acting focus? Did you authentically feel both emotions? Did your feeling of the second emotion,** for which you had no physicalization warm-up and the name of which you may not even have known, **deepen as the second half of the scene progressed?** ◆ [The coach refers to each individual actor.]

Audience, what emotion did you see before the turning point? After the turning point? ◆ Actor, what were the two emotions?

SUMMARY:

We've started our work on emotions with emotion walks and exercises in paralysis and struggle. That is only half of the physicalization process. Physicalizing the emotion will help you to *feel* it but it may not always help you to *communicate* it, especially if there is no dialogue. Emotions that are felt but not communicated are of very little value. The second half of the physicalization process is the emotional handling of props or objects. How you handle your objects shows an audience what you're feeling.

The more attention you pay to communicating an emotional feeling through the handling of your props, the more you heighten the basic physicalization of the feeling itself. You all acknowledged that you felt the second emotion deepen as the second half of the scene progressed. It's like getting two for one: showing the feeling and increasing its source.

You'll notice that in the exercises, improvs, and coaching, there has been an emphasis on, "It (the emotion) chose you; now you choose it." That is about you becoming more self-aware when a feeling appears in the body and then knowing that it is a tool to be employed, not some feeling that just comes up. Once you are aware of the feeling, you seize it, grab it, and then spread it out by physicalizing it through the whole body. This begins a payoff from the initial impetus of the emotion. For instance, you could then go on and heighten the intensity of it and create an arc. These are technical tools that help you to play emotions spontaneously.

The more you employ both aspects of emotional physicalization, the more potential you create for your emotions to change, which is the most interesting aspect of emotional work for an audience. Physicalization keeps you in a state of process, always traveling with your emotions, i.e., improvising with spontaneous emotional playing.

You also had a taste in this exercise of physicalizing a preselected emotion within an improv or scene. Then after the turning point, you went with the spontaneous emotion, applying the same exact tool. With emotion #1, you physicalized a preselected emotion; with emotion #2, you selected the emotion on the run. Both employ the same tools.

In the next class, we will practice more emotions & objects. In addition, we will add dialogue for the first time to the emotional work, get more specific, and begin to practice arc building as a part of the scene, in which you control the use of the emotion.

TO THE COACH: The running time of the improvs usually varies between ten and eighteen minutes each. If an actor is off the acting focus, the coach may use the picture frame device, as in active & still, to create close-ups on an individual actor's handling of the props. During the follow-up, *if there is a big discrepancy between the emotion the audience saw and the emotion the actor said he was doing, ask the actor—* Do you accept that it wasn't communicated?

◆　◆　◆

EMOTION WALK #4

SETUP: All walk around the room responding to the coaching.

RULES: None.

ACTING FOCUS: Respond to the coaching.

COACHING: *[Each ◆ represents 10s.]* Walk around. Observe your breathing. Don't muscle it, just observe how you are breathing. ◆ Select an emotion not used before in the emotion walks. ◆ Physicalize that emotion with your toes and ankles. Have an immediate response, e.g., sad toes and ankles, happy toes and ankles. ◆ Add the knees and move your knees around in that emotion. ◆ Add the pelvis. Complete the physicalization throughout the lower half of your body. ◆ Add the chest. ◆ Shoulders and elbows. ◆ Hands. If you need to heighten it in order to help yourself feel it, do so. Every part of your body, from the neck down, is physicalizing that emotion. ◆ Add the face. Physicalize that emotion with your face. ◆ Heighten the entire physicalization. Check out your body parts. Anywhere you are not physicalizing the emotion, do so now. ◆ Check in with yourself quickly, and observe if you are feeling the emotion. Stay out of the head and just quickly observe. Now, observe your breathing. ◆ **Keep physicalizing the emotion** and reach up into the space and find a space ball, the size of a basketball. ◆ [Coach the **DOUBLE ACTING FOCUS** of simultaneously physicalizing the chosen emotion and playing with a space ball from emotion walk #3, *leading to the following—*] **NEW:** Increase the weight of the ball. More. Extremely heavy. Heavier. Go with it. Keep staying on the emotional acting focus as it becomes heavier. Really heavy. You need the entire body to play with it. Or, even, to move it. And that whole body is physicalizing the chosen emotion. Don't change the emotion. It takes the entire body to throw and catch the ball and keep physicalizing the selected emotion. Especially in the hands and arms. ◆ Change the ball back to its original weight. Keep physicalizing that emotion. Feel that emotion in your fingertips. Physicalize it there. In your palms. In your wrists. ◆ Now keep physicalizing that emotion, and lessen the weight of the ball. More. As light as you can make it. Don't lose the physicalization of the emotion. Focus on playing with a real space ball and not a pretend one. Follow the ball in space with your eyes, taking all the time it needs. Don't change the emotion. Keep physicalizing the emotion with your hands and arms, shoulders, spine. ◆ Change the ball back to its original weight. You've got one minute to play. One minute to heighten the double acting focus of physicalizing that same emotion and playing with the ball in space. ◆ Throw the ball back into the space of the room. Walk around and keep physicalizing the emotion. Observe your feelings. Notice if you have maintained, heightened, or lessened your feeling of the emotion from before you began playing with the ball. ◆ Cut. ◆ Step out.

FOLLOW-UP (as needed): By the end of the physicalization process, before you played with the ball, were you feeling the emotion? Notice that the time we took for that process was shortened from the previous classes. After playing with the ball, was your feeling of the emotion maintained, heightened, or lessened? Did you notice a difference between the two times you observed your breathing?

SUMMARY:

Physicalizing emotions in an acting exercise is one thing, but physicalizing emotions in a scene adds another dimension to the process. When restricted by circumstances, e.g., blocking, the director, no business, then you must physicalize feeling in the body like we do in the emotion walks. However, scenes are often full of doing. *How you do things* is a major reflection and communication of the emotion you're playing. Suppose you have business in the scene where you take a glass of water. In addition to physicalizing the emotion in your body, why not use the glass as a projection device to communicate the emotion? *How* do you drink the glass of water? If you are happy, handle the glass happily. If you're sad, handle the glass sadly.

If your character's emotional state is an important part of a scene, then it's necessary to physicalize the emotion in the body. Given the chance to do more, as Improvisation Technique consistently encourages, make sure you communicate the emotion and heighten the feeling through the business (improvised or preselected and blocked).

Demonstration

Let's do an exercise right now. Stand up. Right in front of you is a space sink. Focus on taking a space glass from a cabinet above the sink, filling it with water, and drinking it. *[Allow time for them to do this.]* **Stop.** Do it again and focus on doing that piece of business *annoyed*. Do that now. Showing the camera that you're annoyed. That's your focus. *[Allow time.]* **Stop.** The left side of the room, watch the right side do a another take. Right side, focus on taking that drink of water and show us that you're annoyed through the taking of the glass, filling it, and drinking it. ✦ Action. *[Allow time.]* ✦ Cut. Now the left side gets another take, and the right side watches them. ✦ Action. *[Allow time.]* ✦ Cut.

Did you all feel annoyed from this little glass of water exercise, which doesn't compare in terms of time or commitment to the emotion walks? When you were watching the other side of the room, did they look annoyed? If you choose to let the body do something with a chosen emotion, you will feel and show the emotion. It's that simple. You don't have to go crazy in the head to feel an emotion. Acting is simple when you know how to do it.

There's not a piece of business in the world that can't be used to score acting points. If you have a piece of business in a scene, why just do the business? Why work single-track monaural when you can work sixteen-track stereo? You're only on screen for x amount of time. Do as much as you can. Don't waste acting potential. You could be showing anything. Some scenes are about a person in an emotional state; other scenes are not. If you've got the latter kind of scene, why not *add the emotional level* of the character? You're only going to make the script better.

We are now playing emotions in two ways, with two rules: (1) Physicalize it with the body. (2) Use all props, all objects, and all business to show how your character feels.

EMOTIONS & OBJECTS #2

SETUP: 2–5 per team. Same as emotions & objects #1, with one exception. In the huddles, the actors privately select one emotion for their character to feel during this activity and also *privately select their second emotion*, which they will feel after the turning point. It doesn't matter that they don't know what the exact turning point will be. It is sufficient that they know there will be a turning point that will cause them to undo the activity.

RULES: Avoid dialogue. ✦ Do your preselected emotion #1 until the turning point. Do your preselected emotion #2 after the turning point. ✦ After the turning point, undo the original activity. ✦ All props, as usual, are in space.

ACTING FOCUS: Physicalize your emotion and communicate it by how you handle the props.

COACHING: [Before the turning point, the coaching is the same as for emotions & objects #1.] ✦ **AS SOON AS TURNING POINT IS COMMU-NICATED: Begin physicalizing your second emotion. No urgency. Stay a part of the whole and take the time you need to physicalize the second emotion. Allow your body to feel what has been selected for it to feel. Physicalize that feeling throughout the whole body. Spread it throughout the body. You chose it before the scene, now choose it**

362

further by physicalizing it throughout the whole body. Now, get on your acting focus and communicate it by how you handle the props, as you undo the original activity. ✦ Coach (as needed): Explore your use of the props with this feeling. Avoid relying on your face. Assume the audience can only see you from the elbows down. Anyone can show with their face, the actor uses his whole body. ✦ [Use coaching from before the turning point as needed.] ✦ **One minute to heighten your acting focus.** When you look at what you are doing, check it out for yourself. Is what you are doing showing us that feeling? ✦ Cut.

FOLLOW-UP (as needed): Same as **essential follow-up** in emotions & objects #1.

SUMMARY:

What if any impact did your emotional handling of the props have on your complete physicalization of the emotion or your feeling of the emotion? It heightened it.

Preselecting choices is the foundation of breaking down a script and preparing yourself for rehearsal and/or performance.

In script acting, preselecting an emotion doesn't preclude the possibility of changing the choice. This might happen in rehearsal or performance by design or improvisation. However, there are occasions when it should not be changed, e.g., it's what the director requires. At those times, as in this improv, you must totally commit to the choice rather than seeking reasons why it's the wrong choice. Assume it fits, go with it, and make it a part of the whole.

TO THE COACH: Same as emotions & objects #1. ✦ For the sake of time, the coach might suggest that, without adding urgency, the actors complete their activity and get to the turning point a little quicker than in emotions & objects #1; about five minutes should be sufficient.

EMOTION ARCS [10]

Using physicalization as the basic tool for doing emotions, we now begin work on playing the emotion scales. *Emotion Arc* is one of the most important tools of acting.

SETUP: 2–4 per team. In huddles, select character, activity, and location. The choices should add up or pertain to a situation that has built-in potential for the characters to experience high-intensity emotions. Also, there should be no built in sense of urgency to the situation. ✦ [The rest of the setup is not revealed until the huddles are completed.] Each actor (1) privately selects an emotion that his character might feel during the improv and then (2) considers what would be the name of the lowest-intensity level of feeling for that emotion. **It must be in the same emo-**

tional family as the originally selected emotion. For example, if *scared* is the first choice, the low-level feeling might be *nervous*. If it's *anger*, then *annoyed*. If it's *happy*, then *pleased*. The actor then (3) reviews the low-level choice to see if it can be lowered further without leaving the original emotional family. For example, nervous lowers further to suspicious; annoyed to displeased; pleased to content. The actor (4) repeats the third step, asking *how low can you go and still be in the same emotional family?* For example, suspicious/aware; displeased/tense; content/calm. ◆ The choices are complete when the actor knows his character, activity, location, and name of the lowest-level feeling. He does not have to remember the names of feelings he considered on his way to the lowest-level feeling choice, only the final choice. ◆ After the actors have set up their location, they will physicalize the low-level choice and then begin the improv. ◆ During the improv, the actors will heighten the physicalization in gradations, creating an arc of the original emotion. They do not have to know the names of the gradation feelings they will be traveling through. They only have to know the name of the starting low-level feeling.

RULES: Usual full improvisation rules concerning physical doing and dialogue.

ACTING FOCUS: Heightening the physicalization of the feeling throughout the course of the improvisation.

COACHING (as needed): Before "Action," the team walks around the stage for one minute. ◆ Physicalize your low-level emotion choice with your whole body. Feet. Knees. Pelvis. Etc. ◆ Places. ◆ Action. **Keep physicalizing that feeling. No urgency. Check out your fellow actors.** Censor nothing. Share your voices. Avoid hanging out. ◆ [The coach must stay alert for any spontaneous escalation of the individual actor's feelings. Upon seeing this, coach the actor to take advantage of that newer, higher feeling state and not return to the previous lower intensity feeling.] ◆ **Physicalize *that* feeling! Escalate the intensity of that feeling. Go with that!** Keep physicalizing that feeling until it goes up again. Raise the intensity one level at a time. ◆ **Don't go backward. Stay on that level until you go higher.** Send that feeling to your whole body. **Sustain that level.** Stay alert for opportunities to heighten it more. Stay available for more heightening. **Never go lower than the level you are on now. That's your new starting place, every-thing from now on will be higher than that.** Use control. You don't want to go too high too soon, but don't back down. ◆ Avoid playwriting. Avoid questions. **Show us what you are feeling; don't tell us.** ◆ **Show how you are feeling through your objects. Heighten that physicalization through your props.** Show it to us. ◆ *If something is happening between two or more actors—* Stay on your acting focus together. Travel up your arcs, together. Go with it. Both, heighten your physicalizations. ✦ You have reached a new level, now use that as a springboard to go higher. You just climbed the arc a little bit. Don't back down. **Never go lower than where you are now. Go with that; that's your new base level. Heighten the feeling from there.** Sustain that until you heighten it more. Take that feeling and heighten it. Intensify it more. Go with it. Take responsibility for being on your acting focus. Don't wait for invitations. **Spread those feelings throughout the body, physicalize it, and heighten it.** Stay on your emotional track. Climb your arc. **Allow your prop handling to help you heighten it. ✦ Check out your fellow actors. Use what is happening around you to help you heighten the feeling.** Don't let anyone distract you from your acting focus. Don't let someone else pull you off your arc. Avoid conflict. **Active & still!** Sustain your physicalization when you go still. Physicalize that thought. Censor nothing. **Choose to stay on your acting focus. Climb your arc.** You are responsible for your own arc. **Stay alert to any opportunity to up the intensity. One minute** to get to the top of the arc. Avoid urgency in the activity. Keep physicalizing. You don't always need to vocalize it. **Use your object handling to help you sustain nonverbally.** Don't let yourself off the hook. **Pull out the cork.** Go through that! **Go with it!** ✦ Cut. ✦ Step out.

FOLLOW-UP (as needed): What was the **character, activity,** and **location?** Did the actors escalate the intensities of their feelings throughout the improvisation? Did they integrate their escalations with what was going on around them, that is, as a part of the whole? At the end, were they communicating much more intense feelings than when they started? Excluding short periods of plateauing were they in a continuous state of escalation, or did they sometimes lessen their feelings and back down the arc? Did any actors approach the top of the arc they were on? When the actors were at the higher ends of their arcs, did they talk excessively? Is verbalization necessary to sustaining or heightening any levels of the arc? Absolutely not. You experienced that when you did the paralysis and struggle exercises. Did you see corks being put in? Did you see any being pulled out? ✦ Actors, do you agree? ✦ [The coach refers to each individual actor.] ✦ **Audience, what emotion family did you see? Did he heighten the physicalization of it?** What were some of the levels of that emotion he passed through? What was the highest level of intensity? **Did he approach the top of the arc?** Did he stay in the same emotional family? **Was there any significant deescalation or backing down the arc?** ✦ Actor, were you aware of that? **What was the name of the low-level feeling you started with? What was your original emotion choice?** ✦ Audience, what might be a lower level choice still?

SUMMARY:

ARCS CREATE DYNAMICS

Notice that each improv built momentum and all had identical dynamics. When you watch plays or movies, notice when you get caught up in a scene. Backtrack from that point and you'll see that you were caught up in the momentum that began when the actors began climbing their emotional arcs. From that point, the whole scene heightened and climbed its own arc, compelling the audience to become more involved. No one went into these improvs with a goal of, "We have to make the scene gain momentum, or involve the audience more." Nevertheless, each improv *achieved* that goal because that's what happens to scenes when actors climb arcs. Audiences are compelled to watch.

ARCS AS SCALES

The traveling of an emotion through gradations of intensity is an emotional scale, similar to a musical scale. You may never have the opportunity to play a complete emotion scale in performance, but learning and practicing them improves the facility and abilities of your instrument.

A complete emotional scale comprises the several levels of any particular emotion. The musical notes of a scale have names. So do the equivalent emotional levels of an emotion arc. Here is a sample *happy arc* or scale:

```
                                JOYOUS
                             JUBILANT
                           ELATED
                         GIDDY
                       HAPPY
                     CHEERFUL
                   GLAD
                 AMUSED
               PLEASED
             CONTENT
           CALM
```

When you know your emotion notes and scales, you can play within the scale, or you can play on multiscales. Just like a musician, you have to know the scales before you can play competently or professionally. It's like any other art form or skill. You have to know the basics. Then you can build on them and get fancy.

LEARNING ARCS

Learn your emotion scales without jumping from one scale to another and you will serve yourself better. Down the line, you will be better prepared to play script choices and to handle switching from one scale to another. In the next class, we'll continue practicing the scales. You'll learn how easy it is to switch scales. The difficult part is what to do after the switch occurs.

The mechanics of executing a preselected emotion arc require choosing the initial low level. When finding the low-level choice, you want to double-check that you haven't moved it into another emotion family. After you've selected the primary emotion and backed it up to the low-intensity level of it, say to yourself, "If I heighten this low-level choice and stay in one emotion family, will I eventually come up to the full intensity primary emotion?" If the answer is no, then your low-level choice has put you into another family. Try again, backing up from the primary emotion choice and staying alert to when you leave its family. The choice just before you left the primary family will probably be the correct low-level choice for you. And of course, every time you arrive at your final low-level choice, ask yourself, "Can I lower it still?"

When you're improvising an emotion arc, you're not labeling the levels you pass through. All you are doing is heightening that feeling in the body. You don't have to know the names of the levels while you are improvising.

The proficient actor not only seizes any opportunity presented in the scene to climb the arc, but also has the skill to initiate his own movement up the arc. With practice, you will develop a skill of spontaneously determining the speed of your ascent up the arc. *When working with scripted material, the length of the beat will greatly influence your rate of ascent.* Generally speaking, whether it's an improv or a script, you don't want to get too high too quick. Regardless of your speed of ascent, you have to keep climbing and never go lower than where you are. When you are learning arcs, you must focus on escalating continually, while sustaining plateaus as speed bumps. This will prevent you from getting too high too quickly. You must never decrease or go backward on the arc. There are only two options: (1) Up, up, up; (2) Up, sustain, up.

Getting too high too quickly robs a scene of momentum and creates a problem for the actor, i.e., sustaining a very high level of intensity once he gets there. When first learning emotion arcs, actors often feel they have to keep speaking at the high end of the arc in order to sustain or heighten it. Excessive vocalization keeps you from expanding the physicalization in the body. It also creates chaos in the improv as everyone is screaming and shouting, totally avoiding the rules of active & still.

Whenever you get to the high end of an arc, whether it's too soon or right on time, allow your previous Improvisation Technique training to pay off for you. You can sustain the very high levels of intensity by physical doing. Do your activities, contact the location, discover objects near you. You can sustain rage, terror, hilarity, despair, or the top of any arc nonverbally for a very long time through the object handling. That would not only fulfill the basic rule of improvisation, *Acting is doing*, it would also sustain the physicalization through object handling, keeping it in the body. Should you choose to speak, respecting your rules—avoid playwriting; active & still—your dialogue will automatically be at that high level of emotional intensity because that's where your body feeling is being sustained or heightened. When you speak, you won't have to pump up to the top of the arc to get back up there. You will already *be* there.

PROBLEMS

In addition to *backing down the arc*, the most common manifestations of being off the emotion arc acting focus are *switching emotion families* and *not approaching the top of the arc.*

While improvising, should you find that heightening the physicalization of the low end you started with is sending you into an emotion family different from the primary one you preselected, go with it. Don't try to correct it back to the original family. Go with the physicalization of what you are feeling and throw out the one you intended. You will still get the benefit of the improvisation exercise, which is the heightening of your feeling. *If you don't go with it* because you have an idea of where you should be going (your preselected primary emotion), you will cripple yourself. That idea is in your head. Your body, which is in the present-tense space, is doing another emotion and is in conflict with that idea. Always go with the body, not the idea. The time to correct the problem is in another improvisation when you can pay more attention to making your low-level choice.

There is a distinction between what I have just mentioned and coming up with reasons for *deliberately* leaving your primary scale, which you must not do. This occurs if you are more concerned with the emerging story of your improv than your acting focus. Responding to the story may be in the moment, but it's not disciplined to being on your acting focus. You must stay on the focus, committing to physicalizing deeper and deeper while you go with the emerging scenario.

The story moments where you want to leave the focus to respond to whatever is happening are the perfect moments to stay on *and heighten* the focus. They offer you the opportunity to escalate your physicalization as a part of the whole. Something is happening in the story, providing you an opportunity to respond. Do so, but at that moment in the story, your challenge is to improvise a response that keeps you on your arc instead of changing the emotion family. Of course, in real life you might respond differently. The more the story (or your fellow actors) gives you something that would normally, in real life, take you off of the continuous heightening of your chosen emotion, the better the exercise. You must find a way to keep everyone and everything you do a part of the whole as you stay on the mission of heightening your arc. This is not real life. This is an acting exercise. It's a drill. Master the scale.

By choosing to stay on your arc, you will come up with your own ways of supporting the choice. That's why it's called Improvisation Technique. It's always about an improvisational challenge. In the heat of the moment, while improvising, while being on the acting focus, you will serve yourself and come up with an answer. Get used to staying on the acting focus no matter what happens in the scene. Your challenge, your *job*, is to integrate the acting focus with what is happening in the moment in the scene.

The other manifestation of being off the acting focus is not approaching the top of the arc. This is usually the result of putting a cork in. If there are no corks, you get to the top. No one is saying that when you act you must play the entire scale, but a well-trained instrument is one that's capable of playing the entire scale *if it's needed*.

You can help yourself remove corks by working in your journal. Ask yourself what level of emotion you got to when you were at the highest level in the improvisation. Then ask yourself if there are higher levels on that primary emotion arc. If you got to anger, what's above anger? Fury and rage. There's a big difference between anger and rage. Continue writing about that. The next time you do this exercise or need to employ an emotion arc, you might find the wherewithal to heighten your physicalization.

If you don't continue heightening, you leave yourself open to all kinds of mental corks, such as, "I can't get angrier because I have to calm her down." That's an *It's-her-fault* cork. Or, "Gee, I don't know what's happening to me, I'm getting too sad here." That's a self-censoring cork. If you want to act, if you want to get better, there are no acceptable reasons to be off your acting focus.

You can always come up with a reason not to do something and it's always irrelevant to the job at hand. The personal growth and expansion of your technique is in choosing not to come up with a reason and *just do it*. Write in your journals about your reasons and then observe that they are only reasons. You'll see the corks start to fly out.

While doing this improv, if you get off the acting focus, start over in midstream. Physicalize any feeling on your primary emotion arc and resume the heightening from that point. Should you go backward on your arc, be aware that you are doing that and renew the acting focus from that point forward. Just start climbing again, from that place. So it won't be a perfect arc. What are you going to do, throw out the whole exercise because you slipped for a moment? Start over at the place you slipped from, and climb. If you find yourself slipping once more, start again from that place and climb. Keep approaching it this way and eventually you'll stop slipping.

The work is now about playing the scales, becoming more aware of the whole process, pulling out the corks, and starting to trust and learn more about what it means to physicalize an emotion.

> **TO THE COACH:** During the setup, emphasize that in considering the lowest level of the feeling, the final choice must stay in the same emotional

family as the original selected emotion. To help do this, the actor should have a sense of which emotion family his original choice is in.

The actor is not the best judge of whether or not he gets to the top of the arc. He should always assume there is another level.

All the actors on the first team will probably speak nonstop when they get high up on their arcs. This is the first emotion improv with dialogue; they won't be used to speaking and physicalizing at a high intensity at the same time. This will create chaos and *they should be coached*— Active & still! Show us the feeling, don't tell us! ◆ In the follow-up with the first team, emphasize that speaking is not necessary to sustain or heighten any level of the physicalization. They can do either of these through physicalization in the body and through how they handle their props.

Stay alert to actors introducing *urgency* to the given circumstances. It makes the arc climbing too easy, deprives the actor of the benefits of the exercise, and it's a special type of a cork, *avoidance*. Urgency makes the actor feel that he's doing a lot. Without it, he'd have been forced to stay on the focus and develop the emotion arc.

Look for the actors who think they are physicalizing but are not. This shows up when the body is inconsistent with the selected emotion, e.g., the emotion choice is *happy*, but a body part reveals tension. If necessary, the following may be helpful—

Demonstration

Coach the whole group, while they are seated— Everyone physicalize pleased. *[Allow 15s.]* ◆ How does your body feel? It's kind of like mashed potatoes. Now, add tension to your left leg only. *[Allow 15s.]* ◆ How does that feel? Pleased? Mashed potatoes? No. Stay alert to how your body is physicalizing.

Sometimes the actors confuse feelings with concepts. For instance, if an actor says his original emotion was *denial*, the coach should point out that denial doesn't tell the actor how he feels. Some people are very angry when in denial, e.g., *(Furiously)* "Damn you, don't tell me I'm a drunk!" Some people feel very pleased, e.g., *(Sweetly)* "Sweetheart, I can quit drinking whenever I want." If you don't know how it feels, how can you back it up to the low level of that feeling? The actor should double-check his initial choice to make sure it's a feeling and not a concept. The vocabulary word for either the first emotion or the low-level version of it can point you in the right direction and help you sustain or heighten the physicalization of it, or it can point you in the wrong direction, your head. If the original choice is a concept, e.g., denial of being an alcoholic, all the actor has to do is ask himself the question, *"How do I feel about* being told I'm an alcoholic?" The answer will be the selected first emotion choice. Playing concepts usually requires playing on multiple scales. It is important to know about concepts and how to play them, but that's for later in the training when we get to *Umbrella Arcs*.

The coach may feel that the information in the summary should be divided and part of it communicated at the end of the *Emotion Arcs (Repeat)* improvs in the next class.

The average time for the preparation walk and improv is 7–10 minutes.

❖   ❖   ❖

EMOTION WALK #5

SETUP: All walk around the room responding to the coaching.

RULES: None.

ACTING FOCUS: Respond to the coaching.

COACHING: Observe your breathing. Select **TWO EMOTIONS** not used before in the emotion walks. Select two emotions not close together, in other words, from two different emotion families. ◆ We start with only one of the two selected emotions. ◆ *[Each ◆ represents 8s.]* Physicalize that emotion with your toes and ankles. Have an immediate response, e.g., sad toes and ankles, happy toes and ankles. ◆ Add the knees and move your knees around in that emotion. ◆ Add the pelvis. Complete the physicalization throughout the lower half of your body. ◆ Add the chest. ◆ Shoulders and elbows. ◆ Hands. If you need to heighten it in order to help yourself feel it, do so. Every part of your body, from the neck down, is physicalizing that emotion. ◆ Add the face. Physicalize that emotion with your face. ◆ Heighten the entire physicalization. Check out your body parts. Anywhere you are not physicalizing the emotion, do so now. ◆ Check in with yourself quickly, and observe if you are feeling the emotion. Stay out of the head and just quickly observe. Now, observe your breathing. ◆ **Keep physicalizing the emotion** and reach up into the space and find a space ball, the size of a basketball. ◆ [Coach the **DOUBLE ACTING FOCUS** of simultaneously physicalizing the chosen emotion and playing with a space ball from emotion walk #3, up to "One minute to play."] ◆ *Then— [No pauses between coachings.]* **NEW:** Keep playing with the ball and immediately **SWITCH TO EMOTION #2,** without thinking about it. While playing with the ball, physicalize the new emotion from the toes up. Pour that emotion into the ball. Play with the ball in ways that show us the new feeling. Keep physicalizing the new emotion while you play. Play with your whole body as you keep physicalizing. Extend your physicalization to the ball. Keep physicalizing and pour it into the ball, especially in the arms and the legs, or any part of the body that comes in contact with the ball. You must physicalize the new emotion into those parts of the body. Out of the head. Into the body and space. Keep the ball in space. Keep your eyes on the ball. Follow the ball in space with your eyes, taking all the time it needs. Keep physicalizing that new emotion. Every time you catch, throw, or kick, you are simultaneously physicalizing that emotion, especially with those body parts making contact with the ball. All of your handling of the ball must be with the physicalization of your second emotion. How you handle the ball is also helping you to feel the emotion more. ◆ **Without hesitation, RETURN TO EMOTION #1.** Complete physicalization of emotion #1. Play with your whole body as your whole body physicalizes emotion #1. —*Allow 30s for playing with emotion #1.* ◆ **SWITCH immediately to emotion #2.** Explore new ways of playing with the ball while physicalizing emotion #2. —*Allow 30s for playing with emotion #2.* ◆ **SWITCH immediately to emotion #1.** —*Allow 15s.* ◆ **SWITCH immediately to emotion #2.** —*Allow 15s.* ◆ **SWITCH to emotion #1.** —*Allow 8s.* ◆ **EMOTION #2.** —*Allow 8s.* ◆ **EMOTION #1. You are on your own. Switch as often and as frequently as you wish. You are on your own!** Keep your eyes on the ball. Follow the ball in space with your eyes, taking all the time it needs. ◆ One minute to play. One minute to practice switching from one emotion to the other. ◆ Throw the ball back into the space of the room. Walk around and keep physicalizing either emotion. ◆ Observe your feelings. Notice if you have maintained, heightened, or lessened your feeling of that emotion from when you first began physicalizing it. ◆ Cut. ◆ Step out.

FOLLOW-UP (as needed): By the end of the physicalization process, before you played with the ball, were you feeling the first emotion? After playing with the ball, prior to switching emotions, was your feeling of the emotion maintained, heightened, or lessened? ◆ **NEW:** Were you capable of switching emotions? Did you feel the second emotion? After you switched to emotion #2 for the first time, did you feel the emotion deepen the more you played with the ball? Did you find that it got deeper still after you started switching between the two emotions but before you were on your own? Were you capable of returning to emotion #1? What happened when you were on your own?

SUMMARY:

You just had an experience of how powerful physicalizing an emotion can be. The ball playing required full body involvement with a full body physicalization.

That heightened physicalization gave you the power to switch emotions suddenly.

When you were on your own, you discovered that it's possible to let the emotion tell you when it wants to change. That is an example of spontaneous emotional changing. You also discovered that it is possible for you to decide in the head that it's time to change the emotions, and the body will follow. You need to be skilled at both options. A skilled actor goes with what is happening and knows how to fulfill it. That means you have the ability to allow whatever comes up to happen, and then exploit it. We are in the process of expanding our understanding of the phrase *go with it*. Many young actors think that the goal of good acting is to be believable. In Improvisation Technique, believability is a given, basic, minimum requirement, but a long way from the goal!

EMOTION ARCS (REPEAT)

SETUP: The same as emotion arcs, except that the actors are asked to preselect their primary emotion from a different emotion family this time.

RULES: Same as original emotion arcs.

ACTING FOCUS, COACHING (as needed), FOLLOW-UP (as needed): Same.

SUMMARY:

By now, we are beyond being concerned with simple believability. We get that automatically through physicalizing. Our concern now is *going with* what comes up. When you have a feeling, whether it's preselected or spontaneously discovered, you know how to heighten it or go up the scale. Then you can go on to the next spontaneous feeling or another previously selected feeling based on a script breakdown.

Some actors climbing an anger arc crossed over into sadness. It takes skill to keep these two families separate. People are seldom angry without there being a previous hurt. There are times when a beginning emotion of frustration will climb through an anger arc and then change to a sad arc, climbing to despair, and then change to an optimism/hope arc, which can change to an embarrassment/funny arc. It is very important for the actor to be adept at the juxtaposition of arcs leading to other arcs. In the end, it's all about body awareness.

ARCING DOWN

No time is spent on exercises in arcing down an emotion. When people come down from any intensity level of an emotion, they switch to another feeling or to a lower level of the same emotion. They don't gradually pass through multiple lower and lower intensity levels of the same emotion. It is not natural human behavior and no scripts ever require it.

TO THE COACH: If there is confusion for any individual actor about the low-intensity-level choice, it will be because the actor is picking an *attitude* as his first choice of an emotion. The coach might suggest that for now, the actor select emotions from the Big Four: happy, anger, fear, or sad.

EMOTION SWITCH[11]

We now explore what it takes to move from one emotion family into another. *Emotion Switch* is one of the most important tools of acting.

SETUP: 2–4 per team. In huddles, select character, activity, and location. ◆ [The rest of the setup is not revealed until the huddles are completed.] Each actor privately selects two emotions that are not from the same emotion family. ◆ At the beginning of the improv, all are physicalizing their emotion #1. At some point in the improv, the actor switches immediately and totally to emotion #2. This is called the turning point. ◆ After the turning point, the actor continues physicalizing emotion #2 until the end of the improv. ◆ Each actor selects his own turning point.

Until the switch, all are absolutely alert to their fellow actors and themselves in order to see and hear an opportunity for switching emotions. The opportunity, or turning point, can come from anywhere in the improv as long as it's spontaneous and not preplanned. It may come from another actor's dialogue, a development in the evolving action of the improv, or from the actor himself. The opportunity to switch may be thought of as an invitation to switch. When the actor spots the opportunity, he unhesitatingly and totally switches to emotion #2, dropping emotion #1. After he switches, he focuses on physicalizing emotion #2 until the improv ends. The amount of attention that had been previously applied to spotting the opportunity to switch is now applied to furthering the physicalization of emotion #2 in the body. No attention is paid to emotion #2 until the moment of the turning point. The actors individually choose their own turning points, and it is not necessary to switch just because another actor has switched. The actors are totally responsible for finding their own opportunities to switch. By this point in the training, their bodies have a sense of how long the improvs usually are. They are encouraged to avoid switching during the first third, but not later than the last third, of the improv.

RULES: While employing physical doing tools of Improvisation Technique for activity, location, relationships, and occupation, actors physicalize emotion #1 in the body and discover a turning point for switching to emotion #2. The switch must be total and immediate, not gradual. The switch is accomplished through changing the physicalization. After the turning point, physicalize emotion #2 until the end. Turning points are not preplanned. Allow the turning point to reveal itself to you. Stay open to seeing it while not going looking for it.

ACTING FOCUS: Switching emotions.

COACHING (as needed): After the location is set up and before "Action," the team walks around the stage for thirty seconds, physicalizing emotion #1. ◆ Places. ◆ Action. ◆ **Totally physicalize the emotion** from head to toes. Physicalize what you are feeling. **Show us the emotion through your objects.** That will help you physicalize it deeper. ◆ Don't let your particular emotion prevent you from playing and using all the previously learned improvisational tools with your fellow actors. Share your voices. ◆ **Stay on your acting focus, physicalizing emotion #1 while waiting for an opportunity for switching. Check each other out. Stay open** to your fellow actors. **Stay alert** for a turning point. Stay open to a turning point revealing itself to you. ◆ After you switch, physicalize emotion #2. Keep physicalizing your emotion in the body. **Take every opportunity to put it further into your body.** Show us what you're feeling through the objects. Respect the space objects. Avoid hanging out. Active & still. Be a part of the whole. Check each other out. ◆ **Physicalize in your body whichever emotion you are in.** ◆ One minute. ◆ Cut. ◆ Step out.

FOLLOW-UP (as needed): Audience, location? Activity? Occupations? Relationships? **Were they on their acting focus?** Did they physicalize their emotions? Did they show us their emotions through the objects? **Did each actor find a turning point and switch?** Did they switch totally and immediately, or was it gradual? **Were the switches accomplished and integrated as a part of the whole scene?** ◆ [The coach refers to each individual actor.] ◆ **What were the two emotions? What was the turning point?** ◆ [To each actor] **Is that right?** ◆ Audience, who was the first actor to switch? Who was the last actor to switch?

SUMMARY:

This is one of the most important acting tools you will ever learn.

CREATING ARCS

If a character is in a scene for more than one beat, that character goes through emotional changes, *or should.* Changing from one feeling to another may be improvised or preplanned and is easily accomplished through an emotion switch. The turning point may be improvised or a designated cue in the script.

If the writer has written a scene of more than one beat for your character and the accumulation of any consecutive beats is designed to reveal something about your character's emotional state, then you will be playing an emotion arc over the duration of those successive beats. *If the arc is in one emotion family, then the emotion arc acting focus is usually the tool of choice.* Sometimes the arc is stretched over long beats and each beat requires sustaining only one intensity level on the arc. On those occasions, the actor can choose emotion switch to go from one level on the arc to the next. The switching will not be as drastic as in these improvisations because both or all of the emotions will be in the same emotion family, e.g., alert, confident, strong, and finally, brave. That would be an example of four successive beats where the writer (and actor) has chosen to reveal that the character finds his courage. In any beats prior to those four beats, the writer has probably chosen to reveal that the character is feeling fear.

UMBRELLA CONCEPT ARCS

Frequently, a skillful writer will create an *Umbrella Arc.* An umbrella arc is an accumulation of separate feelings from different emotion families that adds up to a singular emotional response. This singular emotional response is usually described, or labeled, with conceptual terms, e.g., abandonment, inundation, betrayal, denial. In a script, the actor lists all of the feelings under the singular emotional response, i.e., under the umbrella. If a writer has written three beats to reveal that your character is experiencing abandonment, each beat might require your character to communicate feelings from a different emotion family, e.g., (1) angry, (2) scared, (3) lonely. The accumulation of all three communicates that your character is experiencing abandonment. *When playing an umbrella arc, emotion switch is the acting tool of choice.* It is important to know about umbrella arcs and how to spot them or design them. We'll get to them later in the training, in part 5, "Acting the Script with Improvisation Technique."

WHERE IS THE TURNING POINT?

When employing emotion switch, the primary acting focus is the physicalization of the first emotion while being open to switch to the second. If you turn the primary acting focus into the search for the turning point, you will not automatically physicalize the emotions. By correctly articulating the acting focus, you automatically, because of this training, physicalize the emotions. This is an example of vocabulary assisting you.

If you focus on being open to switching from one emotion to the next, the turning point will reveal itself to you. That's different from you looking for it. There is an old Chinese saying, *Cease striving; then there will be self-transformation.* When you try to make something happen, it seldom does. What is important is that you are prepared, *waiting in readiness* for the opportunity to present itself. When you use the vocabulary word *switch*, there is an inherent openness to spotting the opportunity.

If you focus on looking for the turning point, you are not providing yourself with something to do, *actively*, while looking. If you are on the acting focus of switching from one to the other, you have an active doing called *physicalizing* (the emotion).

Once you have spotted the turning point and switched emotions, that openness transforms into available opportunity for further physicalization of emotion #2 for the remainder of the improv or in a script, for the remainder of the beat. In a script, if there is still another beat to come requiring another emotion, then the acting focus remains the same as you then focus on switching from emotion #2 to emotion #3 at the beat change.

EMOTION SWITCH VS. ATTITUDE LINE SWITCH

Now that you are learning emotion switch, you should employ it wherever you have been using attitude line switch. At this point in the training, it is particularly important not to confuse the two. Although the structure is the same, the process is different. Emotion switch is easier and faster.

Attitude line switch is a meticulous process that requires repeating articulated phrases to yourself while you explore the attitude's impact on different body parts. With emotion switch, you just need the will power to physicalize the emotion. This timesaving aspect of emotion switch is crucial. Emotions can be fleeting and must be worked with very rapidly.

Attitudes are lifelong feelings that have been ingrained in the character's muscles, mind, and personality. Much more securely established than emotions, *attitudes seldom change*. While they may alter over time, attitudes are like a well-made suit. Periodic alterations notwithstanding, the suit is the same suit. The attitude line acting tool takes time and is best used in rehearsal for the exploration of character, not emotions. Emotions, certainly in scripts and improvs, are short-lived and transitory. *Emotions frequently change*. A character can have any attitude or character armoring and still experience any emotion in a transitory way.

Without previous rehearsal of the second attitude line, when you come through the turning point it is very difficult to go into the second attitude thoroughly and when you do, it is usually more superficially embedded in the body compared to the first. With emotion switch, you just go through the turning point and you're there, automatically physicalizing the second emotion without any need for going into the head, the way you would have to with an attitude line.

You may run into another problem with the attitude line switch if you don't know the scripted lines absolutely cold. That little extra element of repeating the attitude line in your head can get in the way of the memorized lines. With emotion switch, you stay out of the head. The memorized lines have the space to themselves!

Attitude line switch certainly has its place in working with scripts and we will explore that later in part 5, "Acting the Script with Improvisation Technique." In the meantime, don't short-change yourself when learning emotion switch by turning it into an attitude line switch or you will never know the difference between the two. It is best to be competent with both emotion switch and attitude line switch so you can freely choose which best serves your needs in fulfilling the different functions of a script.

COMMERCIAL AUDITIONS

Emotion switch is a great tool for commercial auditions, many of which are improvisations. There is no standard setup for them, but almost all of them are built around the character's needs and feelings *prior* to using the product and then *after* using the product. Hello! *The turning point is the product's use.* From whatever improv setup or copy is provided to you, ask yourself, "Is there potential here for an emotion switch?" Be prepared to select an emotional feeling (usually negative) for before the turning point and a second one (always positive) for after using the product. Whether the audition is an improv or from copy, you've got your acting focus.

GENERAL IMPROV AUDITIONS

Whenever you are required to do an improvisation for any audition, emotion switch will serve you well. The setup provided by the director may be minimal, e.g. "You are the only tree in a rock garden. Go!" Or it may be a fully written scenario with way too much information, guaranteed to put all the actors in their heads. Whatever the setup, if you want something quick, easy, and effective, simply choose two emotions and use emotion switch as your acting focus. You will always look better than anyone else out there because you will be the only one who goes through an arc, who has a change.

◆ ◆ ◆

EMOTION WALK #6

SETUP: All walk around the room responding to the coaching.

RULES: None.

ACTING FOCUS: Respond to the coaching.

COACHING: Walk around. Keep breathing. I will select the emotion you are to physicalize. We will do this with a few emotions and each time the coaching will give you less time to physicalize it. ◆ *[Allow 5s between sentences. Each ◆ represents a 20-second pause.]* **SAD.** Physicalize sad with your toes and ankles. Have an immediate response. Go to the knees and move your knees around in that emotion. Add the pelvis. Complete the physicalization throughout the lower half of your body. Add the chest. Shoulders and elbows. If you need to heighten it in order to help yourself feel it, do so. Fingers, knuckles, wrists. Every part of your body, from the neck down, is physicalizing sad. Add the face. Physicalize sad with your face. Heighten the entire physicalization. Check out your body parts. Anywhere you are not physicalizing sad, do so now. Check in with yourself quickly, and observe if you are feeling sad. Stay out of the head and just quickly observe. Now, observe your breathing. ◆ Shake it out as you walk. Lose *sad*. Breathe five long breaths in through the nose and out through the mouth. Then speak nonsense language out loud. ◆ Walk around silently. **JEALOUS.** Physicalize jealous with your toes and ankles. Add the knees. Pelvis. Chest. Shoulders and elbows. Hands. Face. Heighten the entire physicalization. Check out your body parts. Anywhere you are not physicalizing jealous, do so now. Check in with yourself quickly, and observe if you are feeling jealous. Stay out of the head and just quickly observe. Now, observe your breathing. ◆ Shake it out as you walk. Lose *jealous*. Breathe five long breaths in through the nose and out through the mouth. Then speak nonsense language out loud. ◆ Walk around silently. ◆ **SELFISH.** Physicalize selfish with the whole lower half of your body, from the waist to your toes. Physicalize selfish from the waist to the neck, as well. You're now physicalizing selfish from your neck to your toes. Add your face. Physicalize a selfish face. You're now physicalizing selfish with your whole body. Check in with yourself quickly, and observe if you are feeling selfish. Stay out of the head and just quickly observe. Now, observe your breathing. ◆ Shake it out as you walk. Lose *selfish*. Breathe five long breaths in through the nose and out through the mouth. Then speak nonsense language out loud. ◆ Walk around silently. ◆ **TENDER.** Physicalize tender with the whole lower half of your body. Add the upper half of your body, including your face. You're now physicalizing tender with your whole body. Check in with yourself quickly, and observe if you are feeling tender. Stay out of the head and just quickly observe. Now, observe your breathing. ◆ Shake it out as you walk. Lose *tender*. Breathe five long breaths in through the nose and out through the mouth. Then speak nonsense language out loud. ◆ Walk around silently. ◆ **HAPPY.** Physicalize happy with the whole lower half of your body. Add the upper half of your body, including your face. You're now physicalizing happy with your whole body. Check in with yourself quickly, and observe if you are feeling happy. Stay out of the head and just quickly observe. Now, observe your breathing. ◆ Step out.

FOLLOW-UP: Notice that the time we took for each emotion, attitude, or feeling was shortened from the previous classes. Did you feel your selected emotions authentically? When you observed your breathing, did you notice a difference with each emotion?

SUMMARY:

You no longer have to go through all the separate body parts first. By the last two emotions, the body parts were reduced to two groups, lower half and upper half. Your body is learning what to do and is recognizing what you want it to do more quickly.

> **TO THE COACH:** The actors may comment that jealous and selfish did not feel as authentic as tender and happy. The coach can respond that they are not pure emotions and sometimes require a context, e.g., circumstances from a script, in which to place them. *For instance*— How do you feel about your boyfriend looking at another woman? How do you feel about sharing audition information with a competitor?

EXTEND, INTENSIFY, AND ENLARGE (REPEAT)

In order to provide the actors with an experiential sense of the progress they have made with physicalizing emotions, **repeat the first exercise in this chapter.**

> **SETUP, RULES, and ACTING FOCUS:** Same.
>
> **COACHING (as needed):** The coach should not spend a lot of time with **(1) SOUNDS, MOVEMENTS, POSTURES.** Get things rolling with this section and then quickly get to **(2) FEELINGS, EMOTIONS, ATTITUDES.** When commencing **(3) YOU'RE ON YOUR OWN,** *the coach should emphasize*— **Stay alert to what you're feeling and be available to extending, intensifying, enlarging or switching it.**
>
> **FOLLOW-UP (as needed): Same, with the following new questions added. ♦ Did you see actors climbing arcs? Did you see actors switching emotions? ♦ Actors, were you on your acting focus? Did you climb arcs?** Could you have climbed them further? Were you open to sustaining the high end of arcs nonverbally? **Did you switch emotions?**

SUMMARY:

How did this time compare to the first time you played this acting focus? This time was even more spontaneous. You were more aware of the feelings in your body and you knew what to do with them. You heightened your physicalizations of them. You even chose to switch your feelings *arbitrarily* to other feelings instead of waiting for them to switch on their own. All of this was accomplished with less effort and integrated as a part of the whole scene. Knowing what to do, how to do it, and when to do it is technique. Remember, acting is doing and there's always more to do.

Do you see how important it is for your instrument to be open and available for going with it? The more open it is, the more flexible it is. The problem is that as humans we are frequently closed. Our issues, problems, fears, backgrounds, and personal soap operas create a closed system. These keep us somewhat limited in our professional work. It's not a given that just because you're an actor going into the first day of rehearsal, your closed system is going to disappear and you're going to be Mr. Open. If anything, your system gets more closed when you go to work because of peer and career pressure.

It's necessary to stay alert to the corks created by your closed system. If you stop climbing your arc prematurely because it's not *cool* to be that outrageous or it doesn't make sense to you, your closed system is interfering with your openness and creating a cork. You are either open or you are not. The reasons for putting in a cork are irrelevant. Corks prevent the instrument from being tuned up as an organic whole. Comprising body, mind, and spirit, the whole instrument must be freely open to the improvisational world where anything can happen and ready to exploit with technique whatever happens. The instrument is prepared, waiting in readiness to work at maximum efficiency and potential. To achieve this, you must let go of any closed system and be open. With Improvisation Technique training, when you reach that stage the body will take care of business for you. You won't have to do anything except hang onto your body and go for the ride. It's flying time. That's what really *fine* acting feels like. Sometimes, you even have a moment to step outside yourself and have the actor's fantasy of going into the audience and watching your own performance. That is because the performance is taken care of for you, without you, even though it is you. It's a feeling of true freedom.

TO THE COACH: Review "To the coach" for this improv at the beginning of the chapter (p. 332). *If the coaching pertaining to silences isolates the actors, coach—* Enter the silence between you. Focus on the silence between you.

EMOTION SWITCH (REPEAT)

SETUP: Same as emotion switch.

RULES, ACTING FOCUS, COACHING (as needed), FOLLOW-UP (as needed): Same.

SUMMARY:

If emotion is not communicated, ask yourself, "Can I physicalize it more?" Avoid asking yourself, "What else could I have said that would have communicated what I was feeling?" We show our emotions, not tell them. Also, avoid thinking that the size of your physicalization might be too big. When you are concerned about that, you are in your head and censoring yourself. This is an acting exercise, not a finished, polished scene. As long as everything you do is guided by being a part of the whole scene, it will be on your acting focus and sufficient. It is much better for you, in your training, to learn how big your body can be. In practicing this, you extend the range of your instrument and develop further awareness of your corks. Later, when you are accomplished at the work and doing scripted lines, you can adjust your performance.

◆ ◆ ◆

EMOTION WALK #7

SETUP: All walk around the room responding to the coaching.

RULES: None.

ACTING FOCUS: Respond to the coaching.

COACHING: Walk around. Keep breathing. I will select the emotion you are to physicalize. We will do this with a few emotions and each time the coaching will afford you less time to physicalize it. ◆ *[Allow two seconds between sentences. Each ◆ represents a 20-second pause.]* ◆ **PLEASED.** Physicalize pleased with your toes and ankles. Have an immediate response. Go to the knees and move your knees around in that emotion. Add the pelvis. Complete the physicalization throughout the lower half of your body. Add the chest. Shoulders and elbows. If you need to heighten it, in order to help yourself feel it, do so. Fingers, knuckles, wrists. Every part of your body, from the neck down, is physicalizing pleased. Add the face. Physicalize pleased with your face. Heighten the entire physicalization. Check out your body parts. Anywhere you are not physicalizing pleased, do so now. Check in with yourself quickly, and observe if you are feeling pleased. Stay out of the head and just quickly observe. Now, observe your breathing. ◆ Shake it out as you walk. Lose *pleased.* Breathe five long breaths in through the nose and out through the mouth. Then speak nonsense language out loud. ◆ Walk around silently. ◆ **CONFUSED.** Physicalize confused with your toes and ankles. Add the knees. Pelvis. Chest. Shoulders and elbows. Hands. Face. Heighten the entire physicalization. Check out your body parts. Anywhere you are not physicalizing confused, do so now. Check in with yourself quickly. Observe if you are feeling confused. Stay out of the head and just quickly observe. ◆ **NEW:** Are you really doing confused feet or just assuming you are doing it? Look at your feet. Are you sure you want to take the next step? Which foot goes next? Which foot did you use last? Do you remember? Does it make a difference? Now, your feet are physicalizing confused. This is just to remind you that there is a difference between really physicalizing and telling yourself you are physicalizing when you are not. Now, observe your breathing. Keep walking while physicalizing confused. ◆ Shake it out as you walk. Lose *confused*. Breathe five long breaths in through the nose and out through the mouth. Then speak nonsense language out loud. ✦ Walk around silently. ✦ **EMBARRASSED.** Not shame or guilt, but embarrassed. Physicalize embarrassed with the whole lower half of your body, from the waist to your toes. Physicalize embarrassed from the waist to the neck as well. You're now physicalizing embarrassed from your neck to your toes. Add your face. Physicalize an embarrassed face. You're now physicalizing embarrassed with your whole body. Check in with yourself quickly. Observe if you are feeling embarrassed. Stay out of the head and just quickly observe. Now, observe your breathing. ✦ Shake it out as you walk. Lose *embarrassed*. Breathe five long breaths in through the nose and out through the mouth. Then speak nonsense language out loud. ✦ Walk around silently. ✦ **DISGUSTED.** Physicalize disgusted with the whole lower half of your body. Add the upper half of your body, including your face. You're now physicalizing disgusted with your whole body. Check in with yourself quickly. Observe if you are feeling disgusted. Stay out of the head and just quickly observe. Now, observe your breathing. ✦ Shake it out as you walk. Lose *disgusted*. Breathe five long breaths in through the nose and out through the mouth. Then speak nonsense language out loud. ✦ Walk around silently. ✦ **TRIUMPHANT.** Physicalize triumphant with the whole lower half of your body. Add the upper half of your body, including your face. You're now physicalizing triumphant with your whole body. Check in with yourself quickly. Observe if you are feeling triumphant. Stay out of the head and just quickly observe. Now, observe your breathing. ✦ Shake it out as you walk. Lose *triumphant*. Breathe five long breaths in through the nose and out through the mouth. Then speak nonsense language out loud. ✦ Walk around silently. ✦ **SILLY.** Physicalize silly with the whole lower half of your body. Add the upper half of your body, including your face. You're now physicalizing silly with your whole body. Check in with yourself quickly. Observe if you are feeling silly. Stay out of the head and just quickly observe. Now, observe your breathing. ✦ Step out.

FOLLOW-UP: Notice that the time we took for each emotion, attitude, or feeling was shortened from the previous classes. Did you feel your selected emotions authentically? When you observed your breathing, did you notice a difference with each emotion?

SUMMARY:

You are now physicalizing the emotions very quickly. In the next class, we will do our last emotion walk and speed up the process to *instantaneously*. When you notice your breathing, if there is no difference between the emotions, you are probably not physicalizing completely. The difference in breathing between emotions in the same family will be minimal.

EMOTION SWITCH AND ARC

Emotion switch and emotion arc are the two most important tools of emotion work with scripts. Navigating between them is explored in the next group of emotion improvisations.

> **SETUP:** 2–4 per team. In huddles, select character, activity, and location. ◆ [The rest of the setup is not revealed until the huddles are completed.] ◆ After the huddles, each actor privately selects two emotions that are not from the same emotion family and privately considers what would be the name of the lowest-intensity level of feeling for the **second emotion? It must be in the same emotional family as the originally selected second emotion.** ◆ The choices are complete when the actor knows his character, activity, location, names of two emotions, and the lowest-level feeling of the second emotion. He does not have to remember the names of feelings he considered on his way to the lowest-level feeling choice, only the final one.
>
> After the actors have set up their location, they will physicalize the first emotion and then begin the improv. ◆ At the beginning of the improv, all are physicalizing their emotion #1. At some point in the improv, the actor switches immediately and totally to the low-level choice of emotion #2. This is called the turning point. ◆ After the turning point, the actor heightens the physicalization in gradations, creating an arc of the second emotion, until the end of the improv. **They do not have to know the names of the gradation feelings they will be traveling through.** They only have to know the name of the starting low-level feeling. ◆ Each actor spontaneously selects his own turning point in the same way as the basic emotion switch improv (p. 373).
>
> **RULES:** While employing physical doing tools of Improvisation Technique for activity, location, relationships, and occupation, actors physicalize emotion #1 in the body and discover a turning point for switching to the low level of emotion #2. The switch must be total and immediate, not gradual. The switch is accomplished through changing the physicalization. After the turning point, the actor creates the arc of that emotion through heightening the physicalization of emotion #2 until the end. Turning points are not preplanned. Allow the turning point to reveal itself to you. Stay open to seeing it, while not going looking for it.
>
> **ACTING FOCUS:** Switching emotions and heightening the physicalization of emotion #2.

COACHING (as needed): After the location is set up, and before "Action," the team walks around the stage for thirty seconds, physicalizing emotion #1. ◆ Places. ◆ Action. ◆ [Use the standard coaching for emotion switch, **PLUS:**] When you spot your turning point, switch completely to the low-level of emotion #2. **Physicalize whichever emotion you are in, #1 or #2, and if you are in #2, take responsibility for physicalizing it throughout the body and then heightening it. Take responsibility for your own switch and arc.** ◆ [Use the standard coaching for emotion arc, e.g.—] Heighten what you are feeling right now. Go with it. **Sustain your levels until you go higher. You can physicalize without vocalizing.** Don't go backward. **One minute.** ◆ Cut. ◆ Step out.

FOLLOW-UP (as needed): Audience, location? Activity? Occupations? Relationships? **Were they on their acting focus?** Did they physicalize their emotions? Did they show us their emotions through the objects? **Did each actor find a turning point and switch? Were the switches integrated as a part of the whole scene? Did the actors escalate the intensities of their second emotion?** Did they integrate their arc as a part of the whole scene? Excluding short periods of plateauing, **were they in a continuous state of escalation, or did they sometimes lessen their feelings and back down the arc?** When the actors were at the higher ends of their arcs, did they talk or vocalize excessively? *Is verbalization or vocalization necessary to sustaining or heightening any levels of the arc?* Absolutely not. Did you see corks being put in? Did you see any corks being pulled out? ◆ [The coach refers to each individual actor.] ◆ **What were the two emotions? What was the turning point? For the second emotion, did he heighten the physicalization of it?** What were some of the levels of that emotion he passed through? What was the highest level of intensity? **Did he approach the top of the arc?** Did he stay in the same emotional family? **Was there any significant deescalation or backing down the arc?** ◆ [To each actor] Is that right? **What were the two emotions?** What was the name of the low-level feeling of the second emotion, that you started with? ◆ Audience, what might be a lower-level choice still? Who was the first actor to switch? Who was the last actor to switch?

SUMMARY:

PROCESS

When working with scripts, you will always have the opportunity to preselect emotion choices for different beats. The *improvisational aspect* is in what you do with the emotion. **If you choose to arc it, you will be improvising the journey up the arc.**

By climbing the arc of the second emotion, you are adding more to do. The more you add, the more involving it becomes for the audience. *They want to see what you're going to do next.*

When working with emotion arcs, even if your heightening is in tiny steps and doesn't get high up the arc, you're still in a process of adding, changing, and growth. It's more important to add a little bit more than to try and hold onto what you already have. Always assume there's more to do. Don't stop until it's shot or they turn the lights out and tell you to go home. When you act like that and get to the point where you can do that all the time, you become a spontaneous, exciting actor. "She is always doing something, that girl. It is amazing. There is so much variety, so much spontaneity." The actor that they are talking about in this way is someone who knows that there is always more to do, and *does* it.

When improvising an emotion arc by heightening the physicalization of a feeling, you don't have to know the names of the levels of intensity you are passing through. *Dependence on having to know where you are going puts the whole process into the head.* The only mental work involved in this process occurs before you start, when you select the emotion choice.

When switching to an emotion you are then going to arc, switch into it at a low level so that there will be room for climbing up.

It also helps your arc climbing if you are engaged in doing your activity. If you're on the set and they tell you to play the scene without any movement or business, you will still be able to arc the emotion because of these improvisations with the objects. Arcing emotions *without props* is best learned *with props*. In the improvs, the body learns to increase the intensity of the emotion while handling the objects. Once the body experientially learns what it feels like to heighten a physicalization or arc, it will then know what to do without the objects.

Climbing the arcs of fear or anger and not going higher because you don't want to scream is just a reason for not doing what needs to be done. Sometimes, as you remove corks and go higher on your arcs, you add new and more sophisticated corks. When you know you are going to climb an arc, it's important that you *choose* to do it. Regardless of the emotional scale you have selected, you choose to play that scale *without any reason for not doing it.* When you make that breakthrough, your work blossoms immediately in many ways. It's time to notice whether there have been changes in your corks since we began this work with paralysis. Journal work on your thoughts about this will be helpful.

THEATER VS. FILM

In the theater, do you do more in performance, after the play has opened? Yes and no. When you are rehearsing, you are very aware of your technique as you try different things. You use the technique in the rehearsal period to get you to the performance level. Then the curtain goes up, you go out there, and you're performing. You're not thinking technique. Your body has learned what to do in rehearsals. In performance, it just does it. If you have rehearsed well, it does it effortlessly. In performance, you only consciously use technique if you need to fix an unexpected problem, like lack of focus. If you are out there performing and you discover that you don't feel like you *are there* or *involved*, you grab a little technique to get back there. The growth in performance comes from the spontaneity of the live performance, which you achieve from preparing properly in the rehearsal period, and from the high of working in front of an audience. When you're in performance, you're just automatically open to little changes and growth based on being in the moment with your fellow actors. You don't make any big changes in performance without previous rehearsal with the other actors and the director.

In the theater, a performance is a *performance!* In film, if you attempt to give a performance like you do in the theater, you overact. It's too big for the camera. When you're shooting on a set, every take is more like another rehearsal. You'll do three takes and in each take you'll do it brand new, and spontaneously. You're trying something else. When you think of it this way, you'll see that it takes the tension off of you. They give you notes between takes, don't they? "Let's do it again. I'd like you to try something else. Maybe this time you should be angry and not sad." Isn't that a rehearsal-type discussion, not a performance? Nobody stops your theater performance in the middle of a scene and says, "Do it again. I'd like you a little angrier, please."

RESULTS

The structure of emotion switch and arc wins Oscars for actors. There's the night club scene in *GoodFellas,* when Joe Pesci (Best Supporting Actor) says to Ray Liotta, "You're laughing at me? What's so funny?" He switches from emotion #1, which is fun and happy, into emotion #2, which is angry and mean, and then arcs that. Opposite him, Liotta switches from fun and happy to fear, and then arcs that in tandem with Pesci's heightening of anger. From the tops of their arcs, they both switch again: Pesci to happy, when he reveals he was pulling Liotta's leg, and Liotta to relief. Mercedes Ruehl won the Oscar (Best Supporting Actress) for *The Fisher King.* She had a scene where she wakes up the morning after making love with her boyfriend, Jeff Bridges, and she's very happy, emotion #1. He wakes up and says to her, "I'm moving out." That's the turning point and she switches to anger and then proceeds to arc it.

> **TO THE COACH:** If any actors express as a reason for not climbing higher that they thought they would be unbelievable or over the top, the coach can call for a reality check. Ask the audience about actors who did approach the tops of their arcs, whether or not it was authentic?

EMOTION ARC AND SWITCH

Now we practice what frequently happens after climbing an emotion arc.

SETUP: 2–4 per team. In huddles, select character, activity, and location. ✦ [The rest of the setup is not revealed until the huddles are completed.] After the huddles, each actor privately selects two emotions that are not from the same emotion family and privately considers what would be the name of the lowest-intensity level of feeling for the **first emotion? It must be in the same emotional family as the originally selected first emotion.** ✦ The choices are complete when the actor knows his character, activity, location, names of two emotions, and the lowest-level feeling of the first emotion. He does not have to remember the names of feelings he considered on his way to the lowest-level feeling choice, only the final one.

After the actors have set up their location, they will physicalize the low-level feeling of the first emotion and then begin the improv. ✦ During the improv, the actor will heighten the physicalization in gradations, creating an arc of the original emotion #1. They do not have to know the names of the gradation feelings they will be traveling through. They only have to know the name of the starting low-level feeling. ✦ **When the actor is at the high end of the arc, he spontaneously chooses a turning point and switches immediately and totally to emotion #2.** ✦ After they have switched, they focus on physicalizing emotion #2 until the improv ends. The amount of attention that had been previously applied to heightening emotion #1 is now applied to furthering the physicalization of emotion #2 in the body. It is not necessary to arc emotion #2. No attention is paid to emotion #2 until the moment of the turning point. ✦ Each actor is totally responsible for climbing his arc and, only when he approaches the top of it, for finding his own opportunity to switch. The actors individually choose their own turning points in the same way as the basic emotion switch improv (p. 374).

RULES: While employing physical doing tools of Improvisation Technique for activity, location, relationships, and occupation, actors heighten the physicalization of emotion #1 to the top of the arc and then discover a turning point for switching to emotion #2. The switch must be total and immediate, not gradual. The switch is accomplished through changing the physicalization. After the turning point, physicalize emotion #2 until the end. Turning points are not preplanned. Allow the turning point to reveal itself to you. Stay open to seeing it, while not going looking for it.

ACTING FOCUS: Heightening the physicalization of emotion #1 and switching to emotion #2.

COACHING (as needed): After the location is set up and before "Action," the team walks around the stage for thirty seconds, physicalizing the low-level choice of emotion #1. ✦ Places. ✦ Action. ✦ [Use the standard coaching for emotion arcs, **PLUS:**] **Take responsibility for your own arc and switch.** Include the other actors, but don't depend on them. Know that you can go higher and take responsibility. **Keep physicalizing from where you are.** Heighten to the top of the arc. ✦ **Stay open to seeing a turning point. Stay alert to an opportunity to switch. When you see it, switch to the designated emotion #2.** Stay on the acting focus. Keep physicalizing that feeling. **Physicalizing whichever emotion you are in. Handling your objects with that emotion.** Stay alert so that the turning point will reveal itself to you. Avoid hanging out. You won't find the turning point inside you. When you switch, go totally into emotion #2 and physicalize it. Physicalize whichever emotion you are in, #1 or #2; if you are in #2, take responsibility for physicalizing it throughout the body. Keep physicalizing emotion #2 until the end. Share your feelings. ✦ One minute to stay on your acting focus. ✦ Cut. ✦ Step out.

> **FOLLOW-UP (as needed):** Same as for emotion switch and arc, except here the arced emotion is the first emotion. **PLUS:** For the first emotion, could he have heightened the physicalization of it more before switching to emotion #2?

SUMMARY:

The challenge is in climbing your own arc regardless of what's going on with the other actors' arcs and doing it in such a way that you integrate what you and they are doing as a part of the whole scene.

When you are high on the emotion #1 arc, you will feel like you have to switch immediately in order to avoid sustaining the high intensity of feeling. You must be diligent in making your switch a part of the whole scene, and not just an arbitrary one.

When switching to an emotion you are not planning to arc, how do you know what level to switch into? When you designated the name of emotion #2, you did not designate the intensity level of it. It should not be the highest-intensity level. In script acting, you seldom switch from the top of emotion #1's arc to a high-level intensity of emotion #2. Try it on different levels and explore the facility with which you can control the intensity you switch into. Also, do you have a preference for the level you want to switch into? Since it's an improv, and you have the freedom to switch in on any level, allow your body to determine the level it will physicalize. The intensity of emotion #1's arc will greatly influence how you come through the turning point.

COMMON ACTOR PROBLEMS IN ARCING

(1) Starting too high on the arc. This leads to getting to the top too soon and having to sustain the high intensity. (2) Starting low but escalating too fast. (3)

Backing up, or diminishing the intensity. (4) Leaving the emotion family for another emotion. (5) Partial physicalization, i.e., from the neck up. This leads to *indicating*. (6) Not approaching the top of the arc. (7) Attempting an arc not based in a single emotion family, e.g., certain attitudes, or concepts.

If you find yourself off the acting focus, notice it, then coach yourself to get back on the focus and physicalize what you are feeling. Climb from there.

> **TO THE COACH:** The coach should stay alert to actors choosing two emotions that are very close together. The farther apart the emotions, the greater the challenge. It is not necessary to discuss the intensity level of emotion #2 during the setup. It's too much information for the actors to deal with at that time. Save it for the summary. However, if an actor switches into the high end of emotion #2, then the switch will probably not be accomplished with authenticity. The coach may add a follow-up question, "Was the switch authentic?" After the class answers, "No," the coach may point out the problem with switching into the high end of emotion #2.

◆ ◆ ◆

EMOTION WALK #8

We now do the final emotion walk with immediate physicalization of the emotions.

SETUP: All begin walking around the room responding to the coaching.

RULES: None.

ACTING FOCUS: Respond to the coaching.

COACHING: Walk around. Keep breathing. I will select the emotion you are to physicalize. We will do this with a few emotions and each time the coaching will give you less time to physicalize it. ◆ *[No pauses between sentences. Each ◆ represents a 20-second pause.]* ◆ **MEAN.** Physicalize mean with your toes and ankles. Have an immediate response. Go to the knees and move your knees around in that emotion. Add the pelvis. Complete the physicalization throughout the lower half of your body. Add the chest. Shoulders and elbows. If you need to heighten it, in order to help yourself feel it, do so. Fingers, knuckles, wrists. Every part of your body, from the neck down, is physicalizing mean. Add the face. Physicalize mean with your face. Heighten the entire physicalization. Check out your body parts. Anywhere you are not physicalizing mean, do so now. Check in with yourself quickly. Observe if you are feeling mean. Stay out of the head and just quickly observe. Now, observe your breathing. ◆ Shake it out as you walk. Lose *mean.* Breathe five long breaths in through the nose and out through the mouth. Then speak nonsense language out loud. ✦ Walk around silently.

When you are not responding to the coaching, you have time to fill out the physicalization in any parts of the body where it's necessary.

NOBLE. Physicalize noble with the whole lower half of your body, from the waist to your toes. Physicalize noble from the waist to the neck, as well. You're now physicalizing noble from your neck to your toes. Add your face. Physicalize a noble face. You're now physicalizing noble with your whole body. Check in with yourself quickly. Observe if you are feeling noble. Stay out of the head and just quickly observe. Now, observe your breathing. ✦ Shake it out as you walk. Lose *noble.* Breathe five long breaths in through the nose and out through the mouth. Then speak nonsense language out loud. ✦ Walk around silently.

Now, I'm simply going to coach the three parts of the body by numbers: One is the lower half of the body. Two is the waist to the neck. Three is the neck up.

CONCERNED. One. Two. Three. Now, top it off with any body parts you're not physicalizing. You're now physicalizing concerned with your whole body. Check in with yourself quickly. Observe if you are feeling concerned. Stay out of the head and just quickly observe. Now, observe your breathing. ✦ Shake it out as you walk. Lose *concerned.* Breathe five long breaths in through the nose and out through the mouth. Then speak nonsense language out loud. ✦ Walk around silently. ✦ **LOVING.** One. Two. Three. Now, top it off with any body parts you're not physicalizing. You're now physicalizing loving with your whole body. *Just because you are physicalizing by yourself, doesn't mean you can't see your fellow actors. However, avoid getting involved with them.* Check in with yourself quickly. Observe if you are feeling loving. Stay out of the head and just quickly observe. Now, observe your breathing. ✦ Shake it out as you walk. Lose *loving.* Breathe five long breaths in through the nose and out through the mouth. Then speak nonsense language out loud. ✦ Walk around silently. ✦ **RESIGNED.** One. Two. Three. You're now physicalizing resigned with your whole body. Check in with yourself quickly. Observe if you are feeling resigned. Stay out of the head and just quickly observe. Now, observe your breathing. ✦ Shake it out as you walk. Lose *resigned.* Breathe five long breaths in through the nose and out through the mouth. Then speak nonsense language out loud. ✦ Walk around silently. ✦ **FURIOUS.** Immediately physicalize furious with the whole body. Check in with yourself quickly. Observe if you are feeling furious. Stay out of the head and just quickly observe. Now, observe your breathing. ✦ Shake it out as you walk. Lose *furious.* Breathe five long breaths in through the nose and out through the mouth. Then speak nonsense language out loud. ◆ Walk around silently. ◆ **HORRIFIED.** Immediately physicalize horrified with the whole body. Check in with yourself quickly. Observe if you are feeling horrified. Stay out of the head and just quickly observe. Now, observe your breathing. ◆ Shake it out as you walk. Lose *horrified*. Breathe five long breaths in through the nose and out through the mouth. Then speak nonsense language out loud. ◆ Walk around silently. ◆ **EROTIC.** Immediately physicalize erotic with the whole body. Check in with yourself quickly. Observe if you are feeling erotic. Stay out of the head and just quickly observe. Now, observe your breathing. ◆ Step out.

FOLLOW-UP (as needed): Notice that you can now physicalize the emotional feeling *immediately*. Did you feel your selected emotions? Did they feel authentic? When you observed your breathing, did you notice a difference with each emotion?

SUMMARY:

You can practice physicalizing at home. Name an emotion and physicalize it.

TO THE COACH: Some of the choices are really attitudes, but they are treated like emotions when they are temporary. The coach may point out that the actors noticed a minimal change in the breathing when they were physicalizing noble. This is because their response to noble is similar to a feeling of snob, which is not very far from the previous emotion, mean. Emotions in the same family seldom bring about large changes in the breathing patterns.

GO WITH YOUR EMOTION

Now that the actors are skilled at arcing and switching emotions, we broaden the playing field and provide more room for spontaneity.

SETUP: 2–4 per team. In huddles, select character, activity, and location. During the improv, each actor is responsible for recognizing his own feelings and doing something with them, i.e., climbing arcs or switching from one feeling to another. The entire improv is a minefield of potential turning points providing opportunities to switch emotions or to escalate the physicalization of what they are already feeling. The actors should arc or switch emotions continuously. There are no restrictions to the number of emotions they play with.

RULES: While improvising your character, activity, and location, stay open to recognizing feelings and choosing to arc or switch them.

ACTING FOCUS: Go with any feelings.

COACHING (as needed): [Coaching should be minimal to allow the actors the opportunity to take responsibility for their acting focus. However, if the actors are not doing so, employ the coaching for emotion arcs and emotion switch to get them up to speed.] Set up your location. ◆ Places. ◆ Action. ◆ Check out your scene mates. Do something with those feelings. **Keep recognizing your own feelings and choosing to do something with them. Go with that feeling. Heighten that feeling. Switch to another emotion.** Take advantage of the opportunity to do something with it. Go with that. Do something with it. Allow your object handling to help you with these feelings. Avoid censoring yourself. Go with your emotion. Heighten it. See where it leads you. ◆ Active & still. ◆ **One minute.** ◆ Cut.

FOLLOW-UP (as needed): Audience, character? Activity? Location? **Were they on their acting focus?** Did they physicalize their emotions? Did they show us their emotions through the objects? Were the actors open to going with their emotions, or were they guarded and closed? Did they escalate the intensities of their feelings and climb arcs? Did they find turning points and switch out of one emotion into another? Did they integrate their escalations, or switches, with what was going on around them, in other words, as a part of the whole? ◆ Did the actors ever switch into an emotion and then climb its arc? Did they ever climb an arc, and then switch from the arc to another emotion? ◆ Excluding short periods of plateauing or switching to another emotion, were they in a continuous state of escalation, or did they sometimes lessen their feelings and back down the arc? Did any of the actors approach the top of the arc they were on? When the actors were at the higher ends of their arcs, did they talk excessively? *Is verbalization or vocalization necessary to heightening, or sustaining, any levels of the arc?* Absolutely not. ◆ Did you see corks being put in? Did you see any corks being pulled out? ◆ **Was each actor's presence heightened as a result of this acting focus?** ◆ **Actors, were you on your acting focus? Were you aware of your feelings? Did you climb arcs? Did you switch emotions?** ◆ [The coach refers to each individual actor.] ◆ Audience, what emotions did you see him arcing? Did he approach the tops of his arcs? Was there any significant deescalation or backing down the arc? What emotions did you see him switching?

SUMMARY:

While we have been working primarily with preselected emotions, you have just practiced *waiting in readiness for the emergence of spontaneous emotions.* When your emotion appears spontaneously, it may surprise you as well as the audience or the camera. The spontaneous emergence of an emotion is exciting, but it is what you do with it after it comes up that separates the pro from the amateur. Emotion has tremendous power for sustaining itself or for changing, sometimes intensifying or arcing, or transforming into other emotions. You now have the tools for spotting it, grabbing it, and running with it. You know what to do with it when it does emerge. That is technique.

Have you ever completed a take and thought, "Wow! I never thought that at the end of the scene, where I'm beating up on my boyfriend, I would have that laugh moment. And look, it just came and it was great. It was so spontaneous!" But, did you then do something with the laugh? Just like in the improv you just did, you should be so facile, tuned, and so in readiness, that when that little laugh moment appears and surprises you, you can grab the laugh and take it in ten different directions intuitively, instinctively, and with great skill. There's always more to do. It's just like working with a preselected emotion.

When climbing the high ends of arcs, you often *think* you are at the top and there can't be any more levels to get to. You will be wrong. You must assume that there is always one more level. That way you'll always be in the process of climbing. Then, when you discover that you are at that next level, the discovery will surprise you. Anything that is a surprise is at the epicenter of spontaneity, where we always want to be.

The only way to *know* that you have reached the top of an arc is after the fact, when you've come out *through* the top and into another emotion, e.g., rage turns into tears; despair into anger; hilarity into concern. At that point, another feeling has chosen you, and you then choose it by going with it, renewing your acting focus from that point.

If you had known this earlier, you might have used it as a cork cover-up, when you disguise not going to the top of an arc by deliberately changing the emotion. If you deliberately make that change, all you are doing is (1) coming up with another clever reason for putting the cork in and (2) covering it up by switching to another emotion. The only time you really get to the top of an arc is when you spontaneously burst through the ceiling of it into another emotion, and it only happens when you have nothing to do with it beyond the continuous heightening of the physicalization of the original arc. You have to keep climbing until, *surprise*, you come out in the other emotion.

Climbing arcs and switching emotions are tools available to you whenever you are feeling emotions in your acting, improvisational or scripted. It is best to avoid plateauing with one emotional feeling unless it is by design, i.e., a preselected emotional level for the length of a scripted beat. The confidence that accompanies knowing what to do with an emotion and the actual doing of it creates or increases presence. Working with arcs and switches will intensify your presence, making you much more compelling an actor.

TO THE COACH: It is sometimes helpful to remind the actors that these training exercises and improvisations are designed to stretch their acting muscles. They are usually more difficult than anything the actors will face on the set.

ATTITUDE LINE WITH EMOTION SWITCH

Now we see how easily the emotion tools are applied to major character work.

SETUP: 2–4 per team. In huddles, select character, activity, and location. ◆ [The rest of the setup is not revealed until the huddles are completed.] After the huddles, each actor privately selects an attitude line for his character and two emotions that are neither from the same emotion family nor from an emotion family similar to the attitude line. For example: attitude line, "Nobody loves me"; emotion #1, happy; emotion #2, scared. [In this case, due to the attitude line the emotion family to be avoided is *sad*.] ◆ After setting up their location, the actors do an attitude line preparation process with no concern for the emotions. ◆ This process is immediately followed by a one-minute walk for the actors to physicalize emotion #1 while retaining the attitude line. ◆ When the improv begins, the actors are retaining the attitude line, physicalizing emotion #1, and are open to discovering a turning point when they will immediately switch to emotion #2 and still retain the attitude line. ◆ After the turning point, the actor continues physicalizing emotion #2 and retaining the attitude line until the end of the improv.

Each actor selects his own turning point in the same way as the basic emotion switch improv, but does not drop his attitude line.

RULES: While employing physical doing tools of Improvisation Technique for activity, location, relationships, and occupation, the actors retain their attitude line in the body, physicalize emotion #1, and discover the turning point for switching to emotion #2 without dropping the body's retention of the attitude line. The switch must be total and immediate, not gradual. The switch is accomplished by changing the physicalization. After the turning point, physicalize emotion #2 while retaining the attitude line until the end. Turning points are not preplanned. Allow the turning point to reveal itself to you. Stay open to seeing it, while not going looking for it. Never say the attitude line out loud.

ACTING FOCUS: Retaining the attitude line and switching emotions.

COACHING: Before "Action," the team does a complete attitude line preparation process (p. 275). When they get to the part of the process where they say their lines out loud, they will be coached to say it, but they should only mouth it. Their lips form the words, but there is no volume. ◆ *Then*— retain the attitude in your body and on your face, and you have one minute to walk around, physicalizing emotion #1 with this body that is totally retaining the attitude line. Walk around and physicalize emotion #1 with this body. ◆ Places. ◆ You're all physicalizing emotion #1 and retaining the character based on the attitude line. Don't let go of the character. Stay alert for a turning point to reveal itself to you, and then switch to physicalizing emotion #2 while retaining the attitude line. ◆ Action. ◆ **Coach (as needed): Totally physicalize the emotion from head to toes.** Physicalize what you are feeling. ◆ Stay on the acting focus; don't let go of the attitude. Keep it in the face and in the body while you physicalize that emotion. Keep checking out your fellow players. Avoid hanging out. Share your voices. Contact the location. Do your activity. Stay open to helping anyone. Stay open to needing help. Stay on your acting focus. Avoid saying your attitude line out loud. ◆ Show us the emotion through your objects. ◆ Don't let the nature of your attitude line or emotion prevent you from playing and using all the previously learned improvisational tools with your fellow actors. ◆ Stay open to your fellow actors. Stay open to a turning point revealing itself to you. **Keep retaining the character and physicalizing emotion #1 while staying alert for the opportunity to change to emotion #2.** ◆ After you switch, physicalize emotion #2 while retaining the attitude line. Keep physicalizing your emotion in the body. Take every opportunity to put it further into your body. **Keep retaining the attitude line while physicalizing whichever emotion you are in.** ◆ Stay on focus. Keep the attitude in the body and on the face while you physicalize that emotion. Integrate your laughter, tears, etc., with your attitude line. ◆ Show us what you're feeling through the objects. Be a part of the whole. Check each other out. ◆ Keep physicalizing whichever emotion you are in while retaining the attitude line. **Keep retaining your attitude line after you switch** and physicalize emotion #2 until the end. ◆ Active & still ◆ One minute. ◆ Cut. ◆ Step out.

FOLLOW-UP (as needed): Audience, location? Activity? Occupations? Relationships? Did they create characters from their attitude lines? Did they retain the characters throughout the improvisation? **Were they on their acting focus?** Did they physicalize their emotions? Did they show us their emotions through the objects? Were the emotions added to the character work, or did they replace it? Did each actor find a turning point and switch? Were the switches accomplished and integrated as a part of the whole scene? ◆ [The coach refers to each individual actor.] **Describe his character. What were the two emotions? What was the turning point?** ◆ [To each actor] Is that right? **What was your attitude line? What were the two emotions?**

SUMMARY:

Adding emotion work to characterization requires that the character work be done first and be easily retained in the body without your having to think about it. Using the attitude line to create the character will armor the body with that attitude in a way that is similar to having that attitude as a personality core for an entire life. The muscles realign themselves, putting that attitude throughout the body. This differs from physicalizing an emotion, which is transitory and doesn't create body armoring. Attitude lines can contribute to creating the overall character and will not be as immediately facile as physicalizing an emotion. For instance, it is more difficult to arc an attitude line.

The improvisations we just did, attitude line with emotion switch, provide you with an experience of how it feels to do emotion work on top of a body-held characterization. Once the character is in the body, all emotion work is easily applied in the same way it has been presented here.

It's important that the actor understand the difference between an attitude line used to create a character and an attitude that is similar to an emotion and accessible to any character. The latter may be temporary, not lifelong. It does not create body armor and is usually a response to events. It may be treated *like an emotion* and is created through physicalization. We have been doing some of them in our emotion walks.

> **TO THE COACH:** The reason we do not do more work with physicalizing emotions on top of a character has to do with the nature of the workshop. Outside of the time we spent in chapter 7, "Character," the Improvisation Technique character work is restricted to occupation and relationships. Time should be given to creating the character *when the actor is working on a scripted character.* At that point, the actor will find that all of the emotion work we have been exploring in this chapter will come into play.

◆ ◆ ◆

CHAPTER SUMMARY

The professional actor's responsibility is to make choices in preparation for the performance and to be prepared to execute them spontaneously on the set. The choices may change on the set due to rehearsal, the director's input, or the organic chemistry between the actor and his scene mates. In film and TV, he is usually meeting his scene mates for the first time on the day of shooting.

Playing the choice is where the spontaneity comes in. Playing it should be a total improvisation. When your choice is an emotional one, and not all choices are, you need to be equipped to create it spontaneously and to apply some *form* to that spontaneity. This form is provided by sustaining emotion physicalizations, arc climbing from one level to another, or by choosing to switch to another emotion if you desire.

Many inexperienced actors think that the emotion has to arrive magically. In the greenroom or in their trailer prior to going to the set, they say, "Dear God, please let the feelings come on cue!" An actor who works like that isn't very professional. You can feel any emotion any time without divine intervention.

If you do the emotion physically, through physicalization, you will really feel it. When the body does something in a focused manner, it is going to include all the parts of the body: limbs, brain, and heart. Everything within the body comes along for the ride and feelings naturally flow. When the mind works alone, e.g., in an emotional recall, the body *doesn't necessarily come along*. You can't count on it.

Physicalizing

Emotions occur when the body responds to a stimulus. When you physicalize an emotion, the stimulus is doing what the body does when it feels that emotion. You physicalize the emotion *before you feel it*. The body recognizes this specific and familiar behavior and it activates the corresponding emotion. It knows that a particular emotion accompanies a particular physical pattern.

Once in a class, while we were working on physicalization, an actor commented:

> My little baby daughter, who's two, will sometimes pretend to be angry at something. She knows it's a way to manipulate. It's clear she's not really angry. She's only acting like she's angry, but as she does that, there comes a moment when she actually crosses over the line, unconsciously, into real anger.

That's a perfect illustration of physicalization. When the child acts like she's angry, she's physicalizing. She waves her hands, bangs the table, and does all the things that she does when she's angry. She physicalizes anger and it takes her into true anger.

The more you physicalize the emotion in the acting state, the more quickly the emotion will come up. Get the body doing the things that it does when it's in a particular emotional state, even if you're not really feeling it, and the desired emotion will come up. Choose the emotion, physicalize it, and boom! The feeling is there. If it's not—a possible peril with any approach to acting emotions—*at least you look like you're having the feeling*. That's called acting.

Feeling it?

Whether you feel it or not is not the issue. It's a red herring. Feeling an emotion in an *acting context* is not really feeling an emotion as in a *life context*. Real emotions occur without artificiality of circumstances. If someone were *really* furious, or *really* bawling in despair, they wouldn't be able to hit their marks, clip cues, play the subtext, or climb their arcs as actors do when they are feeling emotions.

In performance, the emotions accompanying approval/disapproval issues of self, peers, audiences, directors, coaches, and teachers are very *real*, but they are the actor's emotions and not the character's. They contribute more artificiality to the character's emotions, and the separation created by the artificiality doesn't allow you to really be in the character's emotions. Instead, you experience a secondary version of the emotion, rather like a computer file *alias*. After all, in the heat of any performance, you always know that you are acting and it's not real. So how *really real* can the emotions be?

The physicalization approach allows you to feel it as *authentically as possible within an acting context* and provides you with *the dexterity to do things with the emotion*. And, the camera and the audience see you feeling the emotion. After all, you can feel an emotion authentically, but if you don't have a technique for using your instrument to express it what good is it? It must be in the space for the camera or audience to see. Physicalization will lead you to feelings and makes them available for communication.

Limitations of Traditional American Emotion Technique

The American actor has been held back from his true potential when dealing with emotions. For years, the emotional tool of choice was Strasberg's *affective memory* or *emotion recall*. With affective memory, if the actor wants to arrive at a designated emotion, he consciously reactivates an emotional memory through recalling the sensual surroundings of a parallel event from his past. This recall can evoke the same powerful emotions that helped form them in the body's memory. In reality, the memories are stored in the brain.

A thorough actor should know how to use this tool because it may come in handy on some specific occasion. However, as the actor's basic emotion tool, I suggest this approach is limited, inefficient, and possibly even self-destructive.

These are the problems with emotion recall:

1. Getting it on cue repeatedly and with minimal rehearsal time. To arrive at the emotion on cue requires repetition of the memory exercise in order to reduce the time of the process. However, a performance is not a class situation where everyone is patient and supportive of your process. In performance, you need the emotion on cue and you can't tune out what's going on in the scene in order to do your process. Emotion recall is not a dependable performance tool if you haven't previously perfected the sensual memory process, reduced it to a split second, and can activate it mid-performance.

2. However long it takes for the process, it takes you out of the spontaneous reality of the ongoing scene that you are involved in. You are supposed to be in character, involved in the spontaneous unfolding of a scene, and you are not there. Instead, you are in your head conjuring up your own past. Even if you have reduced your process to a second or two, it's too much time to be out of the moment. It's the death of spontaneity. If another actor changes something or goes with something in that moment, you won't even see them, much less act organically and spontaneously with them in the moment. You're in your own past-tense private moment, unavailable for organic moment-to-moment playing. Emotion recall can lead to isolated acting. Being in the past is not where an actor wants to be. He wants to be in the present where the action is.

3. On top of everything else, it can inauthenticate whatever is authentic and important in your own personal past and growth. Anything you would choose as the subject of your emotional recall is obviously important to you or you wouldn't even remember it. By using that memory as an acting tool, you are not respecting your own primary process.

This is what Academy Award-winning actress Kathy Bates says about this issue. She and her actor friend, Susan Kingsley, worked together in the premiere of Beth Henley's *Crimes of the Heart* at the Actors Theatre of Louisville in 1979:

> My first scene required me to cry on cue. At that age it was still a challenge for me to perform that way. And I used to go upstairs to the stage very early, like 7:45, and sit in the chair and think of horrible things, to get ready. And Susan would sail up at "Places" and go out and be brilliant. I learned from her that I had to do all my preparation during the rehearsal period, and that when it came time to go onstage you had to just leave all that behind and walk to the edge of the cliff and throw yourself off. And trust that you would fly.

She no longer has to dig out some intimate memory whenever she has to cry in a role:

> I've found, for me personally, that that can make the work self-indulgent, and that it can be psychologically harmful to use. Because [emphasis added] *if you continually finger those emotional memories in yourself, you can distort your relationship to them.*[12]

Sanford Meisner, on the other hand, relied on the actor being in the moment and getting in touch with the given circumstances of the scene, trusting that the actor believing himself in those circumstances and in touch with his scene mates would feel the appropriate emotion. He also emphasized the use of Stanislavsky's *As If* tool and [Eugene] Vakhtangov's *Adjustment* tool to aid the actor's imagination. The limitation of this approach is revealed in Meisner's own definition of acting as *"living truthfully under imaginary circumstances."* Certainly, living or behaving truthfully is the most important foundation of acting, but if that's all an actor has to do, where's the art? An actor is an *interpretive artist* whose job is to elevate the truth so that it becomes a part of a whole artistic statement. Acting on the stage or in film is so much more than being believable. Being in the moment and truthfulness are starting points, not the goal. Meisner recognized this limitation when he instructed his students to look at the character, "instead of *merely* the truth." He continues, "The emphasis has been primarily on 'This is what I'm doing and I'm doing it truthfully. Now the question coming up is '*How do I do It?*'"

The limitation of Meisner training as I see it presented in numerous classes in Hollywood and New York is that there is no methodology for the actor to follow in preparing his performance. The training is too dependent on the teachers' pointing out aspects of the given circumstances that the actors are not exploiting in their prepared class scenes. Then the actors are dependent upon being in the moment and traditional acting tools like *As If, Adaptation,* and *Substitution* to stimulate their emotions with imaginary circumstances. This keeps the actor in a position of dependency on: (1) his mind to initiate an imaginary—*as if acting is pretending*—set of circumstances; (2) the hope that imaginary circumstances tools will stimulate the requisite amount of emotion, and on cue; (3) his scene mates' ability to connect in the moment; and (4) the director's assistance.

Stanislavsky, late in his career, discovered with his work on Physical Actions that muscles are more reliable pathways to emotions than is the mind. He found that physical actions released feelings. If Stanislavsky opened the door, Viola Spolin marched through it with theater games designed to teach physicalization.

A true technique is totally self-sufficient with a high degree of success. Too many actors have applied to my workshop after two or more years in some Meisner-oriented class. They declare on the one hand that they don't know how to break down a script so that it leads to choices and they don't feel they have the tools for creating the appropriate emotion efficiently and on cue. On the other hand, they all feel confident that they can act in the moment.

Finally, neither Meisner nor Strasberg ever dealt with tools for technical proficiency in *what to do with the emotion after it arrived.* It's as if just feeling the emotion was sufficient. The actor who simply emotes winds up on the cutting room floor. Uta Hagen says, "There's a tremendous over-emphasis on *emotion,* on riding an emotion—tapping something and starting to cry, and [emphasis added] *going any old where without selection*—that I think is terrible."[13] It's the artist who applies the feelings in a dynamic fashion to his actions in solving the character's problems (traditional technique) and/or reveals emotions the author intended (Improvisation Technique) who is compelling. To do this, the actor must have technical control. He must be able to play on emotional scales at different intensity levels, escalate and climb arcs, and confidently switch emotions on a dime while dealing with the character's problems in the scene. Whether emotions are spontaneously chosen or preselected, the actor should be prepared to do this without depending on a director or teacher to guide him there. Physicalization of emotions is a major tool for achieving this. Not only does physicalization keep the actor in the moment, it enables the actor to make that moment blossom.

CURRICULUM NOTE TO THE COACH

In the curriculum at my workshop, the group does not immediately proceed to the next stage of the training. Instead, we do a script application of the emotion work with a monologue assignment. I'm not sure it is necessary to do this when the actors are not professionals. If the actors are students or amateurs who do not spend their days pursuing their acting careers, it would probably be best to go right into chapter 10.

Professionals can expect a great deal of improvement in their work immediately if they apply what they have just learned to texts. The monologue assignment can be given earlier in this chapter in anticipation of its being performed in the very next classes.

For the assignment and exercise, see chapter 13, "Monologues and Purpose of Scene," (p. 550). As soon as the monologue exercise is completed, my groups go into the conflict part of the training in chapter 10.

ASSIGNMENT: Prepare, in any traditional manner, a one-to-two-minute monologue from a published play. In the designated class, bring it in at performance level and provide copies for everyone in the class. The higher the quality of writing, the better the exercise. Actors may use real or space props. The monologue should not have any changes made to it, e.g., no interior cuts. If it is retyped from its source, include everything, especially stage directions.

10
CONFLICT

A basic difference between Improvisation Technique for the professional script actor and the techniques used in improvisational theater is in the function of *conflict*. Almost every aspect of improvisational theater training requires that there be no conflict. The cardinal rule of all improvisational theater is that the actor must *go with it*. Going with it means that you don't stop, question, object, negate, or deny what is happening. Instead, you accept what is happening and build upon it. While necessary for improvisational theater, this is of minimal use for the actor playing a scene in which the writer has chosen that the characters be in conflict with each other or their environment. This chapter is about how to *go with the conflict*.

Conflict creates tension and confrontation, which are highly dramatic and compelling for an audience. Conflict is usually at the heart of any script. The hero, or protagonist, must do something and there are obstacles in the way. The audience gets caught up in the hero's struggle to overcome these obstacles and in the outcome, whether the hero wins or loses. The nature of the conflict is central to the writer's theme. We don't go into dramatic literature and structure here. It is enough to know that the actor has to play many scenes based on conflict.

CONFLICT SPACE EXERCISE #1[1]

We begin this part of the training with a return to space object exercises.

SETUP: The whole group walks around the playing area.

RULES: Respond to the coaching.

ACTING FOCUS: As designated through the coaching.

404

COACHING: Focus on moving sideways through the space. Now the other side. Move forward. Backward. Feel the space against your body. Move in any direction you wish. Go through the space and feel it with your whole body. Now feel the space moving through you. Focus on moving through the space and feeling the space moving through you at the same time. ◆ Reach up into the space and form a ball of space. It should be the size of a volleyball. Play with that ball and focus on playing with a real space ball and not a pretend one. Always see the ball wherever it is, especially when the ball leaves your hands. Play with it any way you wish. Always see where the ball is, in your hands or moving through the space. ◆ Increase the weight of the ball. More. Extremely heavy. Heavier. Go with it. Stay on your acting focus. Keep it in the space. You need your entire body to play with it. Don't take your eyes off it. ◆ Change the ball back to its original weight. Play with it in new ways. Use the whole playing area. Use different body parts. Lessen the weight of the ball. More. As light as you can make it. Don't take your eyes off of it. Keep playing with it. You need your entire body to play with it. ◆ Change the ball back to its original weight. Don't take your eyes off it. Throw the balls back up into the space of the room. ◆ Everyone on the left side of the playing area face everyone on the right side. Each side of the room is one team for a volleyball game. ◆ [The coach *physically* handles the space net separating the two teams.] ◆ The team on the left serves first. Server, pick up a space ball and begin the game. Keep your eyes on the ball. Stay on the same ball. Only one ball with everyone agreeing on the ball in the space. Who got that point? This side got a point. Server, call out the score. The other team serves now. It came down over here, so this team serves now. Rotate and then call out the score. Five points wins the game. This team wins. Everyone have a seat.

FOLLOW-UP and SUMMARY: None

TO THE COACH: All the actors will be exuberant at the end of the volleyball game. No comments or discussion are necessary. The coach also has the opportunity to refer to the game in the discussions to come on the sports metaphor for conflict.

DISGUISED CONFLICT INFLUENCE[2]

SETUP: 2 (ideally) or 4 per team. In huddles, select characters, activity, location, and a *conflict issue*. A conflict is two opposing wants. A conflict issue occurs when each character in a scene wants something different from and in opposition to what the other character(s) wants. There are very few occasions when two opposing wants do not become a conflict. We will look at these exceptions later. When choosing the conflict issue, the actors should make their selections together so that each actor's selection of what he wants is in opposition to what the other wants. If there are four actors in the improv, then two want one (same) thing and the other two want another (same) thing in opposition to the first two. Example: Husband and wife, packing for vacation, bedroom; he wants his elderly mother to move in with them and she wants his mother to go in a nursing home.

After the huddles, each actor must privately make one more choice, the *private reason*. This is a direct, uncomplicated, private, and personal reason why the character wants what he wants in the conflict issue. The private reason is not shared with the other actor(s). If there are four actors in the improv, even though two actors want the same thing, each actor has his own private reason. Example: Husband wants his mother to move in because he can't afford to pay for a nursing home; wife wants her to go to nursing home because she doesn't want to have to take care of his mother.

After the huddles, all are informed that while improvising they are *never to speak of the conflict or their private reasons*; however, it is the only thing they focus on during the improv.

RULES: While employing physical doing tools of Improvisation Technique for activity, location, relationships, and occupation, the actors must never mention or in any way reveal the conflict issue, including discussion of their private reasons.

ACTING FOCUS: On the conflict issue without speaking about it. (The conflict issue is more than just what you want. It is the fact that you want it and your partner doesn't.)

COACHING (as needed): *After the location has been set up*— Places. Start focusing on the conflict issue. ✦ Action. ✦ **Stay totally focused on the conflict issue.** The only thing on your mind is the conflict issue. Don't speak about it. Don't forget it. **Choose not to talk about it.** Censor nothing except talking about it. Share your voices. The conflict is always present, but never named. Avoid censoring your feelings. Avoid hanging out. Respect your space objects. Stay on your acting focus. ✦ Cut.

FOLLOW-UP (as needed): Audience, characters? Activity? Location? **Did the actors tell or reveal the conflict issue? Did they keep it disguised? Was there conflict in the scene? Was there tension and confrontation? Did you get the feeling that the stakes of the conflict issue were low, medium, or high?** Were the stakes higher or lower for one of the actors than the other? **Did anyone flash on what the conflict issue was?** ✦ *For improvs with four actors, add*— Which actors were on the same side of the conflict? Did they work together against the other side, or did they have conflict between themselves? If not, was the conflict between the two groups watered down because of the conflict within one group? ◆ Actors, **were you on your acting focus? What was your conflict issue?** What were your private reasons? If you don't want to share your private reasons, say, "Pass."

SUMMARY:

Removing the ability to speak about the conflict issue serves two important purposes: (1) It influences the whole scene, informing many aspects of the acting with conflict, regardless of the dialogue. Any dialogue will be informed by what's really going on, the conflict issue. Speaking about the issue allows the actor to compartmentalize it into speech; the whole improv will stay on that one issue. Not speaking about it, while focusing on it, extends the conflict into the total behavior and dialogue of the characters, thereby extending the scene beyond a single-issue verbal argument. (2) The actors experientially learn that playing conflict is not about the discovery of different actions or approaches to getting what you want. It is about the confrontation between the opposing characters.

When playing any scene based on conflict, whether the dialogue is improvised or memorized, articulate the two opposing wants. Once you have done that and know exactly what it is that you want, choose your private reason for wanting it. A private reason anchors the issue in the given circumstances of the scene and makes the conflict more accessible to you. *Private reasons also afford you the opportunity to adjust the stakes of the conflict.* You can raise the stakes of any conflict issue by raising the stakes of the private reason. When the improvisations seem to have higher stakes for one actor than the other, it is usually due to a discrepancy in the stakes of their private reasons.

> **TO THE COACH:** Each improv should last no longer than five minutes. This is a rudimentary exercise designed to introduce unspoken conflict issues with two opposing wants, which have private reasons.

◆　◆　◆

Doing conflict is a full body experience. The purest form of a full body physical conflict, with no violence or ambiguities, is the traditional game of tug of war. The dynamics of this traditional contest will become the foundation for playing conflict.

PULL THE ROPE! #1 [3]

SETUP: 2 actors of fairly similar physical strength per team. No huddles or preparation necessary. The coach chalks a line across the center of the acting area. The actors take their places facing each other, 10' apart, with the line between them. They will play a rope-pulling contest with the space rope.

RULES: Two actors holding the ends of a space rope pull the rope in order to pull the other actor over the center line between them.

ACTING FOCUS: Pulling on the same space rope between you.

COACHING: Get the rope taut. You are going to pull on the rope in order to pull your opponent across the chalk line. Your acting focus is to maintain the same space rope between you. To help you get on the acting focus, look at the rope between your own hands. Let your eyes travel the length of the rope to your opponent's hands and see the rope in your opponent's hands. Let your eyes travel back down the rope to the middle of the rope. That's where you have to focus. Focus on that middle spot between you so both of you are focusing on the rope in the center, where it exists in the space between you. That is what you keep focusing on while you pull the rope as hard as you can. Get ready to pull the other actor over the chalk line. Your acting focus is not your success or failure at pulling the other actor over the line, but your ability to stay on the same space rope, regardless of who gets pulled over the line. ◆ On your mark, get set, pull! **Coach (as needed):** Pull with your whole body. Use your elbows. Use your knees. No pretending. The rope is really there. It's just made out of space. Keep your eyes on the rope! Get your legs into it! Pull the rope! Pull! ◆ [The coach encourages the class to cheer for the actors.] ◆ Pull the rope! You're both pulling the same rope. Pull it! Get your back into it! Get your whole body into it! Pull! Come on! Focus on the rope as it exists in the space. The rope must be in the space, not in your head! Keep your eyes on the center of the rope! Stay up on your feet! Use your back! Pull the rope! Pull! There's only one rope and you're both pulling it. Focus on the one rope connecting you. Keep pulling! Pull with your legs! Pull that other player across the line! You're losing! Pull harder! You're winning! Pull harder! ◆ Cut.

FOLLOW-UP (as needed): Audience, did you see the rope? Did the actors employ only one space rope together or did they each pull a different rope? Did the rope shrink or stretch? ◆ Actors, did you bring the space rope into existence or were you pretending? A rope that's in the space cannot shrink or stretch. Did you pull as hard as you could? Were you able to pull as hard as you could and stay on the acting focus simultaneously?

SUMMARY:

It is difficult to use full body strength to pull the rope and, at the same time, create the rope in the space. However, it is necessary to do this. Maintaining the rope in the space keeps you focused on the connection between you, without which you would be in your heads pretending to pull the rope. Pretending creates isolation and separation from each other. When you were successful at maintaining the space rope, the audience actually saw the rope. More important than the theatricality of the audience seeing something that is invisible is the experiential agreement of the two actors on the space rope as a movable bridge connecting them. When characters are in conflict with each other, there is usually an issue that connects them and operates like a movable bridge.

A rope-pulling contest is the purest kind of conflict there is without violence: two opponents, each one wanting to pull the other over the line, using their full body strength to get what they want. One wins, one loses, or it's a stalemate without a victory for either opponent. There's nothing ambiguous, sophisticated, or clever about it.

Besides conflict in drama and comedy, there are various forms of conflict that are viewed by an audience, e.g., sporting events, trials, political contests. Theatrical conflict is most like a sporting event: (1) Actors are called players and share the thrill of participation with the audience, for their entertainment. (2) The event takes place during a specified and relatively short time span. (3) There is no intentional physical violence, nor do the stakes involved put the participants in any substantial jeopardy. (4) At any time in the contest, one of only three dynamics of conflict will apply: winning, losing, or drawing (stalemating).

From the audience's point of view, which is the most exciting dynamic? When one side does all the winning? When both sides are in stalemate? When one side wins for a while, then the other side catches up and pulls ahead, then the first side recovers and they stalemate for a while, then one side gains the lead for a while, and so on, back and forth, like a seesaw? Theatrically, of course, it is the last option. A certain amount of stalemating along the way heightens the tension and excitement. Theatrically speaking, the best contests, conflicts, even wars, alternate the three dynamics.

In a rope-pulling contest, the most consistent feature is, whatever the dynamic, the opponents are always pulling the rope as hard as they can. When you're winning, you pull as hard as you can to retain the advantage and capitalize on it. When you're losing, you pull as hard as you can to catch up. In a stalemate, you pull as hard as you can to hold your ground, avert loss, and gain advantage.

Athletes engage in conflict to win; that's the goal. Writers, directors, and actors create conflict for dramatic effect. The actor's job is to pull the rope as hard as he can and yet be open to losing or stalemating from time to time. If he is not open to these dynamics, he deprives the audience of the most exciting kind of conflict.

For now, it is important to note that a theatrical rope-pulling contest is the purest form of conflict. When playing it, you must pull as hard as you can at every moment while being open to exploring all three options: winning, losing, and stalemating.

TO THE COACH: A thorough reading and playing of the more sophisticated conflict exercises to come will reveal the importance of this exercise. ◆ It is important that the actors know the proper stance for playing a rope-pulling contest. The coach can lead the following—

Demonstration

Everyone, stand up and hold onto a space rope as if you are going to pull an opponent. Stand sideways. The rope should be parallel with your stomach. Hold the rope with one hand, out in front of you, bent at the elbow. The other hand holds the rope closer to you, and also bent at the elbow. Your feet are 1'–2' apart, with the foot closest to your opponent pointed almost directly at him, while the back foot is perpendicular to the rope. Bend your knees. Everyone, do that and feel how you are maximizing your body strength. Now, try it with your hands close to your body. It feels weaker. Try it with the rope perpendicular to your stomach. Extremely weak.

Sometimes actors play without respecting the space rope in their own hands. Their fists are clenched with no room for the rope. ◆ *Point out—* If you have a clenched fist, you can't possibly be on any space rope let alone the same one as your opponent.

PULL THE CONFLICT #1

Conflict is not about getting what you want. It's about the confrontation between the opposing characters. The next exercise introduces the basic tool for playing conflict and confrontation in scripts.

SETUP: 2 per improv. Same setup as disguised conflict influence. In huddles, select characters, activity, and location. The choice of a sporting event should be avoided as an activity choice. In addition, select a conflict issue for the characters (two opposing wants). Individually, the actors select private reasons for wanting what they want.

The actors are informed that there should be *distance* between their character, activity, and location choices and the choice of the conflict issue. Distance means that the conflict issue should not be revealed by or in any way related to the choices for activity and location so that when the audience receives the communication of the characters, activity and location, they will not automatically assume the nature of the conflict issue. Distance assists the actors to make sure that the scene is not about what it's about. In the same way that an unspoken conflict issue influences a scene or improv based on that conflict issue, working with unrelated activity and location choices spreads the conflict issue's influence further. This makes for a better and more challenging exercise.

CONFLICT ISSUE EXCEPTIONS

There are two kinds of conflict issues that should always be avoided. The first is called a *will-you-marry-me conflict*. This is any conflict issue where one of the opponents would be less inclined to resort to confrontation in order to get what he wants. If a woman doesn't want to marry a man who proposes, the man is unlikely to resort to confrontation to get her to change her mind. Conflict in scripts is always about confrontation.

The second type of conflict issue to be avoided is *unilateral conflict*. This is any conflict issue where the stakes for one of the opponents are minimal or nonexistent. If a character gets what he wants without the other character being deprived by giving in to him, then the choice of conflict issue is unilateral. Or, if one character can do whatever he wants without needing the other character's support, the conflict issue is unilateral. If one character simply wants the status quo and just doesn't want to do what the other character wants to do, for the status quo character there is nothing to pull on. For example: opponent A wants to join the other striking employees and opponent B doesn't want to strike. This unilateral conflict could become an *effective conflict issue* if opponent A wants to join the other striking employees but opponent B doesn't want *anyone* to strike.

RULES: While employing physical doing tools of Improvisation Technique for activity, location, relationships, and occupation, the actors must never mention or in any way reveal the conflict issue, including discussion of their private reasons. The actors employ the dynamics of pull the rope as their active doing acting focus.

ACTING FOCUS: Keep the conflict between you and pull on it! (Pull the rope!)

COACHING:

PULL-THE-ROPE PREPARATION FOR PULL THE CONFLICT

After the actors have set up their location, they go to an empty part of the stage and face each other as if they are about to play pull the rope. ◆ Pick up a space rope and tie the ends around your waists. Put your hands on the rope and get ready to pull on it. On your mark, get set. Really get ready to pull. Get that rope as taut as it can be. Now, keep that tension in the body and look down at the rope you feel in your own hands. Let your eyes travel across the rope to your opponent's hands. Bring your eyes back to the center of the rope. Focus on that rope in the space between you. It's what connects you. See it there between you. Feel its tautness between you. ◆ Now feel the rope transforming into the conflict issue. Substitute the conflict issue for the rope. The rope is the issue of the conflict. What you're now holding between you in the space is the issue of the conflict. Feel it in your hands. Feel it attached to your body and your opponent's body. You are pulling on it and you feel your opponent pulling on it. It is no longer the rope. It is the issue of the conflict.

Now, focusing on the issue of the conflict as the connecting tether between you, slowly remove your hands. Lower your hands from the rope, but feel the issue of the conflict taut and connecting the two of you in the space. In a moment, you will go to places, still feeling the issue of the conflict tied to your bodies between you. Keep this body feeling of tension wherever you are on the stage. If you like the rope image, remember that it is as long as it needs to be, wherever you are in the scene. You are always going to keep that rope taut, no matter where you are on the stage or in the scene. Keep the conflict issue unspoken and in the space between you. You are always attached to it and you're going to use your whole body and being to pull on it to win, just as in a rope-pulling contest. This is going to be war. You must pull to win. If you win, you get what you want. Every time you pull on the rope, you are pulling on the conflict, pulling to get what you want. Pull as hard as you can to pull the other person to what you want. Don't lose this body tension as you go to places.

Places. ◆ Look out at that rope again. Put your hands on it again. What you are holding is the issue of the conflict. The conflict is the rope. Your acting focus throughout the scene is to pull the rope. You've always got the taut rope of the conflict issue connecting you, no matter where you go in the scene. That doesn't mean you're actually doing a rope-pulling contest. From the audience's point of view, there's no rope, just two actors playing the scene. But your acting focus is pulling on that unspoken conflict issue to win. You are always attached to this issue, always pulling as hard as you can on it. Do whatever you have to do to win the war and pull your opponent over to your side, to what you want. ◆ Now, hold onto the rope with your body and *slowly remove your hands*. Keep this body tension. That's the body feeling you must have throughout the scene. Don't let go of it. ◆ Action.

PULL THE CONFLICT IMPROV

Coach (as needed): Keep the rope taut. Play to win. You're pulling on it to win the war. Avoid hanging out. **Play to win!** Win! **Pull the rope!** You've got to destroy the other person to win. You've got to pull them across the line. That takes strength. Use your whole body. **Pull the conflict!** Wherever you go, you carry a taut rope. **Keep the conflict taut!** There are more ways of pulling the rope than just verbal. Use your props to pull. Make contact with your location. Do your activity. Use everything at your command to pull the rope. The conflict is in the space between you all the time and you're pulling on it in a rope-pulling contest. Pull harder! You are losing. Pull back! Win! Don't let go of the rope. You have to pull the conflict to win. You want to win that war at all costs. You must get what you want! ✦ One minute to win the war. ✦ Cut.

FOLLOW-UP (as needed): Audience, characters? Activity? Location? **Was there conflict in the scene? Did the actors tell, reveal, or allude to the conflict issue?** Did you get the feeling the actors were pulling on the same conflict issue? Did they keep the conflict issue taut throughout the scene? **Was there tension and confrontation?** Did you get the feeling that the stakes of the conflict issue were low, medium, or high? **Were the actors cautious? Did they play to win or only to defend their positions?** Did anyone flash on what the conflict issue was? ✦ Actors, **what was the conflict issue? Did you feel you were on the same conflict issue? Did you pull to win or just to defend yourself? Did you pull as hard as you could? Did you feel you were on your acting focus? Did you feel the acting focus was leading you through the scene?** What were your personal reasons? ✦ Audience, did the stakes of each actor's behavior match the stakes of the conflict issue? ✦ Does pulling the conflict always have to be verbal? No.

SUMMARY:

Did you see a difference from the first round of disguised conflict influence, where there was no rope and the acting focus was to simply focus on the conflict without mentioning it, and this improv, where the focus was to make the conflict a rope that you're pulling on to win a rope-pulling contest?

Pull the conflict is more dynamic; there is more rhythm, more confrontation. You could see the opponents scoring on each other in individual battles that were a part of the whole war. There was less thinking, dead time, and intellectualizing. There was less dialogue. There was greater physical involvement in the conflict issue and the characters had a stronger sense of connection as they played off each other more. There was a stronger sense of strategy, the conflicts escalated, and the improvs were much more compelling to watch. In the disguised conflict influence round, without the rope, there was more isolation from each other. When the actors employed the rope-pulling, there was truly a dance in and out of one another's space.

CONFLICT VS. GETTING WHAT YOU WANT

When the actors were on the acting focus, all the improvisations resembled battles with the characters behaving belligerently toward each other. There were arguments and displays of anger and hostility. Is belligerence the best way to get what you want? Aren't there better and more effective ways to achieve your objective? Of course, but when a character is in a conflict situation, which is determined by the author, the scene is not about attaining the character's objective. It is about the clash between two (or more) characters' opposing objectives. If the script dictates a conflict scene, with both characters in absolute opposition, then you must play conflict, and not explore clever attempts at getting what the character wants, e.g., You catch more flies with honey than you do with vinegar. You cannot alter the dynamic of the scene because you think your character would be more successful at getting what he wants by avoiding conflict. *Conflict in scripts is always about confrontation.* Conflict is a form of war.

In some cases, actors will say they don't know what to do during the improv when their scene partner is coming at them with a lot of hostility. They *do* know. They know to stay on their acting focus of pulling the rope. They are simply not choosing to do it. The earlier pull-the-rope exercise with an actual space rope gives you a body experience of how hard you have to pull to win a conflict. When one actor only pulls hard enough to defend himself and keep from being pulled over the line but not hard enough to pull the other actor over the line, it is usually because the conflict issue is a unilateral conflict.

Pulling the conflict is more than just topping the opponent's lines with volume. There are different kinds of strength available to you, other ways of pulling, alternatives to brute force. These are improvisational discoveries that you will make while you stay on your acting focus. Keep pulling as hard as you can and you'll find them.

Conflict is a technical device employed by writers, directors, and actors. We are starting to learn the rules. You do not play conflict by pursuing an objective. While playing conflict, you may be pursuing an objective but this must occur within the dynamic of confrontation.

WILL-YOU-MARRY-ME EXCEPTION

It's because of this confrontational aspect that will-you-marry-me conflict issues are to be avoided. In a will-you-marry-me conflict, the parties are not equal. One party has power over the other party in the situation. The woman being proposed to has more power than the man doing the proposing has. If she says, "No," he can't assert power over her to get her to do what he wants. The only way he's going to get her to change her mind is by being sweet, nice, reasonable, logical, anything but confronting her with hostility. Other examples of this are wanting somebody to be a roommate or go on a date.

PRIVATE REASONS

When you're in a conflict scene, scripted or improvised, your pulling the conflict is more productive if you know why you want something. Why can't your reason be open, aboveboard, and shared with the audience? When improvising conflict with scripted lines, you are not going to add lines, sharing your reason. It will be a private choice. If the reason weren't private, you'd limit your reasons. When the reason is private, you can have the most selfish reason for what you want if it helps raise the stakes for you. The more selfish your reason is, the more likely it is to be private and the more likely it is to have higher stakes. Actors should stay very alert to not picking a private reason that turns the conflict issue into a conflict exception.

> **TO THE COACH:** If the actors forget that they must never physically contact another actor in anger, I wait until one actor does this and immediately coach "Cut." I remind them of it and tell them if it ever happens again, the scene or improv will be stopped on the spot. ◆ If the actors finish a conflict improv having experienced a great deal of anger during it, have them do a step-out prior to the follow-up. ◆ Each improv in the pull-the-conflict series (#1-#4) lasts about 5-8 minutes.

◆　◆　◆

CONFLICT SPACE EXERCISE #2 [4]

SETUP, RULES, and ACTING FOCUS: Same as conflict space exercise #1.

COACHING: Walk around the room. When I clap my hands, turn around and enter the space of the room and feel it with your whole body. [Clap] Move forward. Backward. Feel the space with your body. Move in any direction you wish. Move through the space and feel it. Now, let the space move through you, and feel that. Now feel the space and let it feel you at the same time. ◆ Locate any parts of your body where you feel dead. Take five big breaths and direct them to those body parts. As you walk, look out into the room and name, out loud, at least five different objects with their colors, e.g., "There's a blue chair." ◆ Continue walking quietly. Feel the space with your forehead. Now let the space feel your forehead. Feel the space with your forehead and let the space feel your forehead at the same time. Let your forehead be free of any judgments and censoring. ◆ Reach up into the space and form a ball of space. It should be the size of a basketball. Play with that ball. Focus on playing with a real space ball and not a pretend one. Always see the ball wherever it is, especially when the ball leaves your hands. Play with it any way you wish. Always see where the ball is, in your hands or moving through the space. ◆ *After 1m*— Hold onto the ball with both hands and feel it all over. Extend the ball between your hands, stretching, shaping, thinning it into a rope. Keeping this rope in the space, play with it any way you wish. Allow the rope its place in space. Focus on the rope as you jump with it. Full body energy! Keep the rope in the space and not in your head. It's really there. It's just made out of space. Respect it! ◆ *After 2–3m*— Throw your ropes back into the space of the room. Divide yourselves into two groups and the stage into two playing areas. Two actors in each group become rope turners on the same rope for the rest of the group. Take turns in each group, jumping rope. Take turns as rope turners. Everyone must get a chance to jump and also be a turner. One rope per group. All focus on that same rope in each group, keeping it in the space between you and not in your heads. If you want the rope turned faster or slower, communicate to the turners. You can change turners one or two at a time. Respect the space rope between you. ◆ Cut.

FOLLOW-UP (as needed): Did you all respect the space rope? Did one rope become two ropes? Did the rope stretch or shrink?

SUMMARY:

None.

PULL THE ROPE! #2 (EMPHASIS ON WIN/LOSE/DRAW)

SETUP: Same as Pull the rope! #1. For this round of Pull the rope! #2, they are to focus on being on the same space rope, pulling as hard as they can, and be open to exploring the three dynamics discussed after the first time they played Pull the rope! #1: winning, losing, and stalemating (draw).

RULES: Two actors holding the ends of a space rope pull the rope in order to pull the other actor over the center line between them.

ACTING FOCUS: Pulling on the same space rope between you and being open to winning, losing, or stalemating.

COACHING (as needed): Pick up the rope. Be on the same rope. Agree on its thickness. Get the rope taut. Look at the rope end in your hands. Let your eyes travel the length of the rope to your opponent's hands. Let your eyes travel back down the rope to the middle of the rope. That's where you have to focus. Get ready to pull the other actor over the line. ◆ On your mark, get set, pull! Pull with your whole body. Use your elbows. Use your knees. No pretending. The rope is really there. It's just made out of space. Get your legs into it! **Pull the rope! Pull!** ◆ [The coach encourages the class to cheer for the actors.] ◆ Pull the rope! **You're both pulling the same rope. Are you being outpulled? If you feel you are, show it! If you don't feel you are, show that! Do you feel you are winning? Show that!** There's only one rope! Be on it! **Avoid stretching it! Avoid shrinking it!** Pull it! Get your back into it! Get your whole body into it! Pull! Focus on the rope as it exists in the space. Are you losing? Show that! Now, fight back! You can still win! ◆ **If you are not losing, don't lose! If you are not winning, don't win!** ◆ The rope must be in the space and not in your head! Stay up on your feet! Use your back! Pull the rope! Pull! There's only one rope and you're both pulling it. Focus

416

on the one rope connecting you. It will tell you how you are doing! Keep pulling! Pull that other player across the line! You're winning! Show it! Pull harder! You're losing! Show it! Pull harder! ◆ Cut.

FOLLOW-UP (as needed): Audience, **did you see the rope? Did they employ only one space rope together** or did they each pull a different rope? **Did the rope shrink or stretch?** A rope that's in the space cannot shrink or stretch. The rope shrinks when someone chooses to lose before they are outpulled. ◆ Actors, **did you pull as hard as you could? Did you feel that you were losing and winning battles? Did you put that into the space?** ◆ Audience, **did you see wins, losses, and stalemates?** ◆ Individual actors, **were you open to winning, losing, and stalemating? Did you ever feel outpulled? Did you play that loss? Did you allow yourself to lose a battle during that time? Did you ever feel you were outpulling your opponent? Did you allow yourself to win a battle during that time?** Is it possible to be pulling the rope as hard as you can and still be open to losing a battle? Losing a battle doesn't mean losing the war. Were you truly open to the possibility that you could lose a battle? Were you truly open to the possibility that you could win a battle?

SUMMARY:

When the rope stretches beyond its initial length, one of the opponents is not open to losing a battle. When the rope shrinks, one opponent is not open to winning. *You must never choose to lose a battle if you don't feel you are being outpulled.* You are pretending to lose, and pretending is inauthentic and isolating. That is deadly in a conflict scene where you must be connected in the space with your opponent. Connecting in the space creates a mutual dance on the conflict, which heightens the audience's participation in the scene.

If you don't feel outpulled, you can't lose a battle. Some contests or conflicts just won't include your losing a battle. It's all right if that happens. The real question is *are you open to feeling outpulled.* You may have felt that you were and yet the rope stretched or the contest was one long stalemate. What to do? Consider that you may need to be more open to losing, which means more *willing to lose.* Raise the stakes of your openness and you can cross over to willingness. Being open to losing *leads* to being willing to lose.

There are three things to remember: (1) You are always pulling to win with maximum effort. (2) You are open to losing battles even when you are pulling at your hardest because it's possible your opponent is outpulling you. (3) While you're doing (1) and (2), you are always focused on respecting the same space rope as your partner.

PULL THE CONFLICT #2

SETUP: 4 per team. In huddles, select characters, activity, and location. The choice of a sporting event should be avoided. The actors divide into subteams of two each and select a conflict issue between them. Two characters want the same thing, which is in opposition to what the other two characters both want. Each individual actor selects a private reason for wanting what he wants. In addition, the actors are reminded that there should be distance between their choices of character, activity, and location and their choice of the conflict issue and that they are to avoid the two conflict issue exceptions, will-you-marry-me conflict and unilateral conflict. Unlike pull the conflict #1, in which the conflict issue is unspoken, these characters will speak of the conflict issue. However, the private reasons must never be spoken of.

RULES: While employing physical doing tools of Improvisation Technique for activity, location, relationships, and occupation, the actors employ the dynamics of pull the rope as their active doing acting focus and they include dialogue about the conflict issue. Although the conflict issue is not disguised, the actors must never mention or in any way reveal their private reasons. Whenever an actor feels he has lost a battle or been outpulled by the other subteam, he must mark it by playing the loss as a part of the whole character, activity, and location. An actor must not play a loss if he does not first feel he has been outpulled.

ACTING FOCUS: Keep the conflict between you and pull on it! (Pull the rope!) Mark any moments of being outpulled by playing the loss.

COACHING: *After the actors have set up their location—* **Preparation:** They go to an empty part of the stage and the two subteams face each other as if they are about to play pull the rope with two actors on each side of the rope. ◆ The two actors closest to the center, pick up a space rope, wrap the rope once around your waist, then pass it back to your subteammate behind you. Actors further from the center, tie the ends around your waists. All four of you put your hands on the rope and get ready to pull on it. On your mark, get set. Really get ready to pull. Get that rope as taut as it can be.

In this improv, you have a double acting focus: pull the conflict and play the loss. If you feel you have been outpulled, take that body feeling and transform it into some way of marking for yourself, your teammates, and the audience that a loss has occurred. If we were only playing pull the rope and not doing a conflict improv, when you are being pulled closer to the center line that would be playing a loss. Discover the acting equivalents of that within your improv. Do not play any losses you do not actually feel or experience or we will have the equivalent of a shrinking rope. The moment you feel outpulled, *take the time to play the loss*. **During the time you are playing the loss, do not be concerned with holding onto the conflict issue.** During that time, the rope-as-conflict issue will be slack and not taut. How long you take to play a loss or keep the rope slack is up to you. There may be little losses and there may be major losses. It depends on the extent of your feelings when you feel outpulled. When you have finished playing a loss, get back on the rope/conflict issue and commence the next battle by pulling as hard as you can.

On your mark, get set. Now, keep that tension in the body and look down at the tension you feel in your own hands. Let your eyes travel across the rope to your subteammate's hands, then let your eyes travel down the rope to your opponents' hands. Bring your eyes back to the center of the rope. Focus on that rope in the space between you. It's what connects you. See it there between you. Feel its tautness between you. ◆ Now feel the rope transforming into the conflict issue. Substitute the conflict issue for the rope. The rope is the issue of the conflict. What you're now holding between you in the space is the issue of the conflict. Feel it in your hands. Feel it attached to your body, your partner's body, and your opponents' bodies. You are pulling on it and you feel your opponents pulling on it. It is no longer the rope, it is the issue of the conflict.

Now, focusing on the conflict issue as the connecting tether between you, slowly remove your hands. Lower your hands from the rope, but feel the issue of the conflict taut and connecting the four of you in the space. In a moment, you will go to places, still feeling the issue of the conflict tied to your bodies between you. Keep this body feeling of tension wherever you are on the stage. If you like the rope image, remember that it is as long as it needs to be, wherever you are in the scene. You are always going to keep that rope taut, no matter where you are on the stage or in the scene. The only time it is not taut is when you or your subteammate is playing a loss. Keep the conflict issue in the space between you. **You may talk about it at will.** Make no attempts at disguising the conflict. You are always attached to it and you're going to use your whole body and being to pull on it to win, just as in a rope-pulling contest. This is going to be war. You must pull to win. If you win, you get what you want. Every time you pull on the rope, you are pulling on the conflict, pulling to get what you want. Pull as hard as you can to pull your opponents over the line. **Stay open and willing to play losses.** Don't lose this body tension as you go to places.

Places. ◆ Your acting focus is pulling on that conflict issue to win and playing any losses. You are always attached to this issue and always pulling as hard as you can on it to win. Be open and willing to play any losses. ◆ Action. ◆ **Coach (as needed):** [Same coaching as pull the conflict #1, *then*—] **NEW: Share the conflict issue with the audience. Work with your partner to pull the rope.** Pull in the same direction. You're in it together. Help your partner. Destroy the opposition. Pull together to win. ◆ **Active & still!** ◆ **Was that a loss for you? Stay open to playing any losses that you feel. Stay open to losing a battle.** When you feel the loss, play it. You have to slacken the rope to play a loss. Playing a loss is more than just not pulling back. **If you are feeling a loss, take the time to put it into the space. Show your teammate you are feeling a loss. Show the audience you have lost a battle. Let your opponents see that you have lost a battle.** Slacken the rope. **Be brave and play that loss.** You can come back later and win the war. ◆ *Use your activity, location, and objects to help you play the loss.* ◆ Heighten that feeling of playing the loss. Extend that feeling of loss. Show it to us. ◆ Your partner is playing a loss. Help her to play it. Participate in her loss. Help guide the audience to it. Pulling harder only camouflages your partner's loss. Help your partner show it to the audience. You can get back on the rope soon. It's not the end of the war. It's only a battle. ◆ Come back from that loss. The war isn't over. Get back on the rope! Keep it taut. Pull that conflict! Don't give up. Help your partner come back. Both of you, pull the conflict. Win the war! ◆ One minute to win the war. ◆ Cut.

FOLLOW-UP (as needed): Audience, characters? Activity? Location? Was there conflict in the scene? What was the conflict issue? Did the actors tell or reveal the personal reasons? Did they keep the conflict issue taut through-out the scene when there were no losses? **Did each actor hang on to his side of the issue?** Did they pull on the conflict? Was there tension and confrontation? Did you get the feeling that the stakes of the conflict issue were low, medium, or high? Were the actors cautious? Did they play to win or only to defend their positions? ◆ Does every pull of the rope have to be manifested through dialogue? No. ◆ **Were they on their acting focus?** ◆ Actors, do you agree? Did you pull as hard as you could? Did you allow the acting focus to lead you through the scene? ◆ Audience, **did you see any losses played? When? What caused that loss?** ◆ Actors, **did you play that loss?** What caused that loss? How did that make you feel? **What did you do about it?** Could you have done more to heighten the playing of that loss? Did you play any losses the audience hasn't men-tioned? ◆ *If anyone answers yes, ask*— When? How did you put that loss into the space for the audience to see? You may have felt outpulled but did you add anything to that feeling to turn it into a loss? Could you have enlarged that feeling even more? Could you have further extended it into the space by showing us the feeling through contacting or handling space objects? **Did you ever feel hurt or any other form of loss? What did you do about it?** ✦ Audience, did you see that? What about teammates participating in their partner's losses? Did you see that or did teammates camouflage those losses by ignoring them and simply staying with pulling the conflict? ✦ Actors, were you aware of your partner playing a loss? Could you have helped your partner play the losses more? ✦ If there were no losses played, hopefully it was because there were no losses felt. Did any of you play a loss you didn't first feel? Avoid doing that. Did any of you drop the conflict with your opponents and pull a conflict with your partner?

SUMMARY:

PLAYING THE LOSS

Being frustrated at not winning is not a loss. A loss is when you feel hurt, your heart aches or breaks, or you are stopped in your tracks by something the opponent does or says. For that moment, they have won. The length of the moment is determined by the intensity of the hurt or paralysis. Losses are not ambiguous. You will always know a loss by the authenticity of your feelings. If you have to think, "Is this a loss," it's not a loss. Your body always knows it's a loss because it feels it.

Your body will probably feel it before your head does. Stay alert so that you are aware of the feeling. Say to yourself the equivalent of, "Ouch! That hurt." Then *choose to play that*. Take advantage of that feeling and *explore, extend, or enlarge it*. Put it into the space. Make it stand out more. The feeling is in your heart, or gut, inside of you and not necessarily available to the audience to see. You want to take it out and put it into the space. How you do that is up to you, but you must do it. If you play the loss and the audience doesn't see it, you didn't play it big enough. Extend what you do. Use the location, activity, objects, your teammate, and most importantly, yourself.

We need to see the equivalent of the rope-puller being pulled closer to the center line. Combatants are pulling and we see that. Sometimes combatants are losing for select periods of time and we need to see that too.

A loss is not intellectual. You'll feel it. That's why we practice with space rope-pulling contests. Conflict is very physical and experiential. It's not a question of just topping another's lines. It's life or death. Anything goes to win this war. You'll feel it when the other person has outpulled you. When you do, you have two choices. Immediately pull back as hard as you can to regain the lost ground or play the loss until you get your bearings and then pull as hard as you can to regain your ground. Playing the loss is the equivalent of being inched up to the center line during a rope-pulling contest.

RECOVERING FROM THE LOSS

The opponent has won a battle, but the war isn't over until "Cut" is called. Play the loss until you choose to pull back harder to regain lost ground. You'll provide the audience with the most exciting kind of conflict. One team is winning; the other team catches up. The three dynamics, winning, losing, and stalemating, are in play. The war goes on. The outcome is no longer a sure thing. The audience is more involved than ever.

Although the conflict issue is open and discussed, it doesn't mean the private reasons should be mentioned. Talking about the private reasons creates playwriting, with all its attendant problems. It emphasizes being in the head, not in the body, and will not stretch the muscles needed for improvising with memorized dialogue.

> **TO THE COACH:** This lengthy follow-up should be employed for the first few improvs. For subsequent improvs, a brief follow-up based on the **essential questions** will suffice.
>
> Once in a while, an actor will stop pulling on the conflict issue because something his opponent said made sense to him. The state of conflict is a state of war and presumes that the opponents are past the point of sensible discussion. Feeling a loss involves feeling pain, not opening to reason. When George and Martha go at it in *Who's Afraid of Virginia Woolf?*, do they stop and listen to reason?

PULL THE CONFLICT #3 (DISGUISED & PLAY THE LOSS)

SETUP: 2 per improv. Same setup as pull the conflict #2 except there are only two opponents and the conflict issue is disguised.

RULES: While employing physical doing tools of Improvisation Technique for activity, location, relationships, and occupation, the actors must never mention or in any way reveal the conflict issue, including discussion of their private reasons. They employ the dynamics of pull the rope as their active doing acting focus. Whenever an actor feels he has lost a battle or been outpulled by his opponent, he must mark it by playing the loss as a part of the whole character, activity, and location. An actor must not play a loss if he does not first feel he has been outpulled.

ACTING FOCUS: Keep the conflict between you and pull on it! (Pull the rope!) Mark any moments of being outpulled by playing the loss.

COACHING (as needed): *After the actors have set up their location—* **Preparation:** They go to an empty part of the stage and face each other as if they are about to play pull the rope. ◆ Coach them through the pull-the-rope preparation for pull the conflict (p. 410). If by now the actors fully understand the preparation, *then it is sufficient to quickly coach*— Pick up the rope and square off for a game of pull the rope. Get ready to pull the rope. Keep the rope between you. On the mark, ready, get set! Keep that rope between you. Now, feel the rope transforming into the conflict issue. Substitute the conflict issue for the rope. The rope is the issue of the conflict. What you're now holding between you in the space is the issue of the conflict. That is what you are pulling on.

After the pull-the-rope preparation for pull the conflict, *continue the coaching as follows*— In this improv, you have a double acting focus: pull the conflict and play the loss. If you feel you have been outpulled in any way, take that body feeling and transform it into some way of marking for yourself, and the audience, that a loss has occurred. If we were only playing pull the rope and not doing a conflict improv, it would look like you were being pulled closer to the center line. You are to discover the acting equivalents of that within your improv. Do not play any losses you do not actually feel or experience, or we will have the equivalent of a shrinking rope. The moment you feel outpulled, take the time to play the loss. During the time you are playing the loss, do not be concerned with holding onto the conflict issue. During that time, the rope-as-conflict issue will be slack. How long you take to play a loss, or keep the rope slack, is up to you. There may be little losses and there may be major losses. It depends on the extent of your feelings when you feel outpulled. When you have finished playing a loss, get back on the rope/conflict issue, and commence the next battle by pulling as hard as you can.

Now, focusing on the conflict issue as the connecting tether between you, slowly remove your hands. Lower your hands from the rope, but feel the issue of the conflict taut and connecting the two of you in the space. In a moment, you will go to places, still feeling the issue of the conflict tied to your bodies between you. Keep this body feeling of tension wherever you are on the stage. Keep the conflict issue unspoken and in the space between you. You are always attached to it and you're going to use your whole body and being to pull on it to win, just as in a rope-pulling contest. This is going to be war. You must pull to win. If you win, you get what you want. Every time you pull on the rope, you are pulling on the conflict, pulling to get what you want. Pull as hard as you can to pull the other person over the line. Keep holding onto the rope with your body. Keep feeling the tension between you. Don't lose this body tension as you go to places.

Action. ◆ [Same coaching as pull the conflict #1, *then*—] **NEW:** Keep the conflict disguised. ◆ Was that a loss for you? If not, pull the rope! If it is a loss, play it! **Stay open to playing any losses that you feel.** Stay open to losing the battle. Slacken the rope to play a loss. When you play a loss, play it! Show the audience you are feeling a loss. Show the audience you have lost a battle. Let you opponent see you have lost a battle. Slacken the rope. Be brave and play that loss. **You can come back later and win the war.** Use your activity, location, and objects to help you play the loss. **Reach out and discover an object to help you play the loss. Heighten that feeling of playing the loss. Extend that feeling of loss into the object.** Show it to us. Help guide the audience to your loss. Pulling harder only camouflages your loss. Pull the rope or play the loss! Feeling the loss isn't playing the loss. Feeling the loss is the cue to playing the loss. You can get back on the rope soon. It's not the end of the war. It's only a battle. ◆ Come back from that loss. The war isn't over. **Get back on the rope!** Get back into battle! Keep it taut. Pull that conflict! Don't give up. Win the war! ◆ One minute to win the war. One minute to feel a loss and play it. ◆ Cut.

FOLLOW-UP (as needed): Audience, characters? Activity? Location? Was there conflict in the scene? **Did the actors tell or reveal the conflict issue?** Did you get the feeling the actors were pulling on the same conflict issue? Did they keep the conflict issue taut throughout the scene? Was there tension and confrontation? Did you get the feeling that the stakes of the conflict issue were low, medium, or high? Were the actors cautious? Did they play to win or only to defend their positions? **Were they on their acting focus? Did anyone flash on what the conflict issue was? What was it?** ◆ Actors, what was the conflict issue? Did you feel you were on the same conflict issue? Did you pull to win or just to defend yourself? Did you pull as hard as you could? Did you feel you were on your acting focus? **Did you feel you were letting the acting focus work for you?** What were your personal reasons? ◆ Audience, **did you see any losses played?** When? What caused that loss? ◆ Actors, is that correct? Did you play any losses the audience hasn't mentioned? Did you ever feel outpulled and you didn't add anything to that experience to turn it into a loss? **Did you ever feel hurt or any other form of loss? What did you do about it?** Audience, did you see that? ◆ If there were no losses played, hopefully it was because there were no losses felt. ◆ Actors, did any of you play a loss you didn't first feel? Avoid doing that.

SUMMARY:

DISGUISING VS. NOT DISGUISING THE CONFLICT ISSUE

Aside from the fact that this round was between individual opponents and the previous, between teams, this round of scenes was different in that the conflict issue was disguised (unspoken). What was the impact? Could you feel a difference in your acting? The group's answers are likely to include: (1) less yelling,

(2) more use of space objects, (3) greater concentration on the acting focus, (4) heightened conflict, (5) richer relationships between characters, (6) greater vulnerability in each character.

The conflict was more intense for you when it was disguised in the playing. When it wasn't disguised, some of you lost the intensity of your emotions because the conflict didn't get into the body. You were in the head coming up with arguments in support of your side of the conflict. Because the conflict issue wasn't disguised, the scene didn't build. Your improvs were limited to one issue repeated over and over again. When the conflict issue is in the text, open and undisguised, you are beating a dead horse.

When it was disguised, there was less unnecessary dialogue and playwriting. The conflict moved, and moved around the whole scene, showing up in a continuous stream of developing physical and verbal material. Allowing the acting focus to work for you meant that you traveled throughout the scene in ways that didn't occur when the conflict issue was spoken. In improvisations, a disguised conflict will always produce richer dialogue than an undisguised conflict. Keeping it disguised allows you to feel more comfortable when dealing with the conflict issue. Disguised conflict is to the conflict issue as nonsense language is to text. When you can't say the actual words, you must put whatever you wish to communicate into the body and into the space.

The disguised conflict improvs had more tension in the space between the opponents. Wherever you go on the stage, the conflict is in the space between you, where it should be. When you can talk about the conflict issue, the conflict is relegated to what you say and all the rest of the stage space becomes a safe area instead of an exciting, charged field of conflict landmines.

DISGUISED CONFLICT AND MEMORIZED TEXT

Employing disguised conflicts gives you flexibility with memorized text, allowing you to communicate the textual conflict in a far more spontaneous fashion. With a text conflict, the author has already selected the conflict issue. However, if you improvise while playing the scene, without, of course, changing any text, you may select any conflict issue you wish, *because you will keep it disguised.* You never mention your disguised conflict issue, which is the rule of disguised conflict, so you are free to make it your acting focus while saying the words of the textual conflict issue.

The other actor(s) in the scene doesn't have to know that you are doing this. He'll be in conflict with you because he's playing the conflict issue in the scene that was written. As far as he's concerned, you're playing the same issue, while in fact you are improvising on your disguised conflict. We'll elaborate on *pulling a disguised conflict* with memorized text when we discuss script applications of conflict improvisation.

PLAYING THE LOSS

Did you notice anything further about the impact of playing the loss in this round as compared to the previous times you played pull the conflict? The group's answers will include: (1) In this round, when someone was playing the loss, the other person didn't necessarily let up. (2) It heightened the other person's battle. (3) The rhythms of the scenes changed and there was more variety. (4) It was physicalized a lot more and that took us into an artistic, spontaneous, and dangerous area. (5) It was more compelling to watch as we wonder how they are going to get back into the battle. All of these are instances of spontaneous discovery.

A loss that is internal only and not physicalized in the external space has no significance for anyone else in the scene or the audience. Playing a loss is similar to an acting focus you learned earlier, interrupting the rhythm, where you spontaneously interrupted the rhythms of your activities. The spontaneity of that interruption is equivalent to the spontaneity of feeling a loss. With the rhythm interruption, you did something with it, perhaps improvising a physical reason for the interruption. With playing a loss, you spontaneously feel the loss, then do something with it

In an improv, you must not play a loss that you do not first feel. It is inauthentic because you didn't feel it. It is pretending because you're acting out on it. It creates the acting equivalent of a shrinking rope between the opponents in a rope-pulling contest. Instead of pulling the rope, you are pushing the rope, and that is the same as losing a battle that you didn't feel you'd lost. Feeling the loss is the only cue to playing the loss. If the cue is an authentic feeling, the response will be authentic as well.

TECHNIQUE

You are practicing an art form that deals directly with visible emotions. Your technique elicits your personal emotions and then provides channels for them in the service of your art. Venting your emotions without these channels is exhibitionism and bad art.

Good technique requires respecting the author's blueprint. You have to play what the author intended your character to play. You have to serve your part of the whole scene. If the author puts your character in conflict, it may be your job to get ugly. If you go against that, e.g., "That's too ugly for me," you go against the flow and intent of the script.

It's both challenging and demanding of your acting talents and technique (skills) to explore playing a loss. You get to take an authentic emotional feeling and improvise the enlarging and extending of that feeling during the loss into the playing of your part of the whole scene. When you feel the loss, take the time to feel it, recognize that you are feeling it, and then self-coach, "Show it! Share it!" Then respond to the self-coaching.

There will be times when you get off your acting focus, but you're still taking care of what you have to do in the scene. That's the definition of technique and the success of Improvisation Technique training. Your body experientially knows what to do even if you forget.

When you are accomplished at improvising conflict, you will be able to make any scene in any script a conflict scene. This comes in handy when the writing is bland and needs a little improvement through the actor's contribution, with the director's approval, of course. We are less concerned with your ability to improvise dialogue in front of an audience or camera than we are with your ability to use the Improvisation Technique tools for interpreting and playing memorized scenes spontaneously.

As in any improv, never think about moving the story along. Stay on your acting focus and the story will unfold. Pull on the disguised conflict issue and all the dialogue and acting will be infused with conflict. You needn't go out of your way to invent it.

Losses have nothing to do with you getting to the other actor (opponent) and everything to do with the other actor (opponent) getting to you. In the next class, we explore what to do when your opponent plays the loss and you win a battle.

> **TO THE COACH:** Should any conflict issue, character, activity, and/or location choices require that the conflict resolution be determined by a third party, the conflict will be watered down for the opponents. Examples: beauty contest (I want to win vs. I want to win); job competition (I want the job vs. I want the job). ◆ *If the coach sees an improv where this happens, he can point out—* When choosing a conflict issue for an improvisation in class or an improvisational acting focus to be used in supporting memorized text, choose one that actively involves you in determining whether you get what you want. Avoid a conflict issue that depends on somebody else's choosing the winner for you. Don't add a third party as the judge.

PULL THE CONFLICT #4 (DISGUISED & GO IN FOR THE KILL)

SETUP: Same as pull the conflict #3 (disguised & play the loss).

Introduction: What happens in a pull-the-rope contest when one person starts to outpull the other? The outpulled person is pulled toward the center line, which is the equivalent of playing a loss. What does the winning person do when the losing person is pulled forward? He takes advantage of the fact he is starting to win and pulls even harder to turn this battle's win into a total victory.

In the next round of improvs, you are to practice the various ways of playing losses when you feel them. In addition, whenever your opponent plays a loss, you must do what you would do in a pull-the-rope contest, play more aggressively and *go in for the kill.*

Most people in a real-life conflict situation let up on an opponent who is feeling a loss, especially if it is someone with whom they have a personal relationship. In real life, you are sensitive to the fact that you have hurt someone. You become sympathetic, supportive, apologetic, or, at the very least, you leave them alone to collect themselves.

Going in for the kill is not a real-life, but rather a *theatrical* response. Theatrical conflict has much more in common with sporting events than it has with real life. In theatrical conflict, if your opponent plays a loss, then you have to do what you'd do in a pull-the-rope contest or in any sporting event: you go in for the kill. You keep going in for the kill until you win or the one playing the loss picks himself up, gets back on the rope, and starts pulling again. Then you are back at the neutral place, stalemate, where anything can happen.

In this improv: (1) Practice playing losses when you authentically feel them. If you never authentically feel a loss, you are not empowered to play one. After you have played a loss, choose to get back on the rope again and pull the conflict. (2) If you see your opponent playing a loss, explore and practice going in for the kill. Going in for the kill is the acting equivalent of pulling even harder while your opponent is playing a loss.

RULES: Same as pull the conflict #3 (disguised & play the loss), *with this addition*— Whenever an actor wins a battle, outpulls his opponent, or sees his opponent playing a loss, he must play more aggressively, with more strength, and go in for the kill until his opponent concludes playing the loss in any fashion.

ACTING FOCUS: Keep the conflict between you and pull on it! (Pull the rope!) Mark any moments of being outpulled by playing the loss. Go in for the kill when an opponent plays a loss.

COACHING (as needed): [The first improv should be coached with the complete preparation. The **essential coachings** are for a brief preparation that may be used for second, third, or subsequent improvs.] ◆ **Preparation:** After the actors have set up their location, they go to an empty part of the stage and face each other as if they are about to play pull the rope. ◆ **Pick up a space rope, tie the ends around your waists, and square off for a game of pull the rope. Get the rope taut. Now, feel the rope transforming into the conflict issue.** Substitute the conflict issue for the rope. What you're now holding between you in the space is the issue of the conflict.

In this improv, you have a triple acting focus: pull the conflict, play the loss, and go in for the kill. If you feel your opponent is playing a

428

loss, be open to seeing it and willing to go in with strength and finish the war by destroying your opponent. If we were only playing pull the rope and not doing conflict improv, it would look like you were pulling your opponent closer to the center line. You are to discover the acting equivalents of that within your improv. The moment you feel you are winning, immediately go in for the kill. How long you continue to go in for a kill is determined by the length of time your opponent takes for playing the loss.

Now, focusing on the issue of the conflict as the connecting tether between you, **slowly remove your hands.** The issue of the conflict is what's taut and connecting the two of you in the space. In a moment, you will go to places, still feeling the issue of the conflict tied to your bodies between you. **Keep this body feeling of tension wherever you are on the stage.** Keep the conflict issue unspoken and in the space between you. You are always attached to it and you're going to use your whole body and being to pull on it to win, just as in a rope-pulling contest. This is going to be war. You must pull to win. If you win, you get what you want. Every time you pull on the rope, you are pulling on the conflict, pulling to get what you want. Pull as hard as you can to pull the other person over the line. Keep holding onto the rope with your body. Keep feeling the tension between you. **Don't lose this body tension as you go to places.** ◆

Keep this body feeling of tension wherever you are on the stage. ◆ Action. ◆ [Same coaching as pull the conflict #3 (disguised & play the loss).] ◆ **NEW:** *Is your opponent playing a loss?* Check out your opponent. **Don't miss an opportunity. Stay alert to your opponent. See the loss. Go in for the kill!** Play to win! No Mr. Nice Guy! Avoid backing off! **Kill him. Destroy him.** End this matter once and for all! Do what is necessary. You can change tactics, but don't let him off the hook. Intensify that kill! Enlarge that kill! Heighten the kill! **Keep killing!** Destroy your opponent! ◆ Come back from that loss. The war isn't over. Get back on the rope! Get yourself together and get back into battle! Keep it taut. Pull that conflict! Don't give up. Win the war! ◆ *Had enough of your loss?* Get back on the rope and pull! You don't have to take this. Pull back! You can still win! ◆ Avoid playwriting. Keep it here, don't make it up. [See "Summary" and "To the coach" regarding playwriting coaching.] ◆ One minute to win the war. One minute to feel a loss and play it. One minute to go in for a kill. ◆ Cut.

FOLLOW-UP (as needed): [The first improv should get the complete follow-up. For subsequent improvs, a **briefer follow-up** is sufficient.] ◆ Audience, characters? Activity? Location? Was there conflict in the scene? **Did the actors tell or reveal the disguised conflict issue?** Did you get the feeling that the actors were pulling on the same conflict issue? Did they keep the conflict issue taut throughout the scene? Was there tension and confrontation? Did you get the feeling that the stakes of the conflict issue were low, medium, or high? Were the actors cautious? Did they play to win or only to defend their positions? **Were they on their acting focus?** Did anyone flash on what the conflict issue was? What was it? ◆ Actors, what was the conflict issue? Did you feel you were on the same conflict issue? Did you pull to win or just to defend yourself? Did you pull as hard as you could? Did you feel you were on your acting focus? Did you feel you were letting the acting focus lead you through the scene? What were your personal reasons? ◆ Audience, **did you see any losses played? When?** What caused that loss? ◆ Actors, **is that correct?** [If the audience didn't see any losses] **Did you play any losses?** What caused it? How did that make you feel? **Did you ever feel hurt or any other form of loss? What did you do about it?** ◆ Audience, did you see that? **Did you see any other losses?** ◆ [If the answer is yes, repeat the previous questions regarding losses.] ◆ If there were no losses played, hopefully it was because there were no losses felt. ◆ Actors, did any of you play a loss you didn't first feel? Avoid doing that. ◆ Audience, **did you see the actors go in for kills? When?** Was it always a response to their opponent playing a loss? ◆ Actors, **is that correct? Were you going in for a kill there?** ◆ Audience, **did you see the actors miss or avoid going in for a kill when they had the opportunity?** ◆ Actors, **is that correct? Could you have been more open to seeing your opponent play that loss? Could you have been more willing to go in for that kill? Did you play any kills the audience hasn't mentioned? If so, could you have played that kill stronger?** If there are no losses, you can't go in for the kill. ◆ Audience, was there any playwriting? When? Always avoid playwriting.

SUMMARY:

REAL LIFE VS. ACTING

Personal behavior in a real-life conflict often contradicts the behavior of a character in a theatrical conflict. Most of us in a real-life conflict do not go in for the kill when our opponent is experiencing pain and suffering a loss. Instead, our sympathy is engaged and we let up on the pressure, even if temporarily. This is especially true when we have a personal relationship with our opponent. However, in a dramatic conflict, unless the script indicates otherwise, when your opponent plays a loss you must go in for the kill. This is an Improvisation Technique rule when playing conflict. Conflict is about confrontation.

In real life, when we feel a loss we sometimes behave aggressively. Anger is the Band-Aid we put over hurt. In theatrical conflict, however, aggressive behavior would cancel the effect of the dramatic loss. If you play your loss in anger, the audience will never see that a loss has occurred.

Another difference between real life and acting is that non-actors go through life with one mind; actors, with two. Your performance includes the mind of the character, but you always know that you are acting. That's your second mind. You have often experienced something in your life and said to yourself, "I must remember this experience for my acting." A non-actor has the experience without the acting comment. Your primary response to the experience is with your personal mind, the same as the non-actor's is. Your second mind, the actor's mind, supplies the acting comment.

Much of Improvisation Technique training is about staying alert to the actor's mind and using it to advantage, e.g., "Play this loss!" or "Go in for the kill!" Or, when you are in midperformance and spot that something is not working, allow your actor's mind to coach you, immediately, briefly, to get you back on track, e.g., "Get back on the rope!" Unlike being in the head, dwelling on negative, nonsupportive thoughts and attitudes, this is brief, supportive, and constructive. At times, it's to your advantage to go to your actor's mind in order to get organized, take charge, and get back on your acting focus.

SEEING AND PLAYING THE LOSS

Feeling hurt requires no acting. Playing the loss requires that you extend that authentic feeling out into the space where it can be seen, using your Improvisation Technique tools of physicalizing the emotion, emotional use of objects during activity doing or contacting the location, and so on.

When you feel a loss in a theatrical conflict, you will feel a specific and authentic emotion or attitude. In playing that loss, you have to fill or enlarge that moment, whatever its length, with those feelings that this particular loss created in you. You do this by thoroughly physicalizing the feelings in the body and/or channeling them into the handling of objects or location set pieces. Releasing the rope (conflict) and being silent does not fulfill playing a loss. It isn't big enough. As long as the feelings stay inside of you where they are felt but are not available for communication to your opponent and the audience, the loss dynamic will have been wasted because no one, opponent or audience, will have been aware that a loss occurred. And, your opponent won't know to go in for the kill—another dynamic lost.

In this training stage, perhaps you should look at it from a different angle. Every time you authentically feel a loss, you're given an opportunity to act your socks off. That's what playing the loss is. If you feel sad, betrayed, or confused, go with it! Most of you, at this point in the training, are underplaying the losses. You can afford to "chew scenery" at those moments. If it gets too big, the coach or director will let you know. He will pull you back. Since we are in workshop here, exploring our tools, see what happens when you chew scenery. Overplay the moment, boost the feeling, if that is what is necessary to get a sense of what playing the loss feels like. It's not that risky because you are boosting what is already an authentic initial feeling of loss. *Only enlarge and extend what you are authentically feeling.*

Since you are coming from an authentic feeling, your "chewing scenery," I predict, will simply come out as an appropriate playing of the loss. You will be acting. You will be heightening the feeling. That is what the coaching of playing a loss has been attempting to accomplish. Heighten or enlarge that feeling and share it for all to see. Trust your inner feelings. Recognize "Oh, I feel this hurt, sadness, confusion, betrayal, etc.," enlarge it, and extend it into the space around you, and it will be appropriate. With camera acting, it may be smaller, even as small as an eye flicker, depending on the size of the shot, but you will execute it better if you learn to heighten it here in the training.

SOPHISTICATED LOSS PLAYING

When you are adept at playing losses, doors open up. If you are in the mode of playing a loss and not frightened of enlarging or extending it, you have the opportunity to employ an emotion switch or an emotion arc, all from the starting point of the original authentic feeling. These tools can take you deeper and deeper into the loss. That's when you are on top of your game and playing at a level where you are a witness (the actor's mind) and can see what you are doing at all times. From that vantage point, you might coach yourself, "Look for an opportunity to switch," and go from your original and authentic feeling of, let's say, confusion to sadness. Take a risk. Be brave and reach out into the space. Take a shot at truly playing a loss. Use the objects to show us. It's not sufficient to simply stop pulling the rope (conflict).

GOING IN FOR THE KILL

The point of going in for the kill is to keep the opponent on the hook and to increase the pressure on him as if you are both building to a breaking point where the entire conflict (war) will be decided. Going in for the kill doesn't always have to be through brute strength or through extreme heightening of the voice. Sometimes what you say can be going in for the kill. How you do it is for you discover as you improvise it.

If you have a feeling that your going in for the kill is no more than treading water, change tactics. How can you hurt your opponent more? You can employ becoming more personal, or truth, strength, sarcasm, insult, volume, activity, location, and/or objects. For instance, the truth can raise the stakes of the kill. Calling attention to an actor's weight problem may be a devastating kill. If this happens to an overweight actor, you are actually giving that actor an opportunity to have a genuine, deep, authentic feeling of a loss, which he can then practice playing.

432

Whatever you choose to do, the guiding principle is that your choice must increase the pressure on your opponent. Avoid any tactic that lets him off the hook. For instance, an actor is going in for the kill and is improvising a riff: "It's all your fault. You're selfish, self-centered, narcissistic, and self-indulgent. You want it all. No one counts but you. You don't have a generous bone in your body." The whole riff is a list, but a list is only a list. There may be different complaints on a list, but they are all complaints. This particular list is the worst kind because the complaints are synonymous. A list provides nothing new to heighten the effect of the kill. You're treading water, letting up on the pressure, giving your opponent the chance to get back up again.

Effective kills take us to higher stakes with increasingly devastating ammunition. The ammunition of the kill should springboard from one attack to the next. It's like climbing an emotion arc. You never assume you have reached the top of your kill. There is always somewhere else to go to. If you stay on your acting focus of going in for the kill and keep heightening it, you will springboard to new and unknown levels and tactics for the kill. As you springboard, you keep your opponent reeling. You come up with one killer move after another, giving him no chance to recover. A list works against a pressure buildup because the opponent gets used to it, e.g., "These are all just complaints." Still, a list is better than nothing. It's better than walking away and giving your opponent an opportunity to recover fully, especially if you augment the list with force and pull harder.

In pulling the conflict, you are both attached to the rope (conflict), the basic principle being that *you only have to pull a little bit harder than your opponent and you will win the war.* In going in for the kill, you pull much, much harder because you have the opportunity to win the war at that moment. If there is no loss from your opponent, then simply pulling somewhat harder than your opponent will suffice. If both players are on this acting focus and doing this, the rope will always be taut, the conflict always dynamic.

If you have the slightest suspicion that your opponent is playing a loss, but you are not sure, go in for the kill! You have nothing to lose, even if he isn't playing a loss. The moment you see it, pounce and don't let up. Keep heightening your kill until the other actor picks himself up and pulls back.

Going in for a kill can highlight a loss that was played too small for the audience to see. When an actor spots his opponent playing a loss and goes in for the kill, the audience will see that a loss has occurred. (Not in these words, of course. They perceive the dynamics viscerally.) The other side of that coin is, if an actor is playing a loss and the second actor doesn't go in for the kill, then the first actor is given all the time in the world to dwell in his feelings of loss. The dynamics of effective conflict disappear. The scene treads water, going nowhere. The one playing the loss needs the pressure of the other going in for the kill in order to be pulled back to the conflict.

COMING BACK FROM A LOSS

How long do you play the loss? Until you don't feel it any more. You can't, and shouldn't, anticipate how long that will be. You don't know what the other actor will be doing when he goes in for the kill. What he does will spontaneously shorten or extend your loss time. When you don't feel like playing the loss any more, pull the conflict again.

Discovering the moment when you no longer feel like playing the loss and you return to pulling the conflict is influenced by two considerations: (1) Intuition. Listen to your body and its inner voice; it will tell you when enough is enough. (2) Help your fellow actor. If your opponent is going in for the kill, it takes a lot of energy. The more you play the loss, the more you push him to his limits. Too much of that can be overkill, treading water, and exhausting. Let him (the actor, not the character) get off the hook. Pull back, and balance the conflict again.

TWO LOSSES AT THE SAME TIME

What happens when both opponents play a loss simultaneously? The rope drops to the ground and there is no pulling on the conflict issue. There is no conflict in the scene during that beat. Unless a script indicates otherwise, this must be avoided. When it occurs, it is because the actors are not checking each other out. When you check each other out, the one who has the first loss will be seen by the other and the other will go in for the kill. Checking out is essential to playing conflict. There is no actual rope tied around your waist. The only way you can feel if the other is outpulling you or playing a loss is by seeing, hearing, and feeling it. Stay connected to your fellow actor at all times.

"PLAYWRITING" (LYING)

It is too easy to playwrite while improvising conflict. The actor makes up information to buttress his side of the conflict. Playwriting puts all the actors in their heads, not in the present moment, and must be avoided during conflict or any form of improvisation. Actors should be in the present moment, the realm of spontaneity, artistic danger, and challenge, where you never know what's going to happen next. Discovering dialogue should be similar to discovering objects that you didn't know were there until you reached out and discovered them. The theme in all of our work is getting you to an unknown area rather than someplace where you know all the answers. Acting in the unknown creates presence, which, with technique, is fundamental to an actor's success.

Expressing a fact that something happened, is happening off stage, or is going to happen, that no one else in the improv knows about, is playwriting. Playwriting is lying.

For instance, in the middle of an improv on disguised conflict between a mother and a daughter, Mom says, "Next week is your Uncle Sidney's birthday party. I

434

want you to be there." Where did Uncle Sidney come from all of a sudden, and he is having a birthday next week? The actor playing Mom made that up in her head. She is playwriting. A character may improvise an attitude or an opinion not previously known to the other characters and that is not playwriting. E.g., if Mom says, "You never go out with boys I like," it's fine, but if Mom adds, "I hated that musician you used to see," it is playwriting. It's a lie. The daughter knows nothing about any musician boyfriend in her past. Granted, characters sometimes lie. For instance, Mom's attitude statement, "You never go out with boys I like," can be taken as a lie by the daughter. She might retort, "That's not true. Why haven't you ever said that before?" But if she adds, "You liked Harold, the premed student," it's playwriting. Of course, if an actor playwrites, all other actors in the improv should *go with it!* Whatever the playwriting says happened, happened!

What is the significance of the actor lying? You cannot be authentic when you lie. Your performance becomes a lie. *Giving the lie to your own performance always starts in your head.* If you have a proclivity for playwriting or lying in improvisation, then you also have a proclivity for coming from your head in the creation of a scripted performance. The more you lie, the more you compromise your credibility, making it increasingly difficult for your peers, your audience, and you yourself to believe in your work. Eliminating lies from your improvs is a major step toward eliminating lies from your scripted performances.

Effective dialogue in improvisation is dialogue that arises from the playing between the actors and demands to be said, not what is initiated in your head.

If you have done the Improvisation Technique training up to this point, you do not have a playwriting problem, so don't revert to it now just because it might provide you with ammunition for pulling on the conflict.

> **TO THE COACH:** The first time playwriting occurs in an improv, deal with it in the follow-up, not through coaching. After that, when it occurs, coach the actors to avoid it.

◆   ◆   ◆

CONFLICT & EMOTIONS

Playing effective losses and kills draws upon the ability to heighten, enlarge, and extend the emotions on spontaneous cues. The cue for playing a loss is feeling it first. The cue for going in for a kill is when the opponent plays a loss. During Improvisation Technique training, some actors fail to employ their emotion acting focuses in support of playing their part of the conflict. This suggests that they are also neglecting to use their tools on the set or at auditions where their acting is not structured around improvisations. It is understandable because the training up to this point has included only three direct script application projects. These are: (1) first level script improvisations, chapter 6; (2) improving auditions, chapter 8; (3) the monologue exercise option at the end of chapter 9. (For the complete assignment and exercise, see chapter 13, p. 550.)

The following introduces no new acting focus skills but reminds the actors how much they are capable of doing if they apply the tools they have already experientially learned.

MISTREATMENT #1 [5]

SETUP: 4 per team. In huddles, select character, activity, and location, and a pattern of mistreatment between the characters: three of them will mistreat the fourth, one of them will mistreat the other three, or two of them will mistreat the other two. ◆ The actor or actors who will be mistreated exit the huddle, which continues with the mistreaters only. They decide on a reason (issue) for the mistreatment. They do not tell this to the actor(s) who will be mistreated. ◆ The actors should avoid choices where the mistreatment can be accomplished by simply ignoring the mistreated. There should be distance between the character, activity, and location choices and the mistreatment issue. In other words, don't create a situation that demands approval/disapproval issues, e.g., applying for a job. Appropriate examples: (1) Foreman mistreats three employees, work site, working; mistreatment issue, he thinks they are plotting to get him fired. (2) Three sisters mistreat a new sister-in-law, kitchen, preparing large family meal; mistreatment issue, they think she is vulgar and coarse. (3) A husband and wife mistreat another couple, community center, setting up a rummage sale; mistreatment issue, they think the other couple practice the wrong religion.

In the improvs, the actors focus on either mistreating or being mistreated depending on which roles they have agreed to in the huddles.

RULES: While employing physical doing tools of Improvisation Technique for activity, location, relationships, and occupation, the actors will focus on playing their part of the whole mistreatment setup. The mistreaters should avoid mentioning or revealing the issue, the reason for the mistreatment.

ACTING FOCUS:: Mistreaters: pursuing all forms of mistreatment. Mistreated: experiencing and playing all forms of being mistreated whenever it occurs.

COACHING (as needed): *After the location has been set up—* Places. ◆ Action. ◆ Explore your acting focus. Stay alert; know when something is happening; choose to do something with it. Recognize what is happening and go with it. **Vary your mistreatment. Play your part of the whole mistreatment**

scenario. ♦ Mistreaters, **discover other kinds of mistreatment.** Avoid ignoring the mistreated. How else can you mistreat them? ♦ Mistreated, **how do you feel about that? Show us.** Vary your responses to mistreatment. How else can you show us you feel mistreated? ♦ **Explore other ways of mistreating or being mistreated.** ♦ Avoid hanging out. Active & still. ♦ One minute. ♦ Cut.

FOLLOW-UP (as needed): Audience, character? Activity? Location? **Who were the mistreaters and the mistreated?** Did the actors play their parts of the mistreatment scenario? **Did the mistreaters vary their ways of mistreating? Did the mistreated vary their ways of experiencing mistreatment? Were they on their acting focus?** Did the mistreaters ever treat the mistreated well? If so, they were off their acting focus. ♦ Actors, **were you on your acting focus? Did you feel emotions during the improv? Did you ever feel like you were in conflict?** Are their other effective ways of mistreating or playing the manifestations of being the mistreated? ♦ Mistreaters, what was the mistreatment issue?

SUMMARY:

Organic acting is fundamental to any level of competence in acting, but the place for organic or spontaneous acting is in playing your game plan. In every scene that you play in a script, the author has structured the scene for something to happen for the characters. He may intend them to feel certain emotions, to reveal a particular attitude, to be in conflict, or to respond to a story point. The competent actor must play his interpretation and the director's interpretation of what the author intended. These choices become your game plan for the scene.

The Meisner technique knockoffs give the actor the impression that organic acting is everything. Nothing could be further from the truth. The scene can go out the window if you just play it organically. Your job is to play the game plan organically. Improvisation Technique is a total training in how to do that.

The structure of every improv we do includes an acting focus that you must stay on regardless of what happens during the improv. If you are improvising an emotion arc of happy, you have to stay in the happy family regardless of whether your scene partner is in the sad, anger, or fear families. Improvisationally, you must find the way to include their feelings and issues in what you are doing. It's difficult to play happy against somebody who's angry, but your job in the training is to do that. Staying on an acting focus is what prepares you for playing the game plan, organically and spontaneously.

Mistreatment is a brand new acting focus. Most if not all of you neglected to employ tools that you already possess to be on your focus effectively. You said in the follow-up that you felt some emotions and some conflict. *Did you employ any emotion or conflict tools in the service of playing either side of the mistreatment?* When you felt emotions, did you fully physicalize them, show them to us through your object handling, arc them, or switch them? When you felt yourself in the middle of a conflict, did you keep the rope taut, play the loss if you felt it, or go in for the kill when you saw the other play a loss?

If you felt a little bit of sadness when you felt mistreated, why didn't you heighten or enlarge it and escalate up a sad arc? You could have shown us that you were mistreated and it hurt you very much. If you got irritated during the improv, no matter which side of the mistreatment pattern you were on, why didn't you heighten the physicalization of that irritation and climb an anger arc, showing us that you were really upset? If you got into a little bit of a conflict, why didn't you grab the rope and start playing pull the conflict? Instead, most of you let these feelings go through you, feeling a little bit of this and a little bit of that. You had the opportunity to do more. Ask yourself if you took it or let it slide by. You now have an opportunity to work on this in your journal.

How often when you are working at an audition, rehearsal, or performance do you get a little pang of a feeling and do nothing to augment it? Why not use your tools to make something of that original authentic feeling? Is there a boundary around the organic moment that bars you from employing it or taking it somewhere?

When you are on the set, no one is ever going to ask you, "Please do an emotion arc or switch here." The director might tell you that in this scene you've got to play that you're pissed off at somebody or that you're totally upset when you discover the body. How do you employ your Improvisation Technique at those times? *By being alert to using all of your tools in the service of solving the problem.* In your workshop training, you have a coach who points you to a specific acting focus and coaches you to stay on it. You can't expect that to happen when you're working. Here, you are learning tools. On the set, you have to employ them.

Mistreatment is an acting focus designed to put you right into what it's like to be on a set, solving the problem of a scene. Here, you also have a large problem to solve. You've got to play that you are either mistreating or are feeling mistreated. If it were a scripted scene, that would be why the scene was written and what it's about. The game plan of the scene is for you to play your part of the mistreatment pattern. How about using your tools?

Examples of you already doing this on your own include full body whisper and active & still. Regardless of the acting focus in an improv, whenever one of you feels the urge to whisper, you automatically do it with a full body whisper. You learned it as a specific acting focus and you now employ it on your own without any coaching. If your improvs on any acting focus spontaneously break up into two simultaneous miniscenes, you automatically employ active & still.

Wake up. Not just for this mistreatment improv, but henceforth, stay alert to any moments in your acting when you can apply your improvisational tools. The training has prepared your bodies to execute the tools. All that remains is heightening your alertness so that you (1) choose to employ them and then (2) do so in the service of solving your part of the whole scene's purpose, e.g., the mistreatment game plan. When you are working, things will come up organically and spontaneously. The trick is what to do with them. If something, e.g., an emotion, conflict, attitude, whatever, chooses you, you must respond by choosing it. How? By employing the tools that relate specifically to emotion, conflict, or attitude and then exploiting it, taking advantage of it.

If it isn't second nature to use the tools in your class, it won't be second nature in your work. You now have a chance to practice in another round of mistreatment. Practicing this approach will eventually lead to automatic, spontaneous usage on the set.

> **TO THE COACH:** Should the mistreaters choose to play their mistreatment by continually ignoring the ones meant to be mistreated, *coach*— Avoid ignoring the mistreated. *In the follow-up, add*— Is mistreatment shown only by ignoring?
>
> Mistreatment #1 and mistreatment #2 should always be played back to back. Right after the coach communicates the information in the previous summary, the actors should play mistreatment #2. Avoid splitting up the two exercises over two classes.
>
> Avoid communicating "Conflict & Emotions," the introduction to mistreatment #1, prior to the improvs. It will dilute the intended dramatic effect of the summary. ◆ Each improv lasts about 6-10 minutes.

MISTREATMENT #2

SETUP: The same as mistreatment #1, with new teams and huddles. ◆ *After the huddles have been completed*— In the last round of mistreatment improvs, we saw that there were many opportunities to employ other acting focuses in the service of the general acting focus of mistreatment. In this round, do what you already know to do. You know how to employ physical doing, inner doing, character doing, emotion doing, and pull the conflict. Feel, see, and hear every opportunity to employ another acting focus and then do it! What's important here is that you have a primary acting focus that allows you to use other specific focuses in the service of the primary one.

RULES: The same as mistreatment #1.

ACTING FOCUS: Mistreaters: pursuing all forms of mistreatment. Mistreated: experiencing and playing all forms of being mistreated whenever it occurs. All: using your tools when the opportunities present themselves.

COACHING (as needed): After the team has set up its location, *coach*— Places. ♦ Whenever possible, use your other tools in the service of playing your game plan, that is, your part of the whole mistreatment. Whatever happens to you, take it and do something with it. Become the captain of your instrument. Practice what it's like to have not me, but *you* point you to the tool. ♦ Action. ♦ [Same coaching as mistreatment #1.] ♦ **NEW:** Participate in your partners' mistreatment. Stay on your side of the fence. You are either a mistreater or are mistreated. Show that to us. If you are meant to mistreat, mistreat! Avoid hanging out. ♦ **Stay alert to what you are feeling and be available to physicalize it more.** Physicalize that feeling thoroughly and stay available to arc it. Go into that new feeling. **Heighten it.** Enlarge it. Extend it. Climb its arc. Pour the emotion into the handling of the objects. **Physicalize that emotion with your whole body. Arc it.** Show us the heightened feeling through your handling of the objects. **Climb the arc! Switch it to another emotion. Switch it!** Show it to us through handling your objects. Practice. Stay available for an emotional switch. You are feeling something; switch it to something else. Employ the switch. Take it immediately in the opposite direction. Respond to the coaching! Take the opportunity to explore other emotions in the service of mistreatment. **Take the feeling you have now and switch it** so you can have the opportunity to explore a whole different emotion. Explore that feeling. Take a journey to something you haven't done yet. Enlarge that feeling. Physicalize it! **Show us that feeling by how you handle the objects.** ♦ **You're on the rope. Pull it!** Play to win! Play that loss. Go in for the kill! ♦ You are doing that in the service of playing your mistreatment, not instead of it. Stay focused on playing your part of the whole mistreatment. ♦ Contact the location. Do your activity. Do your part of the game plan. One minute for everyone to stay on the mistreatment focus. ♦ Cut.

FOLLOW-UP (as needed): Audience, character? Activity? Location? Who were the mistreaters and the mistreated? Did the actors play their parts of the mistreatment scenario? **Did the mistreaters vary their ways of mistreating? Did the mistreated vary their ways of experiencing mistreatment?** Is it necessary to be verbal when mistreating or being mistreated? Did actors ever play the wrong part of their game plan, with mistreated actors mistreating each other? **Were they on their acting focus?** Did the mistreaters ever treat the mistreated well? If so, they were off their acting focus. **Did you see the actors employing other acting focuses in the service of their primary acting focus?** Did you see actors employing other acting focuses and losing sight of either their part of the game plan or their part of the whole character, activity, and location, especially their professional relationships? **Which acting focuses did you see them employ?** ◆ Actors, **were you on your acting focus? Did you ever feel like you were in conflict? Did you play it?** Can playing the loss be an effective way to deal with being mistreated? Can pulling the rope and/or going in for the kill be an effective way of mistreating? **Did you feel emotions?** Were you aware of them at the time? **Did you employ any emotion focuses?** Are hurt and anger the only feelings generated from feeling mistreated? What other feelings did you have? **What other acting focuses did you knowingly employ?** Are there other effective ways of mistreating or playing the manifestations of being the mistreated?

SUMMARY:

How did you feel improvising this time compared to the first time? You felt a variety of emotions that you didn't feel in round one. That felt good to you.

In round one, as an actor you felt more of a victim depending on whatever happened to you. In round two, you had more power as an actor. You felt more in control. If something wasn't working, you weren't concerned and you tried something else. That felt good. You took more risks and that definitely felt good. You felt more connected to yourself, your improv mates, and the scene. You were more alert. Improvising was easier. The improv flew because your time on stage was more filled. You found yourselves capable of using various acting tools spontaneously. That felt more alive, freeing, and wonderful. In essence, you felt more confident and powerful.

How did the actors look in round two compared to round one? The actors were more in their bodies and much more present as they filled the space with more energy and presence. Everyone took more risks. The improvs were more colorful, significant, and compelling to watch.

BENEFITS

Obviously, what you are exercising in round two is the playing of your instrument. You have abilities, tools, skills, and control over them. The more you exercise that control, the more you use your instrument to its maximum potential. If you don't do this, you go through the scene being a victim to whatever feelings come up, for however long they last. That's what happens when you don't take the feeling and do something with it. The feeling chose you, but you did not then choose it.

In round two, you essentially said, "Okay, it chose me. I'll choose it back by doing something with it. I'll heighten it. I'll switch it to something else just for the surprise of it. I'll play this loss or kill." That is what it is to be a skilled actor. You can go into a situation and own it because you have the tools and you know what to do with them. Willingness to use the tools is as crucial to your own emerging technique as the tools themselves. If you stay alert and use all your tools all the time, eventually your body will learn to do it as an experiential habit. Then you will always have presence and power.

MORE HOW TO DO IT

In rehearsal or performance, if you notice a feeling coming up, do something with it. You can heighten the physicality or change the intensity of any feeling, you can stay alert to any possibility for switching it to another feeling, all in the service of your game plan—in this case, playing your part of the whole mistreatment—for a scene. Switching emotions is always theatrical: more visible, more fully shared with the audience, more compelling for them, more felt by you, and never left on the cutting room floor. If you notice an attitude emerging, heighten the attitude and hold (retain) it. If you find yourself in conflict, play the conflict dynamics as you have learned them.

This approach should be applied to all feelings and dynamics, not just the ones you think are appropriate to your part of the game plan. For instance, if you are playing the mistreated and you've just completed a pull-the-conflict segment, your character might feel good about the fact that you stood up for yourself. Heighten that feeling immediately. When the next segment of mistreatment comes at you, you'll have that much more dramatic a fall than you'd have had if you had plateaued in the initial good feeling.

LIMITED EMOTION REFERENCES

You can use any acting focus tool as long as you are on the primary acting focus and use it in the service of that focus or the game plan. Does that mean that every time you have a feeling you have to escalate it through the roof? No, but wouldn't you like to know that you have the power to do it if you want to? Then you can spontaneously be the judge of what's most effective. Your workshop is the place where you should always go toward over the top. What's the big deal if you do it here? There is no one to judge you. Take responsibility for exercising your chops and expanding your instrument.

THE POWER OF FOCUSING VS. PLAYING A HOOK

When you truly focus on something, there is such a heightened state of self-awareness that you can't help but be invited by yourself to use the tools. There is a difference between total focusing and merely grabbing a little hook that's only a version of your interpretation of the acting focus. Maybe you interpreted this acting focus as, "Well, let's just pick on so-and-so." It feels right because it feels like you're mistreating them, but you aren't *focusing* on mistreatment and all the places it can lead to. You found a little hook to go with instead of a massive, full body focus on mistreatment.

Never turn an acting focus or game plan into a hook or you deprive yourself of experiencing variations on the acting focus that are yet to be revealed to you.

You feel like you are on your acting focus or serving your part of the whole game plan because that hook is one appropriate response to the game plan. However, the acting focus is set up so that you will always find and reveal new solutions. When you reduce a focus to a hook, you deprive yourself of being in that magical place where all potential exists.

DON'T FEEL IT?

A major benefit of employing all your tools all of the time is that your threshold for an original feeling of an emotion is lowered. When we started playing pull-the-rope conflict, you learned that you only played a loss if you first felt it. That is still true. However, by heightening your alertness, which is what is required when employing all your tools, you will discover it is easier to feel the emotion sooner. The emotion doesn't have to fight its way up to your full, conscious feeling of it. You'll feel it at the pinprick stage. This is of major importance in script work when the scene demands that you play a loss and you don't necessarily feel it. By being more open, alert, and willing to use your tools, you can effectively do what is necessary. Take charge of what you have to do. Don't come up with reasons for not doing it.

PLAYING ANGER VS. BEING IN CONFLICT

Although conflict is always in the anger family, you can be angry without being in conflict. Conflict requires confrontation between two opposing wants. Anger does not. Anger can be played with an emotion acting focus and doesn't require win/loss dynamics.

JOURNAL WORK

For those of you who experience struggle with this, I urge you to start journal work around it. Write about your reluctance to escalate the feelings, switch out of playing the same emotion all the time, or go in for the kill. Start by writing about the experience of what happened. You will raise your self-awareness and maybe next time you won't lock yourself in. You will discover that it is not difficult to stay on an acting focus like this because you are employing all these tools.

Being the ones who were mistreated is the more expansive side to play on. You don't have to be mean. You get to scream, yell, or cry, whatever, while you are being beaten up. That is a fun place for an actor to be in a role, to play all those things and to get to use your tools. You just have to stay alert, know what is going on, and not drop the acting focus to hold onto what you do in your own personal life in those situations.

It is best to assume that you are more limited than any character you are ever going to play. If every time you are in a slight conflict or a situation where someone is mistreating you, you always punch back, that may be all right for you, but will you be cast as someone who has to be sad or vulnerable in those situations?

If you usually avoid sadness or vulnerability, will you be able to show it to us? Your training is your opportunity to do what you don't do in real life. Authors don't create original roles to match you. They create them to serve a purpose in a whole script. Certainly, being a human being with acting talent, training, and technique is sufficient for you to be able to play any part that is written. You don't have to be a con man to play Tartuffe.

Some people run from anger in real life. In the improv, whenever they were mistreated, they did nothing but cry and were full of self-pity. In my journal, I might write, "Isn't there any anger around that? I can play anger. When we did the emotion training, I physicalized anger. Why didn't I select that or go there spontaneously? Why didn't I ever switch into that?" And then I would keep writing. It is your choice. You have the power. Don't be a victim as an actor. These are improvs. The acting focus sets you free to do whatever you want. Why aren't you choosing to want to do more? Consider that for a journal entry: "Why don't I want to do more? Why don't I want to be a better actor?" Then write about it. When you are finished writing, start one more paragraph with the following question, "Where is the lie?" Read over everything you just wrote as you look for answers to that question. When you find lies, write about that.

> **TO THE COACH**: The coach might suggest that actors who have had minimal experience playing losses in the pull-the-conflict improvs choose to play the roles of the mistreated. The coach should stay alert to any team interpreting the mistreatment pattern of two characters mistreating the other two as two teams mistreating each other. That is not the same thing and should be avoided. ◆ Each improv lasts about 6-10 minutes.

◆ ◆ ◆

ADDITIONAL CONFLICT TOOLS

OBJECT STRUGGLE[6]

We return to an acting focus from the emotion chapter.

> **SETUP, RULES, ACTING FOCUS, and COACHING (as needed)**: The same as object struggle (p. 354).

> **FOLLOW-UP (as needed)**: Audience, **what was the struggle?** ◆ Actor, **did you stay on the acting focus, the struggle?** Did you focus on the struggle as it evolved or the struggle as you imagined it should look like? Did you respond to the coaching and heighten the physicalization of your feelings? Could you have gone further?

SUMMARY:

What body feeling did you experience, playing this? Tension, frustration, anger, heat, and tightness. What are other occasions when your body feels like this? Arguments, conflicts, road rage. Struggling with an object is a pure conflict between man and the object. There are two opposing wants: Man, *I want the ring to come off my finger*; Ring, *I don't want to come off your finger*. Woman, *I want to put the slacks on with a correct fit*; Slacks, *I don't want to fit you*. When you are in an effective conflict, your body has these same feelings. No effective conflict is without body tension. The only time a body may feel no tension is if it is not trying to win, e.g., playing a loss.

> **TO THE COACH:** Whether or not the actors have previously practiced object struggle during the emotion work in chapter 9, they should repeat it here because it is necessary experiential preparation for the next two acting focuses. ◆ Each improv lasts about 3-4 minutes.

◆　◆　◆

The following improvs explore new conflict tools and give the actor the opportunity to practice using other acting focuses in the service of the primary acting focus.

ACTIVITY & LOCATION STRUGGLE

SETUP: 2–4 per team. In huddles, select character, activity, and a location that comprises numerous set pieces and objects. The combined choices should not, in and of themselves, necessitate a struggle. They should be neutral so that any struggle arising out of the improv springs from the acting focus, not the given circumstances.

RULES: While employing physical doing tools of Improvisation Technique for activity, location, relationships, and occupation, the actors will focus on struggling with numerous set pieces and objects. Set pieces and objects must be made of space. No real props.

ACTING FOCUS: Struggling with the location and activity set pieces and objects.

COACHING (as needed): *After the location has been set up—* Places. ◆ Action. ◆ **Stay open to exploring the location** and struggling with many objects. **Respect the space objects.** Detail the objects. **Show, don't tell.** ◆ **Heighten the physicalization of the struggle.** Enlarge the struggle. ◆ **Extend what you are feeling into the objects. Heighten what you're feeling in the whole body. Stay focused on the struggle.** Feel the struggle throughout the whole body. Feel the struggle with your neck, your toes, your elbows. ✦ **Check each other out. Censor nothing.** ✦ Take what you are feeling and spread it throughout the whole body. Enlarge the struggle and heighten the feeling. Spread that feeling throughout the body and physicalize it more. Expand that physicalization throughout the whole body. Heighten that feeling as you heighten the struggle! Censor nothing! Keep heightening it! More physicalization! Go with it! ✦ **Stay on your acting focus** and feel it in your body. Focus on the struggle! Use your whole body in the struggle. ✦ **Help your fellow actors. Put the struggle between you. Keep the object between you.** Stay focused on the struggle while you **help each other enlarge the struggle.** ✦ Hinder your fellow actors. **Hinder each other.** Keep the object between you as you hinder each other. Stay focused on the struggle while you hinder each other. ✦ **Focus on the struggle.** Show us your problems; don't tell them to us. Struggle with everything. Stay open to helping each other. Hinder each other. ✦ One minute to discover a new struggle. ✦ Active & still. ✦ Cut.

FOLLOW-UP (as needed): Audience, character? Activity? Location? Did the actors experience struggles or just talk about them? Did they explore the objects they were struggling with? **Did they help each other? Did they hinder each other? Did they enlarge their struggles? Did they contact most of the location?** Did they keep the objects in the space? **Could you spot the actors using other acting focuses in the service of their primary acting focus? Were they still on their primary acting focus?** ✦ Actors, did you discover and experience your struggles or did you plan them ahead of time? **Were you on your acting focus? Did you employ other acting focuses in the service of your primary acting focus? What did you employ?**

SUMMARY:

Until now, the conflict we have been exploring with disguised conflict and pull the conflict pertains to conflict between humans, man vs. man. With location and activity struggle, we begin exploring the conflict between man and his environment. This is a major form of conflict in films and the basis for the entire genre of disaster movies, e.g., *Twister, Jurassic Park, Volcano,* and the last reel of *Titanic.*

The body feelings when struggling with the environment are those of any conflict: tension, frustration, and anger. In addition, high energy accompanies all the acting.

In almost all use of conflict between man and his environment, the high stakes and energy usually bring about additional conflict between characters. In every disaster movie, there are heroes and villains. When you help another actor, all the actors in the scene are working together in conflict against the environmental problem. When you hinder another character, the conflict extends out from the objects and environment and spreads to the characters. In that way, characters are in conflict with the environment and with each other as well, i.e., my way vs. your way.

Personal reasons are seldom necessary in a man vs. environment conflict, since it's always obviously about survival. Conflicts between heroes and villains are enhanced by personal reasons.

> **TO THE COACH**: The coach should stay alert to actors who are selective about which set pieces and objects they choose to struggle with. When they are on their acting focus, they will have to struggle with everything. There is a very high level of improvisational discovery about the nature of the individual struggle and their attempts at solutions. ◆ Each improv lasts about thirteen minutes.

RELATIONSHIP STRUGGLE

The actors have now experientially learned the meaning of struggling with an object and an environment. Now we bring this approach to relationships.

> **SETUP**: 2 per team. In huddles, select characters, activity, and location. The characters should have strong relationships between each other. A casual relationship, e.g., housewife and plumber, will lower the stakes of the improv, although this relationship would be appropriate if they were also lovers.

> **RULES**: While employing physical doing tools of Improvisation Technique for activity, location, relationships, and occupation, the actors will focus on struggling with their relationship.

> **ACTING FOCUS**: Struggling with the relationship.

> **COACHING (as needed)**: *After the location has been set up—* Places. ◆ You know how it feels to be on the acting focus of struggling with an object and struggling with the activity and the location. In this improv, there is no acting focus of struggling with objects and set pieces, though that is still available to you as an acting focus that may be employed in the service of your new primary acting focus, to struggle with your relationship. ◆ Action. ◆ Allow whatever wants to come up to come up. **Check each other out.** No urgency. ◆ **Don't fear the silences. Apply the acting focus to the silences: struggling with your relationship. Silence can be your friend as long as you stay on your acting focus during it.** ◆ **Stay on your acting focus. Let it work for you. Trust the acting focus. Experience the body feelings that accompany struggle.** It's the same

body feeling as struggling with your objects and location. **Let the acting focus solve your problems. Every moment, you are struggling with this relationship. Enlarge the struggle. Take what you get.** Be available for enlarging the struggle. Explore the struggle and heighten it. Keep the struggle in the space between you and explore it there. **Fill the silence with an acting focus.** Apply the focuses to the silences. Experience the struggle in your body just as you did when you experienced struggle with other things. Don't let yourself off the hook. Stay focused on your struggle. **Keep the struggle between you and explore it there.** ◆ Trust the silence and fill it with your acting focus. Trust the acting focus and let it work for you, especially in the silence. Let the acting focus solve your problems. ◆ Avoid hanging out. Use your location. Use your objects. ◆ **One minute to explore the struggle and enlarge it.** ◆ Cut.

FOLLOW-UP (as needed): Audience, character? Activity? Location? Did they struggle with their relationship? Did they heighten their struggle? Could they have used another acting focus in the service of heightening the struggle with their relationship? Such as? **Were they on their acting focus all the time?** When weren't they? Trying to resolve the struggle is off the acting focus. ◆ Actors, **what were some of the struggles in the relationship that you discovered? Did you discover or plan these struggles? Did you heighten your struggle? Did you use other acting focuses in the service of your struggle? Which ones? Were you on your acting focus? Did you allow the acting focus to lead you through the scene?**

SUMMARY:

What did you notice playing or watching the improvs? They were all compelling and especially noticeable for the tension present when there was no dialogue. Because the scenes were continuously tension-filled and occasionally built to explosive confrontation, they resembled strong conflict scenes despite the fact that there was no conflict issue selected. In addition, each improv scene had a great deal of physicality (doing activities and contacting the location) in which the actors used their props to heighten the tension. There were many alternating and compelling beats of dialogue and silence. During the dialogue, no one got bogged down with playwriting. During the silences, the tension never dropped. The actors let the silences work for them. Many times, the silences said much more than when the actors were arguing. The energy surrounding discoveries of new areas for struggle heightened everyone's presence. You could almost see the surprise on the actors' faces. By focusing on relationship struggle, you improvised, or created, as much conflict in every scene as if you had started with a preselected conflict issue.

448

Heightening the struggle is much stronger than simply having the struggle. It thrusts you into a spontaneous level of playing that's loaded with surprises and potential for you and the audience, making it compelling for them. It creates potential for something extraordinary to happen. Without heightening the struggle, the acting focus can too easily translate to, "I don't like you (the scene partner)." That's not it. You must renew the acting focus every second and always stay alert for opportunities to heighten it.

SILENCES

Silences in any scene will work very well for you and serve the purpose of the scene if you just fill them with your acting focus. When you do, you will find many opportunities to do something with the primary acting focus or another acting focus of your choice in the service of the primary one. You just have to choose to actualize those opportunities. If you will yourself to apply all the other acting focuses, there will come a time when your body will, on its own, martial the other acting focuses in the service of the purpose of the scene. That won't happen if you don't practice doing it now, in the training. Do it regularly in class and you will get to a point where your body does it for you. It is called kinesthetic memory. Your body will feel an emotion, a pang of it, even a twinge, and it will know to do something with it, enlarge it, switch it, or arc it. If there is a silence and nothing much is happening, your body will know to fill that with railroad tracks, relationship struggle, whatever. That is a big part of what this training is about, *but you have to choose to do it.* Until the body does it for the first time and then practices doing it more, kinesthetic memory cannot kick in. When it does, the body takes over.

STRUGGLE CREATES CONFLICT

What's the relationship of struggle to conflict? *Struggle creates conflict without a preselected conflict issue.* When you have struggle with an object, it creates conflict with the object. When you have struggle with all the objects in the location, it creates conflict between you and the environment. When you have struggle in a relationship, it emphasizes basic conflict in the relationship. From an actor's point of view, the acting focus of struggle can create conflict where none previously existed. In contrast, all of the conflict work we've done before this exercise was based on the assumption that the conflict (two opposing wants) was in the script or in the given circumstances of the improv. Even when we used a disguised conflict and never spoke of the two opposing wants, the conflict existed and drove the scene as the actors focused on it.

IMPROVING TEXT

With the relationship struggle acting focus, we acquire a tool that will serve us well when the writing in a scene falls short. Have you ever played a scene that seems to be about conflict but the conflict is not there? The author missed something. There are no two opposing wants. Sometimes the scene is exposition and lacks life. The scene is about what it's about, nothing more. There are many poorly written scenes. We get paid to make them work. An undisciplined, technique-free, or lazy actor may try to improve the scene by improvising dialogue, which is a good way to make a bad scene worse.

With Improvisation Technique, before you resort to improvising dialogue, you make every attempt to improve the scene through your acting. The sign of a good professional actor is the ability to deliver a scene as written and at the same time improve it through the acting, bringing a quality to it that heightens the dramatic life of the scene.

Struggle creates conflict, which infuses a scene with the kind of dramatic tension and confrontation that normally accompanies a conflict scene, without replacing the lines with improvised dialogue. It really doesn't matter what the dialogue or the text is saying because we're talking not about what you say but how you play it: the attitude, behavior, emotions, and spontaneity that accompany your improvisational acting approach.

The actor must stay alert to the purpose of the scene or his part of the whole scene prior to choosing the relationship struggle acting focus. Why turn a love scene that's written as a love scene into a conflict scene? If it's a love scene, then the purpose of the scene is clear and your job is to play it as a love scene. On the other hand, if the scene is about the couple in trouble, then relationship struggle is appropriate.

Pay particular attention to poorly written scenes in which you play a supporting role. You're a gas station attendant and you've got one scene with the star. He drives in and there is a six-line exchange: Regular or premium gas? Fill the tank? Where is the pay phone? Do you sell cigarettes? It's written just to show that the hero has to stop for gas for some reason. Maybe, shades of *The Godfather*, there's a gun hidden behind the toilet in the men's room. Not much happens in the scene for you. If you improvise your acting through the relationship struggle acting focus, you'll punch up the scene with more drama and you'll give the star more to play with. He'll have to react to your demeanor and he will get to do more than the simple scene intended. The director and the writer (if he's on the set) may like the added struggle and conflict in the relationship between the two characters, despite there not being any in the dialogue. Without changing any lines, your character puts more pressure on the star's character, providing more drama. You're doing more with the text than the text suggests. That's always your mission as an actor.

If the director doesn't want it, take it out. As always, you don't tell the director ahead of time what you are going to do. Reveal it through your acting in a rehearsal or a take. Your process is your own. Talking about it diminishes it. You certainly don't have to discuss your acting focus with your scene partner. It might be appropriate, prior to a rehearsal or a take, to alert them, "I am going to try something new here." If they are any kind of actor, with or without the heads up they are probably going to go with it.

This is not an extratheatrical acting focus and can therefore be used in front of a camera or an audience You can immediately punch up any scene, creating tension, pain, anger, fear, and confrontation. And in using other acting focuses in the service of the relationship struggle, you have all your emotion focuses to employ as well. You've also got conflict. Many times a scene breaks down into a beat of conflict with two opposing wants. Then you can employ pull the conflict in the service of your relationship struggle. You're not getting off relationship struggle in order to switch to pull the conflict. You do it organically because your body recognizes that now is the time to pull out that specialty tool in order for the primary tool to be more effective.

Play the relationship struggle acting focus, take what you get, and let the focus work for you. Something will happen. When it does, go to town with it.

> **TO THE COACH:** If the form of the struggle seems preplanned, the coach should inquire about their choices in the huddle. The actors may have added an adjective to their character choices, e.g., competitive friends, intrusive mother. It should be pointed out in the follow-up that the adjectives create preplanning. They play out their idea of how their characters should struggle instead of improvising and discovering various forms for their struggle. ◆ Each improv lasts about thirteen minutes.

◆　◆　◆

WHAT TO DO WITH? #I[7]

This improv introduces a new type of acting focus, which will be developed in subsequent improvs as a conflict tool.

> **SETUP:** 2–5 per team. In huddles, select characters, location, and any object that might be found in that location. Then, select an activity (must be a verb) for the team that must be centered on or around that object. Examples: family, garden, tree, planting it; lovers, living room, gift, wrapping it; morticians, mortuary, body, preparing it.
>
> During this improv, the activity is not approached in the usual manner of an ongoing activity with a beginning, middle, and end. Instead, while contacting the location and behaving according to their character choices, the actors should focus on continuously asking themselves one question, "What to do with [the object]?" They frequently ask this question to

themselves silently, in their minds. Every time they ask this question, there is an answer to it, which is the verb selected in the huddle, e.g., "Plant it," "Wrap it," "Prepare it." Despite the frequent repetition in their minds of the same question, the answer is always the same word. While the questions are private and silent, the answer is always shown to the audience.

RULES: While employing physical doing tools of Improvisation Technique for location, relationships, and occupation, the actors continuously ask themselves silently, "What to do with [the object]?" and always show the answer (the verb).

ACTING FOCUS: Continuous silent repetition of the question, "What to do with [the object]," and always showing the answer.

COACHING (as needed) After the location has been set up, do this warm-up. ◆ Walk around. Silently, begin asking yourself the question, "What to do with [the object]?" Ask without urgency. Each time you ask that question is the first time you ask it. Don't simply repeat it like an automaton. Get used to asking the question frequently and with significance, importance, and meaning. During the improv, the answer will always be the verb. Stay alert to the usual process of showing us your character and the location. ◆ Places. ◆ For the first half-minute of the improv, you may not contact the object. Instead, contact the location. ◆ Action. ◆ Contact the location set pieces. Take your time. Check out your fellow actors. **Ask that question. Discover your answer and show it to us. Mean it when you ask the question.** Stay on your acting focus. It's not rote. Every time you ask is the first time. **Interrupt what you are doing. Ask the question. Show us the answer.** Let the acting focus work for you. Share your voices. **Censor nothing.** Keep renewing the question and showing us the answer. **Go with it! Stay on your acting focus.** Trust it. It will work for you. Avoid urgency. Keep asking the question. **Show us the answer, don't tell us.** Keep asking the question and leave room for the answer, the verb. Show it to us. Show us the answer as you discover the answer. Look at the object. **Every time you ask the question, it is the first time you have ever asked it.** Ask that question anew. **Discover your answer for the first time.** Show it to us. It is an important question every time you ask it. Get back on your acting focus. Trust the acting focus and let it work for you. Check each other out. Go with it! Censor nothing. **Ask the question with significance and meaning, and then show us the answer.** Approach this not as an activity but as a response to a specific question that you keep having to ask yourself. Allow room for the question to exist. Ask the question. Discover your answer and show it to us. ◆ One minute to stay on your acting focus. ◆ Cut.

FOLLOW-UP (as needed): Audience, character and location? What was the object? What was the verb? ✦ Actors, is that correct? Did you feel you were on your acting focus? Did you feel you let your acting focus work for you? When you were on your acting focus, did it feel different from what you usually feel when you are on an acting focus? Is it a different feeling from what you normally feel when simply doing your activity? Return to your seats and consider how you let the acting focus work for you. ✦ [Go on to next team.]

SUMMARY:

What did you observe or consider about allowing the acting focus to work for you? If you were on your acting focus, it kept you out of your head and totally focused on what you were specifically doing. Every time you asked the question it put you back to solving the problem, eliminated distractions, and led you to discover new things to do. No matter what went on in the improv or your head, you were always brought back to the present moment in order to solve the problem of *what to do with?* Your relationships were more connected than usual and discoveries were easily made between you. It created a new and varied intensity to these relationships. You experienced a more heightened awareness of the environment and how to use it. The acting focus created a fresh, energetic source of inventiveness that was very freeing and gave you the feeling of just going with it.

If your improvising felt like the usual physical doing of character, activity, and location, you were probably not on your acting focus. Our normal continuous doing of an activity lacks the surprise of the ongoing stream of new discoveries that accompanies the continuous questioning. When you employ this acting focus, regardless of how much you have already done and how many ways you have used an object, *you keep coming up with something brand new to do*, which results in high energy, lots of involvement, excitement, and spontaneity. Each discovery was a springboard for further discovery. That is a very fun trip for you to be on, and it is exciting for the audience as well.

This is all done without any planning on your part. Being on this acting focus requires that you really pay attention to the question, as if it were always the first time you were asking it. Then, take the time to answer it and show us your answer simultaneously. If you simply ask the question by rote, like an endless tape, there is no time built in to answer the question. If you take the time and ask the question, even if it is the twenty-fifth time that you've asked it, you will propel yourself into the unknown where the answer will be discovered in a most spontaneous fashion.

Spontaneity always occurs in the present tense. When you continually ask yourself, "What to do with," you *extend the present tense* because no matter what you do to solve the problem, *you still have to deal with what else to do.* Just when you thought you had completed the present-tense moment, e.g., prepared the body, decorated the present, etc., you had to ask the question again. This acting focus pushes you through the self-imposed boundary of your mind telling you that there is nothing more to do. It forces you into the present tense and then extends it with your discovery of multiple solutions.

When you have an extended present tense, you must fill it with spontaneity, or the present-tense moment ends. It's your job to employ all the tools in your arsenal toward solving the problem, extending the present-tense moment, and filling it with spontaneity.

IN THE SERVICE OF

In all the improvs, everyone experienced authentic emotions. Most of you experienced excitement. There was also joy, fear, and anger.

The exercise also brought out a propensity in some actors to *negate*. When that happened, I coached, "Go with it." Negation, or the impulse to negate, is similar to conflict. So there were many moments, even though I coached you out of most of them, where you had the beginnings of conflict, e.g., "I want to mix beer with the embalming fluid" vs. "I don't want you to do that." In our way of working, you have seen the power of going with it. If you don't go with it and let the guy do it, you will miss the whole, exciting beat that can flow out of the beer being mixed with the embalming fluid, e.g., Everyone proceeds to intoxicate the dead body as a part of their preparing the body. On the other hand, if you didn't go with it, you had the potential for many conflicts.

Given that there were emotions arising and the beginnings of conflict, did you employ your emotion and conflict tools at those times *in the service of* the primary acting focus? What to do with? brings up experiences that create potential for employing other acting focuses in the service of the primary acting focus. Throughout most of these improvs, we had some very exciting present-tense moments. Think how much more exciting they might have been if you had exploited them by using your tools.

When you are working, it must be habit for you to be open to observing, feeling, and then exploiting little moments and feelings that just happen. These moments take you into the heart of the improvisational playing of the scene. The scope of the improvisational playing might be very small, and that is fine. Perhaps you are working on camera and you have a whole beat rehearsed. You are supposed to feel a specific emotion, and you do feel it. Everything is there, but just maybe during one take you get a glimmer of that feeling in a new way. You choose to exploit that by heightening it, even if the heightening only lasts for a second-and-a-half. When they cut the scene, that might be the second-and-a-half they use. You have to be open to using the tools.

ADDITIONAL BASIC TOOLS FOR SERVICE

There are other tools to help you go about solving the problem in new ways. Where are they? In the location. How many of you felt you took advantage of contacting the location in support of your primary acting focus? We know that it is necessary to contact the location in order to communicate what the location is. By going and making physical contact with the set pieces and the props in that location, the audience sees where it is. At the same time, What to do with? is an acting focus that keeps demanding more of you to solve the same simple problem, e.g., plant the seed, fix the car, or blow up the balloon. If you employ contacting the location in the service of the primary acting focus, you solve two for one. One, you communicate to the audience where you are, and two, you've got an entire playground of tools to help you prepare the body, decorate the present, or whatever your object/verb is. Contacting the set pieces and objects doesn't have to be planned ahead of time. It will come to you spontaneously, improvisationally, if your body is already in tune with going and making contacts with the objects in order to serve communicating the location. If you are not making contact with the location, your body has no awareness of those things, and you will have to rely on going up into your head and reminding yourself, "Where am I, and what's in here?" This is a mental process that's only going to distract from what's already a mental process, What to do with?

SHOW, DON'T TELL

Acting on your impulse is at the heart of spontaneous acting. When you have an impulse, go with it. When someone else goes with it, you go with it too. When you come up with a new way of dealing with the object/verb, don't stand around suggesting to others that you all do it. Instead of, "Hey, let's go get the big wrench and fix the car," you go get the big wrench and fix the car! The physical energy of your action invites your fellow actors to join the action. Telling your impulse invites the other actors to go into their heads to consider your suggestion or negate it.

JOURNAL

When we first emphasized employing other focuses in the service of the primary acting focus, we discussed the importance of journal work. Since then, you've had an opportunity to use your journals after learning mistreatment and struggle. How many of you made an entry in your class journal during that time? If you had written about it, you might have been more aware tonight of seizing your opportunities for employing other focuses in the service of the primary acting focus.

Let me explain why the journal does that. Besides everything you learn experientially, you sometimes get an idea or epiphany. You learn something intellectually about your own playing or about the technique. If you don't write it down, it makes no lasting impression upon you. Sometimes you are just taking care of your daily lives and you have a self-realization, "I could have handled that interview differently if I'd done this instead of that." Record the realization and you have a better chance of profiting by it.

If you find that you are still not taking advantage of employing other acting focuses in the service of the primary one or that you could do it to a greater degree, write about it in your journal. Give yourself some private time to review the issue. You will then have a commitment attached to it, because you took time apart to pick up your journal, think about the whole thing, and write about it. Make that higher commitment. You will heighten your self-awareness and with awareness comes potential for change.

> **TO THE COACH:** Keeping the actors from contacting the object for the first half-minute gives them time to adjust to this new type of acting focus. ◆ The coach's main function here is to keep the actors from approaching the object/verb activity in their usual do-an-activity way. To help them make the transition, *coach*— Interrupt what you are doing. Ask the question. Show us the answer. ◆ Plan the classes so that a round of improvs on the next acting focus, What to do with? #2, immediately follows this round of improvs and summary. ◆ Each improv lasts about 5–10 minutes.

WHAT TO DO WITH? #2

SETUP: The same as What to do with? #1, with new teams and huddles ◆ Stay very alert to employing other acting focuses in the service of the primary one. Use your tools to go further into spontaneity. The question is never fully answered because you have to ask and answer it again.

RULES: The same as What to do with? #1.

ACTING FOCUS: Continuous silent repetition of the question, "What to do with [the object]," and always showing the answer; using your tools when the opportunities present themselves.

COACHING (as needed): *After the location has been set up, coach*— Places. ◆ Stay alert to opportunities for employing all of your acting focuses in the service of the primary focus, What to do with [the object]? If you feel like you are in conflict, use your conflict tools. If you feel an emotion, use your emotion tools. Contact your location. For the first half-minute of the improv, you may not contact the object. Instead, contact the location. ◆ Action. ◆ [Same coaching as What to do with? #1.] ◆ **NEW:** Stay alert to your bodies. Use other tools when appropriate. Physicalize that feeling. Show us how you are feeling through the handling of the objects. **Stay on your primary acting focus.** Keep asking the question. Show us the answer. Don't avoid the acting focus. Stay on it. Keep asking the question. Take that feeling and

456

heighten it. **Heighten that feeling. Intensify it. Go with it!** Keep heightening the feeling. Keep asking the question. Show us the answer. Heighten that feeling. **Arc it! Switch it!** Stay alert. You can always switch it to another feeling. ◆ Keep asking the question. Stay on your acting focus. Every time you ask the question, it is the first time you have ever asked it. Trust the acting focus and let it work for you. Stay on the acting focus. Avoid urgency. Ask that question anew. Discover your answer and show it to us. It is an important question every time you ask it. Show us the answer, don't tell us. ◆ Conflict. Pull the rope. **Pull the rope.** Explore the conflict. Pull it. **Pull the conflict.** ◆ **Back on the focus.** Respect the focus. **Trust the focus and let it work for you.** Ask the question and show us the answer. ◆ Avoid muscling the other acting focuses. Use them when called for. Your body will know when that is. Trust your body. ◆ Use your other focuses in the service of the primary one, not instead of it. ◆ Physicalize that feeling. Extend that feeling into the objects. Show us how you feel. Heighten the intensity of it. Censor nothing. Now switch that emotion. Don't think about it, do it. Go with it! Physically switch it. Heighten that feeling. Approach this not as an ongoing activity but as a response to a specific question that you keep having to ask yourself. Bring that feeling to your asking the question. Allow room for the question to exist. Discover the answer. ◆ **Struggle with that relationship! Hinder each other!** Ask the question. Show us the answer as you discover it for the first time. ◆ **One minute to stay on your acting focus.** ◆ Cut.

FOLLOW-UP (as needed): Audience, character and location? What was the object? What was the verb? ◆ **Actors, is that correct? Did you feel you were on your acting focus? Did you feel you let your acting focus work for you?** ◆ **Audience, did the actors employ other focuses in the service of the primary one? Which ones did you see? Did another acting focus ever replace the primary one or was it always in the service of it?** ◆ **Actors, were you aware of employing other acting focuses? How did that make you feel? How did it feel to be on the primary acting focus and let it work for you?**

SUMMARY:

As an audience member, what did you see as the difference between the two rounds of improvs? All the improvisations in the second round were higher energy, full of life, more creative and entertaining. Everyone had a breakthrough due to the use of all the improvisation tools. Characters and relationships emerged more fully. The teams worked better together as everyone more fully played their part of the whole. Even the objects were more real in the space. You saw real improvising and acting with complete authenticity, spontaneity, and heightened presence. That is what acting should feel like. Every improv was a well-focused, exciting, and very theatrical scene.

What did it feel like while playing this round of scenes? The class will answer: (1) Exhilarating; (2) Higher sense of potential; (3) More discoveries; (4) Heightened energy, physical spontaneity, and playfulness; (5) Expanded emotional range; (6) Heightened reality; (7) More risk taking; (8) The focus was truly a springboard.

There were no limitations on what you could do. It was more like playing a game when you were a child, with that complete abandon and inventiveness. It was exciting for you to have an impulse and dive right in. You felt more of a connection with your fellow actors. Spontaneity was heightened. Your bodies responded to themselves without your head's assistance. You cut out the middle-man. Whatever fears you had were diminished; instead, you felt powerful.

When fear is present in your acting, you cannot be a successful actor. Fear comes from lack of confidence, the feeling of not knowing what you are doing. Here, your bodies totally felt like they knew what they were doing as they spontaneously employed the tools of the craft. That is what led you to the feeling of power. That is what it is all about. Power increases your confidence. Confidence feeds back into the playing. The actor has more to do, the character has more to do, and they feed each other. They play reflect the reflector with each other. That confidence/power relationship is a key factor in heightening your presence. When you feel confident and powerful, your body chemistry and aura change. You are bigger, bolder. You have presence.

BODY RECOGNITION AND RESPONSE

You now understand that as you are playing you don't have to consciously know, "Now I am going to heighten the emotion. Now I am going to pull the conflict." The body recognizes what is happening and does it for you. Now that you have body recognition and body response, you don't even have to know that you are doing it. Everyone's presence was heightened in this round. Presence comes from total body involvement in what you are doing. This particular acting focus heightened your openness, alertness, and choosing to commit to the acting focus and take what you get.

ACTING IS TECHNICAL DOING

These results came from your understanding experientially that your improvisational acting is technical. You were just following rules. All you did was play the primary acting focus of asking the question, "What to do with," and show us the answer. When you felt an emotion, you committed to physicalizing it and sometimes heightening it and switching it. You chose to get on a rope with another character and play pull the conflict. You chose to get off the rope when it was time to get off the rope. You chose to go to the location. You chose to do activities. Most importantly, you chose to go with it when not in conflict. Those are all technical tools that you've been learning, one rule at a time, since you started this training. Instead of trying to apply an elusive traditional approach, you are committing to the rules of Improvisation Technique. Self-empowerment and the ability to make choices come from trusting the rules, knowing that rules make things happen.

The more you respect, trust, and let the rules work for you, the more you will take the power and just do it. We are now using *rule* synonymously with *acting focus*. Each rule that you've learned, you first encountered in an exercise where it was introduced as an acting focus. That acting focus became a rule as you moved on to the next acting focus.

Stay alert to not muscling your tools and technique. If you don't first feel an emotion but start to arc it for the sake of arcing it, you are more concerned with displaying your technique than with solving the problem of the scene with the support of your technique. Don't impose strategies and tools before you receive the invitation to do so. Develop selectivity and balance. Your guideline is always being part of the whole, serving the purpose of the scene, not displaying your technique.

> **TO THE COACH:** Until the actors fully understand the acting focus, *keep coaching*— Every time you ask the question is the first time you ask the question. ◆ This keeps the repetition of the question from becoming rote. It forces the actor to keep renewing the acting focus. ◆ This is the acting focus to use when combining traditional technique preparation with Improvisation Technique execution. Reduce the problem of the beat to the question, What to do with [the object in the problem statement]? The verb answer is the same verb chosen as the action that will over-come the obstacle(s) and solve the problem. E.g., the problem is, *I want to make love to the woman.* The obstacle is, *She's married.* The action is, *To seduce.* This reduces to the question, *What to do with the woman?* The answer is, *Seduce.* ◆ Each improv lasts about 5-10 minutes.

◆   ◆   ◆

WHAT TO DO WITH THE CONFLICT?

SETUP: 2 per improv. In huddles, select characters, activity, and location. The choice of a sporting event should be avoided. In addition, they select a disguised conflict issue for the characters (two opposing wants). Individually, they select private reasons for wanting what they want. The actors are reminded that there should be distance between their character, activity, and location choices and the choice of the conflict issue. **Introduction:** The acting focus for this improv is the continuous repetition of the question,

"What to do with the conflict?" Unlike What to do with [the object], there is no preselected answer. Focus on asking the question in the same manner that you did with objects. Every time you ask, allow your body to provide the answer by responding to the question. The answer is a body feeling. The conflict issue was chosen in the huddles, and throughout the improv it is the two opposing wants that you refer to when you ask, "What to do with the conflict?" ◆ When you are in the audience, notice any similarities between improvs.

RULES: While employing physical doing tools of Improvisation Technique for activity, location, relationships, and occupation, the actors continuously ask themselves silently, "What to do with the conflict," and always show the answer. They must never mention or in any way reveal the conflict issue, including discussion of their private reasons.

ACTING FOCUS: Continuous repetition of the question, "What to do with the conflict," and always showing the answer.

COACHING (as needed): After the location has been set up, do this warm-up. ◆ **Walk around. Silently, begin asking yourself the question, "What to do with the conflict?" Experience how the question sounds. Each time you ask that question is the first time you ask it. Don't simply repeat it like an automaton. Get used to asking the question frequently and with significance, importance, and meaning. During the improv, the answer will always be revealed to you by your body. Stay alert to the usual process of showing us the character, activity, and location and employing other acting focuses in the service of the primary one.** ◆ **Places.** ◆ **Action.** ◆ **Stay on your acting focus in order to solve the problem.** Keep repeating the question to yourself. **Every time you ask the question is the first time. Ask the question and trust that the acting focus will take care of you.** Avoid hanging out. **Avoid urgency. Commit to the question. Let the acting focus help you solve the problem. Ask the question. Take the time after you ask the question to feel an answer. Let your body provide the answer.** Check each other out. Censor nothing. Make the question an obsession for you. The question is an obsession. **Take the time to show us the answer.** Trust the acting focus. Let it work for you. **Obsess on the acting focus.** Let the acting focus move you. No urgency, only true commitment to the question. ◆ Keep the conflict issue disguised. ◆ **One minute to ask the question again.** ◆ Cut.

FOLLOW-UP (as needed): Audience, character? Activity? Location? **Was there tension or conflict present?** ◆ **Actors, did you feel like you were on your acting focus? Did you let it work for you?** What was the conflict issue? Private reasons?

SUMMARY:

What did you notice that was consistent for all of the scenes?

SCENES & CHARACTERS

All the scenes were more interesting and compelling to watch than the average pull-the-conflict improvs. The character relationships were very well defined, and the individual characters appeared more actively engaged internally with layers and complexity. As an audience member, you were aware of needing to know more about these characters as they seemed to be hiding issues from each other.

TENSION / CONFLICT

There was a simmering tension in every scene without the heated arguments that we are used to seeing with pull the conflict. Also, there was less dialogue than in other conflict scenes and the beats without dialogue sustained the tension. The actors seemed more willing to take losses and play them. There were more beats of unequal conflict, creating a seesaw effect in the balance of power in any one beat. In some beats, one actor would be more powerful; in other beats, another actor would be more powerful; and in some beats, they would be equal. This maximized the dynamics of conflict, contributed to the tension of how the improv developed, and made it exciting to watch.

The actors found more varied ways of expressing the conflict, and the conflict spread out through more aspects of the scene. It wasn't limited to developing over one specific incident, but continually built while covering many different issues and behaviors. One of the ways it built was through its rhythm, which kept intensifying, like Ravel's "Bolero" or Jefferson Airplane's "White Rabbit," and that really heightened the tension and audience involvement. As in well-written scenes, all the improvs evolved from beat to beat with an artistic structure and were, at the same time, very real. Also, the conflict only came to a head at the end, as if the conflict were being arced by both actors in tandem.

Finally, all the scenes were loaded with interesting business coming from the actors' handling of the location set pieces and objects, and it all seemed to be a part of the whole conflict. This created a sophisticated and totally theatrical level of improvising. Everyone was using the whole instrument in the service of the acting focus. Seeing all these characteristics in play for every improv should be impressive to you.

Did you notice that the conflict in all of these scenes was low-key compared to the rounds of pull-the-conflict scenes? This acting focus brings less intensity to the conflict and is more subdued than pull the conflict. There are still moments of fury, but they are more like peak moments than sustained beats.

How did you feel playing this acting focus? It was easier for you to stay on this focus and not talk about the disguised conflict. It could stay in the back of your mind and color everything else you were doing without your talking about it. In fact, the impulse to speak at all was diminished.

You didn't exert as much effort trying to win. When you tried to win, your attempts were less brutal and more varied, with more colors, as you found new and spontaneous ways to solve the problem.

It was easy to trust the acting focus. You found that as an actor you had no tension improvising, while your character was loaded with tension. Whenever you asked the question, you felt it and things would just start to happen to you because you were so totally engrossed and connected.

It felt more honest to you. You felt the conflict issue getting rejuiced every time you asked the question. When you felt a loss, you were aware of how much more of a full body response you applied to the answer. You really felt losses, just as if there had been a preselected verb, defeated.

All your feelings were amped, and that raised the intensity with which you asked yourself the question. You kept feeling bursts of emotions and your body poured them into the physicalization of handling the objects.

You also felt more connected to your partner than in the other conflict focuses. You were very aware of the active & still moments. You found you went further with using other acting focuses in the service of the primary one, without having to think about it first. The acting focus was taking you to places you hadn't previously considered.

It was exciting for you to spontaneously discover one beat changing to another, and in tandem with your partner. You felt that you accomplished more with less effort. There was a sense that everything was happening to you and for you, and you could almost watch it all go on, like a movie. It was fun.

THE PROCESS

- As in What to do with [the object]? there is a continuous renewal of how many ways there are to deal with the conflict.

- When you ask the question, don't hang out in the head, searching for an answer. Let your body respond. It will reveal the answer. Just go with it.

- Obsessing on the acting focus immediately raises the stakes of the conflict issue and the intensity of the feelings.

- It is important that you really know and feel what the conflict issue is so that when you ask, "What to do with the conflict," you know and immediately relate to what you are asking about.

ON THE SET

What to do with the conflict? adds to our technical acting tools and controls. When you are on the set in a conflict scene, choose pull the conflict for your first improvisational acting focus. If the director tells you, "Way too big," change the acting focus for the next take and use What to do with the conflict? It's like dialing down the intensity control on your conflict amplifier. What to do with the conflict? guarantees a lower-level intensity than pull the conflict, which is always high intensity. Remember that even though you are saying memorized dialogue, you are essentially improvising the scene while they're shooting it.

You now have controls over how big a conflict will be for you. You had some controls with pull the conflict: you could raise or lower the stakes in your choice of a disguised conflict issue or a personal reason. Now you have added controls: you can change the acting focus. If you prefer What to do with the conflict? to pull the conflict, you might make it your first choice for the scene. After a take, if the director says, "Come on, this is an all-out brawl. You're playing it like it's Pinter," you know that your intensity level is way down. Change the acting focus, use pull the conflict, and blow them out of the water.

After we learn the next acting focus, you'll have a complete tool bag of conflict tools and we'll see how a conflict issue can determine which acting focus to employ first.

> **TO THE COACH:** If conflict is missing from the improv, *coach*— The question is what to do with the conflict, not what to do with what you want.
> ◆ Dealing with what you want is not the acting focus. What to do with the conflict? assumes that the conflict already exists and is unresolved. What to do with what you want? forces you to revert to a more traditional approach of playing an objective. When playing a scripted scene that has been analyzed as a conflict scene, pursuing an objective creates problems. There are too many ways of skirting the conflict. *Conflict scenes are about the confrontation over two opposing wants, and not about coming up with new approaches to getting what you want.* ◆ Each improv should last 5–8 minutes. Classes should be planned so that a round of improvs on the next acting focus immediately follows this round and summary.

WHAT TO DO WITH THE CONFLICT, WIN!

> **SETUP:** The same as What to do with the conflict? **Introduction:** The acting focus for this improv is the continuous repetition of the question, "What to do with the conflict?" This time, the question has a preselected answer and it is the same for every actor. The answer is, "Win!" Focus on asking the question in the same manner that you did with the previous improv. Every time you ask, allow your body to show us the preselected answer, "Win!" The conflict issue was chosen in the huddles, and throughout the improv it is the two opposing wants that you refer to when you ask, "What to do with the conflict?" Make no assumptions about how it is going to

play out. ◆ When you are in the audience watching, notice any similarities between improvs.

RULES: While employing physical doing tools of Improvisation Technique for activity, location, relationships, and occupation, the actors continuously ask themselves silently, "What to do with the conflict," and always show the answer, "Win!" They must never mention or in any way reveal the conflict issue, including discussion of their private reasons.

ACTING FOCUS: Continuous repetition of the question, "What to do with the conflict," and always showing the answer, "Win!"

COACHING (as needed): After the location has been set up, do this warm-up. ◆ **Walk around. Silently, begin asking yourself the question, "What to do with the conflict? Take the time to answer it, "Win!" During the improv, the answer will always be "Win!" Experience how the question and answer sounds.** Each time you ask that question is the first time you ask it. Don't simply repeat it like an automaton. Get used to asking the question frequently and with significance, importance, and meaning. During the improv, take the time to show us the answer. Stay alert to the usual process of showing us the character, activity, and location and employing other acting focuses in the service of the primary one. ◆ **Places.** ◆ **Action.** ◆ Ask the question. Let your body show us the answer: "Win!" Take the time to show us that answer. Check each other out. Censor nothing. Stay on your acting focus in order to solve the problem. Keep repeating the question to yourself. Every time you ask it, you answer it. The answer is always, "Win!" ◆ What to do with the conflict? Win! ◆ Every time you ask the question is the first time. **Ask the question and show us the answer.** Trust the acting focus. Let it work for you. Avoid hanging out. **Avoid urgency. Commit to the question. Commit to the answer.** Let the acting focus help you solve the problem. **Obsess on the question and the answer.** Make the question an obsession for you. Keep asking it. Keep showing us your answer. The answer to your question is also an obsession for you. Obsess on the acting focus. Let the acting focus move you. No urgency, only true commitment to the question and answer. Stay on your acting focus. Let it work for you. Ask and answer the question. ◆ One minute to obsess on the answer. Obsess on winning. Keep showing us the answer. ◆ Cut.

FOLLOW-UP (as needed): The same as What to do with the conflict?

SUMMARY:

What did you notice that was consistent about all the scenes, especially compared to the last round when you didn't have the preselected answer? The conflict was heightened and the scenes were all more aggressive. There were fewer losses since the opponents were stronger, more defensive, and quicker to take physical action. Characters were still multilayered and relationships, well defined. The activity doing was consistent, yet more varied and natural. The dialogue was even more spontaneous.

How did you feel playing this acting focus, especially compared to the last round? It was more challenging to keep the conflict issue unspoken. Your emotion levels were higher. You were more aggressive, yet there wasn't a great deal of screaming and yelling. You felt like you were on the edge of something dangerous. Your bodies had a feeling like you were walking a tightrope and could fall at any moment. You felt your relationships were even stronger than before with more connection between you because of a higher level of listening and communicating to each other. It was even more fun.

ON THE SET

This acting focus provides you with one more tool for intensity control in your conflict playing. The most intense conflict focus is pull the conflict, the second most intense is What to do with the conflict, win! The least intense is What to do with the conflict? For scenes where there is no conflict issue, use relationship struggle. Knowing this allows you to preselect your acting focus based on the degree of intensity that you feel is appropriate to the scene. All of them create improvisational acting that fulfills conflict playing. Knowing each will allow you to anticipate the level of intensity your improvising will take you to. You can do each acting focus for different takes or in response to a director's adjustments. If there is time for rehearsals, explore run-throughs of the conflict scene with a different acting focus for each rehearsal. Your body will tell you which is the best choice.

High-intensity conflict ➔ Pull the Conflict!

Medium-intensity conflict ➔ What to do with the conflict, win!

Low-intensity conflict ➔ What to do with the conflict?

No conflict issue ➔ Relationship Struggle

Conflict with the environment ➔ Activity & Location Struggle

TO THE COACH: The coach should always stay alert to follow-up answers that indicate the actor translated the acting focus into an issue of convincing his opponent to give him what he wants. That is not playing a conflict, but playing an objective in the manner of traditional acting. If this occurs, continue the follow-up with more questions to get the actor to reveal that that has happened and that he was not on his acting focus.

◆ Each improv should last 5–8 minutes.

WRITING CONFLICT EXERCISE

Part 1: Written Homework Assignment

I usually assign a writing, discussion, and acting exercise at this point in order to take advantage of all the conflict work that has just been completed and to start preparing the actors for the script analysis work coming up in chapter 12.

Based on your observing and playing a number of conflict improvisations up to this point, do some serious thinking about conflict. For the next class: (1) Everybody is to write a three-page conflict scene, according to the following rule. For the first two pages, the conflict issue must be disguised; on the third page, it must rise into the text. (2) Prepare to discuss what conflict does for a scene.

We are coming very quickly to script breakdown work. It requires a way of reading scripts that you have never done before, and learning the work can be frustrating in the beginning. However, if you do the writing assignments—this is the first of two before we get to script breakdowns—you will be taking care of yourselves by making that work more accessible. I believe you will be surprised to find that even if you have never written a scene, you will enjoy doing it. The assignment is a simple one: a three-page scene with only two characters.

The scenes must be typed, with copies for everyone in the class. Put your name on it. **In the next class, we will cast them and do cold readings.** It will be an excellent opportunity for you to become more knowledgeable about scripted conflict. Conflict is a common writer's device. You will need a clear understanding of it when we get to script breakdown. This assignment will give us an opportunity to find out what you do and don't know about conflict and to clear up any misunderstandings.

Some tips: You might start by picking the characters, activity, location, and a conflict issue, just as we do in the huddles for improvisations. Don't get caught up in major prose descriptions of anything, the characters, their business, or the setting. Write it however you want to write it, but it should essentially be what is happening with the characters through their dialogue and any minimal business you may want to include. You may have specific casting ideas, but have backups in mind because we can't guarantee you will get whomever you had in mind.

Part 2: In Class Performance

Casting Process

Casting can be messy if the coach doesn't control it. Make sure everyone is cast before anyone is cast in more than one scene. If there are too many actors and not enough scenes, the coach can restrict casting to those who accepted the assignment and wrote scenes. I suggest that no actors who are to be cast be permitted to read any scenes prior to casting assignments. You don't want the actors doing quick reads to see if the material is to their liking. That would make the process extremely unwieldy.

The following casting process will allow for casting twenty-five scenes in less than ten minutes. For each member of the class, place a number in a hat. After everyone who wrote a scene draws a number from the hat, the person with number one selects the two actors he wants for his scene. The person with number two selects next, choosing from those who have not yet been cast, and so on, until the person who drew the last number selects. When all the actors, according to appropriate gender, have been cast, and there are still scenes to be cast, actors may be cast in a second scene. No one may be cast in a third scene until all, within each gender, have been cast in a second scene.

Performance

After all the scenes have been cast, the order of presentation is according to the same numbers. The scripts for the first two scenes only are given to the coach and cast members. You don't want everyone missing the work of the class because they are busy, working privately on their scenes to come. As soon as a scene has performed, the script for that scene is handed out to everyone else in the class for the follow-up. At the same time, the writer gives the script for the following scene to the coach and cast and tells the actors which parts they are playing. Other than designating who plays what, there should be no prior discussion between the writer and the actors in a scene. The cast of the next scene looks over their scene during the follow-up discussion of the previous scene. Usually, the actors who are performing next have only had enough time to read the scene to themselves once or twice. They are not to read it together until the actual performance. We want this part of the exercise to be as much like a cold reading as possible.

The actors of the scene about to be performed are given a minute to set up a simple location with chairs and/or space set pieces. Just before they perform, the coach reads to the class from the script's opening description any necessary information about the setting. The coach should not read any information about the characters.

During the performance, there should be no coaching other than *(if necessary)*— Share your voices.

Everyone Reads the Scene

The writer hands out the scripts of the scene they have just watched to the rest of the class. The writer of the next scene gives his scripts to his cast. After everyone has had a few minutes to read the scene they have just watched, the follow-up begins. During it, the actors in the next scene are reading it to themselves and then setting up its location.

FOLLOW-UP (as needed): Is there a conflict issue (two opposing wants)? What is it? Does the conflict issue appear in the text? Does it first appear in the text on page 3? Exactly where, which line? Were the characters in conflict for the entire scene prior to that line? Were they in conflict for the remainder of the scene, after that line? When weren't they in conflict? Did the scene fulfill the assignment? Was the conflict, whether disguised or in the text, always played by the actors? If not, when wasn't it? Did the author provide any losses or kills for the characters? Did the actors play them?

TO THE COACH: The coach should use the follow-up to clarify some common misunderstandings about conflict:

Some actors believe that simply because a character is angry, or two characters are angry with each other, there is conflict. This is not so. Characters may be angry without any conflict issue being present, e.g., when the anger is about something that occurred in the past. True conflict occurs when there is something still to be resolved, i.e., two opposing wants. Without two opposing wants, there is no conflict. The anger is simply an emotional state provided by the writer for the character.

Even though there are two opposing wants, any variation on will-you-marry-me, e.g., "I want you to be my roommate (partner, friend, girlfriend, etc.)," is a conflict exception. If the writer of the scene chose one of these for his conflict issue, he did not fulfill the assignment because these issues are never played according to the dynamics of conflict. It is still valuable to the class to have this conflict exception reminder. Before the scenes are performed, the coach should review for himself all the conflict exceptions. It will help him handle any moments of discussion about the lack of conflict in the performance.

One character doesn't know that there is a conflict issue until it's brought into the text by the other character. This is usually shown when one character in the scene is angry without revealing a reason for his anger, while the other character reveals no tension or anger at all. The actor/character who is angry believes it's a disguised conflict and plays it accordingly, but there can be no disguised conflict unless both characters know it's an issue. When it's only an issue for one character, there is no opposing want. One character is pulling the rope; the other doesn't even know there *is* a rope. A scene like this does not fulfill the assignment because there is no conflict until it arrives in the text on page 3.

What Conflict Does for a Scene

After the last scene has been discussed, the actors are asked their thoughts on what conflict does for a scene.

Conflict enhances scenes with excitement, energy, momentum, mystery, mood, anticipation, and intensified feelings, all of which make the scenes compelling for an audience.

Conflict brings the characters together. The conflict issue is what brings the good guy and the bad guy together. It also can bring two good guys together, as in a tragedy. This coming together over an issue can help further define each character, giving them an opportunity to reveal more about themselves. We learn what each character wants, what they are willing to do to get it, and what provokes them further. The conflict issue provides stakes for the characters. A scene with something at stake is compelling.

Characters in conflict are continuously taking actions, which will require reactions later. The audience knows this and is compelled to watch. They want to know who is going to win and how. When one character does or says something in the service of getting what he wants, i.e., pulls the conflict, the audience is hooked into how the other character will react to that, i.e., pull the conflict back harder. This ongoing struggle between characters gives a scene its momentum. Often, the conflict is not resolved in the conflict scene, which leaves the conflict issue up in the air between the characters and propels the whole script forward with a definite rhythm and thrust, and the audience right along with it.

This momentum has a rhythm and pace seldom found in scenes without conflict, and it is created by the rules of playing conflict: keep the rope taut, play to win, be open to a loss, play any losses, go in for the kill if the other plays a loss. Pauses seldom occur in a high-intensity conflict. As the pace and rhythm quicken, the intensity of feelings for the characters heightens, creating emotion arcs, which in turn further heighten the momentum. Heightening an emotion and pulling the conflict harder follow one upon the other, like two vines making a rope.

The sum of all of these factors guarantees that every conflict scene will have a unified tone and, as conflict scenes are about characters in trouble and not about characters having a good time, *the tone of the scene will be dark.* The mood of the characters in a conflict scene is, at the very least, tense and runs the entire gamut of anger. Once in a while, the anger alternates with fear or sadness. Although a character may feel happy after winning a conflict, a character will not experience happiness or affection for the other character during a conflict scene. Characters may have a history of affection, happiness, and love, but during the conflict scene, those feelings are either not felt, or if they are, not revealed. A happy history will feed the intensity of the negative feelings because the characters have so much more invested in each other. If these are major characters, they will have other scenes in the script that will be about revealing their positive feelings. Scenes serve different purposes in scripts. Conflict scenes are about tension, confrontation, and anger. Conflict can reveal a character's dark side, which may have been hidden from the audience up to that point.

The bottom line is that writers put conflict in a scene in order to move the scene forward with a definite rhythm, intensity, and dark mood.

◆ ◆ ◆

SCRIPT APPLICATIONS OF CONFLICT IMPROVISATION

When you are applying these improvisational acting tools to scripts, the process will be easier for you than it was in any of the conflict improvisations because you won't have to deal with improvising the dialogue. With script work, all your dialogue is memorized and you are free to give full attention to the improvisational acting focus.

After determining that a scene is about conflict, you are ready to employ your conflict improvisation tools. First, define the conflict issue (the two opposing wants) in the scene and decide which side your character is on. Next, determine where the conflict issue begins. This will be the beginning of the conflict beat. Make sure that your choice of where it begins is where it actually begins. It may begin earlier as a disguised conflict and rise into the text at a later point. Sometimes it begins the moment it is first spoken of in the text. Decide where it begins and whether it begins in a disguised fashion. Then, decide whether to use the script's conflict issue or substitute your own disguised conflict issue.

Disguised Conflict

Substituting your own disguised conflict issue for the script's conflict issue is recommended for its improvisational potential. You get to improvise on the disguised conflict while saying the lines about the conflict in the text. This guarantees spontaneity in the playing and gives you access to all of the dynamics and adjustment controls you have learned in Improvisation Technique.

When a beat includes its own disguised conflict, it is not necessary to make this substitution. Not every conflict beat includes a disguised conflict section prior to the conflict issue appearing in the text, but when it does, substituting another conflict issue at the moment it rises into the text will serve you well. In such cases, at the beginning of the beat, employ the script's disguised conflict. When it rises into the text, you could employ pull the conflict with the same conflict issue even though it is no longer disguised or continue to employ a disguised conflict acting focus but change the conflict issue to another one. Then, while saying the text and its conflict issue, you are improvising on another disguised conflict issue. This is not as complicated as it sounds. It simply requires a conflict issue switch. You have been prepared for this abrupt switching through your practice with emotion switch. Only in the theater would you be performing the entire conflict scene without stopping, and that's after a period of rehearsal. In film, they break up the scene into shots and takes, and it's very easy to be prepared to switch.

For an even more effective approach, select a different disguised conflict issue for each and every take. Use any conflict issue other than the spoken one. This totally serves the script as you are playing pure conflict dynamics, and nobody knows you are doing this because you're still saying the conflict lines from the text. The audience is not aware of what you are doing technically. They think you are playing the spoken conflict issue.

Disguised conflict is more potent than dialogue about the conflict issue. Writers know this and in the better-written scripts, most of the conflict dialogue is based on a disguised conflict. The lesser the writing, the more the dialogue will be right on the issue of the conflict. Most conflict scenes are a hybrid of the two approaches. The writer will start a scene in disguised conflict, then more than halfway through the scene the disguised conflict rises into the text for the climax of the scene.

If you're doing a conflict scene in a script and you want to improvise it in front of the camera, give yourself a disguised conflict. In this way, you feed the conflict dialogue with the spontaneous emotions and dynamics of the disguised conflict. It marries with the text and gives you a very spontaneous reading. Disguised conflict creates multiple levels of conflict, which, paradoxically, give clarity to the one conflict issue of the scene. Whenever you can focus on something other than the text, do so. In fact, except for the extratheatrical vocal doing improvisations, Improvisation Technique requires that your acting focus be something other than what you are saying. To play the textual conflict issue is to play a limited version of your instrument. It becomes arguing and shouting from the neck up. With a disguised conflict issue, your entire body comes into play.

Character Conflict or Personal Conflict

Two kinds of disguised conflict are available for substitution. One is person-derived, the other, character-derived. A personal disguised conflict has nothing to do with the script and everything to do with the actors. It might be "I want your dressing room or trailer," "I want bigger billing than you," or "I want you fired." Sometimes a personal conflict issue is not the best choice because it has the potential to take you out of character, out of the scene. The actor pulling a conflict might pull it differently than his character pulling the conflict. However, the tool is available if you feel it's the best choice for a situation.

A character-derived conflict issue requires that it be your character, not you the actor, who wants something in opposition to the other character, and that something is usually related to their relationship and story in the script. You can use a conflict issue that occurs somewhere else in the script for your character or you can devise a conflict issue that might exist in a scene that wasn't written.

Personal Reasons

Anytime you're playing conflict in a scene, you would be remiss if you didn't choose a personal reason for wanting what your character wants or, if you are employing a personal conflict, for what you (the actor) want. After deciding what the two opposing wants are, say to yourself, "I want this because—," and finish the sentence. That automatically makes a stronger connection for you to the conflict issue and gives you a hook into where you are coming from. For a character-driven conflict issue, the personal reason should be anchored in the given circumstances of the script. In addition, the process of thinking about what the personal reason might be will open more doors for your understanding of the character and his position in the script.

In a scene with multiple characters on either side of the conflict, you have the option of selecting your own private reason or agreeing with the other actors on a group private reason. If you opt for the latter, you may add a secondary, individual private reason that the rest of the group knows nothing about. As long as you have a private reason, the option is yours, determined by what's effective for you.

Playing the Loss

What if the script indicates that you play a loss but during the performance, you don't genuinely feel it? During the training in doing conflict, you experientially learned to only play losses from authenticity, that is, when you actually felt a loss, so your whole attachment to playing a loss is grounded in authenticity. In a scripted conflict scene, whenever the script indicates that you play the loss at a particular moment, your execution of that loss will retain that attachment to authenticity and you will spontaneously discover a way of making the moment authentic for yourself.

Controls

Changing Conflict Issue

Through your tools, you can affect the spontaneity and intensity of your conflict playing. As long as you employ an improvisational conflict acting focus, your spontaneity is guaranteed. You can also affect the intensity of your conflict improvising by choosing disguised conflict issues with stakes that are higher or lower than those in the conflict issue in the script. Your first choices should parallel the intensity of the script's conflict issue. If the script's conflict issue is a life-and-death situation, you don't pick a disguised conflict issue with very low stakes, e.g., "I want to line dance" vs. "She wants to frug." If you, or the director, want your conflict intensity to be higher or of greater consequence, select a disguised conflict issue of greater importance than the one provided by the script.

472

You have to do eight takes of the scene? Change the disguised conflict issue for each take. It forces you to improvise each take. In each one you will still be saying the same text lines in a conflict manner. You are giving them conflict, but it's brand new every time. It's easy to adjust to the director's suggestions. If the director says to you, "No. That's way too angry and strong. Bring it down," you say, "Oh, okay, Mr. Director." To yourself you say, "I had better lower the stakes of my disguised conflict issue." If he says to you, "Gee, it's not sinister enough," you say, "Okay, Mr. Director." To yourself you say, "I had better choose another conflict issue. Maybe 'I want to flay your skin' will be sinister enough."

Changing Personal Reason

Another intensity control you have available to you is the personal reason. If for any reason you want to retain the same conflict issue for each take, then change your personal reason for what you want. The choice of a different personal reason for each take will guarantee that each take is brand new and spontaneous. You can also affect the intensity of each take through raising or lowering the stakes of your personal reason.

Changing Acting Focus

You can also guarantee spontaneity and exercise intensity control through your choice of the conflict acting focus. The most intense form of conflict improvisation will be provided with pull the conflict, either the disguised or spoken conflict issue versions. One notch lower in intensity will be What to do with the conflict—win! Still lower intensity is provided with What to do with the conflict? The least intense conflict acting focus, so much so that it will not provoke the dynamics of conflict (and should therefore seldom be used), is the basic disguised conflict with no emphasis on pulling the conflict.

Preparation

When you are preparing your part, you make a choice, evaluating what the script requires. If you decide, "This is a real slam-bang conflict. These people are really going at each other. It's George-and-Martha time," then the acting focus would be pull the conflict. Another scene might require a simpler tension, foreboding, and not raised voices or fury. Then the acting focus might be What to do with the conflict?

It's a good idea to arrive on the set with six or seven different conflict choices (acting focuses, disguised conflict issues, private reasons) for six or seven takes of the same scene. Have them written in your script and keep the script with you, just off camera. Prior to the next take, step over to your script and your alternative choices are right there for you. Change the acting focus, conflict issue, or personal reason for each take. From the director's point of view, each take will appear to be adjusted to his previous suggestion and at the same time, totally spontaneous.

CONFLICT

Working with the Other Actor

In an ideal production situation, there will be discussion and rehearsal time. During that period, the conflict scene should be identified to the extent of specifying the two opposing wants. Discussion about personal reasons is also valuable. The actor using Improvisation Technique should withhold mention of his acting focus choices. That's a personal process and it's nobody's business but his. Of course, if he knows that the other actor in the scene also uses Improvisation Technique, then discussion between them about acting focus choices is valuable. When two actors are pulling the conflict and employing the rules of the dynamics while the camera is running, it's very exciting.

In many professional situations, there will be no discussion, minimal scene rehearsal, and minimal knowledge of the other actor and his technique. On those occasions, you can still do your work without discussing anything with the other actor. If the scene is written as conflict, he will play his side of the written conflict. If you are using disguised conflict, just assume that his conflict playing is based on the same disguised conflict issue you are employing, even though it isn't. In a worst-case scenario where there isn't even discussion about what the conflict issue is, your tools will work for you. Most professionals won't play a conflict scene inappropriately, turning it into a pastoral, sunshine-and-happiness love scene. Your tools are about spontaneity, level of intensity, and full body use of your instrument. That's what you bring to the conflict. The conflict issue in the scene provides that the other actor will play in such a way that you can employ your acting focus and work together. Commit to playing your side of your chosen conflict issue. The other actor will be there for you. If he can't match you, that's his and the director's problem. Never work beneath your potential to meet a lesser actor's abilities. Sometimes integrating the other actor's problem into your acting focus allows you to heighten your own potential.

The more that you are on your acting focus, the more your increased spontaneity and presence will influence the other actor's playing, as if you were pulling him onto your acting focus without his even knowing it. This will be especially true if the other actor has any proclivity at all for playing in the moment.

Watching Films, TV, & Plays

When you watch a film, TV show, or play, notice the conflict scenes. After the work in this chapter, you will spot them easily. First notice how most of the scenes are played as if the actors are playing pull the conflict. Next, observe the rhythm. Conflict scenes demand a particular rhythm. Finally, determine what the two opposing wants are.

Conflict is one side of the coin. *Agreement* is the other. Where conflict is about confrontation and tension, agreement is about playing together, happiness, and going with it. A primary tool of improvisational theater, agreement has a smaller but very specific role in script acting.

REFLECT THE REFLECTOR[1]

We approach agreement by repeating an exercise from chapter 4, "Inner Doing."

SETUP, RULES, and ACTING FOCUS: The same as reflect the reflector, part 1 (p. 154).

COACHING (as needed): The same as reflect the reflector, part 1, with the following added just before "Cut." ◆ **NEW:** Without any hesitation, start walking around the room. Reflect other reflectors. Each of you is reflecting someone else. Walk around the room and reflect any other actors. There's no wrong way to do this as long as you're focusing on reflecting another actor. No one is initiating. Keep walking. It's your choice whom to reflect. Reflect anyone you want. You choose which actor to reflect. You don't have to let them know. They could be across the room. Frequently change the person you are reflecting. Stay actively on the acting focus of reflecting. Reflect everything that you see, nothing that you think you see. You are walking around and on your own, you are selecting whom to reflect. ◆ Cut.

FOLLOW-UP (as needed): When you were doing reflect the reflector, were you truly reflecting or were you sometimes initiating?

SUMMARY:

When doing reflect the reflector, take responsibility for not initiating movement and only reflect what you see your partner doing. Make no assumptions about where the movement may or may not lead. Commit to reflecting whatever you see every moment. Renew your reflection every moment instead of assuming that nothing will change since no one may initiate. This assumption may or may not be true.

SELECT & REFLECT

We now apply the reflect-the-reflector experience to an improvisation.

> **SETUP:** 2–5 (ideally, 3) per team. In huddles, select character, activity, and location. In this improvisation, we will extend the process of reflect the reflector to acting. The necessary components of reflection are the same: see (check out) your fellow actors; focus on them; and stay open to reflecting or going with it. Reflection now means more than simply duplicating body gestures. *All aspects of the improvisational acting, including gestures, are available for reflection.*

> **RULES:** While employing physical doing tools of Improvisation Technique for activity, location, relationships, and occupation, you will be presented with opportunities to reflect the different aspects of each other's improvisational acting. In order for you to reflect, you must be attentive and *open* to going with whatever is happening, including the coaching.

ACTING FOCUS: Reflect the reflector.

COACHING (as needed): After the location has been set up, do a warm-up. ◆ Walk around. Reflect each other. It's your choice whom to reflect. No one is initiating. Reflect the reflector. Reflect any aspect of anyone. Frequently change the person you are reflecting. Keep walking and reflecting. All are focused on reflecting the reflector. **Reflect different aspects. Select and reflect.** ◆ Places. ◆ Action. ◆ Stay open to seeing anything and everything that is available for reflection. Then, **select and reflect.** You are always in the process of reflecting. Avoid coming to a stop. One moment flows into the next. **This is not a duplication focus. Reflect what you choose, and go with it!** Stay on your acting focus. ◆ Share that thought. Speak when you have something to say. Share your voices. ◆ **Check each other out. Stay open to each other.** Reflect the reflector. Show us your reflection. See what there is to see. Allow your body to make the selections of what you are reflecting every moment. **Select and reflect. Integrate your reflections as a part of the whole character, activity, and location. Stay open to reflecting the reflector in new and different ways:** emotionally, physically. Reflect the inside and the outside. Avoid initiation. **Go with what is**

happening. Follow your impulse. You are always reflecting someone, or everyone. See what there is to see. Reflect what there is to reflect. **Avoid hanging out. Explore other aspects for reflection.** In every moment, there is something to reflect. Pursue it. Go with the flow. Avoid hanging out and stay on your acting focus. Reflect each other physically, emotionally, attitudinally, rhythmically, posturally, gesturally. Every moment, you are choosing to reflect something, someone, or some aspect of the playing. Stay totally open, alert, and available for reflecting brand new aspects of different players. Alternate the different aspects you choose to reflect. ◆ **One minute to reflect more and different aspects of the playing.** ◆ Cut.

FOLLOW-UP (as needed): Audience, character? Activity? Location? ◆ **Actors, did you feel like you were on the acting focus?** Were you always in the process of reflecting something or someone? Did you feel like you were reflecting different aspects of each other? **Did you let the acting focus lead you through the improv?** ◆ Audience, were they on the acting focus? Were they willing to give up initiation and make the commitment to reflection? Did one reflection flow into the next reflection? What aspects of the improvisation are available for reflection? You can reflect gestures, attitudes, rhythms, emotions, sounds, ideas, dialogue, vocal qualities, and inner doing. Anything and everything the instrument does or produces is available for reflection. There is always something available for reflection. Could the actors have reflected more aspects than they did? Always. Could the actors have alternated more between the various aspects?

SUMMARY:

Spontaneous selection of whom or what you are reflecting is up to you. Once you start reflecting the reflector, what is meant for you to reflect will be revealed to you. You just have to go with it. In order to reflect each other, you have to see each other. If you stop checking each other out, you stop reflecting and you begin initiating. You must be willing to give up your idea of how a moment should go or develop, how something should happen, or you'll initiate from your idea instead of being open to going with whatever is happening between you and your fellow actors. A mirror reflects everything it sees, not what it wants to see.

> **TO THE COACH:** Coach actors away from hanging out or any stopping of their physicality. The stops kill the energy necessary for the energy flow between the actors. When the actors are on their acting focus, it will look like they are all in the same groove, and the improvising is totally effortless and theatrical.
>
> If the improvisation turns into a dancelike ritual in which all the actors forget about their character, activity, and location and mimic each other's

478

gestures, this is a *transformation dance*. It is all right when it happens because it taps into the spirit of the reflect the reflector acting focus. However, in the follow-up, it should be pointed out that the actors gave up
their abilities for individual spontaneous selection in order to do a group
reflection. The more the actors interpret reflect the reflector as a literal
mirror duplication, the more likely transformation dances are to occur.
Encourage the actors to alternate the aspects of the improvisation they
choose to reflect. When they reflect gestures only, they set themselves up
for transformation dancing. Each improv lasts about ten minutes.

AGREEMENT

SETUP: 2–4 per team. In huddles, select character, activity, and location.
There are two levels of the agreement acting focus. The first level, the
foundation, is to actively agree with anything and everything that happens
during the improvisation. Any form of negation whatsoever is absolutely
forbidden. Being on the acting focus at this level is like seeing, hearing,
and feeling through a filter of *positiveness and communalism*.

The second level builds on the first. You must do something with that
positiveness and communalism. *It is not enough to agree.* What is important
is *how you build upon the foundation of the initial agreement.* How do you
extend every agreement so you take it to a new level? What else can you do
with what you are agreeing with that will extend it? Focused agreement is
not about waiting for setups and then agreeing with them. A setup might
be: "Let's go to the movies." And the response: "Yes, Let's go (I agree)." It
is not about that at all. You must find opportunities and ways of agreeing
that weren't set up. Don't wait for an invitation. You could look across the
stage and see someone focused on doing an activity, and you could choose
to agree with that. They didn't ask you to agree to anything, but you could
choose to agree with that, with another character doing his activity. How?
That is for you to discover on the second level of this improvisational
acting focus. The will to agree without hesitation is the first level. What
you do with your agreement is the second level.

The agreement may be verbal, but should always be physical. There is a
whole world of opportunities within the improvisation for you to select
and agree with. Whatever you see, hear, or feel is an invitation to and an
opportunity for agreement. You are at all times seeking out something to
agree with and to develop further in the spirit of agreement. This requires
maximum openness and willingness to go with it, which translates to
excitement. This is the ultimate go-with-it acting focus.

While select & reflect was an important building block in preparing for
agreement, there are two important differences. In agreement, there is no

requirement to reflect. In select & reflect, there is no law against negation. Your only obligation toward negation was to reflect it if it showed up. In agreement, you cannot have negation of any kind.

A final tip: Avoid questions in your dialogue.

RULES: While employing physical doing tools of Improvisation Technique for activity, location, relationships, and occupation you will be presented with opportunities to agree to anything and everything that is happening on the stage. You must agree. No negation of any kind. In order for you to agree, you must be attentive and *open* to going with whatever is happening, including the coaching. Show us your agreements. Don't just tell them to us. Avoid questions.

ACTING FOCUS: To agree and extend your agreements.

COACHING (as needed): After the location has been set up, do the 40-breath process. ◆ *After the breaths*— Open your toes. Open your legs. Open your chest. No tension. Open your shoulders. Arms. Fingers. Open your spine. Your neck. Open your face. Now, open your heart and whole body toward your fellow actors. ◆ Places. ◆ Action. **Check each other out.** Agree with everything. **Share your voices.** Remove the negativity. Remove the negation from the attitude. ◆ **Agree with that emotion (sound/gesture/ idea).** ◆ Stay open. Keep going forward. **Go with it. Extend the agreement.** Anything can happen, just remove the negativity from around it. No negativity of any kind: past, present, or future. Keep the spirit of agreement. Extend your agreement so it takes you on a trip. You don't have to know where you're going. Every time you agree with it, you go with it. You take it somewhere. Now, take **that** somewhere. Remove the negativity from the experience. Go with it! Stay alert and available for opportunities to agree. Help your fellow actor. **Extend your agreements further** and further. Keep going. There's always another place to take the agreement to. How far can you go with your agreement? How many new ways can you extend an agreement? Go with it. **Go further.** ◆ Everybody contribute to taking the agreement further. Participate in the agreements. Agreement is a team sport. Heighten your spirit of agreement. Help your fellow actor and bring the spirit of agreement with you. Extend your agreement as a team. Add something new. **Go with that!** Are you treading water or going somewhere? **Take a trip on the agreement.** Take it to new levels. **Keep building on your agreements.** ◆ Keep the agreement extensions in the space. **Show, don't tell.** Do it, don't tell it. Avoid announcing what you are going to do. **Physicalize your agreement. Avoid negating.** Avoid tentativeness. **Avoid questions.** Avoid hanging out. Enlarge that gesture and go with it. ◆ One minute to agree further. ◆ Cut.

FOLLOW-UP (as needed): Audience, character? Activity? Location? Were they on the acting focus of agreement? Did you see any negation at all? When? How about emotions? Did you see any fear, anger, or pain? Those are negating emotions. Were the agreements in their heads or in the space? Were agreements limited to responding to setups calling for agreement or negation? **Were they open to agreeing to moments that had not been set up or where there were no invitations to agree?** Are setups essential to agreement? No. **Were agreements limited to duplications?** Duplication is one actor doing exactly the same thing as another. How do duplications limit agreement? Without duplication, the acting focus leads the actors into new areas of playing. Did anyone impose, force, or muscle agreements, either physically or verbally, on the others? Were there any transformations of the characters, activity, or location? **Did the acting focus lead the actors into areas that transcended the characters, activity, or location? When?** Were there moments when agreement could have led them still further into other areas? Could their agreements have gone further? Always. Did you see that a first agreement set in motion a series of agreements, all stemming from the first initiated agreement? Can those series be extended still further? Stay in the process of *there is always more to do.* Each agreement should take the initial impetus a step further. Were the props and costumes made of space? ◆ Actors, did you feel like you were on a trip and you didn't know the destination? Did you explore and contribute to the ultimate destination? Did you feel cautious while improvising? In addition to negation, the greatest enemies of agreement are caution, timidity, and fear. **Did you feel like you were on your acting focus? Did you let it lead you through the improv?**

SUMMARY:

POWER OF AGREEMENT

Agreement is a very powerful acting focus because it is contrary to human nature. All of us have a tendency to negate. We have an idea of how things should be, and we are not enthusiastic about joining anything that contradicts our idea; or we have fears about endeavors that we perceive as challenging.

When people negate new opportunities or challenges, nothing can happen. When you say, "Yes," there is authentic potential for new experiences, events, endeavors, growth, and possibilities. Lots of things can happen! Agreement develops your openness and risk taking. You accept invitations to places that you would never go.

A boy asks a girl out and the girl says, "No, thank you." End of story. But if she says, "Yes," we have potential. They go out and they have a nice time. He says, "Let's go out tomorrow night." She says, "Yes." They go out again, and they have a great time. She says, "Let's go out next week." He says, "Yes." They go out again, and this time they make love. They keep saying yes to each other and before you know it, they are engaged. They keep saying yes to each other, and they get married. They keep saying yes, and they have children. Then their children have children and you end up with people eating at your card table. The point is that *generations spring from that first yes*. If that first invitation had been answered with a no, there would have been no potential. "No" stops things. "Yes" provides potential.

If we are frightened or inauthentic, we are not inclined to say yes. In acting, certainly in your acting workshop, what is there to be frightened of? I'm not dropping you into the middle of a Hell's Angels clubhouse or a war zone and telling you to avoid conflict and go with it. Acting is playing. It is a safe environment. When we bring negation to the playing area, we deprive ourselves of discoveries, momentum, exploration, and energy.

What is the fuel for agreement? Openness, enthusiasm, and excitement. The more enthusiasm and excitement you pour into agreement, the farther and faster you go. If you omit negativity and so, technically fulfill agreement, but you do so without excitement, you are not in agreement. Technically fulfilled agreement, done with words only, has no power. It's lip service. But pour excitement into the smallest of agreements and there is plenty of potential for discovery, for going further. *Excitement is the fuel*.

If you feel cautious, anxious, nervous, or unsure while improvising, it is a sign that you are not on the acting focus. *Agreement does not allow for unpleasant feelings*.

HOW TO DO IT

The first requirement of playing agreement is openness. We have dealt with openness before in other acting focuses, but agreement takes being open to a higher level. If someone comes up to you and wants to do something to you, or with you, that in your real life you may not like and would never do, *in your acting you must be open to it*, so open that you immediately go with it with enthusiasm and joy. In addition, you must reach out to see what you can contribute to the endeavor. What can you bring to the party? How can you take it further, with positiveness, enthusiasm, and invention? Taking it further is the true embodiment of going with it.

The coach may do this *demonstration:*

> The coach asks an actor to walk across the room. Halfway through the walk, the coach joins her in the rest of the walk. ◆ My joining her is an example of just going with it. That is minimal and certainly shows no negation; however, that is not sufficient for true agreement. ◆ The coach asks the actor to take the same walk again. Halfway through the walk, the coach joins her for a step or two and then takes her hand and leads her into a few dance steps, ending up at an empty chair or table. He helps her to

climb up and stand on it. Perhaps on her own, she will do something on the chair or tabletop, or the coach can complete the demonstration by simply bowing to her. ◆ Truly going with it requires joining the other actor and taking both of you further to playing levels neither of you anticipated when the original actor began the equivalent of her walk.

It is not about you thinking ahead of time or planning how you can take it further. It's about an immediate physical response to each moment. If you find yourself thinking about what you can do next, you are off your acting focus. To rectify this, look out into the space of the improv and find something new to agree with. Each moment is a brand new moment of potential. Go right to your location or activity in the spirit of agreement (happiness, enthusiasm, and excitement) and not defeat. When you learned to discover objects near you, you brought yourself to the point of being able to reach out into the space not knowing what you were reaching for, trusting that when your hand arrived at the object you would discover what it was. It is the same with agreement. Reach out and discover your agreements. Dive in, using all your improvisation tools in the service of diving in. If you feel like you are responsible for taking agreements further, and that responsibility creates effort, then you are not on the acting focus. Avoid effort.

In true agreement, you are not even waiting for the invitation; you are initiating as well. This is what it means to be open and not negate. It's not a question of simply saying yes to whatever is suggested. In taking responsibility for initiating your agreements, you can agree with anyone, anything, or any moment. It doesn't have to be verbal. It is always better to show than to tell. You can look out in the location, among your fellow actors, in the same way as when you play reflect the reflector. You can look out there and see anything at all to agree with.

The coach may do this *demonstration:*

The coach should notice any actor in the group who is doing any casual and non-obtrusive gesture during the summary, e.g., playing with her hair. The coach does the following while he talks to the group about it. ◆ I can come over and agree with her by starting to primp her hair, showing her a new way to do her hair. I am not limited to real hair. I have space props available to me. ◆ You can take it in any direction you want. Actually, it is easier to discover something in the space to agree with than to feel you have to invent an agreement with an idea that you tell everybody. Show, don't tell. ◆ Not only am I initiating an agreement moment, I am providing her with an opportunity to respond in agreement by going with it. Then, I'll go with her response and she with mine, and so on. Before you know it, we have created some new hair style that we are both excited about. And, it all started when I looked out into the room and saw her playing with her hair.

The facility to initiate agreement provides you with the power to move the scene forward in any direction. For example, in an improv, some wise guy might say, "Hey, gang, let's all make love to Sheila!" Instead of going with her spontaneous instinct to negate, Sheila must go with it with enthusiasm and excitement. She can move the improv forward, avoiding the sex act, by initiating another agreement that takes the wise guy's original initiation further in another direction. For example, Sheila responds, "Great! I can show you my rash!" (She starts enthusiastically unbuttoning her space pants.) If the guys are on their acting focus of agreement, the improv might now head in the direction of a healing scene. In another example of agreeing further while avoiding the sex, Sheila might say, "Yeah. In Morocco! Let's pack our bags." (She enthusiastically starts contacting the location, gathering her clothes and suitcases.) In both examples, Sheila has not negated the original impetus; she has gone with it, taken it further, and built on it.

Agreement is a magical acting focus because $1 + 1 = 3$, not 2. Each actor is an entity with his own power. When you bring two together in agreement, they create a power greater than the sum of their two individual powers. The added power comes from their commonality. For the magic to work, this commonality must be respected. If one actor muscles agreement issues, the commonality is lost. This is true whether the actor muscles the other actors or himself. The muscling often takes the form of announcements about what is happening or going to happen. Anytime someone says, "I am [a dog, Jesus, the President, etc.]," that will usually be a muscling of the agreement. Everyone else now feels obligated to go with it. When playing agreement, everyone should always feel they have an invitation, not an order, to go with it. Showing instead of telling always precludes this problem. Show that you are a dog, Jesus, or the President with space props and physicalization, and the other actors will feel invited rather than ordered to agree with you. Commonality will be preserved.

EMOTIONS

There is no anger, fear, or pain in the world of agreement. If something happens during the improv that would normally cause pain in real life, the character must not feel pain. He must enjoy it. If he does, it's not pain. It's pleasure. In agreement, a bee sting or broken ankle elicits a positive response. If an object struggle occurs, the emotional response to it determines whether or not the actor is in agreement. If his response is frustration, then he is in conflict with the object and that is a form of negation, as is the emotion of frustration. If his response is joy, then he is in agreement (with the struggle) and he is on his acting focus.

DUPLICATIONS

Going with it and taking it further is often stopped short when other actors simply duplicate the original impetus. If one actor starts barking like a dog and the other actors respond by barking like dogs, we have a pack of dogs barking.

The others have not taken it further. If each actor is on the focus of extending agreement, going with it and taking it further, then the second actor might bark, and then *do something else*. The third actor might bark, but he would also go with what the second actor added, and *add something further still*. By the time each of the four has contributed to the initial impetus, the improv has traveled immensely. Agreement requires that you go with it and take it further.

Verbal duplications will also keep the actors off the acting focus. For example: One actor says, "Look how shiny my hair is." Then the next actor says, "Oh, it is very shiny!" The third actor says, "Oh, it is so shiny!" That is verbal duplication. It is a form of telling, not showing, and it keeps the improv on a plateau with no momentum. If the actors are in the groove of agreement, as soon as it is established that the hair is shiny another actor can discover that it is so shiny, she can use the hair like a mirror and, perhaps, fix her makeup. It is not necessary to use words. You just start doing it. That would be an example of agreeing with the original impetus, "shiny hair," and building upon it instead of duplicating it. The improv now has a sense of new direction instead of a stalled, echo effect. Duplication is a common hurdle when learning agreement because it *seems* to be agreement. The enthusiasm may build and there may be no negating, but the words keep the player from taking the next step into the unknown. When you keep dittoing each other with different words, you stay in the realm of the known. Agreement is designed to take you into the realm of the totally unknown, if you are willing to take the trip.

Duplication is also sometimes used to buy time to come up with an idea for taking the agreement further. Avoid this. It puts you in the head and adds effort to your sense of responsibility for taking things further. This will keep you out of the agreement groove.

IN THE GROOVE

Agreement is always a great deal of fun to play. When you are on the acting focus, it feels like you are in a musical groove. The groove has a unique rhythm, which you ride on a trip, not knowing you are on the trip until you arrive and look back at it. An entire agreement improv consists of moving from one groove to the next. When you are in the groove, initiation of agreements is shared equally between all the actors in the improv.

Being in the groove has a vertical sense to it. The body feels like it is participating in an improvisation that is taking off, going somewhere up and out in all directions. It is a feeling of going up, and all are traveling with it as each person contributes to the next step up in the flight. When you are not in this groove, the body feels like it is stuck on the ground and the improv scene has a horizontal sense to it, like walking on a plateau.

ASKING QUESTIONS

When you ask a question, you're not in agreement. You may not be negating, but you are interrupting the flow of energy that accompanies agreement, the groove, in order to ask the question. The actor who is asked the question has to interrupt his energy flow to come up with an answer, which will probably be from his head.

> **TO THE COACH:** If you are unsure whether the actors were on the acting focus, watch them immediately after "Cut" is coached. If they look relieved, they were not on the acting focus. After "Cut," all actors who were on the acting focus are excited. Agreement should be repeated over the next few classes, each time preceded by some of the next exercises. Each improv lasts about ten minutes.

◆　◆　◆

AGREEMENT WALK

This is an excellent warm-up for the beginning of an agreement class.

SETUP: All the actors walk around the room responding to the coaching.

RULES and ACTING FOCUS: Respond to the coaching.

COACHING: Everybody, start walking around the room. Shake it out. Now, turn around and feel the space against your body as you walk into it. Focus on feeling the space. Feel it with the tip of your nose. Feel it with your chest, your stomach, your knees. Feel it under your feet as you step down and squash it out. Now focus on moving through the space and feel the space moving through you at the same time. ◆ Stand where you are. Reach up and take down a hunk of space. Start to move that space about. Pull it. Twist it. Turn it. Shake it. Extend it. Heighten it. Play with this hunk of space. Move it about. If it turns into something you recognize, you can go with that. If not, fine. It can stay amorphous. Stay up on your feet with your whole body involved. Total body involvement. ◆ Turn to an actor near you. Make eye contact. Approach each other and fuse the two objects together. If there is an odd player, then three can play together. Play together with this hunk of space. Respect each other. Help your fellow actor. Keep twisting and turning the space object between you. Play together with your partner, allowing the object to go wherever it wants to go. Let go of the control. Both focused on the same space, working together. Be aware of your fellow actor and let your fellow actor be aware of you as you both allow the object between you to turn into whatever it wants to turn into. It may be real or amorphous, but allow it to have a life of its own as you work together. Avoid caution. Avoid resistance. Avoid control. Keep going with it. Allow the object to dictate where it wants to go. Nobody knows where it's going. Everybody going together not knowing where we are going to. Keep playing with it. Keep pouring your combined bodies' energy into it. The more you allow your whole body's involvement, the less your head will talk to you. Go with it. ◆

[From this point on, each ◆ represents a 5–20s interval.] ◆ The space disappears right now and you are all playing reflect the reflector in a reflection game with your partner. Just go with it right now. Reflect the reflector. Reflect what you see, not what you expect to see. ◆ Put your focus back on the space object right now. The object is there between you. Go with it. The object leads you. Go with it, focusing on the object between you as the object leads you. Now, you lead the object. Now the object leads you. You lead the object. ◆ Now, the object disappears. Focus on reflecting each other right now. Keep moving. Do not come to a stop. Keep moving. Reflect the reflector. Everybody is reflecting; no one is initiating. ◆ Change again and focus on the space object that is between you right now. Go with it. The object can go anywhere, twisting and turning, keeping the object between you and focusing on the object between you. ◆ Now reflect the reflector. ◆ Now back to the space object. ◆ Now reflect the reflector. ◆ Now back onto the space. ◆ Now reflect the reflector. Just go right into it. ◆ Now back onto the space. ◆ Now reflect the reflector. ◆ Space. ◆ Reflect the reflector. ◆ Space. ◆ Reflect the reflector. ◆ You are on your own. Follow the space. On your own. Follow the space. Heighten your focus. Full body involvement in the space you are following. Follow the space. Keep following the space. Full body involvement. Follow the space. Follow the space. Follow the space. ◆ Cut.

FOLLOW-UP (as needed): Did you respond to the coaching? How did it feel?

SUMMARY:
None.

INVITATIONS TO AGREEMENT, PART I [2]

SETUP: 2 per team. No huddles or preparation. The first actor initiates a pose with his body, any kind of pose. It doesn't have to be a standing pose and his arms and legs can be extended in any way at all. The pose must carry no purpose or intention. It's just a body configuration. Once he takes the pose, he holds it without moving. The second actor takes the first actor's pose as an invitation to join him. He immediately accepts by responding to the first actor's pose with his own gesture, pose, or activity, with or without space props, centered on the first actor's pose. The second actor's response endows the first actor's pose with meaning or purpose. As soon as the second actor completes his response and the purpose or meaning is communicated, the first actor says, "Thank you very much." Both actors return to neutral stances and reverse roles. The second actor initiates a pose with his body, any kind of pose. The first actor accepts the invitation and responds. The second actor says, "Thank you very much." They return to neutral, reverse roles, and continue the game, always reversing roles after the "Thank You" line.

RULES: One actor configures his body into any nonmeaningful pose. The other actor responds by completing the first actor's pose and providing meaning to it. The first actor completes the process, saying, "Thank you very much," as a part of the whole completed purposeful pose or action. No dialogue other than, "Thank you very much."

ACTING FOCUS: Agreement.

COACHING (as needed): First actor, hold that pose. **Avoid having an idea of what your pose represents.** ◆ Second actor, agree and make something of it. Go with it. ◆ First actor, don't change the pose. ◆ Second actor, join him with your contribution, which makes sense or has meaning for both. ◆ **First actor, say, "Thank you very much."** Integrate the "Thank you very much" as a part of the whole you have created. Heighten your "Thank you's" as a part of the whole. Avoid dialogue other than "Thank you very much."

FOLLOW-UP (as needed): Audience, were their "Thank you's" integrated as a part of the whole? Were the first poses invitations to the unknown or did they strongly suggest a purpose? If the first pose is full of purpose, it inhibits the second player from taking it anywhere he wants to, as he feels that he has to complete what the first actor started. **Were they on the acting focus?**

SUMMARY:

You can bring agreement to any moment in any improvisation. With invitations to agreement, the responding player is agreeing with the initiating player by going with the initial pose and taking it further. By doing this, you have experienced true agreement. The bottom line of all agreement is taking whatever is being agreed to, further. In this exercise you have explored agreements that are all physical and without dialogue or setups. You can choose to agree with any moment in any scene. If you are on the acting focus of agreement, you are wearing the *agreement filter*. Whatever you see or hear through this filter presents itself as an invitation to agreement. It is your job to accept the invitation and to go with it.

TO THE COACH: Do the follow-up at the end of each team's playing, not after each "Thank you" line. The "Thank you" lines are important as they allow for total integration of voice and body within the completed pose. Each team plays for 3–5 minutes.

AGREEMENT REPEAT, ROUND 1

After playing the previous agreement improvs, repeat the basic improvisation acting focus of agreement (p. 478). There should now be two consecutive rounds of agreement improvs, presented, played, and coached in the same way as the first time the actors did it. There is no summary necessary after the first round. At that point, coach "Upset," and form new teams for the huddles prior to the second round.

AGREEMENT REPEAT, ROUND 2

SETUP: The same as before, with the following change. ◆ In their huddles, the actors make character, activity, and location choices that allow all the actors to be involved together in their activity. In the past, the actors may have all been a part of the whole activity, but when "Action" was coached, each was in a different part of the stage doing his own activity, separately. In this improv, when "Action" is coached, all should be working/playing together on the activity, and there should be a strong potential for a verbal aspect to the activity choice. Example: preparing a college newspaper.

RULES, ACTING FOCUS, COACHING, and FOLLOW-UP: Same as previous round.

SUMMARY:

By working more closely together at the very beginning of the improvs in the second round, all the actors were more available to going with each other, so more of the actors felt they were in the groove and allowed the acting focus to work for them.

TO THE COACH: The coach may wish to point out that while all improvisational comedy theaters are built, fundamentally, on the premise of agreement, they seldom reach this level of improvisational acting because of their lack of emphasis on the physical aspect of agreement and their over-emphasis on verbal cleverness.

If any actor is still limited in his openness and frequently negates, prior to his team improvising the agreement repeat, coach his entire team in a special warm-up. Have them do an attitude line preparation (p. 289), where each one of them employs the attitude line, "I'm open." ◆ As soon as that warm-up is completed, *coach*— Retain the attitude in the body, as you go to places for agreement repeat. ◆ Action.

◆ ◆ ◆

"YES! AND . . . "

SETUP: 2–5 per team. In huddles, select a type of committee that is planning an event or marketing a product, e.g., PTA/rummage sale. The team places chairs in a semicircle. This is a double acting focus: (1) While you improvise the meeting, everyone is responsible for discovering objects near you, on the table, in your costume, or on the floor. (2) In all dialogue, "Yes! And . . . " must be the first two words.

RULES: You must stay seated. Discover objects near you and take responsibility for sharing the discussion equally. In all dialogue, "Yes! And . . . " must be the first two words.

ACTING FOCUS: Agreement.

COACHING (as needed): Action ◆ Keep discovering objects. Really say yes! More enthusiasm. Build on each other's enthusiasm. Go with it. Share your voices.

FOLLOW-UP (as needed): Audience, what was the original topic or event? Did they discover objects near them? Did they begin their lines with the words, "Yes! And . . . "? Were they on focus? Was there enthusiasm? Did they build on each other's enthusiasm?

SUMMARY:

We play this so you can experience the authentic feelings of enthusiasm and excitement that must always accompany agreement. Also, because of the "And . . . " you always added to your agreement and extended it. It was never just an echo. While "Yes! And . . . " produces the spirit of agreement, it also limits it. You are less inclined to physicalize your agreements. All grooves are aural. The dialogue is all telling with no showing.

> **TO THE COACH:** "Yes! And . . . " is an agreement crutch and promotes the verbal over the physical. Whether improvising in this seated version or one with full character/activity/location, the "And . . . " inherently demands that the agreement extention is announced. An early problem with learning agreement is that too many actors tell their ideas instead of showing them and this may deepen that problem. If the actors are experiencing difficulty learning that agreement must be played with enthusiasm and excitement, "Yes! And . . . " will help. ◆ Improv comedy groups thrive on this acting focus with everyone enthusiastically making humorous suggestions and clever announcements. ◆ Each improv takes about five minutes.

INVITATIONS TO AGREEMENT, PART 2

SETUP: Begin with two actors improvising invitations to agreement, part 1. ◆ After about two minutes, stop the actors and introduce **part 2:** We are going to continue improvising in this manner, except when the first actor is about to say, "Thank you very much," he should not say it. Instead, he is free from his silent pose. He comes to life, responding to the second actor's pose/activity, and both actors go with it, commencing an improvisation scene, which may or may not include dialogue. Both actors focus on agreement. The improv evolves from the completed pose provided by the second actor. The improv is over when the coach says "Cut." The actors return to neutral stances, reverse roles, and repeat the exercise. After this improvisation, the actors return to their seats and the next two begin.

RULES: One actor configures his body into any nonmeaningful pose. The other actor responds by completing the first actor's pose and providing meaning to it. First actor continues the process by coming to life and beginning an improvisation evolving from the whole, completed, purposeful pose or action. Dialogue is allowed.

ACTING FOCUS: Agreement.

COACHING (as needed): First actor, hold that pose. **Avoid having an idea of what your pose represents**. Second actor, agree and make something of it. Go with it. First actor, don't change the pose. Second actor, join him with your own contribution, which makes some sense or has some meaning for both. **First actor, come to life and begin the improvisation.** Integrate your participation as a part of the whole that you have already created. Second actor, **go with it.** Go with it with enthusiasm and excitement. Enlarge your agreements. **Stay in agreement.** Bring your enthusiasm along! Avoid being concerned with the trip you are on. Just go with it! **Build on each other's agreements.**

FOLLOW-UP (as needed): Audience, **did their improvs evolve as a part of the whole from the original poses**? Were the first poses invitations to the unknown or did they strongly suggest a purpose? If the first pose is full of purpose, it inhibits the second player from taking it anywhere he wants to as he feels that he must complete what the first actor started. **Were they on the acting focus of agreement?** Did the improv build in any way after the first actor came to life? Were agreements limited to duplications or setups? Did they avoid questions and playwriting? ◆ **Actors, did you feel like you were on the acting focus? Did it feel like you were in a groove together**?

SUMMARY:

At this stage of the training, the most common hindrances to achieving true agreement or feeling like you hit the groove together are:

STRUGGLE

Struggle is contrary to agreement. Struggling is the opposite of going with it. When you struggle with someone or something, you are demanding that the person or object go with you. There is never struggle in agreement.

BUILDING AGREEMENT

There is no true agreement if the agreements do not build. Saying "Yeah! Great! Terrific!" is the same as saying "Ditto." True agreement goes someplace new because you are adding to it. Agreement is expansion in a positive mode. You expand on what you have. If your agreements don't add expansion, they are limited agreements.

THINKING VS. DOING AND FEELING

When you are in agreement, your body is in a state of going with it, instead of your mind thinking about it. If you stop to think, "What else can I do," or, "What is going on here," you will not be on the acting focus. Agreement is a physical feeling. Happiness, excitement, and enthusiasm always accompany this acting focus. Hesitation replaces those feelings with moments of fear. Words of negation create hesitation.

If you don't know what is going on, go with it. Figuring out what is going on puts you in your head, which is the last place you want to be when you are in agreement. You don't have to know anything. Take a trip into the unknown. Discover adventure and excitement.

> **TO THE COACH:** Actors should pair up with different partners every time they improvise invitations to agreement. The part 2 improv lasts about five minutes.

AGREEMENT REPEAT, ROUND 3

After invitations to agreement, part 2, the actors should improvise a third round of agreement repeat.

> **SETUP, RULES, ACTING FOCUS, COACHING, and FOLLOW-UP:** Same as previous round.

SUMMARY:

We have come a long way since the first time we played agreement. What aspects of agreement did you see in this round that have been strengthened? Actors are more willing to give up their ideas of how things should go. They are more open to seeing what is going on, willing themselves to join in, and taking it somewhere new. Much more enthusiasm accompanies the improvising. There is more physicalizing as the agreements are now coming from body feelings. You are playing with your full bodies, which is necessary for agreement. There is less dependence on inventing ideas of something to do and everybody responding, "Yes, let's." The inspiration to do something now occurs at the same moment that the person does it. That is spontaneity.

AGREEMENT/CONFLICT, PART I

The final level of agreement training combines agreement with conflict.

SETUP: 2 per team. In huddles, select character, activity, and location, and a disguised conflict issue. The improvisation begins with the actors employing the dynamics and acting focus of pull the conflict #4 (go in for the kill). Both actors are pulling to win and staying open to playing losses. If your opponent plays a loss, you go in for the kill. As the improv proceeds, you will be coached to change your acting focus. You must respond to the change immediately, without hesitation or thought.

RULES: While employing physical doing tools of Improvisation Technique for activity, location, relationships, and occupation, the actors employ the dynamics of either pull the (disguised) conflict or agreement. ◆ Actors must respond to the coaching immediately.

ACTING FOCUS: Either pull the conflict or agreement (as coached).

COACHING (as needed): Set up your location. ◆ Places. ◆ Action. ◆ Keep the rope taut and pull on it. **Pull the rope. Pull the conflict. Pull to win.** Play that loss. Go in for the kill. ◆ *After ca. 1m—* **Agreement.** Go with it. Go with the agreements. **Heighten the enthusiasm.** Extend the agreements. **Use your whole body to agree.** Commit to authentic agreement. There is no conflict in agreement. ◆ *After ca. 45s—* **Conflict.** ◆ *After ca. 45s—* **Agreement.** ◆ *After ca. 30s—* **Conflict.** ◆ *After ca. 30s—* **You are on your own. You choose agreement or conflict and practice alternating them. Commit to the acting focus you choose to be on.** Agreement or conflict. ◆ **Change whenever your partner changes.** Stay open to changing your acting focus. **Always know which acting focus you are on and choose to alternate between them.** You are on your own. **When you switch, switch totally and instantaneously.** ◆ When you are in conflict, pull the rope. Keep it taut. ◆ Stay alert to your fellow actor. Go with it. Reflect the reflector when the acting focus changes. Go with the change of acting focus. ◆ Pour your whole body into the agreement. Heighten the agreements and extend them. **Be in one acting focus or the other, no in between.** ◆ **One minute.** ◆ Cut.

FOLLOW-UP (as needed): Audience, did the actors commit to the coached acting focus? Did they integrate their acting focus changes as a part of the whole character, activity, and location? When they were coached to be on their own, did they respond and alternate their acting focus without coaching? **Did they fully commit to their own chosen acting focus?** ✦ Actors, do you agree? **Did you alternate between conflict and agreement as a part of the whole character, activity, and location?**

SUMMARY:

It is important to be on one acting focus or the other. There is no in between. When the acting focus switches, each actor goes with the switch and each other, in a fashion similar to the reflect-the-reflector process. The initiation for the switch comes from either actor; the other actor must go with it immediately. The adventure and journey into the unknown is always heightened at the moment of the change in focuses. If you do not immediately and totally switch, but buy time in some midway area, e.g., apology or concern, you limit your excursions into the realm of spontaneity. The moment of the switch is the penultimate being in the moment. You must dive into it, discovering how to make it a part of the whole. No setups or planning, please! Switch on a dime.

> **TO THE COACH:** Until coaching, "You are on your own," coach the changes at the most unexpected moments. Avoid coaching the changes during easy moments, like lulls or silences. Each improv lasts about 6–10 minutes.

✦　✦　✦

AGREEMENT/CONFLICT, PART 2

SETUP: The same as part 1, until the actors are on their own. ✦ In the on-your-own section, you are to improvise opposite to each other. If your partner switches to agreement, stay in conflict. If your partner switches to conflict, stay in agreement.

RULES: While employing physical doing tools of Improvisation Technique for activity, location, relationships, and occupation, the actors employ the dynamics of either pull the (disguised) conflict or agreement. ✦ The actors must respond to the coaching immediately. ✦ In the on-your-own section, each actor improvises the opposite focus from his partner. Either partner may initiate a change.

ACTING FOCUS: Either pull the conflict or agreement (as coached).

COACHING (as needed): The same as part 1, **UNTIL: You are on your own. Choose your own acting focus and commit to it.** Agreement or conflict. Stay open to changing your own acting focus. **Always know which acting**

focus you are on and initiate a change whenever you want. When your partner initiates one way, you go the other way. When you switch, switch totally and instantaneously. ◆ Stay alert to your fellow actor. Stay on your own acting focus. You must be on one or the other; there is no in between. You are either in conflict or agreement, your choice. ◆ **When you are in agreement, build on your own agreements. You are your own partner in agreement.** Build your agreement with enthusiasm. ◆ **When you are in conflict, pull the rope to win, even when your opponent is not pulling back.** ◆ **Practice alternating between conflict and agreement by yourself.** Spend as much time doing conflict as you do agreement. **Go the opposite way from your partner.** ◆ One minute to stay on your own alternating focus. ◆ Cut.

FOLLOW-UP (as needed): The same as agreement/conflict, part 1. **NEW: Did they alternate acting focuses in opposition to their partner's acting focus choices?**

SUMMARY:

The ability to switch on your own between conflict and agreement despite what your partner is doing provides you with more options and makes the improvising less predictable for you, your partner, and the audience. Ultimately, you may combine parts 1 and 2, sometimes improvising reflect the reflector with each other, switching to the same choice at the same time, and sometimes switching to the opposite acting focus from your partner.

RHYTHM AND INTENSITY

In this improv, you get to experience some aspects of agreement and conflict that are similar and different at the same time. The rhythm and intensity of both are similar in that every moment builds on the previous one. It is the direction that is different. Conflict is horizontal, like a rope-pulling contest. Agreement is vertical, like a rising balloon. This directional difference manifests in the moods of the improvisation, anger vs. joy.

MOMENTUM AND TURNING POINTS

Agreement and conflict always provide forward momentum to a scene and turning points within the scene. On this acting focus, the improvs resemble scripted scenes with all the spontaneity and fun that we associate with our improvisational work. In staying open to, seizing, and actualizing turning points for switching between conflict and agreement, the improv evolves with its own clear, forward, and often logical progression. This provides the momentum that resembles a written scene. What makes it all come together is your taking responsibility for making the switches a part of the whole.

Every time you make a turn, there is a burst of energy and that heightens the audience's interest in what you are doing. We have explored turns off of railroad tracks. Now we have turns available from switching between agreement and conflict.

GROUNDED VS. TRANSFORMATIONAL

Because of the possible transformation of the character, activity, and location, agreement without conflict switches has more potential for improvisational theater. When you alternate between agreement and conflict, the conflict keeps you grounded in the scene. That's why this acting focus should start with conflict prior to the first switch. When you come out of the first conflict section, you are experientially grounded in the reality of the scene and that physicalization remains when you enter the agreement beat.

Extratheatrical transformations are of little use to the camera actor. They are only valuable for avant-garde, improvisational, or story theater. In a film or a traditional play, the actor doesn't magically transform the set through his acting technique.

SCRIPTS

The attitude and spirit of agreement is what is important to the camera actor. If the author has written a scene of agreement, you have to be able to spot that and play it. The most common use of agreement alternating with conflict is found in comedy scripts. Sometimes both characters are in agreement for a five-line beat, then they switch to conflict for four lines, then they switch to agreement, and then they switch to conflict. Sometimes one character is in agreement and the other is in conflict, then it switches. Think of the great comedy teams, real and fictional: Abbott and Costello, Laurel and Hardy, Lucy and Ethel; Felix and Oscar, Vladimir and Estragon.

Playing agreement by yourself while your partner is in conflict means that you have to be the source of what you are agreeing with. You have to be in the groove by yourself and also the source of that groove.

> **TO THE COACH:** Stay alert to actors thinking that they are playing agreement when in fact they are really just not playing conflict. What they think is agreement is manifesting as apology or neutrality. Agreement must always be in the realm of enjoyment, enthusiasm, or excitement. ◆ When the actors are on their own, if one actor initiates all the acting focus changes, *coach*— Help your partner to initiate a focus change. ◆ When creating a format around agreement/conflict, part 2, start with repeats of invitations to agreement, part 2, and agreement.

WRITING CONFLICT/AGREEMENT EXERCISE

Part 1: Written Homework Assignment

I usually assign a writing, discussion, and acting exercise at this point in order to take advantage of all the conflict and agreement work that has just been completed and to start preparing the actors for the script analysis work coming up in chapter 12.

Based on your observing and playing a number of conflict and agreement improvisations up to this point, do some thinking about conflict and agreement. For the next class: (1) Everybody is to write a three-page, two-character scene, according to the following rules. (2) Prepare to discuss the differences and the similarities between agreement and conflict.

Alternate beats of disguised conflict with beats of agreement. For the first two pages, the conflict issue must be disguised; on the third page, it must rise into the text. Once the conflict issue is in the text, it may not be disguised any more and it must still alternate with at least one more beat of agreement. The length of the beats is up to you. There should be at least two beats per page. Do not write beats where one character is in conflict and the other is in agreement. In an agreement beat, both characters are in agreement. In a conflict beat, both characters are in conflict.

This is another chance to prepare for the script breakdown work. Those of you who had difficulty or any misunderstandings with the last writing assignment have an opportunity to show that you now understand what is necessary for disguised conflict.

The scenes must be typed, with copies for everyone in the class. Put your name on it. **In the next class, we will cast them and do cold readings.** It will be an excellent opportunity for you to become more knowledgeable about scripted agreement and conflict. Conflict is a common writer's device. Agreement, although much less common, is another. You will have to understand both very clearly when we get to script breakdowns. This assignment will show us what you do and don't know about agreement and conflict, and let us clear up any misunderstandings.

Some tips: The same as for "Writing Conflict Exercise" (p.465).

Part 2: In Class Performance

Casting Process and Performance

Follow the casting and presentation process for "Writing Conflict Exercise" (p.465).

Everyone Reads the Scene

The writer passes out the scripts of the scene they have just watched to the class. The writer of the next scene gives his scripts to his cast. After everyone has had a few minutes to read the scene they have just watched, the follow-up begins. During it, the actors in the next scene are reading it to themselves and then setting up its location.

> **FOLLOW-UP (as needed): What is the a conflict issue** (two opposing wants)? Does the conflict issue first appear in the text on page 3? What line? **Does the scene contain alternating beats of conflict and agreement?** Are there at least two beats per page? Are the turning points clear? Are there any beats of neither conflict nor agreement? Exactly where, what line? Did the scene fulfill the assignment? **Was the conflict, whether disguised or in the text, always played by the actors?** If not, when wasn't it? **Was the agreement always played by the actors?** If not, when wasn't it?

SUMMARY:

SEGUE TO PLAYING THE SCRIPT

This is the final part of Improvisation Technique training prior to learning script breakdown, choice making, and the application of the training to improvising those choices. Your conflict/agreement scene is a sample of a scripted scene. Most scripts are based on conflict, which is usually very dramatic. When you wrote your conflict beats, you were putting drama into your scenes. When you switched to agreement, you created a turn for the characters and the scene. When you switched back to conflict, you created another turn. Think of the material between those turns as little scenes. When the author is doing, say, conflict, it is a little scene of conflict only that will end when he switches and provides a turning point from conflict to something else, say, agreement. Whole scenes are made up of these little scenes, or *beats*.

When an actor prepares a whole scene, he focuses on these beats one at a time. After solving the individual beats, he strings them together in a run-through. If you encounter a director who doesn't work this way, take responsibility for the preparation on your own.

> **TO THE COACH:** Use the follow-up to clarify the same misunderstandings about *conflict* and *disguised conflict* noted in "To the Coach" (p. 467) after the writing conflict exercise. ◆ The most common misunderstanding about *agreement* will turn up in beats intended as agreement by the writer, but which are in fact simply beats of dialogue without conflict. ◆ Bear in mind that the assignment is designed to help the actors as actors, not as writers. In that regard, it is important that the actors not

only focus on what scripted beats of agreement and conflict look like but also become more aware of *turning points and their function and significance*. The actor must begin playing the conflict or agreement at the moment the beat changes in the text. The coach might point out that in reading a scene in preparation for the performance, the actor should mark the beat changes and label them accordingly. The label, either conflict or agreement, tells him how to play the beat. An agreement beat, for instance, should build with enthusiasm, rather than plateau in conviviality. It must *not* be played with apology or concern. ◆ After the last scene has been discussed, ask the actors what are the differences between agreement and conflict and what are the similarities.

DIFFERENCES

The main differences are the mood and emotions of the scene. Conflict is dark with anger and confrontation. Agreement is light with joy, enthusiasm, and teamwork. When the actor plays conflict, the actor's body is closed, and the muscles, tense. When the actor plays agreement, the body is open to the other actors, and the muscles, relaxed. In conflict, the character has a firm and invincible commitment to how things should be; he wants it his way. In agreement, the character is open to all possibilities; he is excited to try anything. The emotions and attitudes accompanying conflict are: tense, dissatisfied, uneasy, scared, angry, vicious, and sarcastic. The emotions and attitudes accompanying agreement are: pleased, cheerful, fun, serene, happy, enthusiastic, excited, convivial, gay, and joyful. If the actor is feeling or playing happiness, he is not fulfilling the purpose of conflict. If the actor is feeling or playing anger, he is not fulfilling the purpose of agreement. Both conflict and agreement have a feeling of direction in their physicalizations, but the directions are different. In conflict, the body feels horizontally directed; in agreement, vertically directed.

SIMILARITIES

Writers use conflict and agreement to move a scene forward with a definite rhythm, intensity, and mood. A scene is enhanced with excitement, energy, momentum, mood, anticipation, and intensified feelings, which makes the scene compelling for an audience.

Conflict and agreement bring characters together over an issue. In conflict, it's the two opposing wants, the conflict issue. In agreement, it's the subject or issue with which they are agreeing. There is something at stake between them. The more there is at stake, the better the scene.

When characters are in conflict or agreement, they continuously take actions, which will require reactions later. The audience knows this and is compelled to watch. In conflict, they want to know who is going to win and how the character will react to the next obstacle he meets. In agreement, they want to know how the character will build on what has just happened. In both conflict and agreement, the characters fulfill the audience's expectations with reactions that are usually accompanied with some dramatic changes in their emotional intensities. The ongoing struggle between the characters in conflict or the ongoing building of agreements gives a scene momentum and propels the whole script forward, bringing the audience right along with it.

The momentum of agreement and conflict is uniquely categorized by an intensifying rhythm and pace. Pauses seldom occur in a high-intensity conflict or in building agreements. As the pace and rhythm quicken, the intensity of feelings heightens, creating emotion arcs, which in turn heightens the rhythm still more.

◆　◆　◆

CHAPTER SUMMARY

Take away one of the two opposing sides in a conflict scene and you have no conflict. Bring that one side around to join the remaining side and you have agreement, both characters working or playing together in commonality. However, it is only agreement if the characters are working or playing together with joy, enthusiasm, and excitement. Agreement scenes serve a particular purpose in scripts. It is important that you recognize them and know how to improvise the playing of them.

Acting the Script with Improvisation Technique

12

Purpose of Scene

Acting, like anything else, is much easier when you know what to do. Acting with memorized lines is essentially about creating a character, making choices, and playing those choices spontaneously. These are skills. How well you perform these skills is the art.

The skill work for creating a character is covered in chapter 7. The skills for playing choices spontaneously are covered throughout the Improvisation Technique training, especially in chapters 9, 10, and 11. Except for the first level improvisations in chapter 8, however, we have not actually applied these skills to a script. Doing so is part of what this chapter is about. The other part of what this chapter is about is the skill of making choices. The first step is finding out when a choice is necessary.

MAKING CHOICES

Improvisation Technique provides you with a methodology for determining when to make a choice, deciding what kind of choice it should be, and playing the choice spontaneously. Once the skills for making the choices are learned, the quality of your choices will continually improve with practice from breaking down scenes. Throughout your career, you will continue to improve the quality of your choices. The process doesn't end until you're out of the business. You will always be learning to make better choices.

SCRIPTS ARE REWRITTEN

In order to begin, we must understand that scripts are not written. They are rewritten. No one has ever acted in a play, film, or TV show in which the script performed was the script as first created by the author. All professional scripts, even the bad ones, go through a series of rewrites. The author makes choices from draft to draft about what is worthy of remaining in the final draft, which is the finished script. Every scene, every line is scrutinized for emphasis and economy, both artistic and financial. In a finished script, *nothing remains unless it serves a purpose.*

A scene may be crucial to the development of the story: husband walks in on wife cheating on him. A scene may add dramatic tension to the story: divorcing couple argue over responsibility for the kids. A scene may provide comic relief from too much tension: father changes baby's diaper for the first time. A scene may reveal a particular aspect of a character's personality: divorced mother, distraught, watches from afar as father takes their child to first day of school.

PURPOSE OF SCENE

Playing in a scene without knowing its purpose is like doing a 2000-piece jigsaw puzzle without seeing the picture on the box, not very efficient and quite a bit more difficult, especially when you are being paid as a professional to do a great job as quickly as possible. *The actor in any scene should know the purpose of that scene in order to fulfill his part in serving that purpose.* That is the job. An actor who doesn't do that won't last very long in this profession, much less improve his booking average.

Knowing the purpose of the scene you are in allows you to see the picture on the box. Then you know what part of the whole scene you play. Dustin Hoffman says, "As an actor you're trying to get one with the author, and sometimes the only way to do that is to somehow make it your own, as they say. *But you make it your own with the same intent that the author had.*"[1] Once you know *your* part of the whole scene, you can make choices that will actually have you *playing* your part. That is what is really meant by being faithful to the author's intention. When Don Roos was nominated for a Writers Guild of America best screenplay award in 1999 for *The Opposite of Sex*, he said, "Since I was also the director on *Opposite*, I told the cast that the film would be about the script and the performances. It's not really an understood concept in Hollywood, respecting the text. I had actors who really wanted to respect the text; they didn't simply want to use it as a jumping-off point."[2] Discerning the purpose of the scene is what puts you in touch with the author's intent and opens up a whole new approach to making choices.

If the actor must prepare with minimal help from the director, then he must acquire some of the skills of a director in order to shape his performance. The primary skill is to see the scene not from one character's point of view, the way an actor traditionally sees the scene, but from the overall view of all the characters, which is the way the author sees the scene. When the author chose which characters he wanted in a particular scene and what they would do and say, he always had a purpose for these choices. The actor's job is to figure out what that purpose is and to play his part in serving that purpose.

This requires reading the script from the author's point of view and not your character's point of view, which doesn't consider the needs of the whole scene and too easily misses what part you have to play in it. You must *shift your focus from what the character wants, which is traditional acting, to what the author wants.* This means getting close to how the author was envisioning and hearing the scene in his head as he was writing it. Edward Albee says, "When I'm writing a play, I see it and hear it in front of me as a performed piece on stage, not out in some kind of limbo, but as a performed piece on stage by actors. So, I'm sitting in the audience listening to the dialogue—some of it's loud, some of it's soft, some of it's fast, some of it's slow. It's my responsibility to put down very precisely what I hear, to notate, very much the way a composer hears those things and notates them: quarter notes, half notes, dotted eighth notes. I do very much the same thing with punctuation."[3] About actors and directors, he says, "I don't care what anybody does, as long as they end up doing exactly what I intended. *I've also found that the further away actors get in rehearsal from what I have seen and heard, the greater difficulty they have in becoming the character.*"[4]

Writers don't write parts arbitrarily. Everything they write is intended to be as perfectly complete as, for example, a rainbow is. They don't want three reds when they can have red, blue, and yellow. Your job is to know whether you're playing red, blue, or yellow. If the writer intended your character to be blue, you don't want to duplicate red. In an art form that demands efficiency and emphasis, there's no point to a writer's providing multiple reds. Good scriptwriting is not redundant. Lesser writing will have some redundancy, but no writer in the world aims for that. Writers aim for as much variety and interest as possible and for having the different parts complement each other in serving the whole. You've got to find out what they were aiming for so you can play your part. Your art is in serving the whole, not in distorting, detracting from, or usurping it.

For the writer, a scene is defined by what it accomplishes in the service of the whole script. In the rewriting process, writers are scrupulous about cuts and changes, asking themselves, Do I need this scene or beat? For the writer to know if he needs it, he figures out what the scene is doing for the script. If it's not doing anything important, out it goes. If it's doing something that's already being done in another scene, it either gets cut or rewritten to accomplish something new.

CHOOSING THE PURPOSE OF SCENE

The author's choice of what the scene is doing for the script is what I call the *Purpose of Scene (POS)*. It stands for, "What is the author's purpose for putting this scene in the script?" A beat, which is a part of a scene, is the length of script devoted to serving a particular purpose. I use scene and beat interchangeably. No scene or beat exists in a script without a purpose. Academy Award-winning actor Robert DeNiro, when asked what he and Martin Scorsese dig for when they experience that a scene doesn't feel right, replied, "What's the purpose of the scene?"[5]

The purpose of the scene always originates with the author, never the actor. The actor interprets what he thinks the author's purpose is and should arrive on the set ready to serve that interpretation. If the director requests something else, then the actor adjusts. It used to be the director's job to make sure the actor served the purpose. Today, too many directors don't have a clue. The actor who arrives prepared is not dependent on Mr. Clueless.

From the actor's point of view, *a scene can have four possible purposes.*

Conflict

If a beat of the scene is about characters with opposing wants and the mood or tone of the beat is dark, then the purpose of that beat is conflict.

Agreement

If a beat of the scene is about characters playing or working together in commonality with joy, enthusiasm, and excitement, and there is no negating each other, then the purpose of that beat is agreement.

Story

If a beat of the scene includes an event or dialogue that is significant to moving the plot along, called a story point, then the purpose of that beat is story.

Scripts are generally constructed to move from one story point to another. To determine whether the something that happens is significant enough to be a story point, look at what follows it. If what follows it is based on the fact that it occurred, then it is a story point. In other words, without the story point occurring, there would be no reason for the text that follows it.

A beat may include new information and not be a story beat. If the new information is followed by dialogue or behavior that is *not* based on the new information, then the purpose of the beat is not story. If the new information is followed by dialogue or behavior that *is* based on the revelation of the information, then the beat is a story purpose of scene.

Character Revelation

If a beat of the scene is not about conflict, agreement, or story, then the purpose of that beat is to allow a character to reveal a particular emotional or attitudinal state. This purpose of scene is called character revelation. The revelation is rarely accomplished through direct dialogue, e.g., "I'm angry."

PROCESS FOR BREAKING DOWN THE SCENE

I have written a scene to demonstrate the process of breaking down the scene into POS choices. Assume that the scene occurs late in the first act; both characters are principals.

POS Step 1

Read the scene two or three times for simple comprehension.

POS Demo Scene

Husband and wife hang last piece of art on kitchen wall.

          TOM
Straighten the right side.

          SUE
There. It works great next to these curtains.

          TOM
This is a beautiful kitchen. We're done!

          SUE
The whole house is finished! I love it.

          TOM
It's really a showpiece.

          SUE
So let's show it.

          TOM
Party time!

          SUE
Yes! I'll make the guest list.

          TOM
All our friends.

                    SUE
Absolutely. Lois, Pat, Leslie,
Larry, Louise.

                    TOM
Ira, Lisa, Harriet, Lilly, Marty,
Paul.

                    SUE
Shelly, Lyn, Andy, Hal, and Jerry.
We have to plan a menu. What should
we have?

PAUSE.

                    TOM
Yeah. Sure. Whatever.

                    SUE
You think you can trust me to pick
the menu by myself? All right,
you stock the bar. That's your
department.

                    TOM
Thanks a lot. You want me to be the
waiter too?

                    SUE
What's your problem?

                    TOM
Why don't we just call Spago and
have them cater it. Of course we'll
have to sell the house to afford it.

                    SUE
We can afford this party.

                    TOM
    (snapping at her)
Not if you invite the whole phone
book.

                    SUE
Just our friends, Sourpuss.

                    TOM
Jerry?

                    SUE
What's wrong with Jerry?

                    TOM
A sleaze bag.

                    SUE
    (firmly)
He is not. He's extremely charming.

                TOM
           (sneering)
      I'll bet. Forget this party. It's a
      dumb idea.

                SUE
           (angry)
      Forget you. I want a party. And
      Jerry is our friend!

                TOM
           (screaming)
      He's not my friend!

SILENCE.

                SUE
           (softly)
      All right. No Jerry.

                TOM
      That's big of you.

                SUE
      I mean it. I didn't realize you
      don't like him.

                TOM
      HA! That's the point.

                SUE
      Really. I'm sorry. It's no big
      deal. We'll have a nice party with-
      out Jerry.

                TOM
      When's the last time you saw Jerry?

                SUE
      God, I don't know.

                TOM
      You don't know. What do you know?

                SUE
      Come on honey. We've finished deco-
      rating. Everything's so nice. Can't
      you enjoy it with me?

                TOM
      You bitch. We're talking about
      Jerry. Jerry! Jerry and you! It's
      bad enough you're screwing him. Now
      you want to bring him into our
      house . . . With all our friends
      here. What are you going to do,
      PARADE him around the house? SCREW
      him in our bed?!

```
                    SUE
          Oh, Tom, please, honey. Sweetie
          pie, stop this. There's nothing
          going on between Jerry and me.
          Don't be silly. I love you.

                    TOM
             (screaming)
          Silly! God damn you! I hate you. I
          hate you.

                    SUE
             (quietly)
          I'm sorry.
             (pause)
          Maybe if you made love to me once
          in a while. If you only paid atten-
          tion to me . . . you care more
          about this house than you do me.

                    TOM
          Oh, God. Why? Why? Why did you do
          this to me?

                    SUE
          I didn't do anything to you. It
          just happened. Jerry likes me. And
          he shows it. I need affection, Tom.

                    TOM
          Sue. Sue. I can't stand it. Oh,
          God. Please. No. No.

     LIGHTS FADE.
```

POS Step 2—Conflict

Read the scene at least once more with a specific assignment. This time, mark all the conflict beats. Use pencil because you're going to be making changes. Draw a line across the script where you think the conflict beat begins and another line where you think the beat ends. In the left margin, write "Conflict" and name the two opposing wants, e.g., she wants to put mom in nursing home vs. he doesn't.

Labeling the two opposing wants is essential. Do not be lazy and ignore this. If you label the beat as conflict, then you have the responsibility to articulate the two opposing wants. If you can't find the two opposing wants, then the beat is not conflict and you will have to make another choice. Remember that characters who are angry are not necessarily in conflict. They may be angry without any conflict issue being present, as when the anger is about something that has already happened. True conflict occurs when there is still something to be resolved—when there are two opposing wants.

Finding the beginning and ending of a conflict beat: When you spot a conflict section, you will probably spot it somewhere in the middle. Read a couple of more lines so you know it stays in conflict. Then read the section backward until you find where it starts. You are looking for the moment the two opposing wants went into opposition to each other. This is not necessarily the moment when both characters *state* what they want, since the conflict may have begun as a disguised conflict. When you've chosen the moment, draw your line across the page right above it. You have marked the beginning of the conflict beat. Now read forward from there. As you do, keep looking to see whether they are still in conflict. Draw a line there, right after they stop being in conflict.

- There can be successive conflict beats if the two opposing wants change from one beat to the next.

- It is always possible there are no conflict beats in the scene you are working on.

- Go through the scene, mark any beats of conflict, and ignore everything else.

If you have not done the training in part 4, "Improvising Professional Acting Skills," I suggest you read chapter 10, "Conflict," or at least the introductions and summaries. If you skip these and simply assume you know what I mean by conflict, you are missing the essentials and the process will not work for you yet.

POS Step 3—Agreement

When you have marked the beats of conflict, start again at the top of the scene and look for the beats of agreement. Go through the scene, find any beats of agreement, and draw your beat lines where you think the beat of agreement starts and where you think it ends. In the left margin of these beats, write "Agreement." Remember, agreement beats must follow the rules of agreement. The emotional feeling is happiness. There must be no negation of any kind. There is always a certain rhythm, intensity, and momentum; one thing, idea, or action always builds to another. If the beat has these prerequisites, it's probably an agreement beat. If you want further indications, chances are you'll find a lot of words from the "yes" family, such as "sure" or "okay," but these are only indicative. The first three, happiness, no negation, and building momentum, are definitive. If what you think are agreements are simply *echoes* (see chapter 11, "Agreement"), then it's probably not an agreement beat.

Finding the beginning and ending of an agreement beat: Take the same approach as you would with conflict. Find the middle of the beat, read backward to find the beginning, then forward to find the end.

- It is unlikely that you will ever see successive beats of agreement.

- It is always possible there are no agreement beats in the scene you are working on.

- Go through the scene, mark any beats of agreement, and ignore everything else.

POS Step 4—Story Points

Start at the top of the scene and look specifically for any story points. A story point is something significant that happens in view of the audience and moves the story forward, taking it (1) in another direction or (2) in the same direction but raising the stakes or speeding it up. In the left margin, next to the story point, write "Story" and name the story point, e.g., she finds a body. Naming a story point must be factual and not interpretive. If you can't name it factually, it probably isn't a story point. Do not draw beat lines.

A story point has nothing to do with stories about the past unless, and this is most pertinent for soap opera, the telling of the story from the past moves at least one of the characters in a new direction. For example, Aunt Helen tells her niece a story about how, when she was a young unmarried teenager, she gave birth, but the social stigma of the time forced her to give up the child. Her older, married sister raised the child as her own. In other words, the niece is her daughter. That story from the past would be a story point and it would be labeled, *Story: aunt reveals she is the mother.* Notice that the story point is labeled *factually.* Stories about the past that reveal some character background, back story, or exposition, but have no major significance on the characters telling or hearing them in the present are not story purpose of scene. Text about the past must propel the present story forward in order to be a story purpose of scene.

POS Step 5—Story Response

Once you have designated and labeled a story point, you must make an interpretive choice. What is the character's *response* to that story point? The choice is up to you as the interpretive artist. The answer is an emotional or attitudinal choice, and it is *never* what the script has you say in response to the story point. You must add to what the script provides by choosing an emotion, e.g., fear, anger, sadness, or an attitude, e.g., confident, needy, jealous.

Read the dialogue and stage directions for clues to the author's intention for the character's emotional response to the story point. In the example of the aunt/mother's confession to her niece/daughter, the niece/daughter's dialogue might indicate that she is angry when she hears the truth. In that case, the actor interprets that her response to the confession is "angry" and in the left margin under the story point label she writes, "Niece/daughter's response: angry." For the aunt/mother, the actor might interpret from the dialogue and stage directions that she is frightened. She writes, "Aunt/mother's response: fear."

The beginning of the story beat is marked by the moment the character is aware of the story point, e.g., discovers a dead body; sees her father with another woman; confesses something important. If the story point is provided by one character's dialogue, that character's beginning of the story beat is when she knows she is going to provide the story point, not necessarily the moment she actually does so. In the case of the aunt/mother, there will be a point a few or more lines prior to the actual confession when she knows she is approaching the moment when she will make the confession, and that is where her story beat begins. The niece/daughter has no foreknowledge of the confession, so her story beat begins when the confession begins.

The story beat ends when the character stops responding with the chosen emotion and begins a beat of conflict, agreement, or another story beat, or a new chosen emotion. In the latter case, you have found the end of the story beat and the beginning of the next beat, which will be character revelation.

- There can be successive beats of story if one story point follows another.

- It is always possible there are no story beats in the scene you are working on.

- When a story beat has more than one character in it, it requires response choices for all the characters in that beat.

Select your response(s) for the previously selected story point(s). Draw your lines indicating the start and end of any story beats. Any story point(s) and response(s) will be within those lines in the left margin.

POS Step 6—Character Revelation

Again, start at the top of the scene. Every unlabeled section of text that is not included in the conflict, agreement, or story beats is character revelation.

You cannot assume, however, that whatever is unlabeled is *one beat* of character revelation. In any one section of unlabeled text, there may be multiple and successive beats of character revelation. Use the process of elimination after finding the beats of conflict, agreement, and story to point you to the sections of character revelation. Then go into each of those sections and isolate the character revelation beats.

In a character revelation beat the author reveals a character's emotional or attitudinal state to the audience. When labeling a beat as character revelation your choice should be one word, naming the emotion or attitude. Read the dialogue and stage directions for clues left by the author. The clues are always there, and you must decipher them in order to make an interpretive choice of the author's intent.

Character revelation does not mean that the character has a revelation or that he reveals information through the dialogue about himself or anything else. Character revelation means that the character is experiencing a feeling, emotion, or attitude *regardless of what he is saying in the dialogue.*

For example, the character says, "I'm so confused," or, "You make me feel superior." There may not be such straightforward lines, but even if there were, confused or superior would not necessarily be good choices. Depending upon the rest of the dialogue and what's going on in the beats, the character's saying, "I'm so confused," might reveal frustration, not confusion. The character's saying, "You make me feel superior," might be revealing sadness, fear, anger, or happiness rather than superiority.

- The character revelation choice is the feeling that the character experiences while speaking the dialogue in the beat.

- The beat begins when the character commences the emotional or attitudinal state.

- The beat ends when that emotional state changes or another purpose of scene begins. For instance—

   The author is revealing in this beat that my character is confused. The beat ends when the author is choosing to end the character's confusion and a new beat begins right away because now the author is revealing that the character is frightened. That beat of fear ends when a conflict begins, where I have already drawn a line marking the beginning of the conflict beat.

Character revelation is the hardest purpose of scene to decipher because it is pure interpretation and it has the most leeway, the fewest boundaries. Whenever possible, your choice of the emotion or attitude should be a choice not previously used. The author is choosing to reveal something about a character to the audience and this usually means this is being revealed for the first time in this scene and possibly in the entire script.

- When an unlabeled beat becomes labeled as a character revelation beat and has more than one character in it, it requires character revelation choices for all the characters in that beat.

- It is likely that you will see successive beats of character revelation.

- You will seldom see a scene without any beats of character revelation.

Draw your beat lines across the script to indicate where the beats begin and end. In the left margin, write "Character Revelation," followed by your one-word emotional or attitudinal choice.

POS Step 7—Checking Turning Points

Every place you drew a line across the script page is a turning point. Each turning point defines where a scene beat begins or ends. Turning points are provided by the author and interpreted by you.

Since the author chose to begin and end each purpose at a specific turning point, don't you think you ought to know where it is so you can play it? It would be damaging to the scene if you kept playing conflict after he wrote the turn into agreement. Your part of the whole scene is to play conflict where the author wrote it, or agreement, or any purpose of scene the author had in mind

Review every turning point you have chosen. Make sure they designate where you think the beat should begin and end. Be prepared to make changes.

LABELING POS BEATS: COMMON BEGINNING QUESTIONS

Can a story point occur in the middle of a beat of conflict or agreement? Yes, but if it does, consider changing the beginning or ending of the conflict or agreement beat, so it no longer does. Can the beginnings and ends of beats be different for different characters? Yes, but it is not very common. Can a beat have multiple purposes, e.g., conflict and story? Yes. If this occurs, conflict or agreement takes precedence over story or character revelation. We deal with this further in chapter 14.

Demo Scene with POS Choices

Now let's compare choices. If you have not applied the previous steps to the demo scene, do it now, before reading ahead and seeing my breakdown. The process is designed for ease, accessibility, and success if you do the steps in the order they are presented.

```
Husband and wife hang last piece of art on
kitchen wall.
```

AGREEMENT

```
          TOM
Straighten the right side.

          SUE
There. It works great next to these
curtains.

          TOM
This is a beautiful kitchen. We're
done!

          SUE
The whole house is finished! I love
it.

          TOM
It's really a showpiece.
```

                    SUE
          So let's show it.

                    TOM
          Party time!

                    SUE
          Yes! I'll make the guest list.

                    TOM
          All our friends.

                    SUE
          Absolutely. Lois, Pat, Leslie,
          Larry, Louise.

                    TOM
          Ira, Lisa, Harriet, Lilly, Marty,
          Paul.

                    SUE
          Shelly, Lyn, Andy, Hal, and Jerry.
          We have to plan a menu. What should
          we have?

PAUSE.

CONFLICT (disguised)
Sue: Wants to invite Jerry
Tom: Don't invite Jerry

                    TOM
          Yeah. Sure. Whatever.

                    SUE
          You think you can trust me to pick
          the menu by myself? All right, you
          stock the bar. That's your depart-
          ment.

                    TOM
          Thanks a lot. You want me to be the
          waiter too?

                    SUE
          What's your problem?

                    TOM
          Why don't we just call Spago and
          have them cater it. Of course we'll
          have to sell the house to afford it.

                    SUE
          We can afford this party.

```
                    TOM
               (snapping at her)
          Not if you invite the whole phone
          book.
```

```
                    SUE
          Just our friends, Sourpuss.

                    TOM
          Jerry?
```

**(Note: Conflict issue rises into
text; no longer disguised)**

```
                    SUE
          What's wrong with Jerry?

                    TOM
          A sleaze bag.

                    SUE
               (firmly)
          He is not. He's extremely charming.

                    TOM
               (sneering)
          I'll bet. Forget this party. It's a
          dumb idea.

                    SUE
               (angry)
          Forget you. I want a party. And
          Jerry is our friend!

                    TOM
               (screaming)
          He's not my friend!
```

```
     SILENCE.
```

CHARACTER REVELATION:
Tom: jealous
Sue: nervous

```
                    SUE
               (softly)
          All right. No Jerry.

                    TOM
          That's big of you.

                    SUE
          I mean it. I didn't realize you
          don't like him.
```

>   TOM
> HA! That's the point.

>   SUE
> Really. I'm sorry. It's no big
> deal. We'll have a nice party with-
> out Jerry.

>   TOM
> When's the last time you saw Jerry?

>   SUE
> God, I don't know.

>   TOM
> You don't know. What do you know?

>   SUE
> Come on honey. We've finished deco-
> rating. Everything's so nice. Can't
> you enjoy it with me?

STORY: Tom confronts her about affair.

Tom's response: fury

Sue's response: scared

>   TOM
> You bitch. We're talking about
> Jerry. Jerry! Jerry and you! It's
> bad enough you're screwing him. Now
> you want to bring him into our
> house . . . With all our friends
> here. What are you going to do,
> PARADE him around the house? SCREW
> him in our bed?!

>   SUE
> Oh, Tom, please, honey. Sweetie
> pie, stop this. There's nothing
> going on between Jerry and me.
> Don't be silly. I love you.

>   TOM
>   (screaming)
> Silly! God damn you! I hate you. I
> hate you.

STORY: Sue admits affair.

Tom's response: despair

Sue's response: bitter

```
                    SUE
              (quietly)
        I'm sorry.
              (pause)
        Maybe if you made love to me once
        in a while. If you only paid atten-
        tion to me . . . you care more
        about this house than you do me.

                    TOM
        Oh, God. Why? Why? Why did you do
        this to me?

                    SUE
        I didn't do anything to you. It
        just happened. Jerry likes me. And
        he shows it. I need affection, Tom.

                    TOM
        Sue. Sue. I can't stand it. Oh,
        God. Please. No. No.

    LIGHTS FADE.
```

DEMO SCENE CHOICES: DISCUSSION

Agreement

If you did the breakdown on the demo scene, you probably found that this was the easiest beat to spot. The typical mistake is ending the beat too late, after Tom's line, "Yeah. Sure. Whatever." When the actor sees "Yeah" and "Sure," he often assumes that they belong within the agreement beat. They don't. There are two tip-offs. The first is the pause before Tom's line, which interrupts the heightening rhythm that always accompanies agreement. The second is the word "whatever," which communicates a sudden loss of the enthusiasm that Tom sustained throughout the agreement beat.

It is possible to interpret that Sue's line, "You think you can trust me," is said with enthusiasm and not sarcasm, justifying ending the agreement beat after her line. This would not be the best choice. To avoid it, figure that the agreement beat must end, at the latest, by the time Sue says, "What's your problem?" Work backward from there to see where the joy and enthusiasm, which must accompany agreement, really end. This should take you to the pause before Tom's line, "Yeah. Sure. Whatever."

Another way to interpret the end of the agreement beat, which would not hurt the purpose of the scene, would be to keep Sue in agreement until she says, "What's your problem?" However, Tom must start his conflict beat as indicated, before the pause. *Beats do not have to begin and end in the same place for all the characters.* They usually do, but it is not uncommon that they don't.

A third appropriate interpretation of the end of the agreement beat would be to give Sue an additional beat of character revelation, perhaps the emotion "cautious," from any time after Tom's pause until she says, "What's your problem?" During this small beat of character revelation by her, Tom is still in conflict.

Conflict

Missing the beginning of this beat by failing to recognize the disguised conflict is a common mistake. When you spot a conflict beat in the text, e.g., Tom's "I don't want Jerry at the party" vs. Sue's "I do," back up from where it enters the text and see whether the tone of the scene prior to this is as dark. Find the point at which the characters' emotions turn to unhappiness, tension, sarcasm, or anger. Or, find the point when the character *begins* to want what he wants even if he isn't saying it yet. In this scene, it is easy to see that Tom loses his enthusiasm and begins to feel tension as soon as Sue suggests inviting Jerry. That is when Tom begins to want what he wants: to not invite Jerry. The conflict beat begins there, but it is a disguised conflict until it enters the text where I have noted.

It is easier to spot the end of the conflict beat. Sue gives Tom what he wants: Jerry will not be invited. You must always state the two opposing wants when defining a conflict beat or you won't know if one character wins. If you don't know that the conflict is whether or not to invite Jerry, you might miss that the conflict ends when Sue says, "All right. No Jerry." In terms of conflict dynamics, Sue's line is when the actor gets to play the loss. Defining that line as the first line of her character revelation beat, "nervous," tells the actor how to play the loss—nervously.

Not all conflict beats will end with one character winning or losing. Many conflict beats end without the conflict resolved. To find the end of such a beat, look for the start of the next beat, whatever it is.

Story

Let's look at the story beats. Sue's suggesting that Jerry be invited is a story point because the entire rest of the scene flows from that moment. However, the characters' response is to go into the conflict: Invite Jerry vs. Don't invite Jerry. This is a multiple purpose of scene and conflict takes precedence. It is a significant moment when Tom says, "Jerry and you! It's bad enough you're screwing him." This is a turning point in the scene and is usually spotted as a story point. However, a common mistake is in the labeling of it.

Some actors carelessly label this as, "Sue is having an affair," but what is *important* about this moment in the scene, and what the author has actually written, is that Tom *confronts* her about the affair.

Labeling the story point accurately is essential because *what is important in the beat is the character's response to the story point.* If you label the story point, "Sue is having an affair," then the actor playing Sue will ask herself, "What's my response to having an affair?" But what is important is the response to being confronted about the affair. Given the same inaccurate label, the actor playing Tom will be asking himself, "What's my response to Sue's having an affair?" It's the wrong question for this scene. The necessary response is his response to confronting her about it.

Another mislabeling of this beat is calling it conflict. An actor might see Sue's line, "Stop this," and think that she is in conflict with Tom. Searching for the two opposing wants necessary before labeling a beat as conflict, the actor might come up with Tom's "I want you to give up Jerry" vs. Sue's "I don't want to," which would be incorrect because she is still denying there is an affair; or Tom's "I want to shout and be mad" vs. Sue's "I want you to calm down," which wouldn't be conflict because her text, "Honey. Sweetie pie...I love you," is not in conflict tones (which applies as well to the first example).

A possible labeling of this story beat would be to begin the beat earlier, at Tom's line, "When's the last time you saw Jerry?" If you do that, you are interpreting that Tom knows he is going to confront her about the affair at this point or is firmly on the way to doing so. If you start the beat here, it doesn't change what the story point is, or their responses. I interpret the start of the beat later because I interpret that he only goes to the fury and confrontation because she says the lines that suggest they are a happy couple, "Come on, honey. We've finished decorating. Everything's so nice. Can't you enjoy it with me?" Back at, "When's the last time you saw Jerry," I don't think he has decided yet to confront her.

Identifying story points is a skill. They are in the script as dramatic facts, and you have to learn to look for them. The fact is that Tom confronts Sue about the affair. The art is in coming up with your choice of a response. You have to interpret the dialogue and stage directions surrounding the story point, your knowledge of the character's personality, behavior, and arc, and the given circumstances. In this demo scene, it is obvious that your choice should be something from the anger family.

There is more leeway for the choice of a response for Sue when she is confronted. The author clearly chose for the husband to be furious. The nature of her dialogue eliminates anger. I chose scared, but it could be apologetic or loving. Knowing which to choose comes with practice and more information about the process.

When choosing a story point response, remember to *look for what the author chose for the character, not for what you would do in the same situation.* What do you think the author was imagining for the wife's response to this fury? *What was the author's intent?*

At the risk of getting ahead too quickly, I will discuss my choice of scared. It seems a reasonable choice for a wife being confronted by a furious husband. Also, notice the connection between my choice for Sue in the previous beat and my choice for her in this beat. In the former, I chose nervous for her character revelation. By giving her a response of scared in the next beat, I have constructed a fear arc for her character. Does that make sense to you, if you are a woman and your husband is heading toward confronting you and then does accuse you? The fear arc is even more complete if you took the earlier option of adding a little character revelation beat of cautious at the end of the agreement beat. A character playing three consecutive beats, cautious, nervous, scared, is communicating a rising arc of fear. With practice and more tips about the process, you will soon understand how to let the beat choices prior to and following the current beat influence your choice for the current beat.

As the scene continues, Sue stops denying the affair and admits it when she says, "It just happened." The admission is the next story point. Given what this scene is about, and that everything that follows stems from this moment, this is a clear story point. In the simplest terms, when a character goes from denying to admitting something important, it is always a story point. However, the actor must see that the beginning of this story beat occurs earlier. Even though the admission is not actually in the text, it is on her mind and what she is referring to when she says, "*(Quietly)* I'm sorry." The story beat begins here. Everything that follows this moment is about their responses to her admission. Their responses stay consistent and nothing changes for either character from the beginning of this beat until the end of the scene, so the beat doesn't end until the end of the scene.

For Tom, obviously choices in the happy family should be eliminated. I eliminated the anger family because in other beats the author is very clear about when Tom is angry. He uses the stage directions: sneering, angry, screaming. He gives Tom angry dialogue. If he wanted Tom angry in this beat, he would have indicated it. I also considered that Tom is pretty angry for most of the scene prior to her admission. If her admission is a major story point, which it must be, then perhaps the author thinks Tom's anger should change to something else. His response to her admission might be in either the sad or fear families. Looking at his dialogue in the beat, I saw no clues that he was in fear. As I ran the beat in my head with him in fear, trying to capture the author's process, I interpreted that fear was too melodramatic. I ran the beat in my head once more; this time I saw him being sad. The dialogue flowed easily and it worked. Looking at the dialogue the author gave him, I realized the emotion was a very high-stakes sad, which led me to choose despair.

For me, the hardest and most sophisticated choice in the scene is her response to the admission story point. Other than the stage direction, "quietly," and the obvious fact that she is not happy, there are few clues in her dialogue to point the actor in any one direction. She could be self-righteous, angry, terrified, sad, or defiant. How to choose? In my opinion, the author has given her enough fear prior to the admission, so he wants it to change from the fear family. Looking at Tom in despair, I decided to look at the dynamics of the whole beat, reminding myself that this beat is the last beat of the scene. Whatever I choose for this beat must set up what is going to happen in the rest of the script.

Something in the sad family seems appropriate, but with Tom in despair, I think the author's choice of sad for Sue would be redundant. It would read as self-pity, lessening the dramatic potential and leading the audience to care less, not more, about what happens to these characters.

Having eliminated the fear, happy, and sad families, I must consider the anger family. Taking into account the "quietly" stage direction and the fact that Tom is in despair, I look for a low-volatility level of anger and come up with bitter. I run the scene in my mind with Tom in despair and Sue in bitter. There is now a very interesting, dramatic, and authentic dynamic to the beat. I immediately understand that she is bitter that her husband didn't uphold his part of the marriage, that she is in this cheesy position, and that she doesn't know what's going to happen next. It works well. It heightens audience interest in the future of the characters and sets up whatever is going to happen in the next scene.

A story point is a fact. It overrides everything else. While choosing a story point is not an interpretive issue, the choice of responses is interpretive. *A story point is a stop sign in the script that demands: Make a choice here!* Your character has been accused of adultery. How does she feel about that?

Character Revelation

After identifying all of the conflict, agreement, and story beats, there is only one uninterrupted section of the scene left unlabeled. This section will be character revelation. The first choice to be made is whether it is one or more beats of character revelation. Track each character, *individually*, from the beginning to the end of the section. See whether they change their basic emotions or attitudes along the way. If they do, then it will be more than one beat, and the beat will change when they do.

In our demo scene, let's start with Tom. Going into the character revelation section, he is angry and in conflict. His first line in this section, "That's big of you," indicates he is still in the anger family. It may be a lot less volatile then his previous line, "*(Screaming)* He's not my friend," but that's understandable, considering he has just won the conflict. We know that his anger is really about the affair, not just the fact that she wants to invite Jerry to the party, so winning the conflict over Jerry's being invited does not assuage his anger. If you read ahead from that point, *skipping over the other character's lines*, we see that he stays in the anger family. Looking ahead to the next beat, the first story beat, we know he is still angry. So, from the beginning of the character revelation section until the end, there is no change in Tom's emotional or attitudinal state. For the actor playing Tom, this section will be one beat.

Now, let's track Sue. At the end of the previous conflict beat, we know she is angry. However, at the beginning of this character revelation section, she loses the conflict, and the stage directions indicate that she starts the beat with silence and she says her first line "softly." The combination of the conflict loss, played in the silence, and the "softly" stage direction eliminates anger as the emotion choice. According to the rules of playing conflict, if you have a loss, you must play it. Playing a loss in anger would not be playing a loss; it would be continuing the conflict. It's obvious that we can also eliminate happy. Of the four basic emotion families, this leaves sad or fear.

Interpreting between those two *requires that we review the given circumstances*. At this point in the scene, they have just turned a happy time, the agreement beat over finishing their house and planning a party, into a quarrel over whether or not to invite her lover, Jerry, to the party, and she doesn't know if Tom knows about the relationship. Also, later in the scene, when Tom reveals that he does know about the relationship, she at first denies it. Those are the given circumstances. Notice that they are facts, not interpretation.

Do you think that the author chose to have her become sad over the fact that Jerry won't be coming to the party or sad over the state of her marriage? Or do you think the author chose to have her become fearful over the possibility that Tom knows about the relationship? After all, why did Tom get so upset over Jerry's invitation? *The given circumstances will guide you to your interpretive choice.*

I chose that her basic emotion is in the fear family. Knowing that I have already selected that she is going to get scared when Tom confronts her later in the scene only supports my decision. *When making choices, always look at the beat before and the beat after the beat you are working on.* Since she is going to get scared in the next beat, the intensity of her fear in this section, where there is no confrontation yet, must be less than scared. My interpretive choice is nervous. Other appropriate choices might be concerned, aware, or suspicious (of whether Tom knows about Jerry). Any of these choices from the fear family would also be appropriate for playing the loss at the beginning of the section.

If you read her first line in this section as nervous and then read ahead from that point, *skipping over the other character's lines*, you see that she easily stays in the nervous feeling. And when, in the next beat, he confronts her, it raises the stakes of the situation and her nervousness is heightened to scared. These choices, in tandem, also fulfill a natural fear arc. *Constructing natural emotion arcs always makes for dynamic choices.* So, from the beginning of the character revelation section until the end, there is no change in Sue's emotional or attitudinal state. For the actor playing Sue, this section will be one beat, just as it is for Tom.

A more intuitive and simple reading of the beat will reveal that from the beginning of the beat until the end, Sue displays a submissive and supplicating attitude and Tom is obviously upset and/or angry. This might lead you to decide that this section is only one beat, because these attitudes and emotions don't change.

In focusing on whether this section is one beat or more, we have also discovered our character revelation emotion choice for Sue. Now we have to return to Tom and decide what is his specific choice from the anger family.

Looking backward, we know that in the conflict beat the author chose sneering and screaming. Then Tom won the conflict. Looking forward, we know from the dialogue and from our choice that he is furious. What is something from the anger family that would fit between these beats? *Look at the dialogue for a hint.* All of his lines except one, "When's the last time you saw Jerry," are sarcastic, which would be an excellent choice from the anger family. Look closely at that one line, however. The author has placed emphasis on it by not making it not *necessarily* sarcastic when all of the other lines in the beat are clearly sarcastic. Given that line, plus everything else we know about this scene, he sounds jealous to me. Tom's character revelation choice for this beat would be jealous or, if the actor chooses to say the line sarcastically, it could be sarcastic.

After you have made your character revelation choices, double-check them by asking yourself, *What is the character* (emotion choice, i.e., *nervous*) *about?* Or, *Why is the character* (emotion choice, i.e., *jealous*)? If you can answer the question, e.g., *Sue is nervous that Tom will find out about her affair; Tom is jealous of Jerry, his wife's lover*, and the answer makes sense to you, your choice will be all right.

As you make your choices for each of the beats, you become more familiar with the entire scene, and the choice for one beat might cause you to reconsider the choice for another beat. It is totally appropriate to make changes in previously labeled beats. You might discover you mislabeled the beginning and ending of a beat or, if you change an emotion choice in one beat, you will have the character fulfilling a natural emotion arc.

DEMO SCENE CHOICES: SUMMARY

Let's look at what you have accomplished up to this point with a purpose of scene approach. You have a game plan for the scene. You know what your beats are and what you will bring to them, you have selected turning points, and your preselected choices are based on a thorough, reasonable interpretation of the author's intention for each scene.

In the event that there is minimal or no rehearsal time for further exploration or that the director is of no help, you are prepared for every moment in the scene. Should there be rehearsal time, or a helpful director, you are prepared with a solid jumping-off point.

In the theater, your preselected choices give you a game plan for later in the rehearsal process. In film and television, you don't have the four to six weeks of rehearsal you might have in the theater. You arrive on the set on day one expected to give an opening night performance; you *must* preselect your choices. When Kevin Spacey was asked what the difference was between acting in film and acting in the theater, he said, "None. It's about *finding what the writer wanted you to feel and experience and making sure you get that across* in whatever medium it is."[6] Whether you're working in theater or on camera, your choices can always change. As you work with your fellow actors and the director, better choices may evolve. Still, as a professional, you must show up, ready to go, with your own game plan, prepared to spontaneously improvise it on each take.

Directors love actors who show up with preselected choices, as long as the actor is also facile and open to going with other choices. It gives them a chance to see another point of view on the scene from the one person who should be at least as knowledgeable about the scene as they are. If a director is prepared on the technical side but hasn't done the rest of his homework, he sees the actor come in with acting choices and says, "Thank God, she is on the ball. We're covered. I cast the right actor." If he has done the rest of his homework and has made his own preselected choices, he may say, "No, I like my way better," or he may say, "She came up with a better idea. It's great. Keep it." Stella Adler taught a more traditional approach, but she always told her students, "The talent is in the choices."

The actor who doesn't make choices reveals himself as an amateur. In what is an unhealthy trend today, there are actors who say, "I don't have to make choices ahead of time. I have to be totally in the moment. I've learned to go with the flow of honest listening and responding, taking whatever emotions arise from that. I can't be *in the moment* if I make a preselected choice."

These are actors who don't know how to make choices and/or don't want to do the homework. The professional actor knows that once you've made a choice, you can always change. What's more, and this is far more important, *the actor using Improvisation Technique preselects the choices but improvises the playing of those choices.* That is what being in the moment really means: spontaneously playing a preselected choice, incorporating whatever your scene mates provide in the moment, while remaining open to abandoning that choice and going with another should the opportunity for something new and dynamic arise.

IMPROVISING THE CHOICES

The breakdown of the scene into beats and labeling the purpose of the beats is the homework, the creation of your own direction for your part of the whole scene. Having done your homework, you have your text, which you are going to say, and you have your map of what you are going to act, or do. Each beat is approached separately for rehearsal in stage or camera acting. If you are doing camera acting, with or without rehearsals, each beat is prepared separately for performance. *Preparation begins with selecting an improvisational acting focus that will fulfill your chosen purpose of the scene.*

Conflict

Conflict beats are fulfilled by employing a conflict acting focus. The only issues involved with selecting a conflict acting focus have to do with the intensity level of the conflict and whether or not the conflict issue is disguised. *It is recommended that you begin with pull the conflict* (disguised). If the resulting improvisation is too intense, or not intense enough, adjust the intensity through the following approaches, which we examined in chapter 10: (1) Change the acting focus to another conflict acting focus (p. 464). (2) Change the conflict issue to more accurately represent the desired intensity level. This is easily done when you are employing a substitute disguised conflict (p. 471). (3) Adjust the stakes of your private reasons (p.471). (4) Any combination of the above.

Whether you use a disguised conflict to substitute for any conflict issue in the text will be determined by your personal preference and whether or not the conflict issue in the text is disguised by the author prior to bringing it up into the text (p. 469).

In the POS demo scene, I would select pull the conflict as the primary acting focus for the conflict beat, using the actual conflict issue, "I don't want to invite Jerry" vs. "I want to invite Jerry," as the disguised conflict until the conflict issue rises into the text at Tom's line, "Jerry?" At that line, I would change the disguised conflict issue to "I want you to stop sleeping with Jerry" vs. "I want to continue sleeping with Jerry." In that way, I have a new disguised conflict issue to focus on while I say the lines pertaining to whether or not Jerry should be invited, the text conflict issue. In the margin of the conflict beat, under the conflict label and two opposing wants, I would write, "Acting focus: Pull the conflict (disguised/I don't want you to invite Jerry because [add personal reason]) vs. (disguised/I want to invite Jerry because [add personal reason])." At the line, "Jerry," I would write in the margin, "Pull the conflict (disguised/stop sleeping with Jerry because [add personal reason] vs. (disguised/continue sleeping with Jerry because [add personal reason])."

The intensity level of the conflict will be arrived at spontaneously through the combination of your being on the acting focus of pull the conflict and the text you say, listening to your scene mate, any business, and any directorial input. Each rehearsal or take will be improvised spontaneously within the boundaries of the rules and dynamics of conflict. This will fulfill your chosen purpose of the scene, regardless of whether or not there is any rehearsal time or directorial input. *Improvise on the acting focus and you will improvisationally play your preselected choice.*

Agreement

Agreement is the easiest purpose of scene to fulfill. The acting focus choice is always agreement. The level of intensity of the agreement will be arrived at spontaneously through the combination of your being on the acting focus and the text you say, listening to your scene mate, any business, and any directorial input. Each rehearsal or take will be improvised spontaneously within the boundaries of the rules and dynamics of agreement. This will fulfill your chosen purpose of the scene, regardless of whether there is any rehearsal time or directorial input. In the margin of your agreement beat write "Acting focus: Agreement." *Improvise on the acting focus, agreement, and you will be improvisationally playing your preselected choice.*

Story and Character Revelation

Story and character revelation beats use the same type of improvisation acting focuses because they are about emotions and attitudes. The most common choices are physicalize an emotion, emotion arc, emotion switch, and attitude line. On occasion, other acting focuses are very specifically appropriate: off stage; active & still; paralysis; extend, intensify, and enlarge; object (or environment) struggle; and emotions & objects.

After selecting the emotion or attitude for the beat, look at the size of the beat and your choices for the neighboring beats. If the beat is small, less than a third of a page, consider whether your character is plateauing in one intensity of the chosen emotion or escalating the intensities of the emotion in a limited arc. This is an interpretive decision. If the character is plateauing, the improvisation acting focus should probably be physicalize an emotion or, if there is business with props, emotions & objects. Unless the director wants an adjustment, every take is approached like a first level improvisation. Say your lines while improvising on the acting focus, physicalize an emotion or emotions & objects.

If the beat is medium-sized or more, make the same decision about plateauing or arcing. Now, however, strongly consider the possibility of an emotion arc. When you make the interpretive decision to arc the selected emotion, the improvisation acting focus should be emotion arc. Choose the intensity level you will start on and improvise up the arc as you say your lines. You may also choose the highest level of intensity you want to arrive at, your preselected top of the arc, and select the line you want to get there by, usually the last line(s) of the beat. *The improvisation is the traveling up the arc between the designated beginning and ending intensities, while you say your lines and listen to others' lines.* When you do this, you have served your interpretation of the script and every take will be spontaneous because you are improvising the escalation of the emotion arc's intensities. Depending on the director's feedback you can adjust subsequent takes by starting at a lower or higher intensity and escalating to a lower or higher intensity. If the director wants a different emotion, change the emotion to what he wants and arc that. If he wants the emotion to change midbeat to another emotion, use emotion switch and decide if you should arc either or both emotions, or plateau both.

If your character has two or more successive beats of character revelation or story, and you have decided not to use any arcs, then the improvisation acting focus will be emotion switch. You have preselected the turning points for the switches at the beat changes. Stay open to the possibility of choosing different turning points for each take. However, they will all probably be within a few lines of the preselected beat change. In the two short story beats, Sue should use emotion switch: scared to bitter. Tom might do the same with fury to despair. Tom might also employ an emotion arc for the fury beat, starting with anger and escalating to fury.

In the demo scene, the size of the character revelation beat allows for either improvising around one level of intensity or arcing a few levels of intensity. For instance, Sue could improvise physicalizing nervous or she could start improvising around cautious and escalate through nervous and agitated. Either way, she will be in the perfect spot to escalate to scared in the next beat when Tom confronts her.

Tom, on the other hand, has an opportunity to employ a totally different improvisation acting focus in that character revelation beat. Jealous is the kind of emotion or attitude that is difficult to physicalize because it is made up of different feelings. A person may be jealous and actually feeling fear (of abandonment), sad (from abandonment), or angry (from betrayal). Tom could do an umbrella arc (p. 375, 546) including two or three of these feelings. Alternatively, to create an improvisation on the feeling of jealousy, Tom could employ off stage as his acting focus. He might choose to focus on the off stage past or future event of Sue flirting with Jerry. Unless the director wants an adjustment, every take is approached like a first level improvisation. Say your lines while focusing on the off stage event and reflecting it with your body. For subsequent takes, change the location of the off stage event, or its time, past or future, or its stakes. Another improvisation acting focus that would work well for Tom's jealousy would be an attitude line, "I'm jealous." At the turning point into the character revelation beat, Tom would physicalize the attitude line and focus on retaining it in the body while saying his lines and listening to Sue's lines.

For even more spontaneity, the actor playing Tom could mark his script with all these choices and use a different improvisation acting focus for each take. For instance: Take 1, physicalize emotion/sarcastic; Take 2, off stage; Take 3, attitude line; Take 4, off stage/change circumstances.

With all of these improvisations, while you stay on your acting focus you are listening to your scene mates and integrating what they say and how they say it as a part of your whole acting focus.

The choices for the improvisation acting focus should be written in the margin with all the other choices. I suggest, wherever possible, that you have at least four improvisation acting focuses and/or circumstance changes listed for each beat so that you are prepared for multiple takes without directorial input. You won't have to remember them because they'll be listed in your script and you can take a quick look at your script between takes. For theater, these multiple acting focuses are employed at different rehearsals of the same beat.

Final Demo Script

The final demo script should look something like this. Tom's choices are in the left margin and Sue's in the right.

```
Husband and wife hang last piece of art on
kitchen wall.
```

AGREEMENT

Acting focus: Acting focus:
Takes 1 & 2: Agreement   Takes 1 & 2: Agreement
3: Physicalize happy   3: Physicalize happy
4: Arc happy   4: Arc happy

```
                    TOM
         Straighten the right side.

                    SUE
         There. It works great next to these
         curtains.

                    TOM
         This is a beautiful kitchen. We're
         done!

                    SUE
         The whole house is finished! I love
         it.

                    TOM
         It's really a showpiece.

                    SUE
         So let's show it.

                    TOM
         Party time!

                    SUE
         Yes! I'll make the guest list.
```

TOM
All our friends.

SUE
Absolutely. Lois, Pat, Leslie,
Larry, Louise.

TOM
Ira, Lisa, Harriet, Lilly, Marty,
Paul.

SUE
Shelly, Lyn, Andy, Hal, and Jerry.
We have to plan a menu. What should
we have?

PAUSE.

CONFLICT (disguised)

Sue: Wants to invite Jerry

Tom: Don't invite Jerry

Acting focus:	Acting focus:
Take 1: Pull the conflict (disguised/ I don't want to invite Jerry because I'll feel like a fool.)	Take 1: Pull the conflict (disguised/I want to invite Jerry because he makes me feel alive.)
2: (disguised/I don't want a party because we can't afford it.)	2: (disguised/I want to invite Jerry so my girlfriends can see him.)
3: Relationship struggle	3: (disguised/I want your dressing room because it's bigger.)
4: What to do with the conflict?	4: What to do with the conflict? Win!

TOM
Yeah. Sure. Whatever.

SUE
You think you can trust me to pick
the menu by myself? All right,
you stock the bar. That's your
department.

TOM
Thanks a lot. You want me to be the
waiter too?

SUE
What's your problem?

TOM
Why don't we just call Spago and
have them cater it. Of course we'll
have to sell the house to afford it.

> SUE
> We can afford this party.

> TOM
> (snapping at her)
> Not if you invite the whole phone
> book.

> SUE
> Just our friends, Sourpuss.

> TOM
> Jerry?

(Note: Conflict issue rises into text; no longer disguised)

New acting focus:	New acting focus:
Take 1: Pull the conflict (disguised/I want you to stop sleeping with Jerry because it's killing me.)	Take 1: Pull the conflict (disguised/I want to keep Jerry as my lover because I need sex.)
2: (disguised/I want you fired because I hate working with you.)	2: (disguised/I want you to take a long trip because I want to be with Jerry.)
3: Pull the conflict (not disguised)	3: Pull the conflict (notdisguised)
4: What to do with the conflict? Win!	4: What to do with the conflict? Win!

> SUE
> What's wrong with Jerry?

> TOM
> A sleaze bag.

> SUE
> (firmly)
> He is not. He's extremely charming.

> TOM
> (sneering)
> I'll bet. Forget this party. It's a
> dumb idea.

> SUE
> (angry)
> Forget you. I want a party. And
> Jerry is our friend!

> TOM
> (screaming)
> He's not my friend!

SILENCE.

CHARACTER REVELATION

Tom: jealous

Sue: nervous

Acting focus:

Take 1: Off stage/future
  (Sue & Jerry flirting
  during the party)

2: Attitude line/ I'm jealous.

3: Emotion switch (hurt/anger)

4: Physicalize brooding

Acting focus:

Take 1: Physicalize nervous

2: Off stage/future (Tom finding
  Jerry's love letters)

3: Attitude line/ I'm nervous

4: Arc nervous. (cautious,
  nervous, agitated)

                    SUE
                (softly)
          All right. No Jerry.

                    TOM
          That's big of you.

                    SUE
          I mean it. I didn't realize you
          don't like him.

                    TOM
          HA! That's the point.

                    SUE
          Really. I'm sorry. It's no big
          deal. We'll have a nice party with-
          out Jerry.

                    TOM
          When's the last time you saw Jerry?

                    SUE
          God, I don't know.

                    TOM
          You don't know. What do you know?

                    SUE
          Come on honey. We've finished deco-
          rating. Everything's so nice. Can't
          you enjoy it with me?

STORY: Tom confronts her about affair.

Tom's response: fury

Sue's response: scared

Acting focus:

Take 1: Physicalize fury

2: Arc anger to fury

3: Off stage/future (Sue & Jerry
   kissing passionately in front
   of party guests)

4: Attitude line/I'm furious.

Acting focus:

Take 1: Arc fear
   (nervous to frightened)

2: Physicalize fear

3: Attitude line/I'm scared.

4: Paralysis (If I move he'll kill me.)

> TOM
> You bitch. We're talking about
> Jerry. Jerry! Jerry and you! It's
> bad enough you're screwing him. Now
> you want to bring him into our
> house . . . . With all our friends
> here. What are you going to do,
> PARADE him around the house? SCREW
> him in our bed?!

> SUE
> Oh, Tom, please, honey. Sweetie
> pie, stop this. There's nothing
> going on between Jerry and me.
> Don't be silly. I love you.

> TOM
>   (screaming)
> Silly! God damn you! I hate you. I
> hate you.

STORY: Sue admits affair.

Tom's response: despair

Sue's response: bitter

Acting focus:

Take 1: Emotion switch & arc despair
   (fury to sad, miserable, hopeless)

2: Off stage/future (life in prison
   for killing her)

3: Attitude line/It's hopeless.

4: Active & still (Note: keep all
   traveling on sad railroad tracks)

Acting focus:

Take 1: Emotion switch
   (frightened to bitter)

2: Attitude line/I'm bitter.

3: Off stage/past (walking in
   on Tom kissing his secretary)

4: Physicalize bitter

> SUE
>   (quietly)
> I'm sorry.
>   (pause)
> Maybe if you made love to me once
> in a while. If you only paid atten-

```
        tion to me . . . you care more
        about this house than you do me.

                TOM
        Oh, God. Why? Why? Why did you do
        this to me?

                SUE
        I didn't do anything to you. It
        just happened. Jerry likes me. And
        he shows it. I need affection, Tom.

                TOM
        Sue. Sue. I can't stand it. Oh,
        God. Please. No. No.

    LIGHTS FADE.
```

REHEARSAL PREPARATION PROCESS FOR IMPROVISING YOUR CHOICES

Assuming you have time to prepare on your own, you should rehearse after making your choices. Rehearsing means exploring and becoming familiar with the use of your primary acting focus choice with the dialogue, seeing if your choice works or if it is limiting you. Rehearsal is your opportunity to change your choices as a result of your explorations. It is good to rehearse with other actors, even if they are not in the cast. They will play with you and they have an appreciation of and respect for the seriousness of your preparation. It's even better to rehearse with actors experienced with Improvisation Technique because they will be helpful in a follow-up process to determine whether you stayed on your acting focus. If you have to work with a non-pro friend, the process can still work. All the other person has to have is a patient, respectful attitude and the ability to read the other lines on cue. I do not recommend your asking the friend for criticism, and if the friend keeps putting his two non-pro cents in, work with a tape recorder instead. Put the other character's lines on the tape, leaving time for your own lines.

Memorize the lines. All the lines of the scene you are rehearsing must be memorized. You can't improvise on an acting focus if you are struggling with the lines or worse, still carrying the script. The approach used here is essentially the same as for first level improvisations. Working beat by beat, improvise fully on the selected acting focus while saying the memorized lines and seeing and hearing your scene mates. Do not memorize your beat choices.

Rehearse one beat at a time. Look at your beat choices in the script. Approach the beat as a first level improvisation, committing to your chosen and primary acting focus, e.g., physicalize an emotion or pull the conflict, and saying your lines on cue. If you feel you have not been totally on your acting focus, repeat the beat until you can do it thoroughly on your acting focus. Then go on to the next beat in the same fashion. When the second beat is totally on the acting focus, run the first two beats, spontaneously handling the turning point between them. Then, approach the third beat in the same thorough fashion as each of the first two beats. When you are accomplished in the third beat, do a run-through of the first three beats. Continue this process for every beat until the end of the scene you are preparing. The first run-through including the last beat is the final run-through. By now, your body remembers the choices.

Thoroughly improvise each beat rehearsal and run-through. If you improvise on your acting focus, then each beat rehearsal and run-through will be totally spontaneous and within the parameters of your selected purpose of scene choice. This will also prepare you to improvise each take and not settle in to your choice, re-creating what you think works. On the set, if your first take is considered perfect, but for some reason they have to do another take, do not attempt to re-create that first perfect take. Re-creation and creation are two different things. You will only be killing spontaneity. Improvise the second take, either changing or not changing the acting focus or circumstances. This is your opportunity to do the take perfectly in a new way.

FIRST SCENE EXERCISE FOR LEARNING POS

In anticipation of this exercise, the class pairs up, chooses, and prepares five-minute scenes for presentation in class. I assign one scene per class and I alternate classes with a return to emotion acting focus improvisations. The actors must bring copies of the scripted scene for every member of the class. In the first class, purpose of scene is introduced and the actors make their first POS breakdown using the previous demo scene. Then choices are compared and considered using the "Demo Scene Choices: Discussion" portion of this chapter as a guide. In subsequent classes, the actors perform the rehearsed scene at the beginning of the class.

Breakdown

The only discussion after the scene should be the performing actors relating any given circumstances in the script which precede the scene and are important to the breakdown choices. Copies of the scene are distributed and everyone breaks down the scene on their own according to the process used with the demo scene in this chapter. No acting focus choices are made, just POS. The coach also does a breakdown during this time. Allow about one hour.

When everyone has finished, the coach leads a discussion of the choices with questions that parallel the breakdown process.

CONFLICT: Any beats of conflict? How many of you got one beat of conflict? Two beats? Three? More? Let's start with the earliest page where you have a beat of conflict. Anyone have a beat on the first page? If yes, where does the beat begin and end? What are the two opposing wants? ✦ The coach leads a class discussion on whether or not this beat is conflict and whether the beginning and end are accurate. ✦ *When that discussion is over—* Who has found the next beat of conflict? ✦ And so on, until every beat of conflict that the actors have selected has been discussed, agreed to, modified, or rejected. Finally, guided by the coach, the class agrees on the final conflict beat choices.

AGREEMENT: Any beats of agreement? ✦ Follow the same process as for conflict, excluding the two opposing wants. The discussion will be about: (1) Is this beat really agreement? (2) Does it follow the rules and dynamics of agreement?

STORY: Any beats of story? ✦ Follow the same process as for conflict and agreement. ✦ Any story points on the first page? Name it. What is the story point? ✦ The class discusses whether or not that is accurate. If it is, where does the story beat around that story point begin and end? What are the choices for the characters' responses to that story point? ✦ The discussion will generally be about mislabeling a beat as a story point rather than character revelation. Actors tend to do this when they base a story point on interpretive choices rather than factual circumstances.

CHARACTER REVELATION: Any beats of character revelation? ✦ Follow the same process, beginning on the first page and working through to the end. The discussion will be about the exact beginning and endings of these beats, and a comparison of the actors' choices for what feelings the character is revealing.

Since there is only one coach and numerous actors, the coach or the performing actors takes responsibility for designating the ultimate choices to be worked with. Everyone changes his choices on the script pages to the ultimate choices.

Improvising the Scene

The actors in the scene return to the floor. Beginning with only the first beat of the scene, the coach, actors, and class select an acting focus for the beat. (See previous section, "Rehearsal Preparation Process for Improvising Your Choices.")

COACHING: The actors improvise on the acting focus while saying the lines. ✦ *Then the coach asks—* Actors, were you fully on the selected acting focus? ✦ Audience, were they? ✦ If either the actors or the class answers, "No," then the actors do the improv again for as many times as it takes for the actors and the audience to respond to the acting focus question, "Yes." ◆ Every time the actors improvise the beat, they are to start in different parts of the location and improvise new blocking. If necessary, they can rearrange the location floor plan every time.

When the beat has been improvised with the actors fully on their selected acting focus, move on to the second beat. Approach the second beat in the same manner. When the beat has been improvised with the actors fully on their selected acting focus, have the actors run the first and second beats together.

Then approach the third beat in the same manner. When the beat has been improvised with the actors fully on their selected acting focus, have the actors run it from the first beat through the end of the third beat. Keep going through the scene in this manner, one beat at a time, followed by running from the first beat through the beat just improvised. The run-through following the improvisation on the last beat is the final run-through, and except for a brief follow-up, the exercise is over.

FOLLOW-UP: Audience, has the scene improved from the first presentation of it? ◆ Actors, how did it feel playing the final run-through? What felt different and what did you discover?

SUMMARY:

Despite the number of beats in the scene, the labels, and the acting focus choices, the actors have no trouble remembering the choices. If you prepare or rehearse one beat at a time followed by run-throughs, the body remembers the choices for you.

The final improvisational acting is a direct manifestation of the preselected choices. If you have to return to this scene, e.g., for reshoots, you just have to look at your script to see what you did originally.

TO THE COACH: When improvising conflict beats, remind the actors to select their private reasons. ◆ If an actor is having difficulty physicalizing an emotion for character revelation or story beats, *ask the actor*—Why is your character [emotion or attitude]? ◆ This will help him reconnect to the choice selected earlier and marked on the beat in his script. ◆ The coach has an opportunity to discuss the importance of the actor asking himself the follow-up question after each improvisation of each beat. When the actor is preparing for a job by himself, he has no coach or classmates to ask if he was fully on the acting focus for any particular beat. He has to ask that question of himself. He must be totally honest with his answer or his work will suffer.

This is one of the reasons Improvisation Technique training, from the beginning, has a theme of continuously heightening the actor's personal authenticity. The actors should be reminded, when working alone, to ask themselves, "Was I fully on the acting focus," and to be brave enough to answer truthfully. Then, they can continue working on that beat or move on to the run-through and next beat. Keep challenging the actor to improvise his playing of each choice in every run-through instead of re-creating what he did in the final work on a particular beat. This keeps him continuously in the realm of discovery and spontaneity.

This exercise may be done with scenes from any theatrical period. However, I recommend that this first scene exercise with purpose of scene be restricted to the modern period because the early learning approach to POS is difficult enough. This is especially true if the actors have little experience with classical acting.

The actors who are scheduled to perform scenes in subsequent classes should keep preparing in their traditional manner. When they perform in class, they will discover how quickly they are capable of changing from what was prepared to the improvisational playing of totally new choices in an authentic and dynamic fashion.

13

MONOLOGUES AND PURPOSE OF SCENE

Scripts have a built-in rhythm. A structural device employed by the writer to hook the audience, the rhythm carries the audience along as it evolves, moving at its own pace, building to the climax and conclusion. When a character has a monologue, this rhythm can grind to a halt. Why would an author choose to impede his own carefully constructed rhythm? He may deem it a valuable tradeoff to sacrifice some rhythm for the opportunity to reveal something about the character, or he may believe that if the monologue is done the way he conceived it, the rhythm will not be impeded. Not only do many actors (and directors) fail to sustain the rhythm through the monologue, but they also cut their own throats with monologues, especially at auditions, because their understanding of what to do with the monologue is incomplete.

Every monologue is intended to reveal something about the character. If the actor fails to structure his performance around this character revelation, the monologue will be ineffectual and drag the scene down. The better the writing, the likelier it is that what the monologue is intended to reveal will not be mentioned within the monologue text. This presents a problem. If the actor doesn't know what that something is, how can he go about revealing it?

Traditional acting emphasizes playing an action that will overcome obstacles and provide the character with what he wants in the scene. Unfortunately, this emphasis can easily keep the actor from discovering and playing the intended revelation about his character. The actor spends all his time discovering and playing what his character wants in the scene, and pays no attention to *what the author wants* in the scene. This means that the actor sees his character's part as the whole of the scene instead of as a part of the whole, the way the author intended. To see the scene, or monologue, only from the character's point of view, from the character's objective, is to miss the forest for the trees. It is a fallacy to think that by playing the character's objective you automatically reveal what the author intended.

Let's set aside the issue of what the character wants and consider a methodology for determining what the author wants. In Improvisation Technique, we assume that the author has a reason for retarding the rhythm and momentum of his script in order to have a character do a monologue. That reason is always one of only two possibilities.

The first possibility is that the author chooses to reveal something about the character, another part of the puzzle, at that moment in the script. Revealing something about the character is a different and much larger issue than what the character may want at that moment in the scene. The actor who doesn't discern and execute this *character revelation* gains nothing for the production, while trading away the momentum.

The second possibility is that the author has deliberately placed the monologue at a moment in the script where something significant in the evolving story has just occurred. This significant event is called a *story point*. The author is using the monologue to show the audience the character's response to the story point. *How the character responds to the story point is ultimately another form of character revelation.* Authors will have multiple characters respond to the same story point in different ways, thereby revealing the differences between the characters.

METHODOLOGY

In order to begin the work on a monologue, the actor must first determine whether the monologue fits the first or second possibility. This is easy. All you have to do is determine whether a story point occurs around the time of the monologue. If one has occurred just prior to the monologue, within two pages, it is the second possibility, story point. If one is going to occur just after the monologue, within two pages, and the character knows it's going to occur, it is also the second possibility, story point. If no story point occurs near the monologue, then it's the first possibility, character revelation.

Story Point

In the breakdown analysis or choice-making stage of working on monologues, story point monologues are easier to work with than character revelation monologues. Let's become familiar with what a story point is.

When something happens in the script that is crucial to the story, e.g., a crime, discovery, confession, death, opportunity, decision, etc., it's called a story point. A story point is a device to move the plot along. Without it, there would be no reason for all the text that follows the story point. Scripts are generally constructed to move from one story point to the next. If a wife comes home early and discovers her husband in bed with another woman, that's a story point. There may be pages of text until she decides to get a divorce (story point); more pages until she actually moves out (story point); more pages until she meets a new man (story point); and so on.

When working on your monologue, ask yourself if something specific happens near the monologue that's important to the plot development. It must be very specific and you must be able to name the event in a factual statement. Examples of naming a story point: wife discovers her husband in bed with another woman; understudy is told she is going on that night for the star; character witnesses a crime.

Story points never occur in the past. They are always in the present, or the immediate future if the character knows it's about to happen. Suppose a scene is about Charlie being told, for the first time, that his mother committed suicide when he was a child. At the moment he hears this information, there is a story point. However, the story point is not that his mom killed herself, since this is in the past. The story point is that *he hears about it now*. Naming that story point would be: Charlie discovers his mom killed herself.

When you can designate and name a story point near your monologue, you are ready to make an acting choice for the monologue. Ask yourself, "How do I feel about [the story point]?" In other words, determine your character's response to the story point. For example: wife discovers her husband in bed with another woman. That's the story point, and each of the three actors in the scene has to know what their response is. If you are playing: the wife, determine how you feel about this discovery; the husband, determine how you feel about being discovered by the wife; the other woman, determine how you feel about being discovered. Perhaps the other woman didn't know he was married. She still has to have a response to being discovered. Very shortly after that, she will have another story point to react to: discovering that the woman who walked in on them is his wife. In this scene, *each actor's primary purpose is to communicate to the audience the character's response to the story point.* For the wife, it might be shocked, which changes to angry and hurt (betrayal); for the husband, it might be embarrassed to guilty; for the other woman, it might be pleased. Maybe she is his secretary and wants to marry him, and the wife's arrival at this moment just may break up the marriage.

If your monologue occurs near the story point, your job is to *choose how your character feels about the story point and show that to the audience while you say the lines*

544

of the monologue. Obviously, what you say in the monologue will influence your choice, but the monologue is not about what you say in it. The monologue is about your emotional response to the story point. You play that choice, not the words. You get the words, including the information and style, for free the moment you say them. *Your job is to add to what you say by showing how you feel.*

Character Revelation

The choice-making process is more difficult if there is no story point near the monologue. Upon determining that this is the case, you must decide on an emotional choice without the help of the question, "How do I feel about the story point?" Instead, you must *interpret what you think the author is choosing to reveal about the character with this monologue at this point in the script.* As there is room for more interpretation than with a story point, it is more difficult to make this choice.

The clues for making a good choice are in the text of the monologue and in the given circumstances. Like the story point, however, the monologue is not about what you say in it. The monologue is about your revelation of an emotional choice. You play that choice, not the words. *Your job is to add to what you say by showing how you feel.*

For the actor, monologues are always about feelings, not information. Make a decision as to what the author is choosing to reveal about the emotional or attitudinal state of the character during the monologue. What is the character feeling? Decide, then look to see if your choice just repeats information that is revealed in the monologue's text or is it an interpretation of how the character is feeling? Acting is not about what you say. It's about what you do with the words you say; what the character is going through emotionally; the behavior of the character. *Your job is to use the text to lead you to an interpretive choice and then to execute that choice spontaneously while you say the text.*

Allow me to make up a short monologue to demonstrate my point:

Husband and wife at dinner table.

HUSBAND. You won't believe what happened to me today. I come out of lunch with the boss, we get in the car and pull out of the lot, and a dog jumps in front of the car. Splat! There's a little girl standing there and she starts screaming. We get out of the car and the dog is alive but a real mess. There's blood everywhere. A crowd forms and everyone is screaming at me. The little girl is crying hysterically. And, I see my boss just watching me to see what I was going to do.

Is it a story point? Maybe. The husband hit a dog? No. That happened in the past. What's in the present is a husband and wife having dinner. Is that a story point? No. If you interpret that his telling the wife about it is significant to moving the plot along, you might call it a story point. For the sake of demonstration, let's say that is not the case. So, it's a character revelation. Not knowing anything else about the scene, characters, or the whole script, we can't make a choice about what is revealed about the husband.

For *demonstration purposes*, read that monologue to yourself or out loud, and choose to reveal he is *angry*. Just read it while you physicalize anger. If you are female, then it's a wife talking to her husband. That's what the monologue sounds like with the actor's choice being anger. ◆ Now, read it with the choice being *sad*. Physicalize sadness and start reading it. ◆ Try it again with the choice being *amused*. Physicalize amusement and start reading it. ◆ Taking the monologue out of context, you can go in any direction you wish. It's the actor's job to make that choice. Whatever that choice is, the actor has chosen to reveal that his character, in the monologue, is angry, sad, or amused. Knowing more about the characters, scene, and script will guide him in making the better choice.

Pure Arcs

In the monologue example, the choices I suggest are pure emotions, which start, remain, and conclude in the same emotional family. Some monologues are that easy. Now return to saying the monologue three times, each time with either anger, sad, or amused. However, when you do it, increase the physicalization intensities as you go, creating an arc for each emotion. The anger arc version should start at about irritated and end in fury. The sad arc version should start at about confused or lonely and end in grief or despair. The amused arc version should start at amused and end in hilarity.

Notice that each of the three suggested choices is much better when you use an arc. Each is more dynamic, more fun to play, and more compelling to watch. If there were an audience to your readings, they would be caught up in the arc and compelled to see how far you'd go. In addition, if this were a real performance, each of the three versions would be totally spontaneous because you'd be improvising the climbing of the arc.

With this work, you have provided form to the monologue as you serve the author's intention of using the monologue to reveal something about the character. You have revealed the husband is angry, sad, or amused. Also, you have not sacrificed the script's rhythm, because you have brought rhythm to the monologue through the increasing intensities of the arc.

Pure Emotion Switches

Some monologues are not intended to reveal only one emotion, regardless of how many intensity levels of that emotion the actor might choose to travel through in creating the arc. The monologue may comprise several beats, with each beat requiring a different emotion. For instance, read the dog/car monologue as if it comprised two beats. The second beat starts at, "There's a little girl." Read the first beat with an anger physicalization, and the second with a sad physicalization.

It's up to the actor to make the choices that work best, guided by knowledge of the rest of the scene, or even better, of the whole script. With this two-beat approach, the actor makes the choice that the author's intention for the character is to reveal: (1) that he is angry at his misfortune, and then (2) that he is also sad (for himself, the dog, the little girl, or whatever the rest of the script suggests about his character).

If the actor's choice is multiple beats with different emotions, emotion switch is the acting focus to employ. Now read the monologue with three beats of different emotions. Beat #1 ends with "Splat," and the choice is amused. Beat #2 ends at "There's blood everywhere," and the choice is sad. Beat #3 is angry.

It's becoming even more interesting and dynamic as you reveal more about the character. There's room for further fine-tuning by choosing to perform any of the beats with an arc. You could do all three beats with an arc in each. *Acting is doing and there's always more to do.*

Umbrella Arcs

In any scene, writers attempt to accomplish more than what is going on in the scene. How many points can they score with the scene? How many parts of the whole can they serve, instead of just one?

Let's interpret the dog/car monologue as if the author intended to reveal more than the exposition of the story and the revelation of individual emotions. What else might he have intended to reveal about the husband? Depending on the rest of the script and the character's total arc for the whole script, we have many choices. Here are three: (1) The husband is under a great deal of pressure and is not handling it well. As the script proceeds, he is going crazy. We could interpret the monologue as the author's device to reveal at this point in the script that the husband is feeling *tormented, or haunted.* (2) The husband suspects his wife is cheating on him and it's his part of the whole script to be feeling increasingly *betrayed.* The author is choosing to reveal in the monologue that he is feeling betrayed by everything. (3) The husband has been through a great deal of trouble. He is coming back, overcoming adversity, and later in the script, he will do something heroic. The author might be choosing to reveal that he is *back from defeat.*

Now, let's look at the process for executing these choices. First, determine your choice. For the sample, I have determined *tormented/haunted, betrayed,* or *back from defeat.* Next, write your choice at the top of a column. Underneath it, list all the feelings that a person goes through when they are experiencing that choice. The top choice is called an *umbrella* because all the feelings have to fit underneath it. For instance:

TORMENTED/HAUNTED	BETRAYED	BACK FROM DEFEAT
Possessed	Hurt	Defeated
Terrified	Angry	Victorious
Alarmed	Resentful	Happy
Nervous	Hate	Defiant
Wary	Vindictive	Hopeful
Frightened	Suspicious	Courageous
Scared	Bitter	
Confused	Sad	
Distraught	Sarcastic	
Suspicious	Furious	

There is no right or wrong. There are only the feelings you can think of that belong under that umbrella. After making the list, rearrange it in levels of intensity, from least to most intense. If your list includes emotions or feelings from different emotional families, arrange them from least to most intense *within each family*. The order of the families should be determined by your own sense of which comes first when one is feeling the top, or *umbrella*, choice.

TORMENTED/HAUNTED	BETRAYED	BACK FROM DEFEAT
Confused	Hurt	Defeated
Wary	Sad	Hopeful
Suspicious	Suspicious	Courageous
Nervous	Resentful	Happy
Distraught	Bitter	Defiant
Scared	Sarcastic	Victorious
Frightened	Angry	
Alarmed	Vindictive	
Terrified	Furious	
Possessed	Hate	

Look at the text and divide it into beats, labeling the beats from the choices on the list. Assign a different feeling choice to each beat. You do not have to use all the choices on any list and you may add choices you hadn't previously thought of. You are choreographing the speech emotionally so that, if you executed the choices, the audience would see a character going through your umbrella arc choice.

Here are sample choices for the monologue. Try them out in order to experience how you are serving the umbrella choice. Make sure you physicalize each choice. Note that the different umbrellas sometimes create different beat lengths.

TORMENTED/HAUNTED

Beat #1: Suspicious. You won't believe what happened to me today. I come out of lunch with the boss, we get in the car and pull out of the lot, and a dog jumps in front of the car.

Beat #2: Nervous. Splat! There's a little girl standing there and she starts screaming. We get out of the car and the dog is alive but a real mess. There's blood everywhere.

Beat #3: Scared. A crowd forms and everyone is screaming at me. The little girl is crying hysterically.

Beat #4: Possessed. And, I see my boss just watching me to see what I was going to do.

In performance, you would be revealing a character who is tormented and haunted

BETRAYED

Beat #1: Bitter. You won't believe what happened to me today. I come out of lunch with the boss, we get in the car and pull out of the lot, and a dog jumps in front of the car.

Beat #2: Sarcasm. Splat! There's a little girl standing there and she starts screaming. We get out of the car and the dog is alive but a real mess. There's blood everywhere. A crowd forms and everyone is screaming at me. The little girl is crying hysterically.

Beat #3: Hate. And, I see my boss just watching me to see what I was going to do.

In performance, you would be revealing a character who is feeling betrayed.

BACK FROM DEFEAT

Beat #1: Defeated. You won't believe what happened to me today. I come out of lunch with the boss, we get in the car and pull out of the lot, and a dog jumps in front of the car. Splat! There's a little girl standing there and she starts screaming.

Beat #2: Courageous. We get out of the car and the dog is alive but a real mess. There's blood everywhere. A crowd forms and everyone is screaming at me. The little girl is crying hysterically.

Beat #3: Victory. And, I see my boss just watching me to see what I was going to do.

In performance, you would be revealing a character who is back from defeat.

Umbrella arcs are used when the author has chosen to provide a character revelation or story response that is best labeled with a word or phrase other than a single pure emotion or attitude. This label frequently describes a sense of movement or direction for the character, e.g., loss of illusion, celebration of power, or back from defeat. Sometimes the umbrella arc is the name of a unified thematic feeling for the character comprising different emotional feelings, e.g., denial, abandonment, betrayal, or strength. For sample umbrella arcs see Appendix A.

MONOLOGUE SUMMARY:

You see how much is available to you for doing with any monologue. The actor is now making the monologue about more than it is about. There is no mention in the monologue about feeling tormented/haunted, betrayed, or back from defeat. Always assume that the author is choosing to reveal something about the character in addition to what the character says. No matter what your choice is, we are still going to get what the character is saying. This is true whether the monologue is a story point response or a character revelation.

With an umbrella arc, you still have freedom to choose whether you are plateauing or arcing within any one beat. If you plateau, there is room for movement *within that chosen feeling*. As long as you do not leave the chosen emotion, you are free to do whatever you want, unconstrained by an order of intensity levels. You can, and should, spontaneously change your traveling through that emotion choice for every take. You do this by just staying on your acting focus, physicalizing the emotion while staying a part of the whole. That is where the improvisational acting comes in.

In Improvisation Technique: (1) script choices are made ahead of time and (2) the playing of these choices is improvised. How you travel up an arc is improvised. How you physicalize within a selected emotion is improvised. How you switch from one emotion to another is improvised. The improvisational acting focus in all of these samples is either: physicalize the emotion; emotion arc; emotion switch; and since the above monologue takes place at the dinner table, emotions & objects. If you've done the experiential training for Improvisation Technique, this will all be second nature to you.

If you are dealing with character revelation and the choice of what is revealed eludes you, keep breaking down the monologue. *Look for clues and ask yourself questions.* For instance, the monologue seems to be about a car accident. What question can you ask about the car accident? "Well, how do I (the character) feel about the accident?" The surrounding text may yield a clue. In the case of the betrayed husband, "How do I (the character) feel about the fact that I am having dinner with my wife for the first time since I began suspecting she's having an affair?" You can always find something to ask yourself, "How do I (the character) feel about it?"

Once you have picked your character revelation or response to the story point, you must be more specific with what you are going to do. For instance, do you just play that one emotional choice, e.g., anger, the whole way on a plateau? Do you do a spontaneous, organic escalation of the intensities of anger, creating an arc that starts with irritated or annoyed and escalates all the way up to fury and rage? Does the monologue seem to have specific beats in it enabling you to switch around the different aspects of your choice, creating a designed or umbrella arc, in this case, anger? How do you know which way to go, which of these options will serve you best?

Go to the text and look at the rhythm. Does it have a natural rhythm that just keeps repeating itself, getting stronger? That might suggest simply doing an organic arc.

If there are no significant beat changes and it reads like one full-blown feeling, it could be a plateau.

Do you sense from the script that there are shifts in emphatic feelings? That might suggest emotion switching and you should look at it as beats with beat labels.

If you haven't done the work in the emotion chapter, you might think that working this way creates *indicating*. However, if you have done the work, you know it does not do this. Indicating is partial physicalization; only some parts of the body are physicalizing the emotion, e.g., angry hands and angry voice only. Improvisation Technique always demands full body involvement.

> **TO THE COACH:** When leading a group into this monologue section, it is suggested that the work be presented accompanying a monologue exercise, which follows. The exercise can be done after the training in chapter 9, "Emotions," is completed; or, after the entire training has been completed through chapter 11, "Agreement," and as an introduction to chapter 12, "Purpose of Scene"; or, right at this point.

MONOLOGUE EXERCISE

In anticipation of this exercise, the actors should be given an assignment to prepare, in any traditional manner, a one-to-two-minute monologue from a published play. In the designated class, they bring it in at performance level and provide copies for everyone in the class. The higher the quality of writing, the better the exercise. Actors may use real or space props. The monologue should not have any changes made to it, e.g., no interior cuts. If it is retyped from its source, include everything, especially stage directions.

The most efficient and effective approach to the first monologue class requires that the coach, ahead of time, peruse the monologues to be presented in the first class. He can then schedule the order of presentation so that the first monologue will be a *pure emotion, plateau or arc*; the second monologue, *emotion switching;* and the third, *umbrella arc*. In the first class of monologue presentations, I communicate the information at the beginning of this chapter, stopping just prior to the introduction of the sample dog/car monologue. At that point, we begin with the actors' presentations of their monologues.

I wait for the presentation of any actor's monologue that may be interpreted as an umbrella arc, and right after that presentation, I introduce the information about umbrella arcs, replacing the dog/car monologue example with the monologue being presented.

The first actor performs the monologue, then hands out the copies. The actor tells the class what is going on in the whole script around the monologue, especially if there is a story point. The coach has everyone read the monologue and (1) determine if it is a story point or character revelation; (2) determine what the character's story response or character revelation is; (3) and divide and label any beats.

After everyone has done this, the coach moderates a class discussion of (1) whether it's a story point or character revelation, and (2) all the beat choices, going one beat at a time. Since there is only one coach and numerous actors, the coach or the performing actors takes responsibility for designating the ultimate emotion choices to be worked with. Everyone marks his copy according to the ultimate choices.

The actor returns to the stage. If the whole monologue has been determined to be *one beat of one emotion, plateau or arc*, the actor's improvisational acting focus is selected, either physicalize an emotion or emotion arc. The actor does the improvisation with the text and that acting focus. If the actor, coach, and/or class feels the actor is not totally and thoroughly on his acting focus, the actor repeats the improv as many times as necessary until he is thoroughly on the acting focus and physicalizing the selected choice.

If the whole monologue has been determined to have *more than one beat*, the actor does not have to remember all the beat choices, because he is only going to be working one beat at a time. The actor physicalizes the first beat choice, using physicalizing an emotion, emotion arc, or emotions & objects. The actor does the improvisation on the first beat only. If the actor, coach, and/or class feels the actor is not totally and thoroughly on his acting focus, the actor repeats the beat as many times as necessary until he is thoroughly on the acting focus and physicalizing the selected choice.

When the first beat is done, the second beat is approached the same way. When the second beat is finally improvised totally on the acting focus, the actor does a run-through of the first two beats, spontaneously handling the turning point between them.

The actor then approaches the third beat in the same thorough fashion as the first two beats. When he is accomplished in the third beat, he does a run-through of the first three beats. This process is continued for every beat until the end of the monologue. The first run-through to include the last beat is the final run-through.

Even though the actor did not have to remember all the beat choices when he started this process, his body has now learned them because of the work on each beat and each run-through. Even if the actor were asked at the end of the process to name all the beat choices, it would not be necessary for him to remember them mentally. What's important is that in this process, the body will always remember the choices.

The coach moderates a short discussion of the differences between the monologue as brought in and the final run-through. Then it's the next actor's turn.

At the conclusion of the last monologue in the first monologue class (I usually do five or six monologues per four hours of class), I return to communicating the information presented under the heading, "Monologue Summary." [In this summary, replace my references to sample umbrellas from the book with whatever umbrellas were done by the actors in the first class.]

The actors who are scheduled to perform monologues in subsequent classes should keep preparing in their traditional manner. When they perform in class, they will discover how quickly they are capable of changing from what was prepared to the improvisational playing of totally new choices in an authentic and dynamic fashion. This is an important self-discovery about the effectiveness of their Improvisation Technique training in preparing them for employing thorough emotional work with no time needed for any preparation. This is immediately significant in heightening self-confidence. After this exercise is completed, there will be many opportunities for practicing their new approach to monologues.

For earlier success and less frustration in learning this new process, in subsequent classes you may add a step or two to the class readings of the monologue and making their own choices. The coach has everyone read the scene and (1) determine if it is a story point or character revelation; (2) determine what the character's story response or character revelation is; (3) as a class, discuss their choices and select the one that seems best; (4) if it is an umbrella arc, discuss the feelings that would go on the umbrella stem under the arc title; and (5) return to working on the scene on their own, dividing and labeling any beats. After everyone has done this, the coach moderates a class discussion of all the beat choices, one beat at a time.

MONOLOGUE EXERCISE SUMMARY:

At the conclusion of the last monologue in the last class of the monologue exercise— ◆ Do you all feel that this new approach to monologues is accessible to you? Is breaking the speech down easier than what you usually do? If not, was what you were previously doing significantly productive? Is the playing of your choices easier and more productive than what you usually do? Does it bring better results than you usually get? Were all the monologues in this exercise improved when we added this new approach?

Acting requires making choices and spontaneously executing them. The actors who book jobs do this, and the actors who rely on being in the moment and going with the flow do not. If you employ a traditional technique based on objectives, intentions, problems, or actions to arrive at your choices and the spontaneous playing of them, then this new approach can be an additional tool available to you for further exploration. At the very least, the abilities available to you from your own evolving technique have been expanded. I suggest that you employ your traditional technique first, and when you have completed that work, approach it with Improvisation Technique and determine for yourself if you have improved the work.

If you do this, you may discover that working traditionally blinded you to what the author intended the scene to do. The author is the only one who knows what the scene is intended to accomplish. If you don't even stop to consider what the author intended, let alone execute it, you may very well go against what the author intended, which is as labor-intensive and counterproductive as going against the tide. Working in this new fashion will create a feeling of going with the tide: effortless, quick, and productive.

It is worth repeating that one of the benefits of the exercise is the discovery of how quickly you are capable of changing from what was prepared to the improvisational playing of totally new choices in an authentic and dynamic fashion, with no rehearsal time. This is true, regardless of whether the choice was a long beat of a pure emotion arc, like anger, or a complex umbrella, like back from defeat or betrayal, comprising various beats of different emotions.

STUDENT RESPONSE

Here is Emmy and Obie Award-winner, Valerie Mahaffey, commenting on her new tools for monologues:

—I just returned from a new play festival in Montana. I was in a new play by Paul Zindel (*The Effect of Gamma Rays on Man-in-the-Moon Marigolds, Ladies at the Alamo*) that had only two characters. There was a very brief rehearsal period, only one day. All the plays were done as readings. At the end of the rehearsal, Zindel came up to us and said, "Okay, now, you both have these two matching monologues here and you've got to be magnificent! They're the most important monologues in the play. You just have to be magnificent!" And, he didn't say anything else. We had only twenty minutes until the performance! So, I just took the monologue and broke it down the way we do in class. I chose six beats and labeled them with different feelings. In the performance, we got to the monologues and the other actor was a total method actor and he just sort of bathed in one emotion, getting into it, dwelling on it, and so on. It was really slow and just dragged the whole scene down. When my monologue started, I just went boom, boom, boom, hitting each of my emotion choices, and it felt great. It was one of the most successful things I've ever done. Everybody commented on it. All the other actors in the audience who were rehearsing and reading other plays under the same minimal rehearsal conditions said to me, "How the hell did you do all that work on the monologue so fast?"

TO THE COACH: This exercise may be done with monologues from any theatrical period, although if the actors are not that experienced with classical acting, the coach may decide to restrict the exercise to the modern period.

SCRIPT SAMPLES

In the sample monologues from films and TV shows, the actors used this approach in preparing for their performances. The actor's choices are shown in the left margin. In the monologues from widely known theater classics, the choices shown at the left are mine.

Emotion Choices: Film and TV

Film *Miami Rhapsody*[1]

The first selection is a short monologue that requires only one emotion choice with no need to arc it. In the movie, Carla Gugino plays Gwen, who is explaining to her sister, played by Sarah Jessica Parker, why she is having an affair.

Character revelation: Frustrated

Acting focus: Physicalize the emotion

                         GWEN
(Frustrated)

            No, it's weird. Mom always said,
            meet lots of people, don't settle
            down too fast. So I did, I went out
            with a million guys, and then one
            day I thought, Okay, it's time, and
            then there was this ceremony and I
            put on this ring and suddenly I'm
            not supposed to be attracted to
            other men anymore. But I am. And I
            don't just want to flirt with them,
            I want to screw their brains out.

Television Sitcom *Frasier*[2]

This is an example of character revelation with a pure arc of one emotion. Scott Atkinson played Clive, a former boyfriend of Daphne. For various reasons, everyone in the Frasier household has been lying to him and he chooses this moment to tell them all what he thinks of their deceptions.

Character revelation or story: Clive tells the truth.

Revelation or story response: Anger

Acting focus: Emotion arc

                    CLIVE
(Arc Anger)
          Look, I know I'm a guest here so
          I've kept silent so far, but I'm
          sorry, I must speak. You are the most
          appalling family I have ever met.
          (TO FRASIER) You — breaking up with
          your wife over a pair of opera
          glasses. (TO NILES) And you looking
          down your nose at me all the while
          you show off your posh flat. Well,
          for your information, I don't think
          there's anything remotely special
          about your bathrooms. (TO DAPHNE AND
          ROZ) And you two women, flirting
          shamelessly with me right in front
          of your husbands. (TO ROZ, THEN
          DAPHNE) You having just reconciled
          with Frasier, you carrying Niles'
          baby. I pity your child, Daphne...
          and I pity any good Manchester girl
          who comes here to this vile coffee-
          swilling Sodom and lets it change
          her the way it's changed you.

Film *House Arrest* [3]

This sample shows multiple beats and different emotions. Shelley Hack plays a TV psychiatrist promoting her book on the air. It is a one-scene part and because the screenwriter is making fun of the character's superficiality, the choices are more obvious.

Character revelation: A performer and huckster
Acting focus: Emotion switches

```
INT. TALK SHOW SET - DAY
DR. ERICA GILLILAND, a psychologist, holds up
her latest book: Feel the Fear and Go For It.
```

               DR. ERICA GILLILAND

(Chirpy)
          When you're frightened, just do
          like my book says: "Feel the Fear
          and Go For It."

(Sensual)
               (smiles)
          That's right...feel the fear and go
          for it. Go for it like you're an
          Olympic athlete going for the gold
          — because the only way to conquer
          fear is to feel it...know it...then

> break through it and move on!

(Embarrassed)

>> (frowning)
> And who of us isn't afraid? No one,
> that's who!
>> (a beat)

(Fear arc: concerned>scared)

> Let me tell you a little secret...
> I'm scared to death just being on
> TV. All these cameras on me and
> these lights are shining and these
> technicians are staring at me and
> muttering God knows what into their
> headsets — it's a wonder I can
> crawl out of my dressing room and
> face you good people! But I do...
> because

(Earnest)

> I've felt the fear and I've gone
> for it!
>> (peering into the lens)
> What's your biggest fear? Is it
> being rejected? Growing old? Fall-
> ing out of an airplane and tumbling
> sixty thousand feet to your death?
> It could happen...

(Sad)

> it did to a friend of mine. Remem-
> ber — life is hard. Bad things
> happen. Tragedy can strike at any
> moment.

(Patriotic)

>> (sneers)
> So what?! Deal with it! Quit whin-
> ing! Wake up and smell the coffee!
> How? By feeling your fear and going
> for it!

(Triumphant)

>> (shouting now)
> Feel the burn! No pain, no gain!
> JUST DO IT!

(Happy)

>> (Calming down, smiling again)
> Until next week, this is Dr. Erica
> Gilliland. Have a great day.

Umbrella Arcs: Film and TV

TV Series *Star Trek: Voyager* [4]

Martha Hackett played Seska, a spy on the starship. She has been found out, and she confesses, explaining why she was a spy.

Story: Seska confesses.
Response: Defiance/Rebellion (Umbrella arc)
Acting focus: Emotion switches

SEKA

(Oppressed)

> (a long beat, no reason to hide
> it)
> I did it for you. I did it for this
> crew. We are alone here at the
> mercy of any number of hostile
> aliens because of the incomprehen-
> sible decision of a Federation
> Captain.

(Suffocating)

> A Federation Captain who destroyed
> our only chance to get home.
> (with rising frustration)

(Frustration)

> Federation rules. Federation nobil-
> ity. Federation compassion. Do you
> understand if this had been a
> Cardassian ship, we would be home
> now?
> (beat)

(Forceful)

> We must begin to forge alliances
> now... to survive, we must have
> powerful friends... the Kazon-
> Nistrim were willing to be our
> protectors... in return for some
> minor technology...

(Anger)

> That is all that matters at this
> point. Building a base of power to
> control this quadrant.
> (Calmer —)

(Shrewd)

> You're a fool, Captain.
> (To Chakotay)
> And you're a fool to follow her.
> (beat)

(Freedom)

> I can't imagine how I ever loved
> you. Good-bye, Chakotay...
> > (She casually presses a ring on
> > her finger and she DEMATERIAL-
> > IZES away....)

Film *Dogma*[5]

In this satirical and irreverent movie, George Carlin plays Cardinal Glick, introducing to the media a promotional campaign for heightening the motivation of Catholics and increasing attendance at Mass.

Story: Cardinal introduces the new Jesus statue to replace the crucifix.
Response: Back from defeat (Umbrella arc)
Acting focus: Emotion switches

```
EXT. CHURCH - DAY
A thrall of REPORTERS clap as CARDINAL GLICK
takes to the podium. He strikes one as more of
an agent than a man of the cloth. He removes
his Wayfarers.


                    GLICK
```

(Earnest)

> Thank you Ladies and Gentlemen, now
> we all know how the majority and
> the media in this country view the
> Catholic Church.

(Distasteful)

> They think of us as a passé, ar-
> chaic institution. People find the
> Bible obtuse and even hokey.

(Assured)

> In an effort to disprove that, the
> Church has appointed this year as a
> time of renewal— both of faith and
> of style.

> (A few applause ring out. Glick smiles. A dolly
> is wheeled out. It carries a standard crucifix
> and something of equal size, covered with a
> shroud.)

(Reverential)

> For example - the crucifix. While
> it has been a time - honored symbol
> of our faith, Holy Mother Church

has decided to retire this highly
recognizable,

(Gloomy)

yet wholly depressing image of our
Lord, Jesus Christ, crucified.

(Bold)

Christ didn't come to earth to give
us the willies.

(Grateful)

He came to help us out.

(Determined)

He was a booster.

(Commitment)

And it's with that take on our Lord
in mind that we have come up with a
new

(Enthusiastic)

more inspiring sigil. So it's with
great pleasure, that I present you
with the first of

(Knowing)

many revamps that the 'Catholicism
- Wow!' campaign will unveil over
the next year.

(Boastful)

I give you...

(Glick pulls the shroud off the object to his
right - a four foot figure of Christ smiling
and giving the 'thumbs up.')

(Proud)

The Buddy Christ.
(The crowd buzzes)

(False humility)

Now that's not the sanctioned term
we're using for the symbol.

(Confidential)

Just something we've been kicking
around the office.

(Thrilled)

But look at it. Doesn't it pop!

(Victorious)

Buddy Christ!

Umbrella Arcs: Theater Classics

When dealing with quality writers, most long monologues will be umbrella arcs. Here are monologues from theater classics where the choices create umbrella arcs.

The first two monologues are labeled *loss of illusion*. When a character experiences a loss of illusion, he discovers that he has been fooling himself over some important issue and living a significant part of his life as a lie. The most powerful emotional umbrella arc, loss of illusion creates feelings of devastation and will always lead the actor to tears if he thoroughly physicalizes its emotional components. The character feels devastation because he is confronted with the truth about himself. No one made him adopt the lie he has been living. He alone is responsible for his own unhappiness. Loss of illusion is the death of the character's best friend. The character has lived a significant part of his life holding hands with this illusion and running his life in order to serve it. Giving it up creates body feelings similar to giving up one's best friend. Almost every monologue where the author indicates that the character cries will be a loss of illusion.

Three Sisters[6]

In the third act, the brother, Andrei, speaking to his sisters, gives up the double illusions that he is happily married and successful.

Character revelation or story: Andrei confesses he mortgaged the house.
Revelation or story response: Loss of illusion (Umbrella arc)—He is happily married and successful.
Acting focus: Emotion switches and arc

(Angry)

ANDREI. I just want to say this and then I'll go. Now... in the first place you have something against Natasha; I've seen it since the day we were married. I happen to think Natasha is a good, honest person; she's straightforward and honorable. I would like you to understand that I love and respect my wife; I respect her and I demand that respect from others. She is an honest, honorable person, and whatever you imagine are your grievances, I'm sorry, are just pure fabrications on your part. (Pause.)

(Snob/Regal)

Secondly, you are apparently angry that I didn't finish my doctorate and that I'm not in research by now. I happen to serve on the City Council, and I think my work there is just as sacred and noble a calling as science. I'm a member of the City Council, I work hard and I have pride in my work there. (Pause)

(Guilty)

Third, there's something else it's necessary for me to say . . . It is true that I mortgaged the house without your consent . . . that was wrong, I know, and I ask you to forgive me . . . That action was necessitated by my debts . . . thirty-five thousand rubles . . . I don't play cards anymore; I gave all that up long ago; my only justification is that you girls, you received an allotment and I didn't . . . I have (Pause) nothing you could call income at all.

(Defensive)

They're not listening. Natasha is a fine, honest person. (Walks silently up and down, then stops.)

(Arc Sad>Despair)

When I was married I thought we'd be happy . . . but, my God . . . (Cries.) Oh, my dearest, darling sisters, it's not true. Don't believe me. Don't believe me . . . (He exits.)

Measure for Measure

In act 3 of Shakespeare's play Claudio gives up an illusion about his survival.

Story: Isabella tells Claudio that Angelo will only spare him if she sleeps with Angelo and she won't do it. Response: Loss of illusion (Umbrella arc)— His sister (or anyone) will save him from death.

Acting focus: Emotion switches and arc

CLAUDIO

(Confused)

Death is a fearful thing.
… to die, and go we know not where;
To lie in cold obstruction and to rot;

(Bitter)

This sensible warm motion to become
A kneaded clod; and the delighted spirit
To bathe in fiery floods, or

(Defensive)

                    to reside
In thrilling region of thick-ribbed ice;
To be imprison'd in the viewless winds,
And blown with restless violence round about
The pendant world;

(Very frightened)

                    or to be worse than worst
Of those that lawless and uncertain thoughts
Imagine howling:

(Anger)

                'tis too horrible!
The weariest and most loathed worldly life
That age, ache, penury and imprisonment
Can lay on nature is a paradise
To what we fear of death.

(Arc Sad>Despair)

                    Sweet sister, let me live:
What sin you do to save a brother's life,
Nature dispenses with the deed so far
That it becomes a virtue.

561

Long Day's Journey into Night[7]

Since it is a common writer's device to show a character feeling betrayed, betrayal umbrella arcs are widely used. In act 4, Edmund reveals this feeling to his father, James Tyrone. There are different components to different betrayal umbrella arcs. In this particular speech, the feelings are from the anger family. For other examples see Appendix A.

Character revelation: Betrayed (Umbrella arc)
Acting focus: Emotion switches

(Frustration)

> EDMUND. Don't lie about it!
> *(With gathering intensity.)*
> God, Papa, ever since I went to sea and was on my own, and found out what hard work for little pay was, and what it felt like to be broke, and starve, and camp on park benches because I had no place to sleep, I've tried to be fair to you because I knew what you'd been up against as a kid. I've tried to make allowances. Christ, you have to make allowances in this damned family or go nuts! I have tried to make allowances for myself when I remember all the rotten stuff I've pulled! I've tried to feel like Mama that you can't help being what you are where money is concerned.

(Anger)

> But God Almighty, this last stunt of yours is too much! It makes me want to puke! Not because of the rotten way you're treating me. To hell with that! I've treated you rottenly, in my way, more than once. But to think when it's a question of your son having consumption, you can show your-self up before the whole town as such a stinking old tightwad! Don't you know Hardy will talk and the whole damned town will know! Jesus, Papa, haven't you any pride or shame!

(Rage)

> *(Bursting with rage.)*
> And don't think I'll let you get away with it! I won't go to any damned state farm just to save you a few lousy dollars to buy more bum property with! You stinking old miser—!
> *(He chokes huskily, his voice trembling with rage, and then is shaken by a fit of coughing.)*

The Glass Menagerie[8]

At the end of the play, Tom addresses the audience with this monologue. For dynamic effect, it requires an umbrella arc.

Story: The story is over.
Response: Haunted (Umbrella arc)
Acting focus: Emotion switches

(Lonely)

TOM. I didn't go to the moon, I went much further—for time is the longest distance between two places.

(Wary)

Not long after that I was fired for writing a poem on the lid of a shoe-box. I left Saint Louis. I descended the steps of this fire escape for the last time and followed, from then on, in my father's footsteps, attempting to find in motion what was lost in space. I traveled around a great deal. The cities swept about me like dead leaves, leaves that were brightly colored but torn away from the branches.

(Suspicious)

I would have stopped, but I was pursued by something. It always came upon me unawares, taking me altogether by surprise. Perhaps it was a familiar bit of music. Perhaps it was only a piece of transparent glass. Perhaps I am walking along a street at night, in some strange city, before I have found companions. I pass the lighted window of a shop where perfume is sold. The window is filled with pieces of colored glass, tiny transparent bottles in delicate colors, like bits of a shattered rainbow.

(Apprehensive)

Then all at once my sister touches my shoulder. I turn around and look into her eyes. Oh, Laura, Laura, I tried to leave you behind me, but I am more faithful than I intended to be! I reach for a cigarette, I cross the street, I run into the movies or a bar, I buy a drink, I speak to the nearest stranger—anything that can blow your candles out!

   [Laura bends over the candles.]

For nowadays the world is lit by lightning! Blow out your candles, Laura—and so good-bye. . . .

   [She blows the candles out.]

House of Blue Leaves[9]

Artie's girlfriend Bunny is a great cook but has never cooked for him. He has just implored her to cook a meal for them, asking her: "You couldn't give me a little sample right now?" Actors frequently limit this monologue by going for the jokes instead of playing what Guare intended, to reveal that Bunny has great strength. When played according to the following umbrella arc, maximum authentic laughs are achieved.

Character revelation: Strength (Umbrella arc)
Acting focus: Emotion switches

(Resolved)

BUNNY. I'm not that kind of girl.

(Aggressive)

I'll sleep with you anytime you want. Anywhere. In two months I've known you, did I refuse you once? Not once. You want me to climb in the bag with you now? Unzip it —go on—unzip it— Give your fingers a smack and I'm flat on my back. I'll sew those words into a sampler for you in our new home in California. We'll hang it right by the front door.

(Visionary)

Because, Artie, I'm a rotten lay and I know it and you know it and everybody knows it—

(Confidence)

I'm not good in bed. It's no insult. I took that sex test in the *Reader's Digest* two weeks ago and I scored twelve. Twelve, Artie! I ran out of that dentist office with tears gushing out of my face. But I face up to the truth about myself.

(Wise)

So if I cooked for you now and said I won't sleep with you till we're married, you'd look forward to sleeping with me so much that by the time we did get to that motel near Hollywood, I'd be such a disappointment, you'd never forgive me.

(Determined)

My cooking is the only thing I got to lure you on with and hold you with. Artie, we got to keep some magic for the honeymoon. It's my first honeymoon and I want it to be so good, I'm aiming for two million calories.

(Excited)

I want to cook for you so bad I walk by the A&P, I get all hot jabs of chili powder inside my thighs...

(Courageous)

but I can't till we get those tickets to California safe in my purse, till Billy knows we're coming, till I got that ring right on my cooking finger. . . .

(Indestructible)

Don't tempt me. . .

(Invincible)

I love you.

Index of Sample Umbrella Arcs

Sample umbrella arcs are given in Appendix A. They are useful guides in determining umbrella arcs for any scripted monologues or dialogue beats. My students find them to be valuable check lists for preparing script choices. When the actors are learning this approach to monologues or purpose of scene script breakdowns, however, and before they do the monologue exercise, I encourage them to resist going directly to this appendix, which can keep them from developing their own muscles and creating new and unique arcs.

14
Gaining More Finesse with Purpose of Scene

Here are additional notes for increasing your skill at making better purpose of scene (POS) choices. For every POS, I include a sample scene from theater, film, and TV. The film and TV scripts are for scenes in which the actor employed Improvisation Technique with POS choices in preparing for his performance. I include only the choices for one character, my student's/client's. The theater scenes are readily recognizable and include choices for each character. These are strictly my interpretations. The samples were chosen for variety and demonstration value so that the reader can easily see the most commonly used POS and acting focus choices and what they look like on script pages.

READING THE SCENE

The biggest challenge to making better POS choices is to change the way you have always read a scene, which has included you playing your role. In your old way of reading, you're too busy playing the character from the moment you first read the script. You immediately apply your personal frames of reference, explore line readings, and look for objectives. You grab at choices, and then work on the scene to see if it can support those choices. You force the scene to adapt to what you want to do with it. When you find a way to do that, you feel you've done your homework. However, when you bend and shape the scene based on how you know yourself or see yourself playing the part, you limit the script to your own limitations. Your choices keep you from seeing what the author is doing with the whole scene. If you don't see the whole, how can you play your part in it?

The new way of reading the scene requires that you put some distance between you and the script. When you do your scene breakdown, leave yourself as the character out of the process. Instead of thinking of yourself playing the part, think of yourself as the author or director making choices for all the characters. The author was like a puppeteer pulling the strings on all the puppets in the scene. Read the scene as if you were the puppeteer for all the characters, and you will find the necessary distance. This will release you from your personal frames of reference for the character and expand your choice-making ability. You will make clearer, easier, and better choices because you are in the service of the scene instead of what you would do in your life at a parallel moment.

This new way of reading will get you further faster. As professional actors in the new millennium, where there's no rehearsal time and many directors don't direct acting, we must have a way to direct ourselves.

BEAT CHANGES

Beat Connections

No beat is labeled in isolation. Your choices for any beat have to take into account what your choices are for the beats prior to it and after it. Every beat has to come from the beats in front of it and be on its way to the beats after it, i.e., if you want the scene to go somewhere, then you've got to start it somewhere else. You may like your choice for the beat you are working on, and that will call your attention to the limitation of your choice for an earlier or later beat. Sometimes your beat choice must take into account that you are setting up the next beat; at other times, your beat choice must pay off the previous beat. Working this way will frequently cause you to reconsider a choice for an earlier or later beat. That is why working in pencil is best.

Look at the neighboring beats whenever you label a beat with an emotional choice. See if the beat you are working on and the neighboring beats add up to an arc of the emotion that you are considering. E.g., if you select *nervous* for the beat you are working on, look at the neighboring beats to see if you are in the middle of a *fear arc*, where the prior beat might be *suspicious*, and the next, *scared*. If you decide there is no connection between the beats, and so no arc, then approach the beat in a stand-alone fashion.

Behavior and Feeling Changes

While reading over the scene, notice whenever something changes in the character's behavior or feelings. That will probably be a beat change. In your first readings, let your intuition help you.

Notice whether there is a design element. Can you draw a simple diagram of what happens in the scene? For instance, in *boy loses girl*, a couple starts a scene very much together, and by the end of the scene they are apart; in *boy meets girl*, they start apart and come together. The design element would be a sideways V, with the right side down (<) for a couple that increases the distance between them during the scene, and the left side down (>) for a couple that comes together. Each side of the V represents one of the characters. In TV shows and genre movies, formulaic scripts abound. When you have a formulaic script with a design element, your job is to play your part of the formula and your choices have to fulfill that element. In the case of boy loses girl, your choices must increase the estrangement as the scene progresses. They might be excited and happily together at the start of the scene, and move through excited, happy, amused, calm, determined, tense, defensive, and angry to the end of the scene, when they are far apart. Finding the design element of the scene helps you to make sure your choices for each successive beat fulfill it. In scenes like this, make sure that (1) your first beat choices set up the pattern you are going to follow, and (2) your final beat choices complete it.

Dialogue

While changes in the subject of the text may sometimes indicate a beat change, changes in the behavioral aspect of the dialogue will frequently be the indicator of a beat change. For example, if a character starts cursing in the middle of a scene, consider that he has changed his feelings from something else to anger, which may indicate the start of a conflict beat or a character revelation beat around anger. When you see a change in the syntax or the rhythm of the dialogue, look at where the change occurs as an indication of a beat change. Don't be afraid to read your character's dialogue with different rhythms and intensities to see if a better choice emerges. For example, almost any dialogue that can be played angry can also be played hurt or lonely and will have a different rhythm. Try it both ways, physicalizing your choices and line readings as you read it.

Subject changes should seldom be taken as a sign of a beat change. This is a common mistake for beginners in POS work as well as in traditional Stanislavsky work. A subject change may *sometimes* indicate a beat change. You will spot it if the subject change is accompanied by new action or activity, e.g., someone saying, "Let's go get a drink." It means, "Let's get up now and go have a drink and change the subject *and change what we are doing*." A beat change is dictated by changes in behavior and feelings, not by changes in text subjects.

Whenever a character repeats something and there is a beat change anywhere near the two repetitious phrases, consider putting the beat change between the two phrases.

Anytime you have a setup and a payoff as in a joke, experiment with the setup as one beat and the payoff as another beat.

More than one beat or a one-beat arc?

After you have defined and labeled a beat, if you still sense that your character has some changes in his feelings within that beat, you have to make a decision. Should the beat be further divided into more beats to accommodate these changes in feelings, or are your character's changes in feelings accounted for within a single beat, *using an arc?* Look at the other character(s) in the scene. If the other character has no changes during this beat, then it is probably one beat with your character doing an arc.

Character Always Knows

When interpreting beat changes or beat labels, if your process brings you to a question of whether or not your character knows something, your answer should always be yes. For example, in the POS demo scene in chapter 12, when the husband hears that his wife is including her lover, Jerry, on the guest list for the party, he balks and begins a disguised conflict beat: he doesn't want Jerry invited and she does. Since the conflict is disguised and not mentioned in the text at that point, the question is, how does she know that they are in conflict over Jerry's invitation?

> SUE
> Yes! I'll make the guest list.
>
> TOM
> All our friends.
>
> SUE
> Absolutely. Lois, Pat, Leslie,
> Larry, Louise.
>
> TOM
> Ira, Lisa, Harriet, Lilly, Marty,
> Paul.
>
> SUE
> Shelly, Lyn, Andy, Hal, and Jerry.
> We have to plan a menu. What should
> we have?

PAUSE.

CONFLICT (disguised)
Sue: Wants to invite Jerry
Tom: Don't invite Jerry

                    TOM
        Yeah. Sure. Whatever.

                    SUE
        You think you can trust me to pick
        the menu by myself? All right, you
        stock the bar. That's your depart-
        ment.

                    TOM
        Thanks a lot. You want me to be the
        waiter too?

Doing the script breakdown or rehearsing, after she adds Jerry, Tom changes his attitude. The actor playing the wife would have to ask herself, "Do I know he doesn't want to invite Jerry?" The answer should be, "Yes." Then, once she knows that, she can oppose it and commence the conflict. *The character always knows.* Abiding by this rule will make your character smarter and more interesting. In scenes where your character discovers she knows something, rather than enter the scene already knowing it, you have to decide *when she knows it.* There will probably be a beat change for you there.

The exception to this rule is when it is absolutely necessary to the plot, story, or character that your character *not know* something. For instance, in *Othello*, it is necessary that Othello not know that Iago is deceiving him. In comedies, a vein of the humor is often the character's self-blindness, e.g., *Do I know* that I am acting foolishly? rebellious? lying to myself? etc. The answer is *no.* This is common in sitcoms—*Seinfeld*, *Friends*, and *Frasier* for example. In Chekhov, frequently the joke is that a character is very perceptive about the inauthenticity of others, but totally clueless about herself.

Stage Directions

Stage directions usually indicate a POS beat change. POS is based on what the author is doing with a scene, and stage directions are the author's way of communicating to actors to change from what they have been doing and start something new. *The important thing about stage directions is where they occur.* What is more open to interpretation is what he tells you to do within the stage directions. The author knows he can't tell you how to play a scene. He also knows that if you follow the stage direction you will probably experientially discover a beat change and the need for a choice.

If you're interpreting what the author had in his head when he wrote a scene, and he writes that a character laughs, it helps you to see how he imagines the scene unfolding. You may ultimately play the scene without laughing there, but it helps you to get into the interpretive groove of what the author was intending. *POS beat changes often coincide with the placement of the stage directions.*

In the past, some theatrical stage directions about blocking were written into the script by the stage manager of the original production, with the author's approval. Today, almost all the stage directions are purely the author's invention. The better the author, the truer this is. Film and TV script stage directions are only written by the author(s). Forget whatever you've heard about crossing out stage directions. That caveat has deteriorated from the original intent—to keep the actor from arbitrarily executing the stage direction regardless of his overall approach to the scene—to a perverse bravado about disregarding the author's intent. Stage directions are the writer's gift of interpretive clues to the actor.

Nonverbal Beats or Monologues for the Other Character

Nonverbal beats are beats for other characters during which your character has no lines, e.g., when other characters have monologues. In such cases, you do not have to label beat changes for yourself. Go into a nonverbal beat playing your last choice prior to it, and use the beat to improvise a turning point into your next labeled choice when your dialogue begins again, i.e., play a nonverbal emotion switch from your last choice to your next choice. Unless your next choice is dependent on the last word of the other character's lines, improvise your switch at some point *during the other character's lines.* If you choose multiple turning points during his lines, as in improvising active & still railroad tracks, finish by going into your next labeled choice prior to your dialogue beginning again.

Multiple Purposes of Scene

A beat may have more than one purpose of scene. If this occurs, conflict or agreement will usually take precedence. For instance, you may find that a story beat is also conflict or agreement. In that case, playing the conflict or agreement is your character's response to the story point.

Improving Bad Writing

Working with the POS choice-making process, you will become more alert to poorly written scenes that are usually limited because they do too little. Consider improving them by adding a new purpose of scene. If a scene has no purpose other than exposition, or if the purpose of scene is redundant, e.g., a character revelation beat revealing something you've already revealed, add a new purpose. You'll improve the writing and your performance of it without changing the lines. Dialogue rewriting isn't your strong point. Acting is! Sometimes a main character is *under*written. Find maximum variety in your character revelation or story choices and fill out your character.

CHARACTER REVELATION

Umbrella Arcs

Umbrella arcs are frequently used in character revelation or story beats. (Review their description and use in chapter 12.) They are also applicable to dialogue scenes. Instead of going through his umbrella arc during a monologue, a character goes through it during a dialogue beat. As soon as he completes the umbrella arc, his next beat begins. Sometimes two characters in a beat are doing their own umbrella arcs simultaneously.

Character Revelation Beat Endings

When you have difficulty determining the end of a character revelation beat, back up to where it begins. Read it as if it were a monologue for one character; skip over the other character's lines. You will be more alert to when the feelings or behavior for that character change. Mark it at that point, then go back to the beginning of the beat and read only the other character's lines. Mark where you think the beat ends as a result of the other character changing his feelings or behavior. If the end is the same for both characters, you can be sure that is where the beat ends. If there is a different end for each character, reread each character alone and see which one would work ending at the other character's ending. If you can do that, you end the beat at that other's ending. Although it happens more often that different characters have the same beat ending, stay alert to the possibility that different characters have different beat endings. This does happen.

Character Revelation Beat Choices

When selecting your choice for a character revelation beat, you are choosing what you think the author wants the character to be feeling, not what you would feel in that situation. David E. Kelley is the most successful producer/writer in television. His staff has meetings on this subject.

> Since it isn't always easy to interpret the subtleties of a Kelley script, the team developed the "tone meeting," a formal opportunity for Kelley to systematically verbalize his written intents— for example, he might explain what emotional "color" of Ally [*Ally McBeal*] he is going for in a scene.[1]

Your character revelation choices should be emotions or attitudes. If you are stymied when looking for the right one-word emotion or attitude or the name of an umbrella arc, as a last resort use a verb. Verbs are a necessity when doing traditional Stanislavsky work, but not with POS. If you do end up with a verb choice, ask yourself, "How does my character feel about [verb]?" For example, "How does my character feel about [escaping]?" That should make it easier to arrive at an emotion choice.

If your final choice is a verb, then physicalizing it is your acting focus choice. If that doesn't work for you, use What to do with the conflict? (chapter 10) as your acting focus, substituting the verb (gerund or present participle form, "–ing") choice for the conflict.

If your final choice for a beat is a word or phrase that is usually the name of an umbrella arc, e.g., celebrating power or betrayed, but you suspect that, unlike an umbrella arc, the beat has only one feeling to it, ask yourself, "How does my character feel in this beat when she feels [word or phrase]?" The answer will be your choice.

When considering what choice to make, use your body as well as your mind. Read the beat with your prospective choice, make sure that you physicalize the choice as well as imagine the line readings with that choice.

If you are unsure about what is revealed in your character revelation beats, use the following process to help you.

1. Identify the character revelation beats.

2. Determine what's going on in the beat or whose beat it is. This means you should decide whether this beat is in the script to serve your character or another character. If the beat is there to serve your character, then it's your beat. If it's there to serve another character, then your part of the beat is supporting. Remember, not all beats belong to one character or the other; some are shared.

3. If the beat is partially or all yours, read all your lines as a monologue, skipping over the other character's lines as if they were cut, and then ask yourself: "What's the primary emotion my character is experiencing during this monologue?" or "How does my character feel?" Does the script give you any indication of how your character feels? Be careful not to confuse feelings with objectives.

4. Take your answer and imagine it at its height, i.e., at the top of its arc.

5. If you feel that the end of the monologue could never work at the height of that emotion, then you have picked the wrong emotion. Say you've picked *hurt*. Then you imagine the end of the monologue being said in tears and that feels wrong (listen to your intuition), then hurt is the wrong choice. Maybe the choice should be anger. If you see that at the end of the monologue you would be furious and that could work, anger is the better choice. This doesn't mean that after choosing the emotion you will actually play the monologue climbing to the height of its arc. The exaggeration *highlights* your choice. It is a step in the process to help you see if your choice is appropriate.

If you determine that it's not your beat and that your part of it is supporting, consider the POS for the main character. After determining what that character will probably be doing with the beat, ask yourself what should your character be feeling that will best highlight the other character's choice and best serve the scene. For example, if the purpose of the beat/scene is to reveal that Tom (the main character of the beat) is jealous, then Sue (supporting character of the beat) should choose something that will provoke or highlight his jealousy. Examples: indifferent, cold, annoyed; sweet, faux innocence, seductive; nervous, anxious, scared.

In another approach to making a character revelation choice for either the main or supporting role in a beat, notice if the beat is a long one with the supporting role's lines short and succinct, and the main role's, more substantial. That is a tip-off. The main character should probably arc rather than plateau his choice; the supporting role should plateau his choice. E.g., think of the main character climbing an *excitement* arc, and the supporting character plateauing *dubious*. It is the consistency of the supporting character (not being moved off of dubious) that contributes to the main character's heightening of his excitement (perhaps to convince the supporting character of something). The combination of the two has a sense of musicality to it. The character that is arcing provides the melody, which is always the mystery in music. Where is the melody going to go next? Or, in the acting sense, how high will he climb this arc, or will he change to another emotion? The character that is plateauing provides the rhythm, which is always the understanding in music. In the acting sense, the understanding is provided by the character's consistency in plateauing the same emotion and intensity. The unique combination of these two characters provides the harmony, which is always the soul of music.

When you have a long beat revealing only one emotion, review the beat and look for ways to add variety to your choice. First, see if the emotion can be arced throughout the beat. If an arc isn't appropriate, consider holding off the desired intensity of the emotion until as late into the beat as possible and then getting out of it as soon as you can. This will require choosing different varieties of the emotion prior to and following the desired intensity section. If anger is the choice for the whole beat, select where and for how long you absolutely must be angry. Before and after that section, create minibeats selected from bitter, annoyed, irritated, critical, distressed, frustrated, perturbed, etc.

When dealing with comedy, if you suspect your choice should provide humor but you can't see what it should be, approach it as if it weren't a comedy and make a choice. Then experiment with exaggerating that choice, e.g., exaggerate the first choice of nervous to terrified. Evaluate whether terrified is funnier than nervous. Another approach is to consider going opposite to your noncomedy first choice, e.g., nervous becomes amused.

Whenever the character's dialogue includes a list, consider arcing the list.

Mistaking Character Revelation for Story

You are seldom in trouble if you mistake a beat that is character revelation for a story beat, or vice versa. If you mistakenly label a story beat as character revelation, what you choose to be revealed will usually be the same as what you would have chosen for the story response. On the other hand, if you misidentify the beat as having a story point when it doesn't, your response to it will probably equal the choice you should have made for the character revelation.

When you are unsure whether a beat is character revelation or story, it is best to err in the direction of story. It is easier to ask yourself, "What is my character's response to [what you think the story point is]?" than to ask, "What is revealed about my character in this beat?" It is easier because it is so specifically attached to what you are labeling as the story point, rather than the more generalized character revelation question.

SAMPLE SCENES FOR POS

POS Character Revelation: TV

Larry Drake created a memorable character and won two Emmys for his portrayal of Benny Stulwicz on the hit TV series, *L. A. Law*. Eight years after the show concluded its eighth and final season, the cast reassembled for a two-hour reunion movie, *L. A. Law: The Movie*[2] (2002). In this first script example, Benny has seven successive character revelation beats before reaching his first story beat. Due to Benny's unique character, a developmentally disabled file clerk/gofer, Larry Drake made basic, innocent, and straightforward emotion choices consistent with Benny's less sophisticated way of thinking, feeling, and behaving. Also, notice how he uses his objects for physical doing and to physicalize his emotion choice during his big nonverbal beat.

```
INT. RECEPTION AREA - DAY

Seated in the reception area is WARREN MYTELKA,
forties, mentally challenged in the form of
severe learning disability and marginal social
skills; Benny enters with three boxes of Krispy
Kreme donuts - [NOTE: In production, Larry adds
a cardboard tray of coffees.]
```

POS Character revelation: Careful (not to spill coffees)

Acting focus: Physicalize emotion

                         WARREN
             You got Krispy Kreme.

POS Character revelation: Pleasant

Acting focus: Emotion switch

                          BENNY
             Yeah.

                         WARREN
             Can I have one?

POS Character revelation: Polite

Acting focus: Emotion switch

                          BENNY
             They're for the people who work
             here.

        Benny sees Warren withdraw –

POS Character revelation: Compassionate

Acting focus: Emotion switch

                       BENNY (CONT'D)
                 (approaching as he opens the
                 top box)
             You could have one though.
        Warren takes a donut –

                         WARREN
             I get the day-old.

POS Character revelation: Dubious

Acting focus: Emotion switch

                          BENNY
             Day-old donuts?

                         WARREN
             Regular's five dollars and sixty-
             five cents a dozen, day-old's two
             dollars and fifty cents a dozen.

                          BENNY
             Aren't they stale?

                    WARREN
              (as though it's a good thing)
           Yeah.

       Kuzak enters with Yvonne -

POS Character revelation: Preoccupied (with closing donut box and
gathering up the coffees)
Acting focus: Emotions & objects

                    KUZAK
              (going straight to Warren)
           You're Warren?

                    WARREN
           Yeah.

                    KUZAK
              (extending his hand)
           Michael Kuzak.

       Warren shakes hands tentatively -

                    KUZAK (CONT'D)
           Why don't we go into my office?

                    WARREN
           How come?

                    KUZAK
           So we can talk.

                    WARREN
           Can't we talk here?

                    KUZAK
           I think it will be better where we
           could have some privacy.

                    WARREN
              (standing up; panics)
           Maybe I'll come back.

       Warren walks quickly to the elevator, pushes
       the button -

                    KUZAK
              (to Benny)
           Come with me.

POS Character revelation: Bewildered
Acting focus: Physicalize emotions

       Kuzak and Benny go to Warren -

```
                    KUZAK (CONT'D)
        You told the receptionist that
        Belinda told you to come in. Why?
```

```
                    WARREN
        I have to go.

                    KUZAK
        Were you a witness to the murder of
        that cop, Warren?

                    WARREN
            (to Benny, deliberately discon-
            necting from Kuzak)
        To get out to the street do I press
        "One" or "L"?

                    BENNY
        "L." There is no "One."

                    KUZAK
        Benny maybe you want to talk to
        Warren. Tell him a man's life might
        depend on him telling the truth.
```

POS Story: Kuzak enlists Benny's help as a peer and not as an errand man – in a matter of life and death!

Response: Anxious

Acting focus: Emotion switch

```
    A beat; Kuzak waits for Benny to vouch for him—
```

POS: Character revelation: Accepting a challenge (Umbrella arc)

Acting focus: Emotion switch

(Brave)

```
                    BENNY
            (to Kuzak)
        Are you going to stand there?

                    KUZAK
            (takes Benny's point)
        I'll be in my office.

    Kuzak walks back toward the office -

                    WARREN
        He's mean.
```

(Sincere)

```
                    BENNY
        I know him a long time - he's never
        been mean to me.

    The elevator dings, the door opens -
```

POS Story: Warren is leaving!

Response: Accepting a challenge (Umbrella arc continues)

Acting focus: Emotion switch

(Determined)

>   BENNY (CONT'D)
>   He won't hurt you and nobody
>   else'll hurt you.

Warren hesitates, then lets the elevator doors
close.

POS Story: Benny's successful at keeping Warren here.

Response: Pleased

Acting focus: Emotion switch

>   CUT TO:

>   INT. SPARE OFFICE - DAY

>   Amidst the general mess Kuzak sits with Warren
>   who has Benny next to him -

POS Character revelation: Rapt

Acting focus: Physicalize emotion

>   WARREN
>   I saw a flash from a window on the
>   fourth floor across the courtyard.

>   KUZAK
>   Did you see who was in the fourth
>   floor window?

>   WARREN
>   Somebody not Albert Hutchinson.

>   KUZAK
>   Did you tell this to anyone?

>   WARREN
>   First to Belinda only don't be mad
>   at her. She only lied 'cause
>   Dumbledor made her. She wanted me
>   to tell Dumbledor what I saw so he
>   wouldn't make her but he still made
>   her.

>   KUZAK
>   Who's Dumbledor?

POS Character revelation: Helpful

Acting focus: Attitude line, "I know"

>   BENNY
> Like from Harry Potter.
>
>   KUZAK
> Is all this something you read in
> Harry Potter, Warren?
>
>   WARREN
> He was <u>like</u> Dumbledor from Harry
> Potter.
>
>   KUZAK
>   (to Benny)
> Do you know what he's talking
> about?

POS Character revelation: Eager

Acting focus: Physicalize emotion

>   BENNY
> Albus Dumbledor.
>
>   KIZAK
> I don't know who that is Benny.
>
>   BENNY
> He was head of Hogwarts.
>
>   WARREN
> And he was good and nice and the
> man I saw wasn't.
>
>   BENNY
> So he wasn't really like Dumbledor
> then.
>
>   WARREN
> No. His <u>name</u> was like Dumbledor but
> <u>he</u> wasn't like Dumbledor.

> Kuzak drops his head in despair in trying to
> follow these two –

POS Character revelation: Puzzled

Acting focus: Emotion switch

>   WARREN (CONT'D)
> He had no beard and two flags be-
> hind his desk and his name was like
> Dumbledor but not Dumbledor.

```
                    KUZAK
              (on hearing "two flags")
          Diebenkorn?

                    WARREN
          Yeah. Diebenkorn.

                    KUZAK
          Diebenkorn was the District Attorney.

                    WARREN
          I told Diebenkorn.

                                FADE TO BLACK
```

POS Character Revelation: Theater

Here is an example of a character doing a pure emotion arc for his character revelation. David Mamet helps the actor define the length of the beat by starting and ending the beat with pauses. The verb choices after the arc are feelings and are also physicalized. When we pick up the scene in *Glengarry Glen Ross*,[3] office manager Williamson has just made a strategic mistake with a salesman's customer and may have lost the sale. Levene, another salesman, has witnessed it and takes advantage of the situation to get back at Williamson. My choices for Levene are on the left and for Williamson, on the right.

Near end of previous beat:

WILLIAMSON. Mmm.

LEVENE. *Yes.* "Mmm." *Yes. Precisely. Precisely.* 'Cause your partner *depends* on it. (*Pause*)

POS Character revelation:

Levene: Anger	**Williamson: Disbelief**
Acting focus: Emotion arc	**Acting focus: Physicalize emotion**

LEVENE (*Cont'd*). I'm *talking* to you. I'm trying to tell you something.

WILLIAMSON. You are?

LEVENE. Yes, I am.

WILLIAMSON. What are you trying to tell me?

LEVENE. What Roma's trying to tell you. What I told you yesterday. Why you don't belong in the business.

WILLIAMSON. Why I don't . . .

LEVENE. You listen to me, someday you might say, "hey . . ." No, fuck that, you just listen what I'm going to say: your partner *depends* on you. You partner . . . a man who's your "partner" *depends* on you. . . . you have to go *with* him and *for* him . . . or you're shit, you're *shit*, you can't exist alone . . .

WILLIAMSON. *(Brushing past him)* Excuse me . . .

	POS Character revelation:
Levene: No beat change	**Williamson: Tired**
(Still arcing anger)	**Acting focus: Physicalize emotion**

LEVENE. . . . excuse you, *nothing*, you be as cold as you want, but you just fucked a good man out of six thousand dollars and his goddamn bonus 'cause you didn't know the *shot*, if you can do that and you aren't man enough that it gets you, then I don't know what, if you can't take *some thing* from that . . . *(Blocking his way)* you're *scum*, you're fucking white-bread. You be as cold as you want. A *child* would know it, he's right. *(Pause)*

POS Character revelation:	
Levene: Patronizing	**Williamson: No beat change**
Acting focus: Physicalize emotion	

LEVENE *(Cont'd)*. You're going to make something up, be sure it will *help* or keep your mouth closed. *(Pause)*

POS Character revelation:	**POS Story: Levene knows he made it up.**
Levene: Dismissive	**Williamson response: Alert**
Acting focus: Physicalize emotion	**Acting focus: Physicalize emotion**

WILLIAMSON. Mmm. *(Levene lifts up his arm.)*

LEVENE. Now I'm done with you. *(Pause)*

Notice that Williamson has a nonverbal beat change in the middle of Levene's anger arc. The choice of tired is appropriate to the given circumstances and sets up a dynamic transition to his next choice, alert, in the subsequent beat.

POS Character Revelation: Film

In the next scene, we see an umbrella arc, which requires some verb choices. In the movie *What Dreams May Come*,[4] Chris (Robin Williams) dies and goes to heaven. He is escorted around heaven by Leona (Rosalind Chao), a young Asian female flight attendant. In this scene, Leona reveals to Chris that she is really his daughter, Marie, who died when she was a child. I do not include acting focus choices, as my client on the film was the director, Vincent Ward, and these are the choices he brought to the set to assist him in his direction. Leona's choices are on the left and Chris's, on the right.

```
SUMMERLAND - EXT. RIVER - NIGHT
It is fully night now. A shadow from the moon
```

passes over the boat as we emerge from a large
arched mass. As the boat pulls into the night
sky, we pull back to reveal an enormous city
forming a bridge over the river. This is the
same bridge and city Annie painted on each side
of Marie's puppet stage. The clouds in the sky
perfectly match those on Marie's walls.

POS Character revelation

CHRIS

(Sad)

She died three months later.

(Sadly proud)

We played every night, and it meant
the world to me.

His smile has an inner light.
Because maybe he is starting to
realize.

CHRIS

(Sadly prescient)

She never won.

POS Character revelation

Seduces him to the truth (Umbrella arc)

LEONA

(Gently coaxing)

I didn't look like this. In the
body. You know.

(Gently inviting)

We flew to Singapore once. And
my daddy smiled at the flight
attendant.

(Gently embarrassed)

Who looked like this. And wore this
name tag. Leona.

**POS Story: He knows for sure
this is his daughter.
Response: Tender**

Tears stand in his eyes now. Everywhere the
sound of the CHOIR...

(Umbrella arc continues)

LEONA

(Gently beckoning)

> He told me, Asian women are so

> lovely. And so graceful. And
> intelligent.

                                         POS Character revelation: Assured

              CHRIS
He didn't mean onl...

(Umbrella arc continues)

              LEONA

(Forgiving)

> It was just something he said.

(Courageous)

> And what I thought was...I want to
> grow up...

(Lonely)

> to be that.

Tears on her face now. For some reason, that
makes him very happy.

                              POS Story: He lets her know for sure
                                          that he knows.
                              Chris response: Hopeful

              CHRIS
Do you still play chess?

Leona response: Delight switching to tears of joy

              LEONA
I think I waited for my partner.

She slides her arms around her daddy's neck.
Holds him. So tight.

AGREEMENT

In the characters' dialogue, words from the agreement family, e.g., yes, sure, okay, I agree, positively, etc., do not automatically mean that it is an agreement beat. All agreement beats must have one specific characteristic, happiness! If the characters in a beat are not happy during that beat, it cannot be an agreement beat.

If the characters in a beat are using agreement-type words like those listed above, but they are only used as dittos or echoes and the lines don't build on each other, taking the agreement further, then it is probably not an agreement beat.

If there are only two dialogue lines of agreement, it is usually not an agreement beat. The lines are a part of the preceding or subsequent beat or may be split between them.

POS Agreement: Theater

Early in the first act of Arthur Miller's *Death of a Salesman*,[5] Biff and Happy have an agreement beat in the scene in their bedroom. If you crossed out the stage directions, you would miss Miller's intent because of the complaints in Happy's lines.

POS Agreement
Acting focus: Agreement

BIFF. *(With enthusiasm)* Listen, why don't you come out West with me?

HAPPY. You and I, heh?

BIFF. Sure, maybe we could buy a ranch. Raise cattle, use our muscles. Men built like we are should be working out in the open.

HAPPY. *(Avidly)* The Loman Brothers, heh?

BIFF. *(With vast affection)* Sure, we'd be known all over the counties!

HAPPY. *(Enthralled)* That's what I dream about, Biff. Sometimes I want to just rip my clothes off in the middle of the store and outbox that goddam merchandise manager. I mean I can outbox, outrun, and outfit anybody in that store, and I have to take orders from those common, petty sons-of-bitches till I can't stand it anymore.

BIFF. I'm tellin' you, kid, if you were with me I'd be happy out there.

HAPPY. *(Filled with enthusiasm)* See, Biff, everybody around me is so false that I'm constantly lowering my ideals . . .

BIFF. Baby, together we'd stand up for one another, we'd have someone to trust.

HAPPY. If I were around you—

BIFF. Hap, the trouble is we weren't brought up to grub for money. I don't know how to do it.

HAPPY. Neither can I!

BIFF. Then let's go!

POS Agreement: TV

Characters receiving good news will frequently initiate agreement beats. Here is an example from a TV movie, *Presumed Guilty*.[6] Tim Matheson played Nick.

```
                JENNIFER
        That's fifty-fifty net profits,
        right?
```

(Jennifer smiles as they both listen one more time, then:)

POS Agreement
Acting focus: Agreement

           NICK
You're the best, Myron.

(They hang up, and sit beaming at each other a moment before:)

      Shall you do the honors, or shall I?

          JENNIFER
You.

          NICK
Okay.

(They get up and go to their office door. Nick calls out:)

      Everyone listen up.

(Everyone stops working. Bodies appear in office doors. Nick's face gives nothing away until he smiles broadly:)

      We got us a deal.

(Everyone claps and cheers.)

POS Agreement: Film

A frequently used comedy device has two characters playing agreement to the consternation of a third character, who is not playing agreement. Here is an example from the teen comedy movie, *Dangerous Curves*.[7] Tate Donovan and Grant Heslov play Chuck and Wally, who take a road trip to San Diego in a Porsche entrusted to them for safekeeping. When they get there, the Porsche is stolen. In this scene, they scheme to steal it back with the help of their streetwise friend, Bam Bam. Wally and Bam Bam play agreement—the negation at the beginning of Wally's lines is an agreement with Bam Bam—to the consternation of Chuck. Notice the prerequisite components of agreement: the happy state of mind is indicated by the stage direction "amused," and each line builds on the previous line, taking the agreement further.

POS Agreement
Acting focus: Agreement

(Chuck starts to draw in the sand with a stick.
Wally and Bam Bam look on, amused, as Chuck
draws.)

586

              BAM BAM
What is that?

              CHUCK
The Porsche.

              WALLY
No way is that a Porsche.

              BAM BAM
Looks like an aardvark.

              WALLY
You're right, Bam Bam, it does. An
aardvark or an anteater? Which one
has the longer snoot?

              BAM BAM
I thought they were the same thing.

              WALLY
Well, they both eat the same thing.
But one's much bigger and has a
really long, skinny snoot.

              BAM BAM
They have to have skinny snoots. I
mean, how else would they be able
to stick 'em down anthills?

              WALLY
Exactly. And you know, that's something I've always wondered about.
With them always stickin' their
snoots down anthills, you think
they get a lot of ants crawlin' up
their noses?

              BAM BAM
Sure. Must be a common aardvark
problem

(Chuck looks on, getting extremely impatient.
He finally whacks the twig down on the ground,
spraying sand on Wally and Bam Bam.)

              CHUCK
You kids finished?

CONFLICT

Whole Scene is Conflict

Sometimes you will find that an entire scene is one long conflict beat. In this case, it is best to observe the following rule. *Start the actual conflict as late as you can and get out of the conflict as early as you can.* Even though the whole scene or long beat is conflict, find the latest point at which you absolutely must be on the conflict and mark that as the beginning of the conflict beat. Everything prior to that should be approached as a potential beat (or beats) with other purposes of scene, e.g., story or character revelation. (It can't be agreement because these characters will not be happy.) Then return to the conflict beat and find the earliest possible moment that you can get off the conflict. Mark that as the end of the conflict beat. Approach what follows as a potential beat or beats with other purposes of scene, e.g., story or character revelation.

To fulfill the tension requirement that the author had in mind when he wrote the scene as conflict, your choices for these pre- and postconflict beats will probably be from the tense/anger family, e.g., bitter, annoyed, irritated, critical, distressed, frustrated, perturbed, etc. You can choose from beyond the tense/anger family if you create an arc of choices that leads to the tension and anger of the conflict, e.g., casual >weary >burdened (then into the conflict). This provides more variety to the scene choices than one long confrontation or pull-the-conflict contest.

Essentially, you are asking yourself, "How else can I approach this scene for the sake of variety while still staying true to what the author intended?"

Finding Conflict Beats

When you're looking for conflict, look for two features. (1) Do you see any form of tension? If so, make sure that both characters are experiencing the tension; that should be a warning light that calls your attention to the beat as a possible conflict beat. Then, look into that beat and see if you can spot two opposing wants. If you can, it's a conflict beat. If you can't, then it's not. (2) Sometimes you see the two opposing wants and not the tension. If there are two opposing wants and it is not a conflict exception or the beat doesn't require that at least one of the characters not be in tension, then it is a conflict beat. Your job is to provide the tension and rhythm, which you will do when correctly identifying and improvising the beat as conflict.

If there are only two dialogue lines of opposing wants, it is not a conflict beat. The two lines are a part of the preceding or subsequent beat or may be split up into those beats.

Multiple Conflict Beats

You may see multiple beats of conflict on the same conflict issue with other POS beats between them. You may see two consecutive beats of conflict if the conflict issue changes.

Conflict Beat Beginnings

Conflict beats start with the first line of rebuttal. There is no conflict until the second person opposes what the first person wants. However, there is an exception to this rule. If a conflict beat is a return to the same conflict issue from an earlier beat, then the beat starts immediately and not when the second character begins opposing it.

Losses and Kills

Losses are usually marked outside of the conflict beat as the beginning of the next beat. Otherwise, they will have a visceral feeling of having to play them with tension, rhythm, and anger, which will contradict the dynamic of the loss. If the loss is followed by the other character going in for the kill, then the loss and the kill constitute a minibeat, which might be labeled the *conflict tag*. Sometimes losses and kills occur in the middle of a conflict beat but don't end the conflict beat. They should be labeled and played as losses or kills; then resume the conflict.

Conflict Resolution Informs Next Beat

When you have a beat that follows a conflict beat, ask yourself if you won, lost, or stalemated the conflict and how you feel about it. Let the answer inform your choice for the next beat.

Comedy Conflict

Comedy scenes are frequently based on conflict and you should consider if any beats of the conflict are funnier if you play them as a Will-you-marry-me conflict (p. 410), in which one of the combatants uses a carrot instead of a stick. Using a carrot only inflames the other combatant (who is using a stick) even more and can heighten the humor.

POS Conflict: TV

Here is an example of a conflict beat where the conflict is in the text. It's from the TV series *Melrose Place*,[8] and Brooke Langton plays Samantha. At this point in the series, Samantha's father has escaped from jail and is pressuring her to help him get out of the country. When we pick up the scene, Samantha's boy-friend accuses her of lying to him. That is a story point and Samantha's response is to go into conflict.

```
INT. BILLY AND SAM'S APARTMENT - CONTINUOUS

                    BILLY
          Stop lying, alright?!
```
_____

POS Story: He accuses her of lying.

Response: Conflict

POS Conflict: He wants me to tell the truth;

I want him to stop being intrusive.

Acting focus: Pull the conflict!

```
His explosion startles them both. Sam tries to
cover.

                    SAMANTHA
          I don't know why you're yelling at
          me but —

                    BILLY
          I followed you, Sam. Straight to
          some flea bag motel where I guess
          your father's been holed up.

                    SAMANTHA
          You followed me?

                    BILLY
          What else could I do? Between the
          ATM withdrawal and all the hours
          you couldn't account for, I didn't
          know what to think. And then I find
          out you're seeing your dad behind
          my back. I thought you said he was
          in Chicago.

                    SAMANTHA
          Since when do you need to know
          every detail of my family life? I
          mean just because we're together
          doesn't mean everything's your damn
          business.

Samantha tries to sidestep Billy, but he takes
her by the shoulders, makes her look into his
eyes.
```

> BILLY
> Sam, this is crazy. Why are you
> lying to me?

Sam can't deny this anymore, and she doesn't
want to. The pressure gives way to emotion. She
softens, near tears.

(Play the loss)

> SAMANTHA
> Look, he's in trouble, okay? And
> I'm helping him out. I didn't want
> to bring you into it.

Notice that the beat's beginning and end are marked by the two lines directly on the conflict issue.

POS Conflict: Film

In a scene from the movie *Love Potion No. 9*,[9] Tate Donovan plays Paul, a shy scientist being challenged by his friend Jeff to meet an attractive woman in a bar. Here we see a disguised conflict under a different text conflict.

POS Conflict
Text: He wants me to go and talk to the woman; I don't want to.
Disguised conflict: He wants to humiliate me; I want him to stop it.
Acting focus: Pull the conflict!

```
INT. MARINO'S - NIGHT

CAMERA PULLS BACK FROM PAUL'S SWEATY PALMS TO
FULL SHOT.

Jeff takes a $20 from his wallet and places it
on the table.

          JEFF
     I tell you what. I'll pay you $20
     to go and talk to her.

          PAUL
     Why is this so important to you?

          JEFF
     It's not important, I'm just crazy.
     Twenty bucks. Twenty bucks just to
     go and talk to her.

          PAUL
     No.
```

```
        JEFF
    (Places another 20 on other
    20.)
$40.

        PAUL
I don't want to do it.

        JEFF
    (Puts 3 more bills on others.)
ONE HUNDRED Dollars.

(Afraid Jeff will raise the stakes and he'll
become even more humiliated—)
```

(Play the loss)

```
(Paul silently gets up and leaves the table.)
```

Notice that if Paul played the text conflict it would be weak because it is a conflict exception (unilateral conflict). The scene would end with him winning because he doesn't go to the woman. Playing the disguised conflict makes the conflict stronger and he loses, which is how the scene should end in order to fulfill the writer's intent and stage direction.

POS Conflict: Theater

In act 2, scene 2, of Clifford Odets's *Golden Boy*,[10] there is a disguised conflict beat with the conflict rising into the text in the middle of the beat.

POS Conflict. He wants her to leave Moody (her boyfriend); She wants him to stop pushing for that.
Acting focus: Pull the conflict!

JOE. What's on your mind, Lorna?

LORNA. What's on yours?

JOE *(Simply)*. You. . . . You're real for me— the way music was real.

LORNA. You've got your car, your career— what do you want with me?

JOE. I develop the ability to knock down anyone my weight. But what point have I made? Don't you think I know that? I went off to the wars 'cause someone called me a name— because I wanted to be two other guys. Now it's happening. . . . I'm not sure I like it.

LORNA. Moody's against that car of yours.

JOE. I'm against Moody, so we're even.

LORNA. Why don't you like him?

JOE. He's a manager! He treats me like a possession! I'm just a little silver mine for him— he bangs me around with a shovel!

LORNA. He's helped you—

JOE. No, Tokio's helped me.

Conflict rises into text >

Why don't you give him up? It's terrible to have just a Tuesday-night girl. Why don't you belong to me every night in the week? Why don't you teach me love? . . . Or am I being a fool?

LORNA. You're not a fool, Joe.

JOE. I want you to be my family, my life— Why don't you do it, Lorna, why?

LORNA. He loves me.

JOE. I love you!

What allows this conflict beat to avoid being a Will-you-marry-me? conflict exception is: (1) the volatile nature of both characters; (2) the fact that she is involved with another man; (3) the conflict issue is not "Will you marry me," but "Leave Moody" vs. "Stop pushing."

STORY

You must name the story point of every story beat. If you cannot name it, then you have chosen it as story incorrectly. Sometimes a story point occurs, but a character is not aware of it. In that situation, it is not a story point for that character.

Story Beat Beginnings

In the same way that a disguised conflict can indicate the start of a conflict beat even though the actual conflict issue isn't raised into the text until later in the beat, story beats can start before the actual appearance of the story point. In other words, the story beat for the creator of a story point can start prior to the actual lines creating the story point. A marriage proposal, for instance, will be a story point in any script. The story beat that includes the proposal can start earlier than the proposal itself, e.g., "Charlotte, I want to talk to you. We have been together a long time. I think we are soul mates. Will you marry me?" If the man's story response was *nervous*, it would start at the beginning of the beat, not at the actual proposal line, which may be the last line of the story beat. *If the story point is revealed by one of the characters, that story point beat will usually start where the one doing the revealing makes the decision to reveal it.* However, if your character is the one receiving the proposal, the story beat begins for you at the time of the actual proposal, or earlier if you know he is about to propose. Any time you ask yourself if your character knows something, the answer is usually yes unless the script demands otherwise.

Nonverbal Story Beats

Story beats can be nonverbal. If you are in a scene and a story point occurs that you are aware of, then you must have a response to it, with or without lines. For example, the scene has you in a public place. You see an ex-lover across the room (story point); what's your nonverbal response? Then, while you're looking at her, she sees you (story point); what's your nonverbal response to that?

Story Point Response

When considering your response to a story point, it is sometimes helpful to change the question, "What is my (character's) response to the story point," to "How do I feel about that [the story point]?" The answer to that question is almost always the choice that you play. I prefer the question, "What is my (character's) response to the story point," because it makes potential umbrella arcs more accessible.

Surprise should never be your choice of a response to a story point because (1) you get it for free and (2) it only lasts a millisecond and then changes to something else. The something else is your choice of a response to the story point.

POS Story: Film

In the movie *Miami Rhapsody*[11], Carla Gugino plays Leslie, who is having an affair with a dentist. They are sneaking assignations at Leslie's sister's apartment whenever the sister is away. In this scene, the sister, Gwyn, played by Sarah Jessica Parker, unexpectedly walks in on Leslie.

```
INT. BEDROOM.

The music is blasting. Gwyn turns on the
lights. Leslie sits up in bed. She wears her
Victoria's Secret lingerie.
```

POS Story: Gwyn arrives unexpectedly.
Response: Fear and embarrassment
Acting focus: Emotion switch

```
                    LESLIE
(Scared)
        Gwyn.

                    GWYN
        Leslie. Are you all right?

                    LESLIE
        Yeah, I'm fine. I thought you were
        eating at Jordan's.
```

                    GWYN
          So did I. What are you doing here?

(Embarrassed)

                    LESLIE
          God, this is —I didn't think you
          were coming home this early.

     (Leslie glances nervously toward the closed
     bathroom door.)

                    GWYN
          Well, what's the problem? Is there
          someone in the bathroom?

                    LESLIE
          Please don't hold this against me.

                    GWYN
          What?

                    LESLIE
          Maybe you should just go out for a
          few minutes so we could—

     (The bathroom door opens and Mitchell, the
     dentist, appears in his underwear.)

                    MITCHELL
          Get ready, 'cause here I come.

POS Story: TV

In the next story scene, we have an example of two consecutive story beats, each employing its own umbrella arc. The scene is from the TV series, *The Practice*.[12] Michael Monks played George Fogelman, a recurring character in numerous episodes. It has been established that he is a nerd who has been a suspect in different murders including one where the murderer was identified as a nun. He has a serious and unrequited crush on his lawyer, Ellenor, who always believes he is innocent. In the final episode of the season and the climax of George's story on the show, he is revealed as the psychopathic murderer. Ellenor has just returned to her apartment to find her roommate, Helen Gamble, naked and dead in the bathtub.

     INT. GAMBLE/ELLENOR'S APARTMENT - CONTINUOUS
     Ellenor picks up the phone. Tries to dial it,
     sees it's dead. She flicks up the cord, it's
     been cut. She turns toward the front door, her
     path is blocked. By a nun. It's George.

POS Story: *George reveals himself as the murderer.*
Response: *Excitement of teaching (Umbrella arc)*
Acting focus: *Emotion switches*

>   GEORGE
> **(Searching)**
>   *(Calm)* Something wrong, Ellenor?
>
>   (Ellenor is too stunned to even make words.)
>
>   GEORGE (CONT'D)
> **(Baiting)**
>   I changed my mind about dinner.
> **(Disappointed)**
>   But I think Helen is too dead tired
>   to cook.
>
>   ELLENOR
>   Ya...<u>you</u>? (then) Susan Robin?
>   Lindsey?
>
>   GEORGE
> **(Tempting)**
>   You told me you had to work late
>   that night, remember, Ellenor? I
>   had theater tickets, you said you'd
>   be in the office till at least
>   nine, but
> **(Bribing)**
>   when I went there, I found Lindsay.
>
>   ELLENOR
>   Why...why did you hurt <u>her</u>? Or
>   Helen?
>
>   GEORGE
> **(Enjoyment)**
>   Lindsay was there.
> **(Curious)**
>   Helen's not dead, she just inhaled
>   a little chloroform.
>
>   ELLENOR
>   So she's.. she's alive?
>
>   GEORGE
> **(Enthusiasm)**
>   Sometimes I just like to <u>simulate</u>
>   death. I came up on her from be-
>   hind, she doesn't know it was me.
>   When she wakes...she'll find you.

ELLENOR

You're...you're here to kill me?

GEORGE

(Passion)

Know how many times you've killed me?

(There's a cold psychosis to him here. Ellenor's eyes catch her purse on the floor by the fallen groceries.)

GEORGE (CONT'D)

(Excited)

You think you can reach that gun? You think you could use it to kill me, Ellenor?
(A beat)
Let me make it easier for you.

(He kicks the purse over to her.)

(Joy)

I would love to go out that way. With you pulling the trigger.
(There's a psychotic ring to his voice.)

(Satisfied)

Go ahead, Ellenor. Get your gun.

(He then reveals a knife. Ellenor quickly grabs her purse, pulls out the weapon.)

POS Story: Ellenor points gun at him.

Response: Torturing her (Umbrella arc)

Acting focus: Emotion switches

GEORGE (CONT'D)

(Resentment)

Go ahead. Shoot me.

(Bitter)

You'd be doing me a favor, wouldn't you, putting me out of my miserable pathetic existence.

ELLENOR

What you don't know is I <u>would</u>. I <u>will</u> shoot.

GEORGE

(Hate)

Then do it.

(A beat)

(Punishing)

I'll <u>make</u> you do it. I'm going to
kill <u>you</u>. Unless you kill me.

                ELLENOR
George.

                GEORGE

(Anger)

(Screaming) Do it!!

(As he steps toward her—)

                ELLENOR
(Aiming) Don't come any closer.

                GEORGE

(Rage)

Shoot me, Ellenor!

                ELLENOR
(Pointing the gun) Don't make me
pull the trigger, don't make—

                GEORGE

(Satisfied)

You're gonna have to do it,
Ellenor. You'll have to be the
executioner.

                ELLENOR
Just put down the knife...and we
can talk. You and—

___

(But suddenly, George lunges at her with the
knife, Ellenor FIRES TWICE. He staggers
back...with almost a smile on his face.)

POS Story: Theater

In Lillian Hellman's *The Children's Hour*,[13] two young schoolteachers have been
falsely accused of lesbianism and their lives have been shattered. Near the end of
the play is a scene between one of them, Karen, and her fiancé, Cardin. I've
included a part of the scene with three story beats. One of these gives us an
opportunity to see a story beat in which the characters are responding to the
actual story point prior to it appearing in the text. When we pick up the scene,
they have just concluded a conflict beat: she wants him to ask the question that
she knows he wants to ask, and he won't ask it. The question is whether it's true
that she and Martha were lovers. He has been supportive of Karen throughout

the play and has behaved with a presumption that it is not true. My choices for Cardin are on the left and Karen on the right.

Near end of conflict beat:

> KAREN. After a while, in the court, I stopped listening. After a while, It didn't seem to matter what anybody said. Then I began to watch your face. It was the only nice thing I could think of doing. You were ashamed. So was I. But you had trouble worse than that. You were sad at being ashamed. Ask it now, Joe.

> CARDIN. I have nothing to ask. Nothing. (*Then, very quickly, turns to her.*)

POS Story: He asks the question.

His response: Cowardly	Her response: Courageous
Acting focus: Physicalize emotion	Acting focus: Physicalize emotion

All Right. It is—? Was it ever—?

> KAREN. (*Quickly puts her hand over his mouth, stopping him.*) No. Martha and I have never touched each other. That's all right, darling. I'm not mad. I am glad you asked me.

POS Story: She answered the question.

His response: Ashamed	Her response: Somber (lonely)
Acting focus: Physicalize emotion	Acting focus: Physicalize emotion

> CARDIN. My God, what's happened to me? (Embraces her.) I'm sorry, darling, I'm sorry. I didn't want to hurt you— I didn't ever believe— (*Crosses to C.*)

> KAREN. No, of course you didn't really. But after a while, you weren't sure. Maybe there was just a little truth— That's the way these things go. That's the way they are meant to go. You've been a good, loyal friend. (*Turns L.*)

POS Story: She breaks up with him.

His response: Abandonment	Her response: Despair
(Umbrella arc)	(Umbrella arc)
Acting focus: Emotion switches	Acting focus: Emotion switches

(Nervous)   (Durable)

Don't be ashamed of what you felt. You're a fine man.

> CARDIN. (*Crosses to Karen.*) I've asked, you've answered. That's all. Let's go ahead now and—

> KAREN. You believe me?

(Agitated)   **(Nostalgic)**

CARDIN. *(With force.)* You know I believe you.

KAREN. Maybe you do. But I'd never know whether you did. And you're saying it again won't do it. And it doesn't even matter any more whether you do believe me. *(Moves away L.)*

(Lost)

All that I know is that I'd be frightened you didn't. But that's the way it would be. We'd be hounded by it. You don't get over things by just saying you do. I don't believe you could touch my arm without my wondering why you didn't kiss me, and I don't think you could kiss me without my wondering if you really wanted to. And I'd hate myself for all that. And then I'd hate you, too. *(Turns to Cardin.)*

(Sad)

I don't want ruin. I don't like it. *(Softly)* Ah, Joe. You know all that.

(Frustrated)

CARDIN. *(Moves toward her.)* I don't. I don't.

KAREN. (Softly.) Ah, what happens between people, happens, and after a while it doesn't much matter how it started. But there it is. *(Turns U.S.)*

(Bitter)

I'm here. You're there. We're in a room we've been in so many times before. Nothing seems changed. My hands look just the same, my face is just the same, even my dress is old.

(Miserable)

I'm nothing too much: I'm like everybody else, the way I always was. I can have the things that other people have. I can have you, and children, and I can take care of them, and I can go to market, and read a book, and people will talk to me—

(Hopeless)

Only I can't. I can't. And I don't know why. *(Turns L.)* Go home, darling.

(Desperate)   **(Scared)**

CARDIN. *(Crosses to KAREN, puts arms around her. With great force.)* We can't leave each other. We're not going to leave each other. You're tired. I'm tired. I didn't know what I was asking—

KAREN. Don't be sorry. *(Softly.)* You're such a nice man.

CARDIN. You say I helped you. Help me now. Help me. Karen—

(Sorrow)　　　　　　　　　　POS Character revelation:
　　　　　　　　　　　　　　　Brave (for his sake)
　　　　　　　　　　　　　　Acting focus: Attitude line,
　　　　　　　　　　　　　　　　　"I'm brave"

KAREN. *(Turns to him.)* All right. Go away for a little while. Away from me and love and pity, and all the things that mess people up. Go away by yourself. And so will I. Please. Please do it that way. And after a while, I'll know and you'll know, and then we'll see— Please, Joe.

CARDIN. *(After a pause.)* There's nothing for me to know. A few weeks won't make any difference—

KAREN. Please.

CARDIN. I don't want to go.

KAREN. *(Turns L.)* Go now, darling.

CARDIN. What will you do?

KAREN. I'll wait. I'll be all right.

CARDIN. *(Kisses her hair.)* I'll be coming back soon. *(Exits, U. C. leaving door open.)*

Notice the beat where she breaks up with him. The actor has to choose where that beat begins and I suggest Karen decides to do it at the end of her last speech prior to that beat. The clue to making this choice is her sentence, "You've been a good loyal friend," not exactly something you'd say if you were continuing the engagement. If you are playing his part you would have to ask yourself, "Does he know she's breaking up with him when she says that?" As I've previously pointed out, the answer to the question of whether or not your character knows something is almost always yes.

ACTING FOCUS CHOICES

Keep in mind the length of the beat you are working on. Don't pick a focus that is hard for you to do or takes a lot of preparation for a two-line beat. Make sure you are adept at the most commonly used acting focuses with scripted lines: pull the conflict, agreement, physicalize an emotion, emotion arc, emotion switch, off stage, attitude line, and active & still.

REWRITES

If you've done the POS work on a scene that gets changed, you have a complete understanding of what purpose that scene served for your character. When you are handed two new pages, you can see whether those pages serve the same purpose, but with changes in the dialogue. Because you have done all of that analysis work and prepared it in the body, you will know that it is really the same thing, only the dialogue is different. Or, you get to see that it is not the same thing. "I was doing a fear arc in the scene they threw out and now I am taking charge of everything with bravado." What has been changed in the rewrite will stand out to you because it is not what you have planned. Then you only have to make the adjustments to serve the new purpose of the scene. Having done the POS work on the old scene makes it easier to understand the new scene.

Sometimes you will find that the rewrite does not improve the scene for you. Maybe they changed the scene to a new character revelation or story point response, something you've already revealed in a scene that has already been shot. The new scene, while ostensibly serving some purpose the writer, producer or star has in mind, is redundant for you. You are treading water. You can choose to point this out to the director and you will make your point in an intelligent fashion because of your POS knowledge of what the scene was doing with your character and what it is now doing. Or, you can accept the changes and choose to lay in a POS choice that serves the scene and is not redundant regardless of the dialogue. If you do this, don't discuss it with the director first. Show it to him in rehearsal or during the take. A good director will always want you to show him what you are going to do rather than telling him about it ahead of time.

AUDITIONS

POS serves the actor exceedingly well with auditions. I recommend that the actor begin his approach to the material with traditional Stanislavsky work, followed by the first level improvisation process for auditions (chapter 8), and then applying purpose of scene. The resulting audition will be successful and competitive because it will be totally spontaneous and will look like it was directed by the author of the material. This process leads to a high level of success and considerably increases the actor's batting average. Most importantly, the actor will always leave the audition feeling he was totally prepared and did the best he could, which will increase his confidence for the next audition. If the actor does not know or has little confidence in his Stanislavsky technique, skip that step and go directly to the first level improvisation process.

COLD READINGS

If it is impossible to get the sides ahead of time in order to thoroughly prepare and if the actor has done the Improvisation Technique training, he can still shine in a cold reading. All that's needed is the usual short period of time (less than an hour) that the actor has with the sides. Read the sides a few times and then immediately do the POS breakdown. While auditioning, pay attention to your choices and physicalize them as you read, i.e., When you get to a conflict beat, pull the rope (conflict) while you are reading your lines. When you get to an emotion choice beat, physicalize that emotion while you are reading the lines. If you are adept at physicalization, you can even do an emotion arc or switch during a beat you are reading. The resulting audition will never be as good as it might have been had you the time to prepare thoroughly, but it will probably be better than anything else you might have done with the short time you did have.

SUMMARY

When you do POS work, you arrive on the set knowing what you are going to be focused on doing every moment of the scene. If the director doesn't give you any help, you are totally covered. You will really understand what is going on in the scene, know where all your turning points are, and have choices prepared and ready to go. If the director gives you direction, then you become a team with the director, giving and taking, and discussing what is going on; you will know the scene so well that you will adapt to what he is saying much faster. Because of your Improvisation Technique training, your work will always be spontaneous as you are improvising within each choice.

SECOND SCENE EXERCISE FOR LEARNING POS

After the first round of scenes accompanying the introduction of POS, a new round of scenes are rehearsed and presented in class. For these scenes, the actors are encouraged to employ their POS breakdowns in their preparation. The scene copies are handed out in class a week prior to the scene presentation, and the whole class is given the assignment of doing the POS breakdown for the scenes to be presented in the next class.   When handing out the first scene copies, I also tell the class to review the notes on making choices presented in this chapter and to take advantage of the appendix section of this book, using the sample umbrella arcs list and the emotions list for reference.

> **TO THE COACH:** The class is instructed to take advantage of having a week to do the breakdown, unlike the first POS scene exercise for which they only had an hour in class. The extra time for the breakdown will allow them to discover things they have not yet had time to discover. They should work on the scene for as long as they feel confident, according to the steps they have already learned. If they have difficulty making any choices, they should put a *question mark* where they would normally mark their choice. ◆ *Coach them*— Don't force yourself to stay on a beat until you have made a definitive choice for that beat. If you do that, (1) you will take longer than necessary to do the whole thing; (2) you will

get frustrated, crazy, and give yourself a headache; and (3) you will deprive yourself of better choices. In your first pass, make whatever choices are accessible to you, and put question marks where you need other choices. Return to working on the scene at a later time and focus on changing any question marks to choices. Approach the scene in passes, using the second through final passes to address any remaining question marks and to make any changes to previous choices. Take time off between passes. This approach is much more like preparing for professional work. ◆ For this round, I usually have time for two scenes per class. I alternate a week of scenes with a week of further experiential work in emotion doing.

SCENE CLASSES:

1. The actors perform the rehearsed scene.

2. The coach leads a discussion of everyone's POS choices for the scene. (See "First Scene Exercise for Learning POS," p. 536.)

3. During the discussions, the class makes changes in their choices on the script pages, based on the final choices all agree on.

4. The actors in the scene return to the floor and begin improvising on the final selected choices the class has agreed on. (See "Improvising the Scene," p. 537.)

FOLLOW-UP: Audience, did the first presentation of the scene look like it had been directed? Has the scene changed from the first presentation? Describe the change. ◆ Actors, how did it feel playing the final run-through? What felt different and what did you discover?

SUMMARY:

You worked on your own breakdown ahead of time and you saw the scene brought in by the actors who had also made their own choices. You saw that the scene works the way that they brought it in. I assume you believe it also works the way you broke it down and with the choices you made. What does this suggest to you?

There is certainly more than one way to do the scene. POS is simply a methodology for you to make choices to the best of your ability and to bring them onto the set, ready to go. If the director or other actors have a better idea, you are still ready to go. You can shift gears as easily as you did when we improvised the scene with new choices.

Having had a week to work on the scenes, what did you notice about the POS process for breaking down the scenes? Were you more open to the use of question marks in your various passes through the scene?

TO THE COACH: Review the "To the coach" section for the first POS scene exercise at the end of chapter 12. Encourage the actors to write "POS" whenever they are making their choices. When they do, it helps them stay focused and specific. When they don't, it can lead to casualness in their choices.

CONCLUSION

With Improvisation Technique, the training and the tools of the technique are one and the same. During the training period, you will be pleasantly surprised at how the benefits of the training crop up in your career.

One day on the set or in rehearsal you begin noticing, through body feelings rather than thoughts, that you could be doing a lot more. Then you instinctively start doing an acting focus or two, spontaneously selected. This happens because you have been working extensively on creating new experiential levels of how much your body is capable of doing at any one time, e.g., multiple acting focuses. So, when your body recognizes that it is not working up to its capability, it reaches out and chooses some focuses for you, confidently bypassing any time-lag for thinking.

On other days, you notice that you are taking more risks, achieving more spontaneity, and being more authentic in your work, and it's not because you told yourself to do so. It just starts to happen for you.

As you complete the training, you are prepared to arrive on the set ready to work with preselected choices, which are then performed improvisationally. If you are lucky enough to work in an environment with other prepared actors, a competent director, and time for rehearsals, there will be plenty of occasions to leap from the preselected choices into a new discovery based on working with the director and your scene mates. Due to the training, you will not only recognize these potential moments for leaping, you will leap further and with more grace. A new emotion appears, and your body instinctively knows *to do something with that emotion*, e.g., arc it. You will make the new moment blossom.

Improvisation Technique training creates an instrument that explores, discovers, and has the ability to spontaneously make choices and capitalize on them. In a situation with no time for rehearsals, or no help from the director, you have taken care of yourself. You will improvise a carefully prepared performance. Your technique is solid and tangible. Academy Award-winning actor Gary Sinese says, "So much of movie acting is in the preparation. You have to think it through and look for the moments, because you're only there for ten hours or whatever, and that scene is over after that. You have to prepare it the right way to make sure you get everything out of it."[1]

The actor who does little or no homework preparation never works at a level he's capable of. An exceptionally talented and lucky actor may get away with it and even be successful. However, he is still not working at the level he is capable of.

An Improvisation Technique performance has three main components: (1) discovering and becoming the character, (2) making choices, and (3) improvising the choices. When you know how to do these things, successful acting is easy. When it's easy, it's fun. When it's fun, you act at your highest potential.

Breaking scenes down according to purpose of scene (POS) guides the actor to a choice and the selection of an appropriate acting focus. Choosing and playing the acting focus guarantees the improvisational acting, or spontaneous playing, of the choice. Remember, in the theater and sitcoms, the POS choices and acting focuses are for rehearsal process. The actual performance is built upon, and transcends, a thorough rehearsal process; there is no need for a conscious use of tools.

Always approach camera acting as if you are performing in a rehearsal. As long as you stay on the acting focus, the scene will be in the ball park. Some takes will be home runs. Skillfully improvise every take and your batting average will consistently improve.

Always see and listen to the other actor, unless the scene requires otherwise, e.g., a preoccupation. What you see and hear is always integrated into the acting focus as a part of the whole. For instance, you are playing a disguised conflict beat. The other actor changes a line reading or what he's doing with the moment. You hear and see that, but you do not leave your choice. You let your spontaneous response to the new line reading or moment be reflected in what you are doing with your choice. You might pull the conflict harder or slower, but *you don't leave the preselected choice unless the body recognizes an appropriate moment to do so.* The body training has prepared you for spontaneous selection of what works best. If you are thoroughly prepared, on some takes you may choose to throw away your specific preparation choices and just go with it. Doing that will enhance the feeling of improvisationally hitting every beat and emotion you prepared, while leaving you room to discover a new moment with the other actor.

The acting focus is your path through what all are doing together. Stay on your acting focus at the start of any rehearsals prior to the first take. That way the director sees your approach to the scene. If he wants any adjustments, he will tell you, and you can pick another appropriate acting focus. If he says nothing, that means he approves.

Stanislavsky and Improvisation Technique

Those of you well versed in traditional Stanislavsky technique should employ Improvisation Technique as a complement. After an exploration of the character's actions to achieve what he wants, needs, or desires, begin improvising on other aspects of what the character is *doing*. This is the special province of Improvisation Technique.

In acting as in life, what you are doing is not always your objective. Sometimes what you are doing is thinking, feeling an emotion, doing an activity, building an agreement, or participating in a conflict that has gone beyond just wanting something. Improvisation Technique focuses on these aspects and provides you with the tools (acting focus) to turn them into forms of doing influenced by self-awareness, spontaneity, and artistic controls.

Improvisation Technique training is beneficial for the Stanislavsky-oriented actor because of the emphasis on doing. In a letter to his son in 1935, Stanislavsky said:

> What can we rehearse? A great deal. A character comes in, greets everybody, sits down, tells of events that have just taken place, expresses a series of thoughts. Every one can act this, guided by their own life experience. So, let them act. And so, we break the whole play, episode by episode, into physical actions.[2]

In other words, *doing*.

From a selected glossary[3] of Stanislavsky terminology: *Action (Deistvie) - What the actor does to solve the problem or fulfill the task set before his or her character by the play.* In Improvisation Technique, *what the actor does* is changed from the solving of a character's problem to the doing of a technical and improvisational acting focus. Despite this difference, for Stanislavsky as for Spolin, acting is doing. In Improvisation Technique, acting is doing and there's always more to do.

Not all theater is traditional western psychological drama. Stanislavsky technique falls short in these other areas, while Improvisation Technique serves the actor very well.

Ideal Rehearsal Model

An ideal rehearsal period would have four parts.

Part A: Actors who practice the Stanislavsky technique should begin rehearsals with that approach. Exploit it. Get everything that you can from the way you already know how to work. After you have gone through all your scenes in this traditional fashion, go on to the next part. Actors who don't practice, or are not confident with, traditional Stanislavsky technique, skip Part A.

Part B: Do a round of first level improvisations (chapter 6). This will reinfuse spontaneity into the work as well as open doors that you have not previously considered in your traditional approach.

Part C: Do your work on creating a character (chapter 7).

Part D: This is given to purpose-of-scene work (chapters 12-14).

Each part complements the preceding part and builds to the next part. Of course, particularly with camera acting, you seldom find yourself in an ideal rehearsal period. Each actor must decide for himself where to make compromises in this approach. Use the four-part model as a guide.

Why do actors act?

With Improvisation Technique, the actor truly brings himself to the part. The authentic, individual person fuels every acting focus. The actor's being on the acting focus stimulates and conducts his authentic and individual life to the character.

It's a delicious feeling to live a life every moment of which is artistically constructed and serves a purpose. It's an exalted feeling to speak poetry and to communicate effectively with every word. It's a joy to experience life as an artistic creation: to know that that life, *the character*, has meaning and it is a part of a designed whole, *the work of art*, and to feel that that story is actually happening to you.

Closure

TO THE COACH: When a group reaches the end of the training and is about to disband, a ritual is appropriate and useful for easing the path of letting go. I form my group into a seated circle and ask each of them to answer three questions: (1) What did you hope to get from this workshop that you didn't? (2) What did you get that was more than you expected? (3) How did you change as a result of the workshop? After the last actor speaks, I have them all stand in their circle and each actor pats the actor's back to their right: "Let's give ourselves a pat on the back!" A party usually follows.

ABANDONMENT #1
- angry
- scared
- lonely

ABANDONMENT #2
- hurt
- loss
- fear
- sorrow
- anger

ABANDONMENT #3
- nervous
- embarrassed
- frustrated
- needy
- hurt
- bitter
- betrayed
- anger
- despair

ANGER
- fear
- sadness
- hurt
- frustration
- irritation
- rage

ASHAMED
- embarrassed
- defensive
- bitter
- ashamed
- lonely
- hopeless
- despair

AWE
- open
- curious
- attentive
- pleased
- impressed
- amazed
- inspired
- awe
- stupefied
- transcendent

BACK FROM DEFEAT
- defeated
- hopeful
- courageous
- happy
- defiant
- victory

BETRAYED #1
- aware
- suspicious
- frustrated
- resentful
- bitter
- anger - fury

BETRAYED #2
- bitter
- spiteful
- sarcasm
- vindictive
- hate
- punish

BETRAYED #3
- aware
- suspicious
- devious
- confrontational
- angry
- fury
- rage
- satisfied

BRAGGART
- smug
- cocky
- macho
- arrogant
- thrilled

CELEBRATING POWER
- false humility
- enjoy
- savor
- proud
- revel
- brag
- show off

COURAGE #1
- uncertain
- nervous
- calm
- hopeful
- assured
- confident
- arrogant

COURAGE #2
- honest
- hopeful
- confident
- determined
- brave
- bold

COWARDLY-GUILTY
- embarrassed
- weak
- ashamed
- sad
- depressed
- scared
- anger

DEFIANCE - REBELLION
oppressed
suffocated
anger
shrewd
outburst
freedom

DESPAIR
nostalgic
lost
sad
bitter
miserable
hopeless

DESTROYED
confused
embarrassed
sad
grief
despair

ENCOURAGEMENT
hope
excited
humility
proud
love

EVIL
teasing
hurtful
taunting
spiteful
malicious
cruel
vile
vicious

EXCITEMENT OF LEARNING
frustrated
curious
enthusiastic
satisfied
cynical

EXCITEMENT OF TEACHING
disappointed
frustrated
searching
tempting
baiting
bribery
curious
enthusiasm
passion
excited
joy

FACING DEATH
denial/isolation
anger
depression
bargaining
acceptance

FEAR #1
aware
concerned
suspicious
nervous
alarmed
agitated
scared
frightened
terrified
horrified

FEAR #2
cautious
nervous
anxious
apprehensive

GUILT
fear
anxious to be
    forgiven
sad
confusion
remorse
want to please
futility

HAPPY #1
calm
content
pleased
amused
gay/glad
cheerful
giddy
jubilant
happy
elated
joyous

HAPPY #2
content
confident
amused
happy
joyous
euphoric

HAUNTED/ TORMENTED #1
aware
wary
suspicious
nervous
scared
possessed
terrified

HAUNTED/ TORMENTED #2
lonely
wary - cautious
suspicious
apprehensive

HOPEFUL
- aware
- possibility
- risk
- longing

HURT
- defensive
- frustrated
- sarcastic
- angry

INUNDATION
- confusion
- frustration
- disappointed
- irritated
- suffocated
- fear

LIFE FULFILLMENT
- content
- loving
- happy
- careless
- excited
- joyous
- ecstasy

LOSS
- hurt
- anger
- sorrow

LOSS OF ILLUSION #1
- anger
- snob/regal
- guilty/confession
- defensive
- despair

LOSS OF ILLUSION #2
- confused
- embarrassed
- sad
- grief
- despair

MANIC DEPRESSION
- depressed
- euphoria
- irritated

ORGASMIC
- arousal
- stimulation
- pleasure
- tension
- release
- ecstasy

PASSION
- concern
- commitment
- desire
- inspire
- excitement

PREPARATION FOR HARD NEWS
- alert
- caution
- warn
- console
- nurture
- encourage
- inspire

RESENTMENT
- frustrated
- irritated
- sarcasm
- aggravated
- hatred
- bitter
- anger

SADIST/TORTURER
- resentment
- bitter
- hate
- punish
- anger - rage
- power
- satisfaction
- pleasure
- arousal

SELF PITY #1
- resentment
- lonely - sad
- fear - terror
- confused

SELF PITY #2
- lonely
- rejected
- resentment
- confused
- fear
- anger
- terror
- hysteria

SOLICITOUS
- attentive
- caring
- concerned
- anxious (desire)
- eager
- apprehensive
- troubled

STRENGTH
- brave
- proud
- determined
- humility

STRONG		WEAK		HAPPY	FEAR
able	potent	apologetic	unhinged	admire	affrighted
active	powerful	awkward	unstable	aglow	afraid
adequate	productive	confused	useless	alive	aghast
aggressive	quick	considering	vulnerable	amused	alarmed
angry	rage	deathly	wavering	anxious	amazed
arrogant	reliable	defeated	wishy-washy	blissful	anxious
assured	resistant	defective	wobbly	bubbly	appalled
authoritative	respectful	defenseless	worn out	calm	apprehensive
bold	reverential	deficient		cheerful	awed
brave	robust	deflated		compassion	cautious
capable	secure	delicate		content	chicken
challenging	solid	disabled		delighted	concerned
cocky	stalwart	dull		demure	confused
confident	staunch	exhausted		ecstatic	curious
considering	stout	exposed		elated	daunted
consistent	suave	feeble		enthralled	displeasure
correcting	super	fragile		enthusiastic	distrustful
courageous	supportive	frail		excited	dreadful
determined	surviving	frustrated		exuberant	fearful
dismissive	violent	gentle		feel good	foreboding
durable	warn	helpless		felicitous	frightened
enduring	well-being	hopeful		fine	harassed
energetic	zealous	ill		fortunate	horrified
enthusiasm		impotent		full of life	incredulous
everlasting		inadequate		gay	insecure
fierce		incapable		gentle	intimidated
firm		inconsistent		giddy	jumpy
forceful		ineffective		glad	leery
formal		inferior		gleeful	lonely
formidable		insecure		good	meek
forthright		irresolute		grateful	nervous
full of spirit		lacking		great	panic
gentle		languid		happy	stricken
glorious		lethargic		joyful	panicky
hale		lifeless		joyous	petrified
hardy		lost		jubilant	rattled
hate		meager		lighthearted	shaky
healthy		mild		love	shy
helpful		pale		lucky	spooked
herculean		passive		marvelous	startled
hopeful		powerless		memorable	stunned
independent		puny		merry	suspicious
indestructible		quiet		mischievous	terrified
intense		retiring		motherly	terrorized
invincible		run-down		overjoyed	threatened
interrogate		shaky		peaceful	timid
knowing		sickly		pleasant	timorous
loud		soft		proud	tormented
love		spineless		relieved	tremulous
mean		stale		satisfied	uneasy
mighty		submissive		smiley	unpleasant
muscular		subtle		thankful	unstrung
nurturing		timid		thrilled	unsure
opinionated		unable		tranquil	wary
overwhelming		unconvincing		turned on	worried
positive		undernourished		up	
		unfit		uplifted	
				wonderful	

ANGRY		SAD		CONFUSED	LOVE
aggravated	raving	angry	terrible	abashed	affection
agitated	revengeful	apathetic	turned off	addled	desire
anguished	riled	bad	uneasy	amazed	erotic
annoyed	sarcastic	blue	unhappy	anxious	exotic
apoplectic	seething	burdened	unloved	baffled	excited
arrogant	sneering	crushed	unpleasant	befuddled	favor
blustery	sore	defeated	unwanted	bewildered	flirtatious
bothered	spiteful	deflated	upset	bothered	horny
burned up	stormy	dejected		chaotic	intimate
correcting	temper	despairing		confounded	kind
critical	tense	despondent		crazy	longing
cross	threat	depressed		dazed	loving
cutting	troubled	disappointed		depressed	lovelorn
defensive	uncontrollable	disenchanted		deranged	orgasmic
denigrating	unrestrained	disillusioned		disconcerted	passion
disgruntled	warn	distressed		dismayed	release
disgusted		disturbed		disordered	respect
dismayed		down		disorganized	seductive
dismissive		downcast		disoriented	sexy
displeased		downhearted		distracted	stimulated
distraught		downtrodden		distraught	tender
distressed		drab		disturbed	tension
disturbed		dreary		doubtful	willing
enraged		dull		dubious	
exasperated		embarrassed		embarrassed	
fed up		emotional		flabbergasted	
fierce		feel unwanted		flustered	
fiery		forlorn		foggy	
frantic		gloomy		forgetful	
frenzied		glum		frustrated	
frustrated		grave		helpless	
furious		grieved		hopeless	
hateful		hate		incredulous	
hostile		heavy hearted		mistaken	
hot tempered		hopeless		misunderstood	
in a stew		hurt		mixed up	
incensed		lonely		muddled	
indignant		lost		nonplussed	
inflamed		low		obscure	
infuriated		low spirits		out of it	
intense		melancholy		panicky	
irate		miserable		perplexed	
irked		mistrustful		puzzled	
irritated		moody		scatterbrained	
livid		morose		surprised	
mad		mournful		trapped	
madness		negative		troubled	
mean		painful		uncertain	
miffed		pitiful		uncomfortable	
minimizing		plaintive		uncomposed	
outraged		remorseful		undecided	
patronizing		sad		unsettled	
perturbed		self-pitying		unsure	
provoked		sober		untogether	
punishing		somber		upset	
rage		sorrowful		vague	
		sorry		weak	

Painful	>	Joyful
Anger	>	Affection
Sadness	>	Joy
Hate	>	Love
Loneliness	>	Community
Hurt	>	Relief
Boredom	>	Involvement
Frustration	>	Contentment
Inferiority	>	Equality
Suspicion	>	Trust
Repulsion	>	Attraction
Shyness	>	Curiosity
Confusion	>	Clarity
Unfulfillment	>	Satisfaction
Weakness	>	Strength
Guilt	>	Innocence
Shame	>	Pride
Emptiness	>	Contentment
Emptiness	>	Fulfillment

Be careful!	I'm boring.	I'm exotic.
Be honest!	I'm bossy.	I'm fair.
Die, scumbag!	I'm broken.	I'm fancy.
Don't fuck with me.	I'm careless.	I'm fast.
Force me!	I'm caring.	I'm fastidious.
Free me!	I'm casual.	I'm fearful.
Fuck off!	I'm certain.	I'm feeble.
Help me.	I'm chaotic.	I'm fervent.
I am king.	I'm charitable.	I'm fickle.
I can't.	I'm chatty.	I'm flashy.
I don't get it.	I'm clever.	I'm flexible.
I hate men.	I'm cold.	I'm forceful.
I hate women.	I'm combative.	I'm forgiving.
I hate you.	I'm concerned.	I'm fragile.
I hurt.	I'm confident.	I'm frank.
I know best.	I'm cool.	I'm free.
I know better.	I'm crazed.	I'm fresh.
I know it all.	I'm cunning.	I'm fun.
I love everybody.	I'm cynical.	I'm funny.
I love you.	I'm dangerous.	I'm furtive.
I need it.	I'm daring.	I'm generous.
I want help.	I'm decent.	I'm gorgeous.
I want it.	I'm defiant.	I'm grasping.
I want more.	I'm definite.	I'm growing.
I want out.	I'm demanding.	I'm happy.
I'll help.	I'm depressed.	I'm headstrong.
I'm a screw-up.	I'm desperate.	I'm healing.
I'm a winner.	I'm detailed.	I'm honest.
I'm a wreck.	I'm determined.	I'm horny.
I'm abrupt.	I'm devoted.	I'm hot.
I'm adventurous.	I'm direct.	I'm hungry.
I'm afraid.	I'm disgusted.	I'm impatient.
I'm aghast.	I'm distracted.	I'm in control.
I'm agile.	I'm distrusting.	I'm industrious.
I'm alive!	I'm dogged.	I'm insistent.
I'm alone.	I'm driven.	I'm kind.
I'm ambitious.	I'm eager.	I'm knowledgeable.
I'm analytical.	I'm earnest.	I'm lasting.
I'm anxious.	I'm easy.	I'm lazy.
I'm aristocratic.	I'm educated.	I'm limp.
I'm awkward.	I'm efficient.	I'm lively.
I'm bitter.	I'm egotistical.	I'm logical.
I'm bored.	I'm elegant.	I'm lonely.

I'm loud.
I'm loving.
I'm lucky.
I'm manipulative.
I'm messy.
I'm meticulous.
I'm moral.
I'm nervous.
I'm neurotic.
I'm nimble.
I'm noble.
I'm nothing.
I'm old.
I'm open.
I'm opinionated.
I'm organized.
I'm outgoing.
I'm parental.
I'm passionate.
I'm patient.
I'm perceptive.
I'm perky.
I'm perplexed.
I'm phony.
I'm plain.
I'm playful.
I'm pleasant.
I'm pleased.
I'm plodding.
I'm political.
I'm powerful.
I'm pragmatic.
I'm precious.
I'm precise.
I'm prejudiced.
I'm punctual.
I'm pushy.
I'm reasonable.

I'm refined.
I'm relentless.
I'm religious.
I'm resistant.
I'm respectable.
I'm romantic.
I'm rustic.
I'm sassy.
I'm satisfied.
I'm scared.
I'm scrutinizing.
I'm searching.
I'm seasick.
I'm secretive.
I'm selfless.
I'm sensible.
I'm sentimental.
I'm sexy.
I'm shocked.
I'm sincere.
I'm skittish.
I'm slick.
I'm smart.
I'm smarter.
I'm sneaky.
I'm snide.
I'm snotty.
I'm sorry.
I'm spirited.
I'm stern.
I'm stoned.
I'm stubborn.
I'm stuffy.
I'm stupid.
I'm stylish.
I'm superior.
I'm suspicious.
I'm sweet.

I'm the best.
I'm thoughtful.
I'm thrifty.
I'm tired.
I'm tough.
I'm turned on.
I'm unbridled.
I'm uncompromising.
I'm unconscious.
I'm unpretentious.
I'm unruffled.
I'm unyielding.
I'm upright.
I'm vexing.
I'm visionary.
I'm warm.
I'm willing.
I'm winning.
I'm wise.
I'm witty.
I'm worried.
I'm worthless.
I need meaning.
I used to be king.
It's okay.
Keep it neat.
Leave me alone.
Let's party!
Life sucks.
Life's a party!
Look at me!
Love me.
Nobody loves me.
Party down!
Please!
Stay away.
We're all brothers!
Why me?

These formats are for four-hour classes with approxamately twenty-five actors. You can adjust accordingly, but it is recommended that you follow the same order.

#1: Traditional game/Tag
Making Changes, 21
First Focus Walk, 27
Objects in the Space, 33
Activity Doing, 49
Activity Doing/Avoiding Sameness, 53
Traditional game/Poison*

◆

#2: Traditional game/Indians running**
Second Focus Walk, 35
Space Ball/Motion, 37
Activity Doing/Checking Out, 54
Sharing an Object, 58
Activity Doing/Helping, 60
Traditional game/New York (Lemonade)*

◆

#3: Traditional game/Style tag
Third Focus Walk, 41
Space Ball/Weight, 42
Group Blocking, 44
Unfocused/Focused, 46
Activity Doing/Rhythm, 57
Activity Doing/Job Title, 64
Traditional game/New York (Lemonade)*

◆

#4: Traditional game/New York (Lemonade)*
Repeat Activity Doing/Job Title, 64
Activity Doing/Personal Relation-ships, 67
Repeat Activity Doing/Personal Relationships, 67
or Receiving Character, 72

◆

#5: Traditional game/Style tag (add sound)
Physical Discovery of Location, 73
Full Body Whisper, 170

◆

#6: Traditional game/Red light Green light
Physical Contact with the Location, 76
Eating and Drinking while Listening and Speaking, 86

◆

#7: Traditional game/Musical chairs
Location Focus, 80
Discovering Objects Near You, 89
Physical Doing Drill, 93

◆

#8: Traditional game/Swat tag*
Physical Doing Drill Return, 99
Active & Still #1, 108

◆

#9: Traditional game/Who started the motion?*
Active & Still #2, 116
Party Upset, 122

◆

#10: Active & Still Refresher, 124
Turns (Active & Still), 125

◆

#11: Traditional game/Wink
Ad Agency, 92
Active, Still, & Discover, 130

◆

---

*From Spolin, Viola, *Theater Games for the Classroom*, (Evanston, IL: Northwestern University Press, 1986);
**From Spolin, Viola, *Theater Game File*, (St, Louis: Cemrel Inc., 1975).

#12: Traditional game/Puss in the corner
    Multiscene One Acts, 134
    Basic Reflection, 141

◆

#13: Traditional game/SciFi tag
    Full Body Calling, 175
    Physical Contact Speech, 204

◆

#14: Traditional game/Hug tag
    Basic Reflection > Reflection Walk,
      141, 142
    Off Stage Reflection Walk #1, 145
    Off Stage Reflection Walk #2, 147
    Off Stage/Present, 149

◆

#15: Traditional game/Movie star upset
    Reflection Walk Return, 155
    Off Stage Kitchen, 157
    Off Stage/Past,159
    Assign first Scripted Scene Exercise
      (chapter 6), 217

◆

#16: Traditional game/Puss in the corner
    Basic Reflection > Reflect the
      Reflector, 141, 154
    Off Stage/Future, 187
    Nonsense Language Presentation
      Party, 179
    Nonsense Language Commercials,
      183
    Nonsense Language/Teaching and
      Learning, 183

◆

#17: Traditional game/Red light Green
    light
    Nonsense/English, 185
    Basic Reflection > Reflect the
      Reflector, 141, 154
    Nonsense Speech Translation, 187

◆

#18: Traditional game/Animal blind
    man's bluff
    Fear Discussion, 191
    Full Body Singing, 193
    Stretching Speech, 194

◆

#19: Traditional game/Puss in the corner
    Parts of Speech, 196
    Soundless Stretching Speech, 200
    Basic Reflection > Reflect the
      Reflector, 141,154, 475
    Reflection Listening, 206

◆

#20 – #25 Begin First Level Improvisa-
    tions for Scripted Scenes (chapter
    6), 218

◆

#26: Traditional game
    Reformed Bodies in Space, Part 1,
      240
    Animals, 247

◆

#27: Traditional game
    Reformed Bodies in Space, Parts 1
      & 2, 240, 243
    Body Center, 252
    Homework assignment for Script-
      Influenced Animal or Body
      Center, 263

◆

#28: Traditional game
    Extension Bumps, 263
    Script-Influenced Animal or Body
      Center, 266
    Homework assignment for Attitude
      Lines, 273, 283

◆

#29: Traditional game
    Attitude Lines, 274

◆

#30: Traditional game
    Attitude Line/Character, Activity,
      Location, 285
    Party Mingle Attitude Lines, 287
    Homework assignment for Attitude
      Line Switch, 294

◆

#31: Traditional game
    Attitude Line Switch, 295
    Repeat Party Mingle Attitude Lines,
      287

◆

#32: Traditional game
    Physical Catalyst + Attitude Line,
        302
    Multiple Reflection, 305

    ◆

#33: Traditional game
    Camera and Stage Auditions: First
        Level Improvisation Applications
        (chapter 8), 313

    ◆

#34: Traditional game
    Extend, Intensify, and Enlarge, 330
    Emotion Walk #1, 333
    Paralysis/Alone, 336

    ◆

#35: Traditional game
    Emotion Walk #2, 339
    Paralysis/Group, 342
    Silence, 345
    Scene Silence, 346

    ◆

#36: Traditional game
    Emotion Walk #3, 352
    Object Struggle, 354
    Emotions & Objects #1, 356

    ◆

#37: Traditional game
    Emotion Walk #4, 359
    Emotions & Objects #2, 361
    Emotion Arcs, 362
    Homework assignment for Mono-
        logue Purpose of Scene Exercise,
        401

    ◆

#38: Traditional game
    Emotion Walk #5, 370
    Emotion Arcs (Repeat), 372
    Emotion Switch, 373

    ◆

#39: Traditional game
    Emotion Walk #6, 377
    Extend, Intensify, and Enlarge
        (Repeat), 379
    Emotion Switch (Repeat), 380

    ◆

#40: Traditional game
    Emotion Walk #7, 381
    Emotion Switch and Arc, 383
    Emotion Arc and Switch, 387

    ◆

#41: Traditional game
    Emotion Walk #8, 389
    Go with Your Emotions, 391
    Attitude Line with Emotion Switch,
        394

    ◆

#42 – #47: Monologue Purpose of Scene
        Exercise (chapter 13), 550

    ◆

#48: Traditional game
    Conflict Space Exercise #1, 403
    Disguised Conflict Influence, 404
    Pull the rope! #1, 406
    Pull the Conflict #1, 409

    ◆

#49: Traditional game
    Conflict Space Exercise #2, 414
    Pull the rope! #2, 415
    Pull the Conflict #2, 417
    Pull the Conflict #3, 421

    ◆

#50: Traditional game
    Repeat Pull the Conflict #3, 421
    Pull the Conflict #4, 426

    ◆

#51: Traditional game
    Mistreatment #1, 435
    Mistreatment #2, 438

    ◆

#52: Traditional game
    Object Struggle, 443
    Activity & Location Struggle, 444
    Relationship Struggle, 446

    ◆

#53: Traditional game
    What to do with? #1, 450
    What to do with? #2, 455

    ◆

620

#54: Traditional game
What to do with the conflict?, 458
What to do with the conflict, Win!,
462
Homework assignment for Writing
Conflict Exercise, 465

◆

#55: Writing Conflict Exercise, 465

◆

$56: Traditional game
Reflect the Reflector, 154
Select & Reflect, 476
Agreement, 478

◆

#57: Traditional game
Agreement Walk, 485
Invitations to Agreement, Part 1,
486
Agreement Repeat, 488

◆

#58: Traditional game
Invitations to Agreement, Parts 1 &
2, 486
Agreement Repeat, 488

◆

#59: Traditional game
"Yes! And...", 489
Agreement Repeat, 488
Agreement/Conflict, Part 1, 492

◆

#60: Traditional game
Agreement Repeat, 488
Agreement/Conflict, Part 2, 493
Homework assignment for Writing
Agreement/Conflict Exercise, 495

◆

#61: Writing Agreement/Conflict
Exercise, 496

◆

#62: Begin Purpose of Scene (chapters
12–14), 503-604

Here are descriptions of some traditional children's games for quick reference. There are many other published sources; the following are among my favorites:

Spolin, Viola. *Theater Games for the Classroom.* Evanston, IL: Northwestern University Press, 1986.

Boyd, Neva. *Handbook of Recreational Games.* New York: Dover Publications, 1975.

Bancroft, Jessie. *Games for Playground, Home, School and Gymnasium.* New York: The Macmillan Company, 1919.

Children's Games. New York: Award Books, 1970.

Mason, Bernard, and Elmer Mitchell. *Active Games and Contests.* New York: A.S. Barnes and Company, 1936.

The New Games Book. Edited by Andrew Fluegelman. Garden City, New York: Doubleday/Dolphin Books, 1976.

STYLE TAG Played as any basic tag game, with this difference: Each new player who is *it* initiates any style of movement, which all must maintain until a new *it* is tagged. No running allowed. Typical styles: skipping, hopping, monster limp. In the middle of the game, sound should be added.

PUSS IN THE CORNER The group divides in two, with one half having one extra player. The larger half are players. The smaller half are corners spread throughout the playing area. Each player must stand by a corner. The extra player is Puss. Puss approaches any player and says, "Puss wants a corner." The player responds, "Not here. See my neighbor." Puss goes to another player at another corner and they repeat the dialogue. Meanwhile, all the players are slyly and overtly communicating to each other to swap corners. When a player leaves his corner and runs to another, Puss attempts to get into the vacant corner. The person caught without a corner is the new Puss. Players are to take risks, continuously changing corners while trying to avoid becoming Puss. Halfway through the playing time, the corners become the players and the players become the new corners.

HUG TAG A basic tag game except players may not be tagged if they are hugging another player. No hug may be held for more than three seconds. The coach is the referee and counts out the time.

SciFi tag (Chain tag)   Basic tag until the second *it* is tagged. He joins hands with the original *it*. They are now both *it* and must not let go of each other's hand. Either can tag the next *it*, who then joins the chain of tagged people.

Wink   The group divides in two, with one half having one extra player. The smaller half sit on chairs in a large circle; the other half stand behind them. The extra player standing behind an extra vacant chair is *it*. *It* winks at any seated players. When a seated player receives a wink, he must leave his chair and go and sit in the vacant chair in front of *it*. Whenever a person leaves his chair, the person standing behind him, without taking any steps, must tap him on the back or shoulders. If the seated player avoids the tap, then he arrives safely and sits in front of *it*, who now stops being *it*. The person standing behind the newly vacant chair is the new *it*, or winker.

Animal blind man's bluff   All players form a circle around one player, who is *it*. His eyes are closed or covered and he holds a broomstick. The players circle around him until he taps the floor with the stick, stopping the circle. He points the stick anywhere in the circle, and the player being pointed at grasps the other end of the stick. *It* calls out an animal name and the other player must immediately make the sounds of that animal. *It* identifies the other player. If he is correct, the other is the next one to be *it*.

Movie star upset   All players are seated or standing in a circle around *it*. Prior to playing, each player names his favorite actor or movie star. *It* calls out the names of two or three of these movie stars, and the players attached to those names must change places. *It* attempts to get to one of their spots or chairs. If he does, the player left standing without a spot or chair is now *it*. Whoever is *it* always has the option to call out "Upset," and then everyone has to change chairs.

Red Light Green Light   All players line up at one end of the playing area and one player, who is *it*, stands at the other end. The line faces *it* and *it* faces the line. *It* turns his back to the line and says, "Green light." All advance forward while *it* can't see them. *It* turns around at any time, saying, "Red light." *It* sends back to the starting line any players he sees moving even slightly. When the offenders are back at the starting line, *it* turns around again, saying, "Green light." This continues until one player advances close enough to *it* to tag his back. Then all players run back to the starting line chased by *it*. *It* tags any player before that player is safe at the starting line. The one tagged is the next *it*. If no one is tagged, *it* is still *it*.

Notes

The following abbreviations are used in the notes:

>**IT** = Viola Spolin, *Improvisation for the Theater* (Evanston, IL: Northwestern University Press, 1963).
>**TGF** = Viola Spolin, *Theater Game File* (St. Louis: Cemrel, Inc., 1975).

Introduction

1. Anthony LaPaglia, "Buzz," *Variety*, 8/3/97, p.6.
2. Elia Kazan, *A Life* (New York: Alfred A. Knopf, 1988), 143.
3. Richard Dreyfuss, interviewed on *Inside the Actors Studio*, Bravo Television, 2000.
4. Frank Langella, interviewed by Barbara Eisenberg, *Los Angeles Times*, 5/9/93.
5. Personal notes from Actors Studio sessions moderated by Lee Strasberg, circa November 1972.
6. Viola Spolin, *Improvisation for the Theater* (Evanston, IL: Northwestern University Press, 1963).
7. Robert DeNiro, interviewed on *Inside the Actors Studio*, Bravo Television, 2000.

2. Essential Starters

1. Evolved from *Three Changes*, IT & TGF.
2. Evolved from *Space Substance*, IT, *Space Walk #1*, TGF, *Touching-Touched*, TGF, and *Touch & Be Touched/See & Be Seen*, in Viola Spolin, *Theater Games for Rehearsal* (Evanston, IL: Northwestern University Press, 1985).
3. Evolved from *Space Substance*, IT, and *Space Shaping*, TGF.
4. Evolved from *Space Substance*, IT, and *Space Walk #2*, TGF.
5. Evolved from *Play Ball*, IT, and *Play Ball #1*, TGF.
6. Evolved from *Space Substance*, IT, and *Space Walk #3*, TGF.
7. Evolved from *Play Ball*, IT, and *Play Ball #2*, TGF.
8. Evolved from Spolin's *Stage Picture* (unpublished).
9. Evolved from *Exposure*, TGF.

3. Physical Doing

1. Evolved from *Orientation Game #2*, IT, and *Part of a Whole #2*, TGF.
2. Evolved from *Involvement in Threes or More*, IT, and *Involvement with Three or More*, TGF.
3. Evolved from *Orientation Game #3*, IT, and *Part of a Whole #3*, TGF.
4. Evolved from *Orientation Game #4*, IT, and *Part of a Whole #4*, TGF.
5. Evolved from *Who Game*, IT & TGF.
6. Evolved from *Relay Where*, TGF.
7. Evolved from *Where Exercise*, IT & TGF.
8. Evolved from *The Where Game*, IT, and *Where Game*, TGF.
9. Evolved from *Conversation with Involvement*, IT & TGF.
10. Evolved from *Finding Objects in the Immediate Environment*, IT & TGF.

4. Inner Doing

1. Evolved from *Two Scenes*, IT, and *Give & Take*, TGF.
2. *Ibid.*
3. *New York Times*, 12/6/87.
4. Evolved from *Converge and Re-divide*, IT & TGF.
5. Evolved from *Give and Take Warm Up*, TGF.
6. Michael Caine, *Acting in Film* (New York: Applause, 1990), 25, 59.
7. Evolved from *Two Scenes*, IT.
8. Evolved from *Mirror Exercise*, IT, and *Mirror*, TGF.

9. Evolved from *What's Beyond? A*, IT, and *What's Beyond: Where*, TGF.

10. Evolved from *What's Beyond? C*, IT, and *What's Beyond: Activity*, TGF.

11. Evolved from *What's Beyond? F*, IT, and *What's Beyond: Present Event*, TGF.

12. William Goldman, *Adventures in the Screen Trade* (New York: Warner Books, 1983), 127.

13. Evolved from *Follow The Follower #1*, TGF.

14. Evolved from *What's Beyond? E*, IT, and *What's Beyond: Past or Future Event*, TGF.

15. *Ibid.*

16. *Los Angeles Times*, 3/15/98

5. Vocal Doing

1. Evolved from *Stage Whisper*, IT & TGF.

2. Evolved from *Calling-Out Exercise*, IT.

3. Evolved from *Gibberish Exercise #1–Demonstration*, IT, and *Gibberish Introduction*, TGF.

4. Evolved from *Gibberish: Selling*, TGF.

5. Evolved from *Gibberish #3–Teaching*, IT, and *Gibberish: Teaching*, TGF.

6. Evolved from *Gibberish–English*, TGF.

7. Evolved from *Gibberish Interpreter #1*, TGF.

8. Mel Gussow, obituary for Dorothy Stickney, *New York Times*, 6/3/98.

9. Evolved from *Singing Dialogue*, IT & TGF.

10. Evolved from Spolin's *Extended Speech*, unpublished, and *Extended Sound*, in Viola Spolin, *Theater Games for Rehearsal*

11. Evolved from *Vowels & Consonants*, TGF.

12. Evolved from Spolin's *Soundless Sound*, unpublished.

13. Evolved from *Contact*, IT & TGF.

14. Evolved from *Mirror Speech*, TGF.

7. Character

1. Inspired by Michael Chekhov's *Imaginary Body* exercise, the main difference being Chekhov's emphasis on imagining the new body vs. Improvisation Technique's emphasis on physicalizing it.

2. Evolved from *Animal Images*, IT.

3. Inspired by Michael Chekhov's *Imaginary Center* exercise, the main difference being Chekhov's starting location of the imaginary center in the center of the chest versus the *Body Center* starting location at the base of the spine.

4. Evolved from a Spolin exercise, untitled and unpublished.

5. Alan Ball, interviewed in Jamie Painter's "First Time's a 'Beauty'," *Back Stage West*, 3/16/2000.

6. Evolved from *Hold It! A*, IT, and *Hold #1*, TGF.

7. Evolved from *Hold It! C*, IT.

8. Evolved from *Jump Emotion*, IT.

9. Dana Kennedy, "Nicholson on Age, Acting and Being Jack," *New York Times*, 9/22/2002.

10. Donald Chase, "On the Road with Hoffman and Cruise," *New York Times*, 12/12/1988.

8. Camera and Stage Auditions: First Level Improvisation Applications

1. Debi Manwiller, interviewed in Karen Kondazian's "The Actor's Way," *Back Stage West*, 2/19/1998.

9. Emotions

1 Evolved from *Explore and Heighten (Transformation of Beat)*, IT, and *Explore & Heighten*, TGF.

2. Evolved from an unpublished process by Susana Bloch.

3. Evolved from *Inability to Move A*, IT.

4. Evolved from *Silent Scream*, IT.

5. Alec Guinness, *Blessings in Disguise* (New York: Warner Books, 1985), 155-6.

6. Evolved from *Inability to Move B*, IT.

7. Evolved from *Silent Tension*, IT & TGF.

8. Evolved from *Difficulty with Small Objects*, IT & TGF.

9. Evolved from *Changing Emotion*, IT & TGF.

10. Evolved from *Changing Intensity of Inner Action*, IT.

11. Evolved from *Jump Emotion*, IT.

12. David Sacks, "I Never Was an Ingénue," *New York Times Magazine*, 1/27/91, p. 46.

13. Rob Kendt, "Respect for Uta," *Back Stage West*, 7/10/97, p. 4.

10. Conflict

1. Evolved from *Space Walks*, TGF, *Play Ball*, IT & TGF, and *Playground*, IT & TGF.

2. Evolved from *Hidden Conflict*, IT.

3. Evolved from *Tug-of-War*, IT & TGF.

4. Evolved from *Space Walks*, TGF, *Play Ball*, IT & TGF, and *Jump Rope*, TGF.

5. Evolved from *Rejection*, IT.

6. Evolved from *Difficulty with Small Objects*, IT & TGF.

7. Evolved from *What To Do with the Object?*, IT.

11. Agreement

1. Evolved from *Follow the Follower #1*, TGF.

2. Evolved from *Blind Offers* in Keith Johnstone, *Impro* (New York: Theatre Arts Books, 1979), 101.

12. Purpose of Scene

1. Dustin Hoffman, *Los Angeles Times*, 2/14/99.

2. Don Roos, *Daily Variety*, 2/4/99, p. 16.

3. Edward Albee, interviewed on *South Bank Show*, Bravo Television, 1999.

4. *Ibid.*

5. Robert DeNiro, interviewed on *Inside the Actors Studio*, Bravo Television, 2000.

6. Kevin Spacey, interviewed on *Inside the Actors Studio*, Bravo Television, 2000.

13. Monologues and Purpose of Scene

1. Excerpts from the script based on Hollywood Pictures' copyrighted feature film *Miami Rhapsody* are used by permission from Disney Enterprises, Inc.

2. *Frasier.* Courtesy of Viacom Consumer Products.

3. *House Arrest.* Courtesy of Viacom Consumer Products.

4. *Star Trek: Voyager.* Courtesy of Viacom Consumer Products.

5. *Dogma.* Courtesy of STK LLC.

6. From *The Three Sisters* by Anton Chekhov, translated by Lanford Wilson, © 1984 by Lanford Wilson. Reprinted by permission of International Creative Management, Inc.

7. From *Long Day's Journey into Night* by Eugene O'Neill, copyright © 1956

8. From *The Glass Menagerie* by Tennessee Williams, copyright © 1945 by The University of the South and Edwin D. Williams, renewed © 1973 by The University of the South. Reprinted by permission of New Directions Publishing Corp. and The University of the South, Sewanee, Tennessee. Published by New Directions.

9. From *House of Blue Leaves* by John Guare, © 1968, 1971, 1972 by St. Jude Productions, Inc. Published by arrangement with the author.

14. GAINING MORE FINESSE WITH PURPOSE OF SCENE

1. Rita Street, "Uncommon Practice: In Chambers with David E. Kelley," *Film & Video*, 3/1999, p. 72.

2. Screenplay excerpt from *L. A. Law: The Movie*. Courtesy of Twentieth Century Fox Television. Steven Bochco, Terry Louise Fisher, and William M. Finkelstein. All rights reserved.

3. From *Glengarry Glen Ross* by David Mamet, © 1982, 1983 by David Mamet. Used by permission of Grove/Atlantic, Inc.

4. *What Dreams May Come*. Copyright © 2002 by Universal Studios. Courtesy of Universal Studios Publishing Rights, a Division of Universal Studios Licensing, Inc. All rights reserved.

5. From *Death of a Salesman* by Arthur Miller, © 1949, renewed © 1977 by Arthur Miller. Used by permission of Viking Penguin, a division of Penguin Putnam Inc.

6. Excerpt from *Target of Suspicion* (aka *Presumed Guilty*). Courtesy of Ellipseanime.

7. *Dangerous Curves*. Excerpt courtesy of Artisan Entertainment.

8. *Melrose Place*. Courtesy of Viacom Consumer Products.

9. Screenplay excerpt from *Love Potion No. 9*. Courtesy of Twentieth Century Fox Film Corporation. All rights reserved.

10. From *Golden Boy* by Clifford Odets, © 1937 by Clifford Odets, renewed © 1965 by Nara Odets and Walt Whitman Odets. Used by permission of Grove/Atlantic, Inc.

11. Excerpts from the script based on Hollywood Pictures' copyrighted feature film *Miami Rhapsody* are used by permission from Disney Enterprises, Inc.

12. Screenplay excerpt from *The Practice*. Courtesy of Twentieth Century Fox Television. David E. Kelley and Christopher Mack. All rights reserved.

13. From *The Children's Hour* by Lillian Hellman, © 1934 by Lillian Hellman Kober, © 1942, 1953 by Lillian Hellman, renewed © 1961, 1981 by Lillian Hellman. All rights reserved.

Conclusion

1. Gary Sinese, in "Actors We Love," *Back Stage West*, 6/22/00, p.14.

2. Letter 332, to I.K. Alekseev, 12/1935, K. S. Stanslavski, VIII (1961), 421–422, in Sharon M. Carnicke, *Stanislavsky in focus* (The Netherlands: Harwood Academic Publishers, 1998), 154.

3. Sharon M. Carnicke. *Stanislavsky in focus*, 169.

Appendices

1. Appendix B Sample Emotion & Attitude Choices
The source of the original version of this list, which I have made additions to and subtractions from over the years, is unknown to me.

2. Appendix C Sample Character Arcs
Compiled in part from A. L. Rose et al., *The Feel Wheel* (La Jolla, California: Center for Studies of the Person, 1972). As "Some feelings and their opposites," in *Healing the Child Within* (Deerfield Beach, Florida: Health Communications, Inc., 1987), 84.

3. Appendix E
*From Spolin, Viola, *Theater Games for the Classroom*, (Evanston, Ill.: Northwestern University Press, 1986);
**From Spolin, Viola, *Theater Game File*, (St, Louis: Cemrel Inc., 1975).

Key: ✱ = Exercise   ✱✱ = Process

Active & Still Refresher, 124
Active & Still #1, 108
Active & Still #2, 116
Active, Still, & Discover, 130
Activity & Location Struggle, 444
Activity Doing, 49
Activity Doing/Avoiding
    Sameness, 53
Activity Doing/Checking Out, 54
Activity Doing/Helping, 60
Activity Doing/Job Title, 64
Activity Doing/Personal
    Relationships, 67
Activity Doing/Rhythm, 57
Ad Agency, 92
Agreement, 478
Agreement Repeat
    Round 1, 488
    Round 2, 488
    Round 3, 491
Agreement Walk, 485
Agreement/Conflict, Part 1, 492
Agreement/Conflict, Part 2, 493
Animals, 247
Attitude Line Preparation,✱✱ 275
Attitude Line Switch, 295
Attitude Line with Emotion
    Switch, 394
Attitude Line/Character, Activity,
    Location, 285
Attitude Lines, 274
Basic Off Stage Reflection Preparation
    Coaching,✱✱ 146
Basic Reflection, 141
Body Center, 252
Conflict Space Exercise #1, 403
Conflict Space Exercise #2, 414
Discovering Objects Near You, 89
Disguised Conflict Influence, 404
Eating and Drinking while Listening
    and Speaking, 86

Emotion Arc and Switch, 387
Emotion Arcs, 362
Emotion Arcs (Repeat), 372
Emotion Switch, 373
Emotion Switch (Repeat), 380
Emotion Switch and Arc, 83
Emotion Walk #1, 333
Emotion Walk #2, 339
Emotion Walk #3, 352
Emotion Walk #4, 359
Emotion Walk #5, 370
Emotion Walk #6, 377
Emotion Walk #7, 381
Emotion Walk #8, 389
Emotions & Objects #1, 356
Emotions & Objects #2, 361
Extend, Intensify, and Enlarge, 330
Extend, Intensify, and Enlarge
    (Repeat), 379
Extension Bumps, 263
First Level Auditions,✱✱ *314*
First Level Improvisations for
    Scripted Scenes,✱ ✱✱ 218
Focus Walk, First, 27
Focus Walk, Second, 35
Focus Walk, Third, 41
40-Breath Process,✱✱ 26
Full Body Calling, 175
Full Body Singing, 193
Full Body Whisper, 170
Go With Your Emotions, 391
Group Blocking, 44
Huddles,✱✱ 59
Improv Process for Creating the
    Script Character,✱✱ 306
Invitations to Agreement, Part 1, 486
Invitations to Agreement, Part 2, 490
Location Focus, 80
Magic Finger-Snap Location
    Disappearance,✱✱ 75
Making Changes, 21

627

628

Mistreatment #1, 435
Mistreatment #2, 438
Monologue Exercise (POS),* 550
Multiple Reflection, 305
Multiscene One Acts, 134
Nonsense Language
  Commercials, 183
Nonsense Language Presentation
  Party, 179
Nonsense Language/Teaching and
  Learning, 183
Nonsense Speech Translation, 187
Nonsense/English, 185
Object Struggle, 354, 443
Objects in the Space, 33
Off Stage Kitchen (Past or
  Future), 157
Off Stage Reflection Walk #1, 145
Off Stage Reflection Walk #2, 147
Off Stage/Future, 162
Off Stage/Past, 159
Off Stage/Present, 149
Paralysis/Alone, 336
Paralysis/Group, 342
Parts of Speech, 196
Party Mingle Attitude Lines, 287
Party Upset, 122
Physical Catalyst + Attitude Line, 302
Physical Contact Speech, 204
Physical Contact with the
  Location, 76
Physical Discovery of Location, 73
Physical Doing Drill, 93
Physical Doing Drill Return, 99
Picking Up,* ** 113
POS, First Exercise for
  Learning,* 536
POS, Second Exercise for
  Learing,* 602
Pull the Conflict #1, 409
Pull the Conflict #2, 417
Pull the Conflict #3 (Disguised &
  Play the loss), 421
Pull the Conflict #4 (Disguised &
  Go in for the kill), 426
Pull the Rope! #1, 406

Pull the Rope! #2 (Emphasis on win/
  lose/draw), 415
Question & Answer Railroad
  Tracks,* ** 109
Receiving Character, 72
Reflect the Reflector, 154, 475
Reflection Listening, 206
Reflection Walk, 142
Reflection Walk Return, 155
Reformed Bodies in Space, 240
  Part 1, 240
  Part 2, 243
Relationship Struggle, 446
Scene Silence, 346
Script-Influenced Animal or Body
  Center, 266
Select & Reflect, 476
Shake-out,** 242
Sharing an Object, 58
Silence, 345
Soundless Stretching Speech, 200
Space Ball/Motion, 37
Space Ball/Weight, 42
Step-out, 335
Stretching Speech, 194
Tag, 20
Traveling,* ** 108
Turns, 125
Umbrella Arcs,** 375, 546
Unfocused/Focused, 46
Upset, 32
Vocal Warm-up, Special
  Group,* ** 336
What to do with the conflict,
  Win!, 462
What to do with the conflict?, 458
What to do with? #1, 450
What to do with? #2, 455
Writing Agreement/Conflict
  Exercise,* 496
Writing Conflict Exercise,* 465
"Yes! And...", 489

Many thanks to: Professor William Sharp for his friendship, scholarship, and support in beginning my teaching and directing career; the late John Houseman and Alan Schneider for their continual support and encouragement when we worked together at Juilliard; the faculty and my classmates in the graduate program of the drama department at Stanford University for providing me with so many opportunities for directing, acting, learning, and teaching; the administration and faculty of Sarah Lawrence College for introducing me to the experience and meaning of real education and bringing me together with Viola Spolin; my Esalen colleagues, Jack Rosenberg and Beverly Kitaen-Morse, for their wisdom, especially in the areas of authenticity, character styles, and journal work; John de Lancie for insistently bugging me to open the Stephen Book Acting Workshop; the staff of the Spolin Theater Game Center—Robert Martin, Mary Ann Brandt, Patricia Ruskin; Elliot Feinberg, DDS, friend and role model; Jacqueline and Françoise Koster for graciously providing my second home at La Poubelle; my family for their consistent support.

Special thanks for particular contributions to this book: Gwen Feldman, publisher, for her skill and dedication to doing it just right; Judith Rudnicki, editor; Al D'Andrea for editorial comments on the first draft; Leo Braudy for special editorial advice and guidance; Adam Ferrara for his hilarious comments and for always being there; my workshop assistant, Elizabeth Dement, for numerous efforts on behalf of this book; my dedicated student typists—Tom Sunstrom, Brent Suddeth, Keith Levy.

Other friends whose support for this book came in many forms—Conan Berkeley, Terry Berland, Stephen Breimer, Zane Buzby, Ronnie Chasen, Bill Gotti, Boz Graham, Dan Gunther, Crystal Hardison, Adria and Donald Hillman, Rick Levy, Michael Losmandy, Cheryl Peterson; and most importantly, all my students over the years, especially at my acting workshop, The Juilliard School, Bread Loaf School of English, Stanford University, Brown University, University of Southern California, Spolin Theater Game Center, and the Esalen Institute, for their enthusiasm, support, and excitement—that was always the juice that kept me exploring further.